GARLAND STUDIES IN APPLIED ETHICS
VOL. 2

ETHICAL ISSUES
IN SCIENTIFIC
RESEARCH

GARLAND REFERENCE LIBRARY
OF SOCIAL SCIENCE
VOL. 814

GARLAND STUDIES IN APPLIED ETHICS

ALAN GOLDMAN
Series Editor

**JUSTIFICATION AND
EXCUSE IN THE
CRIMINAL LAW**
A Collection of Essays
edited by
Michael Louis Corrado

**ETHICAL ISSUES IN
SCIENTIFIC RESEARCH**
An Anthology
edited by Edward Erwin, Sidney
Gendin, and Lowell Kleiman

**DRUGS, MORALITY,
AND THE LAW**
edited by Steven Luper-Foy
and Curtis Brown

ETHICAL ISSUES IN SCIENTIFIC RESEARCH

An Anthology

edited by

Edward Erwin
Sidney Gendin
Lowell Kleiman

GARLAND PUBLISHING, INC.
New York & London / 1994

Library of Congress Cataloging-in-Publication Data

Ethical issues in scientific research : an anthology / by
Edward Erwin, Sidney Gendin, and Lowell Kleiman.
     p.   cm. — (Garland studies in applied ethics ;
vol. 2) (Garland reference library of social science ;
vol. 814)
   ISBN 0–8153–0641–5 (alk. paper)
   ISBN 0–8153–1790–5 (pbk.)
   1. Research—Moral and ethical aspects. 2. Fraud in
science.   I. Erwin, Edward, 1937– . II. Gendin,
Sidney.   III. Kleiman, Lowell, 1942– . IV. Series:
Garland studies in applied ethics ; v. 2. V. Series:
Garland reference library of social science ; v. 814.
Q180.55.M67E83   1994
174'.95072—dc20   93–37482
                                     CIP

Printed on acid-free, 250-year-life paper
Manufactured in the United States of America

For Benjamin and Johanna
E. Erwin

In memory of my beloved Natalie (1936–1990)
S. Gendin

To Sheila
L. Kleiman

Contents

Series Editor's Preface

The aim of this series is to make available texts and collections of essays on major moral issues. Each volume will be devoted to a single issue of contemporary interest. Such in-depth treatment will transcend the usual superficial presentation of such topics in general applied ethics texts. Background will be provided by classic statements in articles or detailed definitions in texts of the problems, and opposing sides on the issues will be given ample development.

The series will include authored texts on topics that have not been discussed extensively in the philosophical literature before, as well as contemporary advances on earlier treatments. Collections of essays will bring together articles that have previously been scattered in the recent proliferation of journals that address these issues.

Since the National Institutes of Health have mandated a course on ethics in research training for all applicants for research funds, the present volume fills an obvious need. The requirement for such courses expresses the recognition that the ethical dimensions of various types of scientific research greatly affect the general population and therefore require serious study and debate. This collection of essays addresses the major areas of moral debate regarding research: fraud and deception, controlled experiments on humans, animal and genetic research, IQ and military research.

These issues present both conceptual problems (for example, how to define fraud in reports of experimental results) and fundamental moral questions (for example, how to weigh the interests of future medical patients against those of present patients). The issues arising from new kinds of research such as gene therapy challenge basic philosophical concepts (for example, those of personal identity and individual rights) as well as the viability of traditional moral theories for answering new questions (for example, regarding the rights of future generations).

The essays collected here represent the best efforts to date of philosophers and scientists to grapple with these interesting and difficult issues.

Alan Goldman

Ethical Issues in Scientific Research

Science and Values

Is ethics a science? Are any of its hypotheses true? Do we know which ones are true? Skeptics say no, moralists yes, while others, call them "cognitivists," try to have it both ways. For example, some cognitivists distinguish between moral and other value judgments and hold that only the latter can be known to be true. We can determine, for example, that a certain athlete is a *good* track runner or that one university has a *better* chemistry department, but not be able to prove that athletic discipline itself is a moral virtue or that manipulating experimental data a moral vice. So one need not be skeptical of all values to be skeptical of morality.

Skepticism of moral belief, judgment, and theory is a dominant motif in Western philosophy, at least since David Hume in the eighteenth century. Hume admitted that moralists argue for their moral beliefs just as theists argue for their religious beliefs. But just as religious premises have no support outside of other religious assumptions, so moral premises have no support outside of other moral assumptions. The field of ethics might suitably be compared not to a science but to eighteenth-century metaphysics as described by Immanuel Kant:

> We do not find men confident of their ability to shine in other sciences venturing their reputations here, where everybody however ignorant in other matters may deliver a final verdict, as in this domain there is as yet no standard weight and measure to distinguish sound knowledge from shallow talk. (*Prolegomena to Any Future Metaphysics*)

But Kant was not a skeptic; rather, he argued that moral principles could be known through pure reason. Other cognitivists appeal to intuition, arguing that in logic and mathematics we also rely on intuitions. Others argue that even without special intuitions, we can observe when something is wrong. For example, we can see that torturing a human being is immoral.

Carl Hempel, in his paper "Science and Human Values," criticizes the cognitive approach. Hempel agrees that a hypothetical judgment of value, such as "If our children are to become happy, then it is better to raise them in a permissive manner," can be confirmed by scientific evidence. He denies, however, that this is possible for a categorical judgment, such as "Killing is evil." He claims that such a sentence fails to express an assertion that is either true or false. Despite his moral skepticism, Hempel agrees that the acceptance of scientific judgments presupposes certain value judgments, and that science can play a role in clarifying and resolving problems of moral valuation.

Michael Scriven, in "The Exact Role for Value Judgments in Science," argues that even categorical value judgments can be confirmed. He claims that science itself is essentially evaluative, that the practice of good science requires the evaluation of experimental designs, theories, observations, explanations, and estimates. Science, according to Scriven, is neither value-free nor morally neutral.

Within the broader issue of the relation between science and values is the conflict between consequentialists, those who believe that the morality of an action is determined solely by its effects and deontologists, theorists who believe otherwise. For example, a deontologist would condemn the use of placebos in human experimentation if experimenters have an obligation not to deceive their subjects. By contrast, the utilitarian (a consequentialist who emphasizes social well-being) would overlook the deception if the use of placebos did more good than harm.

Although traditional utilitarian and deontologist approaches seem to conflict, Nicholson, Hare et al. suggest a way for bringing both sides together. At the practical level, the deontologist can appeal to moral principles about people's rights and duties. Thus, an ethics committee can reject a proposal for research that ignores the patient's right to give informed consent. However, at the theoretical level, principles of obligation that otherwise appear intuitive can conflict. For example, in AIDS research we have a duty to try to help current patients, as well as an obligation to help future victims. But we cannot always do both, especially if helping current patients compromises the interests of future victims, for example, by relaxing experimental standards in order to bring a drug more quickly to market. Here Nicholson, Hare et al. suggest a utilitarian resolution: relax the standards if that would save more lives and relieve more suffering. The problem, however, is, if we are willing to rely on utilitarian standards at the theoretical level, why turn away from those same standards at the so-called practical level? More must be said about the "theoretical/practical" distinction before a genuine resolution can be achieved.

Science and Human Values

Carl G. Hempel

1. The Problem

Our age is often called an age of science and of scientific technology, and with good reason: the advances made during the past few centuries by the natural sciences, and more recently by the psychological and sociological disciplines, have enormously broadened our knowledge and deepened our understanding of the world we live in and of our fellow men; and the practical application of scientific insights is giving us an ever increasing measure of control over the forces of nature and the minds of men. As a result, we have grown quite accustomed not only to the idea of a physico-chemical and biological technology based on the results of the natural sciences, but also to the concept, and indeed the practice, of a psychological and sociological technology that utilizes the theories and methods developed by behavioral research.

This growth of scientific knowledge and its applications has vastly reduced the threat of some of man's oldest and most formidable scourges, among them famine and pestilence; it has raised man's material level of living, and it has put within his reach the realization of visions which even a few decades ago would have appeared utterly fantastic, such as the active exploration of interplanetary space.

But in achieving these results, scientific technology has given rise to a host of new and profoundly disturbing problems:

The control of nuclear fission has brought us not only the comforting prospect of a vast new reservoir of energy, but also the constant threat of the atom bomb and of grave damage, to the present and to future generations, from the radioactive by-products of the fission process, even in its peaceful seus. And the very progress in biological and medical knowledge and technology which has so strikingly reduced infant mortality and increased man's life expectancy in large areas of our globe has significantly contributed to the threat of the "population explosion," the rapid growth of the earth's population which we are facing today, and which, again, is a matter of grave concern to all those who have the welfare of future generations at heart.

Clearly, the advances of scientific technology on which we pride ourselves, and which have left their characteristic imprint on every aspect of this "age of science," have brought in their train many new and grave problems which urgently demand a solution. It is only natural that, in his desire to cope with these new issues, man should turn to science and scientific technology for further help. But a moment's reflection shows that the problems that need to be dealt with are not straightforward technological questions but intricate complexes of technological and moral issues. Take the case of the population explosion, for example. To be sure, it does pose specific technological problems. One of these is the task of satisfying at least the basic material needs of a rapidly growing population by means of limited resources; another is the question of means by which population growth itself may be kept under control. Yet these technical questions do not exhaust the problem. For after all, even now we have at our disposal various ways of counteracting population growth; but some of these, notably contraceptive methods, have been and continued to be the subject of intense controversy on moral and religious grounds, which shows that an adequate solution of the problem at hand requires not only knowledge of technical means of control, but also standards for evaluating the alternative means at our disposal; and this second requirement clearly raises moral issues.

There is no need to extend the list of illustrations: any means of technical control that science makes available to us may be employed in many different ways, and a decision as to what use to make of it involves us in questions of moral valuation. And here arises a fundamental problem to which I would now like to turn: Can such valuational questions be answered by means of the objective methods of empirical science, which have been so successful in giving us reliable, and often practically applicable, knowledge of our world? Can those methods serve to establish objective criteria of right and wrong and thus to provide valid moral norms for the proper conduct of our individual and social affairs?

2. Scientific Testing

Let us approach this question by considering first, if only in brief and sketchy outline, the way in which objective scientific knowledge is arrived at. We may leave aside here the question of *ways of discovery*, i.e., the problem of how a new scientific idea arises, how a novel hypothesis or theory is first conceived; for our purposes it will suffice to consider the scientific *ways of validation*; i e., the manner in which empirical science goes about examining a proposed new hypothesis and determines whether it is to be accepted or rejected. I will use the word 'hypothesis' here to refer quite broadly to any statements or set of statements in empirical science, no matter whether it deals with some particular event or purports to set forth a general law or perhaps a more or less complex theory.

As is well known, empirical science decides upon the acceptability of a proposed hypothesis by means of suitable tests. Sometimes such a test may involve nothing more than what might be called direct observation of pertinent facts. This procedure may be used, for example, in testing such statements as 'It is raining outside,' 'All the marbles in this urn are blue,' 'The needle of this ammeter will stop at the scale point marked 6,' and so forth. Here a few direct observations will usually suffice to decide whether the hypothesis at hand is to be accepted as true or to be rejected as false.

But most of the important hypotheses in empirical science cannot be tested in this simple manner. Direct observation does not suffice to decide, for example, whether to accept or to reject the hypotheses that the earth is a sphere, that hereditary characteristics are transmitted by genes, that all Indo-European languages developed from one common ancestral language, that light is an electromagnetic wave process, and so forth. With hypotheses such as these, science resorts to indirect methods of test and validation. While these methods vary greatly in procedural detail, they all have the same basic structure and rationale. First, from the hypothesis under test, suitable other statements are inferred which describe certain directly observable phenomena that should be found to occur under specifiable circumstances if the hypothesis is true; then those inferred statements are tested directly (i.e., by checking whether the specified phenomena do in fact occur); finally, the proposed hypothesis is accepted or rejected in the light of the outcome of these tests. For example, the hypothesis that the earth is spherical in shape is not directly testable by observation, but it permits us to infer that a ship moving away from the observer should appear to be gradually dropping below the horizon; that circumnavigation of the earth should be possible by following a straight course; that high-altitude photographs should show the curving of the earth's surface; that certain geodetic and astronomical measurements should yield such and such results; and so forth. Inferred statements such as these can be tested more or less directly; and as an increasing number and variety of them are actually borne out, the hypothesis becomes increasingly confirmed. Eventually, a hypothesis may be so well confirmed by the available evidence that it is accepted as having been established beyond reasonable doubt. Yet no scientific hypothesis is ever proved completely and definitively; there is always at least the theoretical possibility that new evidence will be discovered which conflicts with some of the observational statements inferred from the hypothesis, and which thus leads to its rejection. The history of science records many instances in which a once accepted hypothesis was subsequently abandoned in the light of adverse evidence.

3. Instrumental Judgments of Value

We now turn to the question whether this method of test and validation may be used to establish moral judgments of value, and particularly judgments to the effect that a specified course of action is good or right or proper, or that it is better than certain alternative courses of action, or that we ought—or ought not—to act in certain specified ways.

By way of illustration, consider the view that it is good to raise children permissively and bad to bring them up in a restrictive manner. It might seem that, at least in principle, this view could be scientifically confirmed by appropriate empirical investigations. Suppose, for example, that careful research had established (1) that restrictive upbringing tends to generate resentment and aggression against parents and other persons exercising educational authority, and that this leads to guilt and anxiety and an eventual stunting of the child's initiative and creative potentialities; whereas (2) permissive upbringing avoids these consequences, makes for happier interpersonal relations, encourages resourcefulness and self-reliance, and enables the child to develop and enjoy his potentialities. These statements, especially when suitably amplified, come within the purview of scientific investigation; and though our knowledge in the matter is in fact quite limited, let us assume, for the sake of the argument, that they had actually been strongly confirmed by careful tests. Would not scientific research then have objectively shown that it is indeed better to raise children in a permissive rather than in a restrictive manner?

A moment's reflection shows that this is not so. What would have been established is rather a conditional statement; namely, that *if* our children are to become happy, emotionally secure, creative individuals rather than guilt-ridden and troubled souls, then it is better to raise them in a permissive than in a restrictive fashion. A statement like this represents *a relative, or instrumental, judgment of value.* Generally, a relative judgment of value states that a certain kind of action, M, is good (or that it is better than a given alternative M_1) if a specified goal G is to be attained; or more accurately, that M is good, or appropriate, for the attainment of goal G. But to say that is tantamount to asserting either that, in the circumstances at hand, course of action M will definitely (or probably) lead to the attainment of G, or that failure to embark on course of action M will definitely (or probably) lead to the nonattainment of G. In other words, the instrumental value judgment asserts either that M is a (definitely or probably) sufficient means for attaining the end or goal G, or that it is a (definitely or probably) necessary means for attaining it. Thus, a relative, or instrumental, judgment of value can be reformulated as a statement which expresses a universal or a probabilistic kind of means-ends relationship, and which contains no terms of moral discourse—such as 'good,' 'better,' 'ought to'—at all. And a statement of this kind surely is an empirical assertion capable of scientific test.

4. Categorical Judgments of Value

Unfortunately, this does not completely solve our problem; for after a relative judgment of value referring to a certain goal G has been tested and, let us assume, well confirmed, we are still left with the question of whether the goal G ought to be pursued, or whether it would be better to aim at some alternative goal instead. Empirical science can establish the conditional statement, for example, that if we wish to deliver an incurably ill person from intolerable suffering, then a large dose of morphine affords a means of doing so; but it may also indicate ways of prolonging the patient's life, if also his suffering. This leaves us with the question whether it is right to give the goal of avoiding hopeless human suffering precedence over that of preserving human life. And this question calls not for a relative but for an *absolute, or categorical, judgment of value* to the effect that a certain state of affairs (which may have been proposed as a goal or end) is good, or that it is better than some specified alternative. Are such categorical value judgments capable of empirical test and confirmation?

Consider, for example, the sentence 'Killing is evil'. It expresses a categorical judgment of value which, by implication, would also categorically qualify euthanasia as evil. Evidently, the sentence does not express an assertion that can be directly tested by observation; it does not purport to describe a directly observable fact. Can it be indirectly tested, then, by inferring from it statements to the effect that under specified test conditions such and such observable phenomena will occur? Again, the answer is clearly in the negative. Indeed, the sentence 'Killing is evil' does not have the function of expressing an assertion that can be qualified as true or false; rather, it serves to express a standard for moral appraisal or a norm for conduct. A categorical judgment of value may have other functions as well; for example, it may serve to convey the utterer's approval or disapproval of a certain kind of action, or his commitment to the standards of conduct expressed by the value judgment. Descriptive empirical import, however, is absent; in this respect a sentence such as 'Killing is evil' differs strongly from, say, 'Killing is condemned as evil by many religions', which expresses a factual assertion capable of empirical test.

Categorical judgments of value, then, are not amenable to scientific test and confirmation or disconfirmation; for they do not express assertions but rather standards or norms for conduct. It was Max Weber, I believe, who expressed essentially the same idea by remarking that science is like a map: it can tell us how to get to a given place, but it cannot tell us where to go. Gunnar Myrdal, in his book *An American Dilemma* (p. 1052), stresses in a similar vein that "factual or theoretical studies alone cannot logically lead to a practical recommendation. A practical or valuational conclusion can be derived only when there is at least one valuation among the premises."

Nevertheless, there have been many attempts to base systems of moral standards on the findings of empirical science; and it would be of interest to examine in some detail the reasoning which underlies those procedures. In the present context, however, there is room for only a few brief remarks on this subject.

It might seem promising, for example, to derive judgments of value from the results of an objective study of human needs. But no cogent derivation of this sort is possible. For this procedure would presuppose that it is right, or good, to satisfy human needs—and this presupposition is itself a categorical judgment of value: it would play the role of a valuational premise in the sense of Myrdal's statement. Furthermore, since there are a great many different, and partly conflicting, needs of individuals and of groups, we would require not just the general maxim that human needs ought to be satisfied, but a detailed set of rules as to the preferential order and degree in which different needs are to be met, and how conflicting claims are to be settled; thus, the valuational premise required for this undertaking would actually have to be a complex system of norms; hence, a derivation of valuational standards simply from a factual study of needs is out of the question.

Several systems of ethics have claimed the theory of evolution as their basis; but they are in serious conflict with each other even in regard to their most fundamental tenets. Some of the major variants are illuminatingly surveyed in a chapter of G.G. Simpson's book, *The Meaning of Evolution*. One type, which Simpson calls a "tooth-and-claw ethics," glorifies a struggle for existence that should lead to a survival of the fittest. A second urges the harmonious adjustment of groups or individuals to one another so as to enhance the probability of their survival, while still other systems hold up as an ultimate standard the increased aggregation of organic units into higher levels of organization, sometimes with the implication that the welfare of the state is to be placed above that of the individuals belonging to it. It is obvious that these conflicting principles could not have been validly inferred from the theory of evolution—unless indeed that theory were self-contradictory, which does not seem very likely.

But if science cannot provide us with categorical judgments of value, what then can serve as a source of unconditional valuations? This question may either be understood in a pragmatic sense, as concerned with the sources from which human beings do in fact obtain their basic values. Or it may be understood as concerned with a systematic aspect of valuation, namely, the question where a proper system of basic values is to be found on which all other valuations may then be grounded.

The pragmatic question comes within the purview of empirical science. Without entering into details, we may say here that a person's values—both those he professes to espouse and those he actually conforms to—are largely absorbed from the society in which he lives, and especially from certain influential subgroups to which he belongs, such as his family, his schoolmates, his associates on the job, his church, clubs, unions, and other groups. Indeed his values may vary from case to case depending on which of these groups dominates the situation in which he happens to find himself. In general, then, a person's basic valuations are no more the result of careful scrutiny and critical appraisal of possible alternatives than is his religious affiliation. Conformity to the standards of certain groups plays a very important role here, and only rarely are basic values seriously questioned. Indeed, in many situations, we decide and act unreflectively in an even stronger sense: namely, without any attempt to base our decisions on some set of explicit, consciously adopted, moral standards.

Now, it might be held that this answer to the pragmatic version of our question reflects a regrettable human inclination to intellectual and moral inertia; but that the really important side of our question is the systematic one: If we do want to justify our decisions, we need moral standards of conduct of the unconditional type—but how can such standards be established? If science cannot provide categorical value judgments, are there any other sources from which they might be obtained? Could we not, for example, validate a system of categorical judgments of value by pointing out that it represents the moral standards held up by the Bible, or by the Koran, or by some inspiring thinker or social leader? Clearly, this procedure must fail, for the factual information here adduced could serve to validate the value judgments in question only if we were to use, in addition, a valuational presupposition to the effect that the moral directives stemming from the source invoked *ought* to be complied with. Thus, if the process of justifying a given decision or moral judgment is ever to be completed, certain judgments of value have to be accepted without any further justification, just as the proof of a theorem in geometry requires that some propositions be accepted as postulates, without proof. The quest for a justification of *all* our valuations overlooks this basic characteristic of the logic of validation and of justification. The value judgments accepted without further justification in a given context need not, however, be accepted once and for all, with a commitment never to question them again. This point will be elaborated further in the final section of this essay.

As will hardly be necessary to stress, in concluding the present phase of our discussion, the ideas set forth in the preceding pages do not imply or advocate moral anarchy; in particular, they do not imply that any system of values is just as good, or just as valid, as any other, or that everyone should adopt the moral principles that best suit his convenience. For all such maxims have the character of categorical value judgments and cannot, therefore, be implied by the preceding considerations, which are purely descriptive of certain logical, psychological, and social aspects of moral valuation.

5. Rational Choice:
Empirical and Valuational Components

To gain further insight into the relevance of scientific inquiry for categorical valuation, let us ask what help we might receive, in dealing with a moral problem, from science in an ideal state such as that represented by Laplace's conception of a superior scientific intelligence, sometimes referred to as Laplace's demon. This fiction was used by Laplace, early in the nineteenth century, to give a vivid characterization of the idea of universal causal determinism. The demon is conceived as a perfect observer, capable of ascertaining with infinite speed and accuracy all that goes on in the universe at a given moment; he is also an ideal theoretician who knows all the laws of nature and has combined them into one universal formula; and finally, he is a perfect mathematician who, by means of that universal formula, is able to infer, from the observed state of the universe at the given moment, the total state of the universe at any other moment; thus past and future are present before his eyes. Surely, it is difficult to imagine that science could ever achieve a higher degree of perfection!

Let us assume, then, that, faced with a moral decision, we are able to call upon the Laplacean demon as a consultant. What help might we get from him? Suppose that we have to choose one of several alternative courses of action open to us, and that we want to know which of these we *ought* to follow. The demon would then be able to tell us, for any contemplated choice, what its consequences would be for the future course of the universe, down to the most minute detail, however remote in space and time. But, having done this for each of the alternative courses of action under consideration, the demon would have completed his task: he would have given us all the information that an ideal science might provide under the circumstances. And yet he would not have resolved our moral problem, for this requires a decision as to which of the several alternative sets of consequences mapped out by the demon as attainable to us is the best; which of them we ought to bring about. And the burden of this decision would still fall upon our shoulders: it is we who would have to commit ourselves to an unconditional judgment of value by singling out one of the sets of consequences as superior to its alternatives. Even Laplace's demon, or the ideal science he stands for, cannot relieve us of this responsibility.

In drawing this picture of the Laplacean demon as a consultant in decision making, I have cheated a little; for if the world were as strictly deterministic as Laplace's fiction assumes, then the demon would know in advance what choice we were going to make, and he might disabuse us of the idea that there were several courses of action open to us. However that may be, contemporary physical theory has cast considerable doubt on the classical conception of the universe as a strictly deterministic system: the fundamental laws of nature are now assumed to have a statistical or probabilistic rather than a strictly universal, deterministic, character.

But whatever may be the form and the scope of the laws that hold in our universe, we will obviously never attain a perfect state of knowledge concerning them; confronted with a choice, we never have more than a very incomplete knowledge of the laws of nature and of the state of the world at the time when we must act. Our decisions must therefore always be made on the basis of incomplete information, a state which enables us to anticipate the consequences of alternative choices at best with probability. Science can render an indispensable service by providing us with increasingly extensive and reliable information relevant to our purpose; but again it remains for us to *evaluate* the various probable sets of consequences of the alternative choices under consideration. And this requires the adoption of pertinent valuational standards which are not objectively determined by the empirical facts.

This basic point is reflected also in the contemporary mathematical theories of decision making. One of the objectives of these theories is the formulation of decision rules which will determine an optimal choice in situations where several courses of action are available. For the formulation of decision rules, these theories require that at least two conditions be met: (1) Factual information must be provided specifying the available courses of action and indicating for each of these its different possible outcomes—plus, if feasible, the probabilities of their occurrence; (2) there must be a specification of the values—often prosaically referred to as utilities—that are attached to the different possible outcomes. Only when these factual and valuational specifications have been provided does it make sense to ask which of the available choices is the best, considering the values attaching to their possible results.

In mathematical decision theory, several criteria of optimal choice have been proposed. In case the probabilities for the different outcomes of each action are given, one standard criterion qualifies a choice as optimal if the probabilistically expectable utility of its outcome is at least as great as that of any alternative choice. Other rules, such as the maximin and the maximax principles, provide criteria that are applicable even when the probabilities of the outcomes are not available. But interestingly, the various criteria conflict with each other in the sense that, for one and the same situation, they will often select different choices as optimal.

The policies expressed by the conflicting criteria may be regarded as reflecting different attitudes towards the world, different degrees of optimism or pessimism, of venturesomeness or caution. It may be said therefore that the analysis offered by current mathematical models indicates two points at which decision making calls not solely for factual information, but for categorical valuation, namely, in the assignment of utilities to the different possible outcomes and in the adoption of one among many competing decision rules or criteria of optimal choice. . . .

6. Valuational "Presuppositions" of Science

The preceding three sections have been concerned mainly with the question whether, or to what extent, valuation and decision presuppose scientific investigation and scientific knowledge. This problem has a counterpart which deserves some attention in a discussion of science and valuation; namely, the question whether scientific knowledge and method presuppose valuation.

The word 'presuppose' may be understood in a number of different senses which require separate consideration here. First of all, when a person decides to devote himself to scientific work rather than to some other career, and again, when a scientist chooses some particular topic of investigation, these choices will presumably be determined to a large extent by his preferences, i.e., by how highly he values scientific research in comparison with the alternatives open to him, and by the importance he attaches to the problems he proposes to investigate. In this explanatory, quasi-causal sense the scientific *activities* of human beings may certainly be said to presuppose valuations.

Much more intriguing problems arise, however, when we ask whether judgments of value are presupposed by the body of scientific *knowledge*, which might be represented by a system of statements accepted in accordance with the rules of scientific inquiry. Here presupposing has to be understood in a systematic-logical sense. One such sense is invoked when we say, for example, that the statement 'Henry's brother-in-law is an engineer' presupposes that Henry has a wife or a sister: in this sense, a statement presupposes whatever can be logically inferred from it. But, as we noted earlier, no set of scientific statements logically implies an unconditional judgment of value; hence, scientific knowledge does not, in this sense, presuppose valuation.

There is another logical sense of presupposing, however. We might say, for example, that in Euclidean geometry the angle-sum theorem for triangles presupposes the postulate of the parallels in the sense that that postulate is an essential part of the basic assumptions from which the theorem is deduced. Now, the hypotheses and theories of empirical science are not normally validated by deduction from supporting evidence (though it may happen that a scientific statement, such as a prediction, is established by deduction from a previously ascertained, more inclusive set of statements); rather, as was mentioned in section 2, they are usually accepted on the basis of evidence that lends them only partial, or "inductive," support. But in any event it might be asked whether the statements representing scientific knowledge presuppose valuation in the sense that the grounds on which they are accepted include, sometimes or always, certain unconditional judgments of value. Again the answer is in the negative. The grounds on which scientific hypotheses are accepted or rejected are provided by empirical evidence, which may include observational findings as well as previously established laws and theories, but surely no value judgments. Suppose for example that, in support of the hypothesis that a radiation belt of a specified kind surrounds the earth, a scientist were to adduce, first, certain observational data, obtained perhaps by rocket-borne instruments; second, certain previously accepted theories invoked in the interpretation of those data; and finally, certain judgments of value, such as 'it is good to ascertain the truth'. Clearly, the judgments of value would then be dismissed as lacking all logical relevance to the proposed hypothesis since they can contribute neither to its support nor to its disconfirmation.

But the question whether science presupposes valuation in a logical sense can be raised, and recently has been raised, in yet another way, referring more specifically to valuational presuppositions of scientific *method*. In the preceding considerations, scientific knowledge was represented by a system of statements which are sufficiently supported by available evidence to be accepted in accordance with the principles of scientific test and validation. We noted that as a rule the observational evidence on which a scientific hypothesis is accepted is far from sufficient to establish that hypothesis conclusively. For example, Galileo's law refers not only to past instances of free fall near the earth, but also to all future ones;

and the latter surely are not covered by our present evidence. Hence, Galileo's law, and similarly any other law in empirical science, is accepted on the basis of incomplete evidence. Such acceptance carries with it the "inductive risk" that the presumptive law may not hold in full generality, and that future evidence may lead scientists to modify or abandon it.

A precise statement of this conception of scientific knowledge would require, among other things, the formulation of rules of two kinds: First, *rules of confirmation* which would specify what kind of evidence is confirmatory, what kind disconfirmatory for a given hypothesis. Perhaps they would also determine a numerical *degree* of evidential support (or confirmation, or inductive probability) which a given body of evidence could be said to confer upon a proposed hypothesis. Secondly, there would have to be *rules of acceptance*: these would specify how strong the evidential support for a given hypothesis has to be if the hypothesis is to be accepted into the system of scientific knowledge; or, more generally, under what conditions a proposed hypothesis is to be accepted, under what conditions it is to be rejected by science on the basis of a given body of evidence.

Recent studies of inductive inference and statistical testing have devoted a great deal of effort to the formulation of adequate rules of either kind. In particular, rules of acceptance have been treated in many of these investigations as special instances of decision rules of the sort mentioned in the preceding section. The decisions in question are here either to accept or to reject a proposed hypothesis on the basis of given evidence. As was noted earlier, the formulation of "adequate" decision rules requires, in any case, the antecedent specification of valuations that can then serve as standards of adequacy. The requisite valuations, as will be recalled, concern the different possible outcomes of the choices which the decision rules are to govern. Now, when a scientific rule of acceptance is applied to a specified hypothesis on the basis of a given body of evidence, the possible "outcomes" of the resulting decision may be divided into four major types: (1) the hypothesis is accepted (as presumably true) in accordance with the rule and is in fact true; (2) the hypothesis is rejected (as presumably false) in accordance with the rule and is in fact false; (3) the hypothesis is accepted in accordance with the rule, but is in fact false; (4) the hypothesis is rejected in accordance with the rule, but is in fact true. The former two cases are what science aims to achieve; the possibility of the latter two represents the inductive risk that any acceptance rule must involve. And the problem of formulating adequate rules of acceptance and rejection has no clear meaning unless standards of adequacy have been provided by assigning definite values or disvalues to those different possible "outcomes" of acceptance or rejection. It is in this sense that the method of establishing scientific hypotheses "presupposes" valuation: the justification of the rules of acceptance and rejection requires reference to value judgments.

In the cases where the hypothesis under test, if accepted, is to be made the basis of a specific course of action, the possible outcomes may lead to success or failure of the intended practical application; in these cases, the values and disvalues at stake may well be expressible in terms of monetary gains or losses; and for situations of this sort, the theory of decision functions has developed various decision rules for use in practical contexts such as industrial quality control. But when it comes to decision rules for the acceptance of hypotheses in pure scientific research, where no practical applications are contemplated, the question of how to assign values to the four types of outcome mentioned earlier becomes considerably more problematic. But in a general way, it seems clear that the standards governing the inductive procedures of pure science reflect the objective of obtaining a certain goal, which might be described somewhat vaguely as the attainment of an increasingly reliable, extensive, and theoretically systematized body of information about the world. Note that if we were concerned, instead, to form a system of beliefs or a world view that is emotionally reassuring or esthetically satisfying to us, then it would not be reasonable at all to insist, as science does, on a close accord between the beliefs we accept and our empirical evidence; and the standards of objective testability and confirmation by publicly ascertainable evidence would have to be replaced by acceptance standards of an entirely different kind. The standards of procedure must in each case be formed in consideration of the goals to be attained;

their justification must be relative to those goals and must, in this sense, presuppose them.

7. Concluding Comparisons

If, as has been argued in section 4, science cannot provide a validation of categorical value judgments, can scientific method and knowledge play any role at all in clarifying and resolving problems of moral valuation and decision? The answer is emphatically in the affirmative. I will try to show this in a brief survey of the principal contributions science has to offer in this context.

First of all, science can provide factual information required for the resolution of moral issues. Such information will always be needed, for no matter what system of moral values we may espouse—whether it be egoistic or altruistic, hedonistic or utilitarian, or of any other kind—surely the specific course of action it enjoins us to follow in a given situation will depend upon the facts about that situation; and it is scientific knowledge and investigation that must provide the factual information which is needed for the application of our moral standards.

More specifically, factual information is needed, for example, to ascertain (a) whether a contemplated objective can be attained in a given situation; (b) if it can be attained, by what alternative means and with what probabilities; (c) what side effects and ulterior consequences the choice of a given means may have apart from probably yielding the desired end; (d) whether several proposed ends are jointly realizable, or whether they are incompatible in the sense that the realization of some of them will definitely or probably prevent the realization of others.

By thus giving us information which is indispensable as a factual basis for rational and responsible decision, scientific research may well motivate us to change some of our valuations. If we were to discover, for example, that a certain kind of goal which we had so far valued very highly could be attained only at the price of seriously undesirable side effects and ulterior consequences, we might well come to place a less high value upon that goal. Thus, more extensive scientific information may lead to a change in our basic valuations—not by "disconfirming" them, of course, but rather by motivating a change in our total appraisal of the issues in question.

Secondly, and in a quite different manner, science can illuminate certain problems of valuation by an objective psychological and sociological study of the factors that affect the values espoused by an individual or a group; of the ways in which such valuational commitments change; and perhaps of the manner in which the espousal of a given value system may contribute to the emotional security of an individual or the functional stability of a group.

Psychological, anthropological, and sociological studies of valuational behavior cannot, of course, "validate" any system of moral standards. But their results can psychologically effect changes in our outlook on moral issues by broadening our horizons, by making us aware of alternatives not envisaged, or not embraced, by our own group, and by thus providing some safeguard against moral dogmatism or parochialism.

Finally, a comparison with certain fundamental aspects of scientific knowledge may help to illuminate some further questions concerning valuation.

If we grant that scientific hypotheses and theories are always open to revision in the light of new empirical evidence, are we not obliged to assume that there is another class of scientific statements which cannot be open to doubt and reconsideration, namely, the observational statements describing experiential findings that serve to test scientific theories? Those simple, straightforward reports of what has been directly observed in the laboratory or in scientific fieldwork, for example—must they not be regarded as immune from any conceivable revision, as irrevocable once they have been established by direct observation? Reports on directly observed phenomena have indeed often been considered as an unshakable bedrock foundation for all scientific hypotheses and theories. Yet this conception is untenable; even here, we find no definitive, unquestionable certainty.

For, first of all, accounts of what has been directly observed are subject to error that may spring from various physiological and psychological sources. Indeed, it is often possible to check on the accuracy of a given observation report by comparing it with the reports made by other observers, or with relevant data obtained by some indirect procedure, such as a motion picture taken of the finish of a horse race; and such comparison may lead to the rejection of what had previously been considered as a correct description of a directly observed phenomenon. We even have theories that enable us to explain and anticipate some types of observational error, and in such cases, there is no hesitation to question and to reject certain statements that purport simply to record what has been directly observed.

Sometimes relatively isolated experimental findings may conflict with a theory that is strongly supported by a large number and variety of other data; in this case, it may well happen that part of the conflicting data, rather than the theory, is refused admission into the system of accepted scientific statements—even if no satisfactory explanation of the presumptive error of observation is available. In such cases it is not the isolated observational finding which decides whether the theory is to remain in good standing, but it is the previously well-substantiated theory which determines whether a purported observation report is to be regarded as describing an actual empirical occurrence. For example, a report that during a spiritualistic séance, a piece of furniture freely floated above the floor would normally be rejected because of its conflict with extremely well-confirmed physical principles, even in the absence of some specific explanation of the report, say, in terms of deliberate fraud by the medium, or of high suggestibility on the part of the observer. Similarly, the experimental findings reported by the physicist Ehrenhaft, which were claimed to refute the principle that all electric charges are integral multiples of the charge of the electron, did not lead to the overthrow, or even to a slight modification, of that principle, which is an integral part of a theory with extremely strong and diversified experimental support. Needless to say, such rejection of alleged observation reports by reason of their conflict with well-established theories requires considerable caution; otherwise, a theory, once accepted, could be used to reject all adverse evidence that might subsequently be found—a dogmatic procedure entirely irreconcilable with the objectives and the spirit of scientific inquiry.

Even reports on directly observed phenomena, then, are not irrevocable; they provide no bedrock foundation for the entire system of scientific knowledge. But this by no means precludes the possibility of testing scientific theories by reference to data obtained through direct observation. As we noted, the results obtained by such direct checking cannot be considered as absolutely unquestionable and irrevocable; they are themselves amenable to further tests which may be carried out if there is reason for doubt. But obviously if we are ever to form any beliefs about the world, if we are ever to accept or to reject, even provisionally, some hypothesis or theory, then we must stop the testing process somewhere; we must accept some evidential statements as sufficiently trustworthy not to require further investigation for the time being. And on the basis of such evidence, we can then decide what credence to give to the hypothesis under test, and whether to accept or to reject it.

This aspect of scientific investigation seems to me to have a parallel in the case of sound valuation and rational decision. In order to make a rational choice between several courses of action, we have to consider, first of all, what consequences each of the different alternative choices is likely to have. This affords a basis for certain relative judgments of value that are relevant to our problem. If *this* set of results is to be attained, this course of action ought to be chosen; if *that other* set of results is to be realized, we should choose such and such other course; and so forth. But in order to arrive at a decision, we still have to decide upon the relative values of the alternative sets of consequences attainable to us; and this, as was noted earlier, calls for the acceptance of an unconditional judgment of value, which will then determine our choice. But such acceptance need not be regarded as definitive and irrevocable, as forever binding for all our future decisions: an unconditional judgment of value, once accepted, still remains open to reconsideration and to change. Suppose, for example, that we have to choose, as voters or as members of a city administration, between several alternative social policies, some of which are designed to improve certain material conditions of living, whereas others aim at satisfying cultural needs of various kinds. If we are to arrive at a decision at all, we will have to commit ourselves to assigning a higher value to one or the other of those objectives. But while the judgment thus accepted serves as an unconditional and basic judgment of value for the decision at hand, we are not for that reason committed to it forever—we may well reconsider our standards and reverse our judgment later on; and though this cannot undo the earlier decision, it will lead to different decisions in the future. Thus, if we are to arrive at a decision concerning a moral issue, we have to accept some unconditional judgments of value; but these need not be regarded as ultimate in the absolute sense of being forever binding for all our decisions, any more than the evidence statements relied on in the test of a scientific hypothesis need to be regarded as forever irrevocable. All that is needed in either context are *relative* ultimates, as it were: a set of judgments—moral or descriptive—which are accepted at the time as not in need of further scrutiny. These relative ultimates permit us to keep an open mind in regard to the possibility of making changes in our heretofore unquestioned commitments and beliefs; and surely the experience of the past suggests that if we are to meet the challenge of the present and the future, we will more than ever need undogmatic, critical, and open minds.

The Exact Role of Value Judgments in Science

Michael Scriven

0. Introduction

If there is one set of arguments worse than those put forward for 'value-free science', it is those put forward against it. Both sets have one common characteristic, besides a high frequency of invalidity, and that is the failure to make any serious effort at a plausible analysis of the *concept* of 'value judgment', one that will apply to some of the difficult cases, and not just to one paradigm. Although the problem of definition is in this case *extremely* difficult, one can attain quite useful results even from a first step. The analysis proposed here, which goes somewhat beyond that first step, is still some distance from being satisfactory. Nevertheless, we must begin with such an attempt, since any other way to start would be laying foundations on sand. And we'll use plenty of prescientific examples, too, to avoid any difficulties with irrelevant technicalities. As we develop the definitions and distinctions, we'll begin putting them to work, so that we will almost complete the argument while seeming to be just straightening out the concepts. For this is really an area where the problem is a conceptual one, rather than an empirical or inferential one.

1. The Nature of Value Judgments

It is presumably a truism that a value judgment is a judgment of value, merit, or worth. From this basic meaning, other uses of the term are often generated by adding some extremely questionable philosophical position to the basic definition. For example, there are many contexts in which 'value judgment' is used as a synonym for 'dubious, unreliable, or biased judgment'. In *Webster's Third International Dictionary*, the illustrative quotation identifies it with prejudice or intolerance, although the definition given has no such implication. This can hardly make sense unless one assumes the truth of the view that all judgments of merit or worth are in fact biased, unreliable, intolerant. It is a measure of the extent to which the doctrine of value-free science has received support, that social scientists in introductory lectures, as well as in writing, typically make this assumption. One of the aims of this paper will be to demonstrate why the philosophical position just mentioned is unsound: but whether the reader's conclusions are the same or not, it would obviously be inappropriate to *begin* by begging the question, i.e., by accepting the identification of value judgments as a sub-species of unsubstantiated or unreliable judgments.

Again, one sometimes encounters usages which make it clear that people are even prepared to mingle the sense of 'value' in the mathematical descriptive phrase 'the value of a variable' (which refers to a number) with the sense of 'value' which is essentially equivalent to 'merit': we shall in general disregard this 'quantitative' sense of 'value' as an irrelevant ambiguity, though we shall indicate how it can be included in a comprehensive taxonomy of the term 'value'.

A related misconception involves the identification of the results of *any* act of judgment as a value judgment. This is sometimes related to the quantitative sense of 'value', e.g., when what is judged is the magnitude of a variable. But it is sharply distinct from the qualitative sense. There is a great difference between the assertion of a highway patrolman that you are going 'too fast for the conditions', which can reasonably be translated as 'faster than you should or ought to', i.e. (approximately) 'faster than it is right or good or proper to travel in these conditions'; and his judgment that you are traveling above the legal limit, which is 55 mph on this stretch of road. If he has just read a higher figure off a radar device, one probably wouldn't even use the term judgment in the latter case; but highway patrolmen have been known to give someone a ticket after passing them in the opposite direction, because, 'in their judgment', it was obvious that the pilgrim in question was traveling substantially above the speed limit. That's not a *value* judgment in the sense of concern to us here, although it *is* a judgment of the value of a variable, of course. The extreme form of this position takes judgments of *any properties*, e.g., color, as value judgments. This does not seem to be a useful generalization of the term's sense and we will operate with the idea that value judgments are a *sub*-species of judgments. To avoid some of the confusion due to the 'judgment' element, we'll generalize to talk about value *claims* most of the time.

2. Real-Value Claims

Claims about the *real* value, merit or worth about something—or its 'true' value—often mean something quite different from market value. They refer to 'absolute' value, in one sense. They may indeed be *contrasted* with market value, thereby demonstrating the difference. For example, we may say that the market 'undervalues' used Chrysler Imperial cars because of the prestige appeal of Cadillacs: obviously this only makes sense as a reference to a kind of value that goes beyond describing what people actually value. We may say that antique Bentleys aren't worth that much although they *cost* a lot; thereby thrusting the distinction into an alien context—but no one has difficulty understanding it. These real value claims are what the fight is all about. The great question is what kind of objectivity *they* can have.

What *do* we mean when we say that something isn't worth what we paid for it? Often we would support this claim if it was challenged, by saying things like this:

- "Look at what else you could have done with the money—you could have got some things you really need, . . ."
- "Those prices are just faddist—you could lose half your investment within days. . . ."
- It just isn't well *made*; look at the poor joinery work, the low grade of teak, etc."

These remarks remind us of the standards of 'true worth'—life and health and satisfaction, money (because of its translatability into other useful goods), constancy, reliability, utility, etc. Far from being ephemeral, subjective, like tastes and the market, *real* value is tangible, durable, useful, multifunctional—which doesn't mean that it's always easily measured, any more than forces and fields. Now these qualities—tangibility, etc.—are not so much values in themselves as guarantors of the reality of whatever the valued properties or objects are to which they are attached. Thus—for many people—good life insurance coverage is very valuable. To assert of such a policy that it really *is* a good one, that is, to make a real value claim about it, requires support in terms of evidence that the company will not go bankrupt, that the cost is not higher (without corresponding increases in benefits) than competitors, etc. For these considerations provide safeguards that increase the probability your investment will bring the most return in *your* currency; in this case, security for yourself and perhaps for others. In these commonsensical examples, it is easy to see just how the process of verification of real-value claims goes on and it seems absurd to suppose that no such claims are beyond reasonable doubt. Is there a general model of real-value claims that will enable us to see how they can be objectively confirmed?

    A simple way to conceptualize the logic of confirmation of real-value claims is to see them as representing the result of combining two kinds of evidence; the first being value-base evidence, the second performance data. To determine the merit of a particular life-insurance policy, we examine the needs, performances, and economic abilities of the purchaser; and we also examine the alternative policies he or she can purchase, for their performance on these dimensions. Often we can obtain a simple weighted sum of the performance variables (the weights representing the importance of each dimension of performance, inferred from the value-base) as an indicator of merit and the entry with the highest score is the winner. Or one may have to make a synthesizing judgment that cannot be reduced to a simple weighted-sum, as happens to be the case with life insurance where the fine print varies for each of the companies that deserve serious consideration. (See *Consumer Reports*, January, 1974.) Here indeed is a true judgment of value. But there is nothing arbitrary about it, any more than in the judgment of speed. Arguments can be given and assessed for the judgments made, and they can easily have the status of very reliable conclusions. This is what one might call the Consumers Reports (CR) approach.

The degree of generality of such a conclusion of merit will depend on the degree of commonality of the value bases of prospective policy holders, and on the size of the 'winner's' performance advantage. Naturally, conclusions will have to be phrased so as to reflect these constraints; "For young, single, securely employed people, the five-year term policy from X company is the best because. . . . " Even where there are huge disparities in the values base, they may be swamped by huge differences in the performance profiles of the candidates; thus, one may be able to conclude "Geico is the best company for automobile insurance, whatever your needs" (so long, of course, as they don't include the need to have Allstate write your insurance). Hence, very great differences in 'taste' or needs are perfectly compatible with a universally true (across all *people*) real-value claim.

The model so far described is sometimes said to provide inadequate foundation for real-value claims on the grounds that it only supports claims of the form "X is what this person will *think* is the best choice" (the rational decision-making model). But the CR model does *not* make predictive claims, since it is not committed to the further assumption predictions would required, the assumption that people are in fact rational. It is a normative model; it tells us what people *should* buy, prefer, etc. And it really can tell us what they *should* buy, not "what someone should buy *if* they have such and such preferences." For we can, as social scientists, determine whether they do in fact have those preferences, hence we can make a categorical and not just a conditional assertion about the 'Best Buy' for them, a typical real-value claim.

The only really serious threat to the objectivity of value judgments generated by the CR model is sometimes put as follows: "The model generates true value judgments only if the values that people have in their value bases are themselves *correct*. But *those* values cannot be shown to be correct by the CR model, since that would involve an infinite regression (to support them, we'd have to appeal to yet other values held by these people, which could in turn be called into question). And clearly the values people actually have are *not* always correct; certainly not morally, but also not even prudentially; i.e., egocentrically. So the CR model only does produce conditional evaluations, and the conditions are very questionable. Moreover, there is no *other* way to certify the rightness of the value-base values—at least no way that has any claim to scientific objectivity. So the CR approach simply fails to do what you claim it can do."

If we had to choose the one argument that has had the most effect on the most intelligent of those self-styled 'empiricists', 'behaviorists', or neo-positivists who have continued to believe in the ideal of value-free science, this argument is it. The argument is completely wrong, but not because of a formal fallacy. It is wrong in the way most common with philosophical arguments—it misrepresents a point of philosophical interest as one of practical significance (cf. the arguments about certainty, the external world, etc.). In this case, the argument is of sufficient importance to be criticized in two ways; first by *reductio ad absurdum*, and then by detailed analysis.

First, then, it will be argued that the same argument would destroy the descriptive part of science. Given that the argument is put forward by those who view the descriptive part of science as the paradigm of well-founded knowledge, this constitutes a reduction of the form of argument.

Such an application of the argument would go as follows. In order to support any descriptive conclusion in science that is not directly observable, we often attempt to construct an argument for it using premises that *are* observable, and we believe this can be done in all such cases. But it is well known that even observations can be mistaken, especially since we are well aware that what we call observation-statements are quite often impregnated with theoretical language and implicit assumptions. Thus circularity or infinite regression are involved. Since these built-in assumptions are not themselves reliable, and since there is no other way to establish descriptive assertions besides observation and inference from observations, it follows that there is no room in science for descriptive statements: for descriptive statements are either observably true or not, and we have just demonstrated weakness in both kinds.

The refutation of *this* argument rests on the fact that one can *increase* the probability of statements, to the point where they are beyond reasonable doubt, by *accumulating* observations and inferences that bear upon them. Only if one was engaged in a search for certainty that transcends the *logical* possibility of error could one complain about the reliability of well-supported scientific claims: and the search for *that* kind of super-certainty is irrelevant to the quest for scientific knowledge which has never laid claim to infallibility. Hence the argument does not show that descriptive claims have no place in science, only that they share with all scientific claims the possibility of error.

Applying the analogy to the attack on real-value claims, let's take a simple case. Suppose that we are evaluating methods of resuscitation and we conclude that the mouth-to-mouth method is the best one. This conclusion would be based on synthesizing the data on the relative performance in restoring the vital signs of alternative methods such as the Schaefer method; and the value-base data about the relative strength of people's desire to live versus their antipathy to catching a cold from the germs in the would-be deliverer's lungs, etc.

The skeptic's attack involves reminding us that these values may be in error. It is possible, he might argue, that it is better for the nearly drowned victim to die than to live since it is possible that the victim will live only to contract an agonizing and ultimately fatal disease, etc. Hence one cannot *assume* that *survival* is good, as the victim and rescuer both do. And without that assumption, one can't conclude that mouth-to-mouth is a *better* treatment here.

But one *can* make that assumption, indeed one should; *exactly* as—in the descriptive area—one should assume that the man whom you believe you have just seen shoot a policeman is dangerous. For assumptions should be made when the evidence strongly supports them. It will never do more than that, and it is a complete mistake to suppose it could and hence to suppose that assumptions should only be made when they are infallible.

The nature of all scientific inference and legal inference is to proceed via what are sometimes called *prima facie* cases, i.e. arguments that establish a *presumption* of something being the case, arguments (or observations) that make it 'reasonably probable'.

And that is all we do in the values are. 'Smoking is bad for (harmful to) your health' is value judgment and it's fallible—but only like any other scientific claim, including the 'pure performance' claims about carcinogens on which this claim is partly based. The other part of the basis is no more fallible; it's simply a series of value-base claims about the physical states people prefer to be in, from which the concept of health is constructed by combination with medical knowledge.

Skepticism about real-value claims is not more appropriate than skepticism about any other claims. When the coroner determines the cause of death, there always *might* be something else that's overlooked. But part of good medical (scientific) practice is exactly to search for the presence of other possible causes. When the physician recommends a certain treatment, there may of course be a side effect not yet identified, which will prove serious for this patient. What appears to be for the best may deceive us. Science can only reduce uncertainty, not eliminate it.

Now *one* subspecies of real-value claims is the set of moral judgments, the field of ethics. Another is aesthetics. Another is wine connoisseurship. The credentials of those fields require separate investigation, but the objectivity of real-value claims in general is in no way dependent on them. There is a moral version of the question whether any particular person's life or health should be saved, but that in no way shows that there isn't a nonmoral values issue involved, what one might call the purely medical issue; and the question of the 'best treatment' that we have just discussed is of that kind.

Naturally enough, there are borderline cases in medicine where the moral issues become deeply intertwined with the medical ones. But in general it is easy (and even there it is possible) to separate off not the scientific from the values issues, but the medical values issues from the moral ones. Eventually both must be recombined prior to justified action, but the evidence and expertise for each is different and it's usually helpful to work on them separately.

Let's look back at the line of argument in this subsection for a moment, to see if we've committed any obvious logical crimes. The most threatening candidate is the possibility that we've extracted 'ought' from 'is', i.e., value claims from factual ones, which Hume argued is always fallacious. And it's true that we've argued real-value claims are synthesized out of value-base and performance claims. That is, they have no other evidential base, and need none. But his doesn't violate Hume, though it's often thought to, since our synthesizing process may include a value premise as long as it's true by definition. For example, it might include the premise that whatever is valued is valuable, which is false, but useful to illustrate the point. If that premise were analytic (i.e., definitionally true) then we could legitimately perform the proposed synthesis, and produce conclusions about what is valuable from premises about value-bases.

The *actual* synthesizing principle to which we are committed does not admit of complete condensation into a brief formula—but it can be *approximated* by 'Being valued establishes a prima facie case for being valuable'. That is, unless countervailing considerations can be produced and substantiated, the fact that Smith wants to live provides a sound basis for the prima facie (real-value) conclusion that he should give up smoking.

The 'raw values' of a person or group are of course often inconsistent or inappropriate in view of the facts. The resources of logic and science are often severely strained to determine what *is* the best law to pass concerning, e.g., heroin pushers, even if we already know that 95% of the population favors the death penalty for this. But our difficulties in coming to the value conclusion in such a case do not for a moment show that we are appealing to some other basis for our values besides the value-bases of the people involved. We are simply taking into account *all* of the value-base of the people involved, and the relevant evidence from penology, physiology, etc. A doctor can justify his or her recommendation to the patient to give up a favorite recreation, thereby rejecting an element in the patient's value-base, simply by appeal to other elements in that same value-base—plus medical knowledge. The appeal may be to a single other element which is held more strongly or it may be several others of the same or less importance; or it may simply be to the facts, "Do you really know what it means to become addicted to barbiturates/to have a mongoloid child/to undergo irreversible sterilization? If you did know, you wouldn't continue to do what you've been doing—you wouldn't think the immediate gratification was worth it."

There are, of course, vicious forms of the argument that Doctor Knows Best, and part of the charm of the value-free ideal for some people is that it appears to leave the choices more squarely in the hands of the individual. But our concern here is not with the problem of minimizing the abuses of the correct position; it is only in determining that position. And just as people have long recognized the possibility that a great spiritual leader may lead them to see what is called 'the error of their ways', i.e., of their values, so it is entirely appropriate for a scientist, in certain circumstances, to identify errors of attitude, practice, and judgment in the values domain.

3. Value Judgments in Science

The groundwork we have laid can quickly provide an answer to the main question about the occurrence and role of value judgments in science. We can sum it up by saying that in the sense of the term 'value judgment' that is used in the strongest non-trivial arguments for a value-free science, the fact is that science is *essentially* evaluative, would not be science if it could not make and thoroughly support a whole range of value judgments.

Value judgments were classified . . . in terms of their logical characteristics. They can also be classified in terms of subject-matter, or general type of backing—one might say, domain. Thus there are practical value judgments ("You should never cross the leads when jump-starting an alternator-equipped automobile."), moral value judgments, and etiquette value judgments ("You should never smoke in the ring at sheep-dog trials."). The value language is not, properly speaking, ambiguous just because it can be used to express value judgments from such different domains with such varied force. It is simply context-dependent. The terms 'large' and 'small' are not ambiguous—even though they may be somewhat imprecise—just because a very large mouse is smaller than a very small elephant. Value-language, like size-relative language, should be thought of—understood—in terms of its *function* rather than some specific content. Its function is the same in all contexts, its specific content varies. (Cf. 'it', 'him', 'now'.)

Now one subject-matter category of value judgment is the methodological value judgment, that is the assessment of the merit or worth of methodological entities, such as experimental designs, theories, observations, explanations, estimates, (curve-) fits; and we will extend this concept to cover the hardware and software of method, so it will include the assessment of instruments, computers, and programs. A closely related category of value judgments, which I separate off only to avoid shudders from humanists, consists of judgments of the scientific merit of scientific performances, including the writing of articles, the presentation of papers, the doing of an experiment, etc. Of course, there are methodological value judgments in areas other than science, for example, the dance and the law; and there are extra-scientific performances. It is a natural step from performance to performer, and the scientific sub-species include the Great Scientist Game, the Nobel selection and the activities of other award and appointment committees.

I submit that learning to be a scientist involves learning to distinguish between good theories and bad theories, between good experimental designs and bad ones. Someone who could not make such discriminations could not distinguish good science from bad science, science from nonscience; and therefore could not be a scientist. Science itself is an evaluative term, in one of its principal uses: but even if it were not, the practice of science is an evaluative activity. Nor are the scientific evaluations only methodological: performance evaluations and performer evaluations, evaluations of projects, proposals and personnel by scientific standards are an essential part of the scientific activity.

Faced with these charges, it is a temptation for the value-free enthusiast to react by saying that that position never involved denying that *this* kind of activity went on. It was rather that *moral* value judgments, or *ultimate* value judgments, or some other special kind of value judgment were being disbarred.

Charitable we should be, but it is well to remember that *the reasons* usually given for the value-free position belie this defense. The reasons given were usually something about the impossibility of getting value judgments from facts, which was combined with the assumption that science's natural basic concern was with facts. We have now argued not only that in the relevant sense one *can* get value judgments from facts, but also that some facts are valuational, *and* that science is necessarily involved in making value judgments as part of its *basic* concerns. So that position looks a little tatterdemalion. Alternative versions speak of science as concerned with *descriptions*, which cannot yield *recommendations;* or of science as concerned with *means* and not with *ends*—and perhaps this one deserves direct comment.

First, science *is* concerned with ends; value-base claims describe them and have always been conceded to be scientifically legitimate. The claim must be refined to read: "Science is concerned only with the *assessment* of means, not that of ends. Ends can only be judged by reference to further ends; and to do this is to judge them as means. Ends which can't be thus judged cannot be judged scientifically. It is the evaluation of these ultimate ends which must be excluded from science."

The best reply to this is to roll with the punch and simply add; there are no ultimate ends, hence science can assess all ends as well as all means. Hence this distinction imposes no limits on science. There *are* no ends which cannot be related to, assessed in terms of their consequences for other ends. Of course, justice and art are often, in fact, pursued by a particular person as "ends in themselves. But science or—in the more general case—reason is not restricted by the limitations of one person. Justice can be assessed in terms of its contributions to social harmony, individual safety, and so on." (And the reverse is true.) So all ends are assessable.

Some people have a very strong sense that systems of knowledge must have a basically axiomatic or hierarchical structure. There *must*, they feel, be some *basic* ends or axioms from which all the rest follow. The power of this model has driven philosophers to phenomenology and logical empiricism, and ultimately to skepticism, in the epistemological area—and to relativism in axiology (value theory). The defects of the model are well known. If the axioms are definitional, they can't lead to knowledge about the world; if empirical, they need further justification ad infinitum. It is clear that the hierarchical reconstruction of knowledge, though a useful artifice for some purposes, is fundamentally misleading. One must adopt a 'bootstraps' model, or—as I prefer to call it—a network model of mutually interconnecting and reinforcing nodes of knowledge, linked by both analytic and empirical connections, both to the ground (reality) and to other nodes. This extremely vague picture is nevertheless sometimes enough to break the hold of the hierarchy model, which—even when one can see that it won't work, for the reasons given a moment ago—still has a bewitching force. But justification, in science and in law, is not a linear process; indeed, it is not in mathematics either, except within an *artificial* system.

So science has no need to assume ultimate ends to justify value judgments, since they *can* be justified in other ways. Justification is always a context-dependent process, only making sense insofar as it can connect the acceptable with the debatable, and we are never concerned in science to provide justifications whose premises are infallible, only those whose premises are acceptable to the rational person, i.e., immune to the sources of error that we are trying to avoid by means of a justification. So we justify claims about the carcinogenic properties of cigarettes by appealing to data that is more reliable; and similarly we can justify claims about the harmfulness of smoking. In neither case do we need to find premises that are beyond all possibility of error for eternity.

Hence, *even if* science were unable to justify claims about ultimate ends, it could justify value judgments in just the way it justifies non-value judgments.

But in fact science can also provide some ultimate premises from which value judgments can be inferred: and these are *definitionally true value judgments*. For example, it can reasonably be argued that a watch is a time-keeping device by definition and hence that being an *accurate* timekeeper will be a *merit* in a watch. (Similarly with regard to portability, legibility, etc.) We need only combine this value-premise with some performance data to generate value judgments. The whole idea that value judgments must be built—ultimately—on an *arbitrary* assumption becomes absurd with regard to such cases. Nor are they unusual. Methodological value judgments are *typically* built on definitional or quasi-definitional premises. The 'ultimate values' lying behind assertions about the merit of a particular hypothesis are claims such as "Good hypotheses explain or predict or summarize more phenomena, or do it more simply, than bad ones." Even if we have to elaborate this under the pressure of counterexamples, it's a pretty close approximation to a definitional truth.

Quite apart from its use as a basis for value judgments about specific hypotheses—for which purposes, of course, we have to combine it with 'performance' data about the latter—the simple fact is that propositions like the one just given are value judgments themselves and definitionally true. Hence they constitute an exceptionally powerful counter-example to the skeptical view about the objectivity of value judgments.

Both the specific and the definitional false judgments we are now discussing thus provide an independent line of attack on the doctrine of value-free science. And a simpler line than the one we elaborated as the CR model, where the 'ultimate value' was an empirical value-base claim. We covered that case first because it shows us much more about the real logic of evaluation than the present rather 'lucky' cases where the chain of justification strikes gold in the form of a definitional premise.

Another justification procedure besides the theoretical regress, the CR model, and the definitional one is the functional one. If one can identify the function of a device or social institution, then one can argue that the better it is performed, the better the device (etc.) is—other things being equal. The functional analysis will usually not be a matter of definition itself—though in the case of the watch it is—but it may be possible to establish it beyond reasonable doubt. It is easier with artifacts, harder with social institutions, as long experience in anthropology has shown; but it is a proper task of science to do functional analysis.

We can conclude this section with a few other brief arguments about the role of value judgments in science. The examples we have been discussing so far apply just as well to the purest of pure science as to applied science. Even the mathematician has to make methodological and performance value judgments. But one should of course add that the applied scientist must often make many more. When the cancer researcher has to evaluate proposed treatments, he or she gets into what should be a scientific procedure of identifying relevant criteria from value-base and general performance considerations. Then these criteria are combined with the specific performance data on the treatments, to yield value judgments. What is evaluated here is not itself a component of science; and the value-base data here do not refer to the values of scientists qua scientists, as they do when we are evaluating, e.g., the relative merit of bubble against cloud chambers for a particular kind of investigation. But—'external' to science though the object under evaluation may be—the *process* is (should be) entirely scientific.

It is of particular interest that in some few cases of applied science—medicine (especially psychiatry) and education are perhaps the most obvious examples—the evaluative criteria apparently *must* include some moral considerations. It doesn't make much sense to talk of the patient's overall improvement after psychotherapy, no matter how much better the patient feels, if his behavior towards others has become totally ruthless, even if he can get away with it; or to talk of a successful outcome of a remedial reading program which has incidentally indoctrinated the students with violent racist attitudes. These cases appear to be quite different from the commonplace situation in which the application of science, e.g., to pest control or breeder reactor design, will (probably always) raise moral problems. The apparent difference is that in these latter cases the criteria for scientific success, the definition of the problem in scientific terms, does not necessarily involve moral issues. The scientific problem, it appears, can be separated from the social problem of when to employ the scientific solution.

The distinction will not really hold up, but the correct way to treat the matter is not the traditional one. We could define a 'purely scientific' problem in the psychotherapy or education case, as in the reactor or agricultural case. But to do so is immensely inefficient, for it leads to the development of solutions—at great expense—that either cannot be used, or require expensive modification to be used. Applied science *involves* the skill of problem-specification. It takes a good applied scientist to identify and conceptualize all the relevant considerations that make up the problem. And since the effects of a pesticide on farm workers, crop-dusting pilots, river and bay aquatic life, and city water drinkers are serious, the *problem* is to create or discover one that minimizes these (and other) undesirable side-effects while maximizing the destruction of pests affecting the crops. In determining how heavily to weight the effects to be minimized, the scientist is entering the moral domain and *there is no one who can do that for him*. The value-free ideal presented a picture of the applied scientist as receiving the value judgments from a shadowy figure in the wings, adding these to the scientific parameters to get the specification of the problem, and then bringing in his or her scientific skills to create the solution. Now what of course happened in practice was that the scientist ignored any external values unless someone was yelling about them very loudly, specified what looked like the 'practical' problem ('kill pests') in scientific terms and solved that, if possible. I am not recommending getting the scientist into the moral issues on the grounds that they otherwise get under-emphasized, though that might independently be a good reason, but because the previous procedure was incompetent. The problem to be solved had been incorrectly specified, and the error did not lie with the 'layman', whoever that might be, but with the scientist, who knows very well from many sad experiences that one cannot usually rely on 'outsiders'' specifications of problems, whether the outsider is lay or a specialist in another area; one must understand the problems and analyze them oneself as part of the scientific project. True, there can sometimes be minions who can be given micro-problems to solve without being expected to check on the formulation, but we are talking about huge university research departments (in the agricultural case, for example), mostly working independently of each other. More of *them* should have been criticizing the over-limited formulation of the problems being proposed by industry even if such formulations could not be questioned by the chemists actually on the industries' payrolls.

It is, then, an (applied) scientific necessity to look into the moral dimension of problems because that dimension is part of the problem: it will be so, even if morality is just an arbitrary system of conventions.

The behavior modification enthusiasts in education could probably solve the 'scientific problem' of classroom discipline, by wiring students to an electro-shock network controlled from the teacher's desk, but this is simply not the correct formulation of the problem—and for moral reasons.

Bomb design and chemical-biological warfare provide extreme examples of the same point; but it should not be confused with the moral but not—in the same sense—scientific problem of whether such work is ever justified. Deciding *that* is an obligation on any person, scientist or not, engaged in such a project. Deciding how to conceptualize and weight destructive power of a bomb, a morally significant variable, is—on the other hand—part of the scientific problem.

An extreme case of great interest affects political science, although the 'empiricist' political scientists kept wishing it wouldn't. This is the problem of justification and criticism of the forms of government, such as democracy. It would take a book to document the conceptual confusion surrounding this issue over the past four or five decades, most of it stemming from the clash of the two facts: (a) justification involves values and hence on the prevailing views could have no place in political science,

(b) if political science in a political system called a democracy wasn't prepared to discuss the question of the merits of political systems, including democracies, it could in no way deserve its title. After all, the noblest talk of physics has always been the critical scrutiny of the prevailing system of physics, of psychiatry the prevailing concept of mental health, etc. The touching idea that such matters could be left to political philosophy didn't seem quite satisfactory; after all, had Einstein or Schrödinger left the questions of the foundations of their subjects to philosophers of science? Should they have? Obviously not. The justification of basic positions in a science is a task for *both* the scientist and the philosopher.

Thus I am here suggesting a considerable broadening of the scope of science, compared to the neo-positivist conception. It could be illustrated with a dozen different examples. It is nothing short of tragic to read van der Graaf's farewell to welfare economics, a subject he abandoned after making significant contributions because he saw that the basic problems could not be handled without leaving the realm of science for the realm of value theory, which he took to be forbidden territory. The literature of theoretical psychiatry is rent by the cleft between people like Szasz who see the moral dimension as an essential part of the problem, and those who see it as scientifically irrelevant.

4. Ethics as a Science

The most powerful way to prove that value judgments have a place in science is to prove that ethics is a science. I believe it is, potentially at least, though not for the usual reasons. Given the preceding arguments, it is clear that one can construct a type of ethics by addressing the applied social science problem of determining the optimal set of social rules and attitudes for a society facing given economic, psychological, and environmental constraints, where 'optimal' is defined pre-morally, i.e., only with regard to the value bases of the elements in the society. Since the system resulting will probably cover about the same domain of behavior, etc., as what is traditionally called ethics, and will involve about as many of the traditional moral precepts as any two traditional ethical systems share, and since it will not involve anything notably different, it is entitled to be called ethics. And since it can be scientifically justified, it's entitled to be viewed as the only defensible system of ethics, alternative justifications for ethics having been long since exposed as untenable. (Detailed support for this long string of controversial assertions is suggested in *Primary Philosophy*, McGraw-Hill, 1966.)

Put the matter another way. It is part of science, especially sociology and anthropology, to do functional analysis of social institutions. Very well; let one be done of the ethical system of a given society. It is part of science to identify the value-base of social beings; let this be done for the same society. It will now be *entailed* that some of the ethical rules of that society cannot be justified with regard to their needs/wants/values; or that other parts can; or both. If, for example, their rule against killing is functional, then it's justified and it *is* wrong to kill in that society. (Note that any society interacting with others cannot have the functionality of its rules determined only by considering its own value-base, since disregard of the other value-base may well lead to disastrous results.)

Of course, there are many troublesome details that could turn into disasters for the above account, though in fact I believe they do not (and so argue in the reference given). But I would stress the following warning. The crudest common-sense consideration makes it obvious that there is an excellent justification for a society to have a system of law. The simplest science reveals that much of a given system of ethics can be treated as an internalized extension of law. Hence, unless a clear proof of impossibility can be given, it's obvious that a good slice of ethics can be social-scientifically justified and (probably) another slice rejected, which also can be justified. Incidentally, the justification for, e.g., accepting or banning adultery and homosexuality, certainly requires scientific investigation of their consequences. Conversely, that scientific investigation plus one into the value-base of the society, provides a *prima facie* reason for (or against) the existing moral rule, i.e., a scientific justification for (a part of) ethics. I repeat that this isn't a proof, it's a sketch. My criticism is that scientists have for decades been trained in a way that made them incapable of seeing the possibility of such an argument, *even though* they were not trained to see what was wrong with it. That is, they thought the idea of ethics as a science was absurd, but had no good reasons for the position. It is no wonder that, without cracking a smile, without any sense of absurdity, without ever looking at the possibility of self-refutation, they taught their students: "It is scientifically improper to make value judgments." They might as well have said, "Thou shalt not ever say: 'Thou shalt not ever say'."

One should not close this section without stressing that philosophers were not much better off. In the fifties, the 'in' view was emotivism or non-cognitivism, the doctrine that value judgments were mere expressions of feeling, lacking any propositional content at all, and hence incapable of verification or falsification. Even today, tawdry 'refutations' of pragmatism or utilitarianism are bandied about without serious examination, and most philosophers still think the so-called naturalistic fallacy of Moore and the classic argument of Hume make the facts/value or ought/is distinction secure. But John Searle's crusade has shaken this stance lately (in *Speech Acts*, Oxford, 1971) and to some extent Rawls' *Theory of Justice* (Harvard, 1972) and the 'good reasons' school in ethics have provided an alternative approach.

5. The Bad Reasons

In the end one has to ask how it came about that scientists should have accepted a view of their own subject which is so patently unsound. There are, I think, many contributory factors. One major factor is the very poor training in self-scrutiny that characterizes most scientists' background, something that becomes embarrassingly obvious when they move beyond their own specialty without noticing that useful precepts of scientific practice in quantum physics are not 'the scientific method' and do not apply at all in certain other areas of science or non-science. (I have in mind here the particle physicist's tendency to assume the universal merit of the frequency theory of probability, or the macro-physicist's insistence upon repeatability as a criterion which makes para-psychology unscientific.) The lack of concern with the history of e.g., psychology, in which many issues fought over later were comprehensively disposed of (the 'puzzle' of inversion of the retinal image, for example) is another index of lack of self-scrutiny by the scientists.

Allied with this innocence was the powerful pressure of the desire that science be value-free, a desire held for much the same reasons that Weber had when he first proposed the thesis. The values area is messy, controversial, and you can get on the wrong side and hurt yourself politically. Why rock the boat? The society has treated science well, or tolerated its extravagances. Why start criticizing *it*?

Of course, to concede on values in science is not to concede on politics in science; but perhaps scientists instinctively felt it was better to defend the forward position and fall back if necessary. But when the enemy gets the momentum of attack going, he doesn't wait for you to regroup or even prepare the long-neglected yet defensible position. And indeed you find that you have forgotten exactly where it is.

On the other side, the arguments were at least as bad. If the doctrine of value-free science is now in considerable disrepute amongst the intelligentsia, it is mainly for an irrelevant reason. That is, what has brought it down is the recognition of the huge social costs and commitments of science. "Science is not value-free," the radical is fond of saying: "Its values are those of the establishment." True enough, true of scientists, and of science as a social phenomenon. But never denied by the value-free supporter, who was only arguing that the *content* of science is value-free, not that its *effect* has no social significance. Nor was the claim ever made that scientists could somehow choose to be scientists (or physicists, etc.) without having and thereby exhibiting their values; the claim was that *after* that choice had been made, while they were in the laboratory, they were free of the need (or possibility) of making value judgments *in the name of science*.

Many crimes have been committed in the name of science, but none so serious as this withholding of that name.

The Structure of the Argument

Richard Nicholson, Richard Hale, et al.

Our talk in this report is not merely to make recommendations but to give reasons for them. It is therefore necessary to offer some account of how we think one can argue for conclusions in this field. Since the conclusions are about what ought or ought not to be done or permitted, the arguments will be moral or ethical arguments; and the discipline which assesses such arguments is moral philosophy, or ethics in the narrow philosophical sense. As we shall see, however, the two main approaches to moral argument which have been advocated by philosophers are, both of them, more sophisticated versions of ways of thinking which suggest themselves quite naturally to non-philosophers when they have to think about moral questions. This is in part because the thinking of ordinary people has been deeply, if unconsciously, influenced by what philosophers have said in the past; but more because those philosophers themselves were making explicit certain tendencies which were already there in everyday thinking. Our problem will be to find a way of combining both these approaches in a consistent procedure which could be used by, say, an ethics committee when considering a particular research project. But first we must explain each approach separately.

The first approach bases itself on rights and duties. Most of us think that people have rights which it is the duty of other people to respect. We also think that there are other duties besides the duty to respect people's rights. In our present field we need not look far for examples. If we think of any doctor and

51

any patient of his, we shall be in no doubt that the doctor has the duty to do what he can to cure or alleviate the patient's trouble; not to cause harm to the patient unless that is required for the purpose of achieving some greater good for him, and then only with his consent; not to use his professional relationship to secure for himself advantages which lie outside the implied contract with his patient (for example, he may rightly expect to be paid for his services, but ought not to seek to obtain sexual favours or a place in the patient's will); not to divulge information given in confidence; and so on. These duties are commonly expressed in another way, by saying that the patient has a right to have or not to have this or that done to him.

In a research project the subject is sometimes the patient of the researcher and sometimes not. If he is, then all the above duties will be held to apply, and there may be a conflict between them and the furtherance of the research. If he is not, some of these duties may be absent (for example, the researcher has no duty to try to cure the subject) but those duties will remain which anybody, whether he is a doctor or not, owes to his fellow human beings: for example, not to subject him to physical interventions without his consent; not to lie to him, or make promises that he is not going to fulfil.

The researcher may also think that he has, as a scientist, other duties not so far mentioned. In becoming a scientist, he has dedicated himself to the increase of knowledge, and thus to the duty of pursuing the truth even at considerable cost to himself. If he is a medical scientist, it will not be merely truth for truth's sake that he is pursuing; he will be inspired by the hope that his discoveries may benefit mankind by making possible new therapies, and he will think that this lays on him a duty to make every effort to further his research. This applies to many other kinds of scientist—indeed, to any researcher, for example, a physiologist or a psychologist or a chemist or an engineer— whose discoveries might be of practical use. It is easy to see how in clinical research this duty can conflict with others that we have mentioned. For example, an intervention which is necessary for the research may risk harming the subject without hope of any compensating benefit to him.

Rights and duties are the main preoccupation of the so-called deontological school of moral philosophers. They usually base themselves on the common moral convictions that most of us have, using them as data in much the same way as empirical science uses the facts of observation. In the words of Sir David Ross, 'The moral convictions of thoughtful and well-educated people are the data of ethics just as sense-perceptions are the data of a natural science. Just as some of the latter have to be rejected as illusory, so have some of the former; but as the latter are rejected only when they are in conflict with other more accurate sense-perceptions, the former are rejected only when they are in conflict with other convictions which stand better the test of reflection.'[1] The method employed is thus intuitive: it consists in an appeal to moral intuition of a sort that can dispense with argument. As H.A. Prichard, one of the leaders of the school, said, 'If we do doubt whether there is really an obligation to originate *A* in a situation *B*, the remedy lies not in any process of general thinking, but in getting face to face with a particular instance of the situation *B*, and then directly appreciating the obligation to originate *A* in that situation.'[2]

As well as being intuitionists, such philosophers are usually pluralists: they claim to find in our common moral convictions a plurality of principles which cannot be reduced to one another or to some higher single principle. Thus, the duty not to interfere with other people's bodies is a different principle from the duty not to deceive them, and both are different from the duty to be just in apportioning punishments and rewards. These duties are independent of one another and independently recognized. Most deontologists., however, try to reduce their principles to a manageable number—a list of duties from which the rest can be derived. Among those relevant to our enquiry we may mention duties of beneficence and non-maleficence; the duty to act justly or fairly; and the duty not to deceive. Virtues and principles of these four kinds are made the basis of his moral system by G.J. Warnock, who, however, gives as his reason for commending them that their recognition would 'work towards amelioration of the human predicament'.[3] This is in substance a utilitarian reason and therefore would bring him within the scope of the second approach to be considered below, although he does not call himself a utilitarian.

Besides these principles which apply generally to everybody, there are also thought to be particular duties which attach to certain roles. We have already mentioned the doctor's particular duty to his own patients to promote their health and respect their confidences, and the scientist's duty to pursue the truth. And, as we have seen, to some of these duties there correspond rights: thus the patient has a right that his doctor should give promotion of the patient's health priority over the interests of other people who might eventually be benefited by discoveries made in the course of research on the patient; and those who are paying the scientist have a right that he should pursue his research (indeed, this will often be in his contract of employment).

This kind of deontology or pluralistic intuitionism is tailored to fit the convictions of ordinary people; and consequently it accords so well with them that it has with good reason been called 'the moral philosophy of the man in the street'. However, it does face certain difficulties, to which we shall return. If the duties it lays on us are treated as absolute and admitting of no exceptions, there will be a problem of what we ought to do if they conflict in particular cases, as they seem often to do. On the other hand, if they are treated as only prima-facie obligations (Ross's term), any of which can be overridden by another in cases of conflict, then an account has still to be given of how to decide which is to override which. Usually, deontologists at this point make a further appeal to intuition to settle the conflict: one of the duties will be perceived on reflection as more stringent than the other. But if a doctor who is also a researcher is in doubt whether he may properly take a blood sample at some small risk to his patient in order to further an important piece of research, his intuitions may not give a firm answer, and different people's intuitions may give different answers.

There is also the general problem of how we should justify the moral convictions on which we are to place so much weight. In the past, people have had some moral convictions which most of us would now repudiate, such as the conviction that wives ought to obey their husbands in all things. And at the present time, if children say that the sexual morality of their parents is a set of irrational taboos, can the parents quash this objection by appealing to their own moral convictions? Our common moral convictions may be sound, but it would be good to have a way of showing why they are.

In contrast to this deontological approach via rights and duties, we find in the literature, alongside it, much said about calculations of the risks and benefits attached to particular pieces of research. The idea is that if the benefits likely to be achieved (either to the patient, or to our knowledge of his disorder, or to medical science in general) are greater than the risks incurred, then the research is justified.

This kind of calculation is often called risk/benefit or cost/benefit analysis, and is used in many fields. It is, as we shall see, far from being generally accepted as a safe way of making moral decisions. But, like the deontological approach, it has a natural appeal. What could be more obvious, it might be said, than that we ought, when engaging in any activity involving risk to ourselves and our fellow men and women, to balance the risks against the likelihood of benefit, not incurring any risk that is not justified by the benefits to be expected. In more technical language, and in fields such as economics where it is thought that the risks and benefits can at least in theory be quantified, it is said that the product of the probability of an outcome and its utility (positive or negative) should be taken as its 'expected utility', and that action chosen which maximizes the 'expectation of utility', i.e., the sum of those products over all possible outcomes of an action.

This is in accord with a simple version (too simple to be acceptable) of the philosophical position known as utilitarianism. Positive and negative utility (benefit and harm) are now commonly defined in terms, not of pleasure or even happiness, as the classical utilitarians often did, but of preference-satisfaction.[4] It is important, however, to specify *who* expects the utility or disutility (hopes for the benefit or faces the risk of harm). A completely selfish risk/benefit analysis might be done by an individual purely in his own interest. Or someone (for example, a doctor) might do such an analysis purely in the interest of another individual (his patient). Suppose, for instance, that he balances the risk of death from an operation against the hope of a complete recovery. Only probabilities of benefits and harm to that individual will then be considered. Groups as well as individuals can reason in this way: such, perhaps, were the strategic analyses done by the American forces in Vietnam, which were concerned only with benefits to American policy, not to the Vietcong.

On the other hand, there could be a completely impartial risk/benefit analysis in which the risk of harm or the benefit to *anybody* counted equally. It is the second, impartial kind of analysis which utilitarianism prescribes. It has, indeed, been attacked on precisely this ground, that it bids a doctor treat his professional duty to his own patients as of no greater weight than benefits he might confer on all and sundry by his researches.

This is only one example of a kind of criticism of utilitarianism which has been extremely common and has seemed conclusive to many. It proceeds by bringing utilitarianism into conflict with common moral convictions (the same as form the basis of deontological systems). Cases are adduced in which a utilitarian, seeking to maximize the expectation of utility, would have not merely to condone but to prescribe actions which most people would agree to be manifestly wrong. A common example in the literature is that of the surgeon who arranges to waylay and murder an innocent person, extracts his kidneys and other organs, and transplants them into his own patients, thereby saving several lives at the expense of one. Such a course, it is said, should be prescribed by a utilitarian, because the benefit to the greater number outweighs the cost to the one. The same might be said if the victim, instead of being quarried for transplants, were made the subject of scientifically useful experiments which benefited mankind in general. Most such criticisms rely on the rights of people which everybody recognizes, not to have this kind of thing done to them, and on our duty to respect such rights.

There has thus seemed to be a tension between utilitarian thinking, with its risk/benefit analyses and its stress on the consequences of actions and on impartiality between the interests of everybody, and deontological thinking, with its appeals to rights and duties irrespective of consequences, and to duties to particular people in accordance with those people's rights, which are not owed to others. Yet both approaches have a firm basis in our ordinary moral thinking: we do attach importance to risks and benefits, and we do treat certain rights as sacrosanct, quite regardless of the benefits to be secured by infractions of them.

It is important to notice that this tension exists even *within* deontology, if it admits duties of beneficence and non-maleficence. These duties are, indeed, a kind of fragment of utilitarianism inside deontology, and conflicts can arise as well between them and the deontologist's other principles as between deontology and utilitarianism as a whole. These moral conflicts are at the centre of the dispute between the schools, and our working group has had to consider whether there could be any way of reconciling the two approaches in a practical procedure for addressing them which would retain the insights of both.

One way that has been suggested is to treat certain entrenched rights as side-constraints upon our utilitarian calculations, or, as R.M. Dworkin puts it, as 'trumps'.[5] That is to say, if to do the best for all considered impartially would involve infringing one of these rights, the rights are to prevail. That, it is suggested, is why we are not to commit murder however great the balance of benefits over costs. Although in that case the suggestion is attractive, it does not overcome all the difficulties. It does not tell us how to decide *which* rights ought to be entrenched in this way. And it does not allow us to say, as we may often want to say, that some rights can be overridden when great disasters will ensue if they are respected, but that lesser benefits will not justify their infringement. An example is where we undoubtedly infringe people's rights to liberty by confining them in quarantine in order to control epidemics. In the field of our present enquiry, shall we not want to say that some relatively minor interventions, which everybody would think justified if the benefits to medical science were enormous, would be unjustified if the benefits were small or uncertain? But the black-and-white character of the 'trumps' theory does not allow it to make such distinctions.

A more sophisticated suggestion relies on the separation of moral or ethical thinking into at least two levels. At the practical level at which most of us operate for most of the time, what the deontologists and pluralists and intuitionists say is largely correct. We do have a plurality of intuitive principles, many of them concerned with people's rights and duties, and we do treat these principles as having great authority. We react instantly and with strong repugnance to proposed breaches of them by ourselves or others; for practical purposes we treat some of them as sacrosanct, and all as of dominant importance. Many are enshrined in codes of ethics and lists of human rights. And it is a good thing that we think like this, because if we allowed ourselves to carry out elaborate risk/benefit analyses on particular occasions, we should nearly always get them wrong, either from a human inability to predict the consequences of our actions, or from an equally human tendency to deceive ourselves about the probabilities of benefit and harm. A researcher may convince himself that he will revolutionize the treatment of cancer by carrying out some questionable experiment, when his more judicious and less involved colleagues could tell him that the risks were much greater than he thinks and the likelihood of a major breakthrough very small. That is why we have ethics committees to sanction research projects, and why they should have firm guidelines such as we shall propose.

However, though it is right that we should think like deontologists in the normal course of our life and practice, it may be suggested that something has been left out of the account. Intuitive thinking is, as we have seen, not self-sustaining. We need a way of deciding what principles we should entrench, what intuitions we should cultivate, and what to do when they conflict. What is to be the content of the education of the 'thoughtful and well-educated people' who are Ross's court of appeal (see above)? When people are training to be doctors, or becoming researchers, what ought their seniors to say to them? And how are they to know whether their seniors are giving the best advice, when so much in medicine is changing that different principles may be appropriate to new conditions? To cope with this problem, it is suggested that a higher, 'critical', level of thinking is needed, by which we can criticize the principles and intuitions used at the lower level, and adjudicate between them in particular conflicts.

This higher level, it is suggested, is utilitarian. We should have, and teach, and cultivate in ourselves, those intuitions and those intuitive principles whose general acceptance in the profession and outside it will do the best, all in all, for those affected, considered impartially. (For discussion of this proposal, see Griffin, op. cit.) The advocates of this view will often go on to say that nearly all the traditional principles and rights, including those mentioned earlier, could be justified, in general, by this kind of thinking. It *is* for the best, for example, that doctors should acknowledge special duties to their own patients, including the duty to respect their privacy and bodily integrity, unless the patients consent to invasions of them. If people, and doctors in particular, were not brought up to respect these principles, much more harm than good would result in the field of health care.

It will, however, sometimes happen, as we have seen, that sound general principles conflict with one another in particular cases. Most people would agree that research leading to the advancement of medical knowledge ought not to be hampered. And most people would agree that patients and other subjects have a right not to be experimented on without their consent. Deontologists may say that these common convictions need no justification. Utilitarians will say that they can be justified by the obvious utility of accepting them. We do not need much imagination to see the harm that would come of allowing researchers to shanghai people against their will and cut them up: confidence in the medical profession would be diminished, to put it mildly. And yet the benefits of increased medical knowledge are immense. So what is an ethics committee, to which a particular research project is submitted for approval, to do when, if it blesses a project, patients' rights will be infringed, but if it does not, important and useful research will be inhibited? This dilemma confronts us even when the proposed research subjects are adults; with children there are, as we shall see, further complications.

To some extent these problems can be coped with in advance by adopting general guidelines which attempt to hold a balance between the principles. Our enquiry will suggest guidelines of this sort. We shall assume, for example, that the requirement of consent to an experiment should be treated as sacrosanct in the case of competent adult subjects, because of the harm that would come of any weakening of this principle, the discussion and justification of which is outside our terms of reference. And, in extending the principle to children, we shall propose that proxy consent by parents or guardians should be allowable, subject to severe restrictions on the extent of the risks to which children may be thus submitted.

In determining the precise degree of risk, those of different philosophical persuasions will proceed differently. If we think that our common convictions need no justification, we shall appeal to general consensus, among those who have reflected on the problem, that that is the limit of acceptable risk. If, on the other hand, we either cannot find any such consensus, or do not regard mere consensus as enough of an argument (because people might come to think differently) we shall seek deeper foundations for the same practical prescriptions by pointing out the evil consequences that would result if the limits were put higher, or lower, than we propose. If they are put lower, then research which could be of value will be stopped in order to preserve the rights of children in cases where the preservation of those rights would make a negligible difference to the children's welfare or safety. To use the same example as before: the taking of small blood samples by pricking children's fingers, with consent of their parents and assent by the children, might be forbidden, even if the research project were likely to be of appreciable value. On the other hand, if the limits were put higher, then there would be danger that potentially quite harmful experiments would be allowed just because researchers with gleams in their eyes had prevailed on parents who did not fully understand what was being proposed, or upon gullible or perfunctory or complaisant ethics committees.

A case we have already mentioned illustrates the type of decision that may face us in framing or applying guidelines. A researcher asks to be allowed to perform a renal biopsy for research purposes on a child who is undergoing an abdominal operation. We have expressed the opinion . . . that the risk from this is more than negligible. Should it nevertheless be permitted if very great benefits are expected from the research? In the example reported we doubt whether this was so. We have similar doubts whether it would ever be the case in practice that the benefits justified the risk. We think that the likelihood that *both* the benefits would be very great *and* there would be no other way of obtaining them is small. Therefore, we think that sound guidelines would forbid such an intervention. The deontologist will justify such guidelines on the basis of the rights of the child, and claim that these rights themselves require no further justification. The utilitarian will agree that the child should be accorded these rights, but justify the according of them, and the actual guidelines, by appeal to the evil consequences that will ensue if the rights are not safeguarded: loss of confidence in the medical profession being only one of these.

The different approaches of deontologists and utilitarians to problems such as we face can be further illustrated by a more extreme, but hypothetical, example which is unlikely actually to confront an ethics committee, but is typical of the imaginary cases adduced by deontologists in their arguments with utilitarians. The utilitarians, if they know the ropes, will protest that such unlikely examples are a bad guide to practice in more usual cases ('hard cases make bad law'). We have not found any actual examples in which a utilitarian of the sort we are considering would be committed to approving flagrant violations of commonly accepted human rights. In all the actual cases of high risk known to us, either the research was of insufficient value to be justified by a risk/benefit analysis, or there were other less dangerous ways of completing the research. Since our task is to find guidelines for use in actual cases not imaginary ones, the latter are irrelevant to our practical problem.

However, waiving this objection by utilitarians, suppose that a brain physiologist, on the basis of highly supportive animal experiments, made a scientifically sound proposal for direct experiments on the brains of psychotic infants using implanted microelectrodes, direct brain biopsy and other invasive but only moderately life-threatening methods; and suppose that there was not much doubt, on the evidence, that such experiments would be quite likely to afford a basis for important advances in medical understanding of the biophysical basis of these disorders and thus in their treatment and prevention. Should the rule against harming the individual then be obeyed, or should it be ignored in favour of the course of action judged to give the greatest expectation of utility; namely, allowing the experiment? Should the children's parents be even *asked* for consent to such procedures?

A utilitarian of the sophisticated sort we are considering might seek to avoid this commitment. He might say that if ethics committees are to act for the best, they ought to form for themselves strict guidelines and stick to them. It is, he might say, very unlikely that any set of guidelines that was acceptable even from a purely utilitarian point of view would permit such experiments. For if it were known that ethics committees permitted this sort of thing, there would be widespread public revulsion prejudicing not merely medical research but the entire standing of the medical profession, to the great detriment of health care. People would cease to trust their doctors.

It would be of no use to the deontologist to suggest that the experiments might be kept secret; for this is not the sort of thing that can be concealed for long, and the research would be of little value unless published. Nor would it do for him to suggest that in a different sort of society (Nazi Germany, for example) arrangements could be made to carry out such experiments without interference from the public; for the utilitarian has good grounds for condemning such regimes in general, as likely to do much more harm than good to their subjects and the world. The deontologist might, however, claim that the utilitarian's argument has only succeeded on the basis of an assumption that the public's sentiments are unalterable; they are disposed to be outraged by such practices, and the outrage would rebound on the entire system of health care; so the practices should be forbidden. But what if the public itself could be converted to utilitarianism? Could not public and researchers then approve such experiments and worse?

To this the utilitarian might reply that this would not be 'a conversion to utilitarianism', because such a change in attitudes would be itself undesirable from the utilitarian point of view. If the public and doctors could approve such procedures, it would be a sign that there was something radically wrong with their attitudes—something that would lead to much greater harm than good in society as a whole. One could not, he might say, treat children (any children) as disposable in this way without entirely altering one's attitude to children in general and even to adults as well. One would be on a slippery slope which might really lead to support for a regime like that of the Nazis. The data for moral thinking include facts about what attitudes are humanly combinable; if *in practice* to let one principle go will lead to the sacrifice of a whole lot more, that is a reason for stopping earlier rather than later. Precisely where one should stop can be a matter for debate; but the utilitarian is allowed by his theory to have as strong views about this as anybody else, provided that the facts of our actual situation support them. The 'slippery slope' argument has, no doubt, often been abused, because not all slopes are *in practice* slippery (there are firm resting-places on many of them); but this one clearly is.

It is only apparently paradoxical for our sophicated utilitarian to say that ethics committees should not, in considering individual cases, always think in terms of utilities, or that the public ought not to be encouraged to do likewise. It will be remembered that the kind of utilitarian that we are considering thinks morally at two levels. It is perfectly self-consistent for him to recognize the utilitarian basis of all thinking, but to recognize also that this itself requires him, when considering practical proposals, to be guided by firm principles (of the same sort as the deontologist has adopted for his own kinds of reason), because that is the most likely way on the whole of acting for the best.

However, for the deontologist who is unconvinced by such argument and who finds reliance upon an overriding appeal to welfare maximization abhorrent—there are many, including members of the working group—the same working principles are derivable from other moral premises. Thus, those who hold as morally fundamental the Kantian principle that people should not be treated merely as means but always also as ends, and interpret this principle, unlike utilitarians, as ruling out such an appeal, will in practice—if they are not absolutists—find themselves upholding the same working rules as the utilitarian who supports such working rules on the grounds that they maximize welfare.

It is beyond the scope of this enquiry to pursue further this philosophical dispute. We have perhaps said enough to show that thoughtful utilitarians and deontologists, who have taken good cognizance of the relevant facts, may well agree in practice, as we have, on the guidelines to be adopted by ethics committees, and agree also in insisting that they should be firmly adhered to. That, at any rate, is the hope that has governed our detailed discussion of the issues. The two schools of thought will differ about the reasons to be given for these guidelines, or about the necessity for giving reasons at all; but into these further differences it is for our purposes unnecessary to enter.

NOTES

1. Ross, W.D. *The Right and the Good*, p. 41, Oxford University Press, Oxford (1930).

2. Prichard, H.A. Does Moral Philosophy Rest on a Mistake? *Mind* XXI, 21–37 (1912), reprinted in H.A. Prichard, *Moral Obligation*. Oxford University Press (1949).

3. Warnock, G.J. *The Object of Morality*, pp. 87 and 163. Methuen, London (1971).

4. Griffin, J.P. Modern Utilitarianism. *Revue internationale de philosophie, Bruxelles* 147, 331–75 (1983).

5. Dworkin, R.M. *Taking Rights Seriously*, p. xv. Harvard University Press, Boston (1977).

Fraud and Deception in Scientific Research

Allegations of misconduct in science made national headlines in 1988 when a congressional committee investigated charges that a research assistant to the Nobel laureate David Baltimore fabricated data in a paper published in the journal *Cell*. Although federal prosecutors decided not to charge the assistant with civil or criminal misconduct, the question of prime concern to members of the congressional committee remained unresolved: do scientific research programs, especially those funded by the National Institutes of Health (NIH) and other agencies of government, contain adequate sefeguards against fraud?

How widespread is the practice of manipulating data? If misconduct is rare, established methods of scientific review may be adequate to protect the integrity of science. But if manipulating data is "endemic," as William Broad and Nicholas Wade argue in "Fraud and the Structure of Science," the lead paper in this section, then the issue runs much deeper. Fraud, of course, is wrong. But what exactly *is* fraud? At one extreme is the investigator that makes egregious errors but does not attempt to deceive, which may be sloppy science but apparently not fraud. At the other extreme is the researcher who plagiarizes someone else's work and portrays it as his or her own. Baltimore's assistant, however, was not accused of sloppy science or of plagiarism, but of "fabricating data," which can be more difficult to establish. Federal investigators decided not to prosecute the researcher in part, because jurors might have been required to understand fine points of immunological research that could trouble even specialists in the field.

Moreover, not all attempts at manipulating data are fraudulent. The Nobel laureate Robert Millikan, for example, omitted publishing data that would have modified the results of his famous oil-drop experiments. Galileo exaggerated the outcome of experimental results; Newton "fudged" data to increase the apparent predictive power of his views; Gregor Mendel published statistical results that nowadays seem "too good to be true." Did these scientists have a special intuition that guided them toward the truth even in the absence of empirical evidence? And if they did, does that excuse what otherwise might appear to be scientific misconduct? Ullica Segerstrale addresses this question in her paper "The Murky Borderland Between Scientific Intuition and Fraud." Part of her point is that the criteria for good science are field-specific. For example, because the environment in physics is more carefully controlled, surprises are more suspect than in biology. Legitimately discounting data in physics may count as "fudging" in one of the other branches of science.

Segerstrale's methodological point helps to underscore the difficulty in prosecuting a case of alleged fraud before a jury of nonscientists. It also raises a problem with the idea of a single "fraud team" investigating alleged misconduct in various sciences.

But the problem of fraud is not just that it is field-specific. Fraud implies deception which can cut across all disciplines. Moreover, not all deception in science appears to be wrong. The use of placebos in drug testing is common, and so is the practice of misinforming subjects of social and psychological studies. Stanley Milgram's experiment in obedience is a classic example. The subjects were told (falsely) that they were to serve as "teachers" in a study of learning and punishment, although their own willingness to follow orders was the actual subject of investigation.

Can deceptions of this kind be justified in the name of science? The issue is complex although most ethicists have focused on the need for informed voluntary consent. Deontologists (see introduction to "Science and Values"), those who emphasize respect for the individual, tend to insist that subjects be made aware of the harm that might befall them.

Steven C. Patten goes further, suggesting that subjects be informed of the true nature of the experiment.

By contrast, Alan C. Elms proposes a "consequentialist" approach which minimizes the need for consent. Like the utilitarian (see introduction to "Science and Values") who argues that an act or practice is acceptable if it serves a social good, Elms emphasizes the benefits of studies such as Milgram's. But unlike the utilitarian, Elms admits a variety of constraints, including "an ongoing process of informed consent." We leave the reader to decide whether Elms would satisfy the deontologist.

Both Patten and Elms agree that any use of deception should be justified. They differ on the extent to which informed consent should be part of the justification. J. David Newell argues that deception is morally neutral and that informed consent is irrelevant. Part of his point is that deception is not lying. Rather, like bluffing in poker, or secrecy in undercover criminal investigation, deception in scientific research is integral to the practice.

Where does this leave us? We sought to distinguish fraud from other forms of data manipulation by focusing on deception. But deception may be morally neutral. If this is so, deception by itself would not prove fraud. Something more is needed. We leave the reader to decide what that may be.

Fraud and the Structure of Science

William Broad and Nicholas Wade

The conventional ideology of science cannot satisfactorily explain the phenomenon of fraud. It deals with fraud only by denying it to be a problem of any prevalence or significance. In point of fact, fraud is a significant phenomenon that has occurred throughout the history of science and is no less in evidence today. It is not fraud that must be dismissed, but the conventional ideology.

The analysis of fraud sheds considerable light on how science works in actual practice. It illuminates both the motivation of the individual researcher and the mechanisms by which the scientific community validates and accepts new knowledge.

From its earliest days, science has been an arena in which men have striven for two goals: to understand the world and to achieve recognition for their personal efforts in doing so. This duality of purpose lies at the foundation of the scientific enterprise. Only through recognition of the double goal can the motives of scientists, the behavior of the scientific community, and the process of science itself be properly understood.

The scientist's two purposes for the most part work hand in hand, but in certain situations conflicts arise. When an experiment does not come out exactly as expected, when a theory fails to win general acceptance, a scientist will face a spectrum of temptations that range from improving the appearance of his data in various ways to outright fraud. Some who commit fraud do so to persuade their refractory colleagues of a theory they know is right. Newton manipulated the fudge factor to confound the critics of his theory of gravitation. Mendel's statistics of his pea ratios, for whatever reason, are too good to be true. Millikan was outrageously selective in his use of data to describe the charge on the electron.

If history has been kind to scientists such as these, it is because the theories turned out to be correct. But for the moralist, no distinction can be made between an Isaac Newton who lied for truth and was right, and Cyril Burt who lied for truth and was wrong. Newton and Burt each lied for what he thought he knew to be truth. Probably each turned to fraud also in part for reasons of personal vindication, for the vanity of having his professional colleagues acknowledge the validity of his theory.

Most scientists, no doubt, do not allow the thirst for personal glory to distort their pursuit of the truth. Yet the temptation to which even Ptolemy, Gallileo, Newton, Dalton, and Millikan succumbed grew even stronger as science became professionalized in the nineteenth and twentieth centuries. The remarkable career of Elias Alsabti illustrates how completely the desire for credit can vanquish the honest search for truth. Alsabti's behavior is by no means typical. But it demonstrates in extreme form the ambition and careerism that are regular ingredients of modern scientific life. More importantly, Alsabti's success shows how ineffectually the social mechanisms of science operate to check the excesses of ambition and careerism.

Much of science does not work in this way, and most scientists do research because they like it, not because they are trying to climb some career ladder to scientific stardom. There is no single social organization of science but rather a spectrum of structures that range from the ideal community of equal colleagues to the hierarchically organized research mill. Perhaps the prevalence of fraud is an indication of how well these various structures work. No sure generalization can yet be made, but an apparent pattern is that fraud seems to be committed most often either by loners, such as Alsabti and Burt, or by members of research mills.

If anything, the social mechanisms of science are designed to promote careerism. The hierarchically structured research mills, in which the lab chief often takes an automatic share of the credit for the work done by his junior colleagues regardless of how insignificant his own contribution may have been, allow one scientist to amass glory at the expense of others. Those whose efforts are exploited go along with the practice because they see it as an unchangeable part of the system, from which they too hope to profit in their turn.

The lab-chief system encourages not only careerism but also cynicism because, by its structure and organization, it tends to force a disjunction between the scientist's two goals, the pursuit of truth and the desire for credit. The system, with its heavy emphasis on results, on producing papers, on winning the next research grant, sets up pressures that favor glory-getting and credit-grabbing over the dispassionate pursuit of truth.

Science to a large extent is hard and discouraging work. For every second of cognitive exaltation at a pretty idea or an experiment that finally works, the researcher must put in hours of frustrating labor at the laboratory bench, trying to master a new technique, to iron out the bugs, to wrest a clear answer from the confusing substance of nature. To persevere in research requires a high degree of motivation, for which glory is often the incentive, denial of grant money the goad. But that motivation can easily turn to cynicism if younger researchers see that their elders are more preoccupied with chasing of scientific honors than in dispassionate examination of nature.

Sociologists have emphasized the community of science, portraying it as a band of colleagues dedicated to a common goal, the pursuit of truth. But this is only part of the picture. Science is also a race, an often furious competition in which individuals strive to be first—for without priority, discovery is a bitter fruit. Under the pressure of competition, some researchers yield to the temptation of cutting corners, of improving on their data, of finagling their results, and even of outright fraud.

Science may in one sense be a community, but in another, equally important, it is a celebrity system. The social organization of science is designed to foster the production of an elite in which prestige comes not just on the merits of work but also because of position in the scientific hierarchy. Members of the scientific elite control the reward system of science and, through the peer review system, have a major voice in the allocation of scientific resources.

Like the paper factories of the lab chiefs, the celebrity system favors the search for personal glory over the search for truth. It also interferes with the normal mechanisms for communal evaluation of results, because it gives undue prominence and immunity from scrutiny to the work of the elite. Members of the scientific elite cannot be held directly responsible for the cases of fraud that occur quite regularly in the elite institutions of science, but they are the product and beneficiaries of social organization that fosters careerism and creates the temptations and opportunities for fraud. William Summerlin, Vijay Soman, and John Darsee were members of laboratories where a large number of articles were produced, in part for the greater glory of the lab chief. John Long traded on the prestige of his institution and scientific affiliations to spin a research career out of nothing.

Fraud is revealing not only of the sociological structure of science but also of scientific methodology. Fraud and self-deception generate incorrect data that pose a challenge to the self-corrective mechanisms of science, in particular to the verification of scientific results. As is shown by many of the frauds discussed here, the replication of an experiment is often undertaken only as a last resort, and usually to confirm suspicions arrived at for other reasons. Exact replication is not a regular part of the scientific process. The reason is simple: there is no credit to be gained from replicating someone else's experiment.

Replication is not the engine of scientific progress. A closer description of the central validation method of science would be to say that recipes that work are adopted into the general cuisine. Science is in some respects a profoundly pragmatic enterprise. Theory may get the attention but the working scientist depends on his ability to make experiments work. If a new experiment or technique is successful, it will be adapted by other scientists to their own ends. It is by a continuous succession of small improvements on existing recipes that the scientific juggernaut inches forward. Only rarely are bad recipes demonstrated to be the product not of chefs but of charlatans. More often they just fall by the wayside, to be ignored along with a great mass of other forgettable, insignificant, or somehow erroneous research.

Science is pragmatic, but scientists are also as susceptible as others to all the arts of persuasion, including flattery, rhetoric, and propaganda. The careerist will make full use of these weapons to aid in the acceptance of his ideas. No one showed better how the scientific method could be wielded as a purely rhetorical weapon than did Cyril Burt. By merely claiming to be more scientific than his adversaries, by his mastery of statistics and brilliantly lucid exposition, Burt hoodwinked the community of educational psychologists in both England and the United States for some thirty years.

To the extent that rhetoric is persuasive in science, it can be so only at the expense of objectivity. The study of fraud indicates that the ideal of objectivity is often departed from. Objectivity is perhaps best thought of as a retrospective virtue of science. That accumulation of dispassionate fact in the scientific textbooks seems to stand quite independently of its human originators. Yet the attitude of detachment, however highly applauded by the philosophers and sociologists, is one that is hard to maintain in the competitive, results-oriented atmosphere of modern science. Nor is it evident that objectivity is a necessary qualification for the practicing scientist. Most researchers believe passionately in their work, in the techniques they rely on and the theories they are trying to prove. Without such an emotional commitment, it would be hard to sustain the effort. When the technique proves to be ambiguous or the theory untenable, the researcher learns to pick up the pieces and start over anew. Many scientists want passionately to know the truth. It is only the literary conventions of scientific reporting that compel scientists to feign detachment and pretend that when they put on a white coat they turn into logical automatons. Objectivity is an abstraction of the philosophers, a distraction for the researcher.

How is scientific knowledge validated, if not by replication and objective analysis? The economist Adam Smith explained in his classic work how private greed leads to public good. Even though everyone in the marketplace strives only to maximize his personal gain, the public good is served because an efficient market brings supply and demand into equilibrium at the lowest prices. A similar mechanism operates in science. Each scientist in the research forum tries to win acceptance for his own ideas or recipes: on balance, over time, the better recipe for dealing with nature generally prevails, so that the stock of useful knowledge grows steadily greater. The more vigorously that scientists pursue their own personal goals, the more efficiently does truth emerge from the competing claims.

In the realm of economics, Adam Smith invoked the "Invisible Hand" as the miraculous mechanism that produced public good out of private gain. The analogous mechanism that operates in science might be called the "Invisible Boot." The Invisible Boot kicks out all the incorrect, useless, or redundant data in science. It tramples over almost every scientist's work without discrimination, treading down into oblivion the true and the false, the honest and the dishonest, the keepers of the faith and the betrayers of the truth. Over time it stamps out the nonrational elements of the scientific process, all the human passions and prejudices that shaped the original findings, and leaves only a desiccated residue of knowledge, so distant from its human originators that it at last acquires the substance of objectivity.

The philosophers have described logical deduction, objective verification of results, and the construction of theories as the pillars of the scientific method. The analysis of fraud suggests of different picture. It shows science as pragmatic and empirical, something of a trial-and-error procedure in which the competitors in a given field try many different approaches but are always quick to switch to the recipe that works best. Science being a social process, each researcher is trying at the same time to advance and gain acceptance for his own recipes, his own interpretation of the field. He will use all rhetorical techniques that are likely to be effective, including appeal to scientific authority, emphasis on the thoroughness of his own methods, explanation of how his recipes agree with or support current theory, and other approved modes of discourse.

It would be extreme to state that science is nothing but recipes and rhetoric, with the Invisible Boot kicking out the useless and incorrect research over the course of time. But it is equally extreme to portray science as an exclusively logical process, guided by objective tests of verification and motivated solely by the search for truth. Science is a complex process in which the observer can see almost anything he wants provided he narrows his vision sufficiently. But to give a complete description of science, to understand the process as it really works, the temptation to seek out ideals and abstractions must probably be avoided.

The chief abstraction, of course, is the philosopher's search for the scientific method. It may be that there is no one scientific method. Scientists are individuals and they have different styles and different approaches to the truth. The identical style of all scientific writing, which seems to spring from a universal scientific method, is a false unanimity imposed by the current conventions of scientific reporting. If scientists were allowed to express themselves naturally in describing their experiments and theories, the myth of a single, universal scientific method would probably vanish instantly.

For a rounded understanding of how science works, the disciplinary abstractions of the philosophers, sociologists, and historians of science must be recognized as single aspects of a multifaceted object, not taken for the whole picture, as the conventional ideology assumes. Science is first and foremost a social process: the researcher who discovers the secret of the universe and keeps it to himself has not contributed to science. Secondly, it is a historical process: it moves forward with time, it is an integral part of civilization and history, and cannot properly be understood when wrested out of its context. Thirdly, science is the cultural form that allows fullest opportunity for the expression of the human propensity for rational thought.

It is the third aspect of science that has perhaps been subject to the greatest amount of misinterpretation. The presence of a strong rational element in science has been taken to mean that that is the only significant element of scientific thought. But creativity, imagination, intuition, persistence, and many other nonrational elements are also essential parts of the scientific process, and other less vital qualities such as ambition, envy, and the propensity to deception also play a role. The existence of fraud in science is proof of nonrational elements at work, both on the part of the individual who fakes data and the community that accepts them.

The rationality evident in science has also been misinterpreted to mean that science is the only rational exercise of intellect in society, or at least the highest and most authoritative. Some scientists, in their public appearances, can be noticed playing up to this role, which seems to invest them as cardinals of reason propounding salvation to an irrational public. It is probably a misperception to think of science as different in kind from other exercises of the human intellect. At the least, the burden of proof should be on those who make special claims for science, and any claim founded solely on what the philosophers say about science must be rejected as partial.

In addition, scientists are put in a false position by those who would make them the sole guardians of rationality in society. Historians who have attempted to arrogate to science all credit for social or material progress, or for the triumph of reason over the forces of darkness and ignorance, also render science vulnerable to blame for all the deficiencies of modern societies. To a probably insalubrious degree, science has replaced religion as the fundamental source of truth and value in the modern world.

The rigidity imposed by consciousness of such a role is perhaps evident in the typical response of the scientific establishment to fraud. Establishment spokesmen generally find it difficult to suggest that a certain background level of fraud should be expected in science as much as in any other profession. They are also disinclined to concede that the practices or institutions of science should shoulder any part of the blame for fraudulent behavior. Only by abandoning the conventional ideology of science would it be possible for them to accept fraud for what it most probably is, a small, but not insignificant, endemic feature of the scientific enterprise.

The rejection of fraud as a serious issue leaves the profession of science in an awkward position, most especially when the implications of scientific fraud move beyond the world of pure research to the realm of public policy. Here fraud can become a matter of immediate practical significance. The testing of drugs and food ingredients is a case in point. Government agencies, not the institutions of science, have taken the initiative in trying to control the wide-scale fraud that has occurred in biological testing.

Another significant impact of fraud has been in the unhappy field of measuring human abilities. Fraud and self-deception have played major parts in studies that have influenced public attitudes on matters of class and race, and in shaping public action on issues such as immigration and education. Scientists' deception of themselves and others in this context illustrates the more general principle that objectivity is often the first victim when scientists enter battle on social issues.

Besides the practical damage done by some scientific frauds, there is the harm done by each new revelation of laboratory legerdemain to the public credibility of science. Without a serious effort on the part of scientists to address the issue, pressure will build for Congress to take action of some sort, perhaps by instituting a laboratory police force modeled on the inspection system of the Food and Drug Administration.

Congress would probably take such a step only with great reluctance, because of its deep belief that scientific research and universities should be autonomous from government. But at a period when initiatives against waste and fraud are being pursued in all other areas of government, Congress is unlikely to indulge science as a haven where fraud can continue just as usual.

Political considerations aside, it would in any case be in the interests of science to remedy the causes of fraud. In general, there is no absolute defense against fraud that would not bring the whole machinery of science grinding to a halt. But the detection of fraud is of far less importance than its prevention. What is required first and foremost are steps to diminish the inducement to fraud.

By and large, those features in the social organization of science that encourage and reward careerism also create the incentive for fraud. The excesses of the careerist system spread cynicism among young researchers, who sometimes respond to pressure by imitating the worse aspects of their elders' behavior. This is the atmosphere in which the finagling of data or the wholesale invention of results is perhaps most likely to occur.

Scientists should be more skeptical of elitism, and particularly of young superstars in elite institutions who seem to do too much too fast. A branch of knowledge that claims to be universal should ensure that its own internal tests are evenly applied.

A simple but valuable reform would be for the scientific community to set itself more formal guidelines for the assignation of credit, in particular for that critically important part of a scientific paper—the authorship line. Two principles might be established. First, all people named as authors should have made a definably major contribution to the work reported. Any minor contribution should be explicitly acknowledged in the text of the article. Second, all authors of a paper should be prepared to take responsibility for its contents in precisely the same measure as they stand to take credit.

Such steps, if generally accepted, would curtail the inherently dishonest practice of lab chiefs signing their name to work in which they have been only peripherally involved, if at all. It would also spare the public the ludicrous spectacle of lab chiefs who hog credit for everything that goes well but disclaim responsibility when fraud is discovered. If a lab chief is not close enough to a research project to know whether data is being falsified, he should not put his name on the paper. For the papers he does sign, he should take full responsibility. To most nonscientists, such principles probably seem too obvious to be worth stating.

A specific area in urgent need of reform is that of medical research. The pressures put on students trying to enter medical school encourage and reward a kind of competition that often includes deception. "Stories of cheating among premedical students are common, and the race for high grades so as to insure admission to medical school is hardly designed to encourage ethical and humanitarian behavior," says the former dean of the Harvard Medical School, Robert H. Ebert. When those accustomed to cheating experience the fierce competitive pressures of the medical world and the prestige that attaches to doing research, they do not find it too unnatural to clean up data or even invent experiments. The "bad apples" who commit fraud in medical research are a special fruit of the system. One solution would be a wider degree of separation between medical research and medical education.

A problem that affects research in general is the excessive proliferation of scientific papers. Too many scientific articles are published. Many are simply worthless. Moreover the worthless papers clutter up the communications system of science, preventing good research from receiving the attention it deserves and protecting bad research from scrutiny. Alsabti and his fellow plagiarists were able to achieve success only because of the shelter given them by the ocean of unread and unreadable articles of which the scientific literature is so largely composed.

As the system now stands, researchers are rewarded for extracting the maximum number of separate articles out of a single piece of research, so as to amplify the list of their published work. This pernicious habit makes reviewing the literature almost impossible. Scientists who fragment their results should be criticized rather than rewarded.

The root of the publication problem lies in a system that is carefully protected from market constraints. The research journals that publish the articles that no one needs to read are twice subsidized, both times by the taxpayer. Their publishers levy page charges on authors to defray the printing costs. The scientific libraries that buy the journals are also subsidized. Both the page charges and the library funds come from researchers' government grants. The subsidies underlie the ease with which almost any scientific article, however poor, can get into print.

Attempts to tighten up the refereeing process are seldom successful, because a paper turned down by one journal will eventually be published in another. What is needed is greater competition brought about by a sharp reduction in the number of journals, especially in medicine and biology. Many of these journals serve as little more than what publishers call a vanity press, with the taxpayer supporting the vanity through the grants given to researchers. The practice of page charges should be sharply curtailed. Market forces of supply and demand should be introduced wherever possible into the game of academic publishing.

Just as the emphasis in publication should be shifted from quantity to quality, so promotions and grant renewals should not be handed out on the basis of a long list of seemingly important publications. Administrators should develop sophisticated means of reading and evaluating a research record, such as citation analysis, where the influence of a scientist can be measured by the number of times his work is cited by other researchers. Such techniques tell much more about the real worth of a scientist than a long list of publications on a curriculum vitae.

A reduction in the number of scientific articles of course suggests a more radical kind of surgery, that of a reduction in the number of scientists. The available evidence indicates that the great majority of research responsible for the advance of science is produced by a small number of scientists. This small elite depends overwhelmingly on the research of other members of the elite, not on that of the wider majority. The pace of scientific advance would not obviously be slowed if this majority did not exist. It might even be enhanced if pursued by a leaner and fitter community of researchers. Perhaps there are too many scientists. Perhaps basic scientific research would be more appropriately supported by private patrons, as economist Milton Friedman has suggested, instead of by the government.

In his book *The Decline of the West*, the philosopher Oswald Spengler cited fraud by scholars as one of the signs of a decadent civilization. It is not necessary to believe Spengler's thesis to be alarmed by the persistent, even if minor, presence of fraud in science. The idea of progress is a sustaining value of Western societies, and scientific research is an important means to that end. Scientists are professionally committed to ascertain the truth on society's behalf; when they betray the truth for personal gain, the signs of a possibly serious corrosion of principle should not be ignored.

For the public, a better understanding of the nature of science would lead to their regarding scientists with less awe and a dash more skepticism. A more realistic attitude would be healthy for both. But a proper understanding of science must begin with scientists themselves, and should embrace the concept that there is no discontinuity between scientific and other modes of intellectual creation. The phenomenon of fraud underlines the importance of the human side of science. It suggests that the logical structure of scientific knowledge is not a proper basis for placing science in a different category from other intellectual activities. Science is not removed from the wellsprings of art or poetry, nor is it the only cultural expression of rationality.

Science is not an abstract body of knowledge, but man's understanding of nature. It is not an idealized interrogation of nature by dedicated servants of truth, but a human process governed by the ordinary human passions of ambition, pride, and greed, as well as by all the well-hymned virtues attributed to men of science. But the step from greed to fraud is as small in science as in other walks of life. Usually the misrepresentation amounts to no more than a sweetening or prettification of the data; less often, to outright fraud.

"Truth is the daughter," Bacon remarked, "not of authority, but time." Time and again, the truth has been betrayed by scientists, whether unintentionally, or for their own ends, or because they presumed to lie on truth's behalf. Scientific authorities deny that fraud is anything more than a passing blemish on the face of science. But only by acknowledging that fraud is endemic can the real nature of science and its servants be fully understood.

Appendix

Known or Suspected Cases of Scientific Fraud

"Strangely enough, deliberate, conscious fraud is extremely rare in the world of academic science. . . . The only well-known case is "Piltdown Man."
—J.M. Ziman, *Nature*, 227, 996 (1970)

"Indeed, a number of old stories are being exhumed and revived, as though to reveal a pattern of habitual falsehood

in the process of science. . . . These can, if you like, be made
to seem all of a piece, part of a constantly spreading blot on
the record of science. Or, if you prefer (and I *do* prefer), they
can be viewed as anomalies, the work of researchers with
unhinged minds, or, as in the cases of Newton and Mendel,
the gross exaggerations of the fallibility of even superb
scientists."

—Lewis Thomas, *Discover* (June 1981)

Following is a list of cases of known or strongly suspected fraud
in science, from ancient Greece to the present day. The list
represents merely those cases that have come to our attention,
and is not the result of an exhaustive search. Each case is
described in summary form, with a single reference for the
reader to obtain further information.

We would be glad if those knowing of cases not cited here
would bring them to our attention, c/o Simon & Schuster, 1230
Avenue of the Americas, New York, N.Y. 10020.

Case: Hipparchus (Greek astronomer)
Date: Second century B.C.
- Published star catalog taken from Babylonian sources as
  if it were the result of his own observations.
Reference: G.J. Toomer, "Ptolemy," *Dictionary of Scientific
Biography* (Charles Scribner's Sons, New York, 1975), p.
191.

Case: Claudius Ptolemy (Egyptian astronomer whose theory of
the solar system held sway for 1,500 years)
Date: Second Century A.D.
- Claimed to have performed astronomical measurements
  which he did not.
Reference: Robert R. Newton, *The Crime of Claudius Ptolemy*
(Johns Hopkins University Press, Baltimore, 1977).

Case: Galileo Galilei (physicist and founder of scientific method)
Date: Early seventeenth century
- Exaggerated the outcome of experimental results.

Reference: Alexandre Koyré, *Metaphysics and Measurement: Essays in Scientific Revolution* (Harvard University Press, Cambridge, 1968).

Case: Isaac Newton (first modern physicist)
Date: 1687–1713
- Introduced fudge factors into his magnum opus so as to increase its apparent power of prediction.

Reference: Richard S. Westfall, "Newton and the Fudge Factor," *Science*, 179, 751–758 (1973).

Case: Johann Beringer (German dilettante and collector of fossils)
Date: 1726
- Hoaxed by rivals in publishing book of fake fossils.

Reference: Melvin E. Jahn and Daniel J. Woolf, *The Lying Stones of Dr. Johann Bartholomew Adam Beringer* (University of California Press, Berkeley, 1963).

Case: Johann Bernoulli (mathematician who refined calculus)
Date: 1738
- Plagiarized his son's discovery of the "Bernoulli equation," backdating his own book so it appeared to have been issued before his son's.

Reference: C. Truesdell, in introduction to Euler's *Opera Omnia*, Ser. II, Vol. II, p. xxxv.

Case: John Dalton (father of modern atomic theory)
Date: 1804–1805
- Reported experiments that cannot now be repeated, and which probably could not have happened as described.

Reference: Leonard K. Nash, "The Origin of Dalton's Chemical Atomic Theory," *Isis*, 47, 101–116, 1956.

Case: Orgueil (a meteorite shower that fell on France)
Date: 1864
- Unknown hoaxster tampered with piece of meteorite so it seemed to bear organic remains, implying the existence of extraterrestrial life.

Reference: Edward Anders et al., "Contaminated Meteorite,"
Science, 146, 1157–1161, 1964.

Case: Gregor Mendel (father of genetics)
Date: 1865
  • Published statistical results too good to be true.
Reference: Several papers in Curt Stern and Eva R. Sherwood,
The Origin of Genetics: A Mendel Source Book (W.H.
Freeman and Co., San Francisco, 1966).

Case: Admiral Peary (American explorer)
Date: 1909
  • Alleged he had reached the geographic North Pole when
in fact he knew he was hundreds of miles away.
Reference: Dennis Rawlins, *Peary at the North Pole: Fact or
Fiction?* (Robert B. Luce, Washington–New York, 1973).

Case: Robert Millikan (American physicist and winner of Nobel
prize)
Date: 1910–1913
  • Kept unfavorable results out of published papers while
publicly maintaining that he had reported everything.
Reference: Gerald Holton, "Subelectrons, Presuppositions, and
the Millikan-Ehrenhaft Dispute," *Historical Studies in the
Physical Sciences*, 9, 166–224, 1978.

Case: Piltdown
Date: 1912
  • Hoaxster planted fake fossils in gravel pit, presumably
to cast Britain as birthplace of the human race.
Reference: J.S. Weiner, *The Piltdown Forgery* (Oxford University
Press, London, 1955).

Case: Adriaan van Maanen (American astronomer at Mount
Wilson Observatory)
Date: 1916
  • Misreported the reliability of key astronomical
observations.

Reference: Norriss S. Hetherington, *Beyond the Edge of Objectivity*, unpublished book MS.

Case: Paul Kammerer (Viennese biologist)
Date: 1926
- Kammerer or assistant faked breeding results with toads.

Reference: Arthur Koestler, *The Case of the Midwife Toad* (Hutchinson, London, 1971).

Case: Cyril Burt (English psychologist)
Date: 1943(?)–1966
- Fabricated data to support theory that human intelligence is 75 percent inherited.

Reference: L.S. Hearnshaw, *Cyril Burt, Psychologist*, Hodder and Stoughton, London, 1979, 370 pp.

Case: James H. McCrocklin (president of Southwest Texas State College from 1964 to 1969)
Date: 1954
- Pirated parts of old report in Ph.D. thesis.

Reference: *Texas Observer*, March 7, 1969, pp. 6–8.

Case: "Traction" (pseudonym)
Date: 1960–1961
- A young researcher falsified work at Yale, then was hired by Fritz Lipmann at the Rockefeller Institute, where he published falsified work with Lipmann and was eventually found out.

Reference: William J. Broad, "Fraud and the Structure of Science," *Science*, 212, 137–141, 1981.

Case: P.G. Pande, R.R. Shukla, and P.C. Sekariah (at Indian Veterinary Research Institute)
Date: 1961
- Claimed to have discovered parasite in hens' eggs, but photomicrographs had been lifted from another publication.

Reference: The editorial board of *Science*, "An Unfortunate Event," *Science*, 134, 945–946, 1961.

Case: "Fraley" (pseudonym)
Date: 1964
  • A visiting professor in David E. Green's University of Wisconsin lab faked several important experiments, leading Green to announce retractions at a national meeting.
Reference: Joseph Hixson, *The Patchwork Mouse* (Doubleday, New York, 1976), pp. 146–148. Hixon refers to the perpetrator of the frauds as Fraley.

Case: Robert Gullis (biochemist from Birmingham University)
Date: 1971–1976
  • Faked series of experiments on messenger chemicals used by the brain.
Reference: Mike Muller, "Why Scientists Don't Cheat," *New Scientist*, June 2, 1977, pp. 522–523.

Case: Walter J. Levy (parapsychologist and protégé of father of parapsychology, J.B. Rhine)
Date: 1974
  • Faked results of experiment in which rats were to influence equipment by brain power, a phenomenon known as psychokinesis.
Reference: J.B. Rhine, "A New Case of Experimenter Unreliability," *Journal of Parapsychology*, 38, 215–255, 1974.

Case: William Summerlin (immunologist)
Date: 1974
  • In an attempt to bolster research that was under fire, Summerlin faked results of skin transplants with mice.
Reference: Joseph Hixson, *The Patchwork Mouse* (Doubleday, New York: 1976).

Case: Stephen S. Rosenfeld (undergraduate researcher at Harvard)

Date: 1974

- Forged letters of recommendation and allegedly faked series of experiments in biochemistry.

Reference: Robert Reinhold, "When Methods Are Not So Scientific," *The New York Times*, December 29, 1974, p. E7.

Case: Zoltan Lucas (surgeon at Stanford University)
Date: 1975

- Admitted to faking citations to research papers of his that did not exist. Some of the fakery was aimed at winning NIH grants.

Reference: Series of news releases put out by Stanford University News Service, August 1981.

Case: Wilson Crook III (graduate student in geology at University of Michigan)
Date: 1977

- Regents at the university in 1980 rescinded Crook's master's degree, saying he had fraudulently claimed to have discovered a natural mineral called "texasite," which in reality was a synthetic compound. Crook denied the charges.

Reference: Max Gates, "Regents Rescind Student's Degree, Charging Fraud," *The Ann Arbor News*, October 18, 1980, p. A9.

Case: Marc J. Straus (cancer researcher at Boston University)
Date: 1977–1978

- Group of Straus's researchers and nurses admitted falsifying data in clinical tests and charged that some of the fakery was done on Straus's orders. Straus denied any wrongdoing.

Reference: Nils J. Bruzelius and Stephen A. Kurkjian, "Cancer Research Data Falsified; Boston Project Collapses," *Boston Globe*, five-part series starting June 29, 1980, p. 1.

Case: Elias A.K. Alsabti (Iraqi medical student who worked at several research centers in the United States)
Date: 1977–1980

- Plagiarized scientific papers, perhaps sixty in all.
Reference: William J. Broad, "Would-be Academician Pirates Papers," *Science*, 208, 1438–1440, 1980.

Case: Stephen Krogh Derr (radiation chemist at Hope College in Holland, Michigan)
Date: 1978
- Published allegedly invented results of remarkable treatment said to remove plutonium from the bodies of poisoned workers.
Reference: Lawrence McGinty, "Researcher Retracts Claims on Plutonium Treatment," *New Scientist*, October 4, 1979, pp. 3–4.

Case: John Long (research pathologist at the Massachusetts General Hospital)
Date: 1978–1980
- Forged data in the course of a research career spent studying cell lines that turned out to come not from humans but from a brown-footed Columbian owl monkey.
Reference: Nicholas Wade, "A Diversion of the Quest for Truth," *Science*, 211, 1022–1025, 1981.

Case: Vijay R. Soman (biomedical researcher at Yale)
Date: 1978–1980
- Falsified results in three papers, threw away raw data in others, forcing retraction of twelve papers in all.
Reference: Morton Hunt, "A Fraud That Shook the World of Science," *The New York Times Magazine*, November 1, 1981, pp. 42–75.

Case: Mark Spector (rising young biochemist at Cornell University)
Date: 1980-1981
- A series of elegant experiments by Spector that pointed to a unified theory of cancer causation turned out to be fakes. Spector denied any wrongdoing, saying somebody else spiked the test tubes.

Reference: Nicholas Wade, "The Rise and Fall of a Scientific Superstar," *New Scientist*, September 24, 1981, pp. 781–782.

The Murky Borderland between Scientific Intuition and Fraud

Ullica Segerstrale

1. Introduction

In this paper I want to point out that scientific fraud and fudging of data may not be as clear-cut a thing as one might believe. What I want to show is that "good science" is often hard to describe explicitly, since it is partially dependent on intuition and tacit knowledge. Scientists themselves have a difficult time answering questions about it. They have to trust intuition to give their research any direction at all, and also because of limited time and resources. They often seem to believe they "know" when something is right or wrong. Sometimes this stubborn belief that they know the truth may lead scientists to cut corners or fudge data, and may even lead them to outright fraud.

I will begin with the role of intuition in science. Then I will examine the notion of "tacit knowledge." I will go on to a particularly interesting aspect of scientists' judgments concerning "good science": this I will call "The Importance of Being Earnest vs. the Importance of Being Right." Here I will draw on my own interviews with practicing physicists. After taking the discussion of "good science" one step further, by suggesting that the criteria are field-specific, I will conclude by addressing the question: Can "good science" be taught?

2. Scientific Intuition

Scientific intuition sometimes leads scientists right, sometimes wrong. Famous stories of good scientific intuition include chemist Kekule's discovery of the structure of the benzene ring while dozing in front of his fireplace, and the mathematician Henri Poincare's solution of the Fuchsian functions while he stepped onto a bus. There are also many stories about scientists putting their intuition first and data second. The classic example is Einstein: he openly stated that he was not particularly interested in facts, since he knew that his theory was right.

Galileo is another scientist with great intuition. There are many stories about Galileo's rhetorical or other maneuvers to save what he so strongly believed in: the Copernican heliocentric theory. Galileo was convinced that the Copernican theory was right, but he knew that he had no good evidence. So, in order to make his case more compelling, he invented a theory of the tides which he connected to the motions not of the moon but of the sun. Richard Morris explains:

> Galileo must have been aware that the evidence for a moving earth was, as yet, inconclusive. Otherwise he would not have introduced the tidal theory at the end of his Dialogue in an effort to make the case more convincing. Galileo really had no convincing proof, but he was a firm believer in the heliocentric theory. Like Copernicus, he did not believe that a theory as complicated and inelegant as the Ptolemaic could possibly be an accurate description of nature.
>
> This sounds a little like intellectual dishonesty. But it is not. It is a sign that Galileo possessed the penetrating intuition that is the mark of a great scientist. He could peer behind appearances and see that the Copernician theory was true, even though he had no conclusive evidence.[1]

I find this way of excusing Galileo fascinating. As we shall see later, this may well illustrate the way many scientists think.

But there are some well-known cases where scientific intuition or belief has led scientists into error. A famous example of a powerful but mistaken intuition is Johannes Kepler's great "insight" that there was a numerical relationship between the planetary orbits. He was struck by the idea that the (then) six orbits fit the series of the five perfect geometrical solids. Since he also believed that the orbits were circular, the first orbit became a sphere that fit into a tetrahedron, which nicely fit into the next orbit, a sphere, which just fit into a cube, and so on, and everything came out just right. The only problem was that he was wrong.

Esthetic and religious preconceptions guided Kepler's great "insight." He wanted order in the cosmos. Kepler himself apparently did not consider his famous third law, the one stating that the orbits of planets are elliptical, not circular, as central a finding as his great idea of the solids. He very reluctantly gave up the notion of circular orbits, which had been the prevalent one since the Greeks.[2]

Scientific intuition has led other scientists to discover facts or effects that were not really there. Examples include the discovery of the planet Vulcan in 1859, and the discovery of N-rays in the early 1900s. In both these cases, it was not a single scientist who reported seeing the non-existent phenomenon but many. There was good reason to believe in the existence of Vulcan. The presence of another planet would have explained the puzzle of Mercury's deviation from its expected orbit. So there were many observations of Vulcan, and it even got into science textbooks. N-rays were "discovered" in France; it was in a sense a response to German X-rays. Famous scientists from the French Academy got involved in N-ray research and various effects were reported—until it was proved that N-rays simply don't exist. Still, some scientists stubbornly continued believing in them.[3]

Scientific belief may also lead to the refusal to believe even "hard" facts—like meteorites. The idea that stones could come down from the sky was ridiculed for a long time. Scientists were at one point even removing meteorites from museums because they could not "really" have fallen from the sky.[4]

The idea of scientists jumping on a bandwagon and "seeing" the same effects as their colleagues is also evident in more recent experimental data. According to one physicist this is quite common: he calls it "the herd instinct." He describes it this way: In standard cases where people are trying to measure a certain physical constant by several different methods, there is an expected mean value and all the measures tend to converge around it. If the perceived mean value changes (for example, because of some change in theory), the reported results all shift to values around the new mean. A good example is the sudden change in everybody's measurement of the velocity of light. In 1949 it took a sudden jump. The measurements all shifted by a margin that was outside any previous experimental error.[5]

The results of many experiments in science are dependent on interpretation by a trained eye. One has to know what to look for and be able to discern the signal from the noise. The "herd instinct" shows how the eye may be trained to see the expected thing in the expected place. Through the "experimenter effect" scientists may directly influence the outcome of their experiments in subtle ways. A well-known case of this involved so-called maze-dull and maze-bright rats. Measuring the rats' performance with a stopwatch after having been told that some rats were bright and some dull, experimenters recorded significant differences between the rats. In fact, all the rats came from the same stock. Another case is the so-called Pygmalion effect—making children perform better by raising teacher expectations.[6]

In his *Mismeasurement of Man*,[7] Stephen J. Gould presents an interesting reconstruction of how belief in a particular theory may affect the way measurements are made. He discusses the case of Samuel Morton's measurements of human skulls in the mid-1800s. Morton set out to test a hypothesis about a relationship between skull size and intelligence, and a certain rank order of the races, with Caucasians on top. Morton was a conscientious scientist and measured an enormous number of skulls. He documented all his results in detail. He got the result he expected.

How might Morton have obtained his results, which we know are wrong? Gould imagines that Morton trusted his scientific intuition. For instance, Morton threw out "bad subsamples" of Caucasian skulls (for instance, the Hindu skulls that were "too small"). Gould also imagines how the procedure of measuring the volume of skulls by packing them with mustard seed could have been unconsciously manipulated:

Morton may have packed some skulls more tightly and others more loosely, according to what the results "ought to" be. It was, in fact, easy for Gould to reanalyze Morton's data, since they were all there.

Some scientists have stretched their scientific intuition even further. A famous case is Sir Cyril Burt who was so convinced of the high heritability of IQ through his early experiments with twins, that when more data were not forthcoming—because he had no more twins to study—he invented further twin studies. Still, it is not clear whether his intuition was right or wrong. Some scientists continue to believe IQ is highly heritable while others think it much less so, and others again think the concept of IQ heritability is meaningless.[8]

The problem with scientific intuition is that if we allow it to enter as a post-hoc rationalization for dubious practices in cases where scientists have been right, there is nothing to prevent invoking it to rationalize minor or major fudging of results in other research. One might always claim that if it turns out to be right, the fixing of data was justified. As we shall see later, this is exactly the way some physicists appear to argue!

3. The Role of Tacit Knowledge in Science

Michael Polanyi long ago wrote about the importance of what he called "tacit knowledge" in science. It is fruitless to demand strict criteria for scientific truth, according to Polanyi, because science is actually founded on tacit principles.

> A vital judgment practiced in science is the assessment of *plausibility*. Only plausible ideas are taken up, discussed and tested by scientists. Such a decision may later be proved right, but at the time that it is made, the assessment of plausibility is based on a broad exercise of intuition guided by many subtle indications, *and thus it is altogether undemonstrable. It is tacit.*[9]

Polanyi gives an example of an experiment by Lord Rayleigh published in the *Proceedings of the Royal Society* in 1947. According to Polanyi, no one could find any fault with the experiment, but the results were implausible, and no one believed them. So the scientific community just ignored them. Polanyi's conclusion is that Lord Rayleigh himself should also have ignored them. Polanyi shows how seriously he means this conclusion by observing that the scientific community was also correct in ignoring *his* own "implausible" theory (on absorption of gases on solid surfaces) for about half a century, even though it turned out the theory was right.

This is an example of intuition keeping science on the right course. Though Polanyi here relies not on the individual scientist's intuition that he is right but on *other* scientists' intuitions of plausibility, invoking "tacit knowledge" still does not seem to give any clear guide to truth. In the case of Vulcan or N-rays, lots of scientists were taken in by the plausibility of the idea. Morton's data also sounded eminently plausible. And for a long time, no one thought of asking how Cyril Burt attained such consistency in his highly plausible results. The problem thus seems to be that the very same intuitive or tacit processes that lead to major correct insights may also lead to incorrect ones.

There is another tacit component of scientific practice, the phenomenon of "golden hands," a knack for getting experiments to work. Scientific knowledge depends on craft knowledge. Both types of tacit knowledge, "good intuition" and craft skills, are passed on from master to apprentice in the overall learning of "good science." The belief in a young apprentice's "golden hands" fooled senior researchers in some famous fraud cases.

I have no doubt that "golden hands" exist; some scientists are just better experimentalists than others. This know-how seems very hard to transmit. Experiments, particularly in biomedical research and chemistry, are often hard to replicate. The methodology in published papers is often insufficient and replication may fail even when more detailed instructions are provided. Sometimes the experiments work only when supervised by or done by the initial investigator.

One reason for the difficulty in replication may be that practices in different laboratories differ in subtle ways. An interesting example from physics is a laser experiment that no one could replicate based on written descriptions until the researchers who had initially published the result were present and got the apparatus to work.[10] Chemistry appears to recognize this problem most explicitly. There are two journals, one of organic synthesis and one of inorganic synthesis, where the refereeing includes an independent laboratory attempting to reproduce the results. If the referee cannot reproduce the results, he asks for more information. As one of the journal editors recently reported, 50% of the results initially cannot be reproduced.[11]

4. The Importance of Being Earnest vs. the Importance of Being Right

If we take scientists seriously and listen to their actual judgments of the behavior of other scientists, we shall find at least some more concerned that they came to the *right* conclusion than with exactly *how* they came to it. There seems to be an imbalance: if you got the "right" answer (i.e. a correct, positive result), it is ascribed to "good science" in the sense that you followed your scientific intuition, even though you may not have been totally "earnest." On the other hand, if you are "wrong," no one cares about how earnest you were: the important thing is that you didn't get the right result. I do not know how prevalent this attitude is, but it certainly exists and I have encountered it in more than one science and at more than one school.

One of the problems with this attitude is that, if negative results are not valued, published, or shared, the sciences will not accumulate information about what might go wrong. This attitude offers no encouragement to find out what can go wrong; rather time ought to be spent on producing more "correct" results. Now, if this is the attitude conveyed to students and junior researchers by their mentors, what do students and juniors make of it?

I got my first inkling of this scientific attitude when I was a graduate student in organic chemistry in Finland. Part of the master's degree consisted in doing three months of research guided by the professor. I was assigned to do a difficult reduction experiment that my professor hoped would yield a particular end product. This was obviously his baby, so I followed his guidelines as well as I could, trying to improve the apparatus in different ways. I eventually got it to work and got a product. My professor was very happy. The substance looked and smelled right to him. So, I analyzed the substance and reported to him various features as soon as I had identified them.

I remember my excitement trying to characterize this product. But the more features I found and reported to him, the angrier he got. "Impossible!" he said. Finally, when I had gotten firm evidence of what the thing was, he got really angry. This glorious product turned out to be a common chemical substance, one that must have been in the initial "soup" to be distilled! The professor couldn't believe me. He sent the stuff out for expensive external analysis. The analysis confirmed my result. For a couple of days my professor went around miserably staring into the bowl containing my substance.

How does one write a research report in such a case? I documented my research and methods. I tried to figure out what could have gone wrong, suggesting improvements, and even ventured a theoretical criticism of the whole experiment. I had done my utmost within the limited time I had. I thought I had earned an A. When I got a B+ I asked why. I still remember my amazement at my professor's answer: "You did not get any result!" This answer started my interest in the reasoning of scientists. Obviously the professor and I had different conceptions of "good science."

This may be a common experience of graduate students: their supervisors get impatient with negative results or experiments that don't work. One graduate student at MIT was surprised when his supervisor got angry at him for spending time trying to find out what was wrong with the assay he was using. Another researcher in the same lab learned to refrain from reporting negative results to this supervisor. Of course, there existed a number of good reasons why things might not have worked. But the point is that the students learned not to ask too many questions—to go forward with the research and meanwhile, to follow their professor's motto: "Put your best foot forward."

There seems to exist a principle among some practicing scientists which could be called "Right is Might."[12] Recently, I discussed the famous example of Nobel laureate Robert Millikan's oil-drop experiments with some physicists. I wanted their reaction to the fact that his article stated that his result for the charge of the electron was based on the average of *all* the oil drops over a period of time, when in fact he had omitted the bad ones. (This is something that Gerald Holton at Harvard found out after studying Millikan's notebooks.)[13] Here is how one physicist judges such lies:

> "People say such things as 'this is the average over the entire period.' That is a lie, but people do make statements like that. I don't think it is a terrible crime."

Another physicist's reaction to Millikan's claim that he had included all the oildrops was:

> That is a misleading, possibly even a false statement, but I wouldn't say it is fraudulent. Things can go wrong with experiments, and sometimes you know some readings are not good but you don't know why. That was probably the case with Millikan. Subsequently, his experiment has been repeated and automated at Argonne by Ray Hagstrom. He didn't find a single droplet that was mysterious, not a single deviation from the unit charge.

So Millikan is exonerated on the basis that he was "right." Interestingly, students I taught at Smith College, many of them science majors and involved in research, spent two hours arguing this case. These women were much less lenient with Millikan than the physicists I interviewed.

It appears that at least some physicists (and I suspect a good number of them) are not so interested in *how* you came by your result, if only it holds up later in the light of new experiments. This attitude has important consequences for whistle-blowing in science. The physicist I just quoted said that if you are going to call a scientist a cheat and a liar, you had better be "right" in *two* senses. You have to show not only that his conclusions are unwarranted based on the data, but also that he in fact is drawing the *wrong* conclusion:

Because if you simply accuse people of throwing away bad data, or of improving the statistics of little bit, or not taking into account systematic errors, etc., and the results are ultimately published as a number, if that number holds up in the future, then no matter how the person came up with the conclusion, he isn't going to look that bad in the public eye. On the other hand, if it is a straightforward experiment and someone in the future gets it to disagree by a substantial amount, then he *will* look bad.

Another physicist explained how he handled data points that do not fit, so-called outliers: "It's a feeling!" But he also emphasized that Nobel prizes and the greatest physics have come from outliers, noise, things that did not fit.

Physicists seem to be the group within science most willing to talk explicitly about the role of intuition. Maybe this is because they are more theory-driven than other scientists. Another possibility is that because of the traditionally high standing of physics within the hierarchy of science, physicists feel they can afford to say exactly what they think. One physicist asked for criteria of "good science" blurted out: "It is like playing the piano!"

5. The Field-Specific Nature of Criteria for "Good Science" and Problems with Fraud Teams

The criteria for "good science" seem to be quite field-specific. One can already see this in scientific controversies where scientists from different fields enter the same discourse. I have studied problems of field-specific criteria in the controversies concerning sociobiology, IQ, and environmental risks of genetically engineered organisms.[14]

Different criteria for error also affect the tolerance for non-replicability and at the same time the possibility of fraud in different fields. The fields of physics and biology provide a good contrast here. In physics these days experiments are increasingly automated. It is not uncommon to take data totally by computer. Biologists are more directly involved with their experiments.

There are further differences. One of the physicists I interviewed put it this way:

> As I understand it, in physics the question is, Under what controlled conditions are you taking the data? How accurately do you make the measurements? What are the sources of random error, what is the signal to noise ratio, and so on? In biology, they don't seem to worry about things like that at all. As I understand it, the important thing [in biology] is whether you have an effect or not. If you see it, it tends to knock you over the head!

According to this physicist, one difference between biology and physics is that the environment of physics is relatively controllable and hence the results are ordinarily not surprising. Physicists are in fact trained to believe that surprising results are usually the consequence of error. In biology, on the other hand, controlling what happens is much more difficult and therefore even correct results are often dramatic or surprising.

Another thing differentiating physics from other fields, according to this physicist, is that physics is seeking fundamental knowledge about simple objects. Physicists try to analyze the simplest of all possible situations, using the simplest of materials. Then they go on to study complexities. This means that the experiments are easily repeatable:

> When one lab made high temperature superconductors and described the procedure, hundreds of people could do the same thing and did it overnight. The minute these people published, the materials were accessible to everybody. So if they hadn't been absolutely careful in their description, credit, Nobel prizes, fame and fortune, funding, would all have gone out of the window. They wanted to be very careful before they announced the result.

The physicist added that if someone makes a significant discovery, people will repeat it, extend it, and try to crack holes in it. And they would ordinarily have the materials and apparatus to do it. The difference between physics and biological fields is that in the latter few would have the desire, material, and training to repeat it. Physics may be a much more unified discipline than chemistry or biology, in the sense that everybody has the same fundamental training. The physicists interviewed also pointed to the different conditions for research in biology and physics: biology deals with intrinsically complex systems, where unpredictable things can happen all the time.

Another physicist suggested that the interest drawing students into physics may be fundamentally different from the interest drawing people into biomedical research. Biomedicine draws students who want to make money. The primary interest for a physicist is to understand the basic laws of nature. A person who goes into physics does it because he believes that there are problems that are soluble, that he will have fun solving them, and that he will not earn a lot of money doing it.

Fields like biomedicine, because of their connection to the drug industry and big money for applicable results (e.g., results relevant for curing cancer) may well attract students who want to get rich and famous quickly rather than being interested in finding out how nature works. There may therefore be more of a temptation for students in these fields to engage in shoddy research to get quick results. Not surprisingly, most of the major fraud cases coming to public attention in the late 1970s and early 1980s were in the field of biomedicine. Typically young promising researchers were involved. The physicist interviewed above said that when he heard about some of these cases, involving researchers from Harvard and Cornell, he could not believe his ears.

While physicists believe that good science is based on intuition, they also believe that it can be taught. Yet, they agree that it takes time to learn. One physicist was appalled at how long it took some graduate students. There are potential problems associated with this. Because graduate students often lack the intuition, they may easily think that the group they work with is engaged in fraud or lesser misconduct.

As one physicist explained, there are graduate students who work with a group for a year and then come out and say: "Those guys were fudging everything!" But there is a distinct possibility that the student may not know enough to know why certain things were done and certain data thrown out. He knows this only too well from his own experience as a skeptical graduate student.

Others besides graduate students may be in this awkward position. Another of my informants suspected that the NIH "fraud team," Ned Feder and Walter Stewart,

> are not using the skill of a professional scientist in distinguishing between small differences which are unimportant and small differences which lead to significant new insights. It is just part of the art of being a good scientist, to know how to spot the differences that are important from the differences that are really not.

According to some scientists critical of Feder and Stewart, the problem is that they are not specialists in the fields that they are investigating and have not done much research themselves. They have an impractical view of the scientific method. As one of my informants said: "Science is the art of the possible, it is not some abstract process driven by some abstract logic of analysis. . . . You have to bring in some engineering and some compromises."

When I asked the physicists whether it would be a good idea to have a fraud board or fraud team in physics, à la Feder and Stewart at NIH, one vehemently rejected the idea, pointing out that people in the funding agencies are usually relatively unsuccessful scientists:

> I would be concerned that a fraud team might attract mediocre researchers and it would be mediocre. If you want to have a fraud team, you want the best. You want a fraud team to be at least as good as the people they are trying to catch. Because presumably the way to detect fraud in science is with science. It would give you a false sense of security if these guys were essentially incompetent.

This rejection points to a different problem, which applies even to fraud investigators *within* a specific field. Since the members of the current fraud team at NIH are investigating error and fraud in science *in general*, they could be doubly suspect. If the reasoning of other scientists is similar to this physicist's, Feder and Stewart would have to be the best in their own field to be considered "competent" to assess error and fraud even in that field.

Interestingly, Feder and Stewart themselves don't admit any legitimate constraints on their competence: they feel they have the scientific background needed to investigate scientific error wherever it is found.[15] They feel that they uphold shared scientific standards. Feder and Stewart evidently believe in a unified community of scientists with *universal standards* for "good science." Any member of the scientific community is in principle "competent" to judge any other's work. If scientists in different fields do have field-specific criteria of "good science," whose criteria should be used?

This question does not exclude the possibility of establishing *minimum* agreed-upon standards for all science. Nor should it distract us from the more pressing problem of setting minimum standards of good science for fields with immediate consequences for the general public, such as biomedical research.

6. Can "Good Science" Be Taught?

Graduate courses explicitly in research ethics are still rare. Among the physicists I interviewed, some try to teach research ethics by tacit example; others try to make the graduate student capable of estimating what results can reasonably be expected based on their knowledge of orders of magnitude. They also maintain that good laboratory practice can be specified and taught to students.

But I think one should start "good science" well before graduate school. The place to start is the teaching of science in primary and secondary schools and in undergraduate university curricula. The problem with much science teaching today is exactly the erroneous message it tacitly conveys about science: science is unproblematic and gives unambiguously "right" answers. Laboratory experiments are typically (simplified) replications of classic experiments or illustrations of already known theories. Students are not put in a *real* research situation and taught how to make an informed judgment. A recent Public Television Nova Program ("Do Scientists Cheat?") revealed that science students in high school cheated on their assignments because they wanted the results to come out "right" to get good grades.

The situation may be worse in universities, where undergraduates are taught in the same erroneous way. Students regularly tell me how they make the experimental data points look right, working backwards from theoretically expected results. The present premiums on being "right" rather than earnest efficiently *teaches* undergraduates to *fake* data! Students should instead be taught to construct intelligent hypotheses about the discrepancy between their results and the expected ones. They should be rewarded for thorough critical analysis!

Is it possible that some of the recent fraud cases in science, particularly those committed by junior researchers, may be the result of learning their high school and undergraduate lessons *too well*? Might they still believe that data have to be close to perfect, no matter what?

I think that training for "good science" has to start early. The great difficulty many graduate students have learning the elusive practice of "good science" may well be due to their high school or undergraduate training having thoroughly destroyed their ability to understand the process of science.

So what can we do? As I said before, there has to be some other method than grading the lab reports according to "correctness" of the results. Part of the undergraduate science education ought to be practical exercises in thinking up various measures that could be taken to avoid self-deception. The importance of controlled experiments and the idea of double-blind experiments in medical research is probably already impressed upon students, but it would be particularly illustrative for them to learn about mistakes that were made because appropriate control measures were not taken. The teachers can surely come up with examples from their own experience or from the body of gossip in science. Perhaps practicing scientists can be invited to discuss their own experience and insights with the students in class.

In their own laboratory exercises, students could be given experiments to perform where they do not know from theory what the results ought to be. They could then be asked to document exactly what they did and to demonstrate in detail how they tried to control for error and self-deception. Finally, they could be asked to compare results and discuss the reasons for possible differences. This would be giving the students a glimpse of the world of "real" research.

In order to aid their imagination as to what may go wrong if proper controls are not taken, students could read and discuss famous cases probably involving self-deception, such as the N-rays case. In this way they would learn to appreciate how easily even well-established researchers may become prey of wishful thinking. One particularly useful classic in this genre is Irving Langmuir's article on "pathological science," where he warns of dangers of self-deception in situations where scientists are dealing with barely detectable effects.[16]

Furthermore, there ought to be discussions about what to do with a set of hypothetical results, part of which would be "bad." The students could then be asked what these data showed, what further experiments or controls would be needed, etc. All this would train the scientific imagination in a useful way and make some now elusive "good science" more explicit. I believe everybody, students as well as teachers, would benefit from this.

Another way to open the students'—and their teachers'—eyes to what good science is would be to expose them to the history, sociology and psychology of science. A famous article in *Science* by Stephen Brush in 1974 was entitled "Should the History of Science Be Rated X?."[17] His ironical point was that learning about the history of science might interfere with current science teaching. Science has indeed too long been presented as a triumphantly progressing enterprise, with errors, wrong leads and dubious practices systematically brushed under the carpet. It is time to challenge the simplistic "storybook image" of science and learn about the intricate realities of scientific research along with the content of science. Instead of interfering with science teaching, such an approach might, on the contrary, impress students with the fact that science seems to work despite all!

NOTES

1. Richard Morris, *Dismantling the Universe: The Nature of Scientific Discovery* (New York: Simon and Schuster, Touchstone Books, 1983), p. 97.

2. I here rely on the account given by Morris, op. cit., chapter 4.

3. For a discussion of Vulcan, see Morris, op. cit., chapter 5. The case of N-rays is one of the standard cases of presumed self-deception and is discussed among others in Morris, op. cit.; and William Broad and Nicholas Wade, *Betrayers of the Truth: Fraud and Deceit in the Halls of Science* (New York: Simon and Schuster, Touchstone Books, 1983). However, the case may not be as clear-cut as some scientists would have it. See, e.g., Mary Jo Nye, "N-rays: An Episode in the History and Psychology of Science," *Historical Studies in the Physical Sciences*, vol. 11, no. 1 (1980), pp. 125–156.

4. Ron Westrum, "Science and Social Intelligence about Anomalies: The Case of Meteorites," *Social Studies of Science*, vol. 7 (1977), pp. 271–302.

5. Interview with Tom Erber, Professor of Physics, Illinois Institute of Technology.

6. Accounts of this can be found among others in Broad and Wade, op. cit., chapter 6. The original source is Robert Rosenthal, *Experimenter Effects in Behavioral Research* (New York: Appleton-Century Crofts, 1966), pp. 158–179.

7. Stephen J. Gould, *The Mismeasure of Man* (New York: W.W. Norton, 1981). Broad and Wade, op. cit., chapter 11, have a good summary of Gould's research.

8. The case of Cyril Burt is discussed among others in Broad and Wade, op. cit., chapter 11. The Burt case has by now become a standard episode to invoke in discussions of scientific fraud. One of the basic sources is L.S. Hearnshaw, *Cyril Burt, Psychologist* (London: Hodder and Stoughton, 1979). The relevance of the findings about Burt for the overall field of IQ research is assessed by John Thoday, "Probity in Science: The Case of Cyril Burt," *Nature*, vol. 291 (1981), pp. 517–518.

9. Michael Polanyi, "The Growth of Science in Society," *Minerva* vol. 4, Summer (1967), pp. 533–545. Reprinted in Edward Shils (ed.), *Criteria for Scientific Development* (Cambridge, MA: MIT Press, 1968).

10. See Harry Collins, "The Seven Sexes: A Study of a Phenomenon, or the Replication of Experiments in Physics," *Sociology*,

vol. 9 (1975), pp. 205–24. Reprinted in Barry Barnes and David Edge, *Science in Context: Reading in the Sociology of Science* (Milton Keynes: Open University Press, 1982).

11. Robert G. Bergman, "Irreproducibility in the Scientific Literature: How Often Do Scientists Tell the Whole Truth and Nothing But the Truth?" *Perspectives on the Professions*, vol. 8, no. 2 (1989), pp. 2–3.

12. Ullica Segerstrale, "Right is Might: Physicists on Fraud, Fudging, and "Good Science," Perspectives on the Professions, vol. 8, no. 2 (1989), pp. 5–6.

13. Gerald Holton, "Subelectrons, Presuppositions, and the Millikan-Ehrenhaft Dispute." In Gerald Holton, *The Scientific Imagination* (Cambridge: Cambridge University Press, 1978).

14. For discussions of the sociobiology and IQ controversies, see Ullican Segerstrale, *Whose Truth Shall Prevail? Moral and Scientific Interests in the Sociobiology Controversy*, Ph.D. dissertation in sociology, Harvard University (1983); Ullica Segerstrale, "Colleagues in Conflict: An 'In Vivo' Analysis of the Sociobiology Controversy," *Biology and Philosophy*, vol. 1, no. 1 (1986), pp. 53–86; Ullica Segerstrale, "The (Re)Colonization of Science by the Life-World: Problems and Prospects," in Hans Haferkamp (ed.), *Social Structure and Culture* (Berlin and New York: Walter de Gruyter, 1989); and Ullica Segerstrale, "The Sociobiology of Conflict and the Conflict about Sociobiology," in Vincent Falger et al. (eds.), *Sociobiology and Conflict* (London: Chapman & Hall, in press). For an analysis of field-specific criteria in the debate about the environmental risks of genetically engineered microorganisms, see Ullica Segerstrale, "Negotiating 'Sound Science': Expert Disagreement about the Risks of Release of Genetically Engineered Micro-organisms," *Politics and the Life Sciences*, vol. 8, no. 2 (1990), pp. 221–231.

15. Stewart told *Science*: "We're not investigators *for* NIH. We look into facts as scientists." Cf. Barbara Culliton, "A Bitter Battle Over Error I," *Science*, vol. 240, 24 June (1988a), pp. 1720–1723; and Barbara Culliton, "A Bitter Battle Over Error II," *Science*, vol. 241, 1 July (1988b), pp. 18–21.

16. For the N-rays case, see references above. Other useful cases to study are the Polywater episode in the 1970s and the recent case of Jaques Benveniste and his "water with a memory." The Polywater case is briefly treated in Morris, op. cit., but for a full understanding of the complexities of the case and the temptation of scientists to jump on the bandwagon, see Felix Franks, *Polywater* (Cambridge, MA: MIT Press, 1982). The Benveniste case is treated among others in the following

articles: Robert Pool, "Unbelievable Results Spark a Controversy," *Science*, vol. 241, 22 July (1988b), p. 407; Robert Pool, "More Squabbling Over Unbelievable Results," *Science*, vol. 241, 5 August (1988b), p. 658; John Langone, "The Water that Lost Its Memory," *Time Magazine*, August 8 (1988), p. 73; and Gail Vines, "The Ghostbusters report from Paris," *New Scientist*, 4 August (1988), pp. 30–31. See also Jacques Benveniste, "Jacques Benveniste replies," *Nature*, vol. 334, July (1988), p. 291. The original Langmuir reference is Irving Langmuir, "Pathological Science," General Electric Research and Development Center Report 86–C–035, April (1968). It is reprinted in the October issue of *Physics Today*, 1989.

17.   Stephen Brush, "Should the History of Science be Rated X?" *Science*, vol. 183 (1974), pp. 1164–1172.

On the Supposed Indispensability of Deception in Social Psychology

Steven C. Patten

1. Indispensability and the Logic of the Experiment

The claim that deception is indispensable to research in social psychology has the status of a canon. Thus, for example, one of the standard treatises on social psychology research methods remarks with easy confidence that ". . . it is sometimes possible to answer particular questions without concealing the true nature of the experiment by the use of deceptive devices. . . . "[1] How does one arrive at such a conclusion? The literature contains two clearly separate arguments, although they are often intertwined and conflated. The first case proceeds by way of reflection on supposed logical features of certain kinds of experiment; the second case points to putatively indisputable facts about experiments in social psychology which make use of deception. We will consider each method of justification in turn.

There is something initially tempting, almost overwhelmingly so, in the suggestion that in at least some instances the need for deception becomes apparent once the description of the experiment is properly appreciated. Thus, Aronson and Carlsmith: ". . . One cannot imagine an experimenter studying the effects of group pressure on conformity (as in the Asch experiment) by announcing his intentions in advance."[2] And similarly, Alan Soble:

Experiments designed to test for the existence of psychological phenomena such as obedience and trustworthiness seem necessarily to involve the use of deception. Telling the subjects that what is being studied is, for example, the extent to which they conform with the judgments of persons who are really cohorts of the experimenter will destroy the attempt to discover the extent of conformity.[3]

Succinctly, Westland: "There exist a set of cases where it is absolutely crucial to the logic of the experiment that the subject should not be able to guess what it is all about."[4]

Despite the obvious popularity of this defense of deception on the basis of the logic of the experiment, it remains curiously unproven. To be sure, proof here, if forthcoming, will differ significantly from the usual stacking of facts: the claim is a logical one, it involves an assertion of entailment or conceptual connection. But nonetheless the justification for the claim that deception is required calls for something more than the bare mention of research topics like reactions to authority or conformity; and it needs to appeal to something deeper than someone complaining that his imagination will not countenance a bit of research proceeding without deception. The history of thought is fraught with confident and thoroughly mistaken claims based on the limited horizons of someone's imagination. What *is* required is nothing more than an explicit statement of the experiment along with a clear demonstration that the very idea that such an experiment could proceed without deception is logically bizarre. This bare minimum has not, I submit, ever been provided.

And, in fact, we should not be entirely surprised that we have yet to be shown that studying, say, obedience or conformity logically requires deception. For certain uncomplicated considerations strongly suggest that no such positive argument can be put together. First, consider the stunningly simple fact that experiments with obedience to authority *have* been done without the use of deception. I am thinking, of course, of the role-playing experiments making use of Milgram's model.[5] It may well be that particular role-playing experiments are more or less good, exact, illuminating, etc., but it is curious if not bizarre to suggest that the studies are *conceptually absurd*, that experimenters who engage in role-playing studies of say, obedience, are attempting something logically amiss.

It would be worthwhile to consider the main features of this counterargument. It moves from an appreciation of the fact that proponents of the logic of the experiment defence of deception cite certain supposed clear cases—exemplars—where deception is said to be entailed in a non-trivial way.[6] Then, or so it seems, an implicit generalization is made: deception in general, or in relevantly similar cases—it is not clear which is claimed to be the right inference—is justified by reflection on the logic of the experiment. The countercase put forward here begins with the factual claim that (a) no one has shown that alternatives to the exemplars which do not make use of deception are logically inconceivable, and (b) role-playing alternatives *are* logically coherent. From these factual claims it does follow that any inference from the acknowledged set of exemplars alone to a general justification of deception is without warrant. Nonetheless, it does not follow that there cannot be some clear cases which have yet to be remarked, discovered or uncovered, where deception is indispensable to the experiment. Still, failure of the standard exemplars to exhibit indispensability must give us pause; for it does give us some inductive warrant for thinking that such instances are going to be very difficult to find.

And, when the richness and complexity of experiments which do not make use of deception are considered, the argument from the logic of the experiment will tempt one all the less. In fact, we are likely to find it claimed that experiments with deception are somehow required to *verify* those based on role-playing. We will be told that no matter how sophisticated the given role-playing experiment one "still must wonder whether the observed behavior is the same as that which a genuine subject would produce." Thus, or so the argument proceeds, ". . . we must still perform the crucial experiment [with deception] to determine whether role-played behavior corresponds to non role-played behavior."[7]

It is essential to note, though ignored in the methodological literature, that the case in favour of the necessity of deception has taken a new turn. The claim is now that deception preserves greater experimental realism than alternatives. And this claim is *inconsistent* with the idea that the logic of the experiment entails the necessity of the method of deception. For, as we have seen, the defence of the use of deceptive practices based on putative logical features of the description of the experiment means that it is *logically* impossible for anyone to aspire to the same or similar results using a methodology other than deception. This is what it means to say that deception is a function of the logic of the experiment. Yet, if a technique or experimental method which does not use deception *is* so impossible, then it is foolishly inconsistent to imagine *testing* the results of (say) a role-playing experiment against the analogue which makes use of deception. For the very act of testing the results of the role-playing experiment against the outcome of the one using deception presupposes that the question of the status of the role-playing experiment is an empirical one and thus not a matter of logic at all. And all of this is to say that the person who does wish to pursue the argument from greater realism must abandon the one which is supposed to move from a bare description of the experiment.[8]

Indispensability and Experimental Realism

But all is not felicitous with this argument from realism once clarified. Taken in one way it is certainly question begging, understood in another way it is based on a false premise. The question-begging feature of the argument comes to light in this way. What one wants to know is whether or not methods like role-playing are as experimentally effective as those which make use of deception. We are told, one will recall, that this is not so since it is a matter of dispute or verification whether role-playing behavior ". . . is the same as that which a *genuine subject* would produce."[9] Yet surely, to assume at the start that the behaviour of a subject in an experiment making use of deception is genuine, the real stuff, whereas that of the role-playing experiment is a weak imitation or is counterfeit, is to beg the question at issue.

The argument from realism can avoid the charge of assuming the conclusion as a premise if we suppose that it makes use of a suppressed premise to the effect that, *in fact*, role-playing behaviour is not as veridical or "genuine" as behaviour elicited from experiments which use deception. There is certainly nothing wild about such a supposition, it is the very viscera of traditional methodological guides such as Aronson and Carlsmith. For example, they cite the telling nature of the behaviour of subjects in Asch's conformity experiments.

> For most subjects this experiment seems to have contained a good deal of experimental realism. Whether subjects yielded to group pressure or stood firm, the vast majority underwent a rather painful experience which caused them to squirm, sweat, and exhibit other signs of tension and anxiety. They were involved, upset, and deeply concerned about this evidence which was being presented to them. We may assume that they were reacting to a situation that was as "real" for them as any of their ordinary experiences.[10]

In contrast it is part of this tradition to be told that "a role-playing situation lacks experimental realism; it has little impact on a subject for the simple reason that nothing is happening to him."[11]

Yet one will not walk far with such a premise. It is a broken stick. It is false. Here is a description of subjects' behaviour in an obedience experiment:

> The video tapes recorded the extent of emotional involvement among the involved participants and, to a lesser extent, the uninvolved. Grimaces, looks of stress, and expressions of empathy or sympathy were common, as were nervous smiles, laughter when the victim screamed, and a wide range of nervous activities and fidgeting.[12]

The quote does *not* come from Stanley Milgram or one of his followers in the use of obedience in studying obedience; rather it comes from the role-playing study of obedience by Daniel Geller. And recall how engaged Zimbardo's subjects were in his role-playing prison studies.[13] Taken together such research shows without doubt that subject involvement in role-playing experiments can be as thoroughly realistic as behaviour in any experiment based on deception. And it is just this fact that shows the falsity of the premise we have supposed suppressed in the argument from experimental realism: Using the acknowledged standard of subject involvement role-playing behaviour can be just as genuine as behaviour generated in experiments using deception.[14]

And one should resist the temptation to shift to a more general premise. One should suppress the urge to declaim that entire role-playing experiments somehow lack corroboration or verification whereas deception experiments do not. Such a premise would, I think, get us closer to the desired conclusion— that role-playing experiments must be measured by runs with deception—but only if we are willing again to assent to a proposition which has been shown false. For the benchmark of corroboration and verification in social psychology has traditionally (and rightly) been replication of subject participation. The role-playing literature shows us that we have it.[15] Thus, our more general candidate for a suppressed premise should be rejected as well.

To be sure, I have been assuming throughout that what one writer refers to as pragmatic usefulness[16] will not prove acceptable as a stand-in for indispensability. Deception might well be quicker, cheaper or less cumbersome than alternatives, but the same could perhaps be true of threats and bullying as an experimental tool—and no one would thereby argue for the general use of threats and bullying. Furthermore, and pressing, it is generally acknowledged that debriefing after deception requires some statement of the necessity of the use of deception.[17] How else is the deceit to be explained to one's subjects? Yet it is not to be expected that invoking expeditiousness will assuage.

The day has long passed that experimenters in social psychology can ask for and expect to receive special dispensation with respect to policy guidelines on deception.[18] Given the agreement of both critics and proponents that indispensability must be shown, and appreciating the weakness of the contemporary crop of arguments for indispensability, the choice seems straightforward: either deception in social psychology should be brought to a halt or some satisfactory case should be produced which establishes the indispensability of deception.[19]

NOTES

*I am grateful to the Social Sciences and Humanities Research Council for assistance. I have enjoyed discussing some of the issues covered in this essay with Hugh Spencer. My thanks to Tom Murray, Diana Baumrind and Barry Allen for critical comments. Versions of this paper were read at the University of Prince Edward Island (May, 1981) and at The Fourteenth Trans-Disciplinary Symposium on Philosophy and Medicine: An International Congress on the Use of Human Beings in Research, Tel Aviv University (September 1982).

1. E. Aronson and J.M. Carlsmith, "Experimentation in Social Psychology," in *The Handbook of Social Psychology*, vol. 2, ed. G. Lindzey and E. Aronson (2nd ed.: Reading, MA.: Addison Wesley, 1968–69), 29. For similar remarks see 34 and 35 as well. And note this confident line from the CPA brief: "Unless the researcher is . . . allowed to measure some kinds of behavior without the subject's consent, or even awareness, little valid research could be carried out." (2).

It might be the case that certain research psychologists do not intend the logic of the experiment argument to be a claim of logical entailment as it is represented here. Nonetheless, or so I would contend, it is clear that they either base their case on some looser sort of a priori reflection that is captured by the criticism of the logic of the experiment case put forward here, or they mean to appeal to a supposed lack of realism in subjects' behaviour. I deal with the question of realism below.

2. Ibid., 30.

3. Soble, "Deception in Social Science Research: Is informed Consent Possible?" *Hastings Center Report* 8/5 (August 1978), 40.

4. Gordon Westland, *Current Crises of Psychology* (London: Heinemann, 1978), 109.

5. To be sure, I have in mind Daniel M. Geller's recent "Involvement in Role-Playing Simulations: A Demonstration with Studies on Obedience." *Journal of Personality and Social Psychology* 36/3 (March 1978), 219–234, but all would acknowledge that Don Mixon has fathered thorough and thoughtful role-playing work in this area. See, for example, "Instead of Deception," *Journal for the Theory of Social Behavior* 2 (1972), 145–177, and "If You Won't Deceive, What Can You Do?" in N. Armistead., ed., *Reconstructing Social Psychology* (London: Penguin, 1974). R.H. Willis and Y.A. Willis, "Role Playing Versus Deception: An Experimental Comparison," *Journal of Personality and Social Psychology* 16/3 (1970), 272–277, put forward a conformity

experiment which makes use of role-playing. H. Tristram Engelhart, Jr. seems confident that the "Pygmalion" experiments of Rosenthal could not have been performed successfully without deception. I know of no similar experiments founded on role-playing or some other alternative, but the key point is that Engelhardt does not provide an analysis which shows that deception is logically necessary in this or any other case. See "Basic Ethical Principles in the Conduct of Biomedical and Behavioral Research Involving Human Subjects," *The Belmont Report: Ethical Principles and Guidelines for the Protection of Human Subjects of Research,* The National Commission for the Protection of Human Subjects of Biomedical and Behavioral Research, DHEW Publication No. (OS) 78-0013 (Washington, D.C.: U.S. Government Printing Office, 1978), Appendix, vol. 1, 8–44, note 47.

6. The requirement that the experiment require deception in a nontrivial way is needed to avoid cases where a description is pieced together so that deception is conveniently made analytic. E.g., from Soble, "Deception in Social Science Research," 41: "the effect of LSD-25 on the behavior of a group of *unsuspecting* enlisted men" (my emphasis).

7. S. Milgram, "Subject Reaction: The Neglected Factor in the Ethics of Experimentation." *Hastings Center Report* 7/5 (August 1977), 22–23, quoted by Soble, "Deception in Social Science Research," 46, note 20. The phrase in brackets is Soble's.

8. This charge of inconsistent conflation applies to certain commentators. It certainly fits Soble (ibid.) and might well be tied to Milgram as well (ibid.), although one cannot be completely certain in the latter case.

9. Milgram, "Subject Reaction," 23, my emphasis.

10. Aronson and Carlsmith, "Experimentation in Social Psychology," 22.

11. Ibid., 27.

12. Geller, "Involvement in Role-Playing Simulations," 231–232.

13. Philip Zimbardo, "The Mind is a Formidable Jailer: A Pirandellian Prison," *The New York Times Magazine,* April 8, 1973.

14. Curiously one research psychologist who is a critic of the use of role-playing experiments on the ground of lack of realism, points out that role-playing experiments can have ethical problems similar to those connected with deception experiments because of the high degree of "real emotions" which can be produced. But how can one have it both ways? How can one question a set of experiments on the genuineness of the subjects' involvement and then fault them once again because the

subjects are too highly engaged? See Milgram, "Subject Reaction," 22–23.

15. See, for example, Geller's tabulation of role-playing results in obedience studies, "Involvement in Role-Playing Simulations," 227.

16. Soble, "Deception in Social Science Research," 41.

17. Aronson and Carlsmith, "Experimentation in Social Psychology," 32.

18. In this respect the fears and responses in developing the U.S. Public Health Service guidelines in application to the behavioral sciences have a certain antiquarian charm. See Mark S. Frankel, "The Development of Policy Guidelines Governing Human Experimentation in the United States: A Case of Public Policy-Making for Science and Technology," *Ethics in Science and Medicine* 2 (Spring 1975), esp. 52–53.

19. I hope that I will not be misunderstood. This paper should not be viewed as a defence of role-playing or any other alternative methodology. Instances of role-playing have been cited as part of a case against a pair of a priori arguments in favour of the indispensability of deception in social psychology. By itself, this use is not sufficient to justify role-playing over alternative methodologies. Also I have not argued that deception experiments should be stopped without further ado. Rather, I have suggested that they should be halted if a justifying case cannot be produced that is better than those surveyed in this paper.

Keeping Deception Honest: Justifying Conditions for Social Scientific Research Stratagems

Alan C. Elms

The Problem of Deception:
A Consequentialist Middle Ground

Deception is a word used to end arguments, not to begin them. To accuse researchers of deception is to remove them from the ranks of those with whom legitimate human relationships can be pursued. The term is so sweeping that it includes Satan's lures for lost souls, the traitor's treachery, the false lover's violation of a pure heart. How could any deception ever be considered ethically justifiable if it keeps such company?

The use of so broad a term as *deception* is itself deceptive when applied without qualification to certain common procedures in social scientific research. It muddies issues, biases ethical debates, lumps together a vast array of practices that differ in intent, execution, and outcome. Because of such radical differences among various practices labeled "deception," social scientists have suggested other terms for the kinds of stratagems used in their research, such as "staging" or "technical illusions."[1]

But stage plays and magic tricks are not quite on the same order as our research stratagems, either. The researcher hopes that subjects will not realize an illusion is being created. If the experiment is to work, they should perceive the stage scenery through which they are walking, the memorized speeches of the actors around them, as genuine. When the curtain falls, they are not likely to break into spontaneous applause—any more than they are likely to call the Bunco Squad or the Consumer Fraud Division. So "staging" and similar terms are as problematic as "deception." In lieu of a better word, I will continue to use "deception" for the practice of misleading research subjects, even though it obliterates important distinctions among forms of deception.

Certain ethicists refuse to differentiate social scientists' attempts to mislead subjects from any other kind of deception, conceptually as well as terminologically. For them, the argument is already over: there are no circumstances under which social scientific deception is ethically permissible. Non-absolutists are likely to find such an absolutist stance worth little attention, and I do not have the space to examine it closely here. For those who are interested, Sissela Bok has summarized the basic philosophical arguments against it.[2]

Certain others—I hesitate to call them ethicists, though they do hold down the other end of the ethical scale from the moral absolutists—insist that normal rules do not apply to science, that the end knowledge fully justifies the deceptive means. In extreme form, these people appear to us as Nazi eugenicists or as the mad scientists of Hollywood—much beloved by the moral absolutists, who need such opponents to justify their own extremist stance. In milder form, they include simple corner-cutters, Machiavellian careerists, and earnest believers in the primacy of scientific truth.

The position in the middle of the scale is the hard one to hold. Here are those who see life as filled with moral conflicts, rarely easy to resolve, and who see social scientific research as a necessary part of their ethical life. They see such research as the best route to certain ethical goals, and an element of deception as essential to certain kinds of research. They do not accept deception easily, and so they are the ones who might ask, and who need to know, what conditions make deceptions sometimes ethically tolerable in social scientific research. They are the ones to whom I am mainly speaking, and whom at the same time I am trying to represent.

In so doing, I am taking what is variously called a consequentialist, risk-benefit, or cost-benefit position. Shakespeare neatly dramatized the classic case for this position in *Measure for Measure*, where he presented a novice nun with a moral dilemma: should she yield her virginity to a rapacious judge in order to save her brother's life, or should she deceive the judge and thereby save both her brother and her sexual virtue? The Duke of Vienna, apparently voicing Shakespeare's own sentiments, counsels her to deceive the judge. He assures her that "the doubleness of the benefit defends the deceit from reproof."[3] The Duke and Shakespeare are making a cost-benefit analysis, and they conclude that in this instance the benefits of deception considerably outweigh the costs. Most people other than the strictest moral absolutists would agree: when the value of honesty conflicts with other values, certain circumstances may make those other values more important than honesty, and deception then becomes tolerable.

"Tolerable" does not mean "ethically neutral." Deception is, as Bok argues, never a neutral practice.[4] It always carries potential harm to the interests of the deceived, in this case to the research subjects who might have chosen to avoid research participation had they been fully and accurately informed. It always carries potential harm to the deceivers, in this case the researchers and their assistants, whose reputation for veracity may be harmed and whose own character may be affected negatively by repeated deceptive practices. It carries potential harm to the deceivers' profession, since social scientists in general may become less trusted as the deceptive practices of part of the profession become well known. And it carries potential harm to society, in that it may contribute to a general lack of trust and to the willingness of nonprofessionals to act deceptively themselves. Perhaps none of these potential harms will be realized, if social scientific deception remains on a small scale and is surrounded by various kinds of constraints and counteractive efforts. But given the potential for harm, deception in social scientific research is not something to be employed casually. It must be carefully justified and any negative effects must be offset as much as possible.

What, then, are the boundary conditions under which deception can be considered ethically justifiable in social scientific research? I will state the major conditions in a single sentence, and then expound upon each term: *Deception is justifiable in social scientific research when (1) there is no other feasible way to obtain the desired information, (2) the likely benefits substantially outweigh the likely harms, (3) subjects are given the option to withdraw from participation at any time without penalty, (4) any physical or psychological harm to subjects is temporary, and (5) subjects are debriefed as to all substantial deceptions and the research procedures are made available for public review.* All of these conditions are by now familiar to researchers and ethicists; some have already been built into federal law. Most social scientists who use deception have accepted the conditions as reasonable and even necessary components of their own ethical decision-making processes. But not all ethicists have accepted the conditions as *sufficient* justification. I would like to argue that these five conditions are both necessary *and* sufficient justifications for the use of deception in social scientific research.

Lack of Feasible Alternatives

Henry A. Murray stated the primary justification for social scientific deception some forty years ago, in the opening pages of his classic work *Explorations in Personality.*[5] Among "the few general principles that our [research] experience invited us to adopt," he lists two that are immediately relevant:

[A]. The experimental session should be as life-like as possible. This is important because the purpose of personological studies is to discover how a man reacts under the stress of common conditions. To know how he responds to a unique, unnatural laboratory situation is of minor interest.

[B]. The subject's mind should be diverted from the true purpose of an experiment. This is usually accomplished by announcing a plausible but fictitious objective. If a subject recognizes the experimenter's aim, his responses will be modified by other motives: for instance, by the desire to conceal the very thing which the experimenter wishes to observe.

Deception is at times necessary, Murray says, in order to create a laboratory situation that will seem life-like rather than artificial, since situations that strike the subject as artificial will tell us little about human behavior and may even mislead us. We need experimental control over relevant variables because neither naturalistic observation nor the subtlest statistical manipulations of available data will in all cases allow us to sort out the crucial psychological variables; but, paradoxically, we must sometimes use deception to make an experimentally created situation *seem* real, so that subjects will give genuine, generalizable responses.

Elliot Aronson and J. Merrill Carlsmith make a useful distinction in this regard between "experimental realism" and "mundane realism."[6] An experiment is realistic in the first sense "if the situation is realistic to the subject, if it involves him, if he is forced to take it seriously, if it has impact on him." It is realistic in the second sense "to the extent to which events occurring in a laboratory setting are likely to occur in the 'real world.' . . . The mere fact that an event is similar to events that occur in the real world does not endow it with importance. Many events that occur in the real world are boring and uninvolving." Thus an experiment may be trivial because it is unrealistic in any sense; or it may be trivial because it merely presents some version of mundane reality. But it may transcend triviality by the "stress of common conditions," through the creation of an invented but emotionally involving experimental reality. The latter kind of experiment may be an important route to valuable information about human behavior (whereas the former kinds will never be); and it may be possible to pursue such a route only through the use of deception.

But what of alternative routes? Why not, for instance, simply approach people honestly and ask them to tell us about themselves? This is in some circumstances the best procedure to follow, and I certainly find it a more *comfortable* procedure than deceptive experimentation. But Murray points out its weakness as an exclusive approach, in his Principle B. Wittingly or unwittingly, a subject's knowledge that particular aspects of his or her behavior are under study will almost certainly lead to modifications of that behavior. Enough data are available on the powerful effects of "demand characteristics," the subtle and unintended cues from researchers concerning their intentions and expectations, to indicate that explicit acknowledgement of such intentions and expectations could seriously disrupt normal behavior patterns. Further, subjects may have less than admirable reasons for trying intentionally to mislead researchers about their behavior—particularly about those aspects of behavior that society might have a strong interest in understanding and perhaps in working to modify. Destructive obedience, child abuse, racial and sexual prejudice, authoritarianism—the list could easily be extended of important psychological patterns that many people would be reluctant to admit, but that we need to understand much better if we wish to build a more satisfying society for all. If individuals will not talk about such matters honestly when they are asked straightforwardly, some form of research deception may be essential in order to gain the information we need.

Moreover, people may simply not know how they would behave in certain socially important but seldom encountered situations. Concerning such matters, it may be useless to ask people what they would probably do, and impossible to observe them in relevant real-life situations where the major variables are sufficiently unconfounded to let us make sense of the psychological processes at work. Once again, some use of deception to create an experimental reality may be the only effective means to collect essential knowledge.

But what about simulation? The word here refers not to creating an experimental reality by artificial means, but to asking research subjects to *pretend* they are participating in a realistic experiment and having them report how they think they would behave if they really were in such an experiment. This kind of simulation has often been recommended by people who do not wish to abandon the strengths of experimental research but who find deception to be an unacceptable aspect of such research. Unfortunately, simulation has proven to be an inadequate alternative both methodologically and ethically. If the simulation is relatively undetailed, it is not much different from simply asking people directly to describe how they would behave in various circumstances in the real world, and it has the same flaws as that approach—people often don't know, or don't want to tell, how they would behave.[7] If the simulation closely reproduces each step of a genuine experiment, however—if for instance, as in Don Mixon's[8] or Daniel Geller's[9] simulations of the Milgram obedience studies, subjects are walked through every stage of the experiment, being given only the information available to genuine experimental subjects at each stage—it may gain in accuracy of subjects' self-reports at the expense of ethical losses. Simulation subjects may undergo stresses similar in quality if not in intensity to those experienced by genuine subjects, and at the end they may feel similarly misled as to the actual scope or intent of the experiment they have helped to simulate. Using another example, the fact that Philip Zimbardo's prison study[10] was a simulation does not divest it of the ethical dilemmas originally confronted in nonsimulation experiments. Further, even though simulation studies rendered sufficiently close in detail to the original experiment may yield similar data from their "as-if" subjects, serious doubt would always remain about the validity of a simulation study if no "real" experiment were available for comparison. The substitution of simulation studies for experiments experienced by their participants as real thus appears to be a commendable but unrealizable dream.

The Harm-Benefit Calculus

Here is where I must take an explicitly consequentialist position. Most social scientists are consequentialists, as least to some degree; otherwise they would not take the trouble to do social scientific research. The difficulty of framing and executing empirical studies, the high level of ambiguity that must be tolerated in the typical results, the ethical distress that never quite goes away—all these must be offset by the hope that some kind of social benefit will derive from the research in the long run. Otherwise, you might as well become a philosopher.

Remarkably little direct harm has ever come to subjects from academic social scientific research. I say "academic" because I am not willing to attempt any general ethical justification for the research programs of the CIA, General Mills, or the Church of Scientology, seem scientific though they may be at times. They are not subject to the same kinds of regulations as academic research, and they are not open to free discussion or to the informal influence of scientific peer pressure. In terms of *academic* research, a potential subject is in far less physical danger during virtually any kind of research participation than in driving across town to an experimental session, or in spending the research hour playing tennis instead. Psychologically, as researchers have often pointed out to institutional review boards, the principal danger to the typical subject is boredom. The individual is at much greater psychological risk in deciding to get married, to have a baby, or to enroll as a college student— all activities typically entered without truly informed consent— than in participating in practically any academic research study ever carried out by a social scientist.

But what of the more notorious examples of psychologically stressful research? I worked behind the scenes of the most notorious of all, the Milgram obedience studies,[11] and I interviewed a substantial sample of the participants later,[12] as did (independently) a psychiatrist.[13] The remarkable thing about the Milgram subjects was not that they suffered great persisting harm, but that they suffered so little, given the intensity of their emotional reactions during the experiment itself. Through a combination of careful debriefing and their own standard coping mechanisms, nearly all subjects were able to process the Milgram experience as interesting but as basically irrelevant to their long-term psychological comfort. Though some commentators refuse to believe this, they must ignore not only the data on the Milgram subjects but also a great deal of evidence about human psychological resilience under much more traumatic conditions—from birth, through adolescence, to terminal illness. It may be possible to find an occasional individual who suffers some kind of lasting distress from an encounter with an inept experimenter, of from some unwanted self-insight induced by research participation.[14] But a botched debriefing cannot be held against the bulk of responsibly conducted studies, and a psychologically fragile individual's reactions to carefully managed research participation are unlikely to be any worse than to an emotionally involving movie, a fire-and-brimstone sermon, or a disappointing job interview.

And what of the indirect harms that might come from a deceptive study? I have already mentioned the possibility that deceptive research will generate a greater distrust of social scientists and of other people in general. Researchers should take such concerns into account in limiting deceptive research practices to a necessary minimum. But these concerns are often exaggerated, at times by elevating social scientists into sacred protectors of the truth who must never be caught in even momentary deception. The general public does not see social scientists that way, according to various public opinion polls. Furthermore, abuses of public trust by politicians, physicians, lawyers, ministers, business leaders, and other supposedly trustworthy individuals touch much more directly on people's lives than the encapsulated deceptions of social scientists. Indeed, if could reasonably be argued that certain social scientific research practices, such as prompt debriefing after deception, should work to *promote* trust, in contrast to the attempts of these other societal leaders to maintain deceptions for as long as possible.

Given the generally minor harms of properly conducted social scientific research, what are the benefits? It must be acknowledged that few social scientific research studies will produce any *immediate* major benefits to participants or to society. Unless the researcher is testing a specific aspect of a carefully formulated social program, itself derived from earlier and more basic research, the findings are likely to be useful only in terms of adding to the broad body of social scientific knowledge, much of it tentative and even contradictory. That is the way of science, and it appears to be the way still more of social science, for reasons which we need not examine here. Any insistence that social science research always meet criteria of immediate utility would make it a mere adjunct of business, government, and military interests and would frustrate forever its development as a source of basic scientific discoveries useful in a broad range of applications.

Such preclusion of basic social scientific research would carry its own long-term ethical costs, usually ignored or dismissed by those intent on eliminating short-range costs. It is on this point that the ethical commitment of many social scientists is often misunderstood by professional ethicists. If your planned research clearly has some short-term ethical costs in terms of subject stress or deceptive practices, say the ethicists, why not use a less intrusive methodology or change your research topic entirely? Were researchers mainly concerned with professional respectability or academic advancement, one of those alternatives would indeed be the sensible course to take, and in fact some researchers have made such a shift—or have quit doing research altogether—in the face of difficulties with critics and IRBs. But other researchers continue to feel ethically obligated to investigate serious human issues in ways that are powerful enough scientifically to contribute to the expansion of basic knowledge, not merely in ways that will generate another journal publication as inoffensively as possible. These researchers are usually concerned with the immediate welfare of their subjects, and with the potentially negative social effects of such practices as deception; their critics have no monopoly on such concerns. But these researchers also perceive the dangers in sins of omission, of failures to do the responsible basic research that may contribute to major long-run social benefits. Such commitment to the active pursuit of usable, slowly cumulative information about human behavior may not be shared either by the more urgently involved practitioner or by the more contemplative philosopher; but its ethical foundations are genuine.

Research projects do differ, however, in their degree of potential benefits, and the differences may be important for our ethical decision making. How do we decide whether a proposed study has enough potential benefits to outweigh its potential harms—given that both are potential rather than actual? If there were easy answers to this question, we would not still be debating it. Our estimates of potential harms and benefits must be very crude at best, informed to some extent by previous experience but retaining a greater margin for error than any of us would like. Unless we decide simply to close down large areas of social scientific research, we must continue making such crude estimates and acting upon them, as individual researchers or as peer reviewers of research by others. Some kind of peer review is essential in assessing potential benefits, though it need not always be as extensive or as formal as certain government agencies now insist. If, by rough estimate, a piece of proposed research may potentially yield minor harms offset by minor benefits, it is not worth much ethical agonizing by anyone. If the rough estimate suggests minor benefits and major harms, we can easily reject the research as ethically unacceptable. If the estimate suggests minor harms and major benefits, most of us would be willing to approve the research, though we might wish to assess its actual harms and benefits later and to revise our judgmental criteria accordingly. It is only when our rough estimates suggest major potential harms *and* major potential benefits that we really begin to worry about the crudity of our estimates—and about what specific meaning to invest in such admittedly ambiguous terms as "major potential benefit."

We have already considered the question of harm with regard to the specific example of the Milgram obedience studies. Let us look at the question of benefit in the same context, since estimates of "major benefit" have been more disputed there than in perhaps any other example. Several of Stanley Milgram's critics appear to assume that his claims for the social value of his research were post-hoc justifications intended to quiet criticisms of his deceptive and stressful experimental practices. But Milgram had made a rather detailed case for substantial potential benefit in his original research proposals, and his research was funded on that basis. He had read widely concerning the events of the Holocaust and the various attempts to explain its origins. He did not propose yet another intellectual analysis, or a psychological study of some phenomenon previously much studied and perhaps vaguely related to the Holocaust, such as conformity to peer pressures. Instead, he proposed a series of studies that would examine specific contextual variables associated with greater or lesser obedience to a realistic command to administer severe physical pain to another individual. Doubtless there are many steps between such displays of individual obedience and the occurrence of a social phenomenon as broad and intense as the Holocaust. But it is reasonable to assume that laboratory research on destructive obedience could make a useful contribution to the understanding of destructive obedience on a large scale, even though it might not be the only way or even the single best way to proceed in elucidating the genesis of Holocaust-like phenomena. Further, it is reasonable to assume that better and wider public understanding of the conditions most likely to promote destructive obedience on a small scale could have a prophylactic effect with regard to destructive obedience on a large scale—although, again, there are surely many forces working in a complex society to strengthen or weaken tendencies toward genocidal Final Solutions. Thus, I think Milgram made a good case concerning potential benefit, on the basis of the issues involved and the means by which he proposed to study them. It is hard to conceive how anyone could make a better case, before the fact, for major benefits from basic social scientific research.

Furthermore, I think a case can now be made that the Milgram research has actually yielded substantial benefits in the years since its publication. Most ethical discussions of deceptive social scientific research heavily stress harm and lightly sketch benefits, as if any negative effects would reverberate through all of human society, while any positive effects would hardly resound beyond laboratory walls. That is not the way the diffusion of knowledge works in our society. I would suggest that Solomon Asch's deception-based research on social conformity helped sensitize a generation of college students to the dangers of conformism. I would suggest that Asch's student, Stanley Milgram, has helped to sensitize another generation, well beyond campus boundaries, to the possibility that they themselves could under certain circumstances be as obedient as the sternest Nazis. As much as Milgram's research offends certain moral sensibilities, it has also dramatized serious ethical choices so provocatively that virtually every introductory psychology and social psychology textbook of the past decade has prominently featured Milgram's findings.[15] Some social scientists and ethicists find it implausible that laboratory studies of individual psychological phenomena could yield any useful understanding of the dynamics of a Holocaust. I find it even more implausible to assume that research with the broad dissemination and emotional impact of Milgram's studies has not already generated enough introspection and discussion to diminish significantly the likelihood of another Holocaust-like phenomenon, at least in this country.

Few social scientific studies are likely to have the individual force of Milgram's obedience research. But judgments about their potential benefit can be made in similar fashion, on the basis of the researcher's serious consideration of factors likely to play a role in major social phenomena, the choice of apt research strategies, and the social implications of anticipated (or unanticipated but possible) research findings. At no time can these judgments be so definitive or so overwhelming as to outweigh certain kinds of research harm. But in combination with the remaining criteria, they may lead to a reasoned decision that limited potential harm deriving from deception and other aspects of the research design are outweighed by the likely long-term benefits of a particular research project as a part of the ongoing social scientific research enterprise.

The Option to Withdraw

One of the objections most often raised against research deception is that it prevents subjects from deciding whether to give their fully informed consent to research participation. "Informed consent" is a concept that grew out of medical experimentation, where the only way for patients to make an effective decision about research participation is to know well in advance what kinds of physical interventions might be imposed upon them. Many medical interventions have potentially serious and virtually irrevocable consequences, and if the patient fails to say "No" before being anesthetized, cut open, injected with cancer cells, infected with bacteria, etc., there may be no way of effectively saying "No" later. The situation is usually very different in social scientific research. As already suggested, the intervention is most often minor and the consequences are temporary or reversible (as by post-research debriefing). Perhaps even more important in an ethical sense is the possibility of an ongoing process of informed consent. Even if, for purposes of conducting a study, subjects must be asked to give their consent to participation partly on the basis of misleading or incomplete information, they can continue their assessment of the study's costs to them as it proceeds, and can be guaranteed the right to quit at any point where they decide that the costs are becoming greater than they wish to bear. This process of "ongoing informed consent" is implicit in many research situations, including interviews and questionnaires where the subject is fully in control of the information he or she supplies. In circumstances where the possible harms are greater—as when a questionnaire deals with particularly sensitive issues, or when an experiment manipulates social or other pressures to continue participation beyond normally tolerable limits of stress—the subject should clearly and emphatically be informed in advance of the right to stop participating at any time without penalty.

In some instances, a research procedure may have the potential to impose upon a subject a psychological harm well outside those encountered in normal social interactions, under circumstances where the subject is misled as to what is about to happen and is unable to withdraw his ongoing consent in time to avoid the harm. Such instances more closely resemble physical intervention without informed consent in medical research than does the usual social scientific study, and they should be placed under the same constraints as medical interventions. I am thinking here of such studies as those in which a subject fills out a personality questionnaire, then is suddenly and falsely told that the questionnaire reveals hidden homosexual tendencies or other characteristics that are highly discrepant from the subject's own self-image. Most subjects appear to accept rather easily, during debriefing, the information that an apparently realistic experimental situation has been fabricated or that a recently introduced stranger is not nearly as bad a person as the experimenter has made him out to be. But I suspect that a false imputation of homosexuality or neurosis, made by a psychologist, may continue to raise self-doubts well after the psychologist has changed stories. The characterization is not a consequence of the subject's own behavior, and its sudden attribution to the subject is made without an opportunity for ongoing informed consent.

The Milgram obedience studies have been criticized on somewhat similar grounds. But I do not see the Milgram studies as falling in the same category, since subjects in those studies were never falsely characterized. Subjects who shocked the "victim" unmercifully did so with little persuasion from the experimenter and much resistance from the "victim." They had the choice throughout the experiment of quitting at any time, and in fact a substantial portion of subjects did quit. A continuing opportunity was provided subjects to make a moral decision, and no force or unusual psychological technique was brought to bear to interfere with that choice. In such instances, where research participation brings unsought self-knowledge, I do feel that the researcher has a responsibility to help the subject cope with such self-knowledge and to give the subject some guidance in integrating it satisfactorily into his or her self-concept over the long run. Milgram's debriefing procedures were designed to do that, and the follow-up research suggests that they were effective in that regard. Self-knowledge in itself, even unsought self-knowledge, does not seem to me an ethically negative "risk." Ethically concerned individuals of many persuasions and cultural roles, including preachers, teachers, novelists, and charismatic leaders, have attempted throughout history to induce such knowledge in anyone whose attention they could momentarily catch, even by deceptive devices (such as embedding lessons about human nature within an apparently innocuous entertainment). The induction of unsought self-knowledge need not be seen as a major mission of social scientists, but neither should it be seen as an evil from which research subjects must be protected at all costs.

Temporary versus Lasting Harm

Though I am primarily a consequentialist rather than a deontologist, I am unwilling to balance the certainty of lasting harm to a misinformed subject against the possibility of general benefits as a result of a particular study. But temporary discomfort, anxiety, or even pain may fairly be weighed among the harms in a harm-benefit ratio, as long as the subject is permitted to cease participation whenever the distress becomes personally intolerable and as long as no lasting scars (physical or psychological) result. The generation of temporarily intense anxiety or pain should not be employed casually, even if these terms are met; it must be more than offset by the potential value of the research. Furthermore, as with unsought self-insight in the previous section, the researcher is obligated to take an active role in restoring the anxious or agitated subject to his or her normal emotional state. The debriefing period is usually the opportune time to do this.

Debriefing and Publicity

The debriefing period, properly used, is a time for limiting or eliminating several potential harms of deceptive research practices. First, it provides the occasion to diminish anxiety and other unpleasant emotional reactions, and to give the subject a sense of the true value of his or her participation as a research subject. Instead of leaving the subject with a sense of having been tricked, the researcher should honestly communicate the difficulty or impossibility of doing research on the topic at hand with full subject foreknowledge, and should describe the efforts necessary to give subjects a realistic—if deceptive—experience in a controlled setting. Second, the debriefing process restores a sense of honesty to the researcher, and by interrupting the role of arch-manipulator, it brings him or her back toward the human level of the subjects. Third, it provides an ethical model to researchers, subjects, and others of how a necessary deception can be limited in its consequences, how deception can be used without destroying the integrity of human social contacts or the autonomy and self-esteem of the individuals involved. Given the vast amounts of deception which occur in ordinary social life *without* any intentional debriefing, the use of deception linked with debriefing might even have a salutary effect upon the public sense of ethical standards, as already suggested, rather than producing the invidious effects predicted by certain critics of deceptive practices.

Finally, the requirement of debriefing is ethically advantageous in that it increases the level of publicity connected with the research. I am not referring to publicity in the usual sense of newspaper headlines and talk-show appearances, but to publicity as the term has been used by John Rawls and subsequently by Sissela Bok. As Bok puts it, "According to such a constraint, a moral principle must be capable of public statement and defense."[16] The general requirement of debriefing means that a researcher must at some reasonable point publicize his or her deceptive research procedures to the individuals most likely to be at risk as a result, namely, the subjects, and must therefore be able to justify the deceptions to them or risk some kind of retaliation from them. But publicity must involve more than the researcher's interactions with the subject, as the latter part of boundary condition 5 suggests.

Peer review and reviews by institutional review boards mean more publicity, more occasions when the researcher must be able to offer an acceptable ethical defense of any deceptive practices he or she feels to be required in the chosen research area. Still other professional practices common in the social sciences involve further publicity: peer reviews for academic promotions; peer review by granting agencies, in addition to IRB reviews; presentations of research procedures and findings at professional meetings; journal review and publication of research papers.

Conclusion: The Salutary Consequences of Publicity

Several years ago I wrote a short piece for *Psychology Today* in which I compared and contrasted experimental social psychologists with professional con artists.[17] The similarities, which were considerable, mainly concerned the practice of deception. The differences, which were also considerable, included such things as the principal motivations of psychologists vs. those of con artists and the attitudes of the two groups toward "subjects" or "marks." The *major* difference concerned the matter of publicity. Con artists avoid publicity as much as possible, and thus their deceptive practices can grow unchecked except by sheer force of law. Social psychologists, however, ordinarily seek publicity in the form of professional presentations, and have also by and large accepted its necessity in such forms as debriefing. Publicity of a perfectly ordinary professional sort was how the Milgram studies and others became the focus of a great deal of professional discussion of ethics, eventually widening to include discussion in the news media, on television drama programs, and in various circles of government. I say "publicity of a perfectly ordinary professional sort" because no scandal was involved, no hidden deceits were dramatically revealed, no damage suits came to court. Milgram talked and wrote about his research, and other people responded with their views on the ethical considerations involved, and Milgram responded in turn with his, and the dialogue continues.

The dialogue has by no means been a useless one. Deception in social science research has become much more constrained over the past fifteen years, in large part as the result of such voluntary publicity rather than through the coercion of federal regulations and financial threats. The federal government may ultimately outlaw deception in social scientific research altogether, in response to political pressures stronger than social scientists can muster—in which case I would not be surprised to see the spread of bootleg deception research on and off university campuses, conducted by researchers who feel they cannot study certain major issues effectively by any other means. That would be the ultimate ethical disaster for deception research, since in secret it would be hardly more constrained than the con artist's trade. The ultimate condition under which deception research is ethically justifiable is *out in the open*, where its practitioners are continually forced to present their justifications to others and where their critics must resort to reason rather than coercion. Ethical decision making is not a closed system in which a set of rules can be ordained once and applied to all situations forever after. I do not have all the answers about deception, its effects, and its reasonable limits; nor does anyone else. Continuing publicity about the kinds of deception social scientists see as necessary, and about the controlled conditions under which deception should be tolerated in research, will feed the ongoing dialogue about deception in such a way as to make our decisions about it increasingly more realistic, more sophisticated, and more ethical.

NOTES

1. Stanley Milgram, "Subject Reaction: The Neglected Factor in the Ethics of Experimentation," *Hastings Center Report* 7, no. 5 (1977): 19.

2. Sissela Bok, *Lying: Moral Choice in Public and Private Life* (New York: Vintage Books, 1979), pp. 34–49.

3. *Measure for Measure*, act 3, scene 1. In William Shakespeare, *The Comedies* (New York: Heritage Press, 1958), p. 267.

4. Bok, *Lying*, pp. 32–33.

5. Henry A. Murray, *Explorations in Personality* (New York: Oxford University Press, 1938), pp. 26–28.

6. Elliot Aronson and J. Merrill Carlsmith, "Experimentation in Social Psychology," in G. Lindzey and E. Aronson, eds., *The Handbook of Social Psychology*, 2d ed. (Reading, Mass.: Addison-Wesley, 1968), vol. 2, pp. 22–23.

7. Jonathan L. Freedman, "Roleplaying: Psychology by Consensus," *Journal of Personality and Social Psychology* 13 (1969): 107–14.

8. Don Mixon, "Instead of Deception," *Journal for the Theory of Social Behavior* 2 (1972): 145–77.

9. Daniel M. Geller, "Involvement in Role-Playing Simulations: A Demonstration with Studies on Obedience," *Journal of Personality and Social Psychology* 36 (1978): 219–35.

10. Philip G. Zimbardo, "Pathology of Imprisonment," *Society* 9, no. 4 (1972): 4–6.

11. Stanley Milgram, *Obedience to Authority* (New York: Harper & Row, 1974).

12. Alan C. Elms, *Social Psychology and Social Relevance* (Boston: Little, Brown, 1972), pp. 153–54.

13. Stanley Milgram, "Issues in the Study of Obedience: A Reply to Baumrind," *American Psychologist* 19 (1964): 848–52.

14. Diana Baumrind, "Metaethical and Normative Considerations Covering the Treatment of Human Subjects in the Behavioral Sciences," in E.C. Kennedy, ed., *Human Rights and Psychological Research* (New York: Crowell, 1975), pp. 37–68.

15. In a recent tabulation of frequency of citations in introductory psychology textbooks, Milgram was found to be twelfth in rank among all psychologists, just below Carl Jung and higher than William James, John B. Watson, Abraham Maslow, or Leon Festinger. Daniel Periman, "Who's Who in Psychology," *American Psychologist* 35 (1980): 104–6.

16. Bok, *Lying*, pp. 97–112.

17. Alan C. Elms, "Alias Johnny Hooker," *Psychology Today* 10, no. 9 (1977): 19.

The Case for Deception in
Medical Experimentation

J. David Newell

Any attempt to argue in favor of deceptive practices is bound to meet with at least initial resistance. In the context of health care activities, where what goes on is often quite literally a matter of life and death, deceptive practices would seem to be totally objectionable. But with a little reflection, we might be led to alter our generally negative attitude toward using deceptive techniques in medical experimentation. One of the aims of this essay is to engage the reader in this sort of reflection. In what follows, I shall argue that deception, when properly understood, can justifiably be used in research involving human subjects—even where informed consent is not obtained.

The case for deception will be presented in two phases. In the first section, I will attempt an analysis of the concept of deception itself, with a view to showing the many and diverse forms which deceptive practices may take. The argument there is designed to show that deception can be understood as a *morally neutral strategy*. I maintain that this is the sense of the term which is needed to establish a moral justification for the use of deception in human experimentation. In the second section, I shall use this sense of the term in presenting an argument for deceiving human subjects in certain circumstances. If my arguments succeed, I hope to have taken some of the edge off our general reticence to approve of deceptive research techniques which could result in monumental gains in medicine for modern man.

I. The Concept of Deception

Discussions concerning the use of deception in research involving human subjects have generally failed to give sufficient attention to an analysis of the concept of deception itself. In this section I shall argue that deceptive practices take many forms, and that there is a perfectly good sense of the term in which deception turns out to be a morally neutral notion. Moreover, the sense in which deception is a morally neutral notion is an important one for a proper consideration of the use of deception in human experimentation—which is the central concern of this essay.

A principal difficulty with trying to say something positive, from a moral point of view, about deceptive practices is the close identification in ordinary thought between deception and lying. Lying is generally thought to be morally wrong, and because lying and deception are closely associated, deception is contaminated by association. But, as we will see, lying and deception are not synonymous notions, however much we may be in the habit to linking them together and no matter how similar our emotional responses to each seems to be. One phase in coming to understand my position, then, is a purely psychological one: we must try to resist the strong temptation to identify all deceptive practices with the practice of clear-cut lying.

The request to resist this temptation is based on a conceptual matter; it involves the claim that while all lying is a kind of deception, many forms of deception are not ways of lying. This claim is neither strange nor startling. In fact, it is a claim made by both consequentialists and deontologists. Sissela Bok, in *Lying*, makes the point in the following way:

> When we undertake to deceive others intentionally, we communicate messages meant to mislead them, meant to make them believe what we ourselves do not believe. We can do so through gesture, through disguise, by means of action or inaction, even through silence. Which of these innumerable deceptive messages are also lies? I shall define as a lie any intentionally deceptive message which is stated. Such statements are most often made verbally or

> in writing, but can of course also be conveyed via smoke
> signal, Morse code, sign language, and the like. Deception,
> then, is the larger category, and lying forms part of it.[1]

The crucial point for our purposes is the claim that lying is a particular part of the larger category of deception. That is, lying is just one among many possible deceptive activities. For Bok, the emphasis is clearly on *telling* (in written or spoken form, broadly understood) lies, as opposed to withholding information, ducking the question, etc. Other forms of deception, for Bok, also involve intentionally communicating messages designed to mislead or to make others believe "what we ourselves do not believe." But unless the message is *stated* in some fashion it is not a case of clear-cut lying. This will seem arbitrary on first blush and Bok's defense of it along vaguely consequentialist lines is not very convincing.

Oddly enough, we can make Bok's view (that *telling* a lie is distinguishable in a morally important respect from other forms of deception) more plausible by appeal to the views of a deontologist like Charles Fried. Fried would agree with Bok in that he holds that "every lie is a deception, but the reverse is not true."[2] Fried argues that lying is an act in which someone asserts something he or she believes to be false *to someone else entitled to the correct information*. In the example of a letter containing a false accusation against someone which is intentionally left where you will find it and read it, Fried argues that

> I have intentionally deceived you into believing the truth
> of the allegations falsely asserted in the letter, but I have
> not lied to you . . . because I have not asserted anything to
> you. Though I have caused a false belief in you and have
> done so intentionally, I have not done so by reference to
> the institution according to which you know and I know
> that you know, and you know . . . that I make assertions,
> inviting belief by you.[3]

For Fried, the key notion is the institution of truth-telling or communication in which both parties participate by making certain assumptions. Fried sees an assertion as a type of promise in which assurances are give by the speaker that his/her assertions are true. In the case of the letter left lying around for you to read, the normal conditions of participation in the institution of truth-telling are not met. You are not someone *entitled* to the correct information. Hence, it is possible for you to be intentionally deceived without being lied to. And hence, being deceived and being lied to are not the same thing.

Fried thinks we have a moral obligation to refrain from doing what will destroy the basic institution of truth-telling. But he does not see any reason for saying that it is wrong to create a false impression. He says that, while lying itself is intuitively wrong, "there is no corresponding intuition that inadvertently (though knowingly) creating a false impression is categorically wrong."[4] Moreover, in Fried's view, we do not even have a moral obligation to promote the truth:

> I have not argued for an obligation to further or promote the truth. To urge such an obligation, to urge that it is wrong to fail to pursue and to promote truth wherever possible, would be absurd . . . but the value of truth must be balanced against all other goods and bads with which it competes.[5]

The bottom line on this issue for Fried is the preservation of the institution of truth-telling, the sanctity of which is only challenged by direct bold-faced lies to persons who are entitled to expect the truth. Perhaps the consequences of undermining this basic institution of truth-telling are among the bad consequences to which Bok alludes. Both Bok and Fried can be seen as joining hands on this issue and on the claim that deceptive practices which do not challenge the basic institution of truth-telling are not automatically unacceptable practices (other things being equal).[6]

We are now in a position to suggest that deceptive practices (exclusive of clear-cut lying) are themselves morally neutral strategies for getting certain jobs done, for accomplishing certain ends. Like any other human instrument, a deceptive practice can be put to both good and bad uses. The instrument itself is morally neutral. It is its use by human agents that makes the moral difference.

Beyond clear-cut lying, we might identify nine forms of deception which humans use as strategies in coping with various situations:

1. *Evasion*: systematically ignoring the request for information while pretending to respond to the inquiry.
2. *Suppression*: deliberately leaving out or withholding relevant information.
3. *Euphemism*: substituting an agreeable or inoffensive response, for one that is disagreeable or offensive.
4. *Exaggeration*: making the truth seem ridiculous by stating it in hyperbolic terms.
5. *Changing the subject*: a more direct form of evasion.
6. *Disguise*: putting on an appearance which masks one's true feelings or condition.
7. *Gesturing*: employing ambiguous body movements to create a misimpression.
8. *Silence*: saying nothing in a context in which such silence is likely to be taken a certain way.
9. *Inaction*: like silence, this involves not doing something in a context in which this has import.

These nine deceptive strategies can be understood as morally neutral *in themselves*. It is the use we put them to that is subject to moral valuations. If we take a purely trivial but widely practiced custom in our society, we can see that almost every adult uses one or more of these deceptive practices in dealing with small children who believe in Santa Claus. Many adults would refuse deliberately to lie to a child, while employing every other means of deception short of lying to protect the child's cherished belief. The same may be said about Aunt Hilda's hideous new Easter hat.

There are other contexts in which the issues are much more serious. For instance, is it really wrong for an ex-convict or a former mental patient to use evasion or silence to conceal a past which, if kept secret, harms no one? Are we prepared to argue that the use of plainclothed detectives, unmarked police cars, undercover narcotic agents, camouflaged armies, and CIA agents (spying for our side) are all morally unacceptable practices? It is not difficult to imagine situations involving these phenomena which are every bit as serious or significant as the use of similar strategies to do good things in medicine. These examples show that deceptive strategies themselves are instruments which can be used for either good or bad purposes.

Like a dinner knife which may be used to cut meat or commit murder, these instruments, as instruments, are morally neutral.

The scrupulous person can make every effort to avoid clear-cut lying and in this regard enjoy considerable success. But no one can avoid altogether the multitude of deceptive maneuvers we make on a day-to-day basis. Some will want to say that smiling at your disagreeable next door neighbor or refusing by evasion or exaggeration to shatter a child's belief in Santa are not really deceptive practices. But if such activities are designed to create or retain a false belief in someone, they are clearly modes of deception and cannot be wished away by re-definition. Of course, the prevalence of such activities in everyday situations is not an argument for their moral acceptability. Yet it is simply question-begging to say that all such practices are deceptive when their use is for bad ends, but not when their use is for good or harmless ends. Hence, our conclusion is that (non-assertional) deceptive practices themselves are morally neutral strategies that can be put to good or bad purposes. The deceptive practice of clear-cut lying is exceptional in that even when done for a good cause, it always damages or threatens the moral order in society created by the institution of truth-telling. We have now to apply these general conclusions to the question of deception in research involving human subjects.

II. Deceiving Human Subjects

One might consistently hold that it is morally acceptable to allow human beings to be used as subjects in experimental research, and that deceptive practices are sometimes morally justifiable in certain situations in life, but deny that it is ever right to use deception on human subjects in research. We will now try to make out a case for saying that deceptive practices are sometimes morally acceptable features of medical research designs, even when informed consent is not obtained.

Strong opposition to the use of deception, such as placebos, come from both consequentialists and deontologists.

Sissela Bok cites some of the principal bad consequences of placebo prescriptions:

> Spending for them runs into millions of dollars. Patients incur greater risks of discomfort and harm than is commonly understood. Finally, any placebo uses that are in fact trivial and harmless in themselves may combine to form nontrivial practices, so that repeated reliance on placebos can do serious harm in the long run to the medical profession and the general public.[7]

The serious long-run harm to the medical profession and the public which Bok has in mind here is the general breakdown of trust in physicians on the part of the public. Bok does not think the prohibition against placebos should be absolute however. She allows that by obtaining the consent of the subjects to the experimental design we can "remove the ethical problems having to do with deception."[8]

Even more enthusiasm is shown for informed consent by the deontologist. Deontological moral theorists advance the principles of autonomy and respect for persons as central theses in their model of ethical reflection. They would urge that nothing will do more to secure personal autonomy and personal integrity than the insistence upon informed consent by all subjects participating in human experimentation, especially where deceptive practices are involved.

On a pluralistic model offered by Childress, "voluntary and informed consent" is a central notion and apparently deceptive practices are allowable where such consent is obtained:

> There is a moral presumption for providing all the information that a reasonable person would want and all that this particular person wants. It is a conclusive presumption in that deception is ruled out; it is a rebuttable presumption in that some information may be withheld, or only partially disclosed . . .[9]

It is clear from this passage that Childress does not see withholding information or disclosing only part of it as forms of deception. He does not offer a definition of deception but there is reason to think that he is using it as synonomous with outright lying. If so, his "conclusive presumption" is against only one form of deception, the clear-cut lie, rather than all forms of deception. The presumption against other forms of deception, however, might be rebuttable for Childress if his criteria can be met. This means that, for Childress, deceptive practices can be used in research involving humans only on the condition that, among other things, voluntary and informed consent is obtained.

The standard approach to obtaining informed consent is by asking the research subject to sign a consent form verifying voluntary and informed participation in the project. But the track record on the actual use of such forms is not very impressive. In an empirical study of the use of consent forms by institutional review boards, Gray, Cooke and Tannenbaum discovered that ten percent of the forms in actual use omitted a description of experimental procedures, twenty-three percent said nothing of the purpose of the research, a whopping forty-five percent omitted the benefits of the research to the subjects, and thirty percent had nothing to say about the risks involved for the subjects.[10] Gray, Cooke, and Tannenbaum also found that

> Consent forms tended to be written in academic or scientific language that may be difficult for the lay person to understand. In more than three fourths of the consent forms, fewer than ten percent of the technical terms were explained in lay language.[11]

And even where the consent forms are actually understood, one cannot overlook the vulnerability of the average patient-subject vis a vis his or her physician-researcher when asked to sign such forms.

It is very doubtful that these problems with consent forms have been solved in the few years since the Gray, Cooke, Tannenbaum report was published. It may be that these problems are themselves insoluble—given the nature of the activity in question. It would not follow from this that informed consent is not a useful and valuable ideal to pursue. On the contrary, every effort should be made to secure genuine informed consent whenever and wherever desirable. We should also continually seek ways of solving the problems associated with this important notion. But once we are aware of its limitations, we might be less inclined to rely so very heavily on securing it as the basis for ethical reflection on these research issues. In fact, toward the end of this essay we make some practical suggestions which make reliance on informed consent, especially where deception is involved, far less significant than Bok and Childress make it.

With or without informed consent, it is not at all obvious that deceptive strategies always harm research subjects. The use of such deceptive techniques in allowing (encouraging, enabling) children to believe in Santa Claus seems not to have done much damage to the hundreds of generations of children who have been subject to it. Charles P. Smith did a study on the effects of deceptive practices used in research experimentation and he found

> that deception per se has a different meaning in the context of scientific research than it has in everyday life. Most subjects understand that deception is a necessary aspect of some kinds of research and find it justifiable under such circumstances.[12]

In other words, the possibilities of deceptive strategies in research were found to be a matter of how the game is played in experimental contexts. We can see certain parallels to bluffing in poker or to faking injury to get a foul called in basketball. Clearly, the stakes are much higher in medical research than they are in these games. Moreover we usually know exactly what kinds of deception we are subject to in a game, though the same cannot always be said for medical experimentation. Furthermore, as players in a game we usually get a chance to be the deceiver as well as the deceived, but in medical research no such equal participation is possible. So the game analogy cannot be pressed too far. Still, the basic idea offered by Smith is that most people expect deceptive techniques to be used in research whenever necessary to achieve a worthy end. Smith found no evidence to support the claim that in cases where no physical harm befell research subjects there was discernible harm to their psyches. A similar finding, based on several such studies, has been reported by Leonard Berkowitz.[13]

If there is evidence to show that deceived subjects suffer psychological harm from being deceived, and if informed consent suffers from the difficulties cited earlier, it would seem that all we really need is clearly established and carefully followed procedures for protecting research subjects from physical and (obvious) psychological harm in order to justify using (non-assertional) deceptive techniques of the sort sketched in section I above. The researcher can evade, suppress, exaggerate, disguise, gesture, and so on, in order to deceive the subject of a medical experiment—without that subject's consent and without telling that subject a single lie. In fact, such forms of deception may be used to avoid outright lies, i.e., to protect or preserve the institution of truth-telling. And their use must always be justified in terms of the beneficial consequences achieved. Outright lies will always have at least the potential consequence of undermining the institution of truth-telling and the consequences of this are in turn simply disastrous. So medical research which requires outright or clear-cut lying may never be morally justified. But the other deceptive techniques, when used, may be understood and accepted as merely part of standard research practice.

A rule Utilitarian might set up the "research game" in such a way as to recognize the validity or deceptive technique in research design.[14] Anyone who participates in any research program could become aware of this aspect of research in much the same way anyone who learns poker becomes aware of the bluff. Clearly stated strategies involving deception could be shown to have potential to contribute greatly to the unbiased nature of the data collected. The recognition that deceptive strategies are part of the way the research is done would preempt the danger that such research activities would undermine the institution of truth-telling. We could say that researchers and their subjects more or less belong to a deception club (a weaker version of Fried's "lying club"):

> My argument is that there is a moral right (non-consequentialist) to enter into lying clubs, so long as these clubs do not have the consequence of undermining the institution of truth-telling.[15]

And as long as such arrangements are productive of maximum benefits for all, we could base our research game ultimately on rule utilitarian grounds.

In establishing procedures for the "research game" which allowed deceptive practices, we could insist on every research proposal being doubly reviewed. First, it would be reviewed by a properly constituted institutional review board.[16] Second, because it involved a deceptive technique, it would also be reviewed by a Surrogate Committee on Deception, the sole function of which would be the screening of research proposals involving deception.[17] The aim of the surrogate committee would be to see that the subjects are not harmed (to whatever extent such determination can actually be made). In addition, every research proposal involving deceptive strategies would be published in some sort of newsletter and made available to diverse audiences.[18] This would conform to what Sissela Bok called "the test of publicity" for justifying the use of deception.[19] We could further insist on a genuine debriefing after the experiment has concluded in which the research subject would be given as much information as he or she might be reasonably entitled to have. Finally we could protect the trustworthiness of the profession (the public's need to trust in it) by requiring that the deceptive techniques be used only by researchers who are not also the physicians of subject-patients. A game played by this set of rules would hardly be a game of chance for the research subject. Such controls on the activities of researchers would seem to make reliance on the voluntary and informed consent of the subject very minimal, and in some cases unnecessary. If, at the same time, research projects involving such deceptive strategies carry us rapidly forward in the cause of curing diseases and improving the condition and quality of human life, what is to be gained by challenging their validity?

Conclusion

I have argued that, if deception is understood as a morally neutral strategy, all forms of deception except clear-cut lying can be justifiably used in medical research. The elimination of clear-cut lying (and the inclusion of the other forms of deception) turns on consequentialist considerations. The frailties of the informed consent notion, however, make the need for special committee reviews, publicity, and follow-up work on deceptive research much more imperative. Given that such procedures are followed carefully, we stand to gain a great deal from allowing research in medicine which employs deceptive techniques.

NOTES

*Research for this paper was done while I was on leave at Indiana University, 1981–82, participating in a seminar on bioethics funded by the National Endowment for the Humanities. An earlier version of the paper was presented to the seminar and I am grateful to the seminar participants for their helpful criticisms.

1. Sissela Bok, *Lying* (New York: Vintage Books, 1978), p. 14.

2. Charles Fried, *Right and Wrong* (Cambridge: Harvard University Press, 1978), p. 58.

3. Fried, *Right and Wrong*, p. 58.

4. Fried, *Right and Wrong*, p. 55.

5. Fried, *Right and Wrong*, p. 69.

6. A case for this point is made in terms of a social contract theory by Joseph G. Ellin, "The Solution to a Dilemma in Medical Ethics," *Westminister Institute Review*, Volume 1, No. 2, May 1981. Ellin distinguishes lying from deception in general and attempts to argue, on the basis of a doctor-patient covenantal relationship, that lying weakens trust whereas deception does not.

7. Sissela Bok, "The Ethics of Giving Placebos," *Scientific American*, Volume 231, No. 5, November 1974, p. 19.

8. Bok, "Placebos," p. 22.

9. James F. Childress, *Priorities in Biomedical Ethics* (Philadelphia: The Westminster Press, 1981), p. 67.

10. Bradford H. Gray, Robert A. Cooke, Arnold S. Tannenbaum, "Research involving Human Subjects," *Science*, Volume 201, September 1978, p. 1098.

11. Gray et al., p. 1098.

12. Charles P. Smith, "How (Un)acceptable is Research Involving Deception?" *IRB: A Review of Human Subjects Research*, Volume 3, No. 8, October 1981, p. 4

13. Leonard Berkowitz, "Some Complexities and Uncertainties Regarding the Ethicality of Deception in Research with Human Subjects," *The Belmont Report*, Appendix, Volume II, January 1976 (DHEW Publications no. (05) 78-0014), Article 24, pp. 9–10.

14. It is important to note the Rule Utilitarians are in no way forced by their moral theory to take such a view. In fact, Diana Baumrind is a Rule Utilitarian who takes a very dim view of deceptive research techniques. See "The Nature and Definition of Informed Consent in Research involving Deception," *The Belmont Report*, Appendix, Volume II, January 1976 (DHEW Publication No. (05) 78-0014), Article 23.

15. Fried, *Right and Wrong*, p. 73 note.

16. Gray et al., pp. 1094–96.

17. Suggestions for such a committee to aid in making decisions for noncompetents are made by Diana Baumrind (see note 14) and Norman Fost, "A Surrogate System for Informed Consent," *Journal of the American Medical Association* 233 (August 18, 1975), pp. 800–803. I am not at all sure that either Baumrind or Fost would find my suggestion of a Surrogate Committee on Deception acceptable.

18. The suggested publishing of research proposals involving human subjects belongs to Calabresi. See his "Reflection on Medical Experimentation on Humans," *Daedalus* 98, No. 2 (1969), pp. 400–401.

19. Bok, *Lying*, pp. 98–112.

Experimentation on Humans

Clinical trials in medical and psychological research that use human subjects assigned randomly to experimental and control groups (let us call such trials "RCTs") have produced substantial scientific benefits. Randomization helps to ensure that both groups are sufficiently alike to enable the researcher to discount differences in outcome as the result of pre-treatment differences in subjects. Without randomization experimental design would prove unreliable; experimental results would remain inconclusive.

But for these methodological benefits, researchers pay an apparently high moral price. Suppose, for example, that investigators find preliminary results favorable on an anti-AIDS drug. Is it fair in the name of science to withhold the drug from AIDS sufferers who happen to belong to a control group? That they were picked arbitrarily seems an inadequate rationale for withholding efficacious treatment from them.

It might be felt that in cases such as AIDS, where the stakes are high and treatment is limited, normal experimental precautions can be suspended. A treatment that passes even preliminary trials should be made available to all sufferers alike. But before making this judgment, we should weigh not only the welfare of current AIDS patients but also that of future victims who may be ill served if we stop the experiment too soon. If present benefits outweigh long-term risks, then the judgment to rely on preliminary results would seem justified, as utilitarians would say. (See introduction to "Science and Values" description of utilitarianism.)

However, not everyone is a utilitarian. The deontologist (see introduction to "Science and Values") argues that we ought to consider the rights of experimental subjects and the duties of physicians toward their patients. As Fred Gifford points out in his paper, the physician has an obligation to do what is best for the patient. There may be no violation of this principle when a doctor recommends participation in a randomized clinical trial and the treatments have an equal probability of success. But this condition is not always met. There is often reason to believe that the therapy to be tested is better than the placebo. Thus, in consenting to random selection, the physician would appear to be violating the obligation to do what is best for the patient. We have what Gifford calls "the RCT dilemma": the use of an RCT appears to violate the physician's obligation to the patient; yet, its non-use runs the risk of sacrificing valuable knowledge. Gifford examines and rejects standard proposals for resolving this dilemma and, in the end, suggests a "contractarian" solution.

In a conventional RCT, informed consent is normally obtained from patients before they are randomly assigned to one of the treatment groups. This often creates a practical problem in signing up an adequate number of experimental subjects. As Don Marquis notes in his paper, some patients are reluctant to participate in a study if they do not know which therapy they will receive, and some physicians are reluctant to approach patients about participating in an RCT. To deal with these problems, *prerandomized* RCTs have been proposed. In these studies, randomization comes first; informed consent comes later, if at all. Although prerandomization promises to be of use, this feature brings with it its own ethical problems. Marquis argues that *all* prerandomized clinical trials are unethical.

Michael Lockwood adds to the criticism of utilitarians, especially those who distinguish between RCTs in which the control subjects receive a risky treatment and those in which they do not. In the second case, the doctor is guilty only of an omission; hence, the behavior is said to be easier to justify than if the doctor had placed the patient at risk. Lockwood replies that the distinction between acting and omitting to act, for example, between killing and letting die, is of no moral significance. Thus, he rejects the idea that the use of an RCT can be justified because the doctor merely withholds treatment.

Despite his reservations about RCTs, Lockwood does not advocate that they be abandoned. Instead, he proposes criteria for distinguishing between justified and unjustified uses of RCTs. In her response, G.E.M. Anscombe discusses the permissibility of RCTs and suggests that the act/omission distinction, which Lockwood and many other theorists in recent literature reject, may nevertheless be relevant.

An Argument That All Prerandomized Clinical Trials Are Unethical

Don Marquis

I

The NSABP [National Surgical Adjuvant Project for Breast and Bowel Cancers] study of simple mastectomy versus lumpectomy with and without radiation began as a conventionally randomized clinical trial. Accrual rates were unacceptably low. After the protocol was modified to permit prerandomization the accrual rate increased substantially. Because enough patients have been enrolled in this study, this prerandomized trial has begun to yield important results (Fisher et al., 1985). Presumably as a consequence of the conversion to prerandomization, many thousands of women as a result of this trial will be able to choose, and will be advised by their physicians to select, less disfiguring surgery for early breast cancer. Apparently prerandomization has been successful, not only in generating medical knowledge, but in producing extraordinarily significant human benefits.

Unfortunately, there is a dark cloud on this bright horizon. An argument exists for the position that all prerandomized trials in medicine are unethical. The purpose of this paper is to lay out that argument. The claim is not merely that there are concerns, or problems, or dangers associated with prerandomized trials. Concerns, problems, or dangers are the sorts of things that can perhaps be dealt with through greater vigilance by IRBs or through better federal regulations. The argument of this paper is that the prerandomized design is *intrinsically* ethically flawed, that *any* prerandomized clinical trial is incompatible with the ethics of therapeutic medicine. In view of the great benefits of at least one prerandomized clinical trial, the conclusion of the argument of this paper is one that any reader should be loathe to accept. Accordingly, the argument will be laid out with the care necessary, if not to convince, at least greatly to concern someone unwilling to accept the conclusion.

II

Some preliminaries are necessary to set the stage for this analysis. A conventional randomized clinical trial is a comparative study of different therapies in which patients in the study are randomly assigned to therapies *after* informed consent to participate in the study is obtained. Although this design has great scientific merit, it is thought to involve substantial disincentives for patient accrual. In the first place, some physicians are uncomfortable approaching patients about participation in a randomized trial because they are reluctant to admit that they do not know which therapy is best or because explanation of the trial to a patient is difficult and time-consuming. In the second place, patients may be unwilling to participate in a study if they do not know which therapy they will receive. Consequently, a conventional randomized clinical trial may accrue patients much more slowly than desirable or necessary.

The purpose of prerandomization, as proposed by Marvin Zelen, is to deal with these problems (1977, 1979, 1981, 1982). In this design randomization *precedes*, rather than follows, consent. Prerandomized clinical trials come in two major versions: a multiple arm consent prerandomized design and a single arm consent prerandomized design.

Consider first *multiple arm consent prerandomized design*. In studies of this design all patients whom their physicians wish to enter in the trial are randomized to an arm of the study and *then* asked for informed consent to participate in the trial as recipients of the therapy to which they have been randomized. The advantages of this design over a conventional randomized design are that physicians are not forced to ask patients to take a leap into the arena of unknown therapy and patients can choose to participate in a trial knowing what therapy they will receive. Hence, the rate of accrual should increase. All major prerandomized clinical trials have used this multiple arm consent design.

Consider now *single-arm consent prerandomized design*. This design is for use in that large subclass of trials in which a promising new experimental therapy is to be compared to a standard therapy. The sole difference between this design and multiple arm consent prerandomized design is that patients who are randomized to the standard therapy arm of the study are *not* asked for consent to participate in the study.

Zelen has argued that this design is superior to multiple arm consent design. He has defended not obtaining informed consent from patients randomized to the standard treatment arm on the grounds that patients who receive the standard therapy are not being treated differently than they would have been treated if they were research subjects whose records are being examined retrospectively or if they were not research subjects at all. If anything, such patients may receive better medical care, since they may be more closely monitored as part of the study. Because the informed consent requirements are weakened, Zelen argues that studies using single arm consent prerandomized design would be completed even more rapidly than studies using a multiple arm consent prerandomized design.

Zelen's view comes to this: studies using single arm consent prerandomized design are preferable to studies using multiple arm consent prerandomized design because the former can be completed more rapidly; studies using multiple arm consent prerandomized design are preferable to studies using conventionally randomized design because the former can be completed more rapidly. More rapid completion of a study is always a virtue; when a trial seems not to be accruing patients rapidly enough to be completed, changing the design so completion is possible is plainly a *great* virtue.

With these preliminaries out of the way, a basis exists for outlining the argument of this paper. Note first that the claims that various prerandomized designs increase accrual depend upon the actual reluctance of physicians and patients to participate in some conventionally randomized trials. Now many conventionally randomized trials are completed; hence, we know that in some cases conventional randomization does not prevent adequate accrual. In other cases, conventional randomization has apparently prevented adequate accrual. The argument of this paper takes the form of what logicians call a dilemma. The sketch of the argument follows. For any particular conventionally randomized clinical trial, either conversion to prerandomization will substantially increase patient accrual or it will not. If prerandomization does not substantially increase patient accrual, then prerandomization is unnecessary. If prerandomization does substantially increase patient accrual, then the mechanism by means of which this increase is achieved involves violations of medical ethics. It follows that for any given trial prerandomization is either unnecessary or unethical.

Worse is to come. A decent argument is available for the view that if prerandomization is unnecessary, then there are good moral reasons for *not* adopting a prerandomized design. Hence, it follows from the argument sketch in this and the preceding paragraph that prerandomization is *always* wrong.

This argument outline will be filled in during the next two sections of this paper. In the next section, an argument will be developed for the view that when single arm consent and multiple arm consent prerandomized designs are compared, single arm consent prerandomized design either is unnecessary or entails a violation of accepted ethical standards. In the section after that, an argument will be developed for the view that when multiple arm consent prerandomized design is compared with conventionally randomized design, multiple arm consent prerandomized design either is not needed to increase the accrual rate or entails violations of medical ethics. The final section will contain some remarks concerning what might be done about this most unfortunate conclusion.

III

The major difference between single arm consent prerandomized design and multiple arm consent prerandomized design is that, in studies of the former design, patients prerandomized to the standard therapy arm of the study are not asked for informed consent to participate in the study. According to Zelen the objection to asking patients on the standard therapy arm for informed consent is:

> If a patient in this group preferred the experimental treatment to the best standard treatment, the physician would have little choice but to give the experimental treatment. Clearly, there would be a serious loss in efficiency in evaluation of the therapies if more than a small fraction of patients decided on the change (1979, p. 1245).

Zelen's argument is based on a special difficulty to which prerandomized trials are subject. In a scientifically sound prerandomized trial, patients who are *randomized* to one arm of the study are compared to patients *randomized* to the other arm of the study just as they are in a conventionally randomized trial. It follows that patients randomized to one arm are compared to patients randomized to the other arm whether each patient receives the treatment to which he is randomized or not. A patient will not receive the treatment to which he is randomized when, after being asked for informed consent to participate in the study on the arm to which he is prerandomized, he refuses, preferring the other arm. Plainly when such procedures of analysis are followed any difference in treatment effect is diluted. The greater the refusal rate the more patients must be enrolled in the study for a statistically significant difference in treatment efficacy to emerge if there is one.

The reason for this seemingly perverse statistical procedure becomes apparent if this procedure is compared to the alternative. If patients who *receive* one treatment are compared to patients who *receive* the other, and these classes of patients are determined in part by the refusals of the patients themselves to accept the treatments to which they were prerandomized, then treatment selection is determined in part by patient choice, and, for all we know, in part by physician suggestion. This, by introducing a possible source of bias, defeats the point of randomization, whether conventional randomization or prerandomization.

Now the force of Zelen's argument should be clear. Obviously, not getting informed consent to participate in the trial from persons prerandomized to the standard therapy arm of the study reduces the likelihood that patients prerandomized to standard therapy will ask for the experimental therapy instead of standard therapy. Since a refusal rate as small as 15% will double the number of patients required to complete the study, the importance of minimizing the refusal rate on both arms of the study is quite apparent.

An ethical objection to single arm consent prerandomized design emerges from an analysis based on Zelen's argument. In the case of any particular single arm consent study there would, no doubt, be a difference of opinion concerning whether conversion to a multiple arm consent prerandomized design would substantially reduce the efficiency of study. For our purposes, however, speculation is unnecessary. For any given trial, either conversion to multiple arm consent design will substantially reduce efficiency or it will not. If it will *not*, then single arm consent design is unnecessary because Zelen's argument that multiple arm consent design would reduce efficiency does not apply to that study. If multiple arm consent design *will* reduce efficiency, then there is some significant proportion of patients who, on a single arm consent design, would be given standard treatment and who would have refused standard treatment in favor of experimental treatment if given a choice. In these cases the effect of the adoption of the single arm consent prerandomized design is to coerce some patients into receiving treatment they would not have otherwise accepted. Now the right of informed consent to what is done to one's body is a well-established legal right. The right of choice regarding one's own life, the right of autonomy, is a well-established moral right. It turns out that the very mechanism by which the merits of a single arm consent prerandomized design are manifested is a mechanism through which these patient rights are violated. Therefore, single arm consent prerandomized design is either unnecessary or unethical.

The force of this argument cannot be avoided through an appeal to the fact that physicians do not have an obligation to give a patient any treatment that patient should choose, no matter how much the provision of that treatment flies in the face of sound medical judgment. Provision of experimental therapy to a patient will not fly in the face of sound medical judgment in an ethical prerandomized trial. In such a trial an ethical physician is willing to have her patient randomized either to the experimental arm or to the standard therapy arm. Accordingly, she must believe, if she is ethical, that there is no good evidence that indicates that one treatment is better than the other; otherwise, she would be willing that her patient receive an inferior treatment. Hence, her sound medical judgment can support giving either treatment. Accordingly, to offer her patient only standard treatment is to deny her patient the right of autonomy for the sake of the social good. This is unethical.

Consider two possible objections to this line of argument. It might be argued that single arm consent prerandomized design does not lead to the violation of the autonomy of patients prerandomized to the standard therapy arm of the trial because these patients have the same right to refuse standard therapy as any other patient.

Analysis of this objection points to the fact that any adequate analysis of autonomy must make reference to alternatives. Consider breast cancer treatment. A woman who is offered only simple mastectomy has the right to refuse that treatment and die of breast cancer in order to save her breast. If there were no other remotely efficacious treatment, then such a woman has *not* been denied her autonomy. But a woman offered only simple mastectomy by a physician who (legitimately) believes that lumpectomy is not known to be inferior therapy is, of course, denied her autonomy. One's right of autonomy can be violated as much by *restricting* one's legitimate choice as by denying it altogether. One who is accosted by a robber who says, "Your money or your life," has had her autonomy violated even though she retains a choice. Accordingly, single arm consent prerandomized design violated autonomy even though patients who receive standard treatment in such a trial retain the right to refuse standard treatment.

Another possible objection to this line of argument grants that single arm consent prerandomized design may violate autonomy, but suggests that a mere violation of autonomy is not sufficient to render clinical trials that may produce much social good unethical. A physician may violate a patient's autonomy by not informing a patient of alternatives that the patient would not have chosen anyway or may violate a patient's autonomy by preventing a patient from choosing utterly irrational courses of action. Some violations of autonomy are arguably trivial. Hence, it might be argued, the mere fact that on some occasions autonomy is violated does not establish that a prerandomized trial is unethical.

This objection has some merit, but it has no force in the present context. The *point* of single arm consent prerandomized design is to prevent patients randomized to the standard therapy from *choosing* the experimental therapy. If that option were merely a hypothetical or an irrational option, single arm consent prerandomized design would not offer a significant accrual advantage. Consideration of the most famous prerandomized study, the lumpectomy vs. simple mastectomy Stage I breast cancer study, supports this analysis. Lumpectomy was the experimental therapy. It was surely neither an irrational nor merely hypothetical treatment alternative. Hence, we have every reason to think that the violation of autonomy involved in using a single arm consent prerandomized design rather than a multiple arm consent prerandomized design in cases where use of such a design will significantly increase accrual is sufficiently serious to render such a trial unethical.

This argument shows that use of a single arm consent prerandomized design is either unnecessary or unethical. Since it will be difficult to tell in advance whether use of a single arm consent design is unnecessary or not in some particular trial, there is always a moral argument against using a single arm consent design. Use of a multiple arm consent prerandomized design will rule out the possibility that, due to unanticipated factors, some patients would refuse the standard therapy arm in favor of the experimental treatment arm. Accordingly, when single arm consent prerandomized design is compared to multiple arm consent prerandomized design, there is a moral reason against *ever* preferring single arm consent prerandomized design to multiple arm consent design.

IV

A defender of prerandomization will not be especially perturbed by the argument so far developed. Single arm consent prerandomized design came in for a good deal of criticism when Zelen first proposed it (Capron, 1979; Cox, 1979; Fost, 1979; Rutstein, 1979; Stuart, 1979; Vawter, 1979). Apparently, no major prerandomized trial has used single arm consent design. Accordingly, the real burden of the argument of this paper involves showing that multiple arm consent prerandomized design is unethical. This can be shown. As before, the argument takes the form of a dilemma. Like the previous argument, the conclusion of the dilemma is that multiple arm consent prerandomized design is either unnecessary or unethical.

According to Zelen, multiple arm consent prerandomized design is superior to conventional randomized design because studies utilizing prerandomization will accrue more patients. One reason for this is that in studies using a conventionally randomized design physicians may be unwilling to enroll patients on a study because they are reluctant to admit they do not know which therapy is best or because explanation of a conventionally randomized trial to a patient is difficult and time-consuming. Another reason is that patients may be reluctant to participate in a conventionally randomized trial not knowing what treatment they will receive. Zelen recommends prerandomization as a device for dealing with these problems.

Are Zelen's arguments sound? On the one hand, the difficulties that Zelen cites with conventionally randomized studies are not so serious that many conventionally randomized trials cannot be completed. Hence, with respect to many trials, prerandomization is unnecessary. On the other hand, it is not difficult at all to understand how the difficulties that Zelen cites could plague studies such as the NSABP early breast cancer study. There is, after all, empirical evidence that pre-randomization increased accrual in that case.

The most important part of the argument of this paper comes to this: there is no mechanism through which enrollment in multiple arm consent prerandomized studies can be significantly greater than enrollment in conventionally randomized studies that is consistent with the ethics of medicine. Some of the evidence for this claim emerges from an analysis of Zelen's description of the virtues of prerandomization. According to Zelen:

> The proposed new design has the desirable feature that the physician need only approach the patient to discuss a single therapy. The physician need not leave himself open, in the eyes of the patient, to not knowing what he is doing and "tossing a coin" to decide the treatment (1979, p. 1243).

Ethical problems leap to the eye. As already argued, any ethical physician who enrolls her patient in a randomized trial, whether conventionally randomized or prerandomized, holds the view that neither arm of the trial involves inferior therapy given available knowledge. By what right does such a physician discuss only a single therapy? Zelen's proposal is tantamount to denying a patient a legitimate therapeutic choice, to denying a patient his autonomy. The wrongness of this is made even more evident by leaving this level of abstraction and focusing on the very study that might be thought to provide evidence for the merits of prerandomization. Zelen's comment supports discussing with a patient with early breast cancer in the NSABP study only the surgery to which she had been prerandomized. That's explicitly illegal in some states and for good moral reasons. There is presumably no serious dispute with the claim that *any* patient with early breast cancer has the moral right to choose less radical surgery on cosmetic grounds or more radical surgery because she is willing to err on the side of caution if her physician believes that there is no good evidence that either procedure yields poorer results. Zelen's mechanism by which an accrual advantage is achieved denies a patient that right.

Furthermore, it seems quite wrong for a physician *not* "to leave himself open, in the eyes of the patient, to not knowing what he is doing and 'tossing a coin' to decide the treatment" if he has enrolled a patient in a randomized trial. If a physician does not make it clear that she does *not* know which treatment is best and that the treatment choice *has* been determined randomly, it is reasonable for the patient to believe that the treatment she is being offered is *the* treatment the physician believes best. A sensible argument for an alternative understanding of the doctor-patient relationship is very hard to imagine. Not to correct this presumption by a patient is tantamount to deception. And a consequence of this deception is that a patient is deprived of a choice to which she is, in the breast cancer case, morally, and often legally, entitled. Accordingly, if Zelen's suggestion is followed, increased accrual in prerandomized studies is accomplished only at the price of a serious breach of medical ethics.

Is there any other way in which prerandomization can result in increased accrual without violating medical ethics? Susan Ellenberg, in an excellent paper, has suggested some of the possible ethical shortcomings of obtaining consent in a prerandomized study:

> Knowledge by the physician of the assigned treatment allows conscious or subconscious tailoring of the study presentation to predispose the patient to accept the assigned therapy. If the patient has been assigned to standard therapy, the physician may stress the experimental nature of the new therapy, its potential risks, and the possibility that the new therapy may be worse than the standard one. If the patient has been assigned to the experimental therapy, the physician may stress the unsatisfactory track record of the standard therapy and the promising earlier studies that indicated that the experimental therapy might be an improvement. The physician may gloss over or even omit the information that treatment has been chosen by a random mechanism and imply to the patient that the assigned therapy has been individually selected for the patient. One must question whether patients receiving such presentations are being completely and honestly informed about the nature and objective of the study (1984, p. 1407).

Ellenberg's conclusion seems to be an understatement. The manipulation of the patient that Ellenberg describes is not as extreme as the manipulation Zelen outlines but it is objectionable and it is objectionable for the same reasons that the manipulation Zelen describes is objectionable. Such a presentation involves deceit; such a presentation deprives a patient of informed consent through the attempt to manipulate her choice.

It is easy to see how conversion of a conventionally randomized study to prerandomization can increase accrual, but at the price of clear violations of medical ethics. Hence, the issue becomes: is there any mechanism by means of which accrual could be increased that does *not* involve unethical practices? Such a mechanism would exist if the reasons that physicians give for not entering patients in a conventionally randomized trial were removed by a conversion to prerandomization. In point of fact Taylor et al. (1984) have done a study to discover what these reasons were in the case of the NSABP early breast cancer study when it used conventional randomization. If the multiple consent prerandomized design is ethical and improves accrual, then the reasons that physicians gave for not asking patients to participate in that conventionally randomized study must be reasons that would not limit the enrollment of patients in a prerandomized study.

A look at the reasons cited in the Taylor study is illuminating. A major obstacle to enrollment in the conventionally randomized study was its perceived interference with the traditional doctor-patient relationship. What Taylor meant by this is the perceived incompatibility of placing a patient in a randomized trial with the view of a physician as having expert knowledge and individualized decision-making power, with her trying to do the best for her particular patient, and with her charismatic authority. It is certainly hard to understand how this obstacle to accrual is removed by prerandomization *if* the patient fully understands what she is agreeing to when she signs the consent form. For to understand that form is to understand that one's treatment is being determined independently of this charismatic power of the physician and her individualized decision-making power. Accordingly, prerandomization will not help with respect to these factors. Of course, both prerandomization and conventional randomization involve a physician doing her best for her patient—at least never choosing an inferior therapy—and having expert knowledge. Hence, prerandomization will not help with respect to these factors either, if informed consent is adequate.

Some physicians cited the difficulty of obtaining informed consent as a barrier to recruitment of patients in a conventionally randomized study. But how is this barrier removed by prerandomization if the trial is conducted ethically? It is hard to imagine what would not have to be explained to the patient if the prerandomization design is used that would have to be explained if a conventional design is used and ethical procedures are followed. Does one leave out an understanding of the disease, the risks of either of the therapies, their anticipated benefits, the nature of the trial itself? The trouble with this difficulty is that if getting informed consent is a barrier to enrolling patients in a randomized trial, the only ways that this barrier might be removed in a prerandomized trial that spring easily to mind involve biasing the informed consent to fit the therapy or not taking the trouble to ensure that the patient understands what she is consenting to. Both are unethical.

In Taylor's study, fifteen investigators said they had difficulty telling patients they did not know which option is better. Since it would be *essential* to tell this to patients if one were getting informed consent to participate in a prerandomized trial, prerandomization does not eliminate this barrier to accrual. Some investigators did not enter patients in the trial because they felt they already knew which treatment was better. Prerandomization obviously offers no balm for an ethical physician whose reluctance to enter patients in the trial is based on this belief. Some physicians felt that they would be personally responsible for the patients randomized to what would eventually turn out to be the inferior treatment and for this reason would not enter patients in the trial. Prerandomization obviously does not remove this barrier either. Physicians who were concerned with the greater difficulties of placing a patient on the trial rather than treating that patient independently of the trial, such as the time involved in getting informed consent, the inflexibility of treatment procedures, or the rigid rules governing eligibility, would not find a more congenial situation if the trial were prerandomized.

To summarize: prerandomization is supposed to be a good thing because it deals with the problem of physician reluctance to ask patients to participate in some conventionally randomized studies. However, a serial review of the possible sources of the alleged reluctance reveals that either prerandomization is of no help in overcoming that source of reluctance or prerandomization helps increase the enrollment of patients on the study only by making it easier for physicians to neglect their moral duties to patients. Hence, from this perspective prerandomization is either useless or immoral.

This line of argument is not yet sufficient. Even though it has been shown that it is not reasonable to believe that prerandomization will reduce the reluctance of the ethical physician to participate in a randomized clinical trial, it does not follow that the reluctance of *patients* to participate in a randomized clinical trial will not be reduced by prerandomization. Zelen argued that patients are reluctant to participate in conventionally randomized studies because they must consent to participate not knowing which therapy they will receive. Now it appears that prerandomization can have an effect on *this* source of slow accrual since when patients are asked for informed consent to participate in a prerandomized study, they *are* told which therapy they will receive.

However, consider the following argument. For any given study, either there will be a significant proportion of patients who will prefer one treatment arm to the other or there will not be. On the one hand, if there is not, then it is hard to see why patients should object to being conventionally randomized since, by hypothesis, a randomly chosen treatment would not conflict with what they prefer. Hence, on this horn of the dilemma prerandomization is unnecessary. Of course, it might be argued that some patients would prefer that their *physician* pick their treatment whatever it might be. If such patients know what they have agreed to, however, then they will be no more likely to agree to participate in a prerandomized trial than in a conventionally randomized trial since their physician chooses their therapy in neither case.

On the other hand, if there is a significant proportion of patients who prefer one therapy to the other, then ethical completion of the prerandomized study will be impossible. As the percentage of patients who decline the treatment to which they are prerandomized grows, the number of patients required to complete the study grows even more. Such a study can succeed only by recruiting considerably more patients than a conventionally randomized trial. But this fact eliminates the advantage that the prerandomized study would have over the conventionally randomized study. This argument appears to show that from the patient's perspective conversion to prerandomization is either unnecessary or doomed to fail, if the trial is conducted ethically.

Is it possible that some patients refuse conventional randomization because of the uncertainty involved in committing themselves to an unknown therapy, even when they do not prefer one therapy to the others? If it were, then prerandomization would be superior to conventional randomization for such patients.

This possibility is most unlikely. There is no evidence at all that patients are sufficiently unwilling to commit themselves to an unknown treatment when they do not prefer one to the other to condemn conventionally randomized clinical trials to incompletion. Many conventionally randomized trials do get completed, after all. It seems to follow that patient avoidance of the unknown is not by itself sufficient to bar the completion of a conventional randomized trial.

What factor, in addition to or supportive of mere patient avoidance of the unknown, might increase the level of patient refusal to participate in a trial to a degree such that the trial could not be completed? An obvious factor in, for example, the mastectomy vs. lumpectomy study, is that patients would have a preference for one treatment over the other and *therefore* wish to avoid the unknown outcome of consenting to randomization. But this other factor, as we have seen, is at least as large a barrier to ethical prerandomization as to conventional randomization.

Finally, it is worth noting that patient uncertainty concerning the treatment to which they will be randomized can be minimized in a conventionally randomized clinical trial. A randomization can be performed within a few minutes after the consent form is signed. Hence, if *mere* avoidance of uncertainty were a significant problem in any actual trials, prerandomization is unnecessary for avoiding it.

The conclusion of this long segment of the analysis is that if multiple arm consent prerandomized design increases accrual as compared with conventionally randomized design, then the trial has violated the canons of medical ethics. Since single arm consent designs already have been ruled out on ethical grounds, this argument shows that prerandomization is either unnecessary or unethical.

A final segment of the argument, although it apparently pertains to no presently conducted trials, will tighten up the logic of the argument. Nothing so far shows that prerandomization is wrong in those trials in which prerandomization is unnecessary to increase accrual. Is it wrong?

Ellenberg's account of how prerandomization may allow bias to creep in (or overwhelm) a physician's presentation when getting consent to participate in a trial has already been noted. Such bias is not possible in a conventionally randomized design. The presentation can hardly be tailored to fit the treatment to which the patient has already been randomized if the patient has not yet been randomized. Since conventionally randomized trials contain important safeguards against this bias that prerandomized trials lack, conventional randomization is always preferable to prerandomization on moral grounds. This, when combined with the previous argument, shows that prerandomization is always wrong.

V

The purpose of this essay has been to lay out with some care an argument for the claim that all prerandomized clinical trials are unethical. If the conclusion of this paper is correct, the NSABP early breast cancer study was unethical. Yet, the results of that study have been, and undoubtedly will be, extraordinarily valuable and presumably could not have been achieved without prerandomization. Therefore, no one should be happy about accepting the conclusion of the previous section. Indeed, all persons interested in medical ethics would seem to have a moral obligation to try to show that the argument of this essay is flawed. If that could be shown, then one could construct a much sounder ethical foundation for prerandomization than presently exists. That would constitute a clear advance in our understanding of medical ethics.

The trouble with attacking the argument of this paper is that it rests upon assumptions about the doctor-patient relationship, about informed consent, and about the wrongness of deceit that appear to be too well entrenched to be overturned. An interesting corollary concerning the adequacy of informed consent in a prerandomized trial has emerged. Consent to be enrolled in a prerandomized study is ethically adequate only if disclosure of the nature of the study and treatment alternatives is at least as comprehensive as the disclosure required for a conventionally randomized study. On the one hand, prerandomization has seemed to be ethically permissible because this doctrine tacitly has been rejected. On the other hand, if the doctrine could be shown to be false, then the argument of this paper would be in serious trouble. Perhaps, therefore, this is the place to attack.

If the above strategy does not work, then apparently, prerandomization can be saved only if some fundamental doctrines of medical ethics are reconsidered. One might argue, for example, that the doctrines in question should be overridden by considerations of great social utility. Such a view is not my view, but there is nothing in this paper to show that this way out of the problem should be rejected.

Finally, prerandomization, throughout this paper, has been compared with conventional randomization and has been condemned by comparison. The argument of this essay should not be construed as implying that conventional randomization is ethical. As I have argued elsewhere, the conduct of many conventionally randomized clinical trials is also incompatible with ethical standards of therapeutic medicine that are both commonly accepted and that seem quite defensible (Marquis, 1983).

NOTES

An ancestor of this paper was presented as a commentary on a paper by Dr. Marvin Zelen at the Second Hannah Conference: "Moral Priorities in Medical Research" at the University of Western Ontario, London, Ontario, in November 1984. I wish to thank Richard DeGeorge, Mary Spratt, Ron Stephens, Bill Bartholome, Barbara Jones, Tony Genova, Mike Young, Jack Bricke, Art Skidmore, and an anonymous referee for the *Journal of Medicine and Philosophy* for their helpful comments on the penultimate draft of this essay.

REFERENCES

Capron, A.M.: 1979, "A new design for randomized trials," *New England Journal of Medicine* 301, 787.

Cox, E.B.: 1979, "A new design for randomized trials," *New England Journal of Medicine* 301, 786.

Ellenberg, S.: 1984, "Randomization designs in comparative clinical trials," *New England Journal of Medicine* 310, 1404–1408.

Fisher, B. et al.: 1985, "Five-year results of a randomized clinical trial comparing total mastectomy and segmental mastectomy with or without radiation in the treatment of breast cancer," *New England Journal of Medicine* 312, 665–673.

Fost, N.: 1979, "Consent as a barrier to research," *New England Journal of Medicine* 300, 1272–1273.

Marquis, D.: 1983, "Leaving therapy to chance: an impasse in the ethics of randomized clinical trials," *Hastings Center Report* 13, 40–47.

Rutstein, D.D.: 1979, "A new design for randomized trials," *New England Journal of Medicine* 301, 786.

Stuart, R.K.: 1979, "A new design for randomized trials," *New England Journal of Medicine* 301, 786.

Taylor, K., Margolese, R., and Soskolne, C.L.: 1984, "Physicians' reasons for not entering eligible patients in a randomized clinical trial of surgery for breast cancer," *New England Journal of Medicine* 310, 1363–1367.

Vawter, D.E.: 1979, "A new design for randomized trials," *New England Journal of Medicine* 301, 786–787.

Zelen, M.: 1977, "Statistical options in clinical trials," *Seminars in Oncology* 4, 441–446.

Zelen, M.: 1979, "A new design for randomized trials," *New England Journal of Medicine* 300, 1242–1245.

Zelen, M.: 1981, "Alternative to classic randomized trials," *Surgical Clinics of North America* 61, 1425–1432.

Zelen, M.: 1982, "Strategy and alternate randomized designs in cancer clinical trials," *Cancer Treatment Reports* 66, 1095–1100.

The Conflict between Randomized Clinical Trials and the Therapeutic Obligation

Fred Gifford

The central dilemma concerning randomized clinical trials (RCTs) arises out of some simple facts about causal methodology (RCTs are the best way to generate the reliable causal knowledge necessary for optimally informed action) and a *prima facie* plausible principle concerning how physicians should treat their patients (always do what it is most reasonable to believe will be best for the patient). I begin with the methodological points.

To show that some experimental treatment is a cause of recovery (or of anything else, such as harmful side-effects), one must compare the result of giving that treatment with the result of some other circumstance, such as the giving of the conventional therapy or a placebo. One hopes for a higher rate of cure in the experimental group than in the control group, and one hopes that the results will be statistically significant, i.e., large enough that one can rule out (with a certain degree of confidence) the possibility that this difference came about by chance. However, in addition to ruling out this 'chance' hypothesis, one must also attempt to rule out the possibility that the results are due to differences in some *other* factor, such as seriousness of the illness prior to the treatment.

This problem can be circumvented by assigning the subjects to the experimental and control groups by a random selection process. One can then be confident that any other factors affecting the outcome will exist in approximately the same proportion in each group, and thus that differences in outcome between the two groups will be a result only of the factor being tested.

This problem of confounding factors can be dealt with to some degree in historically controlled trials (HCTs)—prospective studies without randomization—by explicitly matching the two groups for various characteristics suspected of affecting the outcome (e.g., age, seriousness of the illness, other interventions). But this strategy has important limitations. Controlling for a large number of variables requires a prohibitively large sample size, and one can only control in this way for variables that one has already thought of, a limitation which is particularly severe in areas where we have relatively little background knowledge. Randomization, on the other hand, controls for all variables, whether explicitly considered or not.

Other things being equal, then, RCTs are the optimal methodology for establishing causal claims about the safety and efficacy of drugs or other therapies. Forgoing such trials can be expected to cause the acceptance of various drugs and therapies that are in fact ineffective (as well as the failure to accept certain effective ones), resulting in inferior treatment for future patients.

But of course, other things are *not* equal. The subjects of the experiment are patients seeking medical care. Physicians are typically thought to have an obligation to treat a patient in a way which yields the best chance of recovery. Following Marquis (1983), I will call this the therapeutic obligation (TO).

Now, if the two treatments—or arms of the study—have equal expected outcomes, this does not pose a problem. So in cases where there is no reason for saying which of the treatments is better, randomization will be consistent with the TO. But such conditions are often, if not usually, violated. In particular, the TO will be violated in any trial where it is possible to generate interim data.

For consider a trial that establishes the superiority of one of the treatments, and suppose that at the beginning of the trial we have no basis for saying which of the two alternative treatments is better. At the end of such a trial, there is a large enough difference between the cure rates of the two groups to say with, for instance, 95% confidence that treatment A is better than treatment B. But this means that somewhere part way through the trial, we could have drawn this same conclusion, but at a lower confidence level, such as 75%. This would not be enough for acceptance by the medical community, and it might not be sufficient evidence to merit publication. And there are of course good reasons for not simply accepting such results. We know of many cases where such 'trends' have reversed themselves. And we know of cases where reliance on such preliminary results has resulted in a great deal of harm to patients that could have been avoided had experimentation been continued (Silverman, 1980). Further, stopping 'prematurely' can result in others carrying out their own tests so that in the long run *more* persons are subjected to the risks of the research. On the other hand, it would not be correct to say that the physician faced with the data at the 75% confidence level will be indifferent between the two therapies. If a patient meeting the criteria of the protocol were to come under his or her care at that point (but not in the context of the research protocol), the physician would surely give treatment A, and this would be the only appropriate course of action.

Thus, carrying out the RCTs, whose results are so important to the care of future patients, involves violating the TO with respect to one's present patients. As just seen, this 'RCT dilemma' arises whenever evidence for the superiority of one of the treatments is approaching, but has not yet reached, the significance level. There is clearly, as well, a need to study drugs and procedures that are already in wide use, and are thus in some sense 'accepted', raising the dilemma even at the beginning of the trial. Note that the RCT dilemma can be viewed as one about whether to carry out an RCT at all or as one about determining the point at which the trial should be terminated (the problem of 'stopping rules').

A number of proposals have been offered for solving or avoiding the RCT dilemma. One type of solution might be characterized as a *procedural* solution. For instance, it might be urged that such decisions be made by an IRB. This may be an appropriate suggestion, but it does not resolve the dilemma. For the question of the principles to be applied in evaluating a given case or the general practice of RCTs must be addressed no matter who is making the decision. My concern here is with arguments about the substantive questions of whether and when it is permissible to carry out trials in light of the TO, and what the basis for this is.

This substantive problem has itself been addressed in a number of different ways. Some have tried to show that, contrary to initial appearances, one does not really have to violate the TO, either because the benefits are illusory or because RCTs can be carried out in a manner that does not violate the TO. Others take on directly the task of establishing that such violation can in fact be justified. Other discussions focus on determining ways of minimizing such violation (or the harm or sub-optimal treatment that results). A strategy worth separate mention is that appealing to informed consent.

While not attempting to be exhaustive here, I will try to pull together some of the most significant proposals, and pose certain questions about them, in a manner that will enhance our understanding of the issues and point to what further work needs to be done. I will argue that the conflict between the obligation to the patient (the TO) and the value of the experiments cannot be avoided. I will also emphasize that RCTs can only be accepted as morally permissible if one of the 'direct' arguments for the permissibility of violating the TO can be sustained. Other arguments—involving informed consent and the minimization of harm—are very important for determining a particular RCT policy if we can establish independently that the general policy is morally acceptable; but they cannot by themselves justify such a policy. Further, the overall justification we decide upon is likely to affect the nature of the particular policies concerning informed consent and appropriate mechanisms for minimizing risk, as well as which RCTs are deemed acceptable.

I. Attempts to Avoid the Dilemma

A. *Illusiveness of the Benefits*

There are various ways of trying to *avoid* the RCT dilemma. One is by claiming that we do not really have to carry out RCTs because the benefits are illusory. For instance, it is suggested that the conclusions from RCTs do not hold a privileged position over other sorts of medical information, in part because the individual clinician has to make use of clinical judgment in any case in order to interpret the results, or their implications for appropriate action (Burkhardt, 1983). Relatedly, it is also claimed that *historically* controlled trials can sometimes yield information as reliable as RCTs due to especially good background knowledge (for instance, about the factors that need to be controlled for).

Now, this point about the interpretation of results is important. It may well be that the various tests will have to be evaluated from a perspective that takes into account factors outside the RCT itself and subjective assessments of probabilities. However, I do not believe that this has the intended implications. For we still know that RCTs will generally be more reliable than their historically controlled counterparts, and so there will usually be reason to prefer RCTs from the point of view of providing better care to future patients. Turning to the second argument, that concerning the fact that sometimes we will have especially good background knowledge, I believe that this will only apply in a fairly delimited set of cases, and here only to some extent.

However, it is clear that these considerations, while insufficient as an overall solution, constitute an important element in our attempt to deal with the moral problems we face in human subjects research. I will return to this at the end of the paper.

B. The Knowledge Argument

Another strategy attempts to show that we do not really *know* which treatment is better (since we do not have statistically significant results) and thus that we are not really giving the one group treatment that we know to be inferior.

But, as suggested above, this argument equivocates on the term 'know'. It is true that results that are statistically significant are surely *more* reliable and secure than those which are not (or than results of uncontrolled studies, for example). Still, it is clear that as long as the evidence favors the one treatment over the other *at all*, this would reasonably be used to decide what treatment to give if this is all the information we had and the benefit of the patient was our overriding goal. Unless we think that such judgments are entirely irrational, we must agree that such evidence generates the dilemma.

To clarify, we might like to be able to say what sort of information is reliable and worthy of guiding our action and what is not, and it might be thought that statistically significant results of RCTs may mark this division. But we will not in fact find a sharp dividing line here. Reliability of knowledge comes in degrees, and the particular significance level utilized is only conventionally determined. So we will not be able to appeal to a simple rule that tells us what to do just on the basis of whether certain things are 'known' or not. There appears to be no choice but to weigh the degree of likelihood of harm against the value of the knowledge to be gained, unless we are willing to forgo all trials concerning treatments of any consequence. But such weighing will often result in violation of the TO.

C. Division of Labor

It is often said that the way to alleviate the problem for the physician is to withhold interim data from the physicians who are treating the patients. Assuming that we have no evidence about the superiority of one treatment at the beginning of the trial, this will remain true for the physician throughout the trial. An analogous suggestion is made by Chalmers that such information be withheld from the investigators as well, and that decisions about whether to end the trial be made by an independent committee (Chalmers, 1972).

Following Marquis (1983), I will call this the 'division of labor' solution. Such policies can alleviate the practical problems of psychological tension (on the part of the treating physicians and investigators) and biased samples (that can result if subject inclusion is affected by knowledge of how the trial is proceeding), and this may well justify their utilization. But they do not alleviate the RCT dilemma, the moral question of whether violating the TO is permissible. As argued by Marquis, adding more people to the process does not change the moral permissibility of the actions.

D. Special Study Designs

There are also some particular study designs that attempt to avoid violating the TO. For instance, Beecher (1970) recommends using each patient as his own control, alternating the therapies at certain intervals. Thus no one is (completely) denied the better treatment. This addresses the issue of justice—no one is singled out for inferior treatment—but the TO is still violated. At any point at which there begins to be some information favoring one of the treatments, each patient is given what is believed to be sub-optimal treatment.

Similar things can be said of cross-over studies (Armitage, 1984). Here, a patient is switched over to the other treatment if and when he does not respond appropriately to the treatment to which he is originally assigned. Such patients are better off than if they had been in a traditional RCT, but worse off than if they had not been randomized in the first place.

Each of these designs also suffers to some degree from obvious methodological problems.

II. Determining Ways of Minimizing Harm

None of the above strategies succeeds in avoiding the RCT dilemma, but some—such as the special study designs just mentioned—can be viewed instead as ways of minimizing harm brought about by RCTs rather than actually circumventing the dilemma entirely.

A. *The Two-Armed Bandit*

Another example of a design aimed at minimization of subject harm is the two-armed bandit model. This is a mechanism for minimizing the number of subjects given the inferior treatment (Hill, 1978). Meier (1979) points out, however, that its implausible assumptions make it inapplicable in practice, in part because it increases the overall time before completion of the study and thus lessens benefits to the larger number of individuals *outside* the trial.

B. *Randomization from the Start*

Chalmers (1972) argues that we should randomize right from the first patient. Otherwise, investigators and physicians will inevitably begin to form an opinion prior to the initiation of the RCT, one which is quite difficult to discount. Thus, as argued above, they will no longer be able to say truthfully that there are no reasonable grounds for choosing between the two therapies, and as a result they may decide not to proceed with an RCT. If the trend looks negative, they might inappropriately lose a good therapy; if positive, they might go ahead and use a bad therapy without further formal investigation.

But these problems will arise in any case as the evidence accumulates in an RCT. Chalmers's proposal would not alleviate the problem but only put it off for a short time. Of course, putting off that dilemma for a time, as well as generating reliable information sooner, is valuable, and thus it may be that his suggestion should be followed. But it does nothing to address the question of whether it is permissible to violate the TO in the first place, or what the grounds for doing so might be. Indeed, since the dilemma will arise anyway, perhaps one moral to be drawn is that we should attempt to train physicians in such a way that they are not so susceptible to being inappropriately swayed by such 'anecdotal evidence'. (Note that this is a matter of resolving the *psychological* dilemma, and it *assumes* that we are in fact justified in violating the TO.)

C. Meier's Proposal

Meier (1979) suggests an intriguing and more sophisticated framework for conceptualizing the question of when performance of an RCT is acceptable and when it should be stopped.

Suppose we have a quantitative scale on which we can represent the outcome of a given treatment. At any given time, there is for each treatment a probability distribution of expected outcomes on this scale, and this can be transformed into a discrete range by specifying a confidence level. Similarly, the expected *difference* in efficacy between treatments A and B can be given a range for a given confidence level. We then need to identify two levels: a 'least interesting difference' (LD), such that a smaller level would be deemed an inconsequential research result, and a 'maximum acceptable difference' (MD), the greatest difference such that denying a subject that much would not be unacceptable and thus would not count as 'abuse'. (Note that each of these involves making a value judgment, i.e., assessing the importance of avoiding certain kinds of outcomes.) Meier says that we can then give an appropriate stopping rule with something like the following form: stop the trial if the range of uncertainty (or confidence interval) lies clearly above the MD. The graph in Figure 1 allows one to visualize this; one stops when the 'lowest' point of the confidence interval is higher than the MD line. At least in the case pictured—that is, at least where MD > LD—the RCT dilemma can be resolved.

I think that Meier's general framework is promising, properly identifying the parameters to be taken into account, and in particular, helping us to represent uncertainty in a useful way. But its precision also allows us to conceptualize some serious difficulties with trying to weigh the relevant factors against one another. I do not think that these problems count as criticisms of Meier's model so much as further dilemmas we shall have to face in any case. I will discuss one such problem.

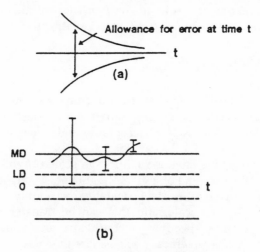

MD—Maximum acceptable difference
LD—Least interesting difference

Fig. 1. Meier's framework for conceptualizing stopping rules for a clinical trial. The curve (b) shows the estimated difference in outcome of two treatments as a function of time. Vertical bars represent the confidence interval.

Consider again the proposed stopping rule: stop if the difference is *clearly* greater than the maximum acceptable difference. This is tantamount to waiting until we are *clearly* above that line, and thus until further treatment is *clearly* 'abusive'. But it is plausible to say that we are concerned to avoid (insofar as is reasonable) the *possibility* of abuse, or to reduce its probability and degree to some specified low level. Perhaps we should be concerned instead with the other end of the confidence interval (thus stopping the trial if any part of the range of uncertainty reaches as high as the MD).

This might seem to be a reasonable modification of Meier's proposal, but it presents the following difficulty. For any reasonable confidence level, the range of uncertainty is going to be very large at the beginning of the trial, and it will almost assuredly extend beyond the MD. So it is clear that the criterion cannot be some simple one like "stop whenever the range of uncertainty extends as high as the MD." Perhaps we could be more tolerant of falling outside the MD range early in the trial, or perhaps we could subtract the extent to which the confidence interval stretches *below* the zero-point. Or we could instead focus our attention on the *mean*. It is not obvious which of these is the correct strategy.

Underlying this difficulty is the problem of weighing or assessing probability *distributions* of possible harms and benefits. This problem is related to that of deciding between different simple decision rules, such as 'maximize expected utility' and 'maximin' (choose that alternative with the best worst outcome). Each alternative seems counter-intuitive. Maximizing expected utility pays no attention to aversion to risk, while maximin is too extreme in the other direction, recommending that we choose as if we knew the worst-case scenario would occur. Further, the latter is somewhat artificial in the present case, since what the 'worst case' is varies with changes in specification of the confidence level. Indeed, this issue is even more complicated in cases like the present one where we are pitting benefits to some against risks to others. Thus one of the difficulties in evaluating RCTs involves this more general problem in ethics and decision theory.

D. More Effective Use of Non-RCT Data

The reference to background knowledge and the fact that HCTs are sometimes very effective in generating causal knowledge can also be appealed to as a mechanism for minimizing harm. More generally, it may be recommended that we develop more sophisticated ways of analysing the data from HCTs and other sources. Perhaps we can then draw reliable conclusions before having to subject so many individuals to the experiment. I will come back to this point at the end of the paper.

It is important to note that each of the proposals in this section *presupposes* that it is permissible to violate the TO, for each involves a certain amount of such violation. Of course, assuming that some such justification can be found (or assuming that the research is going to take place anyway), a next step will be to determine ways of minimizing the cost to subjects. But this cannot substitute for such justification.

III. Informed Consent

An obviously important consideration in thinking about the moral permissibility of RCTs is that of informed consent. One function of informed consent concerns minimization of harm by having the prospective subject make an assessment of the risk, but informed consent also addresses directly the question of the moral permissibility of violating the TO. For it is plausible to say that one should be allowed to choose freely to join a trial even if it is not strictly in one's best interest. For instance, surely one ought to be *allowed* to volunteer from a desire to help others.

It should be kept in mind that informed consent is not really just one of the possible solutions, but must be an element in any plausible solution. On the other hand, I contend that informed consent cannot by itself provide a justification for RCTs, and we cannot *simply* rely on informed consent, allowing any trials to be conducted as long as there are consenting participants. Very briefly, we know that consent is often not well-informed or adequately voluntary. Patients are often extremely vulnerable, and many lack the ability to assimilate the necessary information (Appelbaum, 1983).

I cannot assess here the degree to which patients can make sufficiently autonomous choices in this context without a much fuller discussion. But it is clear that there are limits on this, and that whether or not we rely on informed consent as part of the justification for doing RCTs, we will need to make some assessments about what sort of risks are acceptable in such trials.

But as mentioned above, regardless of whether informed consent can adequately play the roles we are here considering, there is surely an obligation to obtain it as best one can. It is thus important to mention some special problems concerning informed consent in the case of RCTs. For instance, should subjects be given interim data—that is, should they be told that they are entering a trial where they have a 50% chance of being assigned to a treatment that is near the point of statistical significance for being ineffective (or clearly less effective than the other treatment)? It surely seems that subjects have a right to such interim data if they are being asked to participate in the research. But this presents difficulties, perhaps the most important of which is the following. It is said that if the patients are given information such as the above, then they will refuse to become subjects, and trials will be completed much more slowly or not at all.

One solution often suggested is that the prospective subjects could agree beforehand to have withheld from them the information of how much of the trial has already been conducted and what the results have been, and that this will generate a greater consent rate. I believe that this is the most acceptable solution in principle, but in order to assess the acceptability of such 'second-level consent', we need to know what the reason is for the greater consent rate. Is it that subjects see the importance of continuing the trial to the point of statistical significance and do not want to be tempted to refuse to participate? Or is it that, since the facts and proposals described to them are more complicated and abstract, they do not properly comprehend their situation or effectively take into account the risk to themselves? Clearly, it is important to determine which of these is the case before we draw conclusions about the acceptability of this strategy. This underlines the importance of further research on this matter.

IV. Justifications for Violating the Therapeutic Obligation

It appears that we must accept the fact that if we are to gain the knowledge necessary for increasingly high-quality treatment, the TO must be violated. Further, we must be able to give a direct justification for this if we are to perform RCTs. I now turn to some attempts at this.

A. The Utilitarian Justification

The most obvious suggestion is the utilitarian one: we may deny the benefit of optimal treatment to present subjects because this is outweighed by the greater benefit thereby generated for future patients.

However, not only is the correctness of utilitarianism controversial at best, but this is precisely the sort of case that makes it seem implausible. One who takes the RCT dilemma seriously is not going to be moved by the fact that doing RCTs brings about the greatest benefit overall. For this is precisely what creates the dilemma in the first place. This, of course, does not show that utilitarianism is false, but it does suggest that we need to look elsewhere for a justification that will be convincing in the present context. In our current state of uncertainty and unclarity concerning which (if any) moral theory is the correct one, we need to be able to give reasons why we should apply utilitarianism (or some other theory) to this sort of problem.

B. Meier's Argument from Consistency

Meier argues that it is inappropriate to hold ourselves to a principle that requires a physician never to give less than optimal treatment, or that says that "not even a small and uncertain benefit can ethically be denied" (1979, p. 637). As illustrated above, he suggests that we instead define a certain level of risk or sub-optimal treatment as constituting "abuse". Some of the proposals mentioned above could then be used to minimize such risk and keep it below this level.

Meier's argument is one from consistency. It is that in many contexts we carry out policies (or fail to change policies) that we know beforehand will bring harm or risk to certain individuals, and we do not take these decisions to be inappropriate. He suggests that it is not reasonable to require a different set of standards in the case of health care.

One of Meier's examples is the fact that many people risk their lives by driving to work for the convenience of living in pleasant surroundings. There is of course a serious flaw in the use of this particular example. For here the benefit (or convenience) accrues to the same person who takes the risk (and, not incidentally, who seeks out the opportunity in the first place). But in the RCT case, the benefit accrues to *other* patients, while the risk is taken by the present subject who typically does not stand to benefit.

However, Meier can also make his point with other examples where society imposes risks on individuals (or fails to correct for them) for reasons of economy or convenience where the benefit is distributed generally and there is no significant benefit for the person at risk. He uses the example of failing to lower speed limits; one could also mention other sorts of safety standards that are less strict than they might otherwise be for reasons of economy or convenience.

Of course, it might be objected that questions about health care (or physicians' roles) cannot be treated in the same way as the above policy decisions. To respond to this, let us consider an example that concerns health care and sub-optimal treatment, the question of allocation and cost containment.

Increasingly, we are faced with decisions concerning which of a number of patients to give various kinds of medical treatment to, and also whether to put resources in health care or elsewhere. These sometimes result in decisions to stop short of doing everything that is in the interests of a given single patient. For example, the decision to have a system of DRGs [Diagnosis Related Groups] and the decisions by physicians to take these into account in determining what care to give a certain patient involves the decision to give patients sub-optimal treatment.

Of course, one tries as hard as possible in such cost containment measures to leave out only that which is not important, but surely there is some limitation in the use of certain treatments which would in fact provide some significant expected benefit. And the benefit in terms of health care costs that accrues from this is distributed generally, so this is not a case where some single decision-maker prefers to forgo a certain amount of good. So if this policy is acceptable, then perhaps so is violation of the TO for the benefit of future patients.

Still, the appropriateness of this analogy may be controversial. It deserves much more careful attention than I can give it here, but let me mention a couple of points.

First is the distinction between micro- and macro-allocation. It may be claimed that while a general policy decision is made that constrains the decisions of individual physicians in ways that yield sub-optimal treatments for patients, individual physicians still (within that framework) act on the TO to the best of their ability.

But this does not affect the fact that "we" have intentionally made a decision that we have good reason to believe will cause certain people to get less than optimal treatment. Why should creating this sort of "division of labor" be any more morally relevant here than in the case of the physician and the investigator discussed above?

It might be objected that one of the issues at hand is what we want the physician's role and dispositions to be, and thus that this division of labor is in fact important. But I do not claim that the division of labor is unacceptable in either case—only that it cannot itself provide a justification for violating the TO. This must be justified on separate grounds. These facts about division of labor will no doubt be important to what sort of policy we adopt, on the grounds of what is psychologically easier or what is consistent with the physician's role that we want to foster. But the claim now is that the RCT and cost containment cases are on par, so that our judgments about the cost containment case should be carried over to the RCT case.

Another worry concerning this analogy between the RCT and cost containment rationales for sub-optimal treatment concerns the *sorts* of cases in which we would stop short of optimal treatment. In the allocation case, the treatments left out, while not without expected benefit, are typically 'extraordinary', expensive, or ones where the benefit/risk ratio for the patient is lower—this is, no doubt, what makes them seem acceptable. And this surely need not be the case in RCTs.

On the other hand, we are not seeking a rationale that will justify *all* RCTs. So perhaps we can say that violation of the TO will be justified to the extent that the treatments left out fall into this category. For instance, perhaps we can say that being treated strictly by the TO (when the alternative is enrollment in a trial that would probably generate a great deal of important information) is similarly very 'expensive' treatment. And if we cannot give some such rationale, perhaps the RCT is not justified.

C. Contractarian Justifications

Now, the argument so far is one from analogy or consistency with other cases. It would be best if we could provide some further underlying rationale for each of these.

Practices such as those being discussed here are sometimes justified by appeal to the fact that each individual benefits from the presence of the institution, even though this can mean accepting costs or risks in a particular instance. On this strategy, morality and political institutions are conceptualized as (perhaps amongst other things) cooperative ventures for mutual advantage, and each person can see that it is in his interest to have such an institution. I will mention here two different types of such 'contract' models. (There are of course other kinds of ethical theories that could be discussed here. I limit myself to these for reasons of space. I suggest that these can be particularly illuminating for thinking through the present problem, but I am not here asserting that only these theories are plausible.)

First, following Rawls (1971), we might require that the system of rules and procedures for determining whether and when randomized clinical trials are begun and terminated be such that they would be agreed to by rational individuals in the "original position". The latter are individuals who do not know whether they will find themselves on the giving or receiving end, but who know that they have a certain chance of getting various diseases and of being asked to participate in clinical trials. (Of course, we cannot 'pay back' the past generations for the benefit we have gained from them (nor lose the benefit if we decide not to participate). Rawls addresses this problem by arguing that those in the original position choose from a position of not knowing even what generation they are in.

Alternatively, we might appeal to a different strategy, inspired by Nozick (1974), grounding obligations on the basis of what we voluntarily agree or consent to (perhaps implicitly by our actions). Accordingly, we might say that one incurs a duty to participate in research (and thus accept the fact that one may receive sub-optimal treatment) either by (knowingly and willingly) seeking medical care in a research institution or by taking advantage of medical care generally that was based on knowledge generated through such human experimentation.

Note that certain individuals (such as the poor) might in fact not have benefited from past research, and thus might be said not to have such a duty (Caplan, 1984). This of course has important implications for the details of our human experimentation policies.

There is no space to consider in adequate detail the plausibility of each of these proposals, but note that they have the advantage that they give a clear and strong place to the welfare of each individual without requiring that the TO never be violated.

A further question arises concerning the proper way to apply ethical theory to policy. Suppose we decide that some such contract model succeeds, and thus that violation of the TO is acceptable. There would still be good reasons for attempting to minimize risks and for respecting informed consent. So just what sort of practice (say, with respect to informed consent) would be justified? Not trying as hard in informing patients, or not being as sure that their consent is fully voluntary? Using a certain amount of *coercion*? Having third-party payments dependent upon such participation? *Encouraging* people to volunteer—or even *socializing* people in a manner such that they feel a moral duty to do so? (A similar set of questions would need to be addressed concerning how to apply the principle that we should minimize risks.)

The details would require a much more involved argument (and a number of empirical facts about psychology, etc.). But the general contractarian answer would be that the character of the institution would be determined by what it was rational to agree to if one wanted to advance one's own interests but did not know one's particular circumstances (or, in the other version, what we can be said to have tacitly agreed to through our actions). Presumably we would not be willing to agree to give up our right to give informed consent (if only 'second-level') or to be free to withdraw from the trial (at least for a fairly wide range of reasons), but we would be more likely to be willing to impose moral claims to the effect that a certain amount of participation is expected. Such encouragement or requirement would of course have to be such as not to impose an unfair burden on some subpopulation (such as the poor or institutionalized).

This is of course only the outline of an answer to the question with which we began, but I think there is some reason to believe that it leads us in the right direction. It is the *kind* of justification that is needed, it has some plausibility, and it holds the promise of being able to be fleshed out into some particular policies.

V. The Importance of Understanding the Structure of Biomedical Knowledge

I would like now to step back and consider an issue that has been touched on occasionally above and that I believe will be increasingly important as we attempt to deal with the RCT dilemma.

The value of the knowledge for future patients cannot by itself serve as an adequate justification for performing RCTs. Nor can the fact that in certain cases (because of background knowledge) HCTs can yield especially reliable results resolve our dilemma, for this is only applicable in certain cases and, even then, RCTs are likely to be somewhat better.

On the other hand, these considerations are still very important, and we should refine our knowledge about them as much as possible. Indeed, as long as we are committed to the idea that certain large increments in important knowledge justify some greater risk for the subjects than do lesser increments in less important knowledge, we need to be able to measure the value of such information and weigh it against the reasons against doing the trial. And the value of doing the test is in part a function of the increase in reliability gained by doing, say, the RCT rather than the HCT. It is therefore important to have some (roughly quantitative) measure of this difference in reliability.

There is actually a wider set of comparisons we need to be able to make, because there are a number of different and varied sources of biomedical knowledge. In addition to how much more reliability of knowledge is gained by doing an RCT rather than an HCT, we want to know how to compare this to uncontrolled observations and clinical judgment based on such things as background knowledge. We need to know how differences in sample size and specificity of the population affect the reliability of inferences. Finally, we need to know how to draw inferences from *combinations* of trials. (Ideally, all of these could be put on a common scale so that we could compare the significance of different amounts of each of these).

More generally, we need to have a fairly clear account of the various sorts of evidence that we can have for a causal hypothesis, and the degree of warrant each sort of evidence provides.

Of particular importance is a better understanding of clinical reasoning or judgment that a given therapy is the best one to use for a particular patient. Presumably, the various kinds of evidence mentioned above are all considered in making some overall judgment.

Recall that claims about clinical judgment were behind Burkhardt's arguments against RCTs, to the effect that the real judgments about whether to accept the results of any given study require expert clinical judgment anyway. Note that an understanding of clinical judgment would also be relevant to the task mentioned above (in the discussion of Chalmers's proposal) of training physicians in such a way that they are not so susceptible to being inappropriately swayed by 'anecdotal evidence'.

Of course, providing such an overall account of clinical judgment is a tall order, and it might be objected that all of this just shows that we really do not know how to make assessments of the value of RCTs. It is surely the case that 'clinical judgment' remains in important respects a mystery. But I would emphasize instead that significant advances have been made in this regard, and perhaps more importantly, the connection to the present problem reinforces the importance of making further progress here. Studies of clinical judgment and studies of the differential reliability of these various sorts of evidence would no doubt be mutually reinforcing (Engelhardt, 1979).

How are we to obtain this information? Perhaps at some point we will be able to make inferences about these matters on some systematic or theoretical basis, but we could at the start at least make such inferences on an empirical or actuarial basis. That is, having categorized the studies of various types (according to type of control, significance level, amount and type of background knowledge, etc.), we could keep a record of how often the results of a given sort were later overturned by new data, or how often they concurred with any RCTs that might be available (or that were done explicitly for comparison).

Once we have data on the relative reliability of these tests, we can make more informed judgments about the value of carrying out a trial of one sort rather than the other. Perhaps in a given case we could judge that increasing the sample size in an HCT by a certain amount could alter the significance level in such a way as to make up much of the difference in reliability.

If we have an obligation to utilize the various methods which minimize the number of patients at risk in these trials, and to utilize HCTs in those instances where there is good reason to believe that the knowledge gained will be essentially as reliable as that from an RCT, then surely we have an obligation to improve our understanding of the comparative value of these different sorts of studies, for this holds promise of helping us to carry out the above two tasks more adequately.

REFERENCES

Appelbaum, P., Roth, L., and Lidz, C.: 1982, "Letter to the Editor," *New England Journal of Medicine* 308, 344.

Armitage, P.: 1984, "Controversies and achievements in clinical trials," *Controlled Clinical Trials* 5, 67–72.

Beecher, H.: 1970, *Research and the Individual*, Little, Brown and Co., Boston, Mass.

Burkhardt, R. and Kienle, G.: 1983, "Basic problems in controlled trials," *Journal of Medical Ethics* 9(2), 90–93.

Caplan, A.: 1984, "Is there a duty to serve as a subject in biomedical research?" *IRB* 6, 1–5.

Chalmers, T., Block, J., and Lea, S.: 1972, "Controlled studies in clinical cancer research," *New England Journal of Medicine* 287, 75–78.

Engelhardt, H.T., Spicker, S.F., and Towers, B. (eds.): 1979, *Clinical Judgment: A Critical Appraisal*, D. Reidel Publishing Co., Dordrecht, Holland.

Hill, C. and Sancho-Garnier, H.: 1978, "The two-armed-bandit problem: A decision theory approach to clinical trials," *Biomedicine Special Issue* 28, 42–43.

Marquis, D.: 1983, "Leaving therapy to chance," *Hastings Center Report* 13, 40–47.

Meier, P.: 1979, "Terminating a trial—The ethical problem," *Clinical Pharmacology and Therapeutics* 25, 637–640.

Nozick, R.: 1974, *Anarchy, State and Utopia*, Basic Books, New York.

Rawls, J.: 1971, *A Theory of Justice*, Harvard University Press, Cambridge, Mass.

Silverman, W.: 1980, *Retrolental Fibroplasia: A Modern Parable*, Academic Press, New York.

Sins of Omission? The Non-Treatment of Controls in Clinical Trials—I[1]

Michael Lockwood

Most discussions of the ethics of clinical trials have focused on such matters as informed consent and the morality of submitting human subjects to previously untried, and hence possibly dangerous, forms of treatment. What I wish to concentrate on here is the complementary problem, curiously neglected by philosophers and clinicians. Suppose there is some condition for which there exists no generally accepted cure (or prophylactic), but for which some new form of treatment has been mooted; what should then be said of the ethics of non-treatment, of deliberately failing to administer some promising new drug, say, to a control group of patients, with the aim of demonstrating its efficacy, as administered to others? Is it morally acceptable for a doctor to withhold treatment from a subject, for the sake of making him a control, when it is the doctor's opinion, based either on the progress of the study, up to that point, or on prior experiments with animals or tissue cultures, that such treatment, if administered, would be very likely to save the patient from permanent injury or even death?

Some doctors are reluctant to admit that randomized clinical trials, in general, present any ethical dilemma. One frequently encounters an argument that runs more or less as follows: 'Either the doctor knows which of the forms of treatment he is concerned to compare is superior, or he does not. If he does, there is no point in conducting a trial. If he does not, there can be no objection, from the patient's point of view, to the doctor's choosing, on a random basis, which form of treatment to administer.' This line of reasoning is entirely fallacious and must be scotched at the outset. If a doctor was completely agnostic as to which of two forms of treatment was superior, then, to be sure, other things (such as cost) being equal, it would be legitimate, trial or no trial, to choose randomly between them; and likewise, if he *and everyone else in the profession* knew for certain that one was superior, a trial would indeed be pointless. But these are not the only alternatives: the question is what a doctor should do if he thinks it *probable* that one of the treatments is superior, without feeling that he yet knows this for certain, or alternatively where, on the basis of his own first-hand experience, he feels that *he* knows that one of the treatments is superior, but can see that further trials are necessary if he is to convince his colleagues. Under these circumstances, it would either be evading the issue or downright insincere for him to say, by way of justifying a randomized trial, 'But, after all, I don't *know* which is the more effective form of treatment.' Most clinical verdicts are probabilistic anyway, and the usual assumption (embodied in the Hippocratic oath) is that the doctor, when he is unsure, should follow his *judgment* as to what is most likely to be in his patient's best interests. Now the sort of case that we are concerned with in this article is one where the choice is effectively between treatment, of a kind that may turn out to be effective, and non-treatment, where 'non-treatment' may be taken to include placebos or merely palliative measures. Hence, even if the doctor does not rate very high the chances of the new treatment proving effective, he would still judge it to be in the patient's best interests that he receive it, unless he thinks that the risks outweigh the possible benefits. Sometimes the new form of treatment is one that has already been used sufficiently often in relation to other conditions for one to be reasonably confident that it is safe. And then again, the prognosis, in the absence of the new form of treatment, may be simply hopeless. In either case, it may be possible to argue that it is clearly in the patient's best interests that he receive the treatment, because he has nothing to lose.

There is thus a genuine dilemma here. The problem is highlighted in Sinclair Lewis's classic novel *Martin Arrowsmith*.[2]

Experiments with culture plates and laboratory animals lead Arrowsmith to believe that he has discovered a viral agent, or *phage*, capable of killing a variety of pathogenic bacteria, including those responsible for pleural pneumonia and bubonic plague. When there is an outbreak of bubonic plague on an island in the West Indies, the director of the institute for which Arrowsmith works accordingly sends him to the island, with strict instructions:

> If I could trust you, Martin, to use the phage with only half your patients and keep the others as controls, under normal hygienic conditions but without the phage, then you could make an absolute determination of its value, as complete as what we have of mosquito transmission of yellow fever . . .[3]

At first Arrowsmith does as he is told:

> He divided the population into two equal parts. One of them . . . was injected with plague phage, the other half was left without. . . . He began to succeed. . . . The pest attacked the unphaged half of the parish much more heavily than those which had been treated. There did appear a case or two among those who had the phage, but among the others there were ten, then twenty, then thirty daily victims. These unfortunate cases he treated, giving the phage to alternate patients.[4]

As the plague spreads, however, and the phage appears to be proving its worth, the pressure, both from his companions on the island, and within his own conscience, to inject the entire population begins to mount. In the face of the suffering he is forced to witness, Arrowsmith's earlier resolve to 'observe test conditions . . . harden his heart and keep clear his eyes' starts to weaken. In the novel, the dilemma is finally resolved by a deus ex machina in the form of the death from plague of his wife. He then begins to inject everyone, is hailed by the islanders as a saviour as the epidemic dies down, but returns to New York with data which are, from a scientific standpoint, inconclusive at best.

This is a fictional case. But real life examples abound. In 1978, the B.B.C. World Service broadcast an interview with a Dr. Roderick Jones, who had just spent four years conducting a study in India on the victims of severe burns. Suspecting that malnutrition was weakening his patients' resistance to pseudomonas septicemia, which was the major immediate cause of death, he injected alternate patients with a vaccine. The results were dramatic. In one trial, reported in *The Lancet*,[5] all eighteen of the experimental subjects survived, while eight out of twenty controls died. The study continued, however. In 1979–80, Jones experimented with an immunoglobulin prepared from patients who had been vaccinated the previous year. On a random basis, some burn victims were given the immunoglobulin, some a mixture of vaccine and immunoglobulin, some vaccine alone and some, 61 adults and 42 children, given nothing at all to protect them from septicemia. The results were much as before: 36% of those given neither vaccine nor immunoglobulin died (the children apparently being less susceptible than the adults) as compared to only 7% of the vaccinated group. The immunoglobulin proved less effective than had been hoped, less effective than the vaccine though far better than nothing: 10% of those receiving it died. Once again, the trial was written up in *The Lancet*.[6]

There is no evidence, either in Jones's published papers, or from a more recent broadcast interview, that Jones or anyone else saw anything morally problematic in these trials, in particular that there was thought to be anything ethically questionable in conducting a second study that involved withholding, from over a hundred patients, a life-saving vaccine that, though comparatively new, had already yielded such strikingly significant results. In one quite different area of research, however, the prospect of withholding probably beneficial treatment has given rise to widespread misgivings. During the past three years evidence has begun to mount that giving certain vitamins, specifically folic acid, before and shortly after conception, to intending mothers with a history of giving birth to children with spina bifida and related neural tube defects, may be an effective way of preventing a recurrence of such births. Consequently, several researchers have wanted to mount a properly controlled double blind randomized trial, using placebos, in order to put these indications to a rigorous test. One group of researchers, Smithells et al.,[7] had their proposals for such a trial turned down by two research ethics committees, and were eventually forced to fall back on using, as controls, women who were already more than three months pregnant at the time of the trial. This was considered ethically unproblematic, since the administration of vitamins or folic acid beyond that point was thought to be too late to do any good. The results obtained by this group were, however, highly significant, in view of which the Medical Research Council [MRC] has now proposed to sponsor just such a trial as Smithells' group was originally prevented from carrying out.[8] This proposal, which would involve a quarter of the subjects being given no vitamin or folic acid supplementation whatever, has provoked a storm of protest from within the medical profession, led by Labour M.P. Dr. David Thomas; and the controversy has been given a wide airing in the press.[9] Smithells and his co-workers themselves remark that, while they 'regard placebo studies in high incidence areas as still desirable', they consider them, in the light of their own results, to be 'ethically more difficult than before'.[10]

How then, in general, *should* one regard clinical trials that involve the deliberate withholding from patients of treatment believed beneficial? Some doctors appear to favour an approach that is straightforwardly consequentialist. On this view, what is required, morally, of a doctor in Arrowsmith's or Jones's position is that he weigh the immediate benefits to his patients, resulting from his new treatment, against the long-term benefits which might be expected to accrue from a methodologically impressive and widely publicized experiment. If he thinks that there is a fair chance that thousands of lives will ultimately be saved, through other doctors adopting the procedures he has pioneered, then this may fully justify his withholding potentially life-saving treatment from a hundred or so patients here and now. Indeed, the very progress of medicine would be seriously hindered were doctors never to act in this way. This, of course, is precisely the way Arrowsmith reasons. If his experiment is successful, he thinks, he might 'perhaps end all plague for ever'. He sees 'far-off India, with its annual four hundred deaths from plague, saved by his efforts'.

Whether Jones's recent trial, or that proposed by the MRC, could *in fact* be argued for on such grounds as these, is a question into which I do not propose to enter. I simply do not know how many lives might be saved, or neural-tube defects, such as spina bifida, prevented, by further papers published in *The Lancet* or the *Archives of Disease in Childhood* (except that it is almost certainly more than by a paper in the *Proceedings of the Aristotelian Society*); nor do I know how to compare these with the benefits of treating those who would otherwise be controls (assuming, perhaps unrealistically, that this would be the alternative to carrying out a randomized trial). These are questions for the actuary or the sociologist of medicine, rather than the philosopher.

The philosophical question is this: Suppose it *were* possible for Jones or the MRC to argue convincingly that their respective trials would result in more burn victims being saved or more neural tube defects being prevented, in the long run. Would that *automatically* justify their conduct? Do utilitarian considerations of this sort really constitute the last word on the matter, morally speaking? The trouble is that anyone who answers 'Yes' to this question would seem, in effect, to be giving doctors a license to kill and maim their patients, in the name of medical research. Consider the following imaginary case. A hospital doctor is convinced, on the strength of his clinical experience, that a certain drug, commonly prescribed for asthma but no more effective than others on the market, is liable to induce fatal heart attacks in those already suffering from hypertension. He has voiced his belief to his colleagues, only to be met with near-universal scepticism. He therefore runs a clinical trial. Alternate hypertensive asthma sufferers are prescribed the suspect drug over a period of five years. Out of 50 patients in the experimental group, 16 suffer fatal heart attacks within six months of receiving the drug, 25 within a year and 32 within three years. Of the controls, treated with an alternative drug, the corresponding figures are 1, 3 and 8. These results the doctor triumphantly publishes in *The Lancet*. Is the man to be regarded as a benefactor to mankind, or as a monster? Do we condemn him for the murder of literally dozens of patients, or do we congratulate him for having saved many others from being inadvertently killed by their doctors in the same fashion? The consequentialist, or at any rate the utilitarian,[11] is, it would seem, in consistency bound to regard the doctor's behaviour as wholly admirable.

There is, of course, the point that if doctors were routinely to carry out this sort of study, patients would be afraid to consult them. And this is a consequence that no one would welcome. Even the most hard-line act utilitarian would have to recognize the crucial importance of a patient's being able to trust his or her doctor. But all that follows from this is that doctors should not make a general *habit* of killing or injuring their patients in order to further the progress of medicine. The act utilitarian could have no basis for regarding *occasional* behaviour of this kind as wrong, especially where potential patients never found out about it. (After all, who but doctors read *The Lancet*, anyway?) Certainly, he could not regard it as wrong *in principle*.

I suppose there may be doctors who would be prepared to embrace the utilitarian's logic. The following case, which I quote from Campbell's *Moral Dilemmas in Medicine*, seems to reflect this sort of outlook:

> In the early 1950's medical scientists began to accumulate evidence that the treatment of premature infants with high concentrations of oxygen was causing retrolental fibro-plasia, a condition leading to blindness. Three American doctors set up an experiment to prove that this was the case [not, note, to discover *whether* this was the case] by giving 36 premature infants high concentrations of oxygen for two weeks. (A control group of 28 infants was given low concentrations.) The experiment established the connection, but at the cost of permanent blindness for eight of the subjects (Lanman *et al.*, 1954).[12]

Once again, the experiment may well be justified in consequentialist terms. But it seems, nevertheless, a horrifying thing to have done.

The trouble with act utilitarianism, in the present context, as with consequentialism in general, is that it allows of no distinctions as between individuals. It requires people to think and act as though they had a kind of undifferentiated, godlike responsibility for the whole of mankind, down to the last generation: a mode of thought into which Arrowsmith perhaps falls when he reflects on his hundreds of thousands of plague victims in 'far-off India'. Commonsense morality would hold that this just is not true, that our responsibilities are both more specific and more circumscribed than this. Parents, for example, have a unique responsibility for their children, such that it would be positively wrong for them, in their moral deliberations, to give equal weight to the interests of other people's children. And likewise, commonsense morality would regard the doctor as having a special responsibility for his or her patients.[13] This responsibility may not be absolute. But most of us, I think, would find repugnant the idea that our interests, as patients, could be *automatically* overridden for the sake of individuals with whom the doctor had no special ties of obligation at all. That, surely, is the basis of the Hippocratic oath: 'The regimen I adopt shall be for the benefit of my patients according to my ability and judgment, and not for any harm or wrong'. Whoever wrote these words (almost certainly not Hippocrates) was not, I suggest, a consequentialist at all: the doctor is not here being enjoined to subordinate the interests of his patients to the general good.

The question, then, is how far the special responsibility implicit in the Hippocratic oath—if, indeed, one believes that it exists—should be thought of as extending. Is 'harm' or 'wrong', for example, intended to cover only a doctor's acts, or his omissions as well? Doctors nowadays make much of the distinction between killing and letting die. They are apt to quote with approval Arthur Hugh Clough's famous 'modern commandment':

> Thou shalt not kill; but need'st not strive
> Officiously to keep alive.

Most of them, I suspect, are unaware that this was meant satirically. (Another line runs:

> Thou shalt not steal; an empty feat,
> When it's so lucrative to cheat.) . . .

But many a true word, they say, is spoken in jest. Then again, what Clough presumably had in mind by 'officious' striving was striving to prolong the lives of those whose lives were either approaching their end anyway, or were becoming something of a burden to themselves or others. It is hardly officious striving to administer, to an adult in his prime or to a small child, an injection designed to cure or prevent a disease that is likely otherwise to bring worthwhile life to a tragic and premature end. But all the same, perhaps one could argue that it is just this that distinguishes the conduct of Jones and Arrowsmith (before his change of heart) from that of my fictitious doctor with his asthmatic hypertensives. The latter was actually killing his patients, whereas Jones and Arrowsmith were merely letting theirs die. And perhaps what is so horrifying about the Lanman case is that the doctors did not simply let these babies go blind, when it was in their power to prevent it, but actually did something to *make* them go blind.

It is, however, difficult on reflection to see how the distinction between killing and letting die, or between actions and omissions in general, can, as such, have any moral significance. As has frequently been pointed out,[14] deliberately not to rescue a drowning man, when one was in a position to do so at minimal cost to oneself, does not really seem any less bad than pushing him into the water in the first place, knowing that he could not swim, provided the *motive* is the same in each case. And why should it? As Sartre says, 'Not to act is to act'. Standing idly by and watching someone drown may not be a very *energetic* action, but it is an action, of sorts, nevertheless. And so was Jones's in standing by—though not idly (rather, making notes and collecting swabs)—as patients in his care died of a disease that a simple injection would most likely have prevented.

It might be objected that the analogy between a strong swimmer's rescuing or not rescuing a drowning man and a doctor's curing or not curing a sick man is a poor one, and that therefore no particular moral should be drawn for the topic we are here concerned with. In fact, though, there are grounds for thinking that any imperfections in the analogy actually work against the person who would argue that the acts-omissions distinction is, or ought to be, of relevance in medicine. After all, simple humanity seems to demand that the able bystander should jump in and save the drowning man, even if he is a total stranger, with whom, therefore, the bystander has no special ties of obligation. With doctor and patient, though, there would normally be thought to exist a special bond of obligation: it is not simply common humanity that demands that a doctor should endeavour to heal his patients; that is his job. To get a proper parallel, therefore, we should perhaps have made the bystander a lifeguard.

But wait. Could not Arrowsmith, and perhaps Jones, argue that whatever they did they would be letting some people die? If they do not let people die of plague or septicemia here and now, that will just mean letting a greater number die of these diseases in the future: those that will not receive the new treatment, in consequence of their failure to convince enough doctors of its worth. Well yes, perhaps so. This, of course, is just the consequentialist argument over again. But it ignores the fact that the potential beneficiaries of the trial are *not* patients in their care. The point of invoking the acts-omissions distinction was precisely to define what, for the sake of benefiting humanity, a doctor may and may not do to *his* patients. Is letting a patient die in the furtherance of research that may ultimately save lives any *more* permissible, morally, than killing patients for the same end? That is the question. To argue either that they are both wrong, because they violate a doctor's duty to those in his care, or on utilitarian grounds, that they are both right (since the general welfare is best served thereby) is a great deal easier than trying to show that the one is right and the other wrong—even though this is precisely what most doctors seem to believe.

So where do we go from here? Well I certainly would not wish to suggest that randomized clinical trials on human subjects should be abandoned. Nor do I think any such conclusion follows from what I have been saying. As a matter of fact, it seems to me that there are a great many circumstances under which randomized clinical trials should be regarded as morally permissible, even if one takes a very tough line indeed on a doctor's responsibilities to his patients—a line, say, such as Pappworth has defended in his book *Human Guinea Pigs*.[15] Or such as I understand Sir Richard Doll to have defended, in conversation. Pappworth has proposed, as a constraint upon clinical research, what he calls 'the principle of equality'. The researcher is to imagine that some person close to him, such as a wife, son or daughter, were to be a subject in the proposed trial, whether in the experimental or control group. If, under such circumstances, the researcher would still be happy for the research to proceed, then presumably he genuinely thinks that the trial does not seriously jeopardize the subjects' interests, and one necessary condition for the trial's being morally permissible, according to Pappworth, is satisfied. I take it that all the trials, real or imaginary, that we have so far considered fail Pappworth's test. It is no doubt safe to assume that Arrowsmith would have wished his wife to be treated with the plague phage (and would actually have administered a prophylactic dose, had he only realised that she was at risk); and I imagine that Jones, likewise, would have wished his son or daughter to have the pseudomonas vaccine, had either been a burn victim with a susceptibility to septicemia.

Nevertheless, there remain several types of circumstance under which Pappworth's criterion would permit randomized clinical trials. They could be conducted where the researchers were genuinely totally agnostic as to the relative merits of the treatment given in the experimental and control groups. And they could perhaps be conducted where there was genuine informed consent, where the patient was fully aware of the possible risks and benefits, saw that it was not altogether in his own best interests to be, say, in the control group, but was prepared nevertheless to 'do his bit' for medical science: whatever rights a patient may have to expect that a doctor will do his best to cure him are presumably capable of being voluntarily waived. Not only that; although it may be a doctor's duty to *offer* a patient a new treatment, if it is his judgment that it holds more promise than more established remedies, given a choice between that and an older remedy known to have no serious side effects, many patients might express a preference for the latter—on which basis they could then be used as controls (albeit in what would not then strictly be a *randomized* trial). Jones says that all his subjects were 'volunteers'. What he means, no doubt, is that he received the permission of patients, or in the case of the children, their parents, to administer the vaccine or immunoglobulin. Suppose, however, the controls had volunteered to be controls. Suppose he had said: 'Look, with burns such as yours there's about a 40% chance of your dying from blood poisoning. There is, however, a new vaccine that—to judge from earlier trials—might be expected to raise the chance of your survival to over 90%. A simple injection is all that it takes. Do I have your permission *not* to give you the vaccine, for the sake of a further study that I'm conducting?' There could be little objection to that, as far as I can see. But of course, under these circumstances, one would imagine that few, if any, patients would have volunteered to be controls. David Thomas has made a similar observation in relation to the proposed MRC trial of folic acid, discussed earlier: 'If the trial is honestly and fully explained to a woman, all the background information given to her, I think she is going to insist on taking folic acid.'[16] (Since folic acid is freely available, without prescription, at any chemist's, there is in fact nothing to prevent her doing so.)

Of more practical value, perhaps, is the following consideration. A doctor would, presumably, be fully entitled to conduct a randomized trial, in respect of a new form of treatment that he believed to be beneficial, where the treatment either involved the use of some drug that was in short supply— so that it was simply not possible to give it to every patient who stood to benefit by it—or in some other way made demands on available resources that would be intolerable, were it to be administered to every suitable patient. Under these conditions, a researcher is surely entitled to make a virtue out of necessity: given that not all patients can be treated anyway, there is nothing unethical about choosing, on a random basis, which patients are to be treated. Such, as Doll has pointed out, were the circumstances under which the sulphonamide drugs and penicillin were tested, shortly before the war. Today, a similar situation of limited availability obtains in regard to things as diverse as interferon and transplant surgery, though I do not know whether it is being exploited in a similar manner.

Just how large a moral loophole this represents becomes clear when one reflects that any pharmaceutical company, say, is both able and entitled, for the sake of getting a new product tested, to *control* its supply to medical practitioners. A company has the right to do this, because its duties are not to individual patients, but to the public at large; and the public will clearly be best served if the company takes pains to ensure that a product it intends to market is effective and relatively free from harmful side effects. Thus, there could be nothing wrong with a company's making some medication available, in amounts too small to use on every suitable patient, conditional upon its being administered, if at all, only on a random trial basis. Likewise, a charitable body, research foundation or government department might legitimately fund some expensive new form of treatment—some exotic operation, say—in the same manner. For all I know, Jones may have been up against just such strictures in India: there would have been no point, after the first dramatic results, in his having tried to vaccinate everyone, if the only consequence was that the funds for the project, or the supply of the vaccine itself, were prematurely cut off. (Jones and his co-workers must to some extent have been at the mercy of the MRC and the Wellcome Foundation, who respectively provided the money and the vaccine.)

Is this, then, the best that the moral philosopher can do, by way of justifying randomized clinical trials? Well perhaps not. A morality that forbade one to embark on a project that harmed no one, and from which many people stood to benefit, would be just plain silly. One must certainly not lose sight of the fact that, as a result of Arrowsmith's going to his Caribbean island and of Jones's setting up shop in New Delhi, no one can be said to have died who would otherwise not have, and a great many lived who would otherwise have died. In economists' jargon, their conducting their respective projects is *Pareto preferable* to their having stayed at home. If a project is a worthwhile one, harms no one and benefits many, then it *may*, I suggest, be morally permissible, in pursuing the project, to let people die or otherwise omit to save them from harm—when one could do so with the greatest ease—*if doing so would be damaging to the project itself.*

Let me restate this claim, somewhat more rigorously. What I am now suggesting is this: It is a sufficient condition of a project's being morally permissible that (a) under it, nobody, in respect of anything he has a right to expect, is worse off than he would have been under some alternative course of action that is itself permissible, and at least one person is better off—the Pareto condition; and (b) the project has a clear point, such that one can see that departures from the project in the direction, say, of righting evils on the side, at what would otherwise be minimal cost, will actually *in sum* be very damaging to the project's aims. Thus, it is not obviously permissible to embark on a project that provides one with a unique opportunity to help some specific individual out of a jam, at *prima facie* negligible cost, and then not do so; unless it is a worthwhile enterprise which, given its purpose, would be seriously undermined by so doing.

I am not sure that this principle is sound. But it is certainly very plausible, and does appear to justify clinical trials of which the following are true:

> (i) No patient is deprived of beneficial treatment that, were it not for the trial, he would be receiving from another source (or conversely, being made to suffer risks, without compensating benefits, that he would not otherwise have to undergo).

> (ii) The research project promises benefits that can reasonably be expected to outweigh any benefits that would have accrued to the controls had they been in the experimental group instead.

> (iii) It is reasonable to think that a lesser *net* benefit would result from the trial if a larger proportion of the patients were to be given whatever treatment the researcher judges to be more (or more probably) beneficial.

The importance of the Pareto condition, or something closely akin to it, seems already to be recognised by some researchers. Smithells' trial of the effect of folic acid and multivitamin supplements in preventing neural tube defects was in large part a response to an earlier study carried out by Laurence et al. who, albeit with a far smaller sample than Smithells', had already achieved striking results. Laurence and his co-workers reflect as follows on the ethical implications of a further multicentre trial:

> Such a trial would be ethical as we found a probably biological beneficial effect, but the problem might be to consider an alternative regimen. A placebo could be justified by the argument that it is not normal practice to begin supplementation before conception is confirmed.[17]

Their point seems to be precisely that, since the administering of folic acid before conception is not normal practice, the mothers in the control group, or their children, would be no worse, in consequence of the trial's being carried out, than if there had been no trial, whereas those in the experimental group stand a significant chance of being benefited thereby.

What are the implications of these criteria for the other trials we have been considering? Well, in the first place, they would appear to rule out the Lanman experiment, giving high oxygen concentration to premature babies (unless Lanman et al. thought, as I rather think they did not, that the higher concentration of oxygen substantially enhanced their chances of survival). Also, they rule out absolutely my fictitious trial involving the asthma drug. (Clearly, what the doctor would be doing, were he not conducting a trial, would be giving his patients an alternative, safe drug. That would be normal practice and is what his patients would consider that they had a right to expect from him.) Moreover, the criteria do this without—even implicitly, I think—appealing to the dubious acts-omissions distinction.

Whether the Arrowsmith and Jones trials would pass is more difficult to assess. If one thinks that a patient has the right not to be deceived, then what is not permissible is for Arrowsmith and Jones to represent themselves as being guided, in their treatment of their respective patients, solely by these patients' own best interests. That is what their patients would naturally have assumed; and Arrowsmith and Jones had, I would argue, a clear duty to disabuse them of this assumption— to make it clear that they were carrying out a clinical trial. No plague victim and no burn victim could have obtained the phage or vaccine other than from Arrowsmith or Jones. So even the controls lost nothing by being treated by these doctors. Beyond that, it is a matter of weighing probabilities. *Martin Arrowsmith* is just a novel; and that trial would have passed my test, almost certainly, if the facts had been as Sinclair Lewis presents them. As for Jones's project, my own, admittedly lay, opinion is that the trials have continued long beyond the point at which they could be justified on the grounds of usefully adding to medical knowledge. But here is the catch. I learn from Prof. Sydney

Selwyn that the pseudomonas vaccine, in spite of being of greatest value in the relatively ill-nourished, will not, in the foreseeable future, be generally available in India at all! When Jones and his team complete their study, *no one* in India will receive it. Let Jones give the vaccine to as many needy patients as he can. But if the only way Jones can keep the supply of vaccine coming is to run trials with unvaccinated controls, even if it is scientifically completely pointless to do so, then I should be inclined to say: good luck to him.

NOTES

1. This is a substantially redrafted version of a paper first read to a group of doctors and medical students at the Oxford Medical Forum. Occasionally it may betray its origins as something originally intended for a non-philosophical audience.

2. Sinclair Lewis, *Martin Arrowsmith* (London: Jonathan Cape, 1925).

3. Ibid., p. 375.

4. Ibid., p. 414.

5. R.J. Jones, E.A. Roe, J.L. Gupta, 'Controlled trials of polyvalent pseudomonas vaccine in burns', *Lancet* 1978; ii: 977–83.

6. R.J. Jones, E.A. Roe, J.L. Gupta, 'Controlled trial of pseudomonas immunoglobulin and vaccine in burn patients', *Lancet* 1980; ii: 1263–65.

7. R.W. Smithells, S. Sheppard, C.J. Schorah, M.J. Seller, N.C. Nevin, R. Harris, A.P. Read, D.W. Fielding, 'Apparent prevention of neural tube defects by periconceptional vitamin supplementation', *Archives of Disease in Childhood*, 1981, 56.

8. See, e.g., *Nature*, 299 (16 September 1982), p. 198.

9. Cf. *The Times*, 9 October 1982, or *The Guardian*, 10 December 1982.

10. Smithells et al., op. cit., p. 917.

11. By an 'act utilitarian' I here mean a consequentialist who judges the goodness or badness of consequences solely in terms of

aggregate welfare (whether or not 'welfare' is to be equated with happiness). Thus an act utilitarian would not, by this definition, allow considerations of justice, for example, to enter into his assessments. But a (non-utilitarian) consequentialist well might.

12. A.V. Campbell, *Moral Dilemmas in Medicine*, 2nd ed. (Edinburgh, London and New York: Churchill Livingstone, 1975), p. 179. J.T. Lanman, L.P. Guy, J. Dancis, 'Retrolental fibroplasia and oxygen therapy', *Journal of the American Medical Association*, 155 (1954), 223–226.

13. The question of when and how someone comes to stand to a doctor as his patient, in a sense in which this creates special obligations on the doctor's part, is, as Anscombe has recently remarked, a rather neglected one. Cf. G.E.M. Anscombe, 'Focus: current issues in medical ethics. Commentary 2', *Journal of Medical Ethics*, 7 (1981), p. 122.

14. E.g. by James Rachels, 'Active and Passive Euthanasia', *New England Journal of Medicine* (1975).

15. M.H. Pappworth, *Human Guinea Pigs: Experimentation on Man* (London: Routledge and Kegan Paul, 1967).

16. *The Times*, op. cit.

17. K.M. Laurence, N. James, M.H. Miller, G.B. Tennant, H. Campbell, 'Double-blind randomized controlled trial of folate treatment before conception to prevent recurrence of neural-tube defects', *British Medical Journal* 1981, 282, p. 1511.

Sins of Omission? The Non-Treatment of Controls in Clinical Trials—II

G.E.M. Anscombe

> Thou shalt have one God only: who
> Would be at the expense of two? . . .
>
> Do not adultery commit;
> Advantage rarely comes of it.

Certainly Clough's commandments are satirical. No need, then, to seek a respectable sense of 'officiously to keep alive' for him to have had in mind. Sure, there is such a sense. Clough might have circled round it with:

> Strive to maintain your patients' breath
> For doctor's profits cease with death.

As Michael Lockwood observes, doctors are newly fond of the distinction between killing and allowing to die. But we mustn't forget what their bigwigs *call* 'allowing to die': poisoning and starving. So

> The medical profession's rather fussed
> If it can't count on privacy and trust.

This medical line needs to be considered by philosophy with its sights set otherwise than Dr. Lockwood's are. So let us turn to his concerns: omission and positive action. He tells us his topic is omission of treatment of groups of patients chosen to be controls. Yet one of his examples concerns the omission of treatment of

219

premature babies with high concentrations of oxygen. The point of this was not to show that high concentrations did good, but on the contrary to prove that they tended to do harm. For this there was already evidence—for example, premature babies in Russia were not put into oxygen tents and did not tend to go blind. (Personal conversation at the time with the Reader in Ophthalmology at Oxford.)

The medical profession has convinced itself that German measles in early pregnancy is apt to cause various handicaps. This conviction has arisen (has it not?) without giving a lot of pregnant women German measles and abstaining from doing so with a 'control group'.

The first thing we have to note is that in these matters of testing with control groups we have one of Bacon's 'idols of the theatre'.[1] The established church of this idol is so strong that doctors are willing to forget the principle *primum non nocere* in its cult.

> Think not that much of finding out
> For proof's the thing to give you clout.

Dr. Lockwood does momentarily note the difference between trying to find out and trying to prove. But it needed more dwelling on.

The outline of his paper seems to be this: where a doctor is trying to prove something which he already believes, he may aim at this by using a control group to which he does not give a treatment. The ethics of such omission is announced as the question. But in the case of the premature babies, the question is rather the ethics of giving a high concentration of oxygen, not of omitting it. Lockwood loses sight of this fact by sliding weakly away from the omission-commission difference; apparently because it is 'difficult' to make out its 'moral significance'. So after all the topic is *not* what it was announced to be, the ethics of omission. It is simply that of treating your patients as experimental subjects. Hence the difference between trying to prove harm and trying to prove benefit turned out not so important as Dr. Lockwood did obviously feel it was. That is, judging by his sentences. Meanwhile the original question seems to have got lost.

The topic is a tangled one. Our first observation must be that doctors should not sacrifice their patients to that idol. For each patient they should do what they can that they believe is good or at least gives him a better chance. ('Can' here could be lengthily discussed, but that would be a distraction.)

The general dictum doesn't cover the whole ground. For there is the possibility of not so much *believing* that some treatment *would* be good, as *suspecting* that it *might* be. In such a case, one might not have any *very* positive conviction that it would at least do no harm. With or without this, and according to circumstances, one might reasonably try the treatment. First, perhaps, on one patient, then on more than one. The ones it wasn't tried on would then be controls, without need to abstain from the prior preferred treatment and without ritually making them so. This would be a form of trying to find out. If the treatment seemed rather successful, it would be just to give it to all cases not counter-indicated. Further success would be or approach proof. Whether one was inwardly 'trying to prove', or 'trying to do one's best for each patient', or both, might very well be a matter of cast of mind, coming out in whatever showed one's interests.

Here is room for the consideration: 'I've no right to a confident judgment yet and [perhaps] it's not an ailment justifying desperate measures; so I must just go on trying this on some patients until the results are indicative one way or the other.'

This sounds to have been the situation in the example of burns sustained by undernourished Indians. That is, at the first stage. Once the vaccine had been found to reduce the number of deaths greatly, we have a case of sinful omission at the second stage. It might not be wrong to try something further. It is the control group left without treatment either by the vaccine or by the other things that seems to need excuse. But

> Of crowds of very poor you may make use.
> 'Twould be superfluous to require excuse.

The idol demands its sacrifices. But what of the possibility of no supplies, *unless* the idol is served? Here surely Dr. Lockwood is somewhat credulous. People can't know that there won't ever again be supplies of such-and-such a drug, but make it rather come true by their acceptance of such bland assurances. The short term is another matter: a matter which will be just one form of shortage of supplies. In such shortage, and in the absence of any other treatment, you might well make an experiment, having a number of untreated people effectively as control group. In the long term, if supplies seemed to depend on the service of the idol—well, there are questions like: 'How long is this long term?' 'To what extent will you be compromising, fostering rotten attitudes?' 'What about a campaign, making the devil of a shindy, keeping on at it as Plimsoll kept on about the Plimsoll line?'

The variety of possibilities one can imagine (both for what the case is and for what might be done) brings out how impossible it is to lay down a principle beyond that of *primum non nocere*. Once we have said that, we have not said everything; but the matter is subject to Aristotle's leaden rule—the ruler that bends in and out of the many corners, holes and bulges of all sorts of shapes.

Dr. Lockwood has a sort of good-hearted attitude which he cannot turn into a firm statement even where there seems to be room for it, because of his feeble acceptance that there isn't a 'significant' difference between act and omission. If he seriously thinks that, it is puzzling why he felt a special problem about the control groups purposely left without a treatment for the sake of proving its value.

It is easy to construct a case in which a deliberate omission of what was easy to do is (at least on first inspection) quite equivalent to a commission with the same result and for the same motive. A medical attendant, for example, sets up an apparatus necessary for the saving of someone's life, and deliberately omits to turn a certain tap that must be turned, because he wants the person to die. He actually deliberates about it, and decides not to turn on the tap. Or—the case of commission—he sets it all up correctly with the tap on, and then, with similar deliberation and for the same end, he turns the tap off.

It is awfully usual, in discussing the difference between positive act and omission, to think it sufficient to show that there *can* be examples where the moral quality of the deed is the same in the two cases: where, namely, the result is the same, the intention is the same, and the kind of particular responsibility for what happens is the same. I fear that showing this is thought enough to establish that the difference between act and omission is never 'morally significant'. Or is never 'morally significant' where the motive is the same and so is the upshot.

Need I do more than point out that the conclusion doesn't follow? The person who is refuted by the argument is one who holds that 'I didn't actually *do* anything to bring about the (evil) result, I merely omitted to do what would have prevented it' is necessarily always an exonerating plea if it is true. Or at least necessarily prevents guilt from being just the same as if he had done something positive to bring about the evil result.

It is perhaps worthwhile to observe the use that is made of the belief that the difference between positive act and omission is never 'morally significant'. First, it seems to be thought that to omit something is merely not to do it: or not to do it when one could do it. Second, the difference between act and omission *not* being 'morally significant', we are responsible for anything that happens which wouldn't have happened if we had done something which we did not do, though we could have done it. (The qualifications which might be added to this rather crude statement to make it faintly more plausible do not include anything about the matter's being one's business or the like.)

Startling deductions are made from these starting points. If I spend some money on amusement (e.g.) which I might have given to some charitable concern, and if, *if* I had, some life would have been saved, then I have killed someone just as much as if I had cut someone's throat.

The purpose of such arguments seems to be not to arouse an impossible conscientiousness in our conduct, but to loosen our consciences in respect of what would normally be counted as murder.

Dr. Lockwood does not sound as if he favoured any form of consequentialism all that much. But his willingness to simply say 'It's difficult to show that the difference between act and omission is morally significant, at least where the motive is the same' seems to have led him into a swift slide—first, *away* from considering the problem he said he was interested in at the beginning, and second, into a disregard (after all) of a doctor's obligation not to harm his patients.

Non-treatment can amount to willingness to harm: this is a truth which means that if someone is a doctor's patient, the doctor may need special excuse for some non-treatment of that person. It is not the same truth as that which lays it on the doctor *primum non nocere*, for this latter, I take it, refers exclusively to positive action. But the proposition about non-treatment is one that deserves more investigation than either Dr. Lockwood or I have given it. My complaint about him is that he has let himself be deflected from this interesting and difficult task by some easy and spurious reasoning about acts and omissions.

NOTE

1. Novum Organum, Bk. 1.

Animal Research

In the last twenty years, the treatment of animals has become one of the most controversial ethical topics both to the general population and among philosophers. Prior to the early 1970s, one simply did not see essays in philosophical journals dedicated to the rights and wrongs of how we relate to animals. Since then, several journals have devoted entire issues to the matter. Animal advocates have been of two sorts: those who believe animals have moral rights in the same sense that people do, and those who believe that a properly constructed utilitarian theory requires that the same considerations be given to animals that are accorded to humans. Both positions have given rise to heated debates. The issues encompass such practices as killing animals for food, hunting them for sport, keeping them in zoos and circuses, racing them at tracks, and even keeping them as pets. Our interest is confined to the use of animals in scientific research. Carl Cohen's essay, included here, attempts to justify even greater use of animals in research than is now current. Cohen's essay appeals to the pragmatic benefits of such research but is even more philosophically interesting because it challenges the view that animals have any rights. Cohen is also skeptical of the efforts of those who think they can defend animals from a utilitarian perspective.

Each year, throughout the world, close to half a billion animals are killed for scientific purposes. If we are to make an intelligent judgment about the ethics and scientific wisdom of permitting this many animals to be killed in scientific settings, we must begin to inform ourselves about the broad contours of their use. Even before turning to philosophical debate we must

225

discover for what purposes animals are used, and under what conditions.

Types of Use

We may make a modest beginning by briefly categorizing the types of use. The categories include product testing, behavioral research, instructional purposes, pharmaceutical tests, and medical research. Let us consider each of these in turn.

Product Testing

Animals are routinely used to test the safety of consumer products. Acute and chronic toxicity tests are carried out to establish toxic effects of low and high doses of such items as insecticides, antifreeze, brake fluids, bleaches, oven cleaners, deodorants, bubble baths, crayons, zipper lubricants, chemical solvents, and floor cleaners. Besides tests of toxicity there are other sorts of tests of product safety. For example, animals are used in crash tests to analyze the adequacy of seat belts and helmets. At issue for most consumer tests is not whether there is a feasible substitute for them but whether the intended protections are significant enough to justify killing animals.

Behavioral Research

Behavioral research may or may not involve pain. In many cases the experiments are the classic learning experiments in which mice or rats are forced to run through mazes or move levers. Success or failure may bring reward or punishment. Experiments on larger animals differ. A chimpanzee may be taken from its mother, and a soft chimplike toy may serve as surrogate mother. Different chimps experience different discomforts while scientists observe their varying degrees of reliance on the mother-substitutes. Some research may consist of little else than making small modifications in the environment of animals and observing the adaptations these modifications produce in their behavior. Those who base their concern for animals on utilitarian considerations are not likely to object to experiments of the aforementioned kind, but at least a few advocates of animal rights will argue that animals have the right to be let alone, not merely the right not to have pain inflicted upon them. Suffice it to say that there is no area of behavioral research, however apparently benign, that has not been a matter of moral contention.

Instructional Purposes

High school students, learning biology, frequently dissect frogs. Sometimes the students themselves must first deliver the coup de grace. High school students, and particularly college students, are not limited to frogs. Mice, rats, and hamsters are also used. No reliable tabulations are kept concerning how many animals are used, but the lowest estimate is two to three million per year in the United States. Over one million such animals are used annually in the International Science and Engineering Fair alone. Critics point out that since most of these students are not preparing to go into the biological sciences their learning could be confined to videos, texts, slides, and assorted other substitutes. Defenders believe there is no viable substitute for hands-on learning but, more important, ground the practice of student experiments on the belief that any harm to animals is more than compensated by benefit to the students.

Pharmaceutical Tests

Every major pharmaceutical firm tests its new products on animals prior to screening them on people. The thalidomide tragedy a couple of decades ago did more to raise public awareness of these tests than all other tests together. Thalidomide was introduced to treat morning sickness in pregnant women, and it was tested on a wide range of animal species before being made available to humans. Its use by pregnant women caused severe abnormalities in newborn babies.

Why did tragedy happen? For one thing, early tests on thalidomide were for its lethal effects only. No matter how much of the drug animals were given, they didn't die. Also, prior to 1961, that a drug not toxic to those receiving it might nonetheless produce congenital anomalies in their fetuses was not well understood. Finally, teratogenic susceptibility is strain-specific, not species-specific. Abnormalities occurred in a few strains of rabbits and mice but not in most. Animals that might have been expected to suffer the same problems as humans were unaffected by the drug.

As the thalidomide tragedy illustrates, there is an inherent difficulty in trying to predict adverse reactions in humans from studies upon animals. One cannot automatically extrapolate information from animal studies that yields either necessary or sufficient conditions concerning their safety for humans. Drugs that are highly dangerous for some strains of some species of test animals may be valuable for humans, whereas drugs that are harmless on animals may be dangerous for us. Drugs useful for people may be fatal to many animals even in low doses. Some examples are epinephrine, salicylates, insulin, cortisone, and meclizine.

In the final analysis, no matter how many screenings are done upon animals, further preliminary screenings have to be done on humans. Many toxicologists argue that increased reliance on clinical trials coupled with extensive postmarketing surveillance, although not an alternative to animal testing, would sharply reduce the numbers of animals that are now sacrificed.

Medical Research

Animals are used in long-term research on AIDS, heart disease, and every illness and injury known to man, but since the most feared disease of all is cancer, we will focus on it. To a certain extent, the following remarks are generalizable throughout the entire area of medicine.

With the decline of the infectious and nutritive diseases that ravaged people in previous centuries, cancer and heart disease have become the principal killers. Today, about one-third of deaths in middle age are due to cancer. Over the last 35 years or so, the incidence of cancer of the rectum and stomach has decreased but cancers of the breast, lungs, esophagus, and lymph glands have increased. The greatest increase is in lung cancer. In England there was a 136 percent increase just from 1951 to 1975. Smoking is a factor in about 40 percent of all cancers in men and most cancers of the lungs.

Since 1955, the National Cancer Institute (NCI) has screened about half a million chemicals on mice in its search for a useful drug against cancer. It does not merely test chemicals on mice with cancer; it uses them to induce cancer. But most mouse cancers are sarcomas (cancers of the bone and connective tissues) whereas lung cancers are carcinomas (cancers of membranes). Although the screenings have produced some good results, none of the drugs discovered as a result of them is as effective as the ten major anticancer drugs discovered before the screenings began. Biostatistician Irwin Bross makes the controversial claim that even those major drugs owe nothing to animal research. He maintains that the incentive for testing these drugs on animals came only after clinical observations on humans.

Despite the cynicism of Bross and others, the NCI says there has been great progress on "the war against cancer." Vincent DeVita, Director of the NCI, states that thousands of lives are being saved today that could not have been saved 25 years ago. In the 1950s only one-third of cancer victims survived another five years. Today, better than 50 percent survive five years after diagnosis. This improvement is alleged to be due, in part, to animal studies. This claim of the NCI is supported by the American Cancer Society.

Some epidemiologists think otherwise. They claim the statistical analyses of the NCI are flawed. Improvement in the five-year survival rate is the result of sharper diagnostic techniques that now allow physicians to find diseases pathologists classify as cancer but that, in the normal course of events, do not kill most persons within five years. This is particularly true of prostate cancer. Lesions that look bad microscopically do not manifest the biological behavior we associate with cancer. In short, the survival clock now begins to tick earlier than in previous decades.

Some critics of animal research claim that lung cancer can be reduced by 80 percent without medical interventions of any sort. Heart disease can be even more dramatically reduced by simple programs: improved diets, reduced smoking, moderate exercise, reduced stress, and ending airborne pollution. These critics also allege that we should not compare what we stand to gain with what animals stand to lose; rather, it is a matter of comparing what we now lose in human *and* animal life with what we might gain by adopting alternative methods of approaching the causes and treatments of disease.

Critics of the use of animals in science do not argue that we ought to forgo science. They think we ought to rely more heavily on alternatives. Briefly, these include mathematical and computer modeling of anatomy-physiology relationships; the use of lower organisms such as bacteria and fungi for tests of mutagenicity; the development of sophisticated *in vitro* techniques, including the use of subcellular fractions, short-term cellular systems (cell suspensions, biopsies, whole-organ perfusion), and tissue cultures (the maintenance of living cells in a nutritive medium for 24 hours or longer); and finally, more reliance on human studies, including epidemiology, postmarketing surveillance, and the carefully regulated use of human volunteers.

Opponents of animal experiments who cry out for greater reliance on alternatives may be guilty of exaggerating what is available, but those who insist on the current limitations may perhaps be guilty of a failure of the imagination. Defenders of the use of animals in drug tests point out that a drug *must* be metabolized in order to express its toxic effect. They also insist that tissues in the body are integrated in a functional way and that if one raises questions about, say, the transportation of a toxin through the body and does not limit investigation to action on a single cell, then one *must have* a whole biological system. Reasonable as this defense is, total reliance on living creatures may only be a current limitation.

It is of the very nature of scientific revolutions that major advances are unpredictable from the perspective of the old paradigms. There is little doubt that Archimedes would have said it was impossible for a person to whisper in a low voice and be heard instantly by someone else 5,000 miles away. Today that is commonplace. Thus the claim of some animal-based researchers that screening a painkilling drug by in vitro methods is impossible may only point to current technological limitations and may have little bearing on what is or is not physically impossible.

The Future of Animal Research

What is the future of animal research? The animal rights movement is overly sanguine about achieving its goals. It is not inevitable that animal research will one day be obsolescent. It is not clear that the public is on one side or the other as far as the future of animal research is concerned. In the near term animal research will continue. Values are in strong conflict, and the resolution of value conflict lies not within science but is a task for ethical theorists. The following essays are offered as contributions to the debate.

The Significance of Animal Suffering

Peter Singer

Nonhuman animals can suffer. To deny this, one must now refute not just the common sense of dog owners but the increasing body of empirical evidence, both physiological and behavioral (Dawkins 1980; Rollin 1989). My inquiry in this precommentary takes the existence of animal suffering for granted. The question is: Does the suffering of nonhuman animals matter? If so, how much does it matter? When it comes to a choice between human welfare and the suffering of nonhuman animals, how should we choose?

Many people accept the following moral principles:

1. All humans are equal in moral status.
2. All humans are of superior moral status to nonhuman animals.

On the basis of these principles, it is commonly held that we should put human welfare ahead of the suffering of nonhuman animals; this assumption is reflected in our treatment of animals in many areas, including farming, hunting, experimentation, and entertainment. I shall argue the contrary: that the combination of the two principles cannot be defended within the terms of any convincing nonreligious approach to ethics. As a result, there is no rational ethical justification for always putting human suffering ahead of that of nonhuman animals.

Before I defend this claim, a word about religious ethics. It is of course no accident that the principle of human equality and the principle of animal inferiority are widely held in Western society. They reflect a Judeo-Christian view of the human-animal relationship. Genesis tells us that God gave human beings dominion over the beasts. This has generally been interpreted to mean that we human beings have divine warrant for always giving priority to human interests. A clear example can be seen in the work of William Paley, a progressive moral theologian of the late eighteenth century. He wrote that the practice of killing animals to eat them caused them pain and death for our pleasure and convenience; moreover, eating meat was unnecessary, since we could live on fruits and vegetables, as the Hindus do. We are therefore "beholden for it to the permission recorded in Scripture . . ." (Paley 1785). It is true that some Christians have argued for a very different interpretation of the Christian tradition, one much more favorable to nonhuman animals (Attfield 1983; Linzey 1987). But I am putting aside such theological questions, partly because there is no rational foundation for the premises on which they are based, and also because if we are considering public policy in a pluralistic society, we should not take a particular religious outlook as the basis for our laws.

Let us examine the two principles just stated. If they are to be held in combination, we can expect that there is some characteristic possessed by all human beings, but not possessed by any nonhuman animals, by virtue of which all human beings are equal and nonhuman animals are less than equal to humans. But what might that characteristic be?

One possible answer to this question is that the characteristic is simply that of being human. But this merely invites a further question: Why does "being human" matter morally? Here we can go in either of two directions, depending on how we understand the term "human." On the one hand, the term can be used in a strict biological sense, so that it refers to members of the species *Homo sapiens*; on the other, it may refer to a being with those qualities which are distinctive of our species—in particular, the superior mental capacities that are characteristic of our species. Problems arise with both lines of response.

If the claim is that mere membership in the species *Homo sapiens* is enough to entitle a being to special moral consideration, we can reasonably ask why this should be so.

Imagine that, as happens so often in science fiction, a good friend suddenly reveals that she is an alien who was stranded on earth when her spaceship crashed. Although she has been deceiving us all these years about her origins and her species, there was no deception in her visible delight in fresh spring mornings, her sorrow when she felt unloved, her concern for her friends, her dread of the dentist—all these feeling are real. Does our discovery about her species really make any difference as to how she should be treated? To say that it does is to make the mistake made by racists who think that blacks should be treated as inferiors, even though they acknowledge that blacks have the same interest as whites in being treated well. It is significant that there really are few such racists nowadays, and there were very few even when racism was defended more often in public. That is because this type of racism depends so obviously on an arbitrary distinction. Yet a similar type of "speciesism" is still often encountered, either in its naked form, or thinly disguised under the claim that all human beings and only human beings possess some "intrinsic worth" or "dignity" not to be found in members of any other species (Bedan 1967; Frankena 1962). Generally no reasons are given for this claim, which resembles a religious incantation more than an argument. It is, in fact, a slightly secularized descendant of the Judeo-Christian belief that humans, and only humans, are made in the image of God; or the Christian view that only humans have immortal souls.

The term "speciesism" refers to the view that species membership is, *in itself*, a reason for giving more weight to the interests of one being than to those of another. This position, properly understood, is virtually never defended. Some who have claimed to be defending speciesism have in fact been defending a very different position: that there are morally relevant differences between species—such as differences in mental capacities—and that they entitle us to give more weight to the interests of members of the species with superior mental capacities (Cohen 1986). If this argument were successful, it would not justify speciesism, because the claim would not be that species membership *in itself* is a reason for giving more weight to the interests of one being than to those of another. The justification would be the difference in mental capacities, which happens to coincide with the difference in species. (The example of our friend the alien shows the difference; to a genuine speciesist, her mental capacities would be irrelevant; to a defender of the view we are now considering, they would be crucial.) The claim that there are morally relevant differences between all humans and other animals is the second way of understanding what it is to be "human": not the biological sense of membership in a species, but the sense in which to be human is to possess certain characteristics distinctive of our species, such as the capacities for self-awareness, for rationality, and for developing a moral sense.

It is easy to see why such characteristics should be morally relevant to how we treat a being. It is not arbitrary to say that beings with these capacities live fuller lives than beings without them, and that these beings therefore deserve a higher degree of consideration. (Note that I am not saying that this view is necessarily correct, but merely that—unlike the preference for members of a particular species merely on the grounds that they belong to that species—it is not arbitrary.)

There is, however, an obvious problem with any attempt to defend the principle of human equality by reference to superior mental capacities: They are not possessed by *all* humans. Newborn humans, for example, are not rational, appear not to be self-aware, cannot use language, do not share in culture or civilization, and have no sense of morality or justice. No doubt they have the potential to develop these characteristics, but arguing from potential is fraught with difficulties (Singer & Kuhse 1986; Singer & Dawson 1988). Moreover, if infants are to be brought within the scope of the principle of human equality by virtue of their potential, it would seem that human embryos and fetuses must also be included. This would require a significant revision of our attitudes to abortion and embryo research, although that in itself is not a reason for rejecting the appeal to potential. The real difficulty with the attempt to defend the principle of human equality on the grounds of superior mental capacities lies in the fact that even if we include those human beings with potential to develop the requisite mental capacities, some humans will still be outside the scope of the principle of equality—those with profound and irreversible intellectual disabilities.

How are permanently, profoundly, intellectually disabled human beings to be included under the protection of the principle of human equality? One way would be to reduce the level of mental capacity required for inclusion. For example, if we were to require simply a capacity to feel pleasure or pain, to suffer or to enjoy life, almost all of the intellectually disabled could be included; those few who were excluded because they lack even this minimal capacity would be incapable of suffering by their exclusion. But whereas this would be acceptable as far as the principle of human equality is concerned, it would come into direct conflict with the principle of animal inferiority, because so many nonhuman animals would also satisfy the new standard.

No fine tuning of a standard based on mental capacities will eliminate the conflict between the two principles. Because there is an overlap between the capacities of human and nonhuman animals, there is no way of drawing a line that will leave *all* human beings above the line, and *all* non-humans below it.

At this point some observers make a different claim: that the issue should not be put in terms of whether all human beings individually possess mental capacities that dogs lack, but rather whether the essential nature of humanity is different from the essential nature of, say, dogs. Thus rationality, or the capacity for making a moral judgment, or whatever else the capacity might be, is said to be an "essential feature" of humanity, but not of dogs; so even the most profoundly retarded human being is entitled to the respect and moral consideration that we properly deny to the most intelligent dog (Benn 1967: Cohen 1986).

What should we say about this shift of focus from the individual to the species? It is quite unclear what is meant by "essential feature" in this context; the term is redolent of an Aristotelian biology. We should not lose sight of the fact that whatever may be true of the "normal" adult human, there is nothing at all "rational" about the mental processes of some humans with congenital brain defects. It is therefore puzzling why we are supposed to treat them in ways appropriate to rational beings such as "normal" humans, rather than in ways appropriate to nonrational beings, such as some nonhuman animals.

Even if we were given a satisfactory explanation to end our puzzlement here, there is a good deal that should make us suspicious of the suggestion that we ignore individual characteristics and instead judge individuals by the general characteristics of their species. Just over a century ago a similar assertion was made by those who were against proposals to admit women to occupations such as law and medicine, and to the higher education that would qualify them for such professions. It was claimed that women, by their essential nature, lack the capacity for success in these areas. Against this claim, advocates of the feminist cause, John Stuart Mill among them, argued strongly that if the opponents of equality were successfully to make their case, they would have to maintain that "the most eminent women are inferior in mental faculties to the most mediocre of the men on whom those functions at present devolve" (Mill 1970, p. 182). Surely Mill's claim is right; but note that it presupposes that the focus is on the individual rather than on the group. If Mill's opponents were entitled to argue in terms of what is "normal" for men and women, or what is an "essential feature" of the sexes, Mill would have needed a different argument. He would have had to maintain that there are no differences in the essential nature of the sexes that affect the abilities required to succeed in the professions from which women were being excluded. Given the basic presuppositions of Mill's time (and perhaps even of our own), this would have been a much more difficult argument to sustain, and one that goes well beyond what is required for a successful attack on sexual discrimination in employment and education.

An important thrust of movements against discrimination has been the insistence that we consider individuals as such, and not as members of a group. It is curious that some writers want to reverse this in respect of humans and nonhuman animals, especially as they offer no clear reason why, in this particular case, we should focus on the species or kind, rather than on the individual. Indeed, the claim is simply asserted; no argument is presented in its defense. In the absence of any convincing reason for this claim, it should be rejected.

We are now in a position to see why it is so difficult to defend both the principle of human equality and that of animal inferiority. The key to the difficulty is that the combination of principles draws a sharp moral line, whereas evolution and natural variation have left an overlap between human beings and other animals. The solution is to abandon the attempt to draw such a sharp line. Instead, we should be sensitive to both the differences and the similarities between beings. Differences in such qualities as intelligence, self-awareness, and the capacity to make a moral judgment will certainly be relevant in some contexts; in others, similarities will be more important.

Up to this point my argument has had the limited aim of showing that we cannot justify applying sharply different standards to humans and nonhuman animals; but I have, strictly speaking, said nothing about my main subject, the significance of animal suffering. The statement that we should not apply different standards to humans and animals tell us nothing about what standard we should apply to both human and nonhuman animals. Someone might say, as scientists frequently do, that pain and suffering are part of nature, that they have evolved because they have survival value, and that there is no reason why we should be especially concerned with their reduction or elimination. I shall argue that, on the contrary, we should give to the elimination of the suffering of others—humans and nonhumans—the same degree of effort that we give to the elimination of similar suffering when it is our own. This is a demanding standard indeed, and it is only fair to say that although I regard the argument of this precommentary up to this point as one which has proceeded quite rigorously, what follows is more controversial. It is a view that I hold in common with a number of other philosophers, but also one with which many philosophers disagree. Nevertheless, here are my reasons for holding it.

If we make a moral judgment, we must go beyond our own interests and preferences and base it on something more universal: a standard that we are prepared to accept as justifiable even if it should turn out that we lose by doing so. This conception of ethics is at the root of all of the most ancient ethical traditions, but it has been given more precise expression in the work of contemporary philosophers (Hare 1963; 1981; Singer 1979; 1981). Although I may consider my own interests when I first make an ethical judgment, I cannot give them greater weight (simply because they are my own) than I give the interests of those affected by my judgment. If I do not condone robbery when I would lose because of it, then I cannot justify robbing someone if my victim would lose as a result of the robbery—unless there is some morally relevant difference between us that can be expressed in universal terms (that is, without specifying the identity of the individual involved).

This method of ethical reasoning takes as its starting point my own interests. The avoidance of suffering, therefore, receives the same high priority as ethics as it does in all our lives, when it is our own suffering. Other things being equal, it cannot be in my interests to suffer. If I am suffering, I must be in a state that, insofar as its *intrinsic* properties are concerned, I would rather not be in. (I specify intrinsic properties to take account of the objection that I may choose to suffer in order to gain something else that I value; but if I could get that gain without suffering, I would do so—or else it would not really be *suffering* that I was choosing.) Conversely, to be happy is to be in a state that, other things being equal, one would choose in preference to other states. There may, of course, be other things that we value, or disvalue, besides happiness and suffering. The point is that once we understand this method of ethical reasoning, the significance of suffering and happiness is indisputable.

It is consistent both with the method of ethical reasoning just outlined and with the argument presented in the first part of this precommentary that the weight we give to the interests of others should not depend on their race, sex, or species. Suppose that I have suddenly conceived a foolproof method of dramatically improving the lives of profoundly retarded children languishing in state institutions, but to implement it I must evict some poverty-stricken black families from a building I own. To decide whether I ought to do this, I must imagine myself as living the lives of all those affected to any degree by my decision, and ask which *total set of lives* I would prefer—those lives as they will be lived if I do it, or those lives as they will be lived if I do not. Thus, I must imagine myself as a profoundly retarded child, as well as an evicted black parent, and as all the others who will, to a greater or lesser degree, be affected by my decision. Race is not totally irrelevant here. When I imagine myself in the position of the evicted blacks, I must consider what this experience would be like for a black person, whose attitudes have been shaped by a history of slavery and oppression. But having done my best to understand what the experience would be like for them, I do not then give their interests a different weight because they are the interests of black people. Similarly, in putting myself in the place of the profoundly retarded children, I cannot ignore the fact that their mental capacities are different from those of normal children, because this will affect the difference that my scheme will make to their lives. But after considering what experiencing this difference would be like, I do not then discount it because it is a difference made to the life of an intellectually disabled, rather than an intellectually able, person.

We should include animals in our moral reasoning in just the same way. To defend a proposal for improving the housing of battery hens, at the cost of making it more difficult for some families to afford eggs, I would have to put myself into the positions of both the hens and the families. In trying to imagine what is it like to be a hen in a battery cage, compared with being a free-ranging hen, I would have to do my best to grasp what it is like to be a hen, take into account everything we know about how a hen experiences confinement in a battery cage. But having done so (to the best of my ability), I would not then discount the interests of the hen, on the grounds that hens are not human. "The only acceptable limit to our moral concern is the point at which there is no awareness of pain or pleasure, no conscious preference, and hence no capacity to experience suffering or happiness. That is why we need to consider the interests of hens, but not those of lettuces. Hens can suffer, but lettuces cannot. (To the question as to where precisely the limit is to be drawn, I can only plead agnosticism. I presume that fish can feel pain, but I do not know whether shrimps and insects can.)

To resolve such difficult questions as where to draw the boundaries of the capacity to suffer, or what individual animals of different species suffer, we need all the assistance we can get.

242 Ethical Issues in Scientific Research

That is why the pioneering work done by scientists such as Marian Stamp Dawkins (1980; 1989) is so important. There are many methods of trying to assess what an experience is like for a being who cannot describe it to us. Before any empirical attempts at such assessment were made, we could rely on the knowledge of those who knew the animals well and had observed them over long periods. They were often able to understand empathetically what the animals were feeling. But such reports were subjective, based on signs that the observer was perhaps unable to describe. When methods of farm production worth billions of dollars annually were challenged by people concerned about animal welfare, these reports from people with lifetimes of experience were often rejected as "subjective" and "unscientific." But what else could humans do to put themselves in the animals' positions? They could measure productivity, observe instances of abnormal behavior, examine the animals' physical health, or test the levels of hormones in their blood: yet these were all very indirect ways of understanding what the animals themselves felt about different situations. Dawkins's approach has its own methodological problems, as she acknowledges; but it gives us new and valuable information that, perhaps more directly than any other "objective" method, enables us to form some idea of what an experience is really like for the animal at the center of it. And this, as we have just seen, is at the core of ethical reasoning about our treatment of animals. It is because suffering, whether human or non-human, is ethically significant that we must welcome new insights into the existence, and degree, of that suffering.

REFERENCES

Attfield, R. (1983) *The ethics of environmental concern*. Blackwell. [aPS]

Bedau, H.A. (1967) Egalitarianism and the idea of equality. In: *Nomos IX: Equality*, ed. J.R. Pennock & J.W. Chapman. Atherton Press. [aPS]

Benn, S. (1967) Egalitarianism and equal consideration of interests. In: *Nomos IX: Equality*, ed. J.R. Pennock & J.W. Chapman. Atherton Press. [JS]

Cohen, C. (1986) The case for the use of animals in biomedical research. *New England Journal of Medicine* 315:865–70. [aMSD, aPS, MAN]

Dawkins, M.S. (1980) *Animal suffering: The science of animal welfare.* Chapman & Hall. [arMSD, aPS, MM, BER, SFS, TW]

Frankena, W. (1962) The concept of social justice. In: *Social Justice*, ed. R. Brandt. Prentice-Hall. [aPS]

Hare, R.M. (1963) *Freedom and reason.* Oxford University Press. [arPS, SFS].

——— (1981) *Moral thinking: Its levels, method, and point.* Clarendon Press. [aPS]

Linzey, A. (1987) *Christianity and the rights of animals.* Society for the Propagation of Christian Knowledge, London. [aPS]

Mill, J.S. (1970) *The subjection of women.* [First published 1869.] Reprinted in: *Essays on sex equality*, ed. A. Rossi. University of Chicago Press. [aPS]

Paley, W. (1785) *Principles of moral and political philosophy.* Baldwin & Company. [aPS]

Rollin, B.E. (1989) *The unheeded cry.* Oxford University Press. [aPS, BER, ANR, SFS]

Singer, P. (1979) *Practical ethics.* Cambridge University Press. [arPS]

——— (1981) *The expanding circle.* Farrar, Straus & Giroux. [arPS, JD, EAS]

Singer's Intermediate Conclusion

Frank Jackson

Singer's intermediate, and most confidently reached, conclusion is "that we cannot justify applying sharply different standards to humans and nonhuman animals." What exactly does this tell us about how we should treat nonhuman animals? One thing it tells us is that we should not inflict gratuitous suffering on them. But this is, I trust, something we already believed (which is not to say that we should not be forcibly reminded of the point). What about important and controversial questions such as whether it is justifiable to test possibly dangerous drugs on nonhuman animals to protect other animals, both human and nonhuman, and whether it is justifiable for humans to eat nonhuman animals? Although there is no doubting the importance of Singer's conclusion, by itself I think it tells us surprisingly little about how to answer such questions. Let me illustrate this point with the issue of vegetarianism.

The live issue is not whether factory farming is justified. (If animals suffer as much as they appear to—and here work such as Dawkins's is central—factory farming is not justified.) The live issue is whether it is justifiable to eat nonhuman animals that have lived relatively happy lives and have been killed relatively painlessly. We can approach this question by asking. What exactly is bad about the *painless* death of a human? In certain cases the answer is nothing. That is what motivates the debate over euthanasia and mercy killing. Moreover, in those cases where we regard a painless death as a tragedy, we tend to talk about the effect of the death of friends, relatives, and in general on those whose lives will be badly affected, and about the way the death cuts off a life before its time, that is, in terms of the concept of a worthwhile future, a life plan, which premature death terminates.

No doubt much more needs to be said. But for our purposes here, the important point is that if these considerations are at all pertinent, Singer's intermediate conclusion does not help us with the hard question of vegetarianism. Suppose, for instance, that having an articulated life plan is what gives value to continuing one's life and that nonhuman animals do not have articulated life plans, consequently, there is nothing wrong with eating nonhuman animals, provided they are killed painlessly and are not maltreated during their lives. This result will in no way conflict with Singer's intermediate conclusion. The standard being applied to human and nonhuman animals is the same: The answer to the question turns on the very same consideration in *both* cases—whether the creature has a life plan and the associated concept of a worthwhile future.

Our point is not that the moral case for vegetarianism fails—that is as may be: We endeavor only to show how little the (important) line of thought encapsulated in the term "speciesism" and its association with racism and sexism does to establish the moral case for vegetarianism. It shows that we should care about the kinds of lives the nonhuman animals we eat live, but it does not in itself show that we should not eat them.

A similar situation obtains, it seems to us, regarding the question of using nonhuman animals to test drugs. This is a special case of disadvantaging one group of beings in order to advantage another group—something that happens all the time in human society. Every time a freeway is built, the tax laws are changed, a vaccination program is initiated, zoning regulations are changed, or tenure is granted, some people are advantaged at the cost of others being disadvantaged: for example, those who use the freeway are favoured over those who live next to it, and the person who gets tenure is favoured over those who are seeking employment in the department. It is accordingly important to inquire when advantaging one group at the expense of another is morally permissible. It seems to us that the answer to this question as it applies to humans (rather than Singer's intermediate conclusion) will also provide the answer to the question about experimenting on nonhuman animals. The intermediate conclusion does tell us to take into account the same considerations in both cases, but it does not tell us *which* considerations are the key ones.

On Singer: More Argument, Less Prescriptivism

David DeGrazia

Singer's [article] is an excellent discussion of the significance of animal suffering, and I agree with him that there is no characteristic of, or fact about, all humans in virtue of which their interests—including the preference not to suffer—deserve greater moral consideration than the identical interests of animals. I think his article has several shortcomings that are worth examining, however.

Singer's argument against granting humans superior moral status in comparison with animals is fine as far as it goes, but it does not go far enough. First, it ignores the following possible appeal to a putatively relevant difference between humans and animals: Only humans are members of the human community and have special moral relationships to one another because of their social bondedness. Perhaps discrimination on the basis of group membership or social bondedness is not always unjust. Midgley writes:

> The special interests which parents feel in their own children is not a prejudice, nor is the tendency which most of us would show to rescue, in a fire or other emergency, those closest to us. . . . The question is, does the species barrier also give some ground for such a preference or not? (Midgley 1983, p. 102)

This question, and arguments by analogy to an affirmative answer, merit careful consideration. I suspect that the human

249

community argument ultimately fails. It seems true that we may, and should, act preferentially with regard to the welfare of family members, but this seems explicable by the greater long-term efficiency of such partiality. Furthermore, even if discrimination in favor of one's family were justified in terms of social bondedness and not efficiency, to complete the argument one would need to show that favoring human interests over those of animals is relevantly similar to such discrimination, but relevantly different from racism and sexism, where appeals to groups or social bondedness might also be made—and this is a tall order. But the human community approach should not be overlooked.

Singer might also take more seriously what I call the *"sui generis* view," according to which membership in our species per se grants superior moral status. He contends that because no argumentation is offered to demonstrate the relevance of being human, this appeal is arbitrary and therefore unworthy of consideration. But all moral positions ultimately assume that some characteristic is morally relevant—for example, sentience, self-awareness, or, more generally (as Singer and I both hold), the possession of interests—and the *sui generis* view assumes that this characteristic is being human, arbitrary as that may sound.

Moreover, there is at least one good reason to think that this characteristic is morally relevant: Almost all of us, thinking as carefully as we can, feel at least very uncomfortable with the idea that some humans may be used involuntarily in harmful, nontherapeutic research, no matter what capacities they lack. Yet few of us doubt that we may be justified in causing a few rats to suffer if necessary to test a highly promising possible cure for AIDS. Hence the problem of marginal cases, with which all philosophers who take animal welfare seriously struggle: We either (1) justify some use of animals, grounding moral protections in a characteristic they lack, thereby lassoing similarly lacking humans; (2) preclude all use of animals; or (3) identify a morally relevant characteristic of, or fact about, all humans that excludes animals from the protections granted to humans. The *sui generis* view may be a bit mysterious, but it would solve the problem of marginal cases by directing us to possibility (3). Although I consider this view arbitrary, in its favor it may be said that no one has yet dealt very satisfyingly with this problem.

In addressing the problem of marginal cases, Singer focuses too much, I believe, on capacities of individuals. Other facts about individuals might be relevant, though I shall mention only one. If it is in principle permissible to use for research humans (and animals) lacking certain characteristics, this does not prevent us from exempting the humans gratuitously. My giving *A* a gift does not mean that I must give *B* a gift. In addition to protections (e.g., from being harmed needlessly) that are due "naturally" (i.e., in virtue of natural characterisies), there may be protections that are given not as a matter of strict justice, but simply because we care about those affected.

My final objections concern Singer's suggested method for resolving moral problems. After rightly stating that in ethics we must transcend our own interests and adopt a more universal viewpoint, he commences a slide from a description of what ethics is to a very specific moral theory:

> This conception of ethics is at the root of all the most ancient ethical traditions. . . . So, although when I first think about what to do, I may consult my own interests, when I attempt to make an ethical judgment, I cannot give greater weight to my own interests (simply because they are my own) that I give to the interests of others affected by my decision. (ibid.)

According to the view he ends up with, the right action is that which, given one's own preferences (the focus of prescriptivism), one could accept if one were somehow to "stand in the shoes" of all of those affected (utilitarianism). If this position is, as Singer suggests, strongly recommended by an understanding of what ethics is, then few moral philosophers truly understand the subject of their profession, for utilitarian prescriptivists are a minority (and were nonexistent before this century). By begging significant questions in passing from a characterization morality to a discussion of his own moral theory, Singer has, for one thing, ruled out rights views, according to which protections of individuals should be so strong that we may never harm some to benefit others.

In addition, Singer's prescriptivism retains an overly subjective element in moral decision making. He states that "[t]his method of ethical reasoning takes as its starting point my own interests." In considering whether to do something, "I must imagine myself as living the lives of all those affected by my decision, and ask which total set of lives I prefer, those that will be lived if I do it, or those that will be lived if I do not do it." But suppose I am extraordinarily tough and have relatively little concern about pain, nondebilitating injuries, and actions that would humiliate most people. I might then prefer some actions or policies that others would consider too severe. Things would be even worse if I were a sadomasochist! But why should others be subjected to the peculiarities of my own preferences and values?

The Case for the Use of Animals in Biomedical Research

Carl Cohen

Using animals as research subjects in medical investigations is widely condemned on two grounds: first, because it wrongly violates the *rights* of animals,[1] and second, because it wrongly imposes on sentient creatures much avoidable *suffering*.[2] Neither of these arguments is sound. The first relies on a mistaken understanding of rights; the second relies on a mistaken calculation of consequences. Both deserve definitive dismissal.

Why Animals Have No Rights

A right, properly understood, is a claim, or potential claim, that one party may exercise against another. The target against whom such a claim may be registered can be a single person, a group, a community, or (perhaps) all humankind. The content of rights claims also varies greatly: repayment of loans, nondiscrimination by employers, noninterference by the state, and so on. To comprehend any genuine right fully, therefore, we must know *who* holds the right, *against whom* it is held, and *to what* it is a right.

Alternative sources of rights add complexity. Some rights are grounded in constitution and law (e.g., the right of an accused to trial by jury); some rights are moral but give no legal claims (e.g., my right to your keeping the promise you gave me);

and some rights (e.g., against theft or assault) are rooted both in morals and in law.

The differing targets, contents, and sources of rights, and their inevitable conflict, together weave a tangled web. Notwithstanding all such complications, this much is clear about rights in general: they are in every case claims, or potential claims, within a community of moral agents. Rights arise, and can be intelligibly defended, only among beings who actually do, or can, make moral claims against one another. Whatever else rights may be, therefore, they are necessarily human; their possessors are persons, human beings.

The attributes of human beings from which this moral capability arises have been described variously by philosophers, both ancient and modern: the inner consciousness of a free will (Saint Augustine)[3]; the grasp, by human reason, of the binding character of moral law (Saint Thomas)[4]; the self-conscious participation of human beings in an objective ethical order (Hegel)[5]; human membership in an organic moral community (Bradley)[6]; the development of the human self through the consciousness of other moral selves (Mead)[7]; and the underivative, intuitive cognition of the rightness of an action (Prichard).[8] Most influential has been Immanuel Kant's emphasis on the universal human possession of a uniquely moral will and the autonomy its use entails.[9] Humans confront choices that are purely moral; humans—but certainly not dogs or mice—lay down moral laws, for others and for themselves. Human beings are self-legislative, morally *auto-nomous*.

Animals (that is, nonhuman animals, the ordinary sense of that word) lack this capacity for free moral judgment. They are not beings of a kind capable of exercising or responding to moral claims. Animals therefore have no rights, and they can have none. This is the core of the argument about the alleged rights of animals. The holders of rights must have the capacity to comprehend rules of duty, governing all including themselves. In applying such rules, the holders of rights must recognize possible conflicts between what is in their own interest and what is just. Only in a community of beings capable of self-restricting moral judgments can the concept of a right be correctly invoked.

Humans have such moral capacities. They are in this sense self-legislative, are members of communities governed by moral rules, and do possess rights. Animals do not have such moral capacities. They are not morally self-legislative, cannot possibly be members of a truly moral community, and therefore cannot possess rights. In conducting research on animal subjects, therefore, we do not violate their rights, because they have none to violate.

To animate life, even in its simplest forms, we give a certain natural reverence. But the possession of rights presupposes a moral status not attained by the vast majority of living things. We must not infer, therefore, that a live being has, simply in being alive, a "right", to its life. The assertion that all animals, only because they are alive and have interests, also possess the "right to life"[10] is an abuse of that phrase, and wholly without warrant.

It does not follow from this, however, that we are morally free to do anything we please to animals. Certainly not. In our dealings with animals, as in our dealings with other human beings, we have obligations that do not arise from claims against us based on rights. Rights entail obligations, but many of the things one ought to do are in no way tied to another's entitlement. Rights and obligations are not reciprocals of one another, and it is a serious mistake to suppose that they are.

Illustrations are helpful. Obligations may arise from internal commitments made: physicians have obligations to their patients not grounded merely in their patients' rights. Teachers have such obligations to their students, shepherds to their dogs, and cowboys to their horses. Obligations may arise from differences of status: adults owe special care when playing with young children, and children owe special care when playing with young pets. Obligations may arise from special relationships: the payment of my son's college tuition is something to which he may have no right, although it may be my obligation to bear the burden if I reasonably can; my dog has no right to daily exercise and veterinary care, but I do have the obligation to provide these things for her. Obligations may arise from particular acts or circumstances: one may be obliged to another for a special kindness done, or obliged to put an animal out of its misery in view of its condition—although neither the human benefactor nor the dying animal may have had a claim of right.

Plainly, the grounds of our obligations to humans and to animals are manifold and cannot be formulated simply. Some hold that there is a general obligation to do no gratuitous harm to sentient creatures (the principle of nonmaleficence); some hold that there is a general obligation to do good to sentient creatures when that is reasonably within one's power (the principle of beneficence). In our dealings with animals, few will deny that we are at least obliged to act humanely—that is, to treat them with the decency and concern that we owe, as sensitive human beings, to other sentient creatures. To treat animals humanely, however, is not to treat them as humans or as the holders of rights.

A common objection, which deserves a response, may be paraphrased as follows:

> If having rights requires being able to make moral claims, to grasp and apply moral laws, then many humans—the brain-damaged, the comatose, the senile—who plainly lack those capacities must be without rights. But that is absurd. This proves [the critic concludes] that rights do not depend on the presence of moral capacities.[11]

This objection fails; it mistakenly treats an essential feature of humanity as though it were a screen for sorting humans. The capacity for moral judgment that distinguishes humans from animals is not a test to be administered to human beings one by one. Persons who are unable, because of some disability, to perform the full moral functions natural to human beings are certainly not for that reason ejected from the moral community. The issue is one of kind. Humans are of such a kind that they may be the subject of experiments only with their voluntary consent. The choices they make freely must be respected. Animals are of such a kind that it is impossible for them, in principle, to give or withhold voluntary consent or to make a moral choice. What humans retain when disabled, animals have never had.

A second objection, also often made, may be paraphrased as follows:

Capacities will not succeed in distinguishing humans from the other animals. Animals also reason; animals also communicate with one another; animals also care passionately for their young; animals also exhibit desires and preferences.[12] Features of moral relevance— rationality, interdependence, and love—are not exhibited uniquely by human beings. Therefore [this critic concludes], there can be no solid moral distinction between humans and other animals.[13]

This criticism misses the central point. It is not the ability to communicate or to reason, or dependence on one another, or care for the young, or the exhibition of preference, or any such behavior that marks the critical divide. Analogies between human families and those of monkeys, or between human communities and those of wolves, and the like, are entirely beside the point. Patterns of conduct are not at issue. Animals do indeed exhibit remarkable behavior at times. Conditioning, fear, instinct, and intelligence all contribute to species survival. Membership in a community of moral agents nevertheless remains impossible for them. Actors subject to moral judgments must be capable of grasping the generality of an ethical premise in a practical syllogism. Humans act immorally often enough, but only they—never wolves or monkeys—can discern, by applying some moral rule to the facts of a case, that a given act ought or ought not to be performed. The moral restraints imposed by humans on themselves are thus highly abstract and are often in conflict with the self-interest of the agent. Communal behavior among animals, even when most intelligent and most endearing, does not approach autonomous morality in this fundamental sense.

Genuinely moral acts have an internal as well as an external dimension. Thus, in law, an act can be criminal only when the guilty deed, the *actus reus*, is done with a guilty mind, *mens rea*. No animal can ever commit a crime; bringing animals to criminal trial is the mark of primitive ignorance. The claims of moral right are similarly inapplicable to them. Does a lion have a right to eat a baby zebra? Does a baby zebra have a right not to be eaten? Such questions, mistakenly invoking the concept of right where it does not belong, do not make good sense. Those who condemn biomedical research because it violates "animal rights" commit the same blunder.

In Defense of "Speciesism"

Abandoning reliance on animal rights, some critics resort instead to animal sentience—their feelings of pain and distress. We ought to desist from the imposition of pain insofar as we can. Since all or nearly all experimentation on animals does impose pain and could be readily forgone, say these critics, it should be stopped. The ends sought may be worthy, but those ends do not justify imposing agonies on humans, and by animals the agonies are felt no less. The laboratory use of animals (these critics conclude) must therefore be ended—or at least very sharply curtailed.

Argument of this variety is essentially utilitarian, often expressly so;[14] it is based on the calculation of the net product, in pains and pleasures, resulting from experiments on animals. Jeremy Bentham, comparing horses and dogs with other sentient creatures, is thus commonly quoted: "The question is not, Can they reason? nor Can they talk? but, Can they suffer?"[15]

Animals certainly can suffer and surely ought not to be made to suffer needlessly. But in inferring, from these uncontroversial premises, that biomedical research causing animal distress is largely (or wholly) wrong, the critic commits two serious errors.

The first error is the assumption, often explicitly defended, that all sentient animals have equal moral standing. Between a dog and a human being, according to this view, there is no moral difference; hence the pains suffered by dogs must be weighed no differently from the pains suffered by humans. To deny such equality, according to this critic, is to give unjust preference to one species over another; it is "speciesism." The most influential statement of this moral equality of species was made by Peter Singer:

> The racist violates the principle of equality by giving greater weight to the interests of members of his own race

when there is a clash between their interests and the interests of those of another race. The sexist violates the principle of equality by favoring the interests of his own sex. Similarly the speciesist allows the interests of his own species to override the greater interests of members of other species. The pattern is identical in each case.[16]

This argument is worse than unsound; it is atrocious. It draws an offensive moral conclusion from a deliberately devised verbal parallelism that is utterly specious. Racism has no rational ground whatever. Differing degrees of respect or concern for humans for no other reason than that they are members of different races is an injustice totally without foundation in the nature of the races themselves. Racists, even if acting on the basis of mistaken factual beliefs, do grave moral wrong precisely because there is no morally relevant distinction among the races. The supposition of such differences has led to outright horror. The same is true of the sexes, neither sex being entitled by right to greater respect or concern than the other. No dispute here.

Between species of animate life, however—between (for example) humans on the one hand and cats or rats on the other—the morally relevant differences are enormous, and almost universally appreciated. Humans engage in moral reflection; humans are morally autonomous; humans are members of moral communities, recognizing just claims against their own interest. human beings do have rights; theirs is a moral status very different from that of cats or rats.

I am a speciesist. Speciesism is not merely plausible; it is essential for right conduct, because those who will not make the morally relevant distinctions among species are almost certain, in consequence, to misapprehend their true obligations. The analogy between speciesism and racism is insidious. Every sensitive moral judgment requires that the differing natures of the beings to whom obligations are owed be considered. If all forms of animate life—or vertebrate animal life?—must be treated equally, and if therefore in evaluating a research program the pains of a rodent count equally with the pains of a human, we are forced to conclude (1) that neither humans nor rodents possess rights, or (2) that rodents possess all the rights that humans possess. Both alternatives are absurd. Yet one or the other must be swallowed if the moral equality of all species is to be defended.

Humans owe to other humans a degree of moral regard that cannot be owed to animals. Some humans take on the obligation to support and heal others, both humans and animals, as a principal duty in their lives; the fulfillment of that duty may require the sacrifice of many animals. If biomedical investigators abandon the effective pursuit of their professional objectives because they are convinced that they may not do to animals what the service of humans requires, they will fail, objectively, to do their duty. Refusing to recognize the moral differences among species is a sure path to calamity. (The largest animal rights group in the country is People for the Ethical Treatment of Animals; its codirector, Ingrid Newkirk, calls research using animal subjects "fascism" and "supremacism." "Animal liberationists do not separate out the *human* animal," she says, "so there is no rational basis for saying that a human being has special rights. A rat is a pig is a dog is a boy. They're all mammals.")[17]

Those who claim to base their objection to the use of animals in biomedical research on their reckoning of the net pleasures and pains produced make a second error, equally grave. Even if it were true—as it is surely not—that the pains of all animate beings must be counted equally, a cogent utilitarian calculation requires that we weigh all the consequences of the use, and of the nonuse, of animals in laboratory research. Critics relying (however mistakenly) on animal rights may claim to ignore the beneficial results of such research, rights being trump cards to which interest and advantage must give way. But an argument that is explicitly framed in terms of interest and benefit for all over the long run must attend also to the disadvantageous consequences of not using animals in research, and to all the achievements attained and attainable only through their use. The sum of the benefits of their use is utterly beyond quantification. The elimination of horrible disease, the increase of longevity, the avoidance of great pain, the saving of lives, and the improvement of the quality of lives (for humans and for animals) achieved through research using animals is so incalculably great that the argument of these critics, systematically pursued, establishes not their conclusion but its reverse: to refrain from using animals in biomedical research, is, on utilitarian grounds, morally wrong.

When balancing the pleasures and pains resulting from the use of animals in research, we must not fail to place on the scales the terrible pains that would have resulted, would be suffered now, and would long continue had animals not been used. Every disease eliminated, every vaccine developed, every method of pain relief devised, every surgical procedure invented, every prosthetic device implanted—indeed, virtually every modern medical therapy is due, in part or in whole, to experimentation using animals. Nor may we ignore, in the balancing process, the predictable gains in human (and animal) well-being that are probably achievable in the future but that will not be achieved if the decision is made now to desist from such research or to curtail it.

Medical investigators are seldom insensitive to the distress their work may cause animal subjects. Opponents of research using animals are frequently insensitive to the cruelty of the results of the restrictions they would impose.[18] Untold numbers of human beings—real persons, although not now identifiable— would suffer grievously as the consequence of this well-meaning but shortsighted tenderness. If the morally relevant differences between humans and animals are borne in mind, and if all relevant considerations are weighed, the calculation of long-term consequences must give overwhelming support for biomedical research using animals.

Concluding Remarks

Substitution

The humane treatment of animals requires that we desist from experimenting on them if we can accomplish the same result using alternative methods—in vitro experimentation, computer simulation, or others. Critics of some experiments using animals rightly make this point.

It would be a serious error to suppose, however, that alternative techniques could soon be used in most research now using live animal subjects. No other methods now on the horizon—or perhaps ever to be available—can fully replace the testing of a drug, a procedure, or a vaccine, in live organisms. The flood of new medical possibilities being opened by the successes of recombinant DNA technology will turn to a trickle if testing on live animals is forbidden. When initial trials entail great risks, there may be no forward movement whatever without the use of live animal subjects. In seeking knowledge that may prove critical in later clinical applications, the unavailability of animals for inquiry may spell complete stymie. In the United States, federal regulations require the testing of new drugs and other products on animals, for efficacy and safety, before human beings are exposed to them.[19] We would not want it otherwise.

Every advance in medicine—every new drug, new operation, new therapy of any kind—must sooner or later be tried on a living being for the first time. That trial, controlled or uncontrolled, will be an experiment. The subject of that experiment, if it is not an animal, will be a human being. Prohibiting the use of live animals in biomedical research, therefore, or sharply restricting it, must result either in the blockage of much valuable research or in the replacement of animal subjects with human subjects. These are the consequences—unacceptable to most reasonable persons—of not using animals in research.

Reduction

Should we not at least reduce the use of animals in biomedical research? No, we should increase it, to avoid when feasible the use of humans as experimental subjects. Medical investigations putting human subjects at some risk are numerous and greatly varied. The risks run in such experiments are usually unavoidable, and (thanks to earlier experiments on animals) most such risks are minimal or moderate. But some experimental risks are substantial.

When an experimental protocol that entails substantial risk to humans comes before an institutional review board, what response is appropriate? The investigation, we may suppose, is promising and deserves support, so long as its human subjects are protected against unnecessary dangers. May not the investigators be fairly asked, Have you done all that you can to eliminate risk to humans by the extensive testing of that drug, that procedure, or that device on animals? To achieve maximal safety for humans we are right to require thorough experimentation on animal subjects before humans are involved.

Opportunities to increase human safety in this way are commonly missed; trials in which risks may be shifted from humans to animals are often not devised, sometimes not even considered. Why? For the investigator, the use of animals as subjects is often more expensive, in money and time, than the use of human subjects. Access to suitable human subjects is often quick and convenient, whereas access to appropriate animal subjects may be awkward, costly, and burdened with red tape. Physician-investigators have often had more experience working with human beings and know precisely where the needed pool of subjects is to be found and how they may be enlisted. Animals, and the procedures for their use, are often less familiar to these investigators. Moreover, the use of animals in place of humans is now more likely to be the target of zealous protests from without. The upshot is that humans are sometimes subjected to risks that animals could have borne, and should have borne, in their place. To maximize the protection of human subjects, I conclude, the wide and imaginative use of live animal subjects should be encouraged rather than discouraged. This enlargement in the use of animals is our obligation.

Consistency

Finally, inconsistency between the profession and the practice of many who oppose research using animals deserves comment. This frankly ad hominem observation aims chiefly to show that a coherent position rejecting the use of animals in medical research imposes costs so high as to be intolerable even to the critics themselves.

One cannot coherently object to the killing of animals in biomedical investigations while continuing to eat them. Anesthetics and thoughtful animal husbandry render the level of actual animal distress in the laboratory generally lower than that in the abattoir. So long as death and discomfort do not substantially differ in the two contexts, the consistent objector must not only refrain from all eating of animals but also protest as vehemently against others eating them as against others experimenting on them. No less vigorously must the critic object to the wearing of animal hides in coats and shoes, to employment in any industrial enterprise that uses animal parts, and to any commercial development that will cause death or distress to animals.

Killing animals to meet human needs for food, clothing, and shelter is judged entirely reasonable by most persons. The ubiquity of these uses and the virtual universality of moral support for them confront the opponent of research using animals with an inescapable difficulty. How can the many common uses of animals be judged morally worthy, while their use in scientific investigation is judged unworthy?

The number of animals used in research is but the tiniest fraction of the total used to satisfy assorted human appetites. That these appetites, often base and satisfiable in other ways, morally justify the far larger consumption of animals, whereas the quest for improved human health and understanding cannot justify the far smaller, is wholly implausible. Aside from the numbers of animals involved, the distinction in terms of worthiness of use, drawn with regard to any single animal, is not defensible. A given sheep is surely not more justifiably used to put lamb chops on the supermarket counter than to serve in testing a new contraceptive or a new prosthetic device. The needless killing of animals is wrong; if the common killing of them for our food or convenience is right, the less common but more humane uses of animals in the service of medical science are certainly not less right.

Scrupulous vegetarianism—in matters of food, clothing, shelter, commerce, and recreation, and in all other spheres—is the only fully coherent position the critic may adopt. At great human cost, the lives of fish and crustaceans must also be protected, with equal vigor, if speciesism has been forsworn. A very few consistent critics adopt this position. It is the reductio ad absurdum of the rejection of moral distinctions between animals and human beings.

Opposition to the use of animals in research is based on arguments of two different kinds—those relying on the alleged rights of animals and those relying on the consequences for animals. I have argued that arguments of both kinds must fail. We surely do have obligations to animals, but they have, and can have, no rights against us on which research can infringe. In calculating the consequences of animal research, we must weigh all the long-term benefits of the results achieved—to animals and to humans—and in that calculation we must not assume the moral equality of all animate species.

REFERENCES

1. Regan T. The case for animal rights. Berkeley, Calif.: University of California Press, 1983.

2. Singer P. Animal liberation. New York: Avon Books, 1977.

3. St. Augustine. Confessions. Book Seven. 397 A.D. New York: Pocket-books, 1957:104–26.

4. St. Thomas Aquinas. Summa theologica. 1273 A.D. Philosophic texts. New York: Oxford University Press, 1960:353–66.

5. Hegel GWF. Philosophy of right. 1821. London: Oxford University Press, 1952:105–10.

6. Bradley FH. Why should I be moral? 1876. In: Melden AI, ed. Ethical theories. New York: Prentice-Hall, 1950:345–59.

7. Mead GH. The genesis of the self and social control. 1925. In: Reck AJ, ed. Selected writings. Indianapolis: Bobbs-Merrill, 1964:264–93.

8. Prichard HA. Does moral philosophy rest on a mistake? 1912. In: Cellars W, Hospers J, eds. Readings in ethical theory. New York: Appleton-Century-Crofts, 1952:149–63.

9. Kant I. Fundamental principles of the metaphysic of morals. 1785. New York: Liberal Arts Press, 1949.

10. Rollin BE. Animal rights and human morality. New York: Prometheus Books, 1981.

11. Hoff C. Immoral and moral uses of animals. N Engl J Med 1980; 302:115–8.

12. Jamieson D. Killing persons and other beings. In: Miller HB, Williams WH, eds. Ethics and animals. Clifton, N.J.: Humana Press, 1983:135–46.

13. Singer P. Ten years of animal liberation. New York Review of Books. 1985; 31:46–52.

14. Bentham J. Introduction to the principles of morals and legislation. London: Athlone Press, 1970.

15. McCabe K. Who will live, who will die? Washington Magazine. August 1986:115.

16. U.S. Code of Federal Regulations. Title 21, Sect. 505(i). Food, drug, and cosmetic regulations.

17. U.S. Code of Federal Regulations, Title 16, Sect. 1500. 40–2. Consumer product regulations.

On the Ethics of the Use of Animals in Science

Dale Jamieson and Tom Regan

As you read this, animals are being killed, burned, radiated, blinded, immobilized and shocked. They are being locked and strapped into the Noble-Collip Drum, tossed about at the rate of 40 revolutions per minute and thrust against the iron projections that line the drum. This procedure crushes bones, destroys tissues, smashes teeth and ruptures internal organs. Right now, somewhere, animals are in isolation, deprived of all social contact, while others are in alien environments, manipulated into cannibalizing members of their own species. It is not just a few animals at issue. In the year 1978 alone, about 200 million animals were used for scientific purposes, about 64 million of these in the United States. This number includes 400,000 dogs, 200,000 cats and 30,000 apes and monkeys.[1] From anyone's point of view, these are disagreeable facts, but some will say they are the concern of scientists only. We who are not scientists cannot get off the hook so easily, however. The use made of animals in science frequently is carried out in the name of improving the quality of human life: to find cures for cancer, heart disease and a thousand other ailments; to develop safe new products for our consumption; and to instruct others in, and to advance our knowledge of, the world in which we live. Because these things are done in our name, ostensibly to help us live better lives, and because these activities frequently are financed by public monies (approximately $5 billion in federal support in the United States for 1980) we cannot in good faith or with good sense avoid confronting the facts about the use of animals in science, and assessing its morality.

In the past this debate has usually been put in terms of being for or against vivisection. But this term, 'vivisection', is ill-suited for our purposes. To vivisect an animal is to dissect it, to cut it, while it is alive. Not all practices that demand our attention involve vivisection. Animals placed in the Noble-Collip drum or those that are radiated or shocked, for example, are not dissected while they are alive. For this reason it would be misleading at best to pose our central question in terms of whether one is for or against vivisection. Our interest lies in assessing the use made of animals in science in general, not just in those cases where they are vivisected.

Before setting forth our own view regarding the ethics of the use of animals in science, two extreme positions will be characterized and debated. By subjecting their supporting arguments to criticism, we hope to show the need for a more reasonable, less extreme position. We shall call the two positions "The Unlimited Use Position" and "The No Use Position." The former holds that it is permissible to use any animal for any scientific purpose, so long as no human being is wronged. The latter holds that no use of any animal for any scientific purpose is morally permissible. We shall first examine the leading arguments for the Unlimited Use Position.

I

The first argument that we shall consider is the Cartesian Argument. It is named after the seventeenth-century philosopher, René Descartes, who held that animals are mindless machines. Here is the argument.

1. If a practice does not cause pain, then it is morally permissible.
2. Unlimited use of animals for scientific purposes would not cause them any pain.
3. Therefore, the use of any animal for any scientific purpose is morally permissible.

So simple an argument is not without far-reaching consequences. The tacit assumption of the Cartesian Argument by the scientists of Descartes' day helped pave the way for the rapid growth of animal experimentation in the seventeenth and eighteenth centuries. The following passage, written by an unknown contempory of Descartes, gives a vivid and unsettling picture of science at that time.

> They [i.e., scientists] administered beatings to dogs with perfect indifference; and made fun of those who pitied the creatures as if they felt pain. They said the animals were clocks; that the cries they emitted when struck, were only the noise of a little spring that had been touched, but that the whole body was without feeling. They nailed poor animals up on boards by their four paws to vivisect them and see the circulation of the blood which was a great subject of controversy.[3]

It is well to remember this passage whenever we doubt that ideas can make a difference. Clearly Descartes' idea that animals are mindless machines profoundly influenced the course of science. The influence of an idea, however, is not a reliable measure of its truth, and we need to ask how reasonable the Cartesian Argument is.

A moment's reflection is enough to show that some crucial qualifications must be added if the Cartesian Argument is to have any plausibility at all. Inflicting pain is not the only way to harm an individual. Suppose, for example, that we were to kill humans painlessly while they are asleep. No one would infer that because such killing would be painless it would therefore be quite all right. But even if the necessary qualifications were introduced, the Cartesian Argument would still remain implausible. The evidence for believing that at least some animals feel pain (and it is only those animals with which we shall be concerned) is virtually the same as the evidence for believing that humans feel pain. Both humans and animals behave in ways that are simply, coherently and consistently explained by supposing that they feel pain. From a physiological point of view, there is no reason to suppose that there are features that are unique to humans that are involved in pain sensations. Veterinary medicine, the law and common sense all presuppose that some animals feel pain. Though some seem to accept the Cartesian Argument implicitly, it is doubtful that many would try to defend it when it is clearly stated.

The failure of the Cartesian Argument has important implications regarding the moral status of animals. Once we acknowledge the reality of animal consciousness and pain we will be hard pressed indeed to exclude animals from membership in the moral community. Membership in the moral community might be thought of as in some ways analogous to membership in a club, with both qualifications and possible benefits. The key potential benefit of membership is that limits are placed on how others may treat you. For example, as a member, your life and property are protected by moral sanctions. Who belongs to the moral community? Evidently all those individuals who can themselves be treated wrongly qualify as members. But which individuals are these? A variety of answers have been proposed, including the following:

—all and only rational beings
—all and only autonomous beings (individuals having free will).

It will not be possible to discuss these views in detail.[4] It is sufficient to note their common failing: Infants and severely enfeebled human beings, for example, are neither rational nor autonomous, and yet we treat them wrongly if we cause them significant pain for no good reason. Thus, since we can treat these individuals wrongly, they qualify as members of the moral community; and since they qualify as members of this community despite the fact that they are neither rational nor autonomous, neither rationality nor autonomy are requirements for membership in the moral community.

Still, infants and the enfeebled are human beings, and it might be suggested that membership in the moral community is determined by species membership. In other words, it might be suggested that all and only human beings are members of the moral community. This requirement for membership is also unsatisfactory. To restrict membership in the moral community to those who belong to the "right" species is analogous to the racist's attempt to restrict membership to those who belong to the "right" race, and to the sexist's effort to exclude those of the "wrong" gender.[5] Racism and sexism are today recognized as unacceptable prejudices. Rationally, we recognize that we cannot mark moral boundaries on the basis of such biological differences. Yet this is precisely what those who attempt to restrict membership in the moral community to all and only *homo sapiens* are guilty of. They assume that membership in a particular species is the only basis for deciding who does and who does not belong to the moral community. To avoid this prejudice of "speciesism," we must reject this way of setting the boundaries of the moral community, and recognize that when needless pain and suffering are inflicted on infants and enfeebled humans, it is wrong, not because they are members of our species, but because they experience needless pain and suffering. Once this is acknowledged we may then come to see that it must be wrong to cause any individual, human or otherwise, needless pain or suffering. Thus, since many animals are conscious beings who can experience pain, as was argued in response to the Cartesian Argument, we must recognize that we can wrong them by causing them needless pain or suffering. Since they themselves can be wronged, they themselves must be members of the moral community.

The failure of the Cartesian Argument, therefore, does indeed have important implications regarding the moral status of animals. We shall have occasion to remind ourselves later of these implications.

A [second] argument for Unlimited Use is the Knowledge Argument.

1. If a practice produces knowledge, then it is morally permissible.
2. Unlimited use of animals for scientific purposes would produce knowledge.
3. Therefore, unlimited use of animals for scientific purposes is morally permissible.

Here we should balk at the first premise. Torturing suspects, spying on citizens, vivisecting cousins, all could produce knowledge, but surely that alone would not make these activities morally all right. Some knowledge is simply not worth the price in pain required to get it, whether those who suffer the pain are humans, as in the activities just listed, or animals, as in the case about to be described.

The Draize Test is a procedure employed by many manufacturers to determine whether proposed new products, most notably new cosmetics, would irritate the eyes of humans.[7] The most recent Federal guidelines for the administration of the Draize Test recommend that a single large-volume dose of the test substance be placed in the conjunctival sac in one eye of each of six albino rabbits. The test substance is to remain in the eyes of the rabbits for a week, and observations are to be periodically recorded. The guidelines recommend that in most cases anesthetics should not be used. The rabbits are often immobilized in restraining devices in order to prevent them from clawing at their eyes. At the completion of a week, the irritancy of the test substance is graded on the basis of the degree and severity of the damage in the cornea and iris.

The Draize Test is not a very good test by anyone's standards. It is unreliable and crude. In fact, a 1971 survey of twenty-five laboratories employing the Draize Test concluded that the Draize Test is so unreliable that it "should not be recommended as standard procedures in any new regulation."[8] But even if the Draize Test were a reliable test, the most that we would gain is some knowledge about the properties of some inessential new products. Can anyone really believe that there is a scarcity of cosmetics already on the market? The value of whatever knowledge is provided by the Draize Test is insignificant compared to the cost in animal pain required to obtain it. Indeed, no less a figure than Harold Feinberg, the chairperson of the American Accreditation For the Care of Laboratory Animals Committee, has stated that "the testing of cosmetics is frivolous and should be abolished."[9]

A [third] argument seeks to remedy this deficiency of the Knowledge Argument. Here is the Important Knowledge Argument.

1. If a practice produces important knowledge, then it is morally permissible.
2. Unlimited use of animals for scientific purposes would produce important knowledge.

3. Therefore, unlimited use of animals for scientific purposes is morally permissible.

The Important Knowledge Argument fares no better than the Knowledge Argument. Consider an example. Surely it cannot be denied that it is important to know what substances are carcinogenic in humans. But animal tests for carcinogenicity in humans are often inconclusive. For example, in recent years there has been great controversy over whether one can infer that saccharin or oral conceptives are carcinogenic in humans on the basis of data collected in animal tests. Some have argued that because of the methods used in such research, such an inference cannot be made.[10] Massive doses are administered to rats and mice in these studies over short periods of time: there is no reason to believe that human cancers develop in response to similar conditions. Moreover, unlike humans, rats and mice tend spontaneously to develop a high incidence of tumors. One prominent medical journal remarked with respect to the oral contraceptive controversy:

> It is difficult to see how experiments on strains of animals so exceedingly liable to develop tumors of these various kinds can throw useful light on the carcinogenicity of a compound for man.[11]

If, however, we were to adopt the policy of unlimited use of *humans*, we could conclusively determine which substances are carcinogenic in humans. Moreover, such a policy would be sanctioned by the Important Knowledge Argument, since unlimited toxicology testing and experimentation on humans would unquestionably produce important knowledge. If the production of important knowledge makes a practice permissible, then unlimited testing and experimenting on humans is permissible. But again, this is a repugnant conclusion. If we are unwilling to accept it, we must give up the Important Knowledge Argument. If, on the other hand, we are willing to accept it, then most and possibly all toxicology tests and experiments carried out on animals in the name of human interests are unnecessary, since better models, namely humans, are available.

Finally there is the Freedom Argument. The Freedom Argument does not seek to show directly that unlimited use of animals is permissible. Rather it seeks to show that limitations on a researcher's freedom to use animals are wrong. Here is the argument.

1. Outside limits placed on the scientist's right to freedom of inquiry or academic freedom are not permissible.
2. Any outside restriction placed on the use of animals for scientific purposes would place limits on the scientist's right to freedom on inquiry or academic freedom.
3. Therefore, no outside restrictions on how animals may be used for scientific purposes are morally permissible.

This argument focuses attention away from the value of the goal of science (knowledge or important knowledge) to the value of the freedom to inquire. But though this change is noteworthy, and though this freedom is important and ought to be one among a number of factors considered in the course of examining the ethics of the use of animals in science, it is clear that freedom of inquiry is not the only morally relevant consideration. The right to freedom of inquiry is no more absolute than, say, the right to freedom of speech. There are limits on what can be done by individuals in exercising their rights. To say precisely just what these limits are is difficult; but limits there are. Almost no one would say that the right to freedom of inquiry would sanction some of the things that have been done to humans in the name of science. For example, in the eighteenth century "charity children" were infected with smallpox in experiments conducted by Princess Caroline. Early in the twentieth century condemned criminals in the Philippines were injected with plague bacillus. And as recently as the 1960's, black prisoners in Alabama were left untreated to suffer from syphilis after having been intentionally infected. That there are limitations on what can be done in the name of science is a principle that is enshrined in international agreements, including the Nuremberg Code of 1947 and the World Medical Association's Declaration of Helsinki drafted in 1961. Since some limits on the right to freedom of inquiry clearly are justified, the unlimited use of animals cannot be defended by appealing to some supposed absolute right to freedom of inquiry. For this reason the Freedom Argument, like the others before it, fails to provide a rational defense of the Unlimited Use Position.[12]

Although we haven't canvassed all possible arguments that might be given in support of the Unlimited Use Position, we have examined those that seem most common. None of these arguments provides any rational support for this position. It is now time to examine an alternative view.

II

The No Use Position holds that no use of any animal for any scientific purpose is ever permissible. Is this position rationally defensible? We think not. We propose to argue for this conclusion in ways analogous to the case made against the Unlimited Use Position. We shall characterize some representative arguments for this position, indicating where and why these arguments go wrong.

Before addressing these arguments, it is worth noting that the reasonableness of the No Use Position does not follow from the inadequacy of the Unlimited Use Position, any more than it follows, say, that no men are bald because it is false that all men are. Those who accept the No Use Position may take some comfort in our critique of the Unlimited Use Position, but they cannot infer from that critique that their own position is on the side of the truth.

We shall discuss four arguments for the No Use Position. Here is the Pain Argument.

1. If an action causes pain to another being, then it is not morally permissible.
2. The use of animals for scientific purposes causes animals pain.
3. Therefore, no use of any animal for any scientific purpose is morally permissible.

We should note first that not all scientific uses made of animals cause them pain. For example, some experimental uses of animals involve operant conditioning techniques, and most of these do not cause pain at all. Other experiments call for minor modifications in animals' diets or environments. Still others require killing anesthetized animals. The Pain Argument does not provide a basis for objecting to any of these uses of animals. Because the Pain Argument cites no morally relevant consideration in addition to pain, it cannot provide a thorough-going defense of the No Use Position.

More importantly, the Pain Argument is defective from the outset. Contrary to what the first premise states, it is sometimes permissible to cause pain to others. Dentists cause pain. Surgeons cause pain. Wrestlers, football players, boxers cause pain. But it does not follow that these individuals do something that is not permissible. Granted, the presumption is always against someone's causing pain; nevertheless, causing pain is not itself sufficient for judging an act impermissible.

Suppose, however, that, unlike the case of dentists, pain is caused against one's will or without one's informed consent. Does it follow that what we've done is wrong? This is what the Informed Consent Argument alleges. Here is the argument.

1. If an action causes pain to another being without that being's informed consent, then it is not morally permissible.
2. The use of animals for scientific purposes causes animals pain without their informed consent.
3. Therefore, no use of any animal for any scientific purpose is morally permissible.

The second premise is open to the same objections raised against the corresponding premise in the Pain Argument: Not all scientific uses made of animals cause them pain. Thus, one cannot object to every use made of animals on this ground. Besides, animals are not the sort of beings who *can* give or withhold their informed consent. Explanations of what will be done to them in an experiment or test cannot be understood by them, so there is no possibility of "informing" them. Thus, there is no coherent possibility of causing them pain "without their informed consent."

The first premise also falls short of the truth. Suppose that a small child has appendicitis. If not operated on, the condition will worsen and she will die. Scary details omitted, the situation is explained to the child. She will have none of it: "No operation for me," we are told. The operation is performed without the child's consent and causes some amount of pain. Was it to wrong to perform the operation? It is preposterous to answer affirmatively. Thus, we have a counterexample to the basic assumption of the Informed Consent Argument, the assumption that it is not permissible to cause others pain without their informed consent.

Still, one might say that there is a difference between hurting others (causing them pain) and harming them (doing something that is detrimental to their welfare). Moreover, it might be suggested that in the example of the child and appendicitis, what we've stumbled upon is the fact that something that hurts might not harm. Accordingly, it might be held that what is always wrong is not causing pain, or causing others pain without their informed consent; rather, what is always wrong is harming others. This suggestion gains additional credence when we observe that even a painless death can be a great harm to a given individual. These considerations suggest another argument. Here is the Harm Argument.

1. If an action harms another being, then it is not morally permissible.
2. The use of animals for scientific purposes harms animals.
3. Therefore, no use of any animal for any scientific purpose is morally permissible.

This argument, like the ones before it, has gaping holes in it. First, it is clear that it will not even serve as a basis for opposing all animal experimentation, since not all animal experimentation harms animals. More fundamentally, it is simply not true that it is always wrong to harm another. Suppose that while walking alone at night, you are attacked and that through luck or skill you repel your assailant who falls beneath your defensive blows, breaks his neck, and is confined to bed from that day forth, completely paralyzed from the neck down. We mince words if we deny that what you did harmed your assailant. Yet we do not say that what you did is therefore wrong. After all, you were innocent; you were just minding your own business. Your assailant, on the other hand, hardly qualifies as innocent. He attacked you. It would surely be an unsatisfactory morality that failed to discriminate between what you as an innocent victim may do in self-defense, and what your attacker can do in offense against your person or your property. Thus despite the initial plausibility of the first premise of the Harm Argument, no all cases of harming another are impermissible.

The difficulties with the Harm Argument suggest a fourth argument, the Innocence Argument.

1. If an action causes harm to an innocent individual, then it is not permissible, no matter what the circumstances.
2. Animals are innocent.
3. The use of animals for scientific purposes harms them.
4. Therefore, no use of any animal for any scientific purpose is morally permissible.

This argument, unlike the Harm Argument, can account for the case of the assailant, since by attacking you the assailant ceases to be innocent, and therefore in harming him you have not wronged him. In this respect if in no other, the Innocence Argument marks a genuine improvement over the Harm Argument. Nevertheless, problems remain. Again, since animals are not always harmed when used for scientific purposes, the Innocence Argument does not provide a foundation for the No Use Position. It could also be argued that animals cannot be viewed as innocent. We shall return to this issue in the following section. The more fundamental question, however, is whether the basic assumption of this argument is correct: Is it always wrong to harm an innocent individual, no matter what the circumstances?

Here we reach a point where philosophical opinion is sharply divided. Some philosophers evidently are prepared to answer this question affirmatively.[13] Others, ourselves included, are not. One way to argue against an affirmative answer to this question is to highlight, by means of more or less far-fetched hypothetical examples, what the implications of an affirmative answer would be. The use of such "thought-experiments" is intended to shed light on the gray areas of our thought by asking how alternative positions would view far-fetched hypothetical cases. The hope is that we may then return to the more complex situations of everyday life with a better understanding of how to reach the best judgment in these cases. So let us construct a thought-experiment, and indicate how it can be used to contest the view that it is always wrong to harm an innocent individual, no matter what the circumstances. (A second thought-experiment will be undertaken near the beginning of section III.)

Imagine this case.[14] Together with four other friends, you have gone caving (spelunking) along the Pacific coast. The incoming tide catches your group by surprise and you are faced with the necessity of making a quick escape through the last remaining accessible opening to the cave or else all will drown. Unfortunately, the first person to attempt the escape gets wedged in the opening. All efforts to dislodge him, including his own frantic attempts, are unsuccessful. It so happens that one member of your party has brought dynamite along, so that the means exist to widen the opening. However, to use the explosive to enlarge the escape route is certain to kill your trapped friend. The situation, then, is this: If the explosive is used, then it is certain that one will die and likely that four will escape unharmed. If the explosive is not used, it is certain that all five will die. All the persons involved are innocent. What ought to be done? Morally speaking, is it permissible to use the dynamite despite the fact that doing so is certain to harm an innocent person?

Those who think it is always wrong to harm an innocent individual, no matter what the circumstances, must say that using the dynamite would be wrong. But how can this be? If the death of one innocent individual is a bad thing, then the death of considerably more than one innocent individual must be that much worse. Accordingly, if it is claimed that you would be doing wrong if you performed an act that brought about the death of one innocent individual *because it is wrong to act in ways that harm an innocent individual,* then it must be a more grievous wrong for you to act in ways that will bring equivalent harm to a greater number of innocent individuals. But if this is so, then we have reason to deny that it is always wrong to harm an innocent individual, *no matter what the circumstances.* What our thought-experiment suggests is that it is possible that some circumstances might be so potentially bad that morality will permit us to harm an innocent individual. In the thought-experiment it would be permissible to use the dynamite.

Those who incline toward viewing the prohibition against harming the innocent as absolute, admitting of no exceptions whatever, are not likely to be persuaded to give up this view just by the weight of the argument of the previous paragraphs. The debate will—and should—continue. One point worth making, however, is that those who like ourselves do not view this prohibition as absolute can nevertheless regard it as very serious, just as, for example, one can view the obligation to keep one's promises as a very serious moral requirement without viewing it as absolute. Imagine that you have borrowed a chain saw from a friend, promising to return it whenever he asks for it. Imagine he turns up at your door in a visibly drunken state, accompanied by a bound and gagged companion who has already been severely beaten and is in a state of terror. "I'll have my chain saw now," he intones. Ought you to return it, under *those* circumstances? The obligation to keep one's promises can be regarded as quite serious without our having to say, yes, by all means, you ought to fetch the chain saw! There are other considerations that bear on the morality of what you ought to do in addition to the fact that you have made a promise. Similarly, the fact that some action will harm an innocent individual is not the only consideration that is relevant to assessing the morality of that action. In saying this we do not mean to suggest that this consideration is not an important one. It is, and we shall attempt to develop its importance more fully in the following section. All that we mean to say is that it is not the only morally relevant consideration.

There would appear to be cases, then, whether they be far-fetched hypothetical ones or ones that might arise in the real world, in which morality permits us to harm an innocent individual. Thus, even in those cases in which animals used for scientific purposes are harmed, and even assuming that they are innocent, it does not follow that how they are used is morally wrong. Like the other arguments reviewed in this section, the Innocence Argument fails to provide an acceptable basis for the

No Use Position. Assuming, as we do, that these arguments provide a fair representation of those available to advocates of this position, we conclude that the No Use Position lacks a rationally compelling foundation, either in fact, or in logic, or in morality.

III

The previous two sections criticized two extreme positions, one favoring, the other opposing, all uses of animals for scientific purposes. In the present section, and in the one that follows, two different arguments will be developed for less extreme positions, positions which though they place severe limitations on when animals may be used in science, do allow for the possibility that some animals may sometimes be used for some purposes, even some that harm them. The argument of the present section takes up where the argument of the last one ended: with the wrongness of harming the innocent. The argument of the next section is based on the different idea of maximizing the balance of good over evil. The differences between the two arguments will be sketched in section V.

The prohibition against harming innocent individuals is a very serious, but not an absolute, prohibition. Because it is not absolute, it has justified exceptions. The problem is to say under what circumstances an exception is permitted. Perhaps the best way to begin formulating an answer is to again consider the spelunking example. Notice first that in that case we assumed that other alternatives had been exhausted: for example, every effort had been made to find an alternative route of escape and to dislodge your trapped friend. Second, we assumed that you had very good reason to believe that all would be drowned if the only remaining exit was not widened. Very dreadful consequences—death—would obtain, therefore, for five as compared with one person, if the dynamite was not used. These considerations suggest a modified principle concerning the harming of those who are innocent. We shall call this principle the "Modified Innocence Principle" (MIP), and formulate it in the following way.

> It is wrong to harm an innocent individual unless it is
> reasonable to believe that doing so is the only realistic way
> of avoiding equal harm for many other innocents.[15]

The role of this principle can be illustrated by means of another regrettably not too far-fetched thought-experiment.

Imagine that a terrorist has possession of a well-armed tank and is systematically slaughtering forty-five innocent hostages whom he has fastened to a wall.[16] Attempts to negotiate a compromise fail. The man will kill all the hostages if we do nothing. Under the circumstances, there is only one reasonable alternative: Blow up the tank. But there is this complication: The terrorist has strapped a young girl to the tank, and any weapon sufficient to blow up the tank will kill the child. The girl is innocent. Thus to blow up the tank is to harm an innocent, one who herself stands no chance of benefiting from the attack. Ought we to blow up the tank?

MIP would sanction doing so. If, as we argued in the previous section, it is worse that harm befalls many innocent individuals than that an equal harm befall one, then surely it would be worse if all the hostages were killed rather than just the one innocent child. Moreover, we have assumed that other alternatives to the attack have been tried, that they have failed, and that the only realistic way to prevent the slaughter of the remaining hostages is to blow up the tank. Thus MIP should not be understood as sanctioning a policy of "shooting first and asking questions later." It is only *after* other non-violent or less violent alternatives have been exhausted that we are permitted to do what will harm an innocent individual.

Problems remain however. Consider the notion of "equal harm." MIP will not permit harming an innocent just so that others might avoid some minor inconvenience. We cannot, for example, confine innocent vagrants to concentration camps just because we find their appearance aesthetically displeasing. Still, not all harms are equal. It is a matter of degree how much a given harm will detract from an individual's well-being, and problems will arise concerning just how serious a given harm is, or whether two or more different harms are "equal." Moreover, there is also certain to be a problem concerning the number of innocents involved. The thought-experiment involving the terrorist and the tank was a clear case of harming one innocent in order to prevent equal harm to many other innocents. But how many is many? If the only way to avoid the death of two innocents is to kill one, ought we to do this? This question, and others like it, would have to be explored in a comprehensive examination of MIP. We by-pass them now, not because they are unimportant, but because they are less important than another question which cannot be passed over. This concerns the very intelligibility of viewing animals as innocent. The fundamental nature of this issue is clear. If no sense can be made of the idea of the "innocence of animals," then whatever else may be said of MIP, at least this much could be: It simply would be inapplicable to our relations with animals. So let us ask whether sense can be made of the view that animals are innocent.

One argument against the intelligibility of animal innocence is The Moral Agent Argument.

1. Only moral agents can be innocent.
2. Animals are not moral agents.
3. Therefore, animals cannot be innocent.

By "moral agents" is meant individuals who can act from a sense of right and wrong, who can deliberate about what they ought to do, who can act and not merely react, and who thus can be held accountable or responsible for what they do or fail to do. Normal adult human beings are the clearest examples of individuals having the status of moral agents.

The first premise states that only moral agents can be innocent. Why might this be claimed? The most likely explanation is the following. Because moral agents are responsible for their actions, they can be accused of acting wrongly. Individuals who are not moral agents, however, can do no wrong. If a tree falls on someone causing death or injury, it makes no sense to condemn the tree. Since the tree "had no choice," it cannot be faulted. Moral agents can be faulted, however. If a moral agent commits murder, then he has done what is wrong; he is guilty of an offense. Suppose, however, that a moral agent is falsely accused of committing murder; he is not guilty; he is (and here is the crucial word) innocent. Thus it makes perfectly good sense to say that a moral agent is innocent because moral agents can be guilty. It makes no sense to say that a tree is innocent because trees cannot be guilty.

The second premise denies that animals are moral agents. This *seems* true. Granted, we reward and punish animals for their behavior, hoping to incline them towards behaving in ways we prefer and away from those we do not; but it is doubtful that many, if any, animals meet the requirements of moral agency.[17] Thus, if the first premise of the Moral Agent Argument is accepted, and assuming as we shall that the second premise is true, then there would seem to be no way to avoid the conclusion that animals cannot be innocent. If, like trees, they cannot be guilty, then they cannot be innocent either. And if this conclusion cannot be avoided, a conclusive case would have been made against viewing MIP as bearing on the morality of how animals may be treated. Since MIP is concerned with how *innocent* individuals may be treated, it has no bearing on how animals may be treated, if animals cannot be innocent.

An argument has been offered for the intelligibility of the idea of animal innocence. This is a controversial subject, and we shall return to it again at the beginning of the following section. If we assume for the moment that animals can be innocent in a morally relevant way, then we may also assume that MIP does apply to how we may treat them, and thus develop the implications of its applicability to the use of animals in science by means of the following argument, the Modified Innocence Argument.

1. It is wrong to harm the innocent unless we have very good reason to believe that this is the only realistic way to prevent equal harm for many other innocents.
2. Animals are innocent.
3. Therefore, it is not permissible to harm them unless the conditions set forth in premise (1) are satisfied.
4. At least a great deal of the use of animals in science harmful to them fails to meet the conditions set forth in premise (1).
5. Therefore, at least a great deal of this use is wrong.

The first and second premises already have been addressed. The conclusion drawn in step three follows from steps one and two. The step that remains to be examined is the fourth one, and it is to the task of defending it that we shall now turn.

As a minimal condition, MIP requires that it be reasonable to believe that the harming of an innocent will prevent equal harm to many other innocents. Apart from the issue of experimentation, it is clear that not all uses of animals in science harmful to them satisfy this requirement. For example, very many animals are harmed for instructional purposes in school and laboratory settings and in science fairs. The fulfillment of these purposes cannot reasonably be viewed as an essential step leading to the prevention of equal harms for many other innocents.[19] As for experimentation, it is clear that there are many cases in which animals are harmed to obtain trivial bits of knowledge. For example, recently the Canadian Department of Indian Affairs and Northern Development spent $80,000 to determine the effect of oil spills on polar bears.[20] The procedure involved immersing three polar bears in a container of crude oil and water. One polar bear died after licking oil from her fur for 12 hours. A second polar bear was killed for "humane reasons" after suffering intense pain from kidney failure. The third survived after suffering from severe infection that was caused by injections that the bear was given through her oil-stained skin by veterinarians who were attempting to treat her for the kidney and liver damage that was caused by her immersion in oil. The Canadian government, with the cooperation of the American government, is now planning to conduct similar experiments on dolphins.

The polar bear experiment is not an isolated incident. There is a growing body of literature that documents the triviality of much that routinely passes for "original scientific research."[21] The situation in toxicology testing is regrettably similar, as the following test illustrates.

The standard measure of the toxicity of a substance (i.e., the accepted measure of the degree to which a given substance is poisonous to humans) is its median lethal dose. The median lethal dose, or the LD_{50} as it is called, is defined as the amount of a substance needed to kill 50% of the test animals to which it is administered. The United States Government requires that the LD$_{50}$ be determined for each new substance bound for the market. The substances in question are not just exotic life-saving drugs, but include such ordinary products as the latest household detergent, shoe polish, oven cleaner, deodorants and soda pop. There are at least two reasons for believing that these tests, which cause great harm to the test animals, will not prevent equal harm to many other innocents. First, many of the substances for which the LD$_{50}$ is obtained already are known to be relatively non-toxic. As a result, enormous quantities of these substances must be forcibly fed or otherwise administered to the test animals in order to cause 50% fatalities. In such cases it is often very clear long before 50% of the test animals have died, that the substance poses no serious threat to human beings. To put the point baldly: Determining the toxicity of substances which are never likely to harm anyone except the test animals to whom they are initially administered is blatantly impermissible, given MIP. There is no good reason to believe that these tests *will* prevent equal harm to many other innocents.

MIP also requires that other realistic alternatives be exhausted before it is permissible to harm an innocent individual. This requirement does make a difference. If, prior to attempted negotiations with the terrorist, for example, we blew up the tank, we would be morally culpable. We would have resorted to violence, knowing this would harm the innocent child, without having first determined whether we could have acted to prevent harm being done to *all* the innocents. So let us ask whether all scientific uses of animals harmful to them is undertaken only after other realistic alternatives have been tried.

Unfortunately, the answer is no: a great deal of the use made of animals in science clearly fails to satisfy this requirement, though of course we cannot say exactly how much, anymore than we can say exactly how much water there is in the Pacific. What we can say is that the amount in each case is *a lot*. "But there are no alternatives," it is often said. This is an answer that we shall examine more fully shortly. Sometimes, however, there *are* well-established alternatives to the use of animals. These alternatives include tissue and cell cultures, mathematical modeling, chemical analysis, mechanical models, clinical examination and epidemiological surveys.[24] In cases where there are established, scientifically viable alternatives to using animals and other innocent individuals who can be hurt or harmed (e.g., humans), MIP requires that these alternatives be employed and not the innocents.

However, it remains true that sometimes, in some cases, there are no known alternatives that have been proven to be scientifically reliable. What does MIP imply about these cases? Here we must take note of an important disanalogy between the scientific enterprise and our thought-experiments. Those experiments presented us with crisis situations in which the alternatives are clearly defined, in which neither time nor circumstances allow for the investigation of new options, and in which we could not reasonably be expected to have done anything before the crisis developed so that we might have another realistic option at our disposal. (There is nothing we could reasonably be expected to do today, for example, to increase the options that would be available to us in the extremely unlikely event that we should find ourselves in the predicament we imagined in the spelunking example.) There is, however, a great deal that science can begin to do today and could have done in the past in an effort to explore alternatives to the use of animals for scientific purposes. Time and circumstances *do* allow for the scientific investigation of such alternatives; indeed, it is part of the very essence of the scientific enterprise to search for new ways to approach old (and emerging) problems. The longer the life-sciences, including psychology,[25] are delayed in making a conscientious effort to search for alternatives, the greater the wrong, given MIP, since an insufficient commitment in this regard itself offends against the spirit of MIP. To harm the innocent is so *serious* a moral matter that we must do all that we can reasonably be expected to do so that we can avoid causing this harm. If the life-sciences, through lack of will, funding, or both, fail to do all that can reasonably be expected of them in this regard, then we have no reason to assume that the use made of animals in science is justified "because there are no available alternatives." On the contrary, we have reason to deny the moral propriety of such use. To put this same point differently: Since we are justified in believing that it is wrong to harm the innocent unless we can be shown that it isn't, we are justified in regarding the harm caused to animals in science as unjustified unless we can be shown that all that reasonably could be done has been done to avoid causing it. If we cannot be shown that these efforts have been made, then we are right to regard their use as wrong, given MIP.

Viewed from this perspective, *at least most* harmful use of animals in science ought to be regarded as morally unjustified. The "search for alternatives" has been a largely token effort, one that has not been given a priority anywhere approaching that required by MIP. But this is not the fault only of those involved in the life-sciences. As a society we have not seriously thought about the moral status of animals. We have failed to recognize that animals are members of the moral community, or we have minimized the importance of their membership. As a result, we have not funded the search for alternatives sufficiently. Since (as it is well said) "research goes where the money is," the investigation of alternatives has not prospered.

IV

The argument of the previous section relied heavily on the idea that animals are innocent. The attempt to undermine this idea by means of the Moral Agent Argument was considered and found wanting. There are other ways to contest this idea, however. The Rights Argument is one.

1. Only those individuals who have rights can be innocent.
2. Animals cannot have rights.
3. Therefore, animals cannot be innocent.

A defense of the first premise might proceed along the following lines. To speak of individuals as innocent assumes that they can suffer *undeserved* harm. But undeserved harm must be harm that is unjust or unfair, and what is unjust or unfair is what violates an individual's rights. Thus, only those individuals who have rights can be the recipients of undeserved harm. As for the second premise, not very long ago it was assumed to be so obvious as not to require any supporting argument at all.

Recently, however, the idea of animal rights has been debated, and there is a steadily growing body of literature, in an expanding number of prestigious professional journals from scientific and humanistic disciplines, devoted to the reflective assessment of this idea.[26] It will not be possible to review this debate on the present occasion. We mention it only in order to indicate how the idea of the innocence of animals is relevant to the more widely discussed idea of animal rights. A thorough examination of the former idea would have to include a thorough examination of the latter one as well.

It is possible to approach the question of the ethics of animal use in science from a perspective that does not place fundamental importance on innocence and the allied idea of rights. Utilitarianism is one such perspective. It is a view that has attracted many able thinkers, and represents today, in the English-speaking world at least, the primary alternative to views of morality that place central importance on individual rights. Moreover, utilitarianism's most influential advocates, from Jeremy Bentham (1748–1832) and John Stuart Mill (1806–1873) to the contemporary Australian philosopher Peter Singer, have explicitly recognized the membership of animals in the moral community. It will be instructive, therefore, to sketch the utilitarian position in general and to mark its implications for the use of animals for scientific purposes in particular.

Utilitarianism is the view that we ought to act so as to bring about the greatest possible balance of good over evil for everyone affected. Utilitarianism is thus not a selfish doctrine; it does not prescribe that each individual is to act so as to maximize his or her own self-interest. For the utilitarian, your neighbor's good counts the same as yours; in Bentham's words, "Each to count for one, no one for more than one." In trying to decide what ought to be done, therefore, we must consider the interests of everyone involved, being certain to count equal interests equally. The point of view required by utilitarianism is uncompromisingly impartial; we are not allowed to favor our own interests, or those of our friends, or say, White Anglo-Saxon Protestants, over the like interests of others. It is, in the words of the nineteenth-century utilitarian Henry Sidgwick, "the point of view of the universe." For the utilitarian, the ideas of the innocence and the rights of individuals are not independent considerations to be used in determining what ought to be done. They have a role only if they bear on the determination of what the best consequences would be. Utilitarianism recommends a "forward-looking" morality. Results are the only things that matter in the determination of right and wrong.

Utilitarians have disagreed over many points, including the nature of the good consequences they seek and the evil ones they seek to avoid. Classical utilitarians, including Bentham and Mill, viewed goodness as pleasure and evil as pain. Some recent utilitarians understand goodness as the satisfaction of an individual's preferences.[27] On either view, many animals must find a place in the utilitarian calculation of the best consequences, if, following these thinkers, we agree that many animals can experience what is pleasant or painful, or have preferences. For the sake of simplicity, in what follows we shall think of good consequences (utility) as pleasure, and bad consequences (disutility) as pain.

Bentham, in an oft-quoted and justly famous passage, declares the relevance of the pain of animals in the following way.

> The French have already discovered that the blackness of the skin is no reason why a human being should be abandoned without redress to the caprice of a tormentor. It may come one day to be recognized, that the number of the legs, the villosity of the skin, or the termination of the *os sacrum*, are reasons equally insufficient for abandoning a sensitive being to the same fate. . . . [T]he question is not, Can they *reason*? nor, Can they *talk*? but, Can they *suffer*?[28]

If we assume, as we have throughout, that the animals of which we speak can suffer, how might a utilitarian such as Bentham argue against their use for scientific purposes? Clearly no utilitarian would accept the principal assumption of the Pain Argument; the assumption that it is *always* wrong to cause another pain. The permissibility of causing pain, like the permissibility of performing any other act, must depend for the utilitarian on the utility of doing it, and since it could be true in any given case that we will bring about the best consequences for everyone involved by an act that causes pain to some individual(s), the utilitarian will not accept the prohibition against causing pain as absolute (as impermissible at all times, no matter what the consequences).

It remains true, nevertheless, that utilitarians will regard causing pain as a negative feature of an act. Any action which causes pain and fails to bring about a greater amount of pleasure will be ruled out by the utilitarian as morally wrong, except when every other alternative action would bring about an even greater balance of pain over pleasure. Thus one way of formulating the Utilitarian Argument against the use of animals in science is the following.

1. Acts are not morally permissible if they cause pain to some individuals and yet fail to bring about the best possible consequences for everyone involved.
2. A great deal of the scientific use of animals causes them pain and fails to bring about the best possible consequences.
3. Therefore, a great deal of this use is not morally permissible.

There are many reasons for accepting the second premise of this argument. Even in the case of animal-based experimentation or research, much is redundant, and is carried on well beyond the threshold needed for replication. Experimental studies of shock are a good example. As early as 1946 a survey of the literature indicated that over 800 papers had been published on experimental studies of shock. These studies induced shock by various means, including: tournequets, hammer-blows, rotations in the Noble-Collip drum, gunshot wounds, strangulation, intestinal loops, burning and freezing. By 1954 a survey article reported that although "animal investigations in the field of traumatic shock have yielded diversified and often contradictory results," the investigators looked forward to "future experimentation in this field."[29] In 1974 researchers still described their work as "preliminary." Presumably such work will continue as long as someone is willing to fund it.

The utilitarian argument could go even further. John Cairns, Director of the Imperial Cancer Research Fund's Mill Hill

Laboratory in London, has pointed out that during the last 150 years in the Western world, there has been an enormous increase in life expectancy.[37] He notes that this increase in life expectancy began before the advent of "what we would call medical science" and argues that it is primarily due to better nutrition and hygiene rather than to the development of exotic new drugs and surgical procedures. He goes on to say that the chance of dying of cancer in the United States has not altered appreciably in the last 35 years, in spite of intense research activity. Claims to the contrary are based on statistical gimmicks: Since 'cure' is defined as survival five years after diagnosis, the earlier a cancer is diagnosed the greater the likelihood of cure, even if the course of the disease and the time of death are unaffected in any way. In commenting on the eradication of infectious diseases, Cairns claims:

> It is significant, however, that what is often thought of as one of the accomplishments of sophisticated medical science was, in large part, the product of some fairly simple improvements in public health. In the end, history may well repeat itself and the same prove to be true for cancer.[38]

Cairns is not the only prominent figure in the scientific establishment to have made such an argument. Perhaps it goes too far, but it does suggest how thorough-going a utilitarian critique of animal experimentation, or the use of animals in toxicology experiments or in education, can be. If most of our use of animals in these activities are largely irrelevant to producing longer and pleasanter lives, then there is no justification for using animals in ways that cause them pain.

But it is not just the unreliability and redundancy of the data that utilitarians will contest. They can also object to the *kind* of animal used for scientific purposes. Rocks cannot feel pleasure or pain. Only conscious beings can. Nevertheless, there are great differences among conscious beings regarding the degree or level of their consciousness. Some conscious beings have a conception of their own identity, a self-concept: they can make plans for the future, regret the past, and envision their own bodily death. Beings that lack a concept of self might experience something like pleasure, but they cannot anticipate future pleasure, nor regret those pleasures they have missed in the past. It is for this reason that we think of some beings as having more complex, richer and "higher" states of consciousness than other conscious beings. Beings with a sense of self are utility "hot spots," so to speak. Because they have the kind of consciousness they do, they can experience richer, fuller pleasures and pains, and because of this we should take special care to maximize their pleasures and minimize their pains. That would seem to be a winning strategy for bringing about the best consequences.

Where, precisely, we draw the line between animals who do, and those who do not, have a concept of self is unclear. Probably there is no *precise* line to be drawn. That problem is not what demands our attention just now. The point to notice is that utilitarianism will not allow the use of animals having higher levels of consciousness, even if their use would bring about a net balance of good over evil, if these same (or better) results could be obtained by using animals of less highly developed consciousness. Wherever possible, that is, utilitarianism requires that science deal with the most rudimentary forms of conscious life *and* as few of these as possible, or, most preferable by far, with non-conscious beings, living or otherwise. Since there is ample evidence that most chimpanzees, for example, have a sense of self,[39] and growing evidence that some species of Cetaceans do,[40] the case for regarding these animals as having higher consciousness is increasingly reinforced and the utilitarian grounds for cautioning against the use of these animals for scientific purposes is correspondingly strengthened. It is exceedingly doubtful that the 30,000 primates used for scientific purposes in America in 1978 were used justifiably, given the Utilitarian Argument.

In summary, the principle of utility demands that stringent requirements be met before we can be justified in using any animal for any scientific purpose that causes it pain. It must be shown that a proposed use will promote the utilitarian objective of bringing about the greatest possible balance of good over evil for everyone involved. If it does not, then, as premise 2 of the Utilitarian Argument asserts, the procedure is morally wrong. There is ample reason to believe that at least a great deal of the use of animals in science does not satisfy this requirement. Thus, if utility be our guide, there is strong reason to condemn much of the current use made of animals in science.

V

In the two preceding sections we sketched two moral perspectives that converge on the same general conclusion: At least much of the scientific use made of animals is morally wrong and ought to be stopped. Despite their agreement in a broad range of cases however, the Principle of Utility and the Modified Innocence Principle (MIP) support conflicting judgments in some cases.

Recall that MIP will allow harming an innocent only if we have very good reason to believe that this is the only realistic way to prevent equivalent harm to many other innocents. MIP does not sanction harming innocents so that others may reap positive goods (e.g., pleasures); it is limited to the prevention or elimination of harms or evils (e.g., pain). Thus, in principle, MIP will not allow, say, contests between a few innocent Christians and hungry lions so that great amounts of otherwise unobtainable pleasure might be enjoyed by large numbers of Roman spectators. MIP does not permit evil (the harming of innocents) so that good may come. In principle, Utilitarianism could allow this. Classical utilitarianism is aggregative in nature: it is the *total* of goods and evils, for *all* the individuals involved, that matters. Theoretically, then, it is possible that achieving the optimal balance of good over evil in any given case will necessitate harming the innocent. The point can be illustrated abstractly by imagining that we face a choice between two alternatives, A_1 which will harm an innocent individual and A_2 which will not. A utilitarian, we may assume, will assign some disutility, some minus-score, to the harm caused in A_1. Suppose this is -20. Suppose further, however, that A_1 would bring about much better consequences for others than A_2; suppose that the difference is a magnitude of 100 to 1, A_1 yielding benefits that total $+1000$, A_2 yielding only $+10$. A greater balance of good over evil would result if we did A_1 than if we did A_2. Utilitarians, therefore, must choose the former alternative, but not those who accept MIP: they must favor the latter alternative (A_2).

The Principles of Utility and of Modified Innocence do differ in theory, therefore, despite their agreement in many practical cases. Which principle ought we to accept? That is far too large an issue to be decided here. . . . It is enough to realize that utilitarianism theoretically could allow more use of animals in science that harms the animals than MIP allows. Whether or not this difference is a sign of the moral superiority or inferiority of utilitarianism in comparison to MIP, at least this much is clear: there is a difference.

VI

Some general points should be kept in mind as we conclude. First, given either the Principle of Utility or MIP, to harm an animal is in need of moral defense; both principles view the harming of an individual as *presumptively* wrong, as something that is wrong unless it can be shown that it isn't. Given either principle, therefore, the burden of proof must always be on those who cause harm to animals in scientific settings. Unless these persons can show that what they do is morally permissible, we are entitled to believe that it is not. This burden, obvious as it may seem, has not always been recognized. Too often it has been "those who speak for the animals" who have been called upon to shoulder the burden of proof. But it is not the critics, it is the advocates of animal use in science who should bear it. This fundamental point must never be lost sight of in the debate over the ethics of the use of animals in science.

Second, the kind of knowledge (one might better say "wisdom") sometimes required to determine the permissibility of using an animal, especially in experiments in basic research, clearly is not the exclusive property of any particular profession, let alone any particular branch of science. For that reason we should draw upon the expertise of many people, from many fields, to review experimental proposals before they are funded. It is very important that these decisions not be left just to those who have a professional interest in their outcome. Not very long ago in this country experiments were performed on humans with impunity. Today we have recognized the merits of the idea that decisions about the permissibility of research that might harm human subjects must be made on a case-by-case basis, involving the best judgment of persons from diverse areas of expertise: we wouldn't dream of leaving these decisions entirely in the hands of those doing the research. Because animals cannot, except by prejudice, be excluded from the moral community, it is reason, not "mere sentiment," that calls for similar procedural safeguards for their use in science generally and in scientific experimentation in particular. It is not enough, even if it is salutary development, that principles for the care and maintenance of laboratory animals are in place,[44] though even here one should raise questions about how conscientiously these principles are enforced. How often, for example, has a scientific establishment been found in violation of these principles? And how impartial are those in whose hands the business of enforcement rests? One need not prejudge the answers to these questions by insisting upon the propriety of asking them.

At this point someone will accuse us of being "anti-scientific" or, more soberly, perhaps it will be argued that instituting procedural safeguards of the kind we recommend, in which research proposals are considered case by case by a panel of experts from diverse fields, would "rein in science," thus having a chilling effect on important research. The "anti-science" accusation will be answered in this essay's final paragraph. As for the "chilling effect" argument, it is true that adopting the kind of procedural safeguards we recommend *would* place limits on what scientists would be permitted to do. These safeguards would thus restrict the scientist's "freedom to inquire." The right to inquire, however, as was argued earlier, is not absolute; one may not do anything one pleases in the name of this right; it can and should be limited by other, weightier moral concerns. It is no longer possible in this country, for example, to infect poor black males in Alabama with syphilis and to record the development of the disease when left untreated. This *is* a restriction on science, but one which ought to be viewed as welcome and appropriate. An unfortunate consequence of instituting and effectively enforcing procedural safeguards for the use of animals in science, it is true, is that research proposals would have to be screened by another, interdisciplinary committee, requiring that yet another set of forms be filled out and so forth. Both the bureaucracy and the red tape are almost certain to increase if our call for safeguards is heeded. Researchers may see "Big Brother" at work, and decry, in the words of a leader in brain transplant research, Robert J. White, "the ever-present danger of government control of biological research through the limitation of animal availability and experimental design."[45] But the inconvenience "red tape" causes would seem to be a comparatively small price to pay to insure that scientific practice meets the demands of morality. The life-sciences are not physics, and the costs that must be borne in the conduct of biological and psychological research cannot be measured merely in dollars and cents.

In reply it may be objected that the kind of safeguards we propose would be impracticable, and, in any event, would cost too much to implement. Neither objection is well-founded. In July of 1977 some initial procedural safeguards for experimental animals were put into place in Sweden. It has been noted that simply by establishing ethics committees to review research proposals, research designs have been improved; and these designs often require the use of fewer animals than was formerly the rule.[46] In addition, greater use is being made of animals with less highly developed conscious lives, animals which, not surprisingly, are cheaper to procure and maintain; and the employment of less harmful procedures is growing. It has been reported that the Swedish approach has proven satisfactory to many, both in the scientific and in the animal welfare communities. The "Swedish experiment" suggests that it is possible to develop a framework that is practical and financially sound, a framework which, though not a panacea, does go some way toward protecting the interests of animals while at the same time nurturing our interest in the growth and maintenance of science.

Two final points. First, nothing that we have said should be taken as condemning the motives, intentions or character of those engaged in scientific research. We are not saying that these people are nasty, vicious, cruel, dehumanized, heartless, depraved, pitiless, evil people. No one who uses animals in science has been accused of being, in White's terminology, a "monster-scientist, perpetrator of abominable crimes."[47] Neither are we saying that "all scientists" are on an ego-trip, motivated to do their work only to pump out another publication, to be used to secure yet another grant, to be parlayed into yet a bigger name, yet another promotion, yet another raise, and so forth and so forth. These accusations may have powerful rhetorical force in some quarters, but they have no place, and have found none, here, in a reflective assessment of the ethics of the use of animals in science. Our concern throughout has been to assess the ethics of *what* scientists do, not *why* they do it. The point that must be recognized is that people can do what is wrong even though they have the best motives, the best intentions, even though they are "the nicest people." The question of the moral status of animal use in science thus is not to be decided by discovering the motives or intentions of those who do it *or* of those who criticize it. The sooner all the parties to the debate realize this, the better.[48]

Lastly, there is the idea of alternatives again. The search for alternatives to using animals in science is only in its infancy. Many scientists tend to scorn the idea and to believe that the number and utility of alternatives are very limited. One would have thought that recent developments would have put this attitude to rest. To cite just one encouraging example, a promising new bacterial test for carcinogens has been developed by Professor Bruce Ames at the University of California. Whereas animal tests for carcinogenicity typically take two to three years and cost in excess of $150,000, the Ames test takes two to three days, uses no animals, and costs just a few hundred dollars.[49] Ames himself stops short of claiming that his test is 100% accurate, and he does not rule out the present need to use animals as an ancillary part of research into carcinogens. Yet his test does much to suggest the potential benefits to be realized from the search for alternatives, both in terms of the savings in animal pain and in dollars and cents. Those skeptical of "alternatives" ("impossible" it may be said) may hold their ground, but we should not be discouraged. Yesterday's "impossibilities" are today's commonplaces. We must press on despite the skeptics, acting to insure that adequate funds become available to those qualified to search for alternatives. The call to intensify the search is not "antiscientific." In fact, it is just the opposite. It is a call to scientists to use their skill, knowledge and ingenuity to progress toward our common aspirations: a more humane approach to the practice of science. It is a call to *do* science, not to abandon it. The commitment to search for alternatives should be viewed as an index both of our moral *and* our scientific progress.[50]

NOTES

1. For documentation and additional information see J. Diner, *Physical and Mental Suffering of Experimental Animals* (Washington: Animal Welfare Institute, 1979), and R. Ryder, *Victims of Science* (London: Davis-Poynter, 1975).

3. As quoted in L. Rosenfield, *From Animal Machine to Beast Machine* (New York: Octagon Books, 1968) p. 54.

4. These views are discussed more fully in Tom Regan, "The Moral Basis of Vegetarianism," *Canadian Journal of Philosophy* (1975), pp. 181–214. Reprinted in Tom Regan, *All That Dwell Therein: Animal Rights and Environmental Ethics* (Berkeley: University of California Press, 1982).

5. Richard Ryder was the first to argue in this way in *op.cit.*

7. In January 1981 Revlon, Inc. the world's largest cosmetics' manufacturer, announced that it had awarded Rockefeller University $750,000 to research and develop an alternative to the Draize test. The company also granted $25,000 to establish a trust, the purpose of which is to fund further research into alternatives. Thus other cosmetic companies can join Revlon's pioneering move—(this is the first time a commercial firm has funded the search for alternatives to the use of live animals for testing)—by the simple expedient of contributing to the trust. The political realities being what they are, chances are good that Revlon's efforts will soon be imitated by other firms in the cosmetics' industry. Revlon's actions were prompted by an uncommonly well organized campaign, involving more than four hundred separate animal welfare related organizations, conducted over a two year period.

Through meetings with representatives of Revlon, through the media, through petitions to the Congress, through letter writing campaigns, and through protest marches and rallies, the Coalition to Stop the Draize Rabbit Blinding Tests, Inc. helped to persuade Revlon to take its revolutionary step. The Coalition's success gives a clear demonstration of what can be done on behalf of animals and what must be done to succeed. When the money required to seek alternatives is on hand, there will be no lack of persons willing to do it.

8. M. Weil and R. Scala, "A study of Intra-and Inter-Laboratory Variability in the Results of Rabbit Eye and Skin and Irritations Tests," *Toxicology and Applied Pharmacology* 19 (1971), pp. 271–360.

9. Dr. Feinberg made this claim while serving on a panel discussion on animal experimentation, sponsored by the Anti-Cruelty Society of Chicago, in October 1980.

10. Some of these issues are explored in a rather extreme way in S. Epstein, *The Politics of Cancer* (Garden City: Anchor Press/Doubleday, 1979).

11. *British Medical Journal*, October 28, 1972, p. 190. We have taken this example as well as several others from Deborah Mayo's unpublished papers, "Against a Scientific Justification of Animal Experiments."

12. Recently even many scientists have become concerned about the possibilities inherent in certain kinds of research. The interested reader should see the essays collected in the following volumes: G. Holton and R. Morison (eds.), *Limits of Scientific Inquiry* (New York: W.W. Norton and Co., 1978); K. Wulff (ed.), *Regulation of Scientific Inquiry: Social Concerns with Research*, American Association for the Advancement of Science Selected Symposium no. 37 (Boulder, CO: Westview Press, 1979); J. Richards (ed.), *Recombinant DNA: Science, Ethics and Politics* (New York: Academic Press, 1978); and D. Jackson and S. Stich (ed.), *The Recombinant DNA Debate* (Englewood Cliffs, NJ: Prentice-Hall 1979).

13. Baruch Brody is apparently one such philosopher. See his *Abortion and the Sanctity of Life: A Philosophical View* (Cambridge: The MIT Press, 1974).

14. The example is given by the contemporary American philosopher, Richard Brandt in his essay "A Moral Principle About Killing," in Marvin Kohl, ed., *Beneficent Euthanasia* (Buffalo: Prometheus Books, 1972). The philosophical propriety of using more or less unusual hypothetical examples in assessing moral principles is critically discussed by the contemporary English philosopher G.E.M. Anscombe

in her "Modern Moral Philosophy," *Philosophy*, 33 (1958), reprinted in Judith J. Thomson and Gerald Dworkin, eds., *Ethics* (New York: Harper & Row, 1968).

15. MIP would probably have to be reformulated to account for a range of cases (e.g., "innocent threats") with which we are not primarily concerned in this paper. Insane persons can kill just as surely as sane ones and though they are innocent, morality surely allows us to defend ourselves against their threatening attacks.

16. Here we develop an example introduced by Robert Nozick in Chapter 3 of his *Anarchy, State and Utopia* (New York: Basic Books, 1979).

17. The possibility that certain species of animals have a morality of their own, based on mutual sympathy, is explored and defended by James Rachels in "Do Animals Have a Right to Liberty?", Tom Regan and Peter Singer, eds., *Animal Rights and Human Obligations* (Englewood Cliffs: Prentice-Hall, 1976).

19. For a fuller discussion of these issues, see Heather McGiffin and Nancie Brownley, eds., *Animals in Education: The Use of Animals in High School Biology Classes and Science Fairs* (Washington: Institute for the Study of Animal Problems, 1980).

20. The results have not been published in a professional journal. But see the reports published in the Vancouver, B.C. newspapers (*The Province and the Vancouver Sun*) on March 28, 1980 and April 8, 1980. This case and the relevant documentation were brought to our attention by David Rinehart of the *Greenpeace Examiner*.

21. See again, the works by Diner and Ryder referred to in Footnote 1, as well as Peter Singer, *Animal Liberation* (New York: Avon Books, 1975).

24. These methods are reviewed in, for example, Rowan, *op. cit.*, and Ryder, *op. cit.*

25. For a critical assessment of the use made of animals in psychological research, see Alan Bowd, "Ethical Reservations About Psychological Research with Animals," *The Psychological Record*.

26. See "A Select Bibliography on Animal Rights and Human Obligations," *Inquiry*, Vol. Nos. 1–2, 1978.

27. For example, R.M. Hare in "Ethical Theory and Utilitarianism," in H.D. Lewis (ed.), *Contemporary British Philosophy* 4 (London: Allen and Unwin, 1976); and P. Singer, *Practical Ethics* (Cambridge: Cambridge University Press, 1980).

28. Jeremy Bentham, *The Principles of Moral and Legislation* (1789) Chapter 17, Section 1; reprinted in T. Regan and P. Singer (eds.), *Animal Rights and Human Obligations, op. cit.*

29. S. Rosenthal and R. Milliean, *Pharmacological Review* 6 (1954), p. 489. See also Peter Singer, *Animal Liberation, op. cit.*

37. J. Cairns, *Cancer: Science and Society* (San Francisco: W.H. Freeman and Co., 1978).

38. *Ibid.*, p. 7.

39. On chimpanzees, see G. Gallup, "Self-Recognition in Primates," *American Psychologist* 32 (1977), 329–338.

40. On Cetaceans, see the essays collected in K. Norris (ed.), *Whales, Dolphins, and Porpoises* (Berkeley: University of California Press, 1966) and J. McIntyre (ed.), *Mind in the Waters* (New York: Charles Scribner's Son, 1974).

44. These federal regulations are part of the Animal Welfare Act. The physical facilities in which animals used in science are housed and the attention given to some of their basic needs (food, water) have improved as a result of these regulations. Not all animals are covered by the Act, however, rats and mice being notable exceptions; and the regulations apply to, and thus are enforceable only in the case of, federally supported programs.

45. R.J. White, "Antivivisection: the Reluctant Hydra," *The American Scholar*, vol. 40, no. 3 (Summer 1971); reprinted in Tom Regan and Peter Singer (eds.), *Animal Rights and Human Obligations, op. cit.*

46. For a discussion of the Swedish experiment, see M. Ross, "The Ethics of Animal Experimentation: Control in Practice," *Australian Psychologist* 13 (1978).

47. *op. cit.*, p. 166.

48. Some of these matters are discussed in Tom Regan, "Cruelty, Kindness, and Unnecessary Suffering," *op. cit.*

49. See "Bacterial Tests for Potential Carcinogens," *Scientific American* 241 (1979).

50. We wish to thank Barbara Orlans and Andrew Rowan for helpful comments on an earlier draft of this essay. Professor Jamieson's work on this project was assisted by a grant from the University Awards Committee of the State University of New York, while Professor Regan's was assisted by a grant from the National Endowment for the Humanities. It is a pleasure to express our gratitude in a public way to these respective agencies.

Genetic Research

The National Institutes of Health (NIH) and the Department of Energy (DOE) joined forces in 1989 to support an unprecedented scientific effort to reveal the entire human genetic code. If successful, the Human Genome Project will provide geneticists with a fundamental resource for understanding all phases of human development and a powerful weapon for combating human genetic disorder.

The vision of advanced scientific knowledge combined with the prospect of practical social benefit helps to explain, in this era of fiscal restraint, the willingness of members of the NIH and DOE to support a program estimated to cost more than three billion dollars and projected to take 15 years to complete. But can we truly afford this undertaking? The issue is not whether the effort will draw away resources from other scientific programs. Rather, do we want to know what the Human Genome Project promises to reveal?

Biomedical research thus far has proven very successful. Twentieth-century medicine has progressed in understanding and alleviating many bacterial and viral diseases—syphilis, poliomyelitis. Smallpox has been eradicated. So, too, genetic research promises to control and perhaps eliminate a host of painful and debilitating disorders, including sickle cell anemia, Tay-Sachs disease, Lesch-Nyhan disease, and Huntington's chorea. Why should genetic research prove less beneficial than research of the past?

Part of the problem, as W. French Anderson suggests in the final paper of this section, is that biomedical genetic technology may be used not only for therapeutic purposes but also for "enhancement engineering" and eugenics. Genetic

303

information may be used to alter physical traits such as height, or to bring about even more profound changes in personality, intelligence, and character. Do we know enough to decide, for example, if docility is better than aggressiveness or if submissiveness is more desirable than rebelliousness? We are the product of an evolutionary process. Can we improve upon what has taken many generations to create? Developing a new approach to disease is one thing; playing God is something else. This is one reason Anderson states, "We simply should not meddle in areas where we are so ignorant."

However, personality, unlike hemophilia, is likely to be associated with many genes. The complexities are likely to elude complete understanding for a long time. The immediate prospect of successful eugenic engineering, as Anderson points out, is unrealistic. But then it seems equally unrealistic to be concerned about playing God. Perhaps when geneticists discover the conditions that underlie submissiveness and rebelliousness, moralists will have discovered which is more desirable.

But the problem of eugenic engineering runs deeper still. Moral reasoning, like other modes of human activity, has an underlying genetic component. A common genetic core among different people may be necessary for the possibility of successful moral dialogue. What would happen if eugenic manipulation resulted in greater variation of those genes responsible for rational discourse? According to Stephen P. Stich, "human genetic engineering threatens to undermine the foundations of rational ethical dialogue by fragmenting our common nature along social and ideological lines."

Perhaps we should put the brakes on genetic research. Stich thinks the opposite, that more, not less, research is needed. He suggests that an independent body of scientists, ethicists, religious leaders, educators, and lay people should study the issues and help to ensure that decisions that might affect our genetic future will be informed.

But education alone is not enough. Companies today are developing gene-splicing techniques aimed at improving food— a tomato with a flounder gene, for example, that improves the vegetable's resistance to frost. The U.S. government does not require special testing or labeling of all foods produced in this way. Consequently, there might be health risks of which we are unaware. Producers reassure us that the new "sci-fi" foods are as safe and beneficial as were frozen foods when they were first introduced in the 1930s. But many people are troubled by reports of the adverse effects of food additives and special food processing and feel that the rights of entrepreneurs, even in an otherwise free market, should be curtailed to protect the public health.

If we are concerned about genetically altered tomatoes, how much more concerned should we be about genetically altered human beings? What would happen, for example, if parents could choose the gender of their offspring? Some people believe that the result would be a catastrophic sex-ratio imbalance. Moreover, the ability to choose the race, or racial characteristics, of one's children might aggravate the rising problem of race relations.

The issue is not just a matter of assessing public harm, but also one of addressing the deeper conflict between individual rights and the common interest. Just as a producer's right to market a new product may be curtailed in order to protect the public health, so parental rights may be overridden, for example, in order to eliminate the gene for Huntington's chorea. As Robert Wachbroit says, "When the public health is at stake, individual rights are seen as luxuries."

However, sex and race are not matters of public health. Should parental decisions be regulated in these cases as well? We could create a central planning committee to determine the genetic makeup of future generations. But economic central planning, especially in countries of central and eastern Europe, has proven to be unsuccessful. Genetic central planning is not likely to prove any better.

One alternative would be a laissez-faire approach, affording parents maximum freedom to design genetically whatever offspring they want. But parents are not always permitted free reign in making decisions that affect the lives of their children. Courts of law, for example, overrule Jehovah's Witnesses who refuse their children a blood transfusion. If parental authority can be restricted in matters other than genetics, then perhaps it should be curtailed in genetics as well.

Peter Singer and Deane Wells propose, as a way of reconciling individual rights with the public good, a government body with powers limited only to veto parental requests that would harm individuals. Parents would otherwise be free to make decisions that would benefit their children.

The proposed reconciliation, however, might not work. If members of the Singer-Wells committee veto only harmful proposals, the rights of individuals would be protected. But how can we be sure that committee members would veto only harmful proposals? Former Soviet economic planners vetoed many beneficial economic proposals, which is one reason why the Soviet system collapsed. Genetic planners are likely to make similar mistakes. When they do, the rights of individuals will be violated.

It might be suggested that individuals do not lose the right to decide just because a government agency mistakenly prevents them from exercising that right. But if individuals have the right to make decisions independent of government agency, what need is there for government agency? Perhaps parents should be free to decide what they will. But this brings us back to the laissez-faire approach, which we already dismissed.

How can the apparent conflict between individual rights and public interest be resolved? The issue is not new. But the prospect of altering human nature through genetic engineering makes the question particularly compelling. It is apparent, however, especially with the Genome Project now underway, that science is not about to wait for an answer.

Genetic Engineering

Peter Singer and Deane Wells

Genetic engineering is a loose term. Some use it to mean any kind of deliberate tinkering with the human gene pool. So defined, it includes eugenics schemes that go back as far as Plato, whose ideal republic would have encouraged "union between the better specimens of both sexes" while limiting the reproduction of the less desirable types. This form of genetic engineering needs no new technology at all. At the other end of the spectrum there are the latest techniques of manufacturing recombinant DNA and splicing genes to produce entirely new forms of life. We shall describe these techniques later in this chapter.

In between these extremes lie various methods of genetic selection using modern techniques that are less far-reaching than gene splicing. For instance, prenatal diagnosis is now being widely used to detect genetic abnormalities during pregnancy. An abortion is performed if the test shows an abnormal fetus. This will have an effect on the genetic inheritance of future generations; but the main effect will be to restore the process of natural selection that used to operate before modern medicine found the means to save the lives of many genetically abnormal children.

The next step may be the use of IVF [in vitro fertilization] combined with cloning by cell division at the two-cell stage so that one embryo of a genetically identical pair can be examined. An embryo discovered to be defective would be rejected, a normal embryo would be transferred to the womb. With artificial stimulation to produce several embryos, this procedure could easily be taken a step further. Each embryo would be divided, and one of each pair examined. As our ability to "read" the genetic constitutions of the embryo improves, the basis on which parents would be able to select the embryo they would most like to develop into their child will increase. Ultimately this method could be used not just to avoid genetic defects but to select the positive genetic characteristics wanted by the parents.

We shall be more concerned with new methods of manipulating genes than with old-fashioned eugenics—although some of the old issues reemerge with the new technology.

The ability to manipulate genes is not itself a consequence of IVF or any other developments in human reproduction. Splicing bacteria to create new life forms that will devour oil spills; engineering plants that can surpass all existing cereals in the efficiency with which they convert sunlight to nourishment for humans; producing cattle that grow rapidly to twice the normal size—that these things are coming closer has no direct connection with IVF. What IVF has done, however, is to open the way to applying these techniques to human beings; and that, for many people, is the most frightening prospect of all.

Creating new forms of life has traditionally been the prerogative of gods. The dream of discovering this secret is an old one—but so is the thought that this dream could turn into a nightmare. In sixteenth-century Prague, the renowned Rabbi Loew was said to have taken a handful of dust and created a gigantic monster called a golem, which roamed the streets bringing vengeance to those who persecuted the Jews. Early in the nineteenth century, Mary Wollstonecraft Shelley captured the public imagination with a novel that told the tragic tale of Victor Frankenstein, a young scientist who discovered how to create life but unwittingly made a half-human monster. The monster killed all Frankenstein's nearest and dearest and finally drove him to his death in a state of half-mad despair. The moral of the story is made explicit by Frankenstein's response to the ship's captain who serves as narrator of the novel. Frankenstein, now near death, has given the captain a full account of his life, except for one crucial detail:

> Sometimes I endeavoured to gain from Frankenstein the
> particulars of his creature's formation: but on this point he
> was impenetrable. "Are you mad, my friend?" said he; "or
> whither does your senseless curiosity lead you? Would
> you also create for yourself and the world a demoniacal
> enemy? Peace, Peace! learn my miseries, and do not seek
> to increase your own."

Leading scientists now echo the words written by Mary Shelley.
Erwin Chargaff, a biologist who did pioneering work in the
understanding of DNA, has, like Frankenstein, been critical of
following "curiosity" wherever it may take us:

> Have we the right to counteract, irreversibly, the
> evolutionary wisdom of millions of years, in order to
> satisfy the curiosity of a few scientists? The future will
> curse us for it.

Robert Sinsheimer, chairman of the Department of Biology at the
California Institute of Technology and once an advocate of
genetic engineering, also seems to share Victor Frankenstein's
view when he asks:

> Do we want to assume the basic responsibility for life on
> this planet—to develop new living forms for our own
> purposes? Shall we take into our hands our own future
> evolution? . . . Perverse as it may, initially, seem to the
> scientist, we must face the fact that there can be unwanted
> knowledge.

In keeping with the lesson of *Frankenstein*, most people
have grave reservations about scientists dabbling with new
forms of life. A survey carried out in 1980 by the United States
National Science Foundation showed that while most Americans
did not think there should be restrictions on scientific research,
"a notable exception was the opposition to scientists creating
new life forms." Almost two-thirds of those questioned thought
that studies in this area should not be pursued.

Yet there is a different point of view. If the creation of new
forms of life seems a godlike power, what more noble goal can
humanity have than to aspire to it? Like Prometheus, the
mythical Greek hero who defied the gods and stole from them
the secret of fire, should we not challenge the gods and make

their powers our own? Or to put it in more scientific terms, should we allow ourselves to remain at the mercy of genetic accident and blind evolution when we have before us the prospect of acquiring supremacy over the very forces that have created us?

The Ethical Issues

We now turn to the ethical issues raised by modern genetic engineering techniques. What we say will, unless the context rules it out, apply not only to gene splicing, but also to embryo typing and selection, or any other method that can achieve the same results.

The Safety Debate

The first expressions of alarm about research on recombinant DNA had nothing to do with the use of the technique in humans, or indeed with any deliberate application of it. The fear was that bacteria genetically modified for experimental purposes might escape from the laboratory and wreak havoc among living creatures who would have no resistance to it. The danger seemed real enough in 1974 for scientists to accept a self-imposed moratorium on work on recombinant DNA. The United States Government then set up a Recombinant DNA Advisory Committee, which allowed research to go ahead under strict guidelines.

The committee is still in existence, although the guidelines have been relaxed. The general consensus of current scientific opinion is that the original fears were exaggerated. "Crippled" strains of bacteria are now being used, designed to be unable to survive outside the special environment of the laboratory. Careful checks of laboratory workers have failed to reveal infection by the new organisms. No doubt there is still a need for caution and for continued monitoring of this type of research; but opposition to it continuing at all appears to have ceased.

Quite separate from the issue of safety of research into recombinant DNA are questions about the desirabilty of such research, assuming that it can be carried out safely.

Playing God

When the President's Commission for the Study of Ethical Problems in Medicine and Biomedical and Behavioral Research began to examine genetic engineering, it did so at the request of three religious leaders: the General Secretaries of the National Council of Churches, the Synagogue Council of America, and the United States Catholic Conference. In a joint letter, the three general secretaries warned that once genetic engineering was technically possible, "those who would play God will be tempted as never before."

The president's commission asked the three religious leaders to elaborate on any specifically religious objections to gene splicing in humans. They in turn appointed theologians to address the commission. The outcome, as reported by the commission, was hardly what one would have expected from the general secretaries' warnings about "playing God."

> In the view of the theologians, contemporary developments in molecular biology raise issues of responsibility rather than being matters to be prohibited because they usurp powers that human beings should not possess. The Biblical religions teach that human beings are, in some sense, co-creators with the Supreme Creator. Thus, as interpreted for the Commission by their representatives, these major religious faiths respect and encourage the enhancement of knowledge about nature, as well as responsible use of that knowledge. Endorsement of genetic engineering, which is praised for its potential to improve the human estate, is linked with the recognition that the misuse of human freedom creates evil and human knowledge and power can result in harm.

So even from a religious point of view, genetic engineering is not to be rejected outright. It may be used "to improve the human estate."

Rejecting the Wisdom of Evolution

Humans have been interfering with evolutionary process for a long time—ever since they began to breed better cereals or domestic animals. Even breaching the barriers between species is not new: since ancient times horses and donkeys have been crossed to produce mules. True, mules are almost always sterile while gene splicing might lead to new creatures that are not; but all this shows, once again, the need for great caution. It would be one thing to engineer a new species and another to release it upon the world.

Most genetically defective humans used to die in infancy. That may be regarded as the cruel wisdom of evolution. We interfere with this process when we use the latest medical technology to keep defective babies alive. Even treating diabetics with insulin or prescribing spectacles for the short-sighted prevents natural selection from reducing the prevalence of these conditions. Indeed, the entire system of social welfare that now exists in most developed countries is a huge interference with evolution: without it, the children of the poor would be less likely to survive and reproduce. Few people think this a sufficient reason for ending state assistance to the un-employed, single parents, orphans, and the disabled.

All this suggests that there is nothing sacred about the process of evolution. Evolution is not, after all, really wise. The application of such terms to the blind process of natural selection can only be a metaphor, and we should be careful not to be misled by it. Evolution does not minimize suffering. It cannot be relied upon to preserve the existence of our species or any other species. Humans can be wise or foolish: evolution can be neither.

When we first grasp the fact that the course of evolution is utterly indifferent to the well-being or ultimate fate of our species, we may leap to the conclusion that it is easy for us to use our intelligence to improve upon evolution. Perhaps we can; but it is unlikely to prove as straightforward as we first imagine. We should recall the early European settlers in Australia, who thought it would be easy to improve upon the natural environment by bringing over a few rabbits to add variety to the fauna and some blackberries to provide food in the bush. We have now learnt, at immense cost, that the interrelatedness of our ecology makes it impossible to do just one thing—everything has an effect on something else. So, too, when we try to improve upon evolution, we may find that for some quite unexpected reason we have only made matters worse.

This is not an argument for prohibiting genetic engineering, but rather for putting a large warning label on it and taking steps to ensure that the warning is heeded. We need to think about how genetic engineering might properly be used and how it is to be controlled.

Therapeutics or Eugenics?

We can distinguish two major purposes for genetic engineering in humans: to remove defects not present in normal members of the species (therapeutic genetic engineering); and to produce individuals with more desirable qualities than would be the case with normal reproduction (eugenic genetic engineering). Admittedly, the distinction is not clear-cut. We can all agree that sickle-cell anemia is a genetic defect; but what about genetic factors that merely increase the probability of, say, suffering from heart disease later in life? Genetic "markers" that indicate such predispositions are now being discovered, and it seems that there are hundreds of them, covering a wide variety of diseases. Suppose that genetic engineering reached the point at which they could all be eliminated, thereby raising the expected life span of the "corrected" individual from seventy-five years to ninety-five. Or what if the cause of aging were discovered and could be interfered with in such a way that youthful life, free of the diseases of degeneration, was possible indefinitely? Would this be therapeutic or eugenic engineering?

Is this question merely semantic, or does some moral weight hang on the answer? Is therapeutic genetic engineering in a different moral category from eugenic? Many people believe it is. Remedying defects is at the core of medicine. Hence one may conclude that, as the president's commission put it, "the ethical and policy issues do not seem appreciably different from those involved in the development of any new diagnostic or therapeutic techniques." There is no dispute about the initial judgment that, say, sickle-cell anemia is a bad thing. If modern medicine can get rid of it, that will be good, just as getting rid of polio and smallpox was good. To get started on eugenic engineering, however, we need to decide which characteristics it is good to have to a higher than normal degree—intelligence? physical strength? altruism? drive? competitiveness? sensitivity of feeling? physical beauty? emotional toughness? The medical model is no help to us in sorting out these characteristics; hence we can agree on eliminating defects much more easily than we can agree on a moral basis for enhancing someone's genetic constitution above what would normally be expected.

There is some truth in this; but our example of the longer life span that might be achievable by eliminating a range of genetic predispositions indicates that the picture is more complicated. To have twice the normal chance of a heart attack before the age of fifty is, we can all agree, a defect. The same can be said for a quadrupled risk of bladder cancer or a 50 percent greater chance of diabetes. Taken in itself, each predisposition is an abnormality. On the other hand, to have no such predispositions at all is abnormal too—highly desirable as it may be. So while one might regard genetic engineering aimed at raising the expected life span to ninety-five as an attempt at improving things beyond what is normal for our species, and thus as a form of eugenic engineering, this result might come about from eliminating a host of separate conditions. If we were to eliminate each of these conditions separately, we would clearly be doing therapeutic engineering.

Whatever we call it, this form of genetic engineering can be justified on the same basis as cases that are indisputably therapeutic. It does not matter whether the outcome is a life that is or is not better than the statistical norm; the essential element is that no one disputes that, other things being equal, it is better to live longer, in good health, than to die earlier. The acceptability of genetic engineering depends not on whether it falls under the label "therapeutic" rather than "eugenic," but on the ends toward which the engineering is directed. When the goal is something that would indisputably improve the human condition, safe and successful genetic engineering would be a good thing.

Again, however, there is a complication that should lead us to be cautious. Often the gene that predisposes to a disease also has some other, more attractive consequence—otherwise it would have been rapidly eliminated by natural selection. The gene for sickle-cell anemia, for instance, is believed to confer greater immunity to malaria on those who are carriers. Hence carriers of this recessive gene are at an advantage in malaria-prone areas. This particular benefit has lost its value where malaria has been cleared up or can be controlled by tablets. No one is going to oppose eliminating the disease on the grounds that this will also eliminate the benefit. But what are the benefits of other, less disastrous genetic traits? If a certain type of genetic constitution is linked with a doubled chance of a heart attack but is also associated with drive and ambition, is the benefit worth the risk? Is it possible that after eliminating all genetically based above-average risks to health, we would find that we had inadvertently eliminated the characteristics that distinguish many of the most valued members of our species?

This difficulty illustrates two crucial points. The first is simply the need to proceed slowly and cautiously under the watchful eye of an expert committee that can build up a body of information on the long-term outcome of individual attempts at genetic engineering. We shall say more about the need for this kind of committee shortly.

The second point is that, in seeking agreement on the goals to which genetic engineering should be directed, we must take into account possible costs as well as anticipated gains. There are two kinds of cases in which people will disagree about the net benefits of an attempt at genetic engineering. One is the case in which people disagree over the intrinsic desirability of the goal: is it good to have more people with IQs above 150? The other is the case in which an undisputed benefit, like a lowered risk of heart attack, must be balanced against what some see as a cost, like reduced drive. Since the two cases raise similar issues, we shall discuss only the former but our conclusions will be applicable to the latter type of case as well.

Goals and Controls

It would be well to pause here and recognize that what we are talking about is different only in degree, and not in kind, from the human behavior with which we are all familiar. The genetic constitution of our population is determined by human choices to a far greater extent than we like to admit. Whenever people choose one marriage partner rather than another, they affect the gene pool of the future. It would be foolish to deny that tall people often choose other tall people, particularly attractive people often choose others similarly fortunately endowed, sporting people often choose other sporting people, artistic people often choose other artistic people and so on. Sometimes we seek genetic consequences quite deliberately: when we make these choices of marriage partners we often have, decently interred at the back of our minds, the thought that a person with certain characteristics would make a good mother, or father, for our children. But even if this is the last thing in our minds when we choose our spouse, our choices will nevertheless determine the genetic constitution of the next generation.

What is new is the extent of the intervention that genetic engineering will make possible. The genetic lottery, which individuals have deliberately influenced since time began, will become a much less risky game of chance. To a far greater extent than ever before, the procreating generation will be able to determine the constitution of its successors. The question is? who should decide the genetic constitution of the next generation?

There is a central planning approach and a *laissez-faire* approach to handling disagreement over the desirability of a particular form of genetic engineering. The centralized approach would have the government, presumably acting through some expert committee, make the decisions. If the government considered high intelligence desirable, prospective parents would be offered the opportunity to have their embryos treated so as to raise the intelligence of the resulting child.

The government would, no doubt, find it difficult to get consensus on the qualities to be considered desirable, and that is one strong objection to this approach. A still more powerful reason against it, however, is that it puts a frightening amount of power into government hands.

To avoid this, one could take a "free-market" approach. Couples would make their own choices about the genetic constitution of their children. The problem of obtaining agreement about what is desirable is thus overcome, for agreement is unnecessary. All we need is tolerance of other people's choices for their own offspring. Individual freedom would be maximized, the state kept out, and the opportunities for misguided bureaucratic planning, or for something still more sinister, eliminated.

Neither the free-market approach nor the central planning approach seems to us particularly satisfactory. The latter is far too much like Brave New World. Citizens should choose the constitution of their government; governments should not choose the constitutions of their citizens.

The free-market approach is unsatisfactory for a different reason. It puts too much power in the hands of individuals who might use it irresponsibly or even pathologically. It is hard to imagine any parent using genetic engineering to produce a bodyguard of mindless clones, but it is just possible to imagine the sort of parents who might want to genetically engineer a nice, uniform football team.

We don't need to multiply instances to illustrate this point. There is, however, one aspect of individual choice in a competitive society that is worth noticing. If there is pressure on individuals to compete for status and material rewards, the qualities that give children a winning edge in this competition are not necessarily going to be the most socially desirable. For instance, above-average drive and ambition might make a child more likely to succeed—but too much striving for individual success will not make for a harmonious and cooperative society. Now consider the logic of leaving to individuals the choice of the type of children they will have. Suppose that genetic engineering has advanced to the stage at which we could significantly increase the drive and ambition of our children. Then any parents who wished their children to achieve high status and earnings would do well to make use of genetic engineering to produce an above-average level of drive and ambition. If many parents were to have such desires for their children, however, and to take the course that would give their children the best prospects of making it to the top, the result would simply be an increase in the average level of drive and ambition. Since this increase could do nothing to increase the number of winners— by definition, only a few can make it to the top—the result could only be greater frustration all round. So parents might try to engineer an even *greater* increase in drive and ambition for *their* children, thus leading to an upward spiral in these characteristics that would be difficult to reverse. For although the increased emphasis on personal success might so reduce public-mindedness as to endanger the very existence of society as a communal enterprise, no parents could withdraw from this damaging spiral without condemning their own children to the lower ranks of the society. It would not be within the power of individuals to stop the accelerating rush to a society of supremely ambitious individualists. Such is the logic of rational self-interest—or family interest—in a free-market situation.

Those still skeptical about the desirability of any state interference with individual choice in this area should remember that we are talking now of decisions that will (to a much greater degree than contemporary human procreation decisions) alter the public human environment. It is generally acknowledged that a society has the right to exclude certain types of people by the use of immigration laws. Some criteria of selection we do consider wrong—race is the obvious example—but selection on the basis of needed skills or exclusion because of known criminal associations is not considered objectionable If a society is justified in thus selecting those who will become its members, surely it is also justified in excluding certain types of people that its own members are proposing to create.

Our suggestion therefore is this: the genetic endowment of children should be in the same hands it has always been in—the hands of parents. But parents who wished to use genetic engineering to bring about a characteristic that had not previously been sanctioned by the society through its government should have to apply for permission. The public should know what such adventurous parents are proposing to do and should equally have the right to say "no."

The machinery for such a system would not be too hard to devise. A broadly based government body could be set up to approve or reject particular parents' proposals for genetic engineering. It would consider whether the proposed piece of engineering would, if its practice became widespread, have harmful effects on individuals or society. If no harmful effects could be foreseen, the committee would license the procedure. This would mean that parents who wished to use it were free to do so. The committee would keep track of how many people were using each licensed procedure and with what results. It could always withdraw a license if unexpected harmful results emerged. Because the committee would need to agree only on the absence of harm, its deliberations would not be as difficult as they would be if agreement on positive benefit were required—though they would still be difficult enough.

The selective cloning of people with special abilities . . . could be handled in the same manner. In addition to keeping an eye on the problems of adjustment of the cloned individuals, the committee would also place strict limits on the number of clones that could be made from any one person and on the extent of cloning in general. Thus a potentially harmful reduction of the diversity of the human gene pool could be avoided.

What concrete decisions might such a committee make about the genetic engineering procedures it licensed and the individuals from whom cloning would be sanctioned? Presumably it would license proposals to increase intelligence (but cautiously, by small steps) and refuse to license proposals, if there were any, to diminish it. Presumably it would favor proposals that promoted the health of the future member of the society and reject any that put it at risk. It might refuse to allow genetic engineering that would determine even for some positive characteristic (such as physical strength) if it were thought to be associated with some negative characteristic (such as propensity to heart attack). If it happened that scientists found genes associated with altruism or malice, it might license proposals to determine for the former but not the latter. But what it should never do is make positive directions as to what should be done. It should confine itself to exercising the power of veto. In our view, choosing the positive content of the gene pool should remain the preserve of those who have always done it up until now—the parents.

The Genetic Adventure

Stephen P. Stich

Humankind is embarked on an extraordinary adventure, an adventure promising rewards that could barely have been imagined as recently as a generation ago. But human genetic engineering poses moral and social dilemmas every bit as daunting as the rewards are enticing.

It seems clear that in the decades ahead research yielding knowledge relevant to human genetic engineering will continue and accelerate. What is more, I think the acceleration of research in this area is to be welcomed. The medical, industrial, and agricultural applications of genetic engineering research will transform our society in ways even more profound than the computer revolution now well under way. I am enough of an optimist to believe most of these changes will be for the good. However, as we learn more about the mechanisms of human genetics, it is also inevitable that we will start learning how to manipulate the human genome to suit our tastes, or what we perceive to be our needs, in domains far removed from those that traditionally have been the concern of medicine.

At first this ability will be restricted to characteristics under the control of a single gene or a small number of genes. But as our knowledge progresses, we will learn more and more about how to manipulate those characteristics of beings—both physical and mental—under the control of many separate genes. In our current state of knowledge we simply do not know the extent to which aspects of intelligence and personality are under genetic control and thus susceptible to genetic manipulation. But

321

as I read the evidence we now have, there is every reason to think that a substantial component of our mental and moral lives is influenced by our genetic endowment. It would be remarkable indeed if we did not all come genetically equipped with mental strengths and weaknesses just as we come equipped with innate physical strengths and limitations.

As our ability to manipulate the genetic composition of our own offspring grows in sophistication in the decades ahead, the social pressures to use this new technology will become intense. During the last decade we have seen an explosion of interest in home microcomputers; many of the people who buy these wonderful, expensive machines do so in the hope they will give their children a competitive edge in a technologically competitive world. Closer to the fringes of our society we have seen that some women are prepared to have themselves impregnated with the sperm of a Nobel Prize winner in the hope of bearing an intellectually gifted child. Both of these phenomena underscore the fact that the desire to help one's children excel is a powerful and widespread motivational force in our society. When, via genetic engineering, we learn how to increase intelligence, memory, longevity, or other traits conveying a competitive advantage, it is clear that there will be no shortage of customers ready to take their place in line. Moreover, those who are unwilling or unable to take advantage of the new technology may find that their offspring have been condemned to a sort of second-class citizenship in a world where what had been within the range of the normal gradually slips into the domain of the subnormal.

Obviously if history unfolds more or less along the lines I have been predicting, plenty of social problems will be generated. Ensuring equitable access to the new technology and protecting the rights of parents and children who have chosen not to utilize the technology are two that come quickly to mind. These issues, however, are variations on a familiar theme. We already have analogous problems with equal access to high-quality education for children. And in the decades ahead we will increasingly have to worry about the technological illiteracy of people from deprived educational backgrounds. I do not mean to suggest these are unimportant concerns—far from it. Still,

I am inclined to think that if problems of equity and discrimination were the only problems human genetic engineering generated, most people would welcome it as an almost unmixed blessing. Given the enormous increase in knowledge required to function in our increasingly technological society, it might well be argued that the capacity to improve our learning and reasoning abilities by genetic engineering had arrived just in the nick of time.

As we gradually map and learn to manipulate the human genome, however, it will become possible to alter or enhance many traits, not merely those, like intelligence and memory capacity, that are generally desirable and convey an obvious competitive advantage. It is a good bet that tastes, character traits, and other aspects of personality have a substantial genetic component. I do not think it is beyond the bounds of realistic possibility that in the next generation or two—and perhaps very much sooner—prospective parents will be able to choose from a library of genes in redesigning their own offspring. Nor is there any reason to suppose that all people or all societies will make the same choices. However, if different societies, or different groups within our own society, make systematically different choices for several generations, we may begin to see the genetic fragmentation of the human species. The divisions that separate cultural groups may come to include genetic differences so profound that members of different groups will no longer be interfertile.

The Western tradition of moral philosophy has left us unprepared to deal with the dilemmas posed by genetic engineering. Consider first the quandaries that arise when we try to think about such central ethical questions as the nature of the good or moral life, against the background of the emerging genetic engineering technology. From Socrates down to the present, just about everyone who has pondered the question of how men and women ought to live their lives has presupposed that human nature is in large measure fixed. Of course, profound disagreements have arisen about what human nature is like. However, the moral issue has always been conceived of as attempting to determine what sort of life a person should lead, given that a human being is a certain type of creature. This tradition leaves us radically unprepared to think about the questions forced on us by the prospect of human genetic engineering. Sometime within the next century, and perhaps much sooner than that, the age-old presumption of a more or less fixed human nature may begin to dissolve. It will no longer suffice to decide what constitutes the good or moral life for the sort of creature we happen to be; we shall also have to decide what sort of creature (or creatures!) humankind ought to *become*.

A worry of a rather different sort arises when we turn our attention to the processes of moral dialogue and the attempt to resolve ethical disputes. The Western philosophical tradition offers many views about the nature of rational moral dialogue and the quest for ethical agreement. But, I think, a common strand runs through just about all theories on this subject. In one way or another the notion of a shared human nature is rung in to explain how it is possible for people to reach a meeting of the minds on moral matters. When we are able to transcend our cultural and ideological differences, and agree on some ethical principle or judgment, it is because, despite our manifest differences, we share our humanity in common. However, human genetic engineering threatens to undermine the foundations of rational ethical dialogue by fragmenting our common nature along social and ideological lines. How shall I reason with a Moslem fundamentalist or a Marxist or a Moonie if what divides him from me is not merely his traditions and his convictions, but also his genetics? The prospect is at once so staggering and so unprecedented that we hardly know how to begin thinking about it.

Many people are inclined to think that the proper course of action is to put on the brakes in an effort to avoid ever reaching the point where these hard choices will have to be made. Many find it deeply distressing that we should even contemplate significant alterations in the human genome. Others worry that the power quite literally to remake our species is a power humankind will not use wisely, and because of this worry, they urge that we take steps now to ensure that this power will not be acquired. I have considerable sympathy with some of the concerns that underlie the recommendation to put on the brakes, though that is not the recommendation I would make.

I think two rather different arguments have led people to think we ought not to acquire the capacity to manipulate the human genome. One of these arguments is theological. God, it is said, designed humans as He wished them to be, and humans alter God's plan at their peril. Now, I am no theologian, but it seems to me this argument should evoke deep skepticism. For even if we grant for the sake of argument that God has a design or plan for the human species, we must take account of the overwhelming weight of evidence indicating He chose to unfold this plan via the mechanisms of evolution and natural selection. Species are not fixed over time, and each of us alive today had distant ancestors who were far more genetically different from us than we are likely to be from any imaginable genetically engineered descendants. The fallacy of the theological argument is to equate the divine plan with the status quo. Since the Renaissance, this sort of argument has been used repeatedly in an effort to oppose technological or social innovations that threatened to have a major impact on the structure of societies and the way people live. None of us, I would venture, are tempted to think that the technological, social, and economic patterns of the late Middle Ages reflected God's plan for how we should live. Nor do we think anything is sacrosanct about the genetic endowment of our Cro-Magnon forebears. I see no more reason to think God's ultimate genetic plan--if He has one—is reflected in the genetic composition of late twentieth-century humankind.

The second argument against acquiring the capacity to manipulate the human genome rests not on a theological premise but on a scientific one. The current constitution of the human gene pool, it is argued, is no accident. We became the sort of creatures we are as the result of millions of years of natural selection. During those millions of years, many genes disappeared from the gene pool because the characteristics they impart to the organism were less adaptive than the surviving alternatives. Thus in a sense the current genetic makeup of humankind stores a great treasury of information about the sort of design that can flourish in our environment. It is folly, this argument concludes, to fiddle with the hard-won "evolutionary wisdom" bequeathed to us in our gene pool.

Now, although I ultimately disagree with this argument, I have considerable sympathy with the central insight it is urging. Human beings—indeed all currently existing species—are highly evolved, extraordinarily complex, and marvelously well-adapted to their natural ecology. We should be very wary indeed about altering components of this system until we have a good understanding of what role the components play in the overall organization of the system. However, it is one thing to suggest we act cautiously, keeping in mind that there are generally good evolutionary reasons for an organism's genome being the way it is. It is quite another thing to suppose natural selection cannot be improved on. To accept that view is to accept the Panglossian assumption that the status quo is the best of all possible worlds. And that assumption is simply not true. A single example may serve to make the point. It now appears that the gene for sickle cell disease survived and flourished because an individual who carries only one such gene is better able to cope with malaria. In an area where malaria is endemic, the sickle cell gene conveys a selective advantage. However, when the swamps are drained and the mosquito population declines, the sickle cell gene is no longer worth having. What this example illustrates is that genes that may have been useful in the environment in which the species evolved may cease to be adaptive when the species finds itself in a new environment. But, of course, the environment in which humankind now exists is radically different from the environment that shaped the genome of our hunter-gatherer forebears. Thus we have every reason to think that the results of natural selection *can* be improved on.

Let me close with some brief observations on the policy implications of these reflections. As I have already indicated, I think it would be a serious mistake to adopt policies aimed at preventing the development of a technology capable of making major modifications in the human genome. However, it is certainly an area that cries out for ongoing, informed monitoring. Thus I endorse with enthusiasm proposals for an independent body, made up of scientists, ethicists, religious leaders, educators, and lay people whose function would not be to regulate but to study issues as they appear on the horizon. However, I am inclined to urge an even stronger role for education in dealing with the challenge of genetic engineering and other new technologies. Unless the public and the political leaders who represent them come to have a better understanding of the basic science underlying these new technologies, we have little hope that our social decisions will be wise ones. This understanding does not come easy, and it will be expensive. But in the long run the distressingly low level of scientific understanding in our society will be more expensive still.

What Is Wrong with Eugenics?

Robert Wachbroit

Eugenics, as traditionally understood, was an effort to improve the human race by applying the wisdom of animal breeders. If people of good quality were to mate with each other and people of bad quality were not to reproduce, the result would be more people of good quality. As Harvard economist Thomas Schelling nicely puts it, traditional eugenics was an effort to select parents. Of course this effort encountered a number of problems. Illusions about what is inheritable and a failure to calculate how slowly gene frequencies would change by this method are two straightforward problems. Above all, one would like to say, eugenics is morally objectionable since any effective method of selecting parents would involve objectionable intrusions in a private matter if not downright coercion. No one questions the horror of the Nazi eugenic programs, so there is no need to belabor the point.

Traditional eugenics was an effort to select parents. Modern eugenics is an effort to select children. Or better yet, to design them. Biotechnology opens up the possibility of directly altering the genetic makeup of our descendants. This is not a mere possibility: The technology is expected to be available within a couple of decades. When that time comes, a child's genetic makeup will no longer be limited to that of his or her parents and the natural lottery. Parents with Huntington's chorea, beta thalassemia, or sickle cell anemia will be able to stop the inheritance of these diseases and have healthy children. But we need not stop there. Short people can have tall descendants, black people can have "white" descendants, and bald people can have hirsute descendants. Is anything wrong with this?

While some of us might think so, articulating that thought is by no means easy. Certainly the problems with traditional eugenics offer no guidance. No one need be coerced. Indeed, eugenics might appear to be just a part of reproductive and parental autonomy. If we do not object to couples deciding when to have children and how many children to have, should we object to their designing their children?

Two Side Worries

In order to focus the discussion, I would like to mention two worries concerning eugenics only to set them to one side. Eugenics, like any medical therapy, involves some risks. Not only might an actual genetic manipulation fail, causing injury to the patient, sterility, or deformed progeny, unsuspected linkage among genes might have undesired consequences. For example, suppose memory capacity were genetically manipulable, but it was sadly discovered that such manipulation resulted in, say, mentally unstable children. Such worries, by no means unimportant, are worries over cases where eugenics *fails*. Unless we think eugenics is impossible, such worries do not guide us in thinking about cases where eugenics *succeeds*.

A different worry about eugenics concerns its connection with abortion. As things look now, the likely gene therapy techniques would involve detaching a few cells from the embryo within the first week before any cell differentiation occurs, analyzing their genetic composition, and then performing the desired therapy on the remaining cells. As a result of the analysis, the detached cells would be destroyed. Because these detached cells are undifferentiated, they could have developed into a complete fetus on their own. Thus, the procedure of human gene therapy could involve techniques that some people would find morally equivalent to abortion, and they would object accordingly. But the worry here is not so much over eugenics as over a side effect. It is by no means clear that eugenics will have to use such procedures.

The Interests of the Child

How should we think about modern eugenics? If we think about it in one way, eugenics is always in the interests of the child, or at least always believed to be so by the parents. This is plain for the case of removing uncontroversial genetic defects, but it also holds for the so-called enhancement therapies. Given studies showing that 6'3" males do better in our society than 5'3" males, it would clearly seem to be in a male child's interest to be the taller height. In general, any property that is a plausible candidate for eugenics is one that prospective parents reasonably believe confers an advantage to the child. Any advocacy of eugenics will start with this thought.

This thought hardly needs to be argued, for it follows from the definition of "eugenics"—which is, having as its object "the production of fine offspring" (OED). Of course, with developing technology this leaves open the possibility of directly altering the genetic makeup of a child for *non-eugenic* reasons. A couple might want a boy for no other reason than that they have a girl and they want to experience something different, or they might just want to ensure that their child has eyes to match the bedroom walls. These are cases where genetic manipulation is being performed to meet the parents' interests or desires, not the child's. In some cases the manipulation might strike us as innocuous, in others as foolish and irresponsible. But in any case, the reasons behind non-eugenic manipulation will seem weak when compared with the reasons behind eugenic manipulation.

Claiming that eugenics is nearly always in the child's interest may seem too quick. Who is to say what is in that child's interest? How do we know it would not be better for that child to be short and weak or even handicapped with a genetic disease? Despite these shortcomings, perhaps because of these shortcomings, he or she may have a happier life. In fact, what we regard as shortcomings may be no more than local prejudices. After all, it was not that long ago that being left-handed was regarded as a handicap. How can this generation presume what is good for later generations?

Taken out of context, these questions can easily be overwhelming. But placed in their proper context, they are quite mundane. We typically empower parents with the authority to decide what is in their child's interest. For the most part, this authority rests on the belief that parents are the best judges of their child's interest. As an epistemic judgment, parents are held to know, on the basis of presumed intimacy and concern, what is in their child's interest. As a regulative judgment, parents are held to have the authority, derived from the institution of the family, to inform if not determine some of their child's interests. Although parental authority is not absolute and has often been challenged, these challenges are usually against the parents' competency—they have false beliefs about what is in their child's interest—and not against the idea such authority should exist. Even radical challenges to the family question only the placing of this authority, not its legitimacy. Consequently, individual exceptions aside, a eugenics decision on the part of parents is fully in keeping with how we think a child's interests should be acknowledged.

Nevertheless, although eugenics is always in the child's interest, a number of people have tried in various ways to dismiss or deny its benefits. For example, some have objected that eugenics amounts to "playing God." However, without making some controversial assumptions in theology, this protest does not distinguish eugenics from any other medical intervention. Who would object to modern public health efforts, such as the elimination of smallpox, on such grounds? While at various times some people have claimed that an epidemic was God's judgment and that trying to control the disease, by inoculations or other preventative measures, was wrongly trying to avoid God's punishment, such claims are no longer taken seriously.

The secular or naturalistic counterpart of the "playing God" objection is that eugenics amounts to tampering with the wisdom of evolution. The result of millions of years of natural selection is a delicate balance of fragile structures and processes, which direct gene manipulation would upset. The reply to this objection is the same. Under this Panglossian reading of evolution, any attempt to eliminate a disease or affect morbidity rates would be objectionable. Medicine must be viewed as an unnatural and destructive interference. It is difficult to believe that this accurately articulates what worries people about eugenics.

The Interests of Society

Up till now I have tried to present the case for eugenics— eugenics is typically in the interest of the child. Consequently, if we wish to find a way to identify the sort of considerations that oppose eugenics, we need to look beyond the child's interest. A frequent thought has been to point to the consequences of everyone, or at least most people, designing their children. To fix ideas, let us consider choosing the sex of children. If people were allowed to determine the sex of their children, so the worry goes, the result would be a catastrophic sex-ratio imbalance, favoring males.

The reasoning in this worry is weak. The claim that more male children would be born if a choice were available is based on surveys reporting that people prefer their first child to be male. Of course, it does not follow that if someone prefers A over B, then that person would actively bring about A if he or she could. But, for the sake of argument, let us swallow this assumption. Since surveys report that couples prefer having an equal number of boys and girls, the source of sex-ratio imbalance would be from couples who have an odd number of children, with single-child couples having the greatest impact on the imbalance. To get some sense of the numbers involved, suppose that *all* single-child couples use sex-selection techniques and all decide on male children. The resulting sex-ratio imbalance would then be approximately 60 percent males to 40 percent females. What is the harm in that?

One reply might be that, making the obvious assumptions, the number of families would decrease by 10 percent, with the population decreasing accordingly by 10 percent. This is not clearly a bad consequence. Indeed, people who worry about overpopulation would have to regard this result as a good thing.

A different reply might be that having an equal number of men and women is simply an important value for us. But I doubt this is true. Even a casual look at population statistics shows we tolerate all sorts of sex-ratio imbalances. Consider all of the people over the age of 65. Here the sex-ratio imbalance is 60 percent to 40 percent, but of women over men. In fact, if we are looking for striking sex-ratio imbalances, we need only consider the group of single people over the age of 45, for there the sex-ratio imbalance is not 60 percent to 40 percent but rather 80 percent to 20 percent: a four-to-one ratio of women to men! Nevertheless, no one, I think, would suggest that these imbalances should be corrected by direct compensatory actions such as having preferred health care, better Medicare coverage, or even major research specifically in the health problems of elderly males.

I do not wish to suggest that nothing is wrong with choosing the sex of one's children. However, I do not think that what is wrong with it lies in some harmful consequence of the sex-ratio imbalance itself. Rather, what is prima facie wrong with determining that the sex of a child be male is that it insults the dignity of women; it demeans the value of being female. The designer by his or her actions is saying, in effect, that whatever the value of being female is (or whatever the value of the child's original sex is), that value is second-rate.

This objection does not turn on any hypotheses regarding the popularity of eugenics. The other two objections do not identify anything wrong in a single case of sex selection; their worries turn on the consequences of how it could be used and an assumption that its use would likely be widespread. This invites the defender of eugenics to reply that these worries show only that eugenics efforts can be abused, but this hardly distinguishes eugenics from any other technology. Consequently, the most these worries can recommend is that eugenics efforts should be regulated to prevent any harm that might occur from their aggregate use. But if sex selection for make children denigrates the value of being female, then it does so even in a single case.

This objection can be easily generalized to cover cases of genetically altering the racial or ethnic features of one's progeny, and, so generalized, it identifies what we would find troublesome about such cases. This suggests we might generalize even further. Eugenics involves saying that whatever the value of the child's original condition, that value is second-rate.

We can thus see the problem of eugenics as a conflict between two values. On the one hand, we have the value of benefiting the child's interests by altering certain of his or her characteristics; on the other hand, we have the value of the original, untreated condition. How the matter will resolve depends on the particulars. Suppose the original condition were a generally recognized disease, such as Huntington's chorea. Since presumably little if any value can be attached to such conditions, the interests of the child would be decisive. However, in cases where we hold that it is important not to treat the value of the original condition as second-rate, such as sex or racial selection, the interests of the child, unfortunately real though they may be in our society, may not be decisive. We do not want to treat those conditions as being of little value, as if they were diseases. The coherence of our values might not tolerate it.

Old Eugenics versus New Eugenics

Despite the differences, the new eugenics involves the same kind of conflicts that underlay the old eugenics, but with the positions reversed. The old eugenics pitted an alleged state interest in the quality of the genetic composition of the community (the gene pool) against individual rights and liberties over reproduction, that is, the value of improving the gene pool versus the value of individual reproductive autonomy. The case for the old eugenics foundered on false empirical assumptions. Wild claims were made regarding what sort of conditions are inheritable, such as "nomadism," "shiftlessness," and "thalassophilia" (love of the sea). In addition, false claims were made about how much gene frequencies are affected by selective breeding. A standard calculation from population genetics shows that reducing the frequency of a recessive gene from 5 percent to 2.5 percent, even with a vigorous eugenics program, would take more than two hundred generations! I wish I could say that the violation of individual rights was decisive in the downfall of the old eugenics, but neither history nor the courts support that view. When the public health is at stake, individual rights are seen as luxuries. Exposing the false empirical assumptions contributed to the view that the quality of the gene pool is not a public health problem, and so contributed to the repudiation of the old eugenics.

In contrast, the new eugenics pits the alleged interests of an individual against the value the state would find in not having certain human conditions manipulated—against a concern for the stability and harmony of the community. Admittedly, the ways a particular case of eugenics could constitute a threat to that concern will not always be entirely clear. Indeed, when the genetic condition to be altered is unquestionably defective, the state's interest will coincide with the child's interest, since reducing the frequency of such genes is in the interest of public health. There is a danger here, however. If genetic diseases are once again held to constitute a public health *problem*, modern eugenics could very well share the moral collapse of the old eugenics.

Human Gene Therapy:
Scientific and Ethical Considerations

W. French Anderson

There are four potential levels of the application of genetic engineering for the insertion of a gene into a human being (Anderson, 1982):

   (1) Somatic cell gene therapy: this would result in correcting a genetic defect in the somatic (i.e., body) cells of a patient.
   (2) Germ line gene therapy: this would require the insertion of the gene into the reproductive tissue of the patient in such a way that the disorder in his or her offspring would also be corrected.
   (3) Enhancement genetic engineering: this would involve the insertion of a gene to try to 'enhance' a known characteristic; for example, the placing of an additional growth hormone gene into a normal child.
   (4) Eugenic genetic engineering: this is defined as the attempt to alter or 'improve' complex human traits, each of which is coded by a large number of genes; for example, personality, intelligence, character, formation of body organs, and so on.

Somatic Cell Gene Therapy

There are many examples of genes which, when defective, produce serious or lethal disease in a patient. Gene therapy should be beneficial primarily for the replacement of a defective or missing enzyme or protein that must function inside the cell that makes it, or of a deficient circulation protein whose level does not need to be exactly regulated (for example blood clotting factor VIII which is deficient in hemophilia). Early attempts at gene therapy will almost certainly be done with genes for enzymes that have a simple 'always-on' type of regulation.

Ethics

The ethics of gene therapy in humans has been discussed for many years and is being widely debated at present. . . . Essentially all observers have stated that they believe that it would be ethical to insert genetic material into a human being for the sole purpose of medically correcting a severe genetic defect in that patient, in other words, somatic cell gene therapy. Attempts to correct a patient's reproductive cells (i.e., germ line gene therapy) or to alter or improve a 'normal' person by gene manipulation (i.e., enhancement or eugenic genetic engineering) are controversial areas. However, somatic cell gene therapy for a patient suffering a serious genetic disorder would be ethically acceptable if carried out under the same strict criteria that cover other new experimental medical procedures. The techniques now being developed by clinical investigators for human application are for somatic cell, not germ line, gene therapy.

What criteria should be satisfied prior to the time that somatic cell gene therapy is tested in a clinical trial? Three general requirements . . . are that it should be shown in animal studies that (i) the new gene can be put into the correct target cells and will remain there long enough to be effective; (ii) the new gene will be expressed in the cells at an appropriate level; and (iii) the new gene will not harm the cell or, by extension, the animal.

These criteria are very similar to those required prior to the use of any new drug, therapeutic procedure, or surgical operation. The requirements simply state that the new treatment should get to the area of disease, correct it, and do more good than harm. Some flexibility is necessary since the criteria might be altered for a critically ill patient for whom no further conventional therapy is available. The exact definitions of what is 'long enough to be effective', what level is 'an appropriate level', and how much harm is meant by 'harm', are questions for ongoing discussion as more is learned about gene therapy. Ultimately, local Institutional Review Boards and the National Institutes of Health (NIH), the latter through its newly created Working Group on Human Gene Therapy, must decide if a given protocol is ready for human application. Once the criteria are satisfied—that is, when the probable benefits for the patient are expected to exceed the possible risks—then attempts to cure human genetic disease by treatment with somatic cell gene therapy would be ethical. The goal of biomedical research is, and has always been, to alleviate human suffering. Gene therapy is a proper and logical part of that effort.

Safety

A human gene therapy protocol must be safe. Although retroviruses have many advantages for gene transfer, they also have disadvantages. One problem is that they can rearrange their own structure, as well as exchange sequences with other retroviruses. In the future it might be possible to modify non-infectious retroviral vectors in such a way that they remain stable. At present, however, there is the possibility that a retroviral vector might recombine with an endogenous viral sequence to produce an infectious recombinant virus. Properties that such a recombinant would have are unknown, but there is a potential homology between retroviral vectors and human T-cell leukemia viruses so that the formation of a recombinant that could produce a malignancy is a possibility. There is, however, a built-in safety feature with the mouse retroviral vectors now in use. These mouse structures have a very different sequence from known primate retroviruses, and there appears to be little or no

ADA, or PNP are the most likely first candidates for gene therapy.

It is unrealistic to expect a complete cure from the initial attempts at gene therapy. Many patients who suffer from severe genetic diseases, as well as their families, are eager to participate in early clinical trials even if the likelihood is low that the original experiments will alleviate symptoms. However, for the protection of the patients (particularly since those with the most severe diseases and, therefore, the most ethically justifiable first candidates are children), gene therapy trials should not be attempted until there are good animal data to suggest that some amelioration of the biochemical defect is likely. Then it would be necessary to weigh the potential risks to the patient, including the possibility of producing a pathologic virus or a malignancy, against the anticipated benefits to be gained from the functional gene. This risk-to-benefit determination, a standard procedure for all clinical research protocols, would need to be carried out for each patient.

In summary, Institutional Review Boards and the NIH should carefully evaluate therapeutic protocols to ensure that the delivery system is effective, that sufficient expression can be obtained in bone marrow cultures and in laboratory animals to predict probable benefit, even if small, for the patient, and that safety protocols have demonstrated that the probability is low for the production of either a malignant cell or a harmful infectious retrovirus. Once these criteria are met, I maintain that it would be unethical to delay human trials. Patients with serious genetic diseases have little other hope at present for alleviation of their medical problems. Arguments that genetic engineering might someday be misused do not justify the needless perpetuation of human suffering that would result from an unnecessary delay in the clinical application of this potentially powerful therapeutic procedure.

Germ Line Gene Therapy

The second level of genetic engineering, gene therapy of germ line cells, would require a major advance in our present state of will be necessary before somatic cell therapy can properly be judged to be safe and effective. If somatic cell therapy has not become highly efficient with very minimal risks, germ line gene therapy should not be considered.

Second, there should be adequate animal studies that establish the reproducibility, reliability, and safety of germ line therapy, using the same vectors and procedures that would be used in humans. Of greatest importance would be the demonstration that the new DNA could be inserted exactly as predicted and that it would be expressed in the appropriate tissues and at the appropriate times. It should be remembered that gene therapy does not remove or correct the defective genes in the recipient; it only adds a normal gene into the genome. It is not now known what the influence of this combination of defective and normal genes may be on the developing embryo. Might the regulatory signals still associated with the non-functional genes adversely affect the regulation of the exogenous gene during development?

Third, there should be public awareness and approval of the procedure. New drugs, medical regimens, and surgical techniques certainly do not require individual public approval prior to their initiation. There are already regulatory processes in place that insure the protection of human subjects (this issue has been addressed in a previous publication (Anderson and Fletcher, 1980)). Somatic cell gene therapy is receiving widespread public attention, but prior public approval is not being specifically sought. Germ line gene therapy, however, is a different and unique form of treatment. It will affect unborn generations and has, therefore, a greater impact on society as a whole than treatment confined to a single individual. The gene pool is a joint possession of all members of society. Since germ line therapy will affect the gene pool, the public should have a thorough understanding of the implications of this form of treatment. Only when an informed public has indicated its support, by the various avenues open for society to express its views, should clinical trials begin. *In vitro* fertilization, surrogate motherhood, animal organ transplants into humans, holistic treatment of cancer, and other controversial medical procedures can take place based on the decision of the patient (with his/her doctor and/or family) whether society as a whole approves or not. But the decision to initiate germ line gene therapy demands assent from more than the individual involved, since the effects go beyond that individual. If and when germ line therapy is approved by society for clinical trials, then the decision to apply it in any individual case again should be made privately by the patient with his/her doctor.

In conclusion, my position is that germ line therapy, since it is the correction of a genetic defect (albeit in the future), would be ethical and appropriate if the three conditions discussed above were met.

Enhancement Genetic Engineering

The third level of genetic engineering, enhancement genetic engineering, is considerably different in principle from the first two. This is no longer therapy of a genetic disorder; it is the insertion of an additional normal gene (or a gene modified in a specific way) to produce a change in some characteristic that the individual wants. Enhancement would involve the insertion of a single gene, or a small number of genes, that code for a product (or products) that would produce the desired effect—for example, greater size through the insertion of an additional growth hormone gene into the cells of an infant. Enhancement genetic engineering presents a major additional scientific hurdle, as well as serious new ethical issues. Except under very specific circumstances as detailed below, genetic engineering should not be used for enhancement purposes.

Scientific and Ethical Concerns

The scientific hurdle to be overcome is a formidable one. Until now, we have considered the correction of a defect, of a 'broken part', if you will. Fix the broken part and the human machine should operate correctly again. Replacing a faulty part is different from trying to add something new to a normally functioning system. To insert a gene in the hope of improving or selectively altering a characteristic might endanger the overall metabolic balance of the individual cells as well as of the entire body. Medicine is a very inexact science. Every year new hormones, new regulators, and new pathways are discovered. There are clearly many more to be discovered. Most impressive is the enormously intricate way that each cell coordinates within itself all of its thousands of pathways. Likewise, the body as a whole carefully monitors and balances a multitude of physiological systems. Much additional research will be required to elucidate the effects of altering one or more major pathways in a cell. To correct a faulty gene is probably not going to be dangerous, but intentionally to insert a gene to make more of one product might adversely affect numerous other biochemical pathways

We possess insufficient information at present to understand the effects of attempts to alter the genetic machinery of a human. Is it wise, safe, or ethical for parents to give, for example, growth hormone (now that it is available in large amounts) to their normal sons in order to produce very large football or basketball players? Unfortunately, this practice now takes place in this country. But even worse, why would anyone want to insert a growth hormone *gene* into a normal child? Once it is in, there is no way to get it back out. The child's reflexes, coordination, and balance might all be grossly affected. In addition, even more serious questions can be asked: might one alter the regulatory pathways of cells, inadvertently affecting cell division or other properties? In short, we know too little about the human body to chance inserting a gene designed for 'improvement' into a normal healthy person.

An Acceptable Use

There is, however, a set of circumstances under which enhancement genetic engineering may be ethical. This is when it could be justified on grounds of preventive medicine. For example, it is well established that heart attacks and stroke are a direct result of atherosclerosis (i.e., hardening of the arteries). The rate of development of atherosclerosis appears to correlate directly with elevated levels of cholesterol in the blood. The level of blood cholesterol is regulated, at least in part, by its rate of clearance from the blood by the low density lipoprotein (LDL) receptors on body cells (Goldstein and Brown, 1983). LDL is the major cholesterol-transport protein in human plasma. If further research should verify that an increased number of LDL receptors on cells would result in lower blood cholesterol levels and, consequently, in a decreased incidence of heart attacks and strokes, then the insertion of an additional LDL receptor gene in 'normal' individuals could significantly decrease the morbidity and mortality caused by atherosclerosis. In this type of situation, the purpose of the intervention would be the prevention of disease, not simply the personal desire of an individual for an altered characteristic. The concerns expressed above about disrupting the regulatory pathways in the body still should be considered, of course. However, since there is a range for the number of receptors on a cell's surface, shifting a person with a "low normal" number of receptors to a "high normal" number may not be disruptive to other physiological or biochemical pathways.

Eugenic Genetic Engineering

The fourth level is 'eugenic' genetic engineering. This area has received considerable attention in the popular press, with the result that at times unjustified fears have been produced because of claims that scientists might soon be able to remake human beings. In fact, however, such traits as personality, character, formation of body organs, fertility, intelligence, physical, mental, and emotional characteristics, etc., are enormously complex. Dozens, perhaps hundreds, of unknown genes that interact in totally unknown ways probably contribute to each such trait. Environmental influences also interact with these genetic backgrounds in poorly understood ways. With time, as more is learned about each of these complex traits, individual genes will be discovered that play specific roles. Undoubtedly, disorders will be recognized that are caused by defects in these genes. Then, somatic cell gene therapy could be employed to correct the defect. But the concept of remaking a human (i.e., eugenic genetic engineering) is not realistic at present.

Complex polygenic traits may never be influenced in a predictable manner by genetic engineering, but, at a minimum, developing the techniques for producing such changes will take many years. Therefore, there is no point to a scientific discussion of eugenic genetic engineering at present—there is simply no science to discuss. But from a philosophical standpoint, a discussion of the ethics of eugenic genetic engineering is very important. After all, what is it that makes us human? Why are we what we are? Are there genes which are indeed 'human' genes? If we were to alter one of these genes, would we be other than human? These are important questions for us to think about and discuss.

If eugenic genetic engineering were possible today, I would be strongly opposed to its use on philosophical and ethical grounds. Our knowledge of how the human body works is still elementary. Our understanding of how the mind, both conscious and subconscious, functions is even more rudimentary. The genetic basis for instinctual behavior is largely unknown. Our disagreements about what constitutes 'humanhood' are notorious. And our insight into what, and to what extent, genetic components might play a role in what we comprehend as our 'spiritual' side is almost non-existent. We simply should not meddle in areas where we are so ignorant. Regardless of how fast our technological abilities increase, there should be no attempt to manipulate, for other than therapeutic reasons, the genetic framework (i.e., the genome) of human beings.

Conclusion

In summary, somatic cell gene therapy for human genetic disease should be possible in the very near future. The scientific basis on which this new therapeutic approach is founded has been thoroughly documented in a number of publications, as has the ethical justification for its use. Germ line gene therapy is still in the future, but the technical ability to carry it out will almost certainly be developed. Society must determine if this therapeutic option should be used. Enhancement genetic engineering should also be possible and its medical and disturbing ethical implications need continuing discussion. Eugenic genetic engineering, on the other hand, is purely theoretical and will, from a practical standpoint, be impossible for the foreseeable future. The topic is valuable for reflective thinking but not for scientific discussion.

Many of the fears generated by some articles in the popular press that discuss 'gene therapy' or 'genetic engineering' are simply unfounded. Insertion of single functional genes should soon become possible, but claims that new organs, designed personalities, master races, or Frankenstein monsters will be created can be given no credence in the light of what is presently known. Even so, we should be concerned about the possibility that genetic engineering might be misused in the future. The best insurance against possible abuse is a well-informed public. Gene therapy has the potential for producing tremendous good by reducing the suffering and death caused by genetic diseases. We can look forward to the day when, with proper safeguards imposed by society, this powerful new therapeutic procedure is available.

REFERENCES

Anderson, W.F.: 1982, in *Hearings on Human Genetic Engineering Before the Subcommittee on Investigations and Oversight of the Committee on Science and Technology*, 97th Cong. 2d sess., No. 170 (Government Printing Office, Washington, D.C., 1982), pp. 285–292.

Anderson, W.F.: 1984, 'Prospects for human gene therapy', *Science* 226, 401–409.

Anderson, W.F. and Fletcher, J.C.: 1980, 'Gene therapy in human beings: when is it ethical to begin?' *New England Journal of Medicine* 303, 1293–1297.

Brinster, R.L. et al.: 1983, 'Expression of a microinjected immuno-globulin gene in the spleen of transgenic mice', *Nature* 306, 332–336.

Fletcher, J.C.: 1985, 'Ethical issues in and beyond prospective clinical trials of human gene therapy', *Journal of Medicine and Philosophy* 10, 293–309.

Goldstein, J.L. and Brown, M.S.: 1983, 'Familial hypercholesterolemia', in J.B. Stanbury et al. (eds.), *The Metabolic Basis of Inherited Disease*, 5th edition, McGraw-Hill, New York, pp. 672–712.

Hammer, R.E. et al.: 1984, 'Partial correction of murine hereditary growth disorder by germ-line incorporation of a new gene', *Nature* 311, 65–67.

Joyner, A. et al.: 1983, 'Retrovirus transfer of a bacterial gene in mouse haematopoietic progenitor cells', *Nature* 305, 556–558.

Lacy, E. et al.: 1983, 'A foreign ß-globin gene in transgenic mice: integration at abnormal chromosomal positions and expression in inappropriate tissues', *Cell* 34, 343–358.

Miller, A.D. et al.: 1984, 'Expression of a retrovirus encoding human HPRT in mice', *Science* 225, 630–632.

Williams, D.A. et al.: 1984, 'Introduction of new genetic material into pluripotent haematopoietic stem cells of the mouse', *Nature* 310, 476–480.

Willis, R.C. et al.: 1984, 'Partial phenotypic correction of human Lesch-Nyhan (hypoxanthine-guanine phosphoribosyltransferase-deficient) lymphoblasts with a transmissible retroviral vector', *Journal of Biological Chemistry* 259, 7842–7849.

Controversial Research Topics

This final section attains unity, not by substantive theme, but by an aura of taboo that surrounds its two topics. The very motives of the researchers in each area are called into question. It has been claimed that only persons with sinister motives would presume to investigate differences in IQ among persons in different races. It has also been claimed that the quest for money is what drives military research at universities and that universities are institutions that should thrive on openness, not on secrecy.

The acrimony that surrounds the "intelligence controversy" has been due, in large measure, to the suspicion of the critics that the investigators are ill-disguised racists. H.J. Eysenck's critics, for example, point out that he grew up in Berlin during the Hitler years. Some of them have urged that all psychologists should declare their backgrounds when presenting the results of their work. On their view, it is inevitable that a person's background influences not only what he studies but also the findings he comes to. One may wonder, of course, whether it is fair game to ask whether the attack on Eysenck says something about the critics' backgrounds. (By the way, Eysenck left Germany as a teenager when Hitler came to power.)

In 1969 Arthur Jensen published his now celebrated article, "How Much Can We Boost IQ and Scholastic Achievement" (*Harvard Educational Review*), in which he tried to prove that the IQ gap between blacks and whites is mainly genetic. Jensen argued that environmental manipulation could never close more than 20 percent of the gap. Jensen's work has created a veritable industry with hundreds of persons either wanting to show him the error of his ways or coming to his defense.

Critics hold that those engaging in IQ research have a preconceived view that heredity will prove triumphant over the environment as the principal shaper of intelligence. Hereditarians are thought, by their critics, to be advocates of a static society who want to justify unchanging social roles, assignation to which is determined once and for all by forces beyond our control. Worse yet, in their view, intelligence research not only grows out of racial bias but also fosters it because having a low IQ is as stigmatic as being a convicted felon.

These accusations have stunned Jensen, Eysenck, Richard Herrnstein, and others who champion intelligence research. Eysenck denies, of course, that he is a racist and, what is more, denies that racists are chomping at the bit just waiting for the latest results on racial intelligence to be announced. Why should anybody suppose that the results of research would favor the cause of racism rather than undermine it? Moreover, Eysenck states, racists thrive on ignorance not knowledge. Outlandish racist claims flourish where there is no scientific evidence to refute them. Furthermore, Eysenck affirms that intelligence is alterable. He emphasizes that the genetic hypothesis doesn't imply that intelligence is static. Accordingly, he claims that if past research on IQ differences across the races has been flawed, the cure is better research, not "no research."

The essay we have included by Chomsky is directed specifically at Richard Herrnstein but targets all those who believe in the worth of IQ research. Unlike many other critics, Chomsky says that denunciation of Herrnstein as a racist is unwarranted, but he does think that the hereditarian thesis is widely deployed by those who are. Critics such as Chomsky are convinced that research on race and intelligence has no scientific importance, and they call for its immediate cessation. Even if some correlation concerning race and intelligence were discovered, it would be of no greater interest than a correlation between mean height and color of eyes. Further, most research is driven, according to Chomsky, by social malice. Had Nazi scientists investigated the IQs of Jews, we would have condemned them without further ado. Decent societies have no use for this sort of thing. Twenty-three years after Jensen's article first appeared, the controversy continues to generate much heat, but the exchange reprinted here also generates light.

The debate over military research is also vitriolic, and accusations of evil motive have occasionally erupted in near violent confrontations on college campuses. It is commonplace knowledge that the military establishment is an excellent source of funding, and it is fairly well known, too, that many persons derive their principal income from that funding. Critics of military research sometimes assert that researchers have a special interest in assuring that the results of their work find favor with the funding sources. They believe that military research cannot be conducted in the impartial manner that is a *sine qua non* of all science. The two essays brought together here rise above the courtroom level of personal attack and counterattack and consider the matter fully.

Kenneth Kemp, far from being suspicious of military research, thinks of it as a real civic duty and claims that all scientists competent to contribute to it must do a certain amount. He compares it to a lawyer's duty to do *pro bono* work for the indigent. Kemp holds that the intentions of the United States are good and our military powers are focused on deterrence. Kemp does not advocate that scientists should leave the applications of their work to the state. Rather, scientists who live and work in an aggressive and hostile nation ought not to do military research, to ensure that their work will not be used for evil purposes. The responsibility of each scientist extends to making a judgment concerning how this research will be used.

There are legitimate worries about conflicts of interest with respect to funding. These worries, however, are not philosophical, according to Kemp, because he thinks it is obvious that one should not do research merely for money. Actually, the issue is not so easily resolved. If, as Kemp thinks, the intentions of the United States are always noble and research always serves a good purpose, then doing the work for the sake of money seems benign enough.

Another problem surrounding military research is that so much of it is classified. Secrecy in research seems to go contrary to the ideals of the scientific community. Moreover, it seems doubly egregious to carry on this research at universities, since they especially thrive on openness. Kemp is not without interesting responses to this. We leave the reader to decide whether his responses address the criticism adequately.

Douglas Lackey is much less sanguine about scientific involvement in military projects. First, he denies that the United States generally acts nobly when it acts militarily. He thinks it is frequently an aggressor and that every scientist should bear that in mind.

Second, Lackey is more concerned about the funding aspect of military research than is Kemp. It is easy, he thinks, for scientists to take money and to hide behind many excuses. For example, Lackey analyzes such excuses as "We are the good guys," "Star Wars won't work, so the research is benign," "If I don't do it someone else will," and what he calls "the small potatoes" excuse—any single person's contribution is likely to be so small that, even if the goal of the research is not benign, its harmful effect is easily counterblanced by the good it does the researcher. Lackey reminds us that scientists are ordinary men, tempted by all the standard evil. Military research provides financial motivation for a potentially great evil. Consequently, he condemns it categorically.

That the so-called cold war is over does not imply that debate about military research is passé. The use of "smart" bombs and other high-tech devices of destruction in the recent Persian Gulf War demonstrates continued military reliance on scientific research. As the means of waging war become more sophisticated, the issues raised by Kemp and Lackey will prove even more urgent.

Forbidden Research: Limits to Inquiry in the Social Sciences

Dorothy Nelkin

Science is increasingly under public scrutiny. The moral implications of scientific research—its procedures and its immediate and long-range consequences—are subject to vigorous debates. Difficult questions are posed in such debates: Are there moral limits to scientific inquiry? What social or political constraints should be placed on research? Is some research so risky or so reprehensible that it should not be done at all?[1]

While these questions touch diverse areas of science, they are increasingly directed to the social sciences, where research findings have immediate human interest and often carry long-term social policy implications. Moreover, social science procedures pose troublesome ethical dilemmas whenever investigators invade the privacy of individuals and institutions or manipulate the subjects of research.[2] Thus, many areas of social science research are, if not forbidden, at least severely constrained.

A network of control mechanisms is presently in place to protect the rights of human subjects involved in social as well as biomedical research. Federal guidelines for the protection of human subjects and procedures of the local institutional review boards that implement these guidelines have placed effective controls, if not absolute limits, on inquiry. These controls are under debate, as researchers complain of the "medicalization" of social science and decry constraints that they feel are

355

unnecessary, irrelevant, and obstructive. Those who view science as a value-free intellectual activity, "progressing by means of its own norms of consensual validity,"[3] argue that freedom of inquiry is essential for healthy research and is perhaps even a constitutional right. For them, the idea of "forbidden knowledge," or even of external constraints on research, raises the specter of McCarthyism, Lysenkoism, and the Inquisition. They see at stake the freedom of the scientific endeavor from external political control.

While the concept of freedom in scientific inquiry has a venerable history as a basis for the health and integrity of science, there are many cases where the goals of inquiry conflict with prevailing social norms. The premise that scientific freedom overrides other social values would place scientists beyond the judgments of the larger social system.

I will argue that freedom of scientific inquiry is a relative concept that is interpreted and implemented in terms of the prevailing social values and power relationships in a society at a given time. While scientists continually negotiate for autonomy, their work is embedded in a cultural and political context that in fact constrains their choice of research topics and the boundaries of acceptable practice. Some research is questioned because the knowledge pursued is judged to be of dubious social or political merit. In other cases, the ends may be interesting and valued, but the methods of acquiring knowledge—the research procedures—invade privacy, require deception, or pose other problems that are judged to be socially unacceptable. In the following analysis of controversial areas of research, the extent to which such judgments in fact fetter research practices will be seen to vary under different social and political conditions.

Political Acceptability of Research

In 1953 a scholar working under a U.S. Air Force contract published a book on the conditions under which "strategic surrender" is appropriate.[4] Drawing cases from World War II, he concluded that it is a fallacy to expect unconditional surrender in the modern international political context. His study became so controversial that Congress legislated against the use of public moneys for any research dealing with a U.S. surrender. This example is clearly a case where political values have explicitly limited research.

More often, political values impose indirect but nevertheless real limits to inquiry. In 1962 Walter Laqueur observed that in the seventeen years following World War II, scholars in the Soviet Union had not produced a single study of the Nazi regime or of the rise of German fascism, despite a presumably widespread Soviet interest in this topic, and despite its relevance to Soviet political ideology. Laqueur argued that the rise of fascism in a society with a large industrial proletariat contradicted the premises of Soviet political philosophy at the time, and that Soviet scholars therefore avoided the topic.[5]

The political acceptability of social science research is often questioned because of the source of research funding. In the late 1960s the Office of the Secretary of Defense funded a project at Harvard and at MIT to develop a new computer methodology which could handle large quantities of social science data. Project Cambridge became the focus of a heated controversy, with faculty and students seeking to prevent Harvard from doing research which might give the government immediate access to a vast body of social information. In the political climate of the 1960s people were especially wary of social technologies which might be used to collect dossiers on individuals and to suppress dissent. The source of funding for Project Cambridge, the Department of Defense, only reinforced these suspicions. Nevertheless, the funds were accepted and the project launched, although participation in the research was made the responsibility of individual scholars rather than of the university as an institution.[6] Despite intense controversy over the acceptability of research at a time when military policies were widely suspect, no constraints were imposed.

Similar questions about the political acceptability of military sponsored research provoked the famous controversy over Project Camelot. The Department of Defense supported this project to study patterns of revolution and insurgency in developing countries and to find ways to predict and cope with these problems. Described as "insurgency prophylaxis," the project employed many social scientists, not all of whom were aware of its military auspices. Camelot enraged many Latin American scholars who warned that people under its scrutiny would suspect all future research. The ensuing debate hinged on the acceptability of doing academic research to further military goals. Should social scientists under military sponsorship accept the mission of penetrating a culture and investigating the details of its institutions? Critics argued for limiting such research when done by academic scholars. Supporters countered that the research, which would be carried out in any case, would be done better by a "disinterested" community of scientists than by those directly employed by the military.[7] It is important to emphasize here that similar research in collaboration with the military during World War II did not provoke criticism, because of the prevailing political consensus against fascism. For the political limits on research are defined in the context of political goals.

The Potential Misuse of Knowledge

In 1972, UCLA proposed to open an interdisciplinary research center to study criminal violence. The Center for the Study and Reduction of Violence was intended to advance understanding of the sources of pathologically violent behavior, to identify "violent predispositions" in individuals, and to develop techniques of preventing violence and of treating criminal offenders. Among the proposed research projects were studies of the families of disturbed adolescents, investigation of the relationship between chromosomal abnormalities and violent behavior, and evaluation of proposals to improve behavior control therapies. The center's objective was to provide alternatives to incarceration and to reduce violence in society. The researchers regarded their work as a benefit to potential criminals, to victims of violence, and to society as a whole. Critics, however, perceived this project in a different light, attacking the researchers as "racist," "Nazi butchers . . . sprinkling the perfume of scientific legitimacy over the stench of experimentation on prisoners."[8] And they vilified the project as "fascism," "eugenics," and "genocide."

Behavior control can be seen as a way to bring recalcitrant individuals into a more "normal' or productive life, or as a means to maintain order at enormous cost to those who do not conform to establishment expectations. Research on the genetic basis of criminal behavior can be seen as a way to prevent crimes or as a means to facilitate social control. One's judgments on such matters depend on the definition of violent or antisocial behavior that is employed and on normative assumptions about the causes of violence. Depending on one's conceptions and assumptions, research on genetic bases of behavior or on behavior control appears as a public service, or as so pernicious in its potential for abuse that it should not be done at all. In the social climate of the early 1970s, one suffused by a heightened awareness of social injustice and a growing mistrust of authority, the opposition prevailed and the UCLA project was dropped.

The possibilities of pernicious abuse have also supported arguments for restricting studies of the relationship between genetics and intelligence. In response to Jensen's claims that differences in IQ reflect genetic differences more than environmental factors, critics have argued that "the wise scientist will not devote himself to research on the relationship between race and ability; the wise university will not honor those who do, or disseminate their work."[9] Quite apart from the many methodological criticisms of this research, it has been attacked on the grounds that its findings, appealing to racist bias, could result in labeling that would reduce our respect for individuals and promote egregious social policies.

Social scientists often look to hereditary factors to explain human behavior, tracing genetic influences on the development of personality, on criminality, and even on vocational interests.[10] Those who would limit such research maintain that, although causal explanations can never be definitive, emphasis on genetic and therefore intractable bases of human behavior will discourage public policy makers from alleviating existing inequities.[11] Such arguments have had little effect on the direction of research; while few would deny that the results of research can be manipulated and abused, this possibility is generally rejected as a reason for forbidding research.

The extent to which arguments based on the potential social impact of research actually affect the boundaries of acceptable research practice depends on the structure of power relationships in a society. These relationships often impose only subtle constraints—less a question of forbidden research than a discreet avoidance of sensitive topics. Sociologists working in state universities that rely on legislatures dominated by agricultural interests will often study rural and agricultural issues, but avoid the politically sensitive problem of migrant farm labor. Relatively little social science research has focused on the tenure system at universities, or on the decision-making procedures in research foundations.

Analyzing such research biases, Laura Nader has observed that anthropologists always focus on underdogs or the poor.[12] Yet their research methods and their insight could also enrich our understanding of the way power and responsibility are exercised in established elite institutions. Why not study *up* instead of *down*? Nader contends that key institutions—law firms, corporate boardrooms, major agencies, industries—are often "off limits" because they do not want to be examined; they therefore determine practical restrictions on the scope of scientific inquiry. On the other hand, as minority groups have become aware of their rights, they too have imposed limits on research which they feel might have implications for social policy. And, like the elites, minorities have insisted that they must also derive tangible benefits from such research.

These demands and constraints reflect a view of science as a commodity, indeed as a political resource that may be used to enhance the power and control of specific social groups. As various groups either restrict access to knowledge, or conversely seek to employ science to justify their political claims, their vision of science invariably affects the boundaries of research— the issues addressed, the questions raised, and the interpretations of scientific findings.

Science as a Threat to Values

In 1974, protest spread throughout the country against an elementary school course called "Man: A Course of Study" (MACOS).[13] This course was based on contemporary research into animal behavior and on ethnographic studies on human behavior. It explored fundamental questions about the nature of animal and human life, discussing social relations, child-rearing practices, reproductive aggression, and religion. It drew parallels between animals and human beings, and it conveyed a highly controversial message—that neither behavior nor beliefs can be understood and valued independently of their social or environmental context.

MACOS aroused intense opposition from certain groups, who objected to the course on religious and moral grounds. The dispute revealed a social polarization between those who share the outlook of science and those who appeal exclusively to religious and moral considerations that stand opposed to a scientific mode of analysis. Critics of MACOS sought to remove the course from public schools because it promoted "an evolutionary and relativistic humanism." Social science, they argued, is "inseparable from people's beliefs, from their theology, from their morality." They contended that MACOS undermined traditional interpretations of reality, violated sacred assumptions (for example, about the uniqueness of man), and fostered pernicious arguments about cultural relativity. They questioned the validity of such knowledge, claiming that it was based on a dubious belief in "secular humanism," and they sought to forbid its distribution among the "vulnerable" populations of public schools. Social scientists defended MACOS as a well-tested and significant educational advance. The issue, they argued, centered on academic freedom. Can educators' access to the fruits of scholarship be so easily limited? Despite these concerns about educational freedom, federal support for MACOS was eventually withdrawn. The MACOS controversy illustrates how much power "textbook watchers" can wield in the determination of American educational policy.

This dispute and others (over the teaching of evolution theory in public schools or over the books to be used in West

Virginia classrooms) focus less on limitations on scientific research than on science education, less on forbidding the acquisition of knowledge than on limiting its distribution to protect the public against "dangerous" or threatening ideas. But similar arguments based on concern about the religious or moral values threatened by science have limited research as well. Some areas of research are officially off limits in any society at a given historical time; others are simply not perceived as worthy of investigation. Moral norms have always clearly identified certain topics as forbidden. For years sexual behavior, rape, and sexual perversion were not legitimate subjects for research, but even as these areas have emerged as researchable topics, other taboos persist. Incest and childhood sexuality are just now becoming acceptable areas for research. Societies often find it convenient to avoid recognizing certain facts of life, and freedom to conduct research into such facts is accordingly curtailed.

By What Means?

Not long ago, a team of social scientists wanted to evaluate a questionnaire that purported to test people's comprehension of moral principles. They proposed to administer such a test to teen-agers at a male juvenile delinquency rehabilitation center, and then to tempt them to lie or to steal. The test, if valid, would predict the boys' behavior. The methods employed in this research posed a number of problems. The investigators could not elicit the informed consent of the research subjects because the design of the study *required* deception. Moreover, the procedures themselves could cause harm. By tempting boys in a rehabilitation center to lie or to steal, the researchers reinforced the socially undesirable activities that had brought their subjects to the center in the first place. Even in an experimental setting, to tempt youths to steal violates basic values and borders on entrapment. What might be the impact of this test on the rehabilitation of these boys? On their self-image? What, in any case, could be the possible application of the research findings? If a test to judge one's moral understanding were in fact found to correlate with criminal behavior, would this test be administered widely to teen-agers in order to predict who might eventually become a criminal?

This project illustrates several problematic aspects of social science research, but it provides a particularly clear example of the risks to research subjects that may be caused by certain methods of research. These methodological risks may even include legal sanctions. Sociologists study problems such as drug addiction, illegal immigration, criminal behavior, and homosexuality, gathering information that could be used against research subjects. There have yet been no definitive constitutional tests of the legal protection afforded subjects involved in such research.

Some of these problems achieved notoriety in the case of a study of transient homosexual contacts in public restrooms. A sociologist loitered near public urinals, and established himself as a "lookout" willing to watch for police. This gave him a chance to observe people engaged in acts of fellatio. He noted license plate numbers, using them to trace names and addresses of the men involved. Later, he appeared at their homes and secured permission to interview them, ostensibly conducting research for a social health survey. By way of this subterfuge, he accumulated data on their personal characteristics, such as social and economic background, employment status, health conditions, and marital relations. The investigator defended the research as a means to destigmatize homosexual behavior as a social problem. He took great care to protect the identity of the unsuspecting research subjects. Still, the project required considerable deception and invasion of personal privacy, and any lapse in the discretion of the investigator could have brought harm to many of the research subjects. When ethical questions were later raised about the research procedures, the "right of scientists to conduct their work" was vigorously defended by eminent sociologists.[14]

The risks to human subjects in social science research are often vague and difficult to define; they may involve less physical harm than psychological distress, invasion of privacy, or social embarrassment. The research design of many studies requires systematic deception; informing the subject of what is to occur would necessarily invalidate the research results. Research on conformity to group pressure, on individual reactions in emergency situations, on illegal or socially questionable behavior is routinely based on deception. In cases where open research would not be feasible, social scientists often employ techniques of participant observation, which similarly preclude consent. Festinger, Riecken, and Schachter's famous study of "cognitive dissonance" within millenial cults required that psychologists join the cult as believers. Had they identified themselves as social scientists they would not have been admitted to the group.[15]

According to current estimates, between 19 percent and 44 percent of social psychology and personality research involves direct lying to subjects, and one study of psychology experiments suggests that complete information was given in only 3 percent of the cases reviewed.[16] Much of this research would not have been possible without deception. The extension of requirements for informed consent to social research is therefore vigorously opposed within the field. Even when an investigator does seek consent, the vague and intangible nature of psychic risk may preclude informed understanding of the potential consequences of research. Yet much social science research can have a far-reaching impact on the personal lives of research subjects. One of the more dramatic examples is Stanley Milgram's experiment on obedience to authority. Experimenters ordered research subjects to give a series of progressively higher electric shocks to a "subject" (who in fact was a professional colleague) in order to test their obedience to scientific authority. Most subjects obeyed the commands of the researcher and continued to administer apparently dangerous shocks even when the supposed victim appeared to be in pain and losing consciousness. The research created an ethical furor, and a major point of criticism was the personal anxiety and humiliation that subjects could experience following such a graphic demonstration of their willingness to do violence.[17]

In another experiment, Professor P.G. Zimbardo created a prison environment in a building at Stanford University in which students role-played prisoners and guards. Their intense involvement in these roles ("prisoners" became docile and subservient; some "guards" became cruel and abusive) was sufficiently traumatic that the experiment was prematurely terminated because of possible psychological damage to the subjects.[18] For the research subjects, the traumatic nature of both the above experiments resembles that of a psychotherapeutic experience. But in a setting supervised by scientists, not clinicians, this resemblance called into question the moral legitimacy of the experiment.

Research procedures may pose risks to social institutions as well as to individual subjects. In 1952 a team of researchers at the University of Chicago Law School undertook a project to study the way the American jury system actually works. As a part of this broad empirical study, the research team obtained permission to observe a jury by recording jurors' deliberations without their knowledge or consent. The researchers sought to understand how the interaction among jurors influenced both the outcome and the play of deliberation in the legal system. Extending our knowledge about these legal processes is an important research objective, and the Chicago investigation included careful precautions to protect all parties involved. But while the goals of research were important and the quality of results high (two famous books resulted from the study), the means were inherently suspect. The jury is by law inviolate—out of bounds to external intrusion by the public, the press or the research community. The violation of privacy entailed by "bugging" as a research procedure, employed to scrutinize a widely venerated and legally protected American institution, turned this research into a social science scandal. The project became the focus of a Congressional investigation, and legislation was passed prohibiting further studies of its kind. "In effect the jury study sought to lay bare a structure that the society has viewed as indispensable, even sacred . . . and the threat to fundamental values led to a reassessment of the police power of the state."[19]

Such taboos express a society's desire to maintain the sacred quality of certain social arrangements and conventions. Researchers are legally forbidden from placing hidden recorders or cameras in jury rooms or in confessionals, however useful the information obtained might be. Those who violate these fundamental taboos are open to sanction from the scientific community as well as from the law. In effect, our culture considers techniques of scientific investigation inapplicable to certain subjects of unchallenged social importance, regardless of the potential benefit of studying them.

Most constraints, however, affect research done in academic contexts, funded by the government and subject to federal guidelines as well as institutional controls. Considerable research with a similar potential for risk takes place in industrial contexts where proprietary interests preclude public scrutiny.

Recent research, for example, has differentiated the way the brain's two hemispheres process information. As part of this research, psychologists, working for marketing or advertising firms, seek to understand the mechanisms through which the brain remembers images without deliberate effort. Testing is done on television viewers wired to electrodes as they watch proposed commercials. The tester observes brain waves to find out whether the images are registering, and the results are used to help advertisers create images that can be remembered without conscious thought.

Social science research provides significant guidance to the media and its industrial sponsors.

> Psychologists, sociologists, motivation researchers . . . devise ever more sophisticated ways of attracting attention, arousing excitement, and discovering which symbols evoke the kinds of emotions to be packaged with the product image.[20]

Social science research can be employed to develop subliminal techniques of "coercive persuasion,"[21] to influence beliefs, and to break down personal defenses so as to heighten responsiveness to the messages conveyed. The sociological and psychological techniques developed to facilitate media advertising raise ethical questions at least as serious as those projects generating the conflicts and constraints described above. The research violates notions of privacy. It employs procedures that in an academic setting would be promptly subject to criticism and review. Experiments in the psychological manipulation of a television audience are sometimes done without obtaining voluntary informed consent. Moreover, claims of benefit are colored by the fact that support for research in this area often comes from organizations with clearly self-serving purposes—to change consumer behavior, to dull critical sensibilities, or simply to create markets. However, such unquestioned research usually takes place under private auspices and in industrial settings removed from the control and professional sanctions that constrain federally funded research. Thus the ethical questions that would immediately be raised in an academic setting can easily be avoided. As a result, the participation of social scientists in research endeavors involving direct or indirect collaboration with industry remains largely unchallenged and unconstrained.

Conclusion

Political conventions, laws, the availability of funding, and social taboos have long placed many limits on both the ends and the means of research in the social sciences. The choice of research areas and the acceptability of certain procedures are sometimes strongly, but more often subtly, constrained in ways that serve to protect prevailing social values and existing political relationships. But public concerns about the limits of inquiry are increasing. This trend is in part an extension of the preoccupation with the risks of biomedical research; but it also reflects significant changes in the techniques available for social science research and the possibilities inherent in the utilization of research findings.

First, the scope of social research has broadened. Many areas of human behavior formerly out of bounds have become subjects of social science investigation. Second, the technology of data collection has become more sophisticated, increasing the risk to research subjects. Recording devices and one-way screens facilitate violations of privacy; new data-processing techniques permit analysis case by case rather than by aggregation and so enhance the possible abuses of research findings; and the use of computer data banks confers extraordinary power on the organizations controlling them. Third, in the prevailing social climate many activities previously considered acceptable have been challenged. In the early post-Sputnik years it would have been difficult to imagine a serious discussion of limits to scientific inquiry. But by the mid-1970s the "ideology of progress" had given way to an "ideology of limits." Questions of ethics and of individual freedom of choice enter the public evaluation of scientific research just as they enter the assessment of any other social activity, and the unquestioned acceptance of science as an unmitigated benefit has given way to a far more critical view.

Finally, the preoccupation with the limits of social science research reflects the increased use of social science as a basis for social policy. Governments increasingly rely on specialized expertise to meet the complex demands of social planning or to resolve social problems. Social scientists are closely involved in decision making through advisory boards, special commissions, and consultant groups, as well as through increased employment within government bureaucracies. Between 1960 and 1970, federal government employment of social scientists grew by 52 percent (total federal government employment grew by only 30 percent during this period). In this context, social science research itself becomes a source of political power and social control, and its boundaries thus assume increasing social importance.

Despite existing constraints that are seldom questioned by scientists, the very notion of limiting research provokes a defensive response. Scientists continually negotiate for autonomy, arguing that "ethical decisions are best made by educated scientists who understand the value implications of their decisions, carefully consider the moral alternatives when making choices, and then accept responsibility for their actions."[22] But this plea for self-governance is based on an image of science that does not take into account the potential impact of research and its increased use as a political resource. As the role of science changes so does the justification for scientific autonomy. And in this changing context, control over knowledge, its production, and its codification, becomes a focus of political negotiation and public dispute.

NOTES

* This paper has gained enormously from criticism by Rose Goldsen, Rebecca Logan, Michael Pollak, and David Sills.

1. See the issue of *Daedalus* on the "Limits of Scientific Inquiry" (Spring 1978).

2. Edward Diener and Rick Crandall, *Ethics in Social and Behavioral Research* (Chicago: University of Chicago Press, 1978).

3. Morris Janowitz, *The Last Half Century* (Chicago: University of Chicago Press, 1978), p. 324.

4. Paul Kecskemeti, *Strategic Surrender* (Palo Alto, Calif.: Stanford University Press, 1958).

5. Walter Laqueur, "Russia and Germany," *Survey*, nos. 44–45 (October 1962).

6. Harvey Brooks, "The Federal Government and the Autonomy of Science," in Charles Frankel, *Controversies and Decisions* (New York: Russell Sage Foundation, 1976), pp 235–58.

7. Irving Louis Horowitz, ed., *The Rise and Fall of Project Camelot* (Cambridge, Mass.: MIT Press, 1967); Irving Louis Horowitz and James E. Katz, *Social Science and Public Policy in the United States* (New York: Praeger, 1975), chap. 6; and K.H. Silvert, "American Academic Ethics and Social Research Abroad: The Lesson of Project Camelot," *American Universities Field Staff Reports*, West Coast South American Series, 12 (July 1965).

8. See the review of this controversy by Dorothy Nelkin and Judith P. Swazey, "Science and Social Control," in Ruth Macklin, ed., *Research on Violence* (New York: Plenum Press, 1981).

9. In a letter to the *New York Times* (September 21, 1969), p. 4; cited in Lee Cronbach, "Public Controversy over Mental Testing," in Frankel, *Controversies and Decisions*, p. 133.

10. See, for example, Robert Dworkin et al., "Genetic Influences on the Organization and Development of Personality," *Developmental Psychology* 13 (1977): 164.

11. Ann Arbor Science for the People Collective, *Biology as a Social Weapon* (Minneapolis: Burgess, 1977).

12. Laura Nader, "Up the Anthropologist: Perspectives Gained from Studying Up," in Dell Hymes, ed., *Reinventing Anthropology* (New York: Pantheon, 1969), pp. 284–311.

13. Dorothy Nelkin, *Science Textbook Controversies and the Politics of Equal Time* (Cambridge, Mass.: MIT Press, 1978).

14. Laud Humphreys, *Tearoom Trade: Impersonal Sex in Public Places*, enl. ed. (Chicago: Aldine Publishing Co., 1975). See also *Transaction* 7 (January 1970): 10–25; Nicholas von Hoffman, Irving Louis Horowitz, and Lee Rainwater, "Sociological Snoopers and Journalistic Moralizers: An Exchange," *Transaction* 7 (May 1970): 4–9; Letters to the Editor, *Transaction* 7 (May 1970): 12–13 and (July 1970): 7–8.

15. Leon Festinger, Henry W. Riecken, and Stanley Schachter, *When Prophecy Fails* (Minneapolis: University of Minnesota Press, 1956). A review by M. Brewster Smith, "Of Prophecy and Privacy," *Contemporary Psychology* 2(1957): 89–92, first raised the ethical issues involved in the infiltration of an organization.

16. Diener and Crandall, *Ethics in Social and Behavioral Research*.

17. Stanley Milgram, "Behavioral Study of Obedience," *Journal of Abnormal and Social Psychology* 67 (1963): 371–78; and "Issues in the Study of Obedience," *American Psychologist* 19 (1964): 848–52.

18. P.G. Zimbardo, "On the Ethics of Intervention in Human Psychological Research," *Cognition* 2 (1973): 243–56.

19. Gideon Sjoberg, *A Methodology for Social Research* (New York: Harper and Row, 1968), p. 115. For a review of the case, see Ted Vaughan, "Government Intervention in Social Research: Political and Ethical Dimensions in the Wichita Jury Recordings," in Gideon Sjoberg, ed., *Ethics, Politics and Social Research* (Cambridge, Mass.: Schenkman Publishing Co., 1967), pp. 50–76.

20. See Rose Goldsen, "Why TV Advertising Is Deceptive and Unfair," *Et Cetera* (Winter 1977): 355–61.

21. Janowitz, *Last Half Century*, p. 324.

22. Diener and Crandall, *Ethics in Social and Behavioral Research*, p. 5.

The Intelligence Controversy: The Ethical Problem

H.J. Eysenck

A major difference between environmentalists and so-called hereditarians (who should of course more properly be called interactionists) is their view of the ethical consequences of the empirical findings. The argument is usually advanced that even if what I have said in my presentation is *true*, it is socially *undesirable* that I or anyone should say it, or that further research should be done in this field. It is always unfortunate when one side arrogates to itself an exclusive claim to ethical excellence, and accuses the opposite side of callousness, lack of social sensitivity and immorality. It is particularly when ethical questions get tangled up with political preconceptions that passions are brought into play that should have no place in a scientific controversy.

Social Policies Should Be Based on Fact

Let me state categorically that the fact that heredity is twice as important as environment in determining differences in intelligence in our type of society cannot be used as an argument against improving social conditions. The evidence is quite clear-cut that such improvement will raise IQ levels considerably, particularly among the deprived, and I can see no rational argument whatsoever to oppose such a course. What IQ testing does is to pinpoint the groups and the people particularly in need of help, and to monitor whether any of the methods of improvement adopted do in fact have the effects expected of them. This seems to me an entirely benign use of IQ testing, and I can see no ethical objections to it.

When Jensen drew attention to the simple fact that the Headstart movement had largely failed, he was not opposing *realistic* attempts to improve the achievement level and IQ of deprived children; he was concerned to point out that the particular methods adopted by Headstart, and the theories at the basis of the whole operation, were not in line with modern knowledge. Many psychologists, including Jensen and myself, had predicted that Headstart would fail; this does not mean that we would be opposed to more realistic attempts along the same lines, based on proper scientific theories and knowledge. The work of Jensen himself (1972, 1973), Bennett (1976) and Rutter (1979) marks a beginning in the field of rigorous educational research.

The epicentre of the storm over IQ testing has been the racial issue. Are we entitled to label a whole group of people "inferior" on the basis of some form of mental measurement? Can we justify the blow this would be to their self-confidence, their pride and their racial identification? The answer is no, of course, but an additional answer would be that neither Jensen nor I, nor any other responsible psychologist, have ever said anything of the kind. What we have pointed out is that group differences, where they exist, hide a good deal of overlap, and that the existence of this overlap makes it absolutely impossible to use race or social class as an index of intelligence, achievement or competence. Each person has to be treated as an individual, and assessed by means of objective criteria.

Our Duty to Report

It is often argued that while what responsible psychologists say about racial and class differences may be acceptable, the facts and arguments can easily be abused by racists for their own purposes. This is undoubtedly true, but it raises very difficult problems. Should acknowledged facts and correct arguments be kept from the people who pay their salaries by psychologists or other scientists? Should the scientist set up as a censor to keep knowledge from the people? Is there any evidence that racists would be any less extreme in their attitudes if knowledge of such facts as there may be on this issue were to be kept from them? Is their propaganda any more effective because of what science has discovered? There are no certain answers to any of these questions, but it should not be assumed that those who feel that they have a duty to society to make known the results of empirical work are guided by less lofty ethical aspirations than those who hold the opposite view. In my experience, many psychologists interested in the study of genetic influences believe that the obvious social problem produced by the existence of racial and class differences in ability can only be solved, alleviated or attenuated by greater knowledge, and that therefore it is ethically indefensible to refrain from acquiring such knowledge and making it available to society.

To illustrate how the acquisition of genetic knowledge can help in the solution of a problem I will have recourse to an example given by Kamin himself, in connection with quite a different point. Phenylketonuria is a mental disorder produced by a single recessive gene which interferes with the metabolism of phenylanaline, producing toxic substances which lead to a rapid deterioration in mental ability. Recognition of the genetic nature of the defect led to a search for biological causes which was successful, and in turn led to the correct method of treatment, which consists of eliminating analine from the baby's food. The example does not prove, as Kamin suggests, that the environment can alter genetic factors: the individual with this particular hereditary defect possesses a metabolic system which makes it impossible for him to metabolise phenylanaline properly, whatever is done by the environment.

Would it have been ethical to have refrained from investigating the genetic properties of the disorder, and instead proceeded along environmentalist lines—stressing better teaching, more books or better food for the children in question on the assumption that all mental abilities are determined by environmental factors? The recognition of genetic differences leads to an investigation of biological factors, a very necessary step in the logical sequence of investigation which may in the end lead to proper control of intelligence and intellectual differences. The work on evoked potentials already mentioned is a first step in this direction. It would in my review be unethical not to work in this field, because only through such work, I am convinced, will we ever get to grips with the real problems of dullness and low IQ.

The Toll of Misguided Egalitarianism

Beliefs in the determination of intellectual differences by genetic or environmental causes have very important social consequences, and when the beliefs are based on false premises these consequences can be quite serious. One consequence of the widely held belief that environment determines intellectual differences and that all men are equal with respect to intellectual endowment has been the acceptance in many European universities of almost any applicant, regardless of ability or background. Most drastic perhaps has been the effect in Italy, where thousands of ill-prepared and ill-equipped students throng the universities, make normal teaching impossible, and promote a detrimental sub-academic atmosphere and level of instruction. Furthermore, many of the students, unable to achieve examination success at any reasonable level, have produced a situation—by threatening professors, and even taking them prisoner until they agree to the students' proposals—where all are given pass marks (or even awarded first class certificates) for their examinations regardless of the quality of their work. This is now true even in many medical faculties, and the results of this lowering of standards will plague the Italian state for many years to come. Is it not the ethical duty of the scientist to speak out against these false hypotheses in the hope that more appropriate action, based on correct premises, will ensue?

Likewise, the dictates of "affirmative action" have led many American universities and businesses to introduce racist quota systems whereby people are employed or granted studentships on the basis of their race or minority status rather than their ability. This system of "inverse discrimination" has led to problems, including the failure of many blacks admitted under these rules to achieve examination success. It is no kindness to encourage a person to spend years on a university course, only to fail him in the end when that failure was clearly predictable in terms of his IQ scores. Interference in social processes the psychological bases of which are still largely shrouded in mystery is likely to lead to disaster. Our only safeguard is rigorous scientific research, carried out without fear or favour, without prejudice, and without preconceived ideological ideas.

In saying all this I do not wish to give the impression that I am at all certain that the side of the argument I have here presented is right, as far as ethics is concerned, and the other side wrong. I am concerned, rather, to point out that the problem of ethical priorities is a very difficult one indeed, and that any assumption of rectitude on one side or the other should be scrutinised carefully. There are obviously points to support either side, and no one but a fool would assume that one side was wholly right or wholly wrong. My own position was not taken without a great deal of thought and soul-searching, and while I still maintain that in an imperfect world it is probably the most defensible one, and the one most likely to lead to the ultimate advancement of deprived groups, I would not put the point forward with any degree of certainty, nor would I deny my respect to those who disagree with me on conscientious grounds.

The Fallacy of Richard Herrnstein's IQ

Noam Chomsky

Harvard psychologist Richard Herrnstein's by now well-known *Atlantic* article, "IQ" (September 1971), has been the subject of considerable controversy. Unfortunately this has tended to extend the currency of his ideas rather than to mitigate against them! Herrnstein purports to show that American society is drifting toward a stable hereditary meritocracy, with social stratification by inborn differences and a corresponding distribution of "rewards." The argument is based on the hypothesis that differences in mental abilities are inherited and that people close in mental ability are more likely to marry and reproduce,[1] so that there will be a tendency toward long-term stratification by mental ability, which Herrnstein takes to be measured by IQ. Second, Herrnstein argues that "success" requires mental ability and that social rewards "depend on success." This step in the argument embodies two assumptions: first, it is so in fact; and, second, it must be so for society to function effectively. The conclusion is that there is a tendency toward hereditary meritrocracy, with "social standing" (which reflects earnings and prestige) concentrated in groups with higher IQs. The tendency will be accelerated as society becomes more egalitarian, that is, as artificial social barriers are eliminated, defects in prenatal (e.g., nutritional) environment are overcome, and so on, so that natural ability can play a more direct role in attainment of social reward. Therefore, as society becomes more egalitarian, social rewards will be concentrated in a hereditary meritocratic elite.

Herrnstein has been widely denounced as a racist for this argument, a conclusion that seems to me unwarranted. There is, however, an ideological element in his argument that is absolutely critical to it. Consider the second step, that is, the claim that IQ is a factor in attaining reward and that this must be so for society to function effectively. Herrnstein recognizes that his argument will collapse if, indeed, society can be organized in accordance with the "socialist dictum, 'From each according to his ability, to each according to his needs.'" His argument would not apply in a society in which "income (economic, social, and political) is unaffected by success."

Actually Herrnstein fails to point out that his argument requires the assumption not only that success must be rewarded, but that it must be rewarded in quite specific ways. If individuals are rewarded for success only by prestige, then no conclusions of any importance follow. It will only follow (granting his other assumptions) that children of people who are respected for their own achievements will be more likely to be respected for their own achievements, an innocuous result even if true. It may be that the child of two Olympic swimmers has a greater than average chance of achieving the same success (and the acclaim for it), but no dire social consequences follow from this hypothesis. The conclusion that Herrnstein and others find disturbing is that wealth and power will tend to concentrate in a hereditary meritocracy. But this follows only on the assumption that wealth and power (not merely respect) must be the rewards of successful achievement and that these (or their effects) are transmitted from parents to children. The issue is confused by Herrnstein's failure to isolate the specific factors crucial to his argument and his use of the phrase "income" (economic, social, and political) to cover "rewards" of all types, including respect as well as wealth. It is confused further by the fact that he continually slips into identifying "social standing" with wealth. Thus he writes that if the social ladder is tapered steeply, the obvious way to rescue the people at the bottom is "to increase the aggregate wealth of society so that there is more room at the top"—which is untrue if "social standing" is a matter of acclaim and respect. (We overlook the fact that even on his tacit assumption redistribution of income would appear to be an equally obvious strategy.)

Consider then the narrower assumption that is crucial to his argument: transmittable wealth and power accrue to mental ability and must do so for society to function effectively. If this assumption is false and society can be organized more or less in accordance with the socialist dictum, then nothing is left of Herrnstein's argument (except that it will apply to a competitive society in which his other factual assumptions hold). But the assumption is true, Herrnstein claims. The reason is that ability "expresses itself in labor only for gain" and people "compete for gain—economic and otherwise." People will work only if they are rewarded in terms of "social and political influence or relief from threat." All of this is merely asserted; no justification is given for these assertions. Note again that the argument supports the disturbing conclusions he draws only if we identify the "gain" for which people allegedly compete as transmittable wealth and power.

What reason is there to believe the crucial assumption that people will work only for gain in (transmittable) wealth and power, so that society cannot be organized in accordance with the socialist dictum? In a decent society everyone would have the opportunity to find interesting work, and each person would be permitted the fullest possible scope for his talents. Would more be required—in particular, extrinsic reward in the form of wealth and power? Only if we assume that applying one's talents in interesting and socially useful work is not rewarding in itself, that there is no intrinsic satisfaction in creative and productive work, suited to one's abilities, or in helping others (say, one's family, friends, associates, or simply fellow members of society). Unless we suppose this, then even granting all of Herrnstein's other assumptions, it does not follow that there should be any concentration of wealth or power or influence in a hereditary elite.

For Herrnstein's argument to have any force at all we must assume that people labor only for gain, and that the satisfaction in interesting or socially beneficial work or in work well done or in the respect shown to such activities is not a sufficient "gain" to induce anyone to work. The assumption, in short, is that without material reward people will vegetate. For this crucial assumption no semblance of an argument is offered. Rather Herrnstein merely asserts that if bakers and lumberjacks "got the top salaries and the top social approval"[2] in place of those now at the top of the social ladder, then "the scale of IQs would also invert," and the most talented would strive to become bakers and lumberjacks. This, of course, is no argument, but merely a reiteration of the claim that necessarily individuals work only for extrinsic reward. Furthermore, it is an extremely implausible claim. I doubt very much that Herrnstein would become a baker or lumberjack if he could earn more money in that way.

From Herrnstein's data and arguments we can draw no further conclusions about what would happen in a just society, unless we add the assumption that people labor only for material gain, for wealth and power, and that they do not seek interesting work suited to their abilities—that they would vegetate rather than do such work. Since Herrnstein offers no reason why we should believe any of this (and there is certainly some reason why we should not), none of his conclusions follow from his factual assumptions, even if these are correct. The crucial step in his syllogism in effect amounts to the claim that the ideology of capitalist society expresses universal traits of human nature, and that certain related assumptions of behaviorist psychology are correct. Conceivably these unsupported assumptions are true. But once it is recognized how critical their role is in his argument and what empirical support they, in fact, have, any further interest in this argument would seem to evaporate.

Lurking in the background of the debate over Herrnstein's syllogism is the matter of race, though he himself barely alludes to it. His critics are disturbed, and rightly so, by the fact that his argument will surely be exploited by racists to justify discrimination, much as Herrnstein may personally deplore this fact. More generally Herrnstein's argument will be adopted by the privileged to justify their privilege on the grounds that they are being rewarded for their ability and that such reward is necessary if society is to function properly. The situation is reminiscent of nineteenth-century racist anthropology. Marvin Harris notes:

> Racism also had its uses as a justification for class and
> caste hierarchies; it was a splendid explanation of both
> national and class privilege. It helped to maintain slavery
> and serfdom; it smoothed the way for the rape of Africa
> and the slaughter of the American Indian; it steeled the
> nerves of the Manchester captains of industry as they
> lowered wages, lengthened the working day, and hired
> more women and children.[3]

We can expect Herrnstein's arguments to be used in a
similar way and for similar reasons. When we discover that his
argument is without force, unless we adopt unargued and
implausible premises that happen to incorporate the dominant
ideology, we quite naturally turn to the question of the social
function of his conclusions and ask why the argument is taken
seriously, exactly as in the case of nineteenth-century racist
anthropology.

Since the issue is often obscured by polemic, it is perhaps
worth stating again that the question of the validity and scientific
status of a particular point of view is, of course, logically
independent from the question of its social function; each is a
legitimate topic of inquiry, and the latter becomes of particular
interest when the point of view in question is revealed to be
seriously deficient on empirical or logical grounds.

The nineteenth-century racist anthropologists were no
doubt quite often honest and sincere. They might have believed
that they were simply dispassionate investigators, advancing
science, following the facts where they led. Conceding this, we
might, nevertheless, question their judgment, and not merely
because the evidence was poor and the arguments fallacious. We
might take note of the relative lack of concern over the ways in
which these "scientific investigations" were likely to be used. It
would be a poor excuse for the nineteenth-century racist
anthropologist to plead, in Herrnstein's words, that "a neutral
commentator . . . would have to say that the case is simply not
settled" (with regard to racial inferiority) and that the
"fundamental issue" is "whether inquiry shall (again) be shut off
because someone thinks society is best left in ignorance." The
nineteenth-century racist anthropologist, like any other person,
is responsible for the effects of what he does, insofar as they can
be clearly foreseen. If the likely consequences of his "scientific

work" are those that Harris describes, he has the responsibility
to take this likelihood into account. This would be true even if
the work had real scientific merit—more so, in fact, in this case.

Similarly imagine a psychologist in Hitler's Germany who
thought he could show that Jews had a genetically determined
tendency toward usury (like squirrels bred to collect too many
nuts) or a drive toward antisocial conspiracy and domination,
and so on. If he were criticized for even undertaking these
studies, could he merely respond that "a neutral commentator
. . . would have to say that the case is simply not settled" and
that the "fundamental issue" is "whether inquiry shall (again) be
shut off because someone thinks society is best left in
ignorance"? I think not. Rahter I think that such a response
would have been met with justifiable contempt. At best he could
claim that he is faced with a conflict of values. On the one hand,
there is the alleged scientific importance of determining whether,
in fact, Jews have a genetically determined tendency toward
usury and domination (as might conceivably be the case). On the
other, there is the likelihood that even opening this question and
regarding it as a subject for scientific inquiry would provide
ammunition for Goebbles and Rosenberg and their henchmen.
Were this hypothetical psychologist to disregard the likely social
consequences of his research (or even his undertaking of
research) under existing social conditions, he would fully
deserve the contempt of decent people. Of course, scientific
curiosity should be encouraged (though fallacious argument and
investigation of silly questions should not), but it is not an
absolute value.

The extravagant praise lavished on Herrnstein's flimsy
argument and the widespread failure to note its implicit bias and
unargued assumptions[4] suggest that we are not dealing simply
with a question of scientific curiosity. Since it is impossible to
explain this acclaim on the basis of the substance or force of the
argument, it is natural to ask whether the conclusions are so
welcome to many commentators that they lose their critical
faculties and fail to perceive that certain crucial and quite
unsupported assumptions happen to be nothing other than a
variant of the prevailing ideology. This failure is disturbing,

more so, perhaps, than the conclusions Herrnstein attempts to draw from his flawed syllogism.

Turning to the question of race and intelligence, we grant too much to the contemporary investigator of this question when we see him as faced with a conflict of values: scientific curiosity versus social consequences. Given the virtual certainty that even the undertaking of the inquiry will reinforce some of the most despicable features of our society, the intensity of the presumed moral dilemma depends critically on the scientific significance of the issue that he is choosing to investigate. Even if the scientific significance were immense, we should certainly question the seriousness of the dilemma, given the likely social consequences. But if the scientific interest of any possible finding is slight, then the dilemma vanishes.

In fact, it seems that the question of the relation, if any, between race and intelligence has little scientific importance (as it has no social importance, except under the assumptions of a racist society) A possible correlation between mean IQ and skin color is of no greater scientific interest than a correlation between any two other arbitrarily selected traits, say, mean height and color of eyes. The empirical results, whatever they may be, appear to have little bearing on any issue of scientific significance. In the present state of scientific understanding, there would appear to be little scientific interest in the discovery that one partly heritable trait correlates (or not) with another partly heritable trait. Such questions might be interesting if the results had some bearing, say, on hypotheses about the physiological mechanisms involved, but this is not the case. Therefore, the investigation seems of quite limited scientific interest, and the zeal and intensity with which some pursue or welcome it cannot reasonably be attributed to a dispassionate desire to advance science. It would, of course, be foolish to claim in response that "society should not be left in ignorance." Society is happily "in ignorance" of insignificant matters of all sorts. And with the best of will it is difficult to avoid questioning the good faith of those who deplore the alleged "anti-intellectualism" of the critics of scientifically trivial and socially malicious investigations. On the contrary, the investigator of race and intelligence might do well to explain the intellectual significance of the topic he is studying and thus enlighten us as to the moral dilemma he perceives. If he perceives none, the conclusion is obvious, with no further discussion.

As to social importance, a correlation between race and mean IQ (were this shown to exist) entails no social consequences except in a racist society in which each individual is assigned to a racial category and dealt with not as an individual in his own right, but as a representative of this category. Herrnstein mentions a possible correlation between height and IQ. Of what social importance is that? None, of course, since our society does not suffer under discrimination by height. We do not insist on assigning each adult to the category "below six feet in height" or "above six feet in height" when we ask what sort of education he should receive or where he should live or what he should do. Rather he is what he is, quite independent of the mean IQ of people of his height category. In a nonracist society the category of race would be of no greater significance. The mean IQ of individuals of a certain racial background is irrelevant to the situation of a particular individual, who is what he is. Recognizing this perfectly obvious fact, we are left with little, if any, plausible justification for an interest in the relation between mean IQ and race, apart from the "justification" provided by the existence of racial discrimination.

The question of heritability of IQ might conceivably have some social importance, say, with regard to educational practice. However, even this seems dubious, and one would like to see an argument. It is, incidentally, surprising to me that so many commentators should find it disturbing that IQ might be heritable, perhaps largely so.[5] Would it also be disturbing to discover that relative height, or musical talent, or rank in running the 100 yard dash is in part genetically determined? Why should one have preconceptions one way or another about these questions, and how do the answers to them, whatever they may be, relate either to serious scientific issues (in the present state of our knowledge) or to social practice in a decent society?

NOTES

1. He does not specifically mention this assumption, but it is necessary to the argument.

2. Note again Herrnstein's failure to distinguish remuneration from social approval, though the argument collapses if the only reward is approval.

3. Marvin Harris, *The Rise of Anthropological Theory* (New York: Crowell, 1968), pp. 100–101. By the 1860s, he writes, "anthropology and racial determinism had become almost synonymous."

4. See the correspondence in *Atlantic*, November 1971.

5. An advertisement in the *Harvard Crimson* (November 19, 1971), signed by many faculty members, refers to the "disturbing conclusion that 'intelligence' is largely genetic, so that over many, many years society might evolve into classes marked by distinctly different levels of ability." Since the conclusion does not follow from the premise, as already noted, it may be that what disturbs the signers is the "conclusion that 'intelligence' is largely genetic." Why this should seem disturbing remains obscure.

Conducting Scientific Research for the Military as a Civic Duty

Kenneth W. Kemp

Introduction

In recent years, many scientists and other academics have treated scientific research for the military with suspicion. Although few would argue that no such research should ever be done, many are concerned that it (or at least much of it) should, at a minimum, be excluded from the university. (Tela C. Zasloff's article in the *Chronicle of Higher Education*[1] is a recent example of this.) In this paper, I want to argue that that is the wrong way to think about scientific research for the military. The scientist should instead see military research as a kind of civic duty. Although not all scientists will need to act on this civic duty, and there are circumstances under which doing such research would be wrong, some of the most common objections against military research carry less weight than is sometimes given to them.

Scientific Research for the Military as a Civic Duty

I want to begin by making explicit two assumptions that, although they seem to me to be true, are certainly not uncontroversial. Discussing them would be of philosophical valued, but doing so in any detail would keep us from getting to the central concern of this paper. So I will just assert them with only a hint of what would have to be said in their defense.

The first assumption is that war, or at least preparedness for war, is (both in general and in the present political situation) a legitimate means of pursuing just policy objectives. This means that both absolute and modern-war pacifism are false. A defense of the right to go to war would require defense of the view that the duty to see that justice is done (or injustice avoided) sometimes overrides the duty of nonmaleficence.

The second assumption is that it is the duty of the government to protect society from certain kinds of aggression, and it is a duty to do so by waging war if war is the only effective means of providing th..t protection. The duty of the government to wage war follows from a fairly specific right to be rescued. Although the question of whether there is a right to be rescued by passersby is perhaps controversial, the same right as a claim against the government is, I believe, easier to establish. For defense against the threat of force is precisely one of the reasons why a government is worth having. If there is a right to kill in the cause of justice, and a government duty to exercise this right (for example, by protecting its citizens from attack), there will, in certain cases, be a duty to go to war.

Given those two assumptions, there are three reasons for thinking that the scientist has a duty to participate in military research. The first reason, and the one perhaps most properly tied to a *civic* duty, is the government's just-mentioned right and duty to defend its citizens against aggression. Scientific research can improve the government's ability both to wage war, when war is necessary, and to deter war when war is threatened. Improving the government's ability to wage war makes it easier for the government to fulfill this obligation

This claim about the right and duty to wage war, however, is not strictly necessary to my thesis. To the extent that a nation's military forces are primarily (or exclusively) deterrent (as perhaps are those of Switzerland and Sweden), and if the Wrong-Intentions Principle does not apply to deterrent threats (as I have argued that it does not[2]), it might be possible even for a pacifist scientist to support military research. But defense of the legitimacy of military research in the context of nonpacifist views about the moral permissibility of war is surely the more natural way to apprach the issue.

But the government's duty to go to war cannot just be the duty of an institution. It must ultimately become the duty of particular individuals. Those individuals must be either mercenaries, a military caste, or ordinary citizens. Hiring mercenaries raises a host of moral and practical problems. Reliance on a military caste can endanger the principle of civil supremacy over the military. That leaves defense as the duty of ordinary citizens.

The days of the militia are gone, probably forever. There is no alternative but to maintain a permanent standing army. This creates the problem of assuring that the army maintains its allegiance to the ideal of the citizen-soldier, that it does not become a military caste. There are a variety of ways of doing this. For its part, the military can and must keep careful watch on itself, to ensure that officers with Bonapartist views are not promoted to positions of responsibility. If for no other reason, it has this duty because, in the United States at least, it sees itself, and asks others to see it, as a profession and not merely as an occupation. (See, for example, many of the essays in M.M. Wakin's *War, Morality, and the Military Profession*,[3] which is used in the required ethics course at the U.S. Air Force Academy.) But the citizenry also has a part in this. Its responsibility is to ensure that civilians do not shunt the duty of national defense off onto the military as though defense were not a general responsibility. Encouraging those who have no intention of making a career of military service to spend a few years on active duty is one way of keeping the responsibility general. Broadening the involvement of civilian scientists in military research is another.

From the scientist's point of view, doing scientific research for the military will be just one way of fulfilling the rather stronger duty of all citizens to help make the society a better place to live. A scientist could fulfill this duty by being a soccer coach, by feeding the poor, or by raising funds for the symphony. But some scientists must fulfill this duty by doing scientific research when such research is needed. Indeed, because scientific expertise is so scarce, it may be important that many scientists fulfill their duty in this way. If enough scientists take their turn at such research, the burden on any particular scientist need not be too great. (Indeed, because military research has, in recent years, been at least as well funded as other scientific research, the burden of doing such research amounts only to the distraction from what might be intrinsically more attractive lines of research. In comparison to the burden imposed on the conscript, or even the volunteer enlistee, this burden is modest indeed.) Whether the scientist who decides to fulfill his duty to society as a scientist should fulfill it by doing scientific work for the military or by working on some other project will depend, in part, on what work most needs to be done. But the duty imposed by scientific expertise cannot be ignored; it is analogous to the lawyer's duty to do *pro bono* work for indigent clients.

There are two other reasons why scientists have a duty to assist in military research. First, when the nation asks some soldiers to risk their lives in pursuit of certain national security objectives, it has the obligation to minimize those risks by making available to the soldier whatever technological advantages will increase his prospects of survival. That imposes on the government, and consequently on society in general, a duty of research into chemical protective equipment, armor, night observation devices, and the like.

Second, the scientist has a general obligation to minimize the destructiveness of war. Military research aimed at this end will range from increasingly accurate weapons (which reduce collateral damage) to improvements in military medical technology (which the medic is required to use for the benefit of all wounded combatants).

Most of the objections to military research are focused not so much on the rejection of any of the premises of the foregoing argument as on other concerns, concerns which, it might be argued, outweigh those just advanced in favor of broadly based scientific participation in military research.

Unjust Causes, Unjust Means, and Military Research

The right and duty on which the argument in the preceding section was based was the right and duty to wage war, whether in self-defense or in defense of some other right. It goes almost without saying that scientists would have no duty to conduct military research in nations whose foreign policy was dominated by the pursuit of unjust ends. Indeed, ordinarily they would have no right to do so.

The traditional moral rule about cooperation in the wrongful actions of others distinguishes two kinds of cooperation, material and formal. Formal cooperation involves acceptance by the cooperator of the wrongful intentions of the principal agent. An example of such cooperation would be the actions of the conspirators in the Lincoln assassination. Even those who did not actually do the shooting were responsible for the assistance they provided to Booth because they were helping him precisely because they wanted the assassination to succeed. Formal cooperation in the wrongdoing of others is, of course, always wrong. Material cooperation, by contrast, involves cooperation in the *action* of the principal only. It does not involve acceptance by the cooperator of the wrongful intentions of the principal even when he knows of those wrongful intentions. An example would be the action of the mechanic who repaired a getaway car under duress. Such an action would be wrong unless 1) the action was not wrong in itself (as killing an innocent person would be but repairing the car would not) and 2) there was sufficient reason for performing the action despite the fact that it would help in the commission of a crime (as preserving one's life would be, but making a few extra dollars would not).

Scientists who performed military research for aggressive states would surely be doing wrong if they conducted the research in order to further the aims of their government. And although someone *might* be able to think up circumstances in which military research in the service of aggressive nations would be acceptable, on the whole, the *prima facie* duty to avoid even material cooperation in the wrongdoing of others would require avoidance of such activities as well.

The same would have to be said about research into intrinsically objectionable weapons (it would not, of course, be morally objectionable to do research into the means of defense against such weapons), as well as research in violation of treaty obligations.

Military Research and Misplaced Expenditures

Is there a moral obligation to refrain from engaging in military research that should have been put aside in favor of other social needs? Is this also wrongful cooperation in the misdeeds of others? Surely, encouraging unneccessary military spending is blameworthy. For those in positions of influence, even failing to speak up against it may be blameworthy as well. But once the decision to undertake certain research has been made, there is ordinarily no reason why any scientist who believes that he can do the work well should not offer to do it. Here we have a case of merely material cooperation. It is probable that even those who proposed the expenditures did so because they were ignorant, or at worst negligent, of the injustice involved. So, in the ordinary case, there is little likelihood of the cooperating scientist adopting any of the wrongful *intentions* of the principals. Further, engaging in ordinary military research is not wrong in itself. And there are several reasons why the scientist should *not* avoid such material cooperation. First, once the money is allocated, the question becomes one of ensuring that the research is done as well and as economically as possible. Second, if all scientists who favor relatively lower defense expenditures avoid military research on the grounds that military spending is excessive, there will be a kind of concentration of military research in the hands of those who share certain political views. This would create precisely the kind of narrow political base of military work that should be avoided.

Military Research and the Principle of Political Neutrality of Universities

Does participation in military research violate any kind of principle of political neutrality for universities? Would it, in consequence of some such principle, be inappropriate for university scientists to engage in such research? Again, I believe, the answer is no.

Just what a principle of political neutrality requires and forbids is hard to say. Some kinds of activities are obviously forbidden. Hiring faculty on the basis of their political beliefs, endorsing candidates for political office, and conducting political campaigns on behalf of particular candidates are all clearly violations of the principle. Taking sides on particular political issues, at least those far removed from education policy, is only somewhat less controversial. Even those prohibitions have some bite with respect to scientific research for the military, however. A university that conducts military research would, I think, be violating the principle if it waged a lobbying effort in favor of continued funding of that research. For whether such funding is necessary, and whether it is more important than other projects that are competing for the same scarce government money, is a political decision. (This restriction does not, of course, apply to individual academic scientists, who have a right and a duty as citizens to contribute to the debate over these issues. They would also, of course, have a special obligation to be careful lest their personal interest in seeing the funding continue cloud their judgment about its relative merits compared to the merits of other possible uses of government money.)

But in doing military research for a just state, the university only provides the government with the means that the government has chosen to develop for a more effective pursuit of its foreign policy. And although the choice, even among means, may be a political issue, the university could hardly be said to be *making* political choices in virtue of its agreement to help implement choices once they were made.

Classified Military Research and the
Principle of Openness

Some, though not all, military research is classified. Does conducting such research violate a general principle of openness that should characterize either all scientific research, or at least university-based research?

Surely the ideal of an open and unsecretive community of researchers who share results and ideas freely with one another is a noble ideal. The scientific community is at present not such a community, and in part, at least, for reasons that have nothing to do with national security or even with industrial secrecy. James D. Watson's *The Double Helix* offers a good account of the extent to which the eagerness for priority keeps the spirit of provisional secrecy alive in the scientific community. But perhaps what he describes just reflects the vanity of scientists, or the improper pressures imposed by the present institutionalization of science (where continued employment as a scientist requires publication).

Perhaps so, but there are nevertheless good reasons for keeping some scientific results secret. In an ideal world, there would be no knowledge that would be too dangerous to publish, but ours is not that world. In fact, there are things and processes the knowledge of which would enable bad men to pose serious dangers to society. A scientist who stumbles onto such knowledge would have an obligation to restrict access to it or even, under certain circumstances, to suppress it altogether. I think this obligation is analogous to the (unfortunately no less controversial) duty of a journalist not to publish certain kinds of information (for example, gratuitous dirt on public figures). Although there is knowledge that would be dangerous in the hands of some, it does not follow that such knowledge should never be sought at all. It might, after all, provide an important advantage to an honest police force or to an army defending its country. Thus there might remain an important duty to acquire the dangerous knowledge, but to make it known only to those who would not use it for the wrong purposes. If that is true, the only remaining problem is whether there is something distinctive about the university that would make it necessary that this kind of work be done elsewhere.

A recent University of Michigan report suggests that there is something special about universities:

> Research that is secret either in its conduct or its results is directly incompatible with fundamental university goals of the furtherance of knowledge through the discovery and interchange of scientific information and its faithful transmission to the younger generation in the classroom and laboratory.[4]

The report later cites several reasons why openness is important. Surely the most serious is that avoiding secret research "ensures that all members of the university community are free to participate in the research enterprise, including . . . foreign nationals." As long as scientists have the opportunity (both by university policy and in fact) to pursue classified research in laboratories outside the university, it is possible, as the Michigan report suggests, that the separation of classified research and the university may turn out to be the best way of respecting all of the competing values that come into play here. But at this point the question is not whether the scientist will have an opportunity to fulfill his duty, but only of establishing an appropriate institutional setting for his work. (Margaret Schabas[5] has discussed the question of whose right it is to make decisions about the proper institutional setting for such research.) And that, unlike the question of the academic scientist's right or duty to conduct such research, is a question of institutional policy, not of moral principle.

Conclusion

Scientists must avoid the temptation to see military research either as a distraction to be avoided or as an inherently suspect category of work. The defense of the nation continues to require military preparedness, and just states have both the right and the duty to defend themselves. Derivatively, the citizens of those states have the duty to assist in this preparedness when and if their talents are needed. Although the duty to do this can be overridden, it is not overridden as readily as some recent critics of military research have suggested.

NOTES

1. Zasloff, T.C. 1988. The university, by definition, may be the wrong place for military research. Chron. Higher Educ. 34: A52.

2. Kemp, K.W. 1987. Nuclear deterrence and the morality of intentions. Monist 70: 276–297.

3. Wakin, M.M. 1978, 1988. War, Morality, and the Military Profession. Westview Press. Boulder, CO.

4. *Ad Hoc* Committee on Classified Research at the University of Michigan. 1986. Report of the committee. July 14. University of Michigan. Ann Arbor, MI.

5. Schabas, M. 1988. The permissibility of classified research in university science. Public Affairs Q. 2: 47–64.

Military Funds, Moral Demands: Personal Responsibilities of the Individual Scientist

Douglas P. Lackey

Moral Criticisms and Nonmoral Appraisals

I want to begin this essay on a cautionary note. My topic is the ethical implications of the military funding of scientific research, but I want first to get clear in my own mind about what an ethical issue is. It has been my experience that what many people will call an ethical implication does not correspond to what I take to be an ethical implication, and arguments often go at cross-purposes.

I think that we should try to get clear about what ethics is because genuinely ethical judgments are both action-guiding and overriding. It is part of the logic of the terms "ethical" and "moral" that if something is unethical or immoral, it ought not to be done: the immorality of an action provides a conclusive reason for not doing it. The fact that moral judgments override all other judgments stems from the deep connection between what is moral and what is rational for human beings to do, given the social character of human life.[1] So it would be a mistake to think that a moral consideration is one of several considerations for or against a policy or action. On the contrary, a moral judgment is a final consideration about what ought to be done, or what one ought to do, all things considered.[2]

This view of moral judgments, quite common among philosophers, is accepted, for bad reasons, by people who still believe that the moral law is the law of God, but it is quite out of fashion among allegedly educated nonphilosophers. At meetings of the Institutional Review Board of a large metropolitan hospital on which I serve, the board will debate the merits of a research protocol involving human subjects and then turn to me for the "ethical considerations." I supply them, and the committee factors the "ethical consideration" into its decision about whether to sanction the research. I accept the bureaucratic logic of this arrangement, but it appalls my deeper philosophical sensibilities.

Moral judgments—again because of their rational character—are essentially universalizable.[3] What this means is that if a particular action is morally required of a certain person, it is morally required of every other person who stands in the same morally relevant circumstances as the first. A mere difference of persons counts for nothing as regards moral obligations. Two similarly situated persons may rationally adopt two different life-styles, but each cannot consider himself bound by different obligations than the other. Philosophers have made a great deal of the requirement of universalizability, but I am not so much interested in universalizable judgments being moral as I am in nonuniversalizable judgments not being moral; that is, nonuniversalizable judgments cannot express moral requirements.

Given these logical constraints on moral judgments, a distinction naturally emerges between an appraisal based on a political ideal and a moral criticism based on moral principles.[4] We might have certain ideals for ourselves, or others, or for our society, and we might praise those whose conduct serves these ideals. Nevertheless, it remains possible that conduct that falls short of these ideals is not necessarily immoral conduct. To take some examples close at hand:

1. We might argue that it would be better if there were no such thing as the military funding of scientific research because such funding clashes with the desire of nonmilitary researchers to engage in the disinterested pursuit of truth. But the disinterested pursuit of truth is

an ideal, not a moral requirement. Human beings are not obliged to disinterestedly pursue the truth. We may admire those who pursue truth, but we do not number among the wicked all who have no interest in doing so. Thus our appraisal here does not amount to moral criticism.

2. We might argue that the influence of the military establishment on the direction of scientific research in this country, considering the volume of scientific work devoted to military projects and the volume of scientific work sponsored out of the military budget, has had a debilitating effect on the ability of the United States to compete effectively in world industrial markets.[5] But even if we suppose that this is true, and I do suppose this, we must recognize that the economic supremacy of the United States is not something demanded by basic moral principles. American supremacy is not a moral good but a patriotic ideal. Once again, our appraisal is not a moral criticism.

3. We might feel that the scientists and students who signed the petition not to take funds for research budgeted through the Strategic Defense Initiative (SDI) performed a morally admirable action. But unless we are prepared to condemn all those who failed to sign the petition, including those who did not sign the petition but who are in fact *not* working with Defense Department funds, the action of those who signed the petition is not universalizable. We can say that those who signed the petition were pursuing a personal ideal, an ideal that we happen to find admirable, but we cannot say that they were discharging moral obligations when they signed.

What Is Immoral in the Military
Funding of Research

If we concede that the above-mentioned arguments (that the military funding of research is bad for science, bad for the American economy, and bad for the souls of idealistic young researchers) do not amount to a moral condemnation, we might think that the moral slate on military funding has been wiped clean. But in fact I do not think so: I think that the military funding of research is bad, morally bad. I begin my analysis from the standpoint of those who accept the funds.

First, it is obvious that those who accept these funds believe either that the research will in the end yield something that is militarily effective, or it will not. Second, those who believe that their research will in the end yield something effective believe either that this something will be used for good or it will be used for evil.

Case 1

Consider first those who believe that the research is militarily useless. This is a common enough view among those applying for SDI funds because most believe that the goals of the initiative simply cannot be achieved. What I want to say about these people is that they are engaged in a kind of theft: they are taking money from the taxpayers or their representatives on the pretense that they can produce what the taxpayers want for this money, knowing full well they cannot produce it. They are morally akin to meretricious doctors who supply deviant cancer treatments for pay, knowing full well that the treatments will not work.

There is a further error involved in the "Stars Wars won't work, therefore Star Wars research is benign" argument. Even if the goals of SDI cannot be achieved, it may happen that research toward these impossible goals can be diverted for evil purposes. The recent leaks that Star Wars technology will be directed to the destabilizing mission of antisatellite warfare is a case in point.[6]

Case 2

There are some scientists who are willing to concede that their research serves a military function and that this function is evil. In these circumstances there is no moral justification for doing the research: the need for scientific progress provides no argument because scientific research, as I have already urged, is not a moral imperative. Persons in this category usually feel that they have some *excuse*, if not a *justification*, for what they are doing. Whether they have an acceptable excuse will be taken up in the next section.

Case 3

Finally, there are those who believe that their research will serve some military purpose and that this purpose is benign, or perhaps even morally good. I do not wish to challenge the sincerity of those who hold these views, but I do challenge their accuracy. Although the question is daunting, we must ask and seriously try to decide whether the use of military force by the United States in the present era has been morally benign, and we must especially ask whether those aspects of military force that have been developed with the assistance of top-line science and engineering have been morally benign. We must try to approach this problem with at least a minimum of objectivity, defining that minimum as not taking the position that a policy is morally right by definition because it is the United States that has adopted it.

The historical record, at least the record since the Korean War, is not encouraging. In 1953, the American government acted to prevent the realization of legitimate nationalistic aspirations in Iran; likewise, in 1954, it overthrew the Guatemalan government on the pretext that any attempt to regulate the overseas operations of the United Fruit Company was a plot devised by Leninists. In 1956, the United States subverted the 1955 Geneva Agreements by supporting Diem's refusal to hold elections in Vietnam. In Cuba in 1961, in the Dominican Republic in 1965, in Chile in 1973, and in Nicaragua since 1980, the United States has supported forcible attempts to overthrow popular and populist Latin American governments.[7] The late 60s and early 70s were devoted to a foredoomed attempt to block Vietnamese self-determination, and since 1967 the United States has devoted massive resources to blocking Palestinian self-determination. In three of the most violent convulsions of the post-World War II era, the United States tilted to the unjust side: in 1971, in siding against India and the Bengali Independence movement; in 1978, in siding with Pol Pot and the Khymer Rouge against the Vietnamese; and since 1980, in siding with Iraq against Iran, although it was Iraq that invaded Iran, and Iraq that pursued this conflict in vicious disregard of the conventions of war. In all these cases I am prepared to argue that the threat or use of force by the United States was, putting it mildly, not benign.

I am not maintaining that the United States is the Great Satan, the prime offender against international justice. Certainly the record of the United States as regards the use of force since 1953 is not morally worse than that of the Soviet Union, nor is the use of force by the United States, measured by historical standards, uniquely or even especially malevolent. Nevertheless, the record is sufficiently depressing and consistent to make one think that the difficulty is not the result of bad judgment or accidental circumstances but of deeper structural factors, such as the maintenance of global political influence, the needs of the American economy, and the deep-seated myths the American people have about their moral position in history and in the world. There is also the general problem that the use of violence is only justified as a last resort, and politicians, American and non-American alike, rarely have the patience to exhaust all available resources before turning to violence. Hence, it is a safe historical generalization that most uses of violence by states are unjust. If the historical record since 1953 results from such structural factors, we have every reason to expect that uses of force by the United States in the near future will be as immoral as uses of force by the United States in the recent past.

If we turn now to those aspects of the use of American force in which scientists have been especially involved, we find once again structural factors that create a strong probability that scientific research will be used to ill effect. I do not wish to debate the pros and cons of particular weapons systems or to delve into the intricate immoralities of research on chemical, biological, and nuclear weapons. What concerns me is that the application of technology to warfare seems in the present historical phase to create an increasing distance between the killer and the killed, and this increasing separation between the killer and the killed must inevitably lead to bad judgments about the legitimacy of war and bad judgments about how to conduct it. The Vietnam example is the first case that comes to mind, and the last one that anyone should need on this subject. Furthermore, by and large, high-tech armaments in contemporary settings are more suitable to offense than defense, and low-tech armaments are more suitable to defense than offense. Because most offensive wars are immoral wars, research on the high-tech end is more likely to be used for evil than for good. Please note that my argument here is probabilistic, and is not to be overthrown by the example of British radar or the other standard stories of nice technology at work.

My verdict is that those who believe that their research will probably be used for good purposes are mistaken in this belief. If I am right, their participation is not morally justified. Once again, the question of excusability is withheld for the next section.

I have now exhausted the set of possible cases, and the result in the three main cases is that the acceptance of funds is not morally justifiable. But if it is not morally legitimate for anyone to accept the funds, it follows that it is not morally legitimate to offer them either. A policy that encourages immoral action by individuals must itself be an immoral policy.

The Poverty of Excuses

This leaves the residual problem of whether scientists and engineers who participate in research under military auspices have some moral excuse for their participation.

First off, let me note that the traditional excuses supplied by the history of ethics—coercion and ignorance—are ill-suited to the typical case of military research or military funding.

The typical scientist cannot say that he is coerced into doing the research. It might be the case that he will be better off, in financial and career terms, if he does the research than if he does not do it. But the prospect of losing some gain that one might have had, as opposed to suffering some loss of what one already has, has never qualified as an excuse in either morals or law. Of course, there will be exceptions, such as the case of the company scientist who is transferred, on pain of dismissal, from a nonmilitary to a military project. This scientist, in my view, has an excuse, but his is not the typical case.

Likewise, the excuse of ignorance does not come readily to hand. In case 1 and case 2 above, where the scientists know that the research will be ineffective or pernicious, the excuse of ignorance is obviously unavailable. Case 3, in which the research is pernicious but is perceived to be benign, is more difficult, but I rush to point out that the mere belief that one is engaged in a benign activity does not, by itself, excuse the activity unless this belief is reasonable, that is, based on decent evidence decently examined.

It has not been my impression that many scientists involved in defense work or subsisting on the defense dole have undertaken an examination of the historical evidence and the present world scene. On the contrary, one finds, given the educational attainments of these people, a surprising ignorance of history, and an incredible lack of exposure to alternative interpretations of what happened and why. William Broad's account of the political naiveté of young scientists at the Lawrence Livermore National Laboratory describes not the odd case, but the typical ignorance of history and the humanities one finds among these researchers.[8] I am not requesting that everyone slavishly accept the account of recent history that I have sketched here. But, given the impact of science on war, it should at least be possible for those who take defense money to present a modest point-by-point rebuttal of the cases I mentioned, and this they usually cannot do. What we have is culpable ignorance, not the nonculpable ignorance that generates acceptable moral excuses.

There are, however, more exotic excuses available to the scientists and technicians involved.

The Replaceability Excuse

One excuse, which I heard frequently from men of draft age during the Vietnam War, and then once again when the Star Wars pork barrel arrived, was that "If I don't go, someone else will," or "If I don't take the money, someone else will." I call this the replaceability excuse: the argument that if one opts out, one will surely be replaced by someone else who will do the same work, and consequently that it makes no difference to the general outcome whether or not one participates. According to this argument, we can make moral criticisms of the policy choice, but not moral criticisms of those who participate in the operation of the policy, provided that their conduct is consistent with the policy itself and consistent with certain rudimentary moral norms, like the laws of war.

It would be rhetorically unkind of me to mention that the replaceability excuse was offered in the 1950s by staff guards of death camps who were brought to trial, and that the German courts were unmoved by the argument that it was excusable to kill Jews in death camps because someone else was sure to kill them anyway.[9] I will instead offer the more abstract argument that if the replaceability excuse were valid for avoiding the assignment of blame it must also be valid for avoiding the assignment of rewards. But I would be surprised to find a scientist working on a project who would accept the argument that he does not deserve to be paid for his work because, if he had not done it, someone else would have stepped in and done the same work. If the one who does the work deserves the pay, the one who produces the evil deserves the blame, regardless of what others might have done if he had acted differently.

The Small Potatoes Excuse

The replaceability excuse claims that one's contribution makes
no difference. The small potatoes excuse claims that in these
situations one makes a morally negligible contribution to the bad
result. (I used to call this the Eichmann excuse, but I have
stopped using this label because I do not want to accept
Eichmann's self-characterization as a small potato.) Certainly
when one is participating in a large project, it is often difficult to
see the impact of one's contribution to the final result. This is
especially true when the final result is not actual but
probabilistic: for example, an increase in the probability of
nuclear war in a given year from 0.005% to 0.006%. But of course
being unable to see one's contribution is no argument that the
contribution is not there, even if it may be a probabilistic one.

I wish to suggest two different rebuttals to the small
potatoes excuse.

The first rebuttal is that in situations in which many
people contribute to an outcome, it does not necessarily follow
that each bears responsibility for but a small share of the
outcome. On the contrary, it often happens that *each* bears moral
responsibility for the *whole* outcome. This happens when the
work of each is a necessary condition for the success of the
project. This condition is more frequently met than people
realize. For example, each contributor to a project may
mistakenly think that his work was unnecessary because it could
have been done by someone else. This is the replaceability fallacy
again. If a bit of work is a necessary condition for the success of
the whole project—as, for example, designing the exhaust nozzle
for the space shuttle is a necessary condition of the shuttle's
operation—the person who does that bit of work is morally
responsible for the total good or bad produced by the whole
project, even if someone else could have designed the nozzle. In
general, if action A is necessary for result R, and if it is Jones who
is to do A, Jones's action is necessary, even if it could be done by
someone other than Jones. Thus I hold each scientist who did
necessary work on the Manhattan Project responsible for the
entire expectable outcome at Hiroshima and Nagasaki, even if

the scientific work in question could have been done by someone else.

The argument for assigning total rather than partial responsibility for work necessary for an outcome is illuminated by an example from Derek Parfit.[10] Suppose that a building has collapsed and one must choose between (a) saving one person by oneself or (b) participating in a rescue operation in which each rescuer plays a necessary role, and for which only you and nine others are available. If one argued that in (a) one person saves one life while in (b) each person saves half a life, then the rational choice of action is (a). But if one does (a) one life is saved and five lost, whereas if one does (b) one life is lost and five are saved. Obviously the correct moral choice of action is (b), and this shows that each of the ten rescuers is morally responsible for saving five people.

The second rebuttal takes in situations in which the project has a built-in redundancy and in which one's work is not a necessary condition of the project's result. In these cases, I believe, each person is responsible for a fractional share of the total harm or good done, and the fractional share may be a very small fraction. But a small fraction of a big result may itself be a substantial good or harm, and it would be incorrect to argue that every small fraction of an outcome is itself morally negligible. Political scientists claim that each voter in a presidential election has a 1 in 100 million chance of determining the outcome of the election.[11] In all other cases, one's vote is redundant. Certainly it would be fallacious to conclude from this that there is no point in voting. Whoever does get elected president makes a substantial difference to the welfare of a great many people. If one believes that military research, on the whole, does harm in the world, the harm is one that affects a great many people, and it is morally quite serious to play even a small part in this business. As a utilitarian will argue, being responsible for a small fraction of an extensive harm can be as serious as being wholly responsible for a smaller local harm. We should be as reluctant to excuse the former as we are the latter.

NOTES

1. The connection between moral principles and rational principles is usually associated with ethical theories of the Kantian sort. But the link is also obviously present in egoistic systems and in utilitarian systems, if by "rational" one means the efficient choice of means for maximizing the good. Recently, there have been a flurry of non-Kantian attempts to identify moral principles with principles of rational choice.

2. The overriding character of moral principles is comprehensively argued in Baier, K. 1958. The Moral Point of View. Cornell University Press. Ithaca, NY.

3. For a recent discussion of universalizability, see Hare, R.M. 1981. Moral Thinking: Its Methods, Levels, and Point. Oxford University Press.

4. For the differences between political ideals and moral requirements see Beitz, C. 1979. Political Theory and International Relations. Princeton University Press.

5. The main cause of this seems to be the concentration of research on nonmarketable high-tech military products. See Council on Economic Priorities. 1987. Star Wars: The Economic Fallout. Ballinger. Cambridge, MA.

6. At a public meeting sponsored by the New York Academy of Sciences on February 22, 1986, I asked Dr. Gerald Jonas, chief science officer of SDI, what fraction of SDI research could be diverted to an antisatellite mission. Sensible of the congressional moratorium on antisatellite research, Jonas replied "very little." By late 1988, however, satellite destruction was emerging as one of the main missions of strategic defense. See Broad, W.J. 1988. U.S. promoting offensive role for "Star Wars." N.Y. Times, November 27.

7. For background on these and other incidents, see Blechman, B. 1982. Force Without War. Brookings Institution. Washington, DC. See also Prados, J. 1986. The President's Secret Wars. William Morrow. New York, NY.

8. Broad, W. 1985. Star Warriors. Simon & Schuster. New York, NY.

9. Hart, H.L.A. & A.M. Honore. 1960. Causation in the Law. Oxford University Press.

10. Parfit, D. 1984. Reasons and Persons: 67–73. Oxford University Press.

11. Meehl, P. 1977. The paradox of the throwaway vote. Am. Pol. Sci. Rev. 71.

Index

/50

THE MAN FROM NAZARETH

Other Books
by
Harry Emerson Fosdick

★

THE SECOND MILE

THE ASSURANCE OF IMMORTALITY

THE MANHOOD OF THE MASTER

THE MEANING OF PRAYER

THE MEANING OF FAITH

THE MEANING OF SERVICE

CHRISTIANITY AND PROGRESS

TWELVE TESTS OF CHARACTER

THE MODERN USE OF THE BIBLE

ADVENTUROUS RELIGION

A PILGRIMAGE TO PALESTINE

AS I SEE RELIGION

THE HOPE OF THE WORLD

THE SECRET OF VICTORIOUS LIVING

THE POWER TO SEE IT THROUGH

SUCCESSFUL CHRISTIAN LIVING

A GUIDE TO UNDERSTANDING THE BIBLE

LIVING UNDER TENSION

ON BEING A REAL PERSON

A GREAT TIME TO BE ALIVE

ON BEING FIT TO LIVE WITH

THE MAN FROM NAZARETH

As His Contemporaries Saw Him

By

HARRY EMERSON FOSDICK

HARPER & BROTHERS · NEW YORK

THE MAN FROM NAZARETH

Copyright, 1949, by Harper & Brothers

PRINTED IN THE UNITED STATES OF AMERICA BY
KINGSPORT PRESS, INC., KINGSPORT, TENNESSEE

To

My Grandchildren

PATRICIA DOWNS

STEPHEN FOSDICK DOWNS

CONTENTS

Prologue

WHEN one has been fascinated by the personality of Jesus, the desire to see him as one would have seen him had one been his contemporary is inevitable. Even in the earliest records of the New Testament we have an interpreted Jesus, already thought of in current theological and messianic terms. How to pierce behind those interpretations and to recover the Man of Nazareth as he would appear could we moderns directly see him, has been the object of endless research, especially during the last century.

The results of this endeavor have been far from satisfactory. The attempt, as it were, to leap into the self-consciousness of Jesus, to by-pass the Gospel's thoughts about him and to recover the uninterpreted personality, as he was before being set in inherited patterns of theology, is an all but impossible task. Even if Jesus were only a genius, it requires a genius to get inside the mind of a genius. How, then, can we project ourselves into the inner life of the Master, and be sure that we are truly recovering the historic personality and understanding him? The Gospel records themselves are an inadequate basis for such an endeavor, leaving open to endless debate many central questions, such as whether he regarded himself as, in any traditional sense, the Messiah and, if so, what he meant by his messiahship.

[9]

The frustration which one experiences when one tries thus to detour around the first interpretations of the Master and to come immediately into the presence of the "historic Jesus" is made evident in the many diverse ideas of him which have resulted. The difference between the picture of Jesus given us, with only slight variations, in Matthew, Mark and Luke, and the picture presented in the Fourth Gospel is familiar. That, however, is nothing as compared with the difference between Ernest Renan's sentimentalist, Bouck White's social revolutionist, Bruce Barton's expert in salesmanship, Schweitzer's apocalypticist, Thomas N. Carver's economist, Binet-Sanglé's paranoiac, and Middleton Murry's man of genius. That invaluable contributions have been made to our knowledge and appreciation of the Master by attempts to get directly at him, and that such attempts will and should go on, is to be taken for granted. Nevertheless, what each man sees, when he tries this method of direct attack, is what he brings eyes to see, and the portrait he paints is commonly so highly colored by subjective factors that it is more a revelation of himself than of Jesus.

This book is an endeavor to try an indirect method of approach. To project ourselves into the self-consciousness of history's supreme personality may be beyond our power, but to see from the inside the way Pharisees and Sadducees felt and thought, to put ourselves into the places of first-century outcasts and sinners, women and children, patriotic nationalists, believers in God's world-wide kingdom, and even the first disciples, is far more within our range. Moreover, there is a vast amount of specific information, both in the New Testament and outside it, concerning such groups, their convictions and prejudices, their customary ways of thinking, and their personal and social needs. What if we should start with them, identify ourselves with their attitudes, and look at Jesus through their eyes? We might at least see Jesus as they saw him and, in the end, achieve a composite portrait of him as these varied folk, friendly and hostile, looked at him.

Such is the endeavor which this book undertakes. To be sure, I have tried not to let this method enslave and shackle me. The aim is still to see what manner of man the historic Jesus was, what he thought and taught and did, and how he felt. Wherever the insight of his contemporaries makes clear the kind of person they were looking at, I have tried to bring that out; and often, in attempting to portray the way he appeared to them, I have used whatever evidence I could find to show what it was in him that made such appearance possible. Nevertheless, my major approach to the Master has been indirect, by way of the responses to him of the men and women who saw and heard him.

The last half century of research has brought to light revealing information about the life and times of Jesus. For the most part this is known to scholars only, hidden in learned volumes which only specialists are likely to read. Today, however, the desire to know all that we can know about the Man of Nazareth is widespread, and not intellectual curiosity alone but profounder motives of personal and public need awaken hunger for all available information about Jesus. I have hoped, therefore, that a modest volume, such as this, written not by a technical New Testament scholar, might be of use in presenting to the ordinary reader some of the results of recent study.

I am under no illusion that I have avoided the subjective element, which colors all portraits of the Master. Inevitably one's own predilections and biases get in the way of one's endeavor to draw a true picture of him. But I have done my best and, to that end, have tried to make clear by apposite quotations and by specific references the objective evidence on which the opinions of this book are based.

As for my indebtedness, that is far too extensive to be covered by any printed acknowledgment. The list of selected books in the appendix will indicate a portion of it. This list, however, has been compiled mainly with the non-technical reader in mind, and it comprises only books which are available in English. To Dr. John Knox, Professor of Sacred Literature in the Union Theological Seminary, New York City, I owe a special debt. He read the manuscript of this book with painstaking care and, while he must not be accused of holding all the opinions which the book expresses, his critical judgment has made it a much better piece of work than it would otherwise have been.

The material in four of the chapters was used as the basis of the Shaffer Lectures at the Yale Divinity School in 1948; and a few paragraphs in Chapter IV are repeated substantially from an article of mine which appeared in *Life* magazine, entitled, "The Personality That Christmas Celebrates." To Mrs. Dorothy Noyes I am grateful for the tireless care she has expended on the preparation of the manuscript for the publisher. As for the rest, I must trust the imagination of the reader and the evidence of the footnotes to indicate my many and varied obligations.

Quotations from the Old Testament are ordinarily from the Standard Edition of the American Revised Version, issued in 1901. In quoting the New Testament I have regularly used the Revised Standard Version, issued in 1946. Both are published by Thomas Nelson and Sons, New York. Occasionally

Dr. James Moffatt's rendering, published by Harper & Brothers, has been used, and this has been indicated by an "M" after the footnote.

HARRY EMERSON FOSDICK

Boothbay Harbor, Maine
July 1, 1949

THE MAN FROM NAZARETH

CHAPTER I

A Real Man, Not a Myth

THE personality of Jesus, as portrayed in the Gospels, is so vivid, his individual characteristics are so lively and unmistakable, he stands out so distinctively himself and not anyone else, that the story leaves the intense impression of a real man, dealing with real people, in an actual historic situation.

Nevertheless, some have thought that Jesus of Nazareth never lived—that he was only a myth.

Some religions have been built around mythological figures, while others have had historic founders. No reputable scholar now doubts that Gautama founded Buddhism, Zoroaster Zoroastrianism, Mohammed Islam, and that at the source of Judaism stands Moses. Jupiter, Juno, Venus and Mars, however, never lived as real persons; Isis and Osiris, Adonis, Attis and Dionysus were mythological; Mithra was a mythical figure, around whose legends and rituals a religion developed so powerful that, for a time, in the third century, it threatened to outdo Christianity.

To which category, then, does the Christian religion belong? Was Jesus a real historic personality or a myth?

As the record in the Gospels stands—granting the legendary accretions there—the mythical interpretation of Jesus seems

[17]

at first grotesque. Here are people, whose attitudes and prejudices we know from extra-Biblical sources—Pharisees, Sadducees, Romans like Pilate, taxgatherers like Zacchaeus and all the rest—dealing with Jesus in ways so apt to the historic situation, so native to the land and time, so appropriate to their own predilections, that common sense protests that this is not the way a myth is made. Does mythology construct a god by picturing a man like this—a carpenter by trade, loving flowers and children, talking about garments that need patching and about poor folk buying two sparrows for a penny; telling stories in a style so characteristically his own that they cannot be reduplicated; being weary and hungry and angry and out of heart; called "beside himself" by his family, a heretic by his church, a traitor by his government? This is not the way mythical gods are made. Nor can the intense historic realism of the response Jesus called out from the legalism of the Pharisees, from the collaborationist alliance of the Sadducees with Rome, from the spiritual hunger of the outcasts, from the fiery hopes of those who looked for a Messiah, be reasonably fitted in to a process of myth-making with no vivid, vital, powerful personality at the center of it.

Nevertheless, the idea that Jesus never actually lived has been seriously argued, and if we are to see him through the eyes of his contemporaries, we must start with the proposition that they saw him as a real man and not a myth.

At the very end of the eighteenth century a few French writers classed Christianity among the mythical religions, but the first person of acknowledged modern scholarship to deny that Jesus actually lived was Bruno Bauer, who died in 1882. That is a long time to wait for doubt to arise about the existence of a transcendently important historic personality.

Christianity from the beginning had bitter enemies, shrewd and powerful, who sought every available weapon of attack. Had there been factual basis for the supposition that this Christ the Christians worshiped was an invented fable, would they not have used it? Yet, so far as is known, no one thought of such a possibility until close to the beginning of the nineteenth century.

The cogency of this fact is especially evident when one considers Jewish testimony to the reality of the historic Jesus. From the beginning of the Christian church the Jews were hostile to it for reasons whose force any loyal Jew would have felt. To be sure, the powerful Rabban Gamaliel, when the nascent Christian church was less than a decade old and the disciples were still faithful observers of the law, defended the apostles from punishment as heretics. He doubtless saw little peril to Judaism in this futile sect of unimportant folk who called the crucified Jesus the Messiah.[1] Such liberal tolerance, however, soon faded out, and hostility between church and synagogue became bitter. Jesus was a heretic, the Jews thought; claiming messiahship, he had misled the people; and now, the Christian movement, spreading across the Roman Empire, was splitting synagogues asunder, making converts to a false Messiah, inviting persecution from the Romans who might confuse Christians with Jews, and in every way hurting and troubling Israel. In the early documents of the New Testament, such as the letters of Paul, the conflict arising between Jews and Christians is evident.

Had Jesus not really lived, none would have known it better than the Jews and, had it been possible, they surely would have raised that issue. Upon the contrary, all Jewish attacks on Jesus take for granted his life and death in Palestine. Says the Talmud: "On the eve of the Passover Jesus of Nazareth was hung. During forty days a herald went before him crying aloud: 'He ought to be stoned because he has practiced magic, has led Israel astray and caused them to rise in rebellion. Let him who has something to say in his defense come forward and declare it.' But no one came forward, and he was hung on the eve of the Passover.''[2]

In Jewish writings—none contemporary with Jesus, some centuries later—we are told these things about Jesus: he was the illegitimate son of a Roman soldier;[3] his mother's name was Mary, and she was a dresser of women's hair; he was a "revolutionary" and he "scoffed at the words of the wise"; he worked miracles by means of magic brought out of Egypt; he had devoted personal disciples, who healed diseases in his name; he was a heretic who sinned and caused the multitude to sin, and he "led astray and deceived Israel"; he was about thirty-three years old when he was put to death; and he was executed on the eve of the Passover. One thing, however, which the Jewish enemies of Jesus never thought of saying was that he had not existed.[4]

Josephus, the Jewish historian, was born in Jerusalem in the year A.D. 37 or 38, and thus narrowly missed being Jesus' contemporary. In two passages in his *Antiquities*, he mentions Jesus. The first (18,3,3) has so evidently been expanded by later hands that, while it probably started with a bona fide core,[5] its use may be questioned. If an authentic core be granted, as it is by many scholars both Jewish and Christian, then Josephus tells us that Jesus came into prominence about the time a popular uprising opposed Pilate's attempt to use temple revenues to improve Jerusalem's water supply; that Jesus was "a wise man," "a doer of wonderful works"; that "when Pilate, at the suggestion of the principal men among us had condemned him to the cross, those who loved him at the first ceased not to love him"; and that "the race of Christians, so named from him, are not extinct even now." Whatever may be one's judgment concerning this first passage, the second passage (20,9,1) appears so casually and naturally in Josephus' narrative that there is no valid reason to suspect its authenticity: "Ananias called a Sanhedrin together, brought before it James, the brother of Jesus who was called the Christ, and certain others . . . and he caused them to be stoned."

One naturally wishes there were more references to Jesus in early Jewish writings, but the far more important fact is that in whatever references we do have, even when most evidently motived by hostility, Jesus' life, ministry and death in Palestine are assumed as matters of unquestioned fact.

The same is true concerning the evidence from Roman writings. Scanty as that witness is, it might easily have been scantier. The Roman world was filled with religions, big and little, commonly despised by serious minds; and why this Messiah-cult from Palestine, scorned by the Jews themselves, concerned with a crucified felon, and attracting, insofar as it attracted at all, those whom the historians would regard as insignificant people, should claim attention from Roman writers is not evident. Inevitably early references to Jesus are few. Yet Tacitus, writing about A.D. 115, describes Nero's ruse when in A.D. 64 he blamed the burning of Rome on the Christians, and Tacitus adds: "This name comes to them from Christ, whom the Procurator Pontius Pilate, under the rule of Tiberius, had handed over to torture."[6] So few are the references to Jesus in Roman writings—Pliny's letter to Trajan, about A.D. 112, reporting meetings in Bithynia-Pontus where a hymn is sung "to one Christus as a god," and Suetonius' possible reference to Jesus when he reports that the Emperor Claudius, probably about A.D. 50, "banished from

Rome the Jews who made a great tumult because of Chrestus"[7]
—that some say Jesus never lived. The more important fact,
however, is that Jewish and Roman references to him when
they do occur, take for granted his historic existence, confirm,
as Tacitus does, some detail of his life, ministry or death, and
breathe no faintest rumor that he was a myth.

Doubt concerning the historicity of Jesus was a passing
vogue of the nineteenth century; no serious scholarship now
upholds it. After centuries of credulity concerning the infallibility of the Bible, the new historical criticism, glorying in its
scepticism, destroyed one supposed certainty after another,
until even the existence of personalities like Moses and Jesus
was denied, and, as Professor McCown says, "It seemed that
every scholar in Germany who was even remotely connected
with theology had to write a brochure with the title, 'Did
Jesus Ever Live?' "[8]

At the height of this vogue in 1854, Professor Wilson, of
Oxford University, read a paper before the Royal Asiatic
Society of London, maintaining that the supposed life of
Buddha was a myth and "Buddha himself merely an imaginary being." Dr. T. W. Rhys Davids' comment would be generally agreed with: "No one would now support this view."[9]
A similar reversal has taken place with regard to the historicity
of Jesus. The day of Arthur Drews in Germany, John M.
Robertson in England and W. B. Smith in the United States,
with their mythological theory of Christ, has gone, and they
have left no disciples of any importance in the field of scholarship.

The nearest approach, in present-day New Testament
study, to the mythological school of thought is to be found
among certain exponents of "Form Criticism." Scholars of
this school have made notable contributions to the under-

standing of the Gospels. They have analyzed the patterns in which the earliest oral traditions about Jesus were probably transmitted; have subjected these component units to searching examination; have emphasized the way the needs and convictions of the Christian communities, at the time our Gospels were written, must have affected the selection, formulation and transmission of this inherited material; and, in many cases, have thus cast doubt upon the historical reliability of the Biblical record. This approach to the Gospel narratives must now be taken seriously into account in all studies of the historic Jesus, but even the most extreme exponents of "Form Criticism," like Rudolf Bultmann, do not for a moment question that Jesus of Nazareth was a real person, who lived and taught in Palestine, and died on Calvary.

Moreover, the idea toward which the more extreme Form-critics tend, that the later Christian community *created* the major features of Jesus' life and teaching as portrayed in the Gospels, meets increasing incredulity. Communities, as such, are not thus creative—not in music, art, philosophy, science, morals or religion. Communities can furnish favorable conditions for creativity, can help at the start and radically modify and amplify the result afterwards, but it takes creative personalities to account, in all such realms, for the unique, original discoveries. Johann Sebastian Bach's music was largely lost sight of for a century, and then gathered around it an enthusiastic following of those who hailed Bach as the prince of all musicians. To suppose, however, that this fellowship of followers produced the music, and that Bach was a more or less imaginary mouthpiece through which the community spoke, would be preposterous. Nothing like the originality of Bach's music or Jesus' unique contribution to ethical and religious life and thought is ever explicable without creative

[23]

personality. On that matter New Testament scholarship is increasingly agreed.

The idea that Jesus never lived involves the assumption that the New Testament's witness is untrustworthy, and that his existence must be proved, if proved at all, by extra-Scriptural evidence. The fallacy of this assumption becomes clear when one thinks not first of the Gospels but of Paul. No serious scholar now doubts that he really lived, and at least eight letters attributed to him are today taken for granted as authentic. If ever a distinctive personality was revealed in valid, firsthand documents, Paul is so revealed in these vivid letters —with his convictions, traditions, handicaps and repentances, his enthusiasm and downheartedness, his troubles with himself and his tussles with opponents. Moreover, if one still insists on further evidence, we have a long letter written to the Corinthians by Clement of Rome in A.D. 95, reminding them that, only a scant forty years before, Paul had founded their church, and exhorting them to read and reread "the epistle of the blessed Paul," written to them "in the beginning of the Gospel," in which he warned them against divisive party spirit.[10]

Paul was a contemporary of Jesus. He studied under Gamaliel in Jerusalem while Jesus was alive. He was converted probably within three years after the crucifixion. Perhaps he even saw Jesus, although his clause, "Even though we have known Christ after the flesh,"[11] probably has another meaning. Certainly he knew the Christian movement from its very start. Among its first persecutors, he was informed and concerned about it, and bitter with hostility against it. After his conversion and before his Christian ministry began, as his letter to the Galatians, probably written about A.D. 50, tells us, he "went up to Jerusalem to visit Cephas [Peter], and

[24]

remained with him fifteen days," seeing, at the same time, he adds, "James the Lord's brother."[12] In his missionary activity he was allied with Barnabas, an associate of the first disciples, with Silas, another member of that earliest Christian community, with John Mark, whose mother's home in Jerusalem was headquarters for the first disciples, where John Mark himself lived[13] and to which Peter is said to have repaired when he escaped from prison.[14] Probably throughout his ministry, and certainly during the first fourteen years of his ministry, Paul was in communication with men who had known Jesus.

In the extravagant days of mythological interpretation, this Pauline witness was so obviously dangerous to the idea that Jesus was a myth that Paul also had to be liquidated. He too became only a ventriloquist's lay figure, and the real voice was supposed to be some unknown, pseudonymous writer who, long years afterwards, made up these letters to support the myth that had created "Christ." All this, however, has proved too preposterous to last. These letters are too vividly real, too authentically autobiographical, too intensely sincere for any such interpretation. Here a distinctive personality speaks, not out of some late generation but from the middle years of the first century, when eschatological hopes of Christ's immediate return, for example, were still fresh and strong— not yet translated from outward physical into inward spiritual terms as they were later in the Fourth Gospel. At every point the characteristic qualities and ideas of the letters reveal an author who was what Paul was said to be—a Pharisee, born in Hellenic Tarsus, educated in Jerusalem, and converted to a convinced faith that the Messiah at last had come.

That this historic Paul bears witness to an historic Jesus seems clear. Much has been made by the mythologists of the fact that few details of Jesus' life are mentioned in Paul's let-

[25]

ters. Reading them, the charge runs, one would learn only that he was born a Jew, "under the law,"[15] that he ate a last supper with his disciples,[16] that he was crucified and rose from the dead. Paul's Christ, they say, is no such human personality as the Gospels present, but a supernatural deity, awaiting in heaven his second coming and meanwhile mystically dwelling in the hearts of believers.

Paul unquestionably did speak most frequently, not of the Jesus of history but of the coming Messiah, and of the Christ of experience, of whom he could say, "It is no longer I who live, but Christ who lives in me."[17] The real question, however, still remains: Was Paul's idea of this Christ, to whom the future belonged and whose indwelling spirit could take possession of men's lives, dominated by the historic Man of Nazareth?

To argue that the historic Jesus was unreal to Paul because so few details of his life are mentioned in the letters is, like many another argument from silence, dubious business. The life and teaching of Jesus were the common property of the Christian communities. Evangelism started with that. How else could it start, except with the story of Jesus? An indwelling Christ could have had no conceivable meaning unless the career and character, the nature and quality of him who was the Christ, had been made plain. The real explanation of Paul's silence about the details of Jesus' earthly life is not that he was unaware of it or unconcerned with it, but that, writing to Christian churches where it was the basis of all instruction, he took it for granted. The material that later went into the Gospels was already formulated in oral tradition, some of it already written down, all of it cherished, and transmitted to every new convert. Paul's letters were not intended to take the place of that; they started from that and assumed it.

The evidence for this seems convincing. One of Paul's most constant and loyal traveling companions was Luke.[18] Once Paul calls him his "fellow-worker";[19] again he alludes to him as "the beloved physician";[20] once again—if Second Timothy, as seems probable, contains a bona fide passage from Paul— he says, "Luke alone is with me."[21] But Luke wrote the third Gospel. Is it possible to imagine Paul and Luke as fast friends and fellow apostles, and to suppose Paul ignorant of Jesus' earthly ministry and unconcerned about it?

The fact is that Paul's letters are saturated with the ideas of Jesus, and his whole conception of Christ is dominated by the character and teaching of the Man of Nazareth. At this point, the argument from silence breaks down completely. There is no silence about what Jesus was and taught: "I, Paul, myself entreat you, by the meekness and gentleness of Christ";[22] "We who are strong ought to bear with the failings of the weak, and not to please ourselves. . . . For Christ did not please himself";[23] "We all with unveiled face, beholding as in a mirror the character of the Lord, are changed into the same image from character to character."[24] Jesus said, "Every one who exalts himself will be humbled, and he who humbles himself will be exalted."[25] Paul said, "Do not be haughty, but associate with the lowly; never be conceited."[26] Jesus said, "As you did it to one of the least of these my brethren, you did it to me."[27] Paul said, "Who is weak, and I am not weak? Who is made to fall, and I am not indignant?"[28] Jesus said, "Blessed are those who are persecuted for righteousness' sake."[29] Paul said, "For the sake of Christ, then, I am content with weaknesses, insults, hardships, persecutions, and calamities."[30] Jesus said, "Do not be anxious."[31] Paul said, "Have no anxiety about anything."[32] Jesus said concerning the laws of Kosher food, "There is nothing outside a man which by going into him can defile him."[33] Paul said on the same subject, "I know and am persuaded in the Lord Jesus that nothing is unclean in itself."[34] Jesus said, "Judge not, that you be not judged."[35] Paul said, "Let us no more pass judgment on one another."[36] Jesus said, "Whoever says to this mountain, Be taken up and cast into the sea, and does not doubt in his heart . . . it will be done for him."[37] Paul said, "If I have all faith, so as to remove mountains."[38] Jesus said, "Love your enemies and pray for those who persecute you."[39] Paul said, "Bless those who persecute you; bless and do not curse them. . . . Repay no one evil for evil."[40] Jesus said that love of God and one's neighbor is the first of all the commandments.[41] Paul said, "Love is the fulfilling of the law."[42]

These are but samples of the constant reflections of Jesus' ways of thought and life in Paul. When he said, "Be imitators of me, as I am of Christ,"[43] what could he have meant, had he not been thinking of the character whom he and Luke together preached? As he put it in his Ephesian letter: "It is Christ whom you have been taught, it is in Christ that you have been instructed—the real Christ who is in Jesus."?[44]

Paul did emphasize the Christ of experience, but not by eliminating the Jesus of history. He rather distilled the essential quality and meaning of Jesus, and proclaimed the gospel that this same spirit could possess men's souls. What else could he have meant when he wrote: "My little children, with whom I am again in travail until Christ be formed in you"?[45]

Paul did stress the supernatural Messiah who would soon come upon the clouds of heaven, but in all the Jewish portraits of the Messiah there is nothing remotely like the quality which Paul ascribes to Christ. Paul's Messiah is utterly unique and his uniqueness is inexplicable save as we see its cause in the character of the historic Jesus. "Do nothing from selfishness or conceit, but in humility count others better than yourselves. Let each of you look not only to his own interests, but also to the interests of others. Have this mind among yourselves, which you have in Christ Jesus"[46]—for *that* kind of Messiah one looks in vain except among those like Paul, whose Christ was Jesus glorified.

There seems no escaping the conclusion that the historic Paul bears witness to the historic Jesus.

The attack of the mythologists on the factual reality of Jesus was, of course, centered on the Gospels. Presenting in vivid detail, as they seem to do, the characteristic qualities, activities and ideas of a genuine historic person, they had to be brushed aside as untrustworthy if Jesus was to be regarded as a myth. The Gospels were not the honest record of a life humanly lived in Palestine; they were the late, legendary endeavor to build a camouflaged foundation under the symbolic figure of a dying and a rising god—such was the necessary assumption of the mythologists.

Modern scholarship dealing with the Gospels, however, has rendered this position untenable. It nowhere fits the facts.

The very contrasts and contradictions within the Gospels, which at first were used to discredit their reliability now turn out to be a boomerang for the mythologists. To be sure, the Gospels disagree on many points in Jesus' life and teaching, from small matters, like the wording of the placard on the cross—"This is Jesus the King of the Jews," says Matthew; "The King of the Jews," says Mark; "This is the King of the Jews," says Luke; "Jesus of Nazareth, the King of the Jews," says John—to matters of graver import. Matthew's Beatitudes are spiritual—"Blessed are the poor in spirit, for theirs is the kingdom of heaven"[47]—while Luke's are stated in terms of

economic classes: "Blessed are you poor, for yours is the kingdom of God. . . . But woe to you that are rich!"[48] Matthew
says: "Blessed are those who hunger and thirst for righteousness," but Luke thinks the beatitude refers to literal penury:
"Blessed are you that hunger now, for you shall be satisfied."

Such distinctive slants and biases on the part of the writers
do sometimes turn Jesus' reputed sayings to varied meanings;
and, as for his life, so uncertain is the order of events, and so
irreconcilable are some of the narratives, that no biography
of him can be written with confidence about the sequence of
many incidents. Papias, an early Christian writer in the first
half of the second century noted this, and said: "Mark, having
become the interpreter of Peter, wrote down accurately whatsoever he remembered. It was not, however, in exact order
that he related the sayings or deeds of Christ. For he neither
heard the Lord nor accompanied him."[49]

Modern criticism, uncovering these discrepancies in the
Gospels, at first seemed to confirm the impression of their
unreliability, and to make it possible plausibly to say that,
even if there were a person named Jesus, we know little or
nothing trustworthy about him and what we have is only the
myth that grew up around him.

Now, however, the very inconsistencies in the Gospels, puzzling though they often are, turn out to be one reason why the
myth-theory has broken down. No mythological Christ, deliberately created by an adoring group, would ever have been
presented in documents like the Gospels. Their historic realism
is evident in these very differences that distinguish their narratives. This is no concocted myth, but the honest endeavor
to record an actual story, with all the effects of oral transmission involving diverse renderings, and with the writer's dis-
similar backgrounds and temperaments resulting in divergent

interpretations. The total impression now made upon New Testament scholars by these records, with their natural, casual, often explainable contrasts, is one of bona fide authenticity.

These Gospels are genuine historical documents, subject to gaps in information, failures of memory, and individual coloring, with no artificial inspiration saving them from dissimilarities that inevitably sprang from varied authorship, legendary accretions, the vagaries of verbal transmission, and the effect of special needs and interests in the different Christian communities for which they were written. Not the less, but the more because of their inconsistencies, they now appear as valid portrayals of a real personality of whom they are honestly trying to present a true picture.

This becomes the more clear when one turns to details. If Christianity began not with a living person but with a myth created around an allegorical figure, and if the human elements in the tradition were made up later to give it richer content, then one consequence must have followed: the earliest records would have presented a completely deified Christ, and the later records would have introduced for the first time his human qualities.

The precise opposite is true; the earliest Gospel record presents Jesus in the most human terms. Mark, the first of the Gospels, has no story of a virgin birth. Mark even represents Jesus as saying, "Why do you call me good? No one is good but God alone,"[50] which Matthew later tones down: "Why do you ask me about what is good?"[51] In one instance after another, comparing Mark with Matthew and Luke, one finds the miraculous powers of Jesus heightened in the later narratives. In Mark a fig tree denounced in the evening was wilted the next morning, while in Matthew the tree, cursed in the morning, "withered at once."[52] While in Mark one demoniac

[31]

was healed at Gadara, in Matthew two were healed;[53] and two blind men, according to Matthew, were given sight at Jericho, whereas in Mark there was only one.[54] In Mark "one of those who stood by drew his sword, and struck the slave of the high priest and cut off his ear," but only later in Luke do we hear that Christ performed a miracle and restored the dissevered member.[55]

That the early tradition concerning Jesus moved not from a mythological figure toward an historic person but from an historic person into heightened theological interpretations of him becomes unmistakable when one contrasts the Jesus of the first three Gospels with the Jesus of the Fourth Gospel. There not only are hitherto unheard of exhibitions of miraculous power narrated—turning water into wine, curing a man born blind, raising Lazarus from the dead after he had been four days entombed[56]—but the whole concept of Christ is set in terms of pre-existent deity, and the theological interpretation of him dominates the narrative.

At first such facts as these deeply disturbed the faith of Christians, but now they have turned out to be not so much a problem to believers in an historic Jesus, the interpretation of whom deepened with the years, as an insurmountable obstacle to the mythologists. The earliest records start not with a myth but with an authentic person who said things—for example, that the end of the world would come before some of those who heard him speak had died[57]—which no one would have made up two generations later when the situation had turned out otherwise; and who did things, such as submitting to John's baptism, which very much perplexed the next generation of Christians. Facing a bitter conflict with John the Baptist's continuing movement, Christians of the second century would never have concocted the story of the baptism, which could so easily be used, as it was used, to give John priority.

In short, the earliest Christian tradition plainly started with the human personality of Jesus and the position of the mythologists is no longer supported by serious scholarship.

This becomes even more clear when we reconstruct, in the light of such information as we possess, the way our four Gospels came to be written.

At the beginning the Christian community relied on oral transmission of stories about Jesus' life and teaching. Papias, writing in Phrygia, in Asia Minor, sometime before A.D. 135, said: "I shall not be unwilling to put down, along with my interpretations, whatsoever instructions I received with care at any time from the elders, and stored up with care in my memory, assuring you at the same time of their truth. . . . If, then, any one who had attended on the elders came, I asked minutely after their sayings—what Andrew or Peter said, or what was said by Philip, or by Thomas, or by James, or by John, or by Matthew, or by any other of the Lord's disciples: which things Aristion and the presbyter John, the disciples of the Lord, say. For I imagined that what was to be got from books was not so profitable to me as what came from the living and abiding voice."[58]

This oral transmission which Papias so valued was clearly not haphazard and formless. In our written Gospels scholars now perceive the shapes and patterns it took on in a generation accustomed not so much to writing and reading as to listening and remembering. The narrative of Jesus' trial and death was evidently told and retold in ordered form. Illustrative anecdotes with an appended pronouncement by Jesus represent one of the most familiar patterns of recollection in the Gospels. "The sabbath was made for man, not man for the sabbath"[59] is appended to a story about the disciples plucking ears of corn on the sabbath day; "Let the children come to me, and do not hinder them; for to such belongs the kingdom of heaven"[60] is appended to a story about the disciples rebuking parents who brought children to the Master for his blessing; "Those who are well have no need of a physician, but those who are sick; I came not to call the righteous, but sinners"[61] climaxes an anecdote about Jesus eating with publicans and sinners.

The oral transmission of the early disciples' recollections about Jesus thus broke up the narrative into rememberable units, and the result is still manifest in the lack of continuity the reader often feels in our Gospels—for example, in detached narratives introduced by phrases such as, "On another day," "And it came to pass," "He arose from thence." Any thoughtful reader must be aware of these cells of which the body of the record is composed—parables, miracle stories, disconnected anecdotes, sayings of Jesus set in familiar Hebrew poetic forms, such as

If ye love them that love you,
  What thank have ye?
For even sinners love those that love them.

If ye do good to them that do good to you,
  What thank have ye?
For even sinners do the same.

If ye lend to them of whom ye hope to receive,
  What thank have ye?
Even sinners lend to sinners to receive
  again as much.

But love your enemies, and do good, and lend,
   Never despairing!
And your reward shall be great,
And ye shall be sons of the Most High.[62]

Far from invalidating the record, therefore, this period of oral transmission made the record an affair of the whole Christian community. These units of recollection were no matter of individual remembrance only but were used by the church in the winning and instruction of converts, the confuting of opponents, and probably in public worship to keep fresh the Lord's memory.

Nevertheless, while even Papias, with written Gospels in his hands, might prefer personal testimony by word of mouth, written records became inevitable, and their beginning scholars now push back to a date far earlier than used to be supposed. In any case, the period of sole reliance on oral transmission was brief. Within thirty to forty years after Jesus' death Mark's Gospel—the earliest we now possess—was written, and before that the evidence indicates that written records were familiar. Certain sections in Mark are in themselves such distinct, self-consistent units, that they suggest previous narratives, taken over and incorporated in the Gospel. Certainly Luke was acquainted with numerous written accounts of Jesus: "Many have undertaken to compile a narrative of the things which have been accomplished among us."[63]

One such document was almost certainly a record of Jesus' sayings used, along with Mark's Gospel, by both Matthew and Luke. That these two writers had in their hands either an identical or a very similar document, mainly made up of the

[35]

words of Jesus, is so convincingly indicated that few now question it. Papias says that Matthew, the disciple, "put together the oracles of the Lord in the Hebrew language, and each one interpreted them as best he could."[64] This certainly was not our present Gospel of Matthew, which was written in Greek, but it may well have been an early record of Jesus' teaching by one of the first disciples, which in its original form we no longer possess, but which the writers of our first and third Gospels knew and used. At any rate, the evidence is so convincing that written records lay behind our present Gospels and that the authors of the first and third Gospels had in their hands not only Mark and an early collection of Jesus' sayings but other material as well, that the historical reality of Jesus becomes increasingly difficult to question.

That these earlier writings passed out of existence when our four Gospels were at the disposal of the churches was natural. They probably were partial, incomplete, covering distinct areas of Jesus' life and ministry—his Passion, his sayings, stories of his birth, and so on—and the need became urgent for inclusive narratives that would tell the whole story.

Why this need was not felt in the church's earliest years is easy to guess. The immediate return of Christ was ardently expected. Since he so soon would be back again in glory, the need of gathering the detailed memories of his earthly ministry, setting them down in order, and preserving them for future generations was not evident. When, however, Christ did not return, when attention was increasingly centered not so much on the expected end of the world as on the expanding church in the world, that necessity became urgent. The church was making converts whose indoctrination in the truth about the Savior's life, death and resurrection was imperative. The church was facing enemies whose slanders had to be refuted by authentic records of the Founder's life and teaching. The church confronted early Gnosticism, making Christianity an abstract theosophy, and the need of presenting the gospel's factual, historic, personal origin became acute. The church was inwardly perplexed by controversies in dealing with which knowledge of any relevant and applicable words of Jesus was anxiously desired. Our Gospels were not written for the purpose of satisfying historic curiosity; they are in no sense the fruit of academic biographical research; they were called into being by the pressing needs of the churches. Luke undertook the writing of his Gospel with intellectual conscientiousness—"It seemed good to me also, having followed all things closely for some time past, to write an orderly account for you, most excellent Theophilus"—but the motive that drove him to it was one of those practical necessities that confronted the expanding church, the instruction of converts, or perhaps the enlightenment of an influential official: "that you may know the truth concerning the things of which you have been informed."[65]

Thus our four Gospels were written between A.D. 65 and 100. Their authors did the best they could, but despite the rememberable units of oral transmission and many written records, they faced grave difficulties, whose nature reveals an authentic historic situation.

Incidents in Jesus' life had been forgotten. Only one is recorded from the years before his public ministry began, although his brother, James, could have told, and doubtless did tell, how many! The order of events in Jesus' ministry had grown obscure, so that, for example, Luke dates the time when he preached in Nazareth at his ministry's beginning while Mark puts it later;[66] and as between the first three Gospels and

[37]

the fourth, the cleansing of the temple is put by Matthew, Mark, and Luke at the close of his ministry, and by John at the beginning.[67] The setting of Jesus' sayings had in some cases grown uncertain, so that Matthew puts the Lord's Prayer in his first recorded sermon, while according to Luke it was taught to the disciples after the final journey to Jerusalem had begun.[68] The words of Jesus had been variously remembered, as in the case of the Beatitudes; and even the versions of the Lord's Prayer and of the golden rule in Matthew and Luke are not the same.[69] Moreover, legendary elements had been added to the tradition, so that while in Mark we have only the symbolic rending of the temple veil at Jesus' death, in Matthew "the earth shook, and the rocks were split; the tombs also were opened; and many bodies of the saints who had fallen asleep were raised; and coming out of the tombs after his resurrection they went into the holy city and appeared to many."[70]

This realistic situation confronting Jesus' biographers cannot be successfully fitted into the supposition that they were constructing a myth around an allegorical figure. Our Gospels spring from a bona fide historical background, not to be mythologically interpreted.

Mark's Gospel was most probably written in Rome, where all early tradition associates John Mark with the ministry of Peter. So, at least, Clement of Alexandria, in the middle of the second century, understood the facts: "The Gospel according to Mark had this occasion. As Peter preached the word publicly at Rome . . . many who were present requested that Mark, who had followed him for a long time and remembered his sayings, should write them out. And having composed the Gospel he gave it to those who had requested it."[71] Certainly Mark wrote for some Gentile community. He translates every

Aramaic phrase he uses;[72] he explains the Palestinian coinage —the widow's two copper coins equal a penny;[73] he explains the season when ripe figs are to be expected in Palestine;[74] he explains Jewish ceremonial customs which his readers might not understand;[75] and whereas under Jewish law no woman could divorce her husband, while under Roman law she could, Mark citing Jesus' condemnation of divorce, includes the guilty woman as well as the guilty man.[76]

Matthew's Gospel was almost certainly written in some city where the constituency of the Christian community was largely Jewish—perhaps Antioch in Syria, where the disciples of Jesus were first called Christians. Old Testament prophecies, brought to fulfillment in Jesus, are a major concern in this Gospel, and interest in Jesus' attitude toward the Jewish law bulks large. Who the author was we do not know—the writing is anonymous, the present title a late addition—and no early tradition, as in the case of Mark, throws light on the problem. That the author, however, was a Jewish Christian, writing for a church where the relationship between Judaism and the Christian gospel was of front rank concern seems certain.

Luke's Gospel suggests a Gentile author, writing, as a not improbable early tradition says, in some Gentile community in Greece.[77] That "Luke, the beloved physician," Paul's traveling companion, wrote it is far and away the most likely hypothesis. This certainly was the early church's tradition, and this also is the natural inference from the opening words of the Book of Acts: "In the first book, O Theophilus, I have dealt with all that Jesus began to do and teach, until the day when he was taken up." Moreover, according to those passages in the Book of Acts where "we" is used, apparently including the author, Luke had ample opportunity to get at firsthand

[39]

testimony concerning Jesus' life and ministry. Early in Paul's mission he worked for a time in company with Silas, a member of the early Jerusalem church.[78] Later he spent several years in Palestine, mainly in Jerusalem and Caesarea, where he had ample opportunity to meet those who had known Jesus.[79] He was present with Paul at interviews with James, the Lord's brother, and with leaders of the church.[80] At Caesarea he lodged, along with Paul, at the house of Philip the evangelist.[81] Still later at Rome he was the companion of John Mark.[82]

John's Gospel, latest of all, was probably written in Ephesus, not by John, the immediate disciple of Jesus, but by John the Elder, a leader of the Ephesian church. One of the earliest traditions we have about the matter comes from Clement of Alexandria: "Last of all, John, perceiving that the external facts had been made plain in the gospel, being urged on by his friends, and inspired by the Spirit, composed a spiritual gospel."[83]

Our four Gospels, therefore, were written not only by different persons, but in different communities, such as Rome, Antioch in Syria, some city in Greece, and Ephesus in Asia Minor. They were composed to meet the needs of widely separated churches and the marvel is not their differences but their agreement. Seen against the background of the historic situation out of which they came they are authentic endeavors to deal with bona fide recollections of a real personality.

All such evidence as we have canvassed for the historic reality of Jesus comes to its fulfillment when we take into account the impressive mass of information uncovered during the last half century about Palestine in Jesus' day. Whether one thinks of its now familiar geography, of the revelations of archaeology, of the then current estate of Judaism and its various problems and parties, of the meaning of Roman rule, of the prevalent ideas and hopes of the people, or of the social and economic conditions in Galilee and Judea, one faces a situation into which the Gospel record fits with such entire congruity that a mythological interpretation of Jesus is ruled out.

This Palestine, which the visitor sees even yet, is the veritable land where he lived and taught. The incidents narrated in the Gospels, the pictures drawn in the parables, the Master's casual metaphors and similes, the background assumed by the story's outline and filled in by its details, fit the scene like a hand in a glove. Nazareth, the Sea of Galilee, the coasts of Tyre and Sidon, Mount Hermon and the Jordan, Esdraelon and Samaria, Jericho and the Judean wilderness, Bethlehem and Jerusalem—it is all too consistent with the Gospels to leave any doubt about the factual basis of the record.

Here in the Gospels are vineyards, surrounded by hedges and guarded by towers; fields, sometimes beautiful with flowers, sometimes overgrown with thorns. Here are fig trees, needing cultivation, herbs such as mint and rue, and, as well, tares and dry grass for fuel in primitive home ovens. Here are pits into which an animal might fall, and houses, made of clay bricks, in danger from downpouring rain. Along the Jordan are reeds shaken by the wind and on the uplands mustard trees in which birds make their nests. Here are all the typical animals of Palestine—foxes, wolves, dogs, calves, asses, oxen, goats, kids, sheep and lambs. Here vultures gather about their prey, sparrows fall, and ravens, doves, hens and chickens are familiar. Here the farmer, the husbandman, the shepherd go about their daily tasks, businessmen make their investments and artisans ply their trades. Within poor homes are problems of patched garments and cheap food, and by the roadside blindness is a commonplace and beggars flourish. This is Palestine as all the evidence we have, past and present, shows it to have been, and to suppose that such verisimilitude was concocted is incredible.

Moreover, when one turns from the outward scene to the inner thinking of that first band of disciples, one finds in the Gospels ideas which the church two generations afterward would never have invented. Illustrations of this fact we shall repeatedly face in this book. When the Gospels were written, for example, the Gentile mission had long been taken for granted, and the universality of the gospel, including Jew and Greek, Scythian, barbarian, bond and free, was accepted doctrine. Support for that was found in Jesus' teaching, but other sayings of the Master are recorded that never would have been made up, if they had not been set down in the original recollections of the first disciples. Would the later church, predominantly Gentile, have invented a Jesus who said, "I was sent only to the lost sheep of the house of Israel"?[84] That goes veritably back to Palestine, where Jesus, however universal his outlook, faced the practical necessity of concentrating his attention on the immediate task of reaching his own people. So, in one realm after another, one finds in the Gospels ideas and emphases that never could have been invented two generations after Jesus, and, as well, one finds two generations after Jesus prevalent customs and doctrines, from speaking with tongues to the allegorizing of Jewish eschatology, that in the first three Gospels are not found at all.[85]

Here, then, we may confidently start: whatever else his contemporaries saw in Jesus, they saw *him;* he was a real man and not a myth.

[42]

CHAPTER II

As the Crowds Saw Him

THE unpopularity of Jesus among his own people in Palestine had become, by the time the Fourth Gospel was written, a major factor in the portrayal of his life. John retains echoes of the earlier tradition that "a multitude followed him,"[1] and even adds an incident, not elsewhere recorded, that the crowd once sought to "take him by force to make him king."[2] John's main emphasis, however, is on the fact that "he came to his own home, and his own people received him not,"[3] and, attacking the Jews as a whole, John's indictment is sweeping: "The Jews sought to kill him."[4] That the Jewish populace was thus massed in opposition to Jesus is an idea naturally reflecting the harsh hostility between Jews and Christians at the close of the first century, but it does not accord with the earlier records.

According to them, Jesus' popularity was one of his most dangerous problems. When Jesus began his ministry, says Mark, he caused a great stir, and "his fame spread everywhere throughout all the surrounding region of Galilee."[5] When he entered Capernaum, "many were gathered together, so that there was no longer room for them, not even about the door."[6] Once, at the lakeside, he spoke from a boat, "because of the crowd, lest they should crush him";[7] once, when his family came to seek him, "a crowd was sitting about him,"[8] so that they could not reach him; once the crowd so pressed upon the disciples that "they could not even eat";[9] and once, "the whole city was gathered together about the door."[10] When Jesus noted a woman's beseeching touch on his garment and asked who it was, the disciples exclaimed: "You see the crowd pressing around you, and yet, you say, 'Who touched me?' "[11] Indeed, Mark says that "a great multitude from Galilee followed; also from Judea and Jerusalem and Idumea and from beyond the Jordan and from about Tyre and Sidon a great multitude, hearing all that he did, came to him."[12]

These descriptions of throngs crowding about Jesus may involve enthusiastic exaggeration, as, for example, in such phrases as "the whole city," but Galilee in Jesus' day was a populous land. Josephus says that it contained "two hundred and forty cities and villages," the least of which numbered fifteen thousand souls,[13] and while such statistics are questionable, the picture Josephus draws of a rich and fruitful country, thickly settled and busy with varied trades is doubtless true. As late as A.D. 600 Antoninus, the Martyr, visiting Galilee, reported: "The province is like paradise, rivalling Egypt in its grain and cereals, and, while small indeed, it surpasses Egypt in wine and oil and fruit."[14] Gennesaret—the plain, some four miles wide along the lake's western shore—was especially the "garden" of Galilee, and Josephus called it "the ambition of nature." Not only in fishing and agriculture were the lakeside and uplands rich in possibilities, but merchant routes led travelers by way of the lake to varied destinations. Galilee's population, therefore, was not purely Jewish; Judeans commonly condescended to its people as a motley racial mixture. Not only were Roman officers and soldiers there, but Greek colonists, settlers from Phoenicia, emigrants and travelers from

Syria, Arabia and the East.[15] It was in this teeming, busy region that Jesus began his public ministry, and was met by so popular a response that it might easily have cost his life. Far from facing neglect and rejection, he was greeted with a mounting outburst of public favor.

The consequence of this popularity enables us, with some confidence, to reconstruct the order of events in Jesus' early ministry. Impossible as it is, in our modern sense, to write his biography, certain outlines in his career seem evident. He came from Nazareth. At first associated with the movement launched by John the Baptist, he later parted company with it, and began an independent ministry in Galilee. The popular interest which he called out, with crowds attending him, was brought to the attention of Herod Antipas, Tetrarch of Galilee, whose superstitious fears were aroused that John the Baptist, though beheaded, had come back again.[16] Certainly Herod could not allow the public agitation caused by Jesus to continue. A dilemma thus confronted the Master—either to leave Galilee or to be executed. This choice, Luke reports, was plainly presented to him by "certain Pharisees," who said to him, "Get away from here, for Herod wants to kill you."[17] Were those Pharisees really friendly, desiring to protect Jesus? Or did they see a chance to frighten him away and so rid the country of his disturbing presence? Or were they emissaries sent by Herod himself, who hoped to solve his own problem by scaring Jesus into exile? Jesus' reply to the Pharisees suggests that the last was his interpretation. He bade them return to Herod: "Go and tell that fox, 'Behold, I cast out demons and perform cures today and tomorrow, and the third day I finish my course.' "[18]

The dilemma which Jesus faced was a real one. Then was

not the time for him to die, nor was Galilee the place; "It cannot be" he told the Pharisees, "that a prophet should perish away from Jerusalem."[19] Leaving Galilee, therefore, he retired to the Mediterranean coasts at Tyre and Sidon, until the commotion should die down, and even there "he entered a house, and would not have any one know it; yet he could not be hid."[20]

The picture of Jesus, therefore, as a rejected man, with the massed hostility of his people arrayed against him, must be given up. He was, instead, a popularly arresting figure in Palestine. He caught the public imagination. He alienated those who feared him as a heretic and hated him as a disturber of the peace, but large numbers of common people were drawn to him. Even after religious leaders had organized their opposition and political leaders were deciding to get rid of him, he entered Jerusalem in triumph, while "the crowds that went before him and that followed him shouted, 'Hosanna to the Son of David! Blessed be he who comes in the name of the Lord! Hosanna in the highest.' "[21] The Fourth Gospel's representation of the way the Pharisees felt at this evidence of Jesus' acceptance by the masses is not improbable: they "said to one another, 'You see that you can do nothing; look, the world has gone after him.' "[22] As though to leave no doubt of Jesus' popular following that last week in Jerusalem Mark tells us that "the mass of the people listened with delight to him."[23]

A familiar interpretation of this popularity has stressed its fickle nature, and the crowd that cried "Crucify him" at the Passion Week's end has been commonly supposed to be the same crowd that cried "Hosanna" at the week's beginning. There is no evidence for this, and such data as we have casts doubt upon it. The claque that cried "Crucify him" in Pilate's court were most probably the organized hirelings of the high priests, the hangers-on of Judea's collaborationist government. Still the "multitude" stood by Jesus. When his foes plotted to seize him, "they feared the people."[24] When they arrested him they bribed Judas, and through his information chose night-time in Gethsemane, when the people could not intervene. Even when he went to the cross, "there followed him a great multitude of the people, and of women who bewailed and lamented him,"[25] and after the dreadful deed was done on Calvary, "all the multitudes who assembled to see the sight, when they saw what had taken place, returned home beating their breasts."[26]

Who made up this "multitude"? The Jews of Palestine in Jesus' day are now commonly thought of as divided into par-ties—Pharisees, Sadducees, Essenes, Zealots—but parties never adequately describe a population. Parties have their inner core of eager, even fanatical, adherents and their larger circle of more or less loyal followers, but always, there are the vague, uncertain hangers-on, and beyond all parties the gen-eral mass of human beings to whom party lines are of small or no concern.

"It is the task of Gospel Criticism," says a modern scholar, "to make ourselves the contemporaries of Jesus."[27] One who tries to do this faces at the very start these crowds made up of plain folk rather than partisans, who saw in Jesus a challeng-ing personage. As with all crowds, what they saw did not reach the spiritual depths, but it is nonetheless important to the understanding of Jesus. Can we make ourselves one of them, and through their eyes catch at least a glimpse of him?

That they saw him as one of themselves, a Jew of the com-mon people, is clear. He spoke their familiar dialect, drew his similes and parables from their familiar experiences, shared

[47]

with them the current mental categories of his generation, and in his teaching they heard the affirmations of their traditional faith. He dressed as they did, with tassels on the corners of his garment to show he was a Jew—so distinctive a uniform that no Jew was permitted to sell a garment to a Gentile until the tassels were removed.[28] At the height of Jesus' popularity in Galilee we read that "they would lay their invalids in the marketplace, begging him to let them touch even the tassel of his robe."[29]

They saw him as a faithful exemplar of Jewish piety, observing their festivals, going on pilgrimage to the temple in Jerusalem, regularly worshipping in their synagogues.[30] Indeed despite his attacks on Phariseeism, they must have seen that he himself was closer to that most numerous and devout party in Israel than to any other. He certainly was not a Sadducee; he had no kinship with the high priestly group that ruled in Jerusalem, collaborated with Rome to make their tenure secure, and said that "there is no resurrection, nor angel, nor spirit."[31] He was not a Zealot; he stood completely apart from militant hopes of a violent insurrection against Rome. He was not an Essene; they were ascetics—according to early tradition numbering only some four thousand souls—living in communistic communities separate from the general life of Israel, and practicing severe austerities, whereas Jesus was accused by his foes of being "a glutton and a drunkard."[32]

Despite their faults, the Pharisees were the hope of Israel, the Puritans of Palestine, with the deplorable legalism of Puritanism which Jesus condemned, but with its sturdy virtues too, its convinced faith, stubborn conscientiousness, devout loyalty. Of all the parties in Israel Jesus was closest to them. If he visited special censure on them it was because in them he saw the best hope of his people and to their reform dedi-

[48]

cated his attention. What he said in rebuke of the Pharisees, orthodox Jewish literature also said. Among the evils that "destroy the world," the Mishna lists "the plagues of the Pharisees."[33] A very ancient *Baraita* describes seven kinds of Pharisees, of which only one clearly and one other doubtfully are to be admired.[34] Nevertheless, the great heritage of Jewish religion in Jesus' day was in the keeping not of the Sadducees, Zealots, or Essenes but of the Pharisees; to them in criticism and appeal his attention was given; and to them, as the crowds must have sensed, he was closer than to any other group in Israel.

The fascination with which Jesus drew crowds around him, however, is not explicable simply by the qualities and attitudes that made him seem one of themselves. No such phenomena as greeted his appearance beside the Sea of Galilee can be accounted for without presupposing a distinctive personality, vigorous, aggressive, outstanding, challenging. To be sure, the manner of his teaching in parables was familiar. The Jewish rabbis also spoke in parables. Did Jesus tell of a father's mercy toward a prodigal? "A king's son fell into evil courses," runs an ancient rabbinic parable. "The king sent his tutor to him with the message, Repent, my son. But the son sent to his father to say, How can I return? I am ashamed before thee. Then the father sent to him to say, Can a son be ashamed to return to his father? If you return, do you not return to your father?"[35] Such teaching in stories was not strange to the crowds that surrounded Jesus, but never such parables as he told had they heard before. Considered only from the literary point of view, one feels about them still, as about some passages in Shakespeare—not an unfamiliar word in them, yet breathtaking in effect.

One hesitates to use the word "artist" about Jesus, because he was so much more, but one does not understand him and his impact on his contemporaries, if one fails to see him as that too. In his thinking about God, the soul and the profound concerns of religion with which he dealt, he was never a speculative theologian, working out a formal religious philosophy, but an artist, seeing truth with visual vividness and embodying it in similes, metaphors, parables, which mankind has never been able to forget. If the common folk who heard him were to understand serious teaching at all, they would best understand *that*.

This does not imply that the crowds easily grasped the meaning of his parables; we are explicitly told that they did not.[36] Indeed, to many of the multitude he and his teaching mattered not at all. They stood in the presence of one, concerning whom nearly two millenniums later a man like H. G. Wells could say that he is "easily the dominant figure in history," and they saw and heard nothing worth attending to. Like the guests in his parable, invited to a royal banquet, they were busy with their farms, their oxen, and their families, and making their excuses, passed him by.

This, however, is not the whole story. On many of the common folk those parables struck home. Not only what he said but the way he said it—with the impact of a personality whose mysterious, powerful *plus*, though indescribable, they felt—fascinated and challenged them. During the early days of his ministry, so Mark reports, the crowds, watching his deeds and hearing his words, "were all so amazed that they discussed it together, saying, 'Whatever is this?' 'It is new teaching with authority behind it!' "[37]

It is a commonplace in history that while empires fall and all the ostentatious bigness on which contemporary interest is centered proves ephemeral, those things at long last are most treasured and preserved which are beautifully done. Great literature and music far outlast the external settings of the centuries that produced them, and even remnants of creative beauty, such as the Parthenon, and fragile embodiments of supreme artistry, such as great paintings, are preserved when all else perishes. We should not have the parables of Jesus now, had they not been so consummately well told. Even the common people, dull of understanding though they were, felt a uniqueness they could not explain.

To many of the crowd, however, something besides this in Jesus' teaching must have been arresting. The crowd always loves a fight and Jesus provided one. He attacked with unsparing vigor evils that the "multitude" may well have been pleased to hear attacked. The pride of the scribes and Pharisees was not popular, and the outlawing of the *amme ha-arez*, "the people of the land," from the community of faithful Israel, because they did not and often could not keep the minutiae of scribal legalism, was resented. Josephus said of the Pharisees that "they valued themselves highly upon the exact skill they had in the law of their fathers, and made men believe they were highly favored by God."[38] When, therefore, Jesus criticized pharisaical pomp and circumstance, when he hit with hard epithets those who tithed mint, anise, and cummin and neglected the weightier matters of the law, when he called well-known types of religionists whitewashed tombs and blind leaders of the blind, the crowd, with no conscious disloyalty to the nobler sort of Pharisee, was probably with him. He was saying what they commonly felt but did not dare to say.

There is no understanding the impact of Jesus on the

crowds without stressing this hard-hitting vigor of his speech. The "Gentle Jesus, meek and mild," who satisfies the imagination of many moderns, cannot explain what happened in Galilee. In painting and poetry we have sentimentalized him, made him what Thomas Dekker, the English dramatist at the beginning of the seventeenth century, described as,

> A soft, meek, patient, humble, tranquil spirit,
> The first true gentleman that ever breathed.

That some of the qualities Dekker names were his is true, but the total picture is fallacious. No man of merely soft, patient, tranquil spirit did the crowds in Galilee come out to hear. He was exciting, uncompromising, stormy, formidable.

A man's style of speech reveals him. Dekker's lines tell us more about Dekker than about Jesus. Jesus' speech was packed with energy—vehement, vigorous, exuberant, often extravagant. One listening to him saw men straining out gnats and swallowing camels;[39] men with logs in their own eyes trying to take specks from others' eyes;[40] herdsmen offering pearls to swine;[41] men plucking out their eyes and cutting off their hands in order to escape hell;[42] offenders with great millstones about their necks thrown into the ocean.[43] Hyperbole was his native language—a man forgiven a debt of twelve million dollars denies forgiveness to a man who owes him seventeen dollars;[44] a mountain, because a man prayed that it be done, is "taken up and cast into the sea";[45] a sycamine tree, commanded by a man of faith to be rooted up and "planted" in the ocean, obeys the order;[46] the disciples are to be at one and the same time like serpents and like doves;[47] a camel goes through a needle's eye;[48] dead men bury dead men.[49] There is no mistaking the kind of person who speaks like that. Young, dynamic, tremendously in earnest, such a person the crowds heard, and were convinced that something unique in their experience was happening.

To be sure, homelier qualities in Jesus doubtless drew the common people to him, especially his extraordinary gift of being at ease with all sorts of persons. His was a time when caste lines were sharply drawn, but with unembarrassed ease he ate alike with Simon, the Pharisee, and with tax collectors and sinners. It was a time when stiff conventionalities limited social intercourse between the sexes, but alike in public and in private he associated with men and women on equal terms. He was at home with little children in their innocence and strangely enough at home too with conscience-stricken grafters like Zacchaeus. Respectable home-keeping women, such as Mary and Martha, could talk with him with natural frankness, but courtesans also sought him out as though assured that he would understand and befriend them. He lost from his discipleship the "rich young ruler" but Mark says he "loved him"[50] and, as for the poor, his heart was always theirs. He was a loyal Jew, yet in a good Samaritan he portrayed incarnate unselfishness, and in a Roman centurion he found more faith than he had found in Israel.[51]

This inclusiveness of Jesus, his strange unawareness of boundaries that hemmed ordinary people in, is one of his most characteristic qualities. Even in the Fourth Gospel, where his deity rather than his humanity is stressed, the recollection of this human quality is still fresh and strong; he was equally at ease with a learned rabbi, Nicodemus, and with a questionable woman of Samaria. He was, as Dekker said, a "gentleman." The common people would be quick to feel such openheartedness to all sorts and conditions of men and women. Jesus hated pose. Long prayers made for show and ostentatious

[53]

almsgiving "to be seen of men" aroused his indignation. He despised the façades that men built to shut themselves in and others out and, by-passing social, economic and pietistic distinctions, he went straight for people as human beings, and touched a responsive chord in common folk.

Nevertheless, it was not such ingratiating qualities alone that drew the fascinated crowds. There was power in Jesus, force and drive of personality, daring ideas, strong language. He never minced matters. He felt so intensely that he stretched his words into superlatives before he trusted them to carry what he wished to say. Getting good conduct from bad character was like picking figs from thistles;[52] God, in his care for men, counted every hair on their heads;[53] children were imagined asking for bread or fish and receiving from their fathers stones or snakes.[54] As for denunciation, when Jesus faced selfish greed or cruelty or sham his indignation was explosive. To point out that overstatement is characteristically oriental and that some of Jesus' extreme expressions were doubtless current idiom does not change the picture. In the Babylonian Talmud, written in the Euphrates valley where elephants were known, not a camel but an elephant is imagined trying to pass through a needle's eye.[55] That Jesus seized upon such similes and, along with those of his own invention, used such hyperbole to express his thought, reveals the man. He was not restrained, tame, moderate. He intended his words to be taken seriously—but not literally. Like Beethoven, composing music for whose expression no existent instruments were adequate, the drive of Jesus' thought stretched to the limit his available vocabulary and wanted more.

All this, of course, the crowds did not fully comprehend, but the general effect they must have felt. Jesus was not like anyone they had ever heard before. The content of his teaching they might not understand, but the unique power of both teaching and teacher aroused their wonderment: "The crowds were astonished at his teaching, for he taught them as one who had authority, and not as their scribes."[56]

Naturally, however, not so much Jesus' teaching as his miracles first brought the crowds thronging around him. At that point for moderns to become his contemporaries requires a change of mental outlook so radical as to be almost beyond our power. We start with the idea of nature as an ordered system, in which by law-abiding processes everything moves from cause to consequence. Not in all the Bible, however, is there any such concept as natural law. The Old Testament contains no word that can be translated "nature," and in the New Testament the word so rendered refers not to cosmic order but to the specific constitution of some particular thing, such as an olive tree, wild by nature.[57] Whatever happened in the world of Jesus' day was conceived as happening by personal volition; God, Satan, angels, demons, and men did things, sometimes in usual and to-be-expected ways, sometimes in ways extraordinary and marvelous. No organized knowledge of natural laws limited credulity; miracles, challenging attention and awakening wonder, were expected and counted on; the doors were wide open for any unusual event to be taken as a miracle and for its marvelousness to grow with the retelling.

Indeed, our word "miracle," carrying the implication of broken law, completely misrepresents the thinking of Jesus' day. There is no one word in the New Testament for miracles. Extraordinary events are called mighty works, powers, wonders, signs.[58] Such surprising expressions of power, even when mercifully exhibited in healing the sick, might not be divine at all. Jesus' foes said of him, "He casts out demons by Beelzebub, the prince of demons,"[59] and Jesus himself is reported as saying: "False Christs and false prophets will arise and show signs and wonders, to lead astray, if possible, the elect."[60] Nor were such wonderworks so uncommon as to constitute unique authentication; "If I cast out demons by Beelzebub," said Jesus, "by whom do your sons cast them out?"[61] This clear indication in the Gospels of the familiarity of miracles—divine, satanic, angelic, demonic, human—corresponds with what we know of the whole world in Jesus' day. In Greece the god Asclepius was credited with endless feats of healing, and the inscriptions discovered in the ruins of the Asclepieion at Athens or of the temple of Epidaurus in Argolis give long lists of marvelous cures. The wonder-works attributed to Apollonius of Tyana (born about 4 B.C.) by Philostratus, his biographer, are so strikingly like those attributed to Jesus, that the similarity was once widely ascribed to conscious intent, but now is understood to be the reflection of an all but universal way of thinking. As for Palestine, both the Talmud and Midrash describe typical miracles performed by Rabbi Johanan ben Zakkai and his disciple, Rabbi Eliezer ben Hyrcanus, contemporaries of Jesus.[62] Moreover, magicians like Elymas whom Paul defied,[63] and books of sorcery whose spells could even raise the dead, were familiar.

Into such a world came Jesus and, healing the sick as he undoubtedly did, faced in the multitudes who sought his help one of the most embarrassing problems of his ministry.

A contrast seems evident between Jesus' attitude toward "mighty works" and that of his contemporaries. The crowds gathered to see his miracles, partly from curiosity and love of the marvelous, but mostly from desperate need. Beneath Galilee's prosperity were grim factors of poverty and disease.

The oppression of Herod and the Romans was cruel to the bodies and maddening to the minds of the Jews. Resentment seethed; unemployment and mendicancy existed alongside the wealth of a few; and behind bodily ills which no known medicine could cure, mental ills flourished alike on the outward wrongs that seemed to have no end and on inward bitterness that could see no hope. As a result—so Dr. Klausner describes it—"Palestine, and especially Galilee, was filled with the sick and suffering and with those pathological types which we now label neurosthenics and psychosthenics . . . and especially hysterical women and all manner of 'nerve cases'— dumb, epileptics, and the semi-insane—were numerous."[64]

When Jesus, therefore, "healed many," all Galilee soon heard of him and throngs gathered. At the center of his ministry, as they saw it, not his teaching but his "mighty works" were paramount. To them he was first and foremost a miracle man, and this disturbed him. Repeatedly, as Mark records it, he admonished those whom he had healed and those standing by to tell no one.[65] Only in recent years have students of the Gospels begun to take the full measure of that fact. Jesus felt himself in danger, and in danger he surely was. He came with a prophetic message; his was a spiritual mission to redeem Israel and to proclaim a gospel of salvation; and instead of being so understood he was being followed by curious, clamoring crowds as a wonder-worker.

To be sure, Jesus valued his power to heal the sick. "If it is by the Spirit of God that I cast out demons," Matthew quotes him as saying, "then the kingdom of God has come upon you";[66] and to imprisoned John the Baptist, so both Matthew and Luke report, he sent word of his healing ministry.[67] Jesus could not have been himself without rejoicing in his power to help afflicted minds and bodies. One fact of crucial importance to him, however, made the multitudes who followed him solely because of his miracles an unwelcome sight: their amazement at the curing of a sick man was no guarantee that either the healed man or those who saw the healing would be spiritually won to Jesus' message and morally transformed. The crowds might exclaim, "We have seen strange things today,"[68] or "We never saw anything like this!"[69] but with that gaping wonder the whole effect might end, and that was not Jesus' goal. After a certain healing, though "all men marveled," the district's inhabitants thought only of getting rid of this wonder-worker, and "began to beg Jesus to depart from their neighborhood."[70] After another healing, his critics, far from being won to him, "were filled with fury and discussed with one another what they might do to Jesus."[71] Let him do his merciful best in healing the sick, his foes could still ascribe his power to the prince of demons,[72] and despite his miracles, that, as he said, might well have converted Tyre and Sidon, the cities where they were wrought, Chorazin, Bethsaida and Capernaum did not repent.[73]

Jesus saw that wonderworks were not convincing; they proved nothing and did not necessarily lead to any good consequence. They were displays of power that men could marvel at while brushing off the major message of the one who worked them. So from his ministry's beginning he tried to keep them in the background. "He strictly charged them that no man should know this,"[74] was his characteristic word after a miracle of healing.

This attitude of Jesus came plainly out on an occasion, when "the crowds were thronging him,"[75] hoping to see some "mighty work." "This generation is an evil generation," said Jesus. "It seeks a sign [that is, a miracle] but no sign shall be given to it except . . ."[76] Then he pictured Jonah's ministry in Nineveh, preaching the grace of God and the call to penitence, until Nineveh repented, although Jonah wrought no miracle there; and, as well, Solomon, attracting the Queen of the South from the ends of the earth to listen to his wisdom, although no miracle is recorded as wrought by him. Jonah and Solomon in what they were and taught were themselves the "sign," said Jesus—"Jonah became a sign to the men of Nineveh." They and their message *were* God's wonderwork, and no outward marvels were needed to persuade the Queen of Sheba to listen or Nineveh to repent. So, said Jesus, the Queen of the South and the men of Nineveh will rise at the judgment to condemn this "evil generation," clamoring for marvels while impenitently deaf to the message and blind to the person of a "greater than Jonah." Indeed, the earliest Gospel pictures Jesus as profoundly depressed by the crowds' obsession with miracles. When, apparently dissatisfied with Jesus' acts of healing, they pestered him for some more pretentious wonderwork, "he sighed deeply in his spirit, and said, 'Why does this generation seek for a sign? Truly, I say to you, no sign shall be given to this generation.' And he left them."[77]

The contrast between Jesus' attitude toward "mighty works," and that of his contemporaries, therefore, seems clear, and it extended beyond the crowds to his disciples and to the recorders of his life. They, too, were of their own time, fascinated by the miraculous. They played up Jesus' marvelous deeds, and with successive retelling his miracles grew in wonder. In Mark's Gospel there is no record that Jesus revived the dead, for in the healing of Jairus' daughter, the father appealed to him saying, "My little daughter is at the point of death," and while a messenger came later announcing her decease, Jesus himself when he saw her said, "The child is not dead."[78] By the time the Fourth Gospel was written, however, not only was Lazarus, entombed four days, revived by a word from Jesus, but the miracles in general had moved into the center of the church's picture of him, and were used as proof of his divinity. Even in recording Jesus' attack on his generation for demanding a sign, Matthew interpolates a saying, unknown to Mark and Luke, comparing Jonah's deliverance from the sea-monster with Christ's resurrection from the dead—a comparison alien to the argument and almost certainly not a saying of Jesus himself,[79] but a reflection of the post-resurrection church.

The contrast between Jesus' reluctance to be known as a miracle worker and the ancient world's attitude comes out startlingly in the apocryphal lives of Christ, written in the second and third centuries. They undoubtedly intended to exalt and glorify Jesus, but how did they do it? When the Holy Family flees to Egypt dragons assail them, but when Jesus descends from his mother's bosom and stands before them they adore him. Lions and panthers reverently show Mary and Joseph the way, and palm trees bend their branches to furnish fruit. Jesus himself in early boyhood becomes a magician. He makes a dried fish live. He molds sparrows from clay, claps his hands, and they fly away. He slays with a word a boy who accidentally bumps into him, and, when the boy's parents complain, he strikes them blind. When one of Jesus' playmates falls from a roof and is killed, the dead boy's parents accuse Jesus of throwing him down, and Jesus brings the boy to life again just long enough to report that it was an accident. Repeatedly he revivifies the dead. When six years old he breaks his water pitcher at the well, but carries the water home nonetheless in the folds of his cloak. He makes clay animals walk, colors cloths all the hues the dyer wishes by dipping them in one tub of indigo, changes boys to kids and then back to boys again, lengthens and shortens timbers by touching them to make Joseph's work easier, makes a serpent suck back the poison from a boy whom it has bitten so that the boy lives and the serpent dies, and even divides the river Jordan so that he can walk across it.[80]

Some of the miracles in our canonical Gospels tax modern credence but, in comparison with the wild extravagance of these later apocryphal Gospels, their sobriety stands out. To be sure, obsession with thaumaturgy in forms utterly incongruous with Jesus' character, does begin to appear in the later strata of our Gospels, as in Matthew's account of the hungry Jesus cursing a fruitless fig tree, which "withered at once,"[81] or in the late addition to Mark's Gospel where "they will pick up serpents, and if they drink any deadly thing, it will not hurt them"[82] is a sign of the true believer. Against the miracle-madness of his age the dread of Jesus that he might be taken for a wonder-worker and a magician does seem, as one scholar calls it "extremely modern."[83]

Here is one area where, in Matthew Arnold's phrase, we must see Jesus over the heads of his reporters. The passage about the evil generation that demands a sign could never have been made up later. It runs counter to the whole drift of current thought in Jesus' day. It is alien to the development of the early church's thought as evidenced even in the Fourth Gospel. It must be genuinely his. He did not think that a spiritual message could be authenticated by a wonderwork or that men and women, unconvinced by truth's appeal, could be savingly persuaded by a miracle. He said this explicitly and unmistakably: "If they do not hear Moses and the prophets, neither will they be convinced if some one should rise from the dead."[84]

With the coming of modern psychosomatic medicine Jesus'

healings have become increasingly understandable. He did do "mighty works," rejoicing in the succor brought to the afflicted, but he was apprehensive about their effect upon his ministry. His disciples, returning from a mission in Galilee, were jubilant about one thing most of all: "Even the demons are subject to us." Sharing their joy, Jesus confronted them with a warning: "Nevertheless do not rejoice in this, that the spirits are subject to you; but rejoice that your names are written in heaven."[85] Obsession with wonderworks, he saw, could crowd out that deeper matter in his disciples—their inner quality, their transforming spiritual message, their gospel of God's grace and man's salvation.

As for himself, he feared being misunderstood as a magician. Long afterward the Jewish Talmud called him a sorcerer. He dreaded that reputation among the crowds that sought him for his marvels. He was a teacher, a prophet, a savior—not a magician. He wanted his spiritual mission to be indubitably paramount, and even with the common people, despite their clamor for a sign, he did not altogether fail. At Caesarea Philippi he asked his disciples, " 'Who do men say that I am?' And they told him, 'John the Baptist'; and others, 'Elijah'; and others, 'One of the prophets.' "[86]

When the early church had separated from the synagogue, and Christianity had become a heresy dangerously disrupting Judaism, so that there were even "some believers who belonged to the party of the Pharisees,"[87] the division between Jews and Christians became ever more embittered. In Antioch in Syria, where both Judaism and Christianity were strong, Ignatius, bishop of the city near the end of the first century and the beginning of the second, saw no compromise between the two. "It is monstrous to talk of Jesus Christ," he wrote, "and to practise Judaism."[88] As for the Jews, the earliest mention of Christians in their first century literature is the curse contained in their daily prayer, the "Schemonè Esrè," at the century's close: "May the Nazarenes and the Minim perish."[89] In that generation the Jewish multitude was certainly against Jesus, as the Christian multitude was against the Jews. In our present Gospels, therefore, written as that bitter hostility developed, some of the harshest things said against Jews in general, and Pharisees in particular, may well be not historically authentic but reflections from the then raging controversy between church and synagogue. Obviously this is true in the Fourth Gospel;[90] quite probably it may be true of some passages in the first three. The whole trend and temper of the times when the Gospels were written would lead to emphasis on the hostility of the Jews to Jesus, and of Jesus to the Jews.

All the more impressive, therefore, is the witness of the Gospels, reflecting the original tradition, that the common people heard him gladly, and that to the end multitudes attended him. According to their varied interests and their capacities to comprehend they saw in him a wonder-worker, a teacher, a prophet, an understanding friend, a personality of challenging power, until to meet their anxious hopes of national release from humiliation and slavery the rumor spread that he might be the Messiah. At least the High Priest had heard that rumor concerning the popular response to him, and at the last asked him, "Are you the Christ, the Son of the Blessed?"[91]

It was not the Jewish common people by whom Jesus was despised and rejected. In their response, from the start to the end of his ministry, lay his best chance of winning Judaism to his leadership. The evidence seems convincing that at the beginning of his ministry he had hoped for this. When he laments those Galilean towns which would not repent,[92] or exclaims, "O Jerusalem, Jerusalem, killing the prophets and stoning those who are sent to you! How often would I have gathered your children together as a hen gathers her brood under her wings, and you would not!"[93] do we not hear the cry of a disappointed spirit that had hoped for a consummation of his mission now denied him?[94]

CHAPTER III

As the Scribes and Pharisees Saw Him

CONTRARY to common supposition among modern Christians, the Pharisees were Israel's progressive party. The Sadducees were the reactionaries, standing rigidly for the written Scripture as the sole authority for their faith and including in their Scripture only the five Books of Moses. Later innovations in Judaism, such as belief in the resurrection of the dead, they denied, along with the existence of angels and spirits. Precisionists in the interpretation of the law, they were harsh in its enforcement, requiring, for example, that in cases of personal injury the rule, "Eye for an eye," be literally enforced, whereas the Pharisees allowed compensation by a fine. This comparatively small group representing wealth and political power in Jerusalem were orthodox believers of the old school, of whom Josephus said: "Their doctrine reaches only a few men, but those who hold the highest offices."[1]

The Pharisees, however, based their faith and practice not only on the written Scriptures—Torah, Prophets and Sacred Writings—but on oral tradition as well, which they regarded as the true interpretation of the Scriptures. Devoutly faithful to the law, they nevertheless developed its applications, tried to make it relevant to their people's changing life, and wel-

[65]

comed new ideas which had emerged in the generations immediately preceding Jesus: the angelic and demonic world, the resurrection of the dead, the future life, and the hope of a coming Messiah who would redeem Israel.

Judaism in Jesus' day, therefore, was not at peace within itself but was riven by controversy and, as between Pharisees and Sadducees, the former, often alleviating the too strict enforcement of old laws on which the latter insisted, were the more popular. So Josephus says of the two parties that "great disputes and differences have arisen among them," and that "while the Sadducees are able to persuade none but the rich, and have not the populace obsequious to them, the Pharisees have the multitude on their side."[2]

The differences between Jesus and the Pharisees have been stressed in Christian thinking, as they are stressed in the Gospels, but his disagreements with the Sadducees were much more radical. Even when he criticized the Pharisees for displacing the written law by later oral tradition—"You leave the commandment of God, and hold fast the tradition of men"[3]—he did it for reasons quite unlike the Sadducees' reactionary attitude toward the Books of Moses. Jesus shared with the Pharisees doctrines which the Torah does not teach— belief in the resurrection, for example, which to the Sadducees seemed ridiculous. If a man has had seven wives, they asked, which wife would be his in the resurrection?[4] As for the coming Messiah, that expectation had no such place in Sadducean thinking as in the faith of the Pharisees. The Sadducees stressed man's power of choice and saw the nation's future depending on the uncertainties of that, rather than on the predestinating providence of God. The messianic hope, as the Pharisees held it, they could not find in the Torah and, being rich, powerful, on co-operative terms with Rome, they felt no flaming desire for a change in the *status quo* such as was setting the Jewish people, as a whole, afire. That the Sadducean priests at last conspired with Pilate to crucify Jesus was due not so much to theoretical differences with him as to fear of the public unrest he was causing, and to wrath at his cleansing of the temple, with its threat to their prestige and revenues. As between the Sadducees and the Pharisees, Jesus was mainly on the Pharisees' side.

Nevertheless, it was with the "scribes and Pharisees" that his trouble began. The scribes were the official teachers, who specialized in the interpretation of the law. Most of them were Pharisees, although the Gospels link them also with the Sadducean high priestly party;[5] and especially after the cleansing of the temple, "The chief priests and the scribes . . . sought a way to destroy him."[6] The Pharisees, however, were far more numerous than the Sadducees, and "the scribes of the Pharisees," as Mark calls them,[7] belonged to the party and with their revered authority guided the thought and swayed the judgment of this most popularly powerful and progressive religious group in Palestine.

What Jesus thought of the scribes and Pharisees the Gospels enlarge upon. While scholars feel confident that some of his most scathing epithets—"You brood of vipers,"[8] for example, in Matthew only—are not authentically his, but represent the later fierce hostility between Christians and Jews in the early church, yet Jesus' stern dislike of certain aspects of Phariseeism is unmistakable. Not, however, what Jesus thought of the Pharisees, but what they thought of him is at present our concern.

That some of them were attracted to him is evident. The earliest church in Jerusalem contained "some believers who

belonged to the party of the Pharisees,"[9] and Jews like Paul—
"I am a Pharisee, a son of Pharisees"[10]—were among the first
converts. In view of all the enmity between church and synagogue, grown virulent by the time our Gospels were written,
it is natural that in the record hostility between Jesus and the
Pharisaic rabbis should be stressed. All the more authentic,
therefore, must be every indication that some of the scribes
and Pharisees were drawn to him.

One scribe, Mark tells us, so heartily agreed with Jesus
about "which commandment is the first of all," that he exclaimed, "You are right, Teacher," and Jesus answered, "You
are not far from the kingdom of God."[11] In our latest Gospel,
"a man of the Pharisees, named Nicodemus," came to Jesus,
secretly by night, saying, "Rabbi, we know that you are a
teacher come from God."[12] Behind such recollections of Jesus'
appeal to scribes and Pharisees, so alien to the trend of the
times when the Gospels were written, one suspects forgotten
incidents, which, could we recover them, would put into truer
perspective Jesus' relationship with the religious leaders of his
people.

His own brother, James, according to all available data was
an ardent Pharisee, and he became head of the first church in
Jerusalem. Paul's account of him, makes clear his loyalty to
the Pharisaic laws,[13] and the Book of Acts confirms the picture.[14] So loyal a Jew was James, so assiduous in his attendance
at the temple and his practice of the law, that when Annas,
the High Priest, condemned him to death, Josephus says, the
Pharisees themselves protested this perversion of justice and
sent messengers to Agrippa II to complain of it.[15]

Not all scribes did Jesus find alien and hostile. "Every scribe
who has been trained for the kingdom of heaven," he said, "is
like a householder, who brings out of his treasure what is new

and what is old."[16] And, once, we read, "A scribe came up and said to him, 'Master, I will follow you wherever you go.' "[17]

Our accustomed emphasis upon the enmity between Jesus and Israel's religious leaders has obscured the fact that with many things which Jesus said the Pharisees heartily agreed, and that many things they said represented what Jesus thought. "Think not that I have come to abolish the law and the prophets; I have come not to abolish them but to fulfill them. For truly I say to you, till heaven and earth pass away, not an iota, not a dot, will pass from the law, until all is accomplished"[18]—was not that good Phariseeism? "The scribes and the Pharisees sit on Moses' seat; so practice and observe whatever they tell you"[19]—could religious leaders ask for more than that, even though scathing criticism of their deeds did follow?

As for the rabbis' teaching, the Jewish writings which we still possess, composed between 200 B.C. and A.D. 100—the Apocrypha and Pseudepigrapha—bear witness to many elements akin to Jesus' thought. "Blessed is he in whose mouth is mercy and gentleness";[20] "The holy man is merciful to his reviler, and holds his peace";[21] "If anyone seeks to do evil unto you, do well unto him, and pray for him, and you will be redeemed of the Lord from all evil"[22]—such teaching was in the Jewish literature of Jesus' day. He carried the sin of adultery back into lustful desire, but so did the books of his time: "Except my wife I have not known any woman. I never committed fornication by the uplifting of my eyes";[23] "He that has a pure mind in love, does not lust after a woman with a view to fornication; for he has no defilement in his heart."[24] Jesus minimized ceremonial sacrifice in comparison with a devout and righteous life, but so did the contemporary writings: "All sacrifice is little for a sweet savor, and all the fat is very little for a whole burnt offering to Thee; but he that fears the Lord is great continually."[25]

Such selective attention to kindred elements between the teaching of Jesus and the best Jewish religion of his time undoubtedly oversimplifies the situation. Such kinship did exist, however, and the movement of thought and life which he started went victoriously on into the Christian era, not simply despite the scribes and Pharisees, but because at least some of them responded to him and believed. They too were eager for the spiritual renewal of Judaism. They too were praying not simply for the Messiah's coming but for a prophet who should cleanse his people and prepare their hearts for his arrival. They were often men of true piety and profound spiritual life, ready to respond to new insights and to discover new dimensions in their faith.

Nevertheless, as a party, the Pharisees rejected Jesus. They saw him treating with carelessness or with disdain many distinctive practices of Jewish religion. Nation after nation had been absorbed by Persian and Greek conquerors and, losing their separate identity, had perished. The Jews, however, had persisted unassimilated, and it was the Pharisees who had saved them. In the middle of the second century B.C. the revolt, led by the Maccabees, had won a military victory which brought release from Hellenistic Syrian oppressors. The peril in which Judaism stood, however, was deeper than any war could overcome or any change of political regime could guard against. The appeal of Greek culture was pervasive, penetrating, constant. Many Jews ceased being Jews and became Hellenists, in dress and daily customs, in habits of thought and of recreation, in love of the Greek gymnasium and theater, and even in religious practice. The Maccabees won the military battle, but the Pharisees won this more vital war.

To them religion, far more than an individual matter of belief and character, concerned the entire culture of the Jewish people. Orthodoxy with them was not, as is commonly the case with us, a matter simply or mainly of creed. Their religion determined not only how they believed or prayed, but how they dressed and washed and ate, how they observed the sabbath, fasted and kept aloof from all Gentile defilements. From circumcision and phylacteries to Kosher food, therefore, from tassels on their garments to scrupulous observance of the sabbath, the minutiae of the law were to them much more than minutiae. They were the distinguishing marks of a Jew, the indispensable guardians against assimilation. Without them the Jews too would gradually have been absorbed into the powerful, alluring culture of the Hellenistic world.

To study, honor and obey the law, and thus to preserve the distinctive integrity of the Jewish people was the central passion of the Pharisees. The word itself means "Separatists." They were not simply quibblers over legalistic trivialities. They were fighting for a cause they willingly would die for: to save their people from being assimilated by the Gentiles. To achieve that required more than a profound religious faith and a high ethic; it required outward signs and symbols, customs and observances whose practice would make a Jew stand out from all others, unmistakably a Jew.

Then Jesus came. Loyal Jew he might claim to be but he minimized and even treated with disdain ceremonial and legalistic customs which the scribes and Pharisees had pain-stakingly elaborated. He was undoing their work, breaking down the barriers that marked off Jews from all other people. He and his disciples did not keep the appointed fasts.[26] They

[71]

broke the sabbath laws.[27] They failed to observe the appointed ritual washings before eating.[28] They disregarded the rules concerning food, eating with Publicans and sinners at whose tables no Kosher customs were respected.[29] Indeed, Jesus, addressing "the multitude," even said, "There is nothing outside a man which by going into him can defile him; but the things which come out of a man are what defile him."[30] Of course the Pharisees were outraged! At one with Jesus in many of his positive emphases, they were grieved at first, then frightened, then incensed by his failure to understand the necessity to Judaism's future of those distinctive cultural and religious customs which were to them the very commandments of God. Let his ideas obtain ascendancy, let a profound faith in God and a high ethic become the essence of religion and all else relatively negligible, what would any longer distinguish a godly and righteous Jew from a godly and righteous Gentile? Far off and dimly they caught the foreshadowing of a possibility—which from their point of view they were justified in fearing—that some day Jews might say, "Neither circumcision nor uncircumcision is of any avail, but faith working through love."[31]

How far Jesus himself foresaw the implications of a universal religion in the things he said and did against the ceremonial and legalistic differentials of Judaism is open to argument. The instinctive fear of the Pharisees, however, that he was breaking down the distinguishing characteristics of Judaism, has been justified by the event. This new teacher, centering his attention on the spiritual core of Israel's prophetic faith, making it primarily a matter of personal loyalty to God and goodness, and either pushing into a secondary place or quite canceling the scribal rules and regulations, was a peril to Phariseeism's major purpose. "The Judaism of that time," says a modern

Jewish scholar, "had no other aim than to save the tiny nation, the guardian of great ideals, from sinking into the broad sea of heathen culture."[32] How could that be done, if the distinctive ceremonial and legalistic customs of the Jews were not maintained? With a good conscience the Pharisees determined to suppress Jesus, as later Saul of Tarsus, a Pharisee, for the same reason, persecuted his followers.

The Pharisees, however, were only human, and in their case, as in all religions, this program of moral and ritual legalism, justified by a high motive though it was, could not escape deterioration. Religion makes sacred whatever it thinks important. A legal requirement, if it is only *that*, can be treated as a practical matter, easily adjusted, altered or annulled but, if religion adopts it, however minor it may be, it becomes sacred, the will of God, a holy and inviolable commandment of the Most High. It was not an ancient Pharisee but a New England Puritan who said that to hold a wedding banquet or any similar festivity on the Lord's day was "as great a sin as for a Father to take a knife and cut his child's throat."[33] It was not a Jewish rabbi in the first century but a Christian clergyman in the twentieth century who wrote that to eat breakfast before partaking of Holy Communion was a sin comparable with fornication.[34]

This is what "Phariseeism" has now popularly come to mean, and it is a degradation that has afflicted all religions. Behind it is a noble motive—to discover and to do the will of God. That motive was the driving power of the Pharisees in Jesus' day. As they saw themselves, they wanted above all else to learn God's will and to do all of it, in matters great and small. Still in *The Standard Prayer Book* of the synagogue, Rabbi Judah, the Patriarch, is quoted: "Be heedful of a light precept

as of a grave one, for thou knowest not the grant of reward for
each precept." The consequence of this is obvious, not only
in the Gospels but in the literature and continuing practice of
orthodox Judaism. Major ethical obligations and legalistic
trivialities were put upon a common level. Alike they were
the will of God and alike mandatory. Who was man to distinguish in importance between requirements that God himself had laid down?

Then Jesus came, not simply distinguishing between the
religious and ethical profundities of Israel's faith and the legalistic minutiae of Pharisaic rules and regulations, but setting
the two in contrast, and pouring derision on those who, tithing
"mint and dill and cummin," neglected "the weightier matters of the law."[35] He even said that they were straining out
gnats and swallowing camels.[36] These ritualistic and moralistic
rules, however, were to the Pharisees not gnats but the holy
will of God. Where would this teacher stop, thus picking and
choosing among the divine commandments?

Once Jesus dined with certain scribes and Pharisees. Great
matters were on his mind, and here was an opportunity to
announce them. Then the dinner was held up because a cere-
mony of ritual cleansing had been neglected. "Why do your
disciples not live according to the tradition of the elders, but
eat with hands defiled?"[37] asked the Pharisees. To Jesus this
religion of precise etiquette seemed trivial. Did not the Pharisees themselves say that the great commandments were to love
God and one's neighbor as one's self? What right, then, had
this ceremonial peccadillo to stride into the center of the picture when great matters were afoot? So, Mark tells us, Jesus
indignantly condemned their triviality, accusing them of substituting "human tradition" for "God's commands."[38] To the
Pharisees, however, these rules and regulations *were* "God's

commands." "He who lightly esteems hand-washing," says the Talmud, "will perish from the earth."[39]

This conflict emerged again with reference to oaths. "When a man voweth a vow unto Jehovah, or sweareth an oath to bind his soul with a bond, he shall not break his word"[40]— with painstaking care the scribes had amplified that command, prescribed its applications in varied circumstances, "built a hedge around the law," as they described it, with detailed regulations guarding it from any possibility of being broken. Then Jesus swept their accumulated rules and precedents aside: "Do not swear at all. . . . Let what you say be simply 'Yes' or 'No'; anything more than this comes from evil."[41]

To a Pharisee such an attitude was utterly unrealistic. People did take oaths; to this day in the Near East vows are the common expression of strong feeling; in Jesus' time they were a stubborn fact, not to be brushed aside by the ideal of an oathless life, but to be practically dealt with. Moreover, the scribes had dealt with them—often sensibly. Their infinite finesse, however, elaborating rules about the phrasing of an oath if it was to be binding, had run out into absurdity. If a man swore by a great matter, such as the temple, without having the details of the temple, such as its golden adornment, clearly in mind, his vow was not binding, but if, when he swore by the temple, the gold was clearly in his thought, he was bound. To Jesus this was trivial nonsense: "You say, 'Swear by the sanctuary, and it means nothing; but swear by the gold of the sanctuary, and the oath is binding.' You are senseless and blind!"[42] As for a son who, by swearing an oath with technical correctness, avoided responsibility for financial aid to his parents, Jesus was indignant: "You say that if a man tells his father or mother, 'This money might have been at your service, but it is Korban' (that is, dedicated to God), he is exempt, so you hold, from doing anything for his father or mother. That is repealing the word of God in the interests of the tradition which you keep up. And you do many things like that."[43]

In Christian circles today, the popular picture of the Pharisees is mainly composed of such trivial legalisms, especially concerning the observance of the sabbath. Plenty of evidence in the Talmud illustrates this aspect of Pharisaic formalism. A man might walk two thousand cubits on the sabbath, but no more. Some knots and not others could be tied or untied on the sabbath. Vinegar, if swallowed, could be used to relieve a sore throat, but it could not be gargled. No woman was to look in a mirror on the sabbath lest, seeing a gray hair, she might be tempted to pull it out. No fire could be kindled on the sabbath. In case death threatened, a physician could be summoned, but, "A fracture may not be attended to," says the Mishna; "If anyone has sprained his hand or foot, he may not pour cold water on it."[44] The schools of Hillel and Shammai, the two most famous rabbis in the generation immediately preceding Jesus, even discussed and disagreed about the question whether an egg that a hen had laid on the sabbath could be eaten.[45]

Such punctilious legalism did characterize Phariseeism, and on the basis of Jewish testimony itself it is evident that many a Pharisee was, in Mark Twain's phrase, "a good man in the worst sense of the word." Nevertheless, to allow this fact to monopolize attention is as unfair as it would be to see New England puritanism in terms only of its senseless scrupulosities. Both Pharisees and Puritans believed in a theocracy, God sovereign and his will the law alike of the individual and the community; this law they found infallibly revealed in sacred books; to determine the meaning and make possible the observance of this law in daily life, they developed official interpreters, the scribes in one case, the clergy in the other; these interpreters faced the inescapable necessity of all legalism, to define permitted and unpermitted conduct in varied circumstances, to establish precedents and to lay down corollary rules deduced from major laws; and since these deduced regulations were the official definition of God's will, scribes and clergy had to be intolerant of all divergence from them. So, in Boston, Captain Kemple, three years absent on a sea voyage, returning on a Sunday, was greeted by his wife on their front doorsill, and for kissing her there in public was put in the stocks.

The similarity between Puritans and Pharisees is especially notable with regard to the observance of the sabbath. "It has truly and justly been observed," wrote Cotton Mather, "that our whole religion fares according to our sabbaths."[46] So, in the Puritan commonwealth to gather firewood on the sabbath was a sin punished with the same severity meted out to theft and adultery.[47] Indeed, one would think that Increase Mather had deliberately chosen the Pharisees rather than Jesus for spiritual guidance to hear him saying, after the great fire swept Boston in 1711: "Has not God's holy day been profaned in New England? Has it not been so in Boston this last summer? Have not burdens been carried through the streets on the sabbath day? Nay, have not bakers, carpenters and other tradesmen been employed in servile works on the sabbath day? When I saw this, my heart said, 'Will not the Lord for this kindle a fire in Boston?' "[48]

Nevertheless, the Puritans were a sturdy breed, with much more to be said of them than such quotations indicate. Few groups in history, so small in numbers, ever made a more constructive contribution to the building of a nation. The same is true of the Pharisees. The drift of religion toward petty ritualistic and moralistic legalism is universal. All religions exhibit it—Christianity not least of all—and to estimate the real quality and significance of any religious group one must have a wider perspective than its punctilious casuistry affords.

Moreover, there were countermovements among the Pharisees, as there were among the Puritans. Not all were compliant and satisfied with the prevalent casuistry. A Gentile, asking that he be told the whole law while standing on one foot, Shammai scorned; but Hillel answered: "What you would not have done to yourself, do not to another; that is the whole law, the rest is commentary."[49] Orthodox Judaism was no more unanimous than most religions are, and over three hundred dissenting opinions are reported in the Talmud between the schools of Hillel and Shammai.[50] In Jesus' day—when Shammai's influence was probably dominant—Jesus' protest against the rigorous legalism by which one could escape filial obligation by saying "Korban" was doubtless justified. The Jewish Mishna, however, which, while codified much later, may well reflect opinions present in the first century, is all on his side, holding that no vows can release a man from responsibility to support his parents.[51] The precarious basis of Pharisaic legalism was frankly noted by an early rabbi: "The [provisions for] release from vows float in the air, there is nothing to support them; the regulations about the sabbath, and offerings at festivals, and the misappropriation of sacred things are like mountains hanging by a hair, for they are very little Bible and many rules."[52]

Some teachers in Israel were not so blind as to miss seeing what they themselves called "the plagues of the Pharisees,"[53] and not so lacking in humor as to miss observing the ridiculousness of much Pharisaic scrupulosity. The Talmud cari-

[78]

catures one Pharisee who with sham humility drags his feet
along the ground and stubs his toe; and makes fun of another
who, walking with eyes half shut for fear of seeing a woman,
bruises his head against a wall.[54] Moreover, the impression
made by some sabbath laws of utter heartlessness in forbidding
the relief of misery on the sabbath is far from representing the
whole truth. Jesus' saying, "The sabbath was made for man,
not man for the sabbath"[55] is paralleled by the rabbis. "The
sabbath was given into your hand, and ye were not given into
its hand," said R. Jonathan ben Joseph; "The sabbath is delivered to you, and ye are not delivered to the sabbath,"[56] said
R. Shimeon ben Menassia.

Nevertheless, the fact remained that the Pharisees were
thoroughgoing legalists and Jesus was not. "A body of Jews
who profess to be more religious than the rest and to explain
the laws more precisely," is Josephus' description of the Pharisees,[57] and they could not possibly tolerate Jesus. To be sure,
they put the saving of life above the keeping of the sabbath
laws. Says the Talmud, "The saving of human life sets aside
the laws of the sabbath."[58] Jesus, however, went further. He
defended his disciples for plucking corn on the sabbath because
they were hungry;[59] he healed a withered hand on the sabbath,
when no question of life and death was involved;[60] and he
stated the principle of his conduct unmistakably, "Thus it is
right to do a kindness on the sabbath."[61] Any strict Pharisee
could see that such an idea, once gaining general acceptance,
would ruin the whole superstructure of sabbath laws.

This point of conflict came plainly out when Jesus on the
sabbath healed a woman who for eighteen years had been
"bent double" so that she could not "raise herself." "The
president of the synagogue," we read, "was annoyed at Jesus'
healing on the sabbath, and he said to the crowd, 'There are

six days for work to be done; come during them to get healed, instead of on the sabbath.' "[62] That Pharisee could with good logic have argued his case. No question of threatened death was involved. Had death threatened, a reasonable rule of the rabbis, formulated later but in principle quite probably recognized in Jesus' day, would have covered the case: "A man may profane one sabbath in order that he may observe many sabbaths."[63] A disability endured for eighteen years, however, could be borne one day more—there was no need of desecrating the holy day by that woman's healing. Jesus, however, was incensed by such an attitude. "You hypocrite," he said, "does not each of you untether his ox or ass from the stall on the sabbath and lead it away to drink? And this woman, a daughter of Abraham, bound by Satan for all these eighteen years, was she not to be freed from her bondage on the sabbath?"[64] Luke adds that "all his opponents were put to shame, but all the crowd rejoiced over all his splendid doings." It is evident, however, that his opponents were more than "put to shame"; they were affronted and outraged; their whole legalistic system was in danger so long as this man was abroad in the land.

Insult was added to injury, as the Pharisees saw it, when Jesus not only imperiled the peculiar customs that distinguished Jews from Gentiles and threatened their system of ritual observances, but defended his attitude by appeals to their sacred Scriptures. This was, in Shakespeare's phrase, hoisting them with their own petard, and they could not endure it.

Jesus, criticized because his disciples on the sabbath plucked, husked and ate corn in the fields, came back at his critics with an appeal to Scripture: "Have you not read what David did when he and his men were hungry, how he went into the house of God, and there they ate *the loaves of the Presence* which neither he nor his men were allowed to eat, but only the priests?"[65] It was bad enough to face the laxness of Jesus, but to confront a defense of it from their own sacred authorities was infuriating. He was using Scripture to demolish Scripture. When the question of divorce came up, he asked them what the Mosaic law was, and when they replied, "Moses permitted a man *to divorce her by writing out a separation notice*," he answered, "He wrote you that command on account of the hardness of your hearts." He did not leave the matter there, however, as though his disregard of a Mosaic law were his own opinion merely. He appealed to Scripture, going back to God's intent concerning marriage when he first made man and woman:

"From the beginning, when God created the world
Male and female, He created them:
hence a man shall leave his
father and mother,
and the pair shall be one flesh.
So they are no longer two but one flesh. What God has joined, then, man must not separate."[66]

Such setting of Scripture against Scripture was disturbing. According to Matthew, on two occasions—once when he had eaten with publicans and sinners, breaking Kosher laws,[67] and once when his disciples had broken sabbath laws—Jesus appealed in self-defense to Hosea: "I desire goodness, and not sacrifice."[68] The Pharisees used that quotation too. Once Rabbi Johanan ben Zakkai, Jesus' contemporary, heard a friend lament over the ruins of Jerusalem, "Woe unto us, that this, the place where the iniquities of Israel were pardoned, is laid waste." But Rabbi Johanan said to him, "My son, be not distressed; we have another atonement as effective as this.

And what is that? It is deeds of lovingkindness; as it is said,
'For I desire mercy, and not sacrifice.' "[69] All the more, however, because that prophetic passage was holy writ to the
Pharisees, Jesus' use of it was unendurable. He was aligning
Hosea on his side against their sacred laws, using Hosea to
break down the legal system on which depended the future of
Judaism. Nothing more enrages the orthodox in any religion
than this appeal to their own sacred writings against their
orthodoxy.

Luke's Gospel strongly stresses the idea that Jesus turned to
the Gentiles because the Jews rejected him, and this emphasis
in the evangelist's thought may have affected his rendering of
the incident at Nazareth, when Jesus returned there and
preached in the synagogue. There is vivid verisimilitude in
the narrative, however, especially with regard to Jesus' use of
Scripture: "There were many widows in Israel in the days of
Elijah, when the heaven was shut up three years and six
months, when there came a great famine over all the land; and
Elijah was sent to none of them but only to Zarephath, in the
land of Sidon, to a woman who was a widow. And there were
many lepers in Israel in the time of the prophet Elisha; and
none of them was cleansed, but only Naaman the Syrian."[70]
At that point "all in the synagogue were filled with wrath."
To have their racial prejudice called in question was bad
enough, but to have Elijah and Elisha marshaled on the
critic's side, their sacred Scripture used to condemn the very
exclusiveness that saved them from Gentile defilement, was
intolerable. This was "new teaching" indeed, holy writ employed to unholy ends, the devil himself, as it were, quoting
Scripture to his purpose.

Jesus used this same style of argument in dealing with the
Sadducees. They could find no warrant for any hope of resur-

rection from the dead in their sacred canon, the Books of Moses, and so they held no hope. When they confronted Jesus, however, with their skeptical ridicule of the resurrected life, his answer came from their own Scriptures. He brushed aside as senseless their question—to which husband, in the resurrection, would a wife belong who had had seven husbands—and went to the pith of the matter in a passage from Exodus.[71] Centuries after Abraham, Isaac and Jacob had died, God said to Moses: "I am the God of Abraham, and the God of Isaac, and the God of Jacob." So, Jesus argued, on the basis of Mosaic authority itself, God claims the great dead as his living servants still. "He is not God of the dead, but of the living."[72] Whether this reply to the Sadducees from the Sadducean canon of Scripture convinced any we do not know, but that it incensed many we may be sure.

Even if the controversy thus arising between Jesus and the leaders of his people had remained in the theoretical realm, teaching against teaching, it would have been serious. The scribes, however, were used to controversy. They were at variance among themselves; Sadducees and Pharisees radically differed; argument and counterargument about the meaning of Scripture and the observance of the law were their familiar occupation.

In Jesus, however, they faced another phenomenon. Jesus was not primarily a teacher. He was a reformer. He came not only to *say* something but to *do* something—to call his nation to repentance, to cleanse the synagogue of its sterile conventionality and the temple of its abuses, to open the gates of salvation to folk who were forgotten or despised, to usher in a new age of righteousness. Whatever else was in his mind, this much was there, and it made of him not so much a rabbi,

[83]

founding a school, as an active reformer insisting on change. It is easy now to conceive him as a religious philosopher and to arrange his teaching in systematic order, but no contemporary could so have pictured him. He was actively proposing revolutionary changes in the religious life and practice of his people. His offense was not simply "new teaching"; what he said they might with difficulty have endured, but what he did was unendurable. He actually broke the sabbath, ate with the unclean, defied the laws of purification, and called on the people to live by his blasphemous innovations—"It was said to the men of old . . . but I say to you . . ."[73] He was gathering disciples, sending them out on missions, attracting a popular following, launching a movement. This man intended insurrection against the cherished customs of his people, and he said so: "No one puts new wine into old wineskins; if he does, the wine will burst the skins, and the wine is lost, and so are the skins: but new wine is for fresh skins."[74] From the day he first defied the sabbath laws to the day he cleansed the temple in Jerusalem he was a doer, not a speaker only.

This fact, indeed, often makes difficult the recovery of the exact meaning of his teaching. As the Gospels present his doctrine, there is no system or order in it. All his teaching was incidental to what he was doing with some individual or group. A personal conversationalist, what he said was determined, not by the logical development of a thesis, but by the needs of those whom he addressed. When scholars now abstract from his scattered sayings a religious philosophy, there is always a wooden, stereotyped, unreal quality in their systematic classification of his doctrines. What actually happened was that, facing self-righteous Pharisees, he told his parables of the lost sheep, the lost coin and the lost son to show up the evil of their attitude;[75] taking a little child in his arms, he

[84]

spoke his unforgettable words about what real greatness is;[76] confronted by a scribe with a much discussed question as to who one's neighbor is, he told the story of the good Samaritan;[77] when dining with Simon the Pharisee, the presence of a sinful woman called out his startling pronouncement on forgiveness.[78] All his teaching was thus incidental, casual, called out by something he was doing with some individual or group.

To be sure, Matthew's Gospel groups together narratives of Jesus' typical miracles, and, in another section, groups his typical teachings in what we call "The Sermon on the Mount." It is evident, however—as in the case of the Lord's Prayer which Luke assigns to a different setting[79]—that these various sayings were at first separate, and that the original background of circumstance which called them out had been forgotten. If we could know, for example, what occasion elicited his saying—so unlike him, as it is usually interpreted—about casting pearls before swine,[80] what light would be thrown on its meaning!

Such was the man the Pharisees confronted, out to do something radical and revolutionary in Israel. It was no theory they faced but a situation to which indifference was impossible.

In the lush days when faith in progress—even inevitable progress—was prevalent, Jesus was sometimes interpreted as a social reformer, striving by gradual processes to reconstruct society and bring in the divine utopia. That such a picture of him is unjustified modernization has long since been evident. He did not attack "social problems" in our modern sense. He did not conceive his mission as reconstructing the government, dethroning Caesar, changing the economic system, or even abolishing slavery by progressive means. He shared the hope which was real to his people's tradition—a divine intervention in history that would bring the kingdom in. The idea of evolu-

[85]

tionary progress was nowhere present in the ancient world, and not long-drawn-out amelioration but sudden catastrophic intervention was the vivid hope of the Jews in Jesus' generation. Nevertheless, to deny that Jesus was a social reformer and then to substitute the idea that he was a wistful, expectant dreamer, merely awaiting God's apocalyptic action, is to put one falsehood in the place of another. Not a social reformer in our modern sense, he was certainly a reformer. He would not give the *status quo* in Israel a moment's rest. At one point after another he attacked it—the economic evils of proud and greedy wealth, the social evils of class prejudice, the ruthless tyranny of rulers like "that fox," Herod, the blasphemy of commercialism in the temple courts, the unfairness to women of the current laws concerning divorce, and with tireless vigor and insistence the religious failures of Pharisaic legalism. Moreover, wherever the opportunity opened, he not only talked but acted. Apocalyptic hopes suggest to moderns a substitute for energetic action, but among the Jews they were far more commonly a stimulus to energetic action.

That Jesus himself was aware of this real point of conflict seems evident. He even told "the multitudes" to "practice and observe" whatever the scribes and Pharisees bade, as though with the major intent and meaning of their teaching he could make shift to get along. It was "what they do" that troubled him. Their self-righteousness and exhibitionism, their show of broad phylacteries, their outward piety and inward unworthiness, their punctilious scruples alongside their major sins, their withering scorn of outcast folk and moral failures, their misrepresentation of the grace of God and the spirit of humaneness which should be Israel's glory—these were the crux of his attack. The law he too wanted to see fulfilled but in them he saw it misused—

[86]

The meanest man I ever saw,
allus kep' inside o' the law.[81]

Such criticisms, leveled by Jesus against the Pharisees, are paralleled in Jewish literature. They apply not to all Pharisees, but to perverse members of the party. When Jesus charges that "they bind heavy burdens, hard to bear, and lay them on men's shoulders; but they themselves will not move them with their finger,"[82] he is confirmed by the Talmud, which calls a scribe who so interprets the law as to make its rules light for himself and burdensome for others a "subtle knave."[83] Jesus' picture of the Pharisee thanking God in the temple that he is "not like other men,"[84] has its counterpart in a rabbi's prayer, quoted in the Talmud, "I give thanks before thee, O Lord my God, that thou hast set my portion with those who sit in the house of study and not with those who sit at street-corners; for I and they rise early—I to words of Torah, but they to vain matters; I and they labor, but I labor and receive a reward, whereas they labor and receive no reward: I and they hasten—I to the life of the world to come, but they to the pit of destruction."[85] Such self-righteousness is a major temptation of legalism, and it was so understood by the better sort of Pharisee. Not even Jesus himself pled more earnestly for humility than did Hillel: "My abasement is my exaltation and my exaltation is my abasement."[86]

Such recognition of Pharisaic faults by Pharisees, while it brings into the foreground the nobler members of the party, also confirms the fact that Jesus was dealing with a real problem. As a teacher only, he might have been content to argue against scribal exegesis; as a reformer of Israel, he had to attack a way of living, entrenched in the most influential religious group among his people.

[87]

✕ The radical cause of this difference between Jesus and the Pharisees runs deep. They were thinking primarily of saving Judaism in general and the nation in particular; Jesus was thinking primarily of saving individuals. To be sure, the Pharisees would have affirmed that the Jewish nation and religion could not be saved without devout and faithful individuals, and Jesus obviously was thinking of a transformed nation and world as the crown and consummation of transformed persons. The focus in each case, however, was distinctive. Both wanted right living, but the Pharisees, with the protection of Judaism and its people from pagan defilement in the center of attention, could think of its achievement mainly in terms of legalistic discipline, rules and regulations externally imposed; while Jesus, with individual persons central, thought in terms of inward transformation—

A good tree cannot bear bad fruit,
and a rotten tree cannot bear sound fruit.[87]

If one is aiming primarily at the defense of a people and a religion from the corruption of surrounding heathenism, the Pharisaic method is logical and defensible. Distinctive customs, rigidly defined, insisted on as the very will of God, and drilled into a devout and loyal nation, will protect, and did protect the Jews, from assimilation. If one, however, is digging the tunnel from the other end, seeing transformed persons as the only way to a transformed people, such a method is inadequate and self-defeating. Far from making bad people good, rules and regulations externally imposed—as religious history amply proves—commonly lead to mere external conformity, the outside meticulously correct while the inside is all wrong.

[88]

Here was the deepest source of conflict between Jesus and Jewish legalism—"You blind Pharisee! first cleanse the inside of the cup and of the plate, that the outside also may be clean"[88]—and the reason for this conflict lay in a radical difference of predominant aim. Legalism might save a nation but, by itself alone, it never saved a person. Persons, to be made good men and women, must be inwardly transformed, and because this was Jesus' central interest, his distinctive approach to the human problem, he rebelled against the whole Pharisaic system. Whether one takes Matthew's rendering, just quoted, where the contrast lies between cleansing the outside and the inside of a dish, or takes Luke's rendering—"You Pharisees clean the outside of cups and dishes, but inside you are full of greed and wickedness"[89]—where the contrast lies between the external cleansing of dishes and the internal cleansing of human souls, Jesus' essential meaning is the same. He was content with nothing less than transformed life within. What was first with the Pharisees—a people faithfully observing a mass of regulations—was not first with him: "first cleanse the inside of the cup and of the plate."

Far from inwardly redeeming persons to a good life, Jesus saw the Pharisaic method issuing in what he called hypocrisy. That word has come to mean conscious pretense, deliberate play-acting and insincerity, but this almost certainly was not Jesus' meaning. The Pharisees, as a whole, were obviously sincere, ready to lay life down for their law; but they were, said Jesus, "blind," self-complacent about their scrupulosities, depending on the techniques of legalism to do what only inward, personal regeneration can do. Whatever other quality Jesus' ethic and religion had, *inwardness* was at the heart of them. When Dr. Manson says, "For Jesus good living is spontaneous activity of a transformed character; for the scribes

[89]

and Pharisees it is obedience to a discipline imposed from without,"[90] he states the gist of the matter. Those two approaches are not easily reconcilable. In this regard the Pharisees were right in thinking that they faced in Jesus a mortal enemy of their whole system.

This inwardness of Jesus' approach lights up one of the most difficult problems in our Gospels: the seeming contradiction between Jesus' professed intention, on one side, not to abolish but to fulfill the law, and, on the other, Jesus' sustained and vehement attack upon scribal legalism. When all the guesses concerning Matthew's special interest in the sanctity of Jewish law, and concerning the possible reflection in the Gospels of the early church's controversy between Judaistic and Hellenistic Christians, are taken full account of, that contradiction is too tenacious to be easily eliminated, and the question still remains: what if Jesus did say that he came not to abolish but to fulfill the law, and what if he meant it?

There are two ways of fulfilling the great commandments of Judaism. One the Pharisees tried. They drew out corollary rules from major laws, deduced specific regulations from general principles, created detailed precepts applying to endless concrete situations, and so built up their immense and complicated legal system. Jesus, however, used another method. If a man does not hate, he will not kill; if he does not lust, he will not commit adultery; if his word is "simply 'Yes' or 'No,'" he will not break his oath; if evil thoughts do not proceed out of his heart, he will do no evil; if he is a fig tree he will bear no thistles. Jesus did come to fulfill the law, but by a method that could not be reconciled with Pharisaic legalism.

A typical illustration of this difference is provided by the desire of both Jesus and the Pharisees to escape from the old law by which, in cases of personal injury, the victim could demand an eye from the aggressor if his own eye had been destroyed. While the Sadducees called for the law's literal observance, the Pharisaic substitution of financial compensation was almost certainly the general, if not the universal, practice. Nevertheless, the Pharisees were forced by their theory to retain and fulfill the law, and they did so in typical legalistic fashion. The victim could extract the aggressor's eye, they said, but only if it was exactly like his own in size and color; and since this condition is never present, the principle of retaliation was retained without its barbarous expression.[91] Jesus, however, went at that problem in another way by rejecting the law of retaliation altogether—undiscourageable goodwill even toward those who injure us, the vindictiveness that desires an eye for an eye conquered at its source in the heart of the injured man.

This does not mean that Jesus would have denied the function of custom, law and regulation. In any culture they are indispensable to personality, as a trellis is to guide the growth of a living vine. Jesus' concern, however, was centered on the living vine and, as he saw it, the vast elaboration of the Pharisaic trellis endangered the very growth it was intended to assist.

One suspects, therefore, that the seeming contradiction between what Jesus said about fulfilling the law and what he did about it is no real contradiction at all. He had pondered deeply the meaning of the law, as interpreted by the prophets, and with all the passionate devotion of a true Pharisee he wanted it fulfilled. But was it being fulfilled by this multiplication of rules and this insistence on their meticulous observance? Did not the fulfillment of the law demand another method altogether—inward transformation, spiritual rebirth, the cleansing of motive, the creation of a quality in life that prevented and forestalled the evils which the law prohibited? Not legalistic regulation but inward regeneration was the way he chose to the law's fulfillment, and he stated the contrast between the two with merciless clarity.

Inevitably, then, the scribes and Pharisees found him a dangerous enemy. As they saw themselves they were Judaism's hope, and he was putting them to scorn. So, in the end, that "strictest party of our religion," as Paul called the Pharisees,[92] turned against Jesus, convinced that he must be suppressed. They never dreamed that history, watching them in retrospect, would see them facing in the Man of Nazareth a personality too big for their acceptance and understanding.

CHAPTER IV

As the Self-Complacent Saw Him

self-satisfaction

A MAJOR tragedy of legalistic religion is that its rules can be observed and that, like Saul of Tarsus, its devotees can be, "as to righteousness under the law blameless."[1] Self-complacency always dogs the footsteps of legalism. The elder brother of the Prodigal Son incarnated Jesus' idea of Pharisee-ism at its worst; yet that elder brother said to his father: "Lo, these many years I have served you, and I never disobeyed your command."[2] Such self-complacent folk found Jesus a disturbing person.

A man of wealth and station once asked him, "Good Teacher, what must I do to inherit eternal life?" and when Jesus rehearsed certain major commandments, the man replied: "Teacher, all these I have observed from my youth."[3] Then Jesus called on him to sell whatever he had and give to the poor, required of him, that is, an excess of goodness which no one could reasonably expect. Jesus was aiming at that man's self-complacency, showing him dimensions in goodness which no rules and regulations could express, and facing which no man could be self-satisfied. That rich man's "countenance fell, and he went away sorrowful." While some, however, may thus have responded to Jesus' extravagant ethical demands

[93]

with sorrow, there must have been more who responded with resentment.

No record exists that Jesus asked any other individual to sell all his possessions for the sake of the poor. He habitually dealt with persons, one by one, sailing, as it were, around the island of each life until he saw where the real problem was, and then landing *there*. Zacchaeus called out Jesus' praise when he gave only half his goods to the poor and restored his extortions fourfold.[4] Jesus said nothing to Martha about selling her goods, but dealt with her personal problem of overanxiety about small details.[5] In the earliest Gospel one who wanted to do what Jesus required of the rich man—leave all and follow him—was not permitted by Jesus to do it, but was told instead: "Go home to your friends."[6] What Jesus said to an individual about his personal problem may not without due care be generalized as though applicable to everyone. Always, however, Jesus presented to any self-complacent person an ethical ideal that made blamelessness impossible.

What, then, did these morally self-satisfied folk see in Jesus —the rich man in love with his wealth, who had observed all the laws from his youth; men like the elder brother of the Prodigal, who had never transgressed a command; men like the Pharisee, who thanked God that he was not as the rest of men;[7] Simon the Pharisee, unaware of his need of forgiveness, finding himself unfavorably compared with a sinful woman, who, forgiven much, loved much?[8]

To such characters Jesus must have seemed what we would call "perfectionist," asking the impossible, presenting not observable rules but unattainable ideals. "You have heard that it was said to the men of old, 'You shall not kill; and whoever kills shall be liable to judgment.' But I say to you that every one who is angry with his brother shall be liable to judgment"[9]—no one ever lived up to *that*. Indeed, many ancient authorities read, "every one who is angry with his brother *without cause*"—obviously a later addition, written in by someone desiring to mitigate Jesus' unqualified ideal. Such unqualified idealism, however, was the very essence of Jesus' ethical demand. He went far beyond rules, plunged deep into the inner recesses of motive and emotion, and called for a quality of spirit beyond the reach of any man's volition. This distinctive characteristic of Jesus' teaching was his way of dealing with the actual situation which he faced. Self-complacency, inherent in any legalistic system, confronted him on every side, and he deliberately challenged it with an ethic that made self-righteousness impossible.

To be sure, Jesus did not altogether discard legalism, whether moral or ritual. When he condemned the Pharisees for tithing "mint and rue and every herb" and passing over "justice and the love of God," he did not eliminate the tithing: "These you ought to have done without neglecting the others."[10] He himself observed faithfully the more important customs of his people, and far from being a ruthless iconoclast, he told one whom he had healed, "Go and show yourself to the priest, and make an offering for your cleansing, as Moses commanded."[11]

As Jesus would not have discarded all legalism, so the Pharisees would have lifted the Psalmist's prayer for a clean heart and a right spirit.[12] They too remembered Jeremiah, "I will put my law in their inward parts, and in their heart will I write it."[13] Nevertheless, while Jesus and the legalists could each have granted much to the other's position, the practical situation meant controversy. Legalism, dominant, detailed, obsessing, was bringing its inevitable consequence—the self-righteousness of men who thought themselves blameless.

Attempted explanations of Jesus' idealism have gone far afield. He expected the speedy end of the age and the coming of God's victorious kingdom, some have said; his ethic was not intended to be livable in this present evil world; it was the ethic of a heavenly realm soon to come, or an "interim" morality conceivable today only because today would soon be replaced by an ideal tomorrow. The Pharisees, however, also believed in the coming messianic reign. They too were expecting an ideal tomorrow; yet, far from sharing Jesus' so-called "perfectionist" ethic, many of them were contented legalists. While undoubtedly their faith in the coming kingdom was less intense than his, and while they did not feel, as vividly as he did, its imminence, this difference in intensity and vividness should not blind us to the fact that Jesus and the Pharisees shared a basic hope of God's victorious intervention. The unique quality of Jesus' ethic, so sharply in contrast with Phariseeism, demands a deeper explanation than the eschatological expectation which he shared with them.

The essential demand of Jesus for inner rightness was in the Psalms and prophets before messianism became central in Israel's thought, and many noble sayings of the rabbis gave it voice after messianism became peripheral. Jesus' expectation of the speedy coming of the kingdom was neither the profound origin of his inward ethic nor the immediate motive of his insistence on it. The sources of his high ideals must be sought in the depths of his own personality and in his idea of God, rather than in a single category of contemporary thought like messianism. He was an idealist because he was that kind of person, and he would have been that kind of person in the twentieth century with its ideas of progress as well as in the first century with its apocalyptic hopes. Moreover, as the Gospel record stands, his presentation of unattainable ideals was, in part at least, called out by an immediate situation. He confronted self-satisfied moralists. *"Unless your righteousness exceeds that of the scribes and Pharisees"*—with this crucial need his ethical demands in the Sermon on the Mount were dealing.

You say your prayers, he said, but what about your inward life of prayer in secret where no man sees? You do not break your spoken vows, but what about sincerity? You do not commit adultery, but what about lust? You give alms, but what about love? You fast, but what about penitence? The impression made by these searching demands is not at all that of a man constructing a perfectionist ethic in view of a coming messianic reign, but of a man, practically in earnest, speaking to real people who needed these things said to them. Self-righteousness, pride, complacency with kept rules, were prevalent vices. Jesus saw no hope for his people until they confronted God's will in terms of a good life that made such pride impossible.

Legalism in religion is commonly presented as a heavy burden, obedience to whose many rules is difficult and wearisome. There is, however, another side to the matter. To live up to a perfect ideal is impossible, but a rule can be observed. For earnest religious people, seriously wishing to do God's will, there is positive relief in having duty precisely defined, saved thus from vagueness, brought down to earth, translated into detailed commandments which can be obeyed. To be "in the Spirit on the Lord's day,"[14] as the New Testament says, is an ideal that leaves so much to the imagination and inner quality of the individual that many would despair of knowing what it means, but strict sabbatarian regulations simplify the problem; they can be learned and obeyed.

The familiar idea, therefore, that the laws of the Pharisees were an onerous burden to faithful Jews misrepresents the total picture. It was rather their glory, as sons of Israel, to possess the law and, in small matters and large alike, thus to have God's will defined for them. They said that the law is like a garden, all of whose fruits and flowers are cultivated by the son because he loves his father. They said that while an inferior guest at a banquet may have only one dish or one cup of wine, whereas the sons of the house have access to the whole larder and the whole wine cellar, so Israel has the privilege of knowing and obeying all the divine precepts.[15] The best of the Pharisees, therefore, conceiving their multiplied commandments as garden flowers or varied courses at a banquet, were not, as commonly pictured, dour, glum, heavily burdened obeyers of meticulous rules, but often were radiant souls, carrying off their observance of the divine laws as happily as distinguished gentlemen at a royal court might carry off customary ceremonies, to observe which is their pride. As for the common people, wide areas of required observance, especially at the Jewish festivals, were doubtless as joyfully handled as Christmas customs are among Christians now.

Nevertheless, the nemesis of legalism is inescapable. It does become burdensome. A modern Jewish scholar writes, "The requirements of the Law, both moral and ritual, were far-reaching, intricate, manifold. They did not merely affect the great concerns of life, but fussed over the small; they left few things untouched, and their touch was mostly, though far from invariably, a heavy one."[16] Worse than this, however, was the temptation to self-righteousness, to observe laws and then thank God in consequence that one is not as the rest of men.

In the face of this temptation Jesus presented an ethical demand so inward, concerned so deeply with quality of thought, motive and emotion, that being "in every respect . . . tempted as we are,"[17] he said even about himself, "Why do you call me good? No one is good but God alone."[18]

The morally self-satisfied faced in Jesus a demand not only for inward rightness but for positiveness of life and character. It was this that left the "rich young ruler" baffled. An attractive personality—"Jesus looking upon him loved him"[19]—his goodness was negative. The commandments he had obeyed were prohibitions and his virtue was respectability. Jesus demanded of him devotion, enthusiasm, sacrificial loyalty. "So far, so good!" Jesus seemed to say about his conventional correctness, "but now, amount to something! Leave the nest of your comfortable living and give yourself to a cause greater than yourself! Follow me, and find your life not in what belongs to you but in what you belong to!"

That kind of goodness lies beyond the power of law to generate. Laws may help define its expression, but the thing itself is inwardly begotten, and no prohibitions can even touch the fringes of its meaning. Inherent in Jesus' character, illustrated in his mission, it was central also in his message. None could follow him without accepting as the essential constituent of discipleship a positive sacrificial loyalty that burned all bridges behind it. As for self-righteousness, based on the observance of prohibitions, that seemed to Jesus the caricature of goodness.

The morally self-satisfied, therefore, content in their re-respectability, found him an annoying person. Some of his

[99]

sternest condemnations fell on people, not who did something wrong, but who did nothing. The priest and Levite, who went by on the other side and left the victim of the robbers unhelped, fell under his censure.[20] What had they done? Nothing whatever! The condemned in the judgment to whom the Lord said, "I was hungry and you gave me no food, I was thirsty and you gave me no drink, I was a stranger and you did not welcome me, naked and you did not clothe me, sick and in prison and you did not visit me,"[21] faced doom because they had done nothing. The rich man who had fared sumptuously every day, while Lazarus lay starving at his door, was condemned not for doing but for not doing. The son who roughly answered his father's command to "work in the vineyard" by saying, "I will not," but who then went, was praised by Jesus rather than the son who answered, "I go, sir," but who did not go.[22] Negativeness was the disdain of Jesus. Once he told a parable, alike whimsical and urgently serious, about an unclean spirit which, having left a man to roam abroad, came back again to find "the house empty, swept, and put in order"; then into this vacant, decent, respectable habitation that unclean spirit brought seven others, "and the last state of that man becomes worse than the first."[23]

It would be grossly unjust to the Pharisees to represent them as lacking in positive, devoted, sacrificial loyalty. It was they who had refused easy compromise with pagan culture and who labored tirelessly to save Judaism from corruption. They were in deadly earnest about their cause, traversing "sea and land to make a single proselyte."[24] Their furious resistance against any rupture of their laws or profanation of their holy places was the despair of the Romans. Not once but many times—as when Petronius proposed a statue to the emperor in the temple area—the answer of the Pharisees was resolute

[100]

and final: They would all die rather than transgress the law.[25] Seldom in history has a more persistent, sacrificial devotion to a cause been seen than in the long struggle of the Pharisees to save Judaism.

Nevertheless, as Jesus watched the consequences, one factor in it was to him unendurable. This positive devotion was given to the support and maintenance of a legalistic system, too much concerned with prohibitory rules. It was, in too large measure, positiveness dedicated to negativeness. No religious cult altogether escapes this paradox; current Christianity furnishes plentiful illustrations. From being right within, which is very difficult, the emphasis shifts to doing right which is then defined in precepts; but doing right is most easily guarded by prohibitions against doing wrong. So in every religion intense loyalty has been massed around commandments concerning things forbidden. There is nothing peculiar to Phariseeism in the Pharisee who thanked God he was not as the rest of men largely because of what he had *not* done.[26]

Such self-righteousness, as Jesus saw it, was much too cheaply won. Anyone could have it by lowering the standard of goodness to prohibitory rules. From not doing, therefore, he turned his stress to doing, and from doing to being, in part at least because he saw self-righteousness, cheaply bought, as a major problem among his people.

What Jesus wanted was humility. He would have agreed with Rabbi Joshua ben Levi that it is the greatest of the virtues[27]—certainly that without it no genuine virtue is possible —and he came at it by making the criterion of moral excellence so deep, inward and positive that no one could be self-satisfied. What troubled him, as he watched some of the Pharisees, was their pride. They did their deeds to be seen of men, made their phylacteries ostentatiously broad and their tassels

long, loved places of honor at feasts, the best seats in the synagogues, and salutations in the market place;[28] and, worst of
all, they thought of themselves as "righteous persons who need
no repentance."[29]

That the best of the rabbis talked just as Jesus did about
pride and humility is sometimes urged as a reason for thinking
his judgment on Pharisaic self-complacency unjustified. Upon
the contrary, at this point such rabbis confirm Jesus. They too
saw the peril of self-righteousness. God cannot live in the same
world with the proud and arrogant man, they said.[30] It is not
in the Gospels only that we meet "Some who trusted in themselves that they were righteous and despised others."[31] The
rabbis bear witness to the same type of person.

If Jesus could not tolerate such folk, neither could they tolerate him. He disturbed their complacency, upset their equa-
nimity, stole from them the occasion of their pride. What modern psychiatry teaches he discovered as a grim fact, that few
possessions are dearer to men than those claims to superiority
which set them above their fellows. How, then, could the morally respectable and self-satisfied endure one who said to them:
"The tax collectors and the harlots go into the kingdom of God
before you"?[32]

At no point did Jesus state his uncompromising ethical ideal
in more difficult fashion than in his demand for all-inclusive
undiscourageable love, even toward enemies. To this day the
familiar passage in the Sermon on the Mount seems to the
world at large and to honest Christians in particular unattain-
ably perfectionist. What must it have seemed to galled, embittered Jews under the yoke of Rome in a Palestine seething
with incipient revolt?

"You have heard the saying, 'An eye for an eye and a tooth for a tooth.' But I tell you, you are not to resist an injury:
> whoever strikes you on the right cheek,
> > turn the other to him as well;
> whoever wants to sue you for your shirt,
> > let him have your coat as well;
> whoever forces you to go one mile,
> > go two miles with him;
> give to the man who begs from you, and turn
> > not away from him who wants to borrow.

"You have heard the saying, 'You must love your neighbour and hate your enemy.' But I tell you, love your enemies and pray for those who persecute you, that you may be sons of your Father in heaven:
> he makes his sun rise on the evil and the
> > good, and sends rain on the just and
> > the unjust.
> For if you love only those who love you,
> > what reward do you get for that?
> do not the very taxgatherers do as much?
> and if you only salute your friends, what is
> > special about that?
> do not the very pagans do as much?

You must be perfect as your heavenly Father is perfect."[33]

From the uncompromising idealism of this passage some moderns seek escape by calling it the ethic of the coming kingdom, which men now are not expected to observe. To Jesus' contemporaries, however, no such refuge would have been possible. They were then and there facing the indignities which Jesus described—insulted, sued, compelled by Roman law to carry a soldier's burden for a mile, and in every way experiencing the humiliation of their country's occupancy by enemies. Jesus' injunctions were not relevant to any messianic age of heavenly perfection, when they would not be smitten, cheated and coerced by foes, but to the present time when these evils realistically confronted them.

To suppose that Jesus taught undiscourageable love only because he thought that tomorrow the messianic age would come is to miss his meaning, and fail to hear his message as his contemporaries heard it. For centuries the best thought of Judaism about the treatment of enemies had been developing toward Jesus' ideal. Said the Book of Proverbs:

> If thine enemy be hungry, give him
> bread to eat;
> And if he be thirsty, give him water
> to drink;[34]

and Job, asserting his innocence of wrong-doing, pleaded that he had never

> rejoiced at the destruction of him
> that hated me,
> Or lifted up myself when evil found him.[35]

No special form of eschatology is needed to explain such ideas. Jesus could tell a Jew not to resist a Roman soldier's requisition of coerced service, say some, only because so soon the Messiah would put an end to Rome. But Epictetus, the Roman stoic, said: "If there is a requisition and a soldier seizes your ass, let it go! Do not resist or complain, otherwise you will be first beaten, and lose the ass after all."[36] Granted that Jesus' similar demand was based on the nature of God and his mercy, rather than on prudential considerations such as Epictetus cites, nevertheless the messianic expectation is not needed to explain that difference.

If over four hundred years before Christ, Socrates, with no apocalypticism in his thinking, could say that if he had to choose between doing and suffering wrong, he would prefer to suffer rather than do it,[37] why must apocalpyticism be taken as the central and controlling motive of the similar quality in Jesus' ethic? The philosophic background of Buddhism's thinking is utterly different from that of Jesus and nothing remotely like Jewish apocalyptic is in it, but Buddhism says:

> Worse is he who, when reviled, reviles again.
>> Who, when reviled, does not revile again
>>> A two-fold victory wins.
> He seeks the good both of the other and himself.[38]

> We live happily indeed, not hating those who hate us.
> Among men who hate us, we dwell free from hatred.[39]

> If villainous bandits were to carve you limb from limb,
>> even then be it your task to preserve your hearts
>>> unmoved,
>> never to allow an ill word to pass your lips,
> but always to abide in compassion and goodwill
>> with no hate in your hearts.[40]

In Jesus' teaching about all-inclusive love he was talking to contemporaries who shared his messianic hopes but who differed with him concerning legalism. That he had in mind the insurrectionist party in Israel, afterward called Zealots, is highly probable. Not waiting for the Messiah's coming, they were already dreaming of violent revolt against Rome, which a few years after Jesus' death broke out in fury and ended in Jerusalem's destruction. Certainly what Jesus said was relevant to them. The Zealots, however, sprang from the left wing of the Pharisees and, as Matthew's record stands, it is of the Pharisees as a whole and of their legalism that Jesus primarily was thinking when he pleaded for all-inclusive love. Here, too, as when he appealed for inwardness and positiveness of life and character, he was announcing an ideal superior to common practices. The very wording of his plea reveals this motive. The ordinary levels of respectable behavior anyone can reach, he said—"Do not even the tax collectors do the same?" "Do not even the Gentiles do the same?" He was deliberately presenting a way of life so demanding that no legalism could define it, no unredeemed heart practice it, no saint perfectly fulfill it.

To be sure, the messianic hope must have affected Jesus' ethic by heightening the expression of his demands, intensifying his urgency, and thrusting into the background prudential counsels for getting on in this present world. When Jesus, however, pleaded for all-inclusive love, what the morally self-satisfied heard was not some corollary of messianism but the presentation of an ethical standard that made their self-righteousness impossible. This whole range of Jesus' teaching is best understood if the theme with which it started is kept steadily in mind: "Unless your righteousness exceeds that of the scribes and Pharisees."[41]

A common description of Jesus' teaching today is to call it an "absolute ethic," thus suggesting its irrelevance to immediate practical problems whether among his contemporaries or among us. In Hebrew, however, there is no such word as "absolute," and the whole range of theoretical abstractness which in our speech that word connotes is alien to Jesus and to the Jews of his time. We are continually warned against modernizing Jesus, attributing to him ideas and motives at home in our day but not in his; but no modernizing of Jesus is more flagrant than the ascription to him of the concepts which across the centuries have accumulated around the word "absolute." Among the books that Jesus almost certainly read was *The Testament of the Twelve Patriarchs*, written about 100 B.C. "Love one another from the heart," says this book, "and if any man

[106]

sin against you, speak peaceably to him, and in your soul hold not guile; and if he repent and confess, forgive him." Was this admonition ethical absolutism, moving only in the stratosphere above Israel's actual life, irrelevant to and unlivable in the present evil age when enemies were rampant? When Booker T. Washington, the Negro leader, enduring his humiliations, said, "I will not let any man reduce my soul to the level of hatred," was that an "absolute ethic," and not a way of life to be undertaken in the face of actual hostility?

Impressed by the unattainableness of Jesus' ideal of love unlimited, committed to the idea that it is an unlivable, absolute ethic, some interpreters stretch the evidence to make their point. The phrase, "Do not resist one who is evil," can be torn from its grammatical context and from its larger matrix in the speaker's life, and made to mean something not only impossible but undesirable. But Jesus himself did resist evil. All his ministry he fearlessly resisted evil. In this very text he was attacking evil—but, he would have insisted, *not with evil*. Paul understood his meaning: "Do not be overcome by evil, but overcome evil with good."[42] The problem he was dealing with is inherent in a wicked world—the temptation to become a monster when one fights a monster, to meet hate with hate, and violence with violence. Against such moral surrender Jesus protested.

A principle of interpretation is here involved of primary importance in the case of Jesus: *what is said must be understood in terms of the life of the one who said it*. To make nonresistance an "absolute" is to lift a single phrase completely out of the context of Jesus' life. Soft compliance with evil deeds and with unrepentant evil men was no characteristic of his. "Of the teachers of the past, whose sayings have been preserved," said Sir John Seeley, "Mohammed would be regarded by most as the type of unrelenting severity, and yet we may read the Koran

[107]

from beginning to end, without finding words expressive of more vehement condemnation than those attributed to Christ." Indeed, on this point critics of Jesus have insisted that while he taught love to enemies he did not practice it. A modern Jewish scholar, Dr. C. G. Montefiore, grants the beauty of Jesus' demand that we love our enemies and the originality with which he expressed it, but then adds: "Yet how much more telling his injunction would have been if we had *a single story* about his doing good to, or praying for, a single Rabbi or Pharisee! One grain of practise is worth a pound of theory. ... But no such deed is ascribed to Jesus in the Gospels. Toward his enemies, toward those who did not believe in him, whether individuals, groups, or cities (Matthew 11:20–24), only denunciation and bitter words! The injunctions are beautiful, but how much more beautiful would have been a *fulfillment* of those injunctions by Jesus himself."[43]

To Christians such a charge is shocking. Nevertheless, the charge must be faced. In answer to it, we may doubt the authenticity of some of Jesus' wrathful words, and may ascribe them to the later church speaking out of its bitter Jewish-Christian controversy. We may say that this later controversy easily could have caused the remembrance of Jesus' harsh words and the forgetting of others, which critics like Dr. Montefiore wish were in the record. We may say that as Matthew grouped typical miracles in a connected passage and typical teachings in the Sermon on the Mount, so in his twenty-third chapter he grouped Jesus' criticisms of scribes and Pharisees, which originally were not so massed in a prolonged invective, but were individually called out by separate occasions when they were justified. We may say that while Jesus with prophetic indignation attacked Pharisaic evils, in his personal relationships with Pharisees, dining and conversing with them, he met them with friendly goodwill. We may say that while he did condemn cities that rejected him, he also wept with pity over Jerusalem where he experienced his ultimate rejection.[44] We may say that even at the close of Matthew's twenty-third chapter, his mercy went out to the city that killed the prophets, "How often would I have gathered your children together as a hen gathers her brood under her wings, and you would not!"[45] Nevertheless, what we cannot do is to picture Jesus as one who did not resist evil.

The idea that Jesus taught nonresistance as an absolute ethic is part of the sentimentalizing of him which has characterized much modern Christianity. "Tenderness of heart," wrote Renan, "was in him transformed into an infinite sweetness, a vague poetry, and a universal charm."[46] If Jesus was anything like that, one wonders why they crucified him. He stirred some men to loyalty so intense that they willingly died for him and others to hatred so fierce that they would not rest until they killed him. Some called him a blasphemer, some a sorcerer in league with the devil, but apparently they never thought of him in terms of "infinite sweetness, vague poetry, universal charm." Money-changers driven from the temple courts, self-complacent moralists castigated by his stinging condemnation, faced another kind of man than that—a formidable personality who certainly did attack evil. What he meant by "Do not resist one who is evil,"[47] cannot be adequately understood apart from its setting in his life.

This principle, that Jesus' words must be interpreted in terms of his deeds, is illustrated in that most impractical of all passages ascribed to him where, saying, "Do not be anxious,"[48] he used the carefree attitude of flowers and birds as an illustration of what his disciples' unworried life should be. Such teaching can easily be interpreted as utterly unrealistic—until

[109]

one sees it as autobiography. Jesus had plenty to be anxious about. Early in his ministry the cross loomed, and from then until he sweat blood in Gethsemane, anxiety about his disciples, his mission and his own fate was his familiar companion. His injunction against worry sprang from his own inner struggle, accentuated by his sensitiveness, made more acute because he cared so much for the cause he was willing to die for. Even in John's Gospel which minimizes the indications of Jesus' humanness and which, to that end, omits altogether his agony in Gethsemane, this anxious stress and strain in Jesus' life could not be utterly left out: "Now is my soul troubled. And what shall I say? 'Father, save me from this hour'? No, for this purpose I have come to this hour. Father, glorify thy name."[49] Set thus in the matrix of his own life his words about anxiety gain reality. This winning of freedom from fear was his problem. This admonition to live day by day, borrowing no trouble from tomorrow, doing one's best and leaving the consequence in God's hands, he had addressed to himself before he addressed it to his disciples. When one thinks of the many people who have said, "Don't worry," to an unimpressed world that soon forgot, one sees that Jesus' words about anxiety gained their first impact and won their permanence in mankind's memory because his confident, fearless life, lived under terrific tension, drove them home. When words like "Be not anxious" are spoken, it makes all the difference in the world what kind of person says them.

To set Jesus' teaching about love of enemies in the matrix of his life is similarly revealing. His contemporaries, like all the rest of mankind, were used to an average ethic based on reciprocity. If we can count on decency from others, we should be decent to them; we should extend goodwill to those from whom we have received or can expect it—so runs ordinary morality.

Far past *that* went Jesus' thinking. Be decent, he said, whether others are decent or not. Exercise goodwill whether they do or not. Never let your rightness depend upon another's conduct. Do not hate because you are hated, or revile because you are reviled. If two blows must be given prefer taking both to giving one. Never let vindictiveness be the motive or retaliation the standard of your conduct, else your conduct will be at the mercy of others' ill behavior. Keep your own criteria of character intact and independent. Love even when hated, bless even when cursed.

That, too, was Jesus' own problem, and his solution of it went far beyond legalistic rules that could be blamelessly observed. To call it an "interim ethic," however, or to deny its relevancy to this present evil age because it is "perfectionist" and "absolutist" is fantastic. Jesus' ethic was expressly meant for this tough world, where goodwill and fair play from others are often not to be counted on, and where, if because of that we justify our own ill will and inhumanity, there is no hope. For then mankind will go on, evil always met by evil, hatred met by hatred, violence arousing violence, injustice calling out injustice. From that vicious cycle the only escape lies in those who break through it, refusing to surrender their own criteria of conduct to the standards of their enemies. To be sure, Jesus based his plea for such superior living not on the future welfare of society conceived in terms of progress but on the eternal character of God; yet even when this ethic is assayed in hardheaded modern terms, its realism is evident. Until mankind can do better then meet hate with hate, it heads for catastrophe.

This realism in Jesus' teaching some try to deny by stressing the sentence with which, according to Matthew, he concludes it: "You, therefore, must be perfect, as your heavenly Father is perfect."[50] One wishes that the Aramaic word which Jesus used were known. In Luke's account the phrase is not "be perfect," but "be merciful, even as your Father is merciful."[51] Dr. Torrey catches the logical conclusion of Jesus' argument and the probable meaning of the Aramaic words he used, when he translates Matthew's sentence thus: "Be therefore all-including (in your goodwill), even as your heavenly Father includes all."[52] The word "perfect" in our speech has come to mean blamelessness. That, however, was the very thing the proud claim to which Jesus was rebuking. The main point of his teaching concerning inward rightness, devoted character, and all inclusive love, was that such an ethic makes faultlessness and its attendant pride impossible. The Greek word translated "perfect" is variously rendered in the New Testament. "Solid food is for the mature";[53] "until we all attain . . . to mature manhood";[54] "Be babes in evil, but in thinking be mature"[55]— such is its common meaning. It connotes full spiritual growth. Of God only is it used in the complete sense. God's all-inclusive mercy is our ideal, said Jesus; to attain maturity so that our mercy too is all-inclusive should be our aim. That is not "perfectionism," as the word now is used to indicate an absolutist ethic inapplicable to realistic living, but it is a demand for a quality of spirit and a manner of life that rules out self-righteousness. When one puts oneself into the place of Jesus' contemporaries, what they saw in him was no ethical absolutist, but a teacher who with almost maddening directness was attacking one of the commonest evils of their time, insistently saying, in every way he could find to say it, often with the extravagant hyperbole characteristic of his speech, that real goodness must exceed the legalistic righteousness of the scribes and Pharisees.

All this explains Jesus' constant and weighty emphasis on repentance. He called on men not alone to change their behavior but, first of all, to change their minds, to recognize their deep, inward sin, to acknowledge their ingrained self-love, their unjustified pride, their unpayable debt of guilt,[56] and to seek pardon and rebirth. Moreover, he addressed this call for penitence not alone to obvious sinners, guilty of gross iniquity, out-and-out thievery and debauchery, but more especially to the conventionally respectable and self-satisfied.[57] It was they who needed most to see how stained with self-seeking their best goodness was, and with how thin a veneer their obedience to many laws covered their disobedience to God's divine intent for their characters.

The morally self-satisfied, therefore, had to reject Jesus. They might be drawn to him, as the "rich young ruler" was, but they could not follow him. They had to choose between their prized self-satisfaction and his idea of what the good life really is and, preferring the former, they easily could rationalize their choice: his demands were extravagant, no one could live up to them. Their legalistic habit was, starting with a great law, to seek its specific applications in the varied situations life presents, and so alike to define what the law's observance practically implied and to prove its observance practically possible. Let any one try *that* with these ideals of Jesus—turning the other cheek, refusing to resist an injury, surrendering coat and cloak together rather than go to law to protect one's rights, offering to bear a soldier's burden two miles when required to bear it one—and endless concrete situations were imaginable where the literal application of such injunctions would be impossible for the individual and dangerous to the community. This was no ethic for a man of common sense or for a nation whose self-preservation was important to the world. Far better seemed their type of religion, practical, livable, defined in laws that men could learn and observe, and which, when observed, made one a good Jew and a good man. So Li Hung Chang, centuries later, comparing Confucianism with Christianity, sincerely stated his preference for the former because Jesus' ideals were too lofty to be practical.

This conflict between Jesus and the legalists in the ethical realm involved an underlying conflict of temperament. Whatever else Jesus was, he was exuberant. He loved nature, and when the Galilean hills were clothed with flowers, he felt that "Solomon in all his glory was not arrayed like one of these."[58] He loved children, and even on a busy day "was indignant" because the disciples tried to keep them from him.[59] He had little use for the solemn fast days of his people, called his company of friends a bridal party, exempt from fasting,[60] and even when his disciples did fast, bade them, "Do not look dismal."[61] He described his gospel as an invitation to a royal banquet,[62] and when his message was accepted by even a single sinner, he said that the very angels in heaven rejoiced.[63] There is no mistaking Jesus' temperament—vital, dynamic, exuberant— the very kind of temperament that legalistic precisionists least of all could understand.

This superabundant vitality naturally expressed itself in the ethical and religious realm in ways infuriating to precise minds. Jesus' teaching—even in our present Gospels, from which more flagrant contradictions may well have been omitted—is full of paradox and seeming inconsistency. He said that we were not to practice our piety before men in order to be seen by them;[64] but he also said that we were to put our lamps not under a bushel but on a stand, and to let our light so shine before men that they might see our good works.[65] He called to him the heavy-laden, promising them an easy yoke, a light burden, and rest for their souls;[66] but he also said that if any man would

[114]

come after him, he must deny himself, and take up his cross.[67] He said that we were not to be "anxious about tomorrow";[68] but then he told the parable in which foolish maidens, providing no oil with their lamps, were condemned because they had not been anxious enough about tomorrow.[69] He said that his disciples were to "do good . . . expecting nothing in return"; but in the same sentence, as in many another passage, he promised, "your reward will be great."[70] He said, "Blessed are the peacemakers"[71] but he also said, "Do you think that I have come to give peace on earth? No, I tell you, but rather division."[72] He pictured the fatherly God sending his merciful sun and rain on good and evil men alike;[73] but he also said about God, "I will warn you whom to fear: fear him who, after he has killed, has power to cast into hell; yes, I tell you, fear him!"[74] He claimed that he did not come to abolish the law;[75] and yet he cried, "It was said to the men of old . . . But I say to you."[76]

To be sure, the modern reader, considering the way Jesus' sayings were addressed, now to this individual or group and now to that, sees in such contrasting statements not inconsistency but many-sidedness. Some men do need to be warned against pious exhibitionism, and others against hiding their light under a bushel. Jesus saw truth and duty from many angles—his discipleship refreshing, liberating, exhilarating and yet costly and sacrificial too: forethought for the morrow both dangerous and indispensable, goodness for the sake of reward selfish, and yet in God's world goodness without ultimate reward unthinkable; peacemaking both divine and sometimes impossible; God both merciful and stern; the law eternal in its profundities but transient in its forms. To contemporary legalists, however, devoted to clarity and consistency, Jesus must have been difficult to understand. The typical rabbinical mind was scholastic; Jesus' mind was anything but that. The rabbis sought precise definitions of duty; Jesus threw out metaphors and similes in the direction of high ideals.

One feels this temperamental conflict when Jesus is compared with a great rabbi, such as Akiba ben Joseph. Born about A.D. 40 and dying a martyr's death when he was in his nineties, he was a forceful character, whose influence on Judaism is comparable with the influence of his contemporary, the Apostle Paul, on Christianity. He too was vital, sincere, courageous, deeply devout and, within the limits of rabbinism, progressive and forward looking. All the more, modern minds, both Jewish and Christian, wonder at the concerns which habitually occupied his thought. If, said the law, a person was murdered on the highway and the assassin was not discovered, the nearest town must bring a calf as an atonement. If, however, the corpse was found halfway between two towns, where on the dead body should the measurement begin to determine which town must bring the calf? Rabbi Eliezar said one must measure from the navel, but Rabbi Akiba, with elaborate reasons based on man's creation in the image of God, argued that one must measure from the nose.[77]

All his life this really great rabbi dealt with such legalisms. When, with Rabbi Gamaliel and others, he went by ship on a mission to Rome, the question arose whether, since two thousand cubits were the limit of travel for a faithful Jew on the sabbath day, they had to count the distance the ship sailed, and whether or not in addition they could walk about the deck for exercise. Rabbi Gamaliel was sure that they could not. Once, coming into port and discovering that the improvised ladder by which they were to descend to the wharf had been made on the sabbath, they debated whether—since no Jew should profit by work done, even by a Gentile, on the holy day—they could use it. Rabbi Gamaliel resolved their scruples: "Since it was not made in our presence (and therefore was not specially intended for us), we may use it."[78]

That Jesus not only held ideas alien to such punctiliousness, but was essentially the kind of person who could not endure it, is obvious. The difference between him and the legalists was irreconcilable. Especially when he saw the legalists supposing that by such meticulous observance of scruples they gained merit with God, he rose in wrath. Dr. Arthur Marmorstein, himself a loyal Jew, in his volume, *The Doctrine of Merits in Old Rabbinical Literature*, sums up his research by saying that, while obedience to rabbinical regulations is not the only way to obtain merit in the sight of God, "the faithful observance of the law and ceremonies is not unimportant. . . . By performing the commandments man is entitled to a reward. . . . The laws and observances were given to obtain merits."[79]

Against this idea Jesus directed his parable about the servant who, having worked all day in the fields and then having prepared his lord's supper and served him, expects not even thanks. "So you also," said Jesus, "when you have done all that is commanded you, say, 'We are unworthy servants; we have only done what was our duty.' "[80] Here again, Jesus' demand for excess goodness appears. There is no such thing as being good enough, no service which justifies any man in saying, I have done enough; with all the commandments obeyed, no merit has been gained; real goodness lies beyond commandments in willingness to do more than anyone has a right to expect; when the first required mile has been finished, goodness lies in voluntarily going the second mile; the best of men desperately need to repent. Shakespeare caught the spirit of the kind of ethic Jesus stood for in his lines about Desdemona—

"She is of so free, so kind, so apt, so blessed a disposition, she holds it a vice in her goodness not to do more than she is requested."[81]

This quality of exuberance in Jesus' ethic must have puzzled the disciples—he told them that when they were hated, excommunicated, denounced and defamed, they were to "Rejoice in that day, and leap for joy"[82]—but it both puzzled and enraged the precisionists. According to rabbinic teaching one was bound to forgive one's brother three times.[83] Peter was being generous when he asked, "Lord, how often shall my brother sin against me, and I forgive him? As many as seven times?" Jesus, however, pushed the limit out toward infinity: "I do not say to you seven times, but seventy times seven."[84] To be sure, here as always, one must remember the rabbis who would not altogether have disagreed with Jesus. Said one of his contemporaries, Rabbi Johanan ben Zakkai, "If thou hast practiced Torah much, claim not merit to thyself, for thereunto wast thou created."[85] Nevertheless, the rabbi would still have regarded legalism as alone a safe morality for individuals and alone a sufficient defense of Judaism, and would have regarded Jesus' idealism as visionary, unrealistic, extravagant.

Easy as it is, however, to see why legalists—especially those who found in the successful performance of the law's demands their chief self-satisfaction—rejected Jesus, it is easy also to see now what lay beyond their vision then. Jesus' ethic inculcated a spirit, presented a goal; like a compass, it indicated a direction, moving in which through the jungle of this evil world, one often had to make detours. Not always was Jesus himself in a position to choose between courses of conduct, the one ideal and the other utterly wrong. He too had to find his way as best he could *toward* his ideals amid confusing choices between what was better on the whole and what was worse. He said, "Judge not, that you be not judged,"[86] but times came when he had not only to judge but to denounce. He said, "Do not be anxious," but this evil world plunged him into the agony of Gethsemane where he sweat blood. He said that his disciples should swear no oaths, but when the high priest put him under oath— "I adjure you by the living God"[87]—he nonetheless answered.

It is no wonder that his ethic has always been a stumbling block to legalists. Nevertheless, his ideals, which often cannot be taken literally, can be taken seriously. Legalistic rules and regulations are formulated to meet contingencies, and with changing circumstances pass away, but his ideals have gone before the best thinking and living of the race, like a pillar of cloud by day and of fire by night. They are the standard by which even the best conduct is judged and moral progress is measured; and, as the world faces today the consequence of mankind's neglect and defiance of them, Jesus' saying has in it a realistic relevance to practical affairs that his contemporary rejectors could not have dreamed: "Everyone who listens to these words of mine and acts upon them will be like a sensible man who built his house on rock."[88]

CHAPTER V

As Religious and Moral Outcasts Saw Him

TWO familiar groups in first century Palestine were the *haberim* and the *amme ha-arez*. The former were a fellowship of scrupulous Jews, pledged to ceremonial purity and to carefulness in tithing. The members of this fellowship may have been drawn mainly from among the more fortunate and better educated, but their distinction was not so much learning, economic comfort or social station as punctilious piety in the observance of tithing, dietary rules and ritual cleanliness.

Amme ha-arez means literally "people of the land," and by inference "the masses," but it came more specifically to signify religiously negligent Jews, who either did not know the scribal laws or who, knowing them, were indifferent to their observance. An *am ha-arez* was a nonpracticing Jew, who did not recite the formal prayers, omitted the ritual fringes from his garments and the donning of phylacteries at his devotions, who neglected tithing and ritual washing, or, having a son, failed to train him in scrupulous obedience to the law.[1] That the word meaning "the masses" should thus come to signify Jews ignorant or negligent of the scribal laws suggests that such folk for the most part may have come from the underprivileged classes —the poor, the uneducated, the toilers—engaged in trades that made ritual purity difficult, if not impossible, and, in any

[120]

case, too hard pressed to be scrupulous about ceremonial niceties. This is further suggested by the fact that, along with condemnation of the impiety of the *amme ha-arez*, rabbinical literature reveals contempt of them as illiterate, coarse, uncouth.

No such idea of the *amme ha-arez*, however, based solely on class lines, is adequate. A tax collector, or a priest by grace of secular influence, if careless of rabbinical laws, would be to the scrupulous an *am ha-arez*, although the tax collector would not be poor nor the priest socially depressed. As the word "heathen," originally meaning a peasant dwelling on a heath, came later to have almost exclusively an ideological and moral significance, so the phrase, "people of the land," outgrew its origin. Folk of all social classes could be *amme ha-arez*, as folk of all social classes could be heathen. Indeed, an *am ha-arez* could rise to the highest ranks of religious leadership, as did Rabbi Akiba ben Joseph. Born of a lowly family, a shepherd by occupation, he was an out-and-out *am ha-arez*, hating the rabbis, and refusing observance of their casuistry but, later changing his mind, he became a learned student and expositor of the law, and rose to first-rate eminence.

Between the *haberim* and these rebels against rabbinical casuistry no love was lost. Among the pledges taken by the *haberim* when joining their fellowship were vows never to be the guest of an *am ha-arez*, or to entertain one unless the unclean visitor left his cloak outside, never to sell him any products of the soil or buy from him anything that legally could be subject to impurity, never to travel in company with one, or perform purifications in his presence. "Do not be frequently in the company of an *am ha-arez*," ran the admonition, "for in the end he will give you something to eat from which the tithes have not been separated."[2]

Underneath these caste rules which made the *amme ha-arez* an outlawed group, ran hatred and contempt whose expressions are often shocking. One rabbi, describing the kind of girl a good Jew might marry, lists "The daughter of one of the great men," "The daughter of the president of a synagogue," "The daughter of a teacher of children," and then adds: "But let him not marry the daughters of the *amme ha-arez*, for they are loathsome, and their children are abominations, and of them the Scripture says, 'Cursed is he that lies with any manner of beast.' "[3] One rabbi denied all hope of resurrection to an *am ha-arez;*[4] another said, perhaps as a bitter joke, "It is lawful to stab an *am ha-arez* on a Day of Atonement";[5] and even Rabbi Hillel said, "No *am ha-arez* is truly religious."[6]

Such contempt on the part of the *haberim* for this outlawed group was naturally returned in kind. "The hatred of the *amme ha-arez* for the learned class," said one rabbi, "is greater than the hatred of the Gentiles against Israel, and the hatred of their wives exceeds theirs."[7] Were there any doubt of this, the personal testimony of Rabbi Akiba would dispel it. "When I was an *am ha-arez*," he remarked, "I used to say, 'I wish I had one of those scholars, and I would bite him like an ass.' His disciples said, 'You mean like a dog.' He replied, 'An ass's bite breaks the bone; a dog's does not.' "[8]

One of the earliest intimations we have in the Gospels concerning the kind of people attracted to Jesus is Mark's description of him as he "sat at table in his house," with "many tax collectors and sinners" sitting with him.[9] The tax collectors are familiar, one of the most detested groups in Palestine, but who were the "sinners"? To suppose them to be only moral derelicts is surely a mistake. Moral failure doubtless was represented among them, but they were in general nonpracticing Jews, ignorant or careless of the scribal laws, the scorn of the scrupulous, the outcast *amme ha-arez*, concerning whom one rabbi said that only because of them God's punishments fall upon the world.[10]

Few things are more indicative of the kind of person Jesus was than the fact that the *haberim* reacted against him, while these "sinners" responded to him. The Fourth Gospel sums up the contempt of scrupulous Jews for this aspect of Jesus' ministry: "Have any of the authorities or of the Pharisees believed in him?" they said, "But this crowd, who do not know the law, are accursed."[11] What did such outcast contemporaries of Jesus see in him as they sought his company?

Obviously they felt his sympathy. Accustomed to the contempt of the purists, they saw in Jesus a phenomenon they had never faced before—a religious teacher, speaking as "one who had authority, and not as their scribes,"[12] a loyal Jew affirming the great faiths of Israel and concerned for the redemption of his people, a powerful personality whose words and works alike could not be hid, yet who was one with them, who, far from despising them, made himself their champion and broke through one barricade after another of impeding ceremonial laws to get at them and claim their following. The later rabbis were carrying on an ancient tradition when they wrote, "The wise say, Let not a man associate with sinners even to bring them near to the Torah."[13] To that attitude the outcasts were accustomed. Not simply about Jesus' miracles of healing, therefore, but about this other miracle—a towering spokesman of Judaism, who understood, valued, and loved the *amme ha-arez*—it must have been true that "the crowds marveled, saying, 'Never was anything like this seen in Israel.' "[14]

In so far as the *amme ha-arez* were poor, depressed, underprivileged—as many of them doubtless were—Jesus' understanding sympathy went out to them. There, too, he was one with them, and saw their problems from within. More fortunately situated legalistic precisionists could know little about the difficulties a poor man faced in his tithing, or about the sheer impossibility of observing meticulous rules concerning phylacteries and ceremonial washings amid the soil and drudgery of impoverished, laborious days. But Jesus knew. The early church fathers quote a saying of Jesus not in our Gospels: "Because of the weak was I weak, and because of the hungry did I hunger and because of the thirsty did I thirst." This unmistakable quality in Jesus was evident in his treatment of the *amme ha-arez*. He looked at them through no window of privilege; he was one with them. His sympathy with them sprang from intimate understanding of the reasons why many of them were not faithful Jews. What Shakespeare's apothecary who sold the poison said—"My poverty and not my will consents"— Jesus heard from many a guilty conscience among these outcasts. He resented the contempt the precisionists poured out on them, and to his understanding sympathy they responded.

In so far as these *amme ha-arez* were not only poor, but uneducated and ignorant, Jesus understood them. He himself faced as they faced the scorn of the educated: "How is it that this man has learning, when he has never studied?"[15] To be sure, ample evidence indicates that Jesus had studied long and deeply; some scholars even think that, while he spoke Aramaic, he was well versed also in Rabbinical Hebrew, the technical language of the schools.[16] He knew the Hebrew Scriptures— eighty-seven quotations from the Old Testament are attributed to him in our Gospels. Repeatedly he met the rabbis on their own terms and outargued them, and not only did his own disciples call him "Rabbi," but so did the scribes and Pharisees.[17] In his earlier ministry he taught in the synagogues, and the inference is most probable that the years between his boyhood's questioning of the rabbis in the temple and the beginning of his public ministry had been absorbed not in carpentry alone, but in profound study of his fathers' faith.

Nevertheless, from the viewpoint of the technical scholastics he was an untaught, unlearned man, and in that regard also one of the *amme ha-arez*.

The condescension of the learned rabbis toward the unlearned multitude was one of Israel's tragedies, for it was the misuse of one of the noblest elements in Judaism. The Pharisaic ideal was an educated people, loving the law, studying it, intelligent about it, observing it. Josephus wrote only a few years after Jesus' death: "Most of all we are mindful of the education of children . . . so that if anyone ask us concerning the laws, we can tell them all more easily than our own name. Having learned them straightway with our earliest perception, they become engraven in our souls."[18] The rabbis were fighting for the hope of Israel when they thus put education first among their priorities, saying, "The world is saved only by the breath of the school-children"; "Study is more meritorious than sacrifice"; "No one is poor except the man who is poor in knowledge."[19] The emphasis which the rabbis thus put on learning and the devotion with which they tried to spread knowledge of the law among their people were admirable.

Nevertheless, this emphasis when perverted led to pride of learning and contempt for the unlearned. The rabbis thought they had good reason for this contempt. These folk who did not and perhaps would not study the law, who through innate boorishness were incapable of knowledge or through willfulness refused it, were the peril of Israel; nothing too bad could be said about them.

It is not difficult, therefore, to put oneself into the place of a sensitive *am ha-arez*. He knows that he is ignorant of the laws, despised for his illiteracy and boorishness, and regarded as a public menace. To such contempt he reacts with bitterness, but along with resentment go humiliation, a sense of inferiority ill-concealed by hatred, an inner, unacknowledged drift toward self-disdain. Then this *am ha-arez* confronts Jesus, who does not shrink from him, even eats with him, breaks the laws of Kosher food and ritual purity to get next to him, speaks up for him as a champion and appeals for his support. No wonder the scribes and Pharisees were outraged, unable to understand that outreaching sympathy which stirred the *amme ha-arez*, and which the centuries have not been able to forget: "When he saw the crowds, he had compassion for them, because they were harassed and helpless, like sheep without a shepherd."[20]

If Jesus' foes, calling him "a friend of tax collectors and sinners,"[21] had reason to despise the latter, with even better reason they hated the former. Piety and patriotism alike aroused wrath against these Jewish publicans who fleeced their own people to fill the Roman treasury. They were a contaminated class to be avoided; their evidence was not valid in court; a promise made to them was not binding; and even a charitable offering made by a tax gatherer to temple or synagogue was declared unacceptable.[22] The Gospels give clear evidence of their dishonesty, as when John the Baptist said to certain tax gatherers who came to be baptized, "Collect no more than is appointed you,"[23] or when penitent Zacchaeus took for granted the kind of sin he had been guilty of: "If I have defrauded any one of anything, I restore it fourfold."[24] One can understand Jesus' compassion for the poor, illiterate, depressed peasantry who did not keep the scribal laws, but how could he have been the friend of tax collectors?

One reason is evident: to Jesus contempt of a whole class of people was intolerable. He said "Judge not, that ye be not judged," but he himself passed scathing judgment on three things—cruelty, sham and contemptuousness. The last especially he could not stand—not even when directed against so ugly a group as the tax collectors. Luke introduces Jesus' story of the Pharisee and the publican, who prayed in the temple, with this revealing remark: "He also told this parable to some who trusted in themselves that they were righteous and despised others."[25] That aroused Jesus' indignation; no group, as a whole, should be thus gathered up and lumped together in indiscriminate disdain. Jesus scorned such scorn, contemned such contempt, and whenever he saw any group thus despised he instinctively came to their defense and help. If it be said that Jesus himself, as reported in the Gospels, visited upon the Pharisees as a whole just such indiscriminate denunciation, one answer is that they, at least, were not underdogs, outcast and scorned, as were the tax collectors. It was the outcast groups that called out his compassion.

Deeper than his contempt of contempt, however, in making him a friend of publicans, ran Jesus' invincible individualism. He saw men not as groups so much as persons. Some tax collectors were all their enemies said of them—greedy, dishonest, traitors to their people, the scum of the earth. Jesus was not in the least sentimental about them. They ganged up against their victims and co-operatively served their greedy interests—Jesus saw that. "If you love those who love you," he said, "what reward have you? Do not even the tax collectors do the same?"[26] But always his eyes were open to the individual publican as a person, sure that here and there, at least, was one with the stuff in him out of which saints are made.

The Jewish records themselves consent to this, and tell of at least one tax gatherer, the father of a certain Rabbi Zevia, who used his office to lighten the burdens of his countrymen rather than to increase them.[27] That some publicans sought John's baptism of repentance shows clearly that not all of them were of one kind. It took Jesus, however, to make capital of this—to visit Zacchaeus, although "all murmured," with such effect that he could say, "Today salvation has come to this house, since he also is a son of Abraham;"[28] and even to find in Matthew, "sitting at the tax office," the makings of an apostle.[29]

Both the tax gatherers and the *amme ha-arez* in general saw in Jesus, therefore, one who refused to accept the current labels on their class and who insisted on coming at them as persons, one by one. Hillel was wrong when he said that no *am ha-arez* could be truly religious, and Jesus proved it. In Jesus' day no more loyal Jews were in Palestine than some of these plain people whom the rabbis despised. They believed in Israel's God, respected "the weightier matters of the law, justice and mercy and faithfulness,"[30] hoped with all their hearts for the coming kingdom and, though in ways Jesus would not approve were ready, as the event showed, to sell their lives dearly to make it come. Jesus was not going it blind when he saw values in these reprobated groups and, as for them, here one individual and there another responded to him, saw in him what the rabbis could not see, and justified his thanks to God "for hiding all this from the wise and learned and revealing it to the simple-minded."[31] In no small measure the victory of the early Christian movement was due to this appeal of Jesus to the masses, as over against the scorn of the Pharisees. Indeed, Dr. Kaufmann Kohler, a Jewish scholar, says: "There can be no doubt that it was this contemptuous and hostile attitude of the Pharisaic schools toward the masses that was the chief cause of the triumphant power of the Christian church."[32]

So distinctive was Jesus' attitude that his foes eagerly seized on it and, along with calling him "a glutton and a drunkard," because he was not an ascetic like John the Baptist, they nicknamed him "a friend of tax collectors and sinners."[33] To make matters worse, from their point of view, he did not check this outgoing friendship at the point where technical ceremonial negligence and disobedience passed over into moral wrongdoing. It was bad enough, they thought, to appoint—let us suppose—an honest publican, like Matthew, to the inner circle of his disciples, and to champion the *amme ha-arez* in general against the precisionists, but he went far beyond this, exhibiting what seemed to them a shocking care and compassion for flagrantly disreputable characters.

Indeed, he went so far that some records of his mercy toward real sinners apparently embarrassed the writers of our Gospels. How else can one explain the treatment accorded the story of the woman taken in adultery? In our versions John's Gospel contains it,[34] but with a single exception, on which its inclusion in our Bible is based—the Bezan Codex—it is omitted by all the oldest Greek manuscripts. In later manuscripts it is found sometimes at the end of John's Gospel, sometimes after Luke 21:38, and some manuscripts place the story in the margin or on extra leaves. Here was a wandering narrative which, since Papias apparently knew it,[35] went back in all probability to early oral transmission. It rings true to the spirit and method of Jesus; it has all the inner marks of authenticity; it is not the kind of story a later generation would have made up; and the surmise seems justified that we nearly lost it from the written record because not only were the Jews shocked by Jesus' leniency toward an adulteress, but the Christian writers themselves were afraid of its effect. They feared, as St. Augustine said, that because of it "an excuse for sinning might be given to women."[36]

Dangerous or not, the story stands, too typical of Jesus' conflict with the scribes and Pharisees to be left out. When they confronted him with the adulteress their primary concern was to catch him, "that they might have some charge to bring against him," showing up the looseness and leniency of his attitude even toward gross sinners whom the law condemned to stoning. His answer confounded them—"Let him who is without sin among you be the first to throw a stone at her"— and when, "one by one, beginning with the eldest," they had gone out, his treatment of the woman, all too abbreviated in our condensed record, sent her out too, forgiven for the past and challenged to a new future. The sins of the flesh are bad— such is Jesus' typical attitude—but the sins of the spirit are worse: harsh legalism, contemptuous condemnation without trying to understand its victim, concentration on the law's letter with no care for the personality involved and for what may yet by God's grace be done in her, pride without pity, judgment without mercy.

Not simply tax collectors and technical sinners, therefore, but the morally defeated and disreputable saw in Jesus a new phenomenon—a religious leader who when he faced their sin thought first not of condemnation but of cure. "Why do you eat and drink with tax collectors and sinners?" asked the scribes and Pharisees; "And Jesus answered them, 'Those who are well have no need of a physician, but those who are sick; I have not come to call the righteous, but sinners to repent-

[130]

ance.' "[37] No analogy could better express the attitude of Jesus—a physician. A man in sound health is no physician's chief concern; but show a doctor a sick man, with maladies complicated and difficult, and his every faculty is called into play. That extraordinary attitude toward sinners was characteristic of Jesus. Outcast, hurt, despised and disreputable folk called out his intense interest and sympathy. "Ninety-nine righteous persons who need no repentance" aroused him not half so much. No wonder that legalistic precisionists could not understand him!

When legalists of the stricter sort faced a disreputable sinner their instinctive reaction was to assume the function of judges. They established, as it were, a courtroom, announced the law and its prescribed penalties, presented the charge and began a trial. Jesus' instinctive reaction was that of a physician: the sinner is sick, he needs not so much a Doctor of Laws as a Doctor of Medicine, cure is the one aim above all others to be sought. One is tempted at this point to detour and note how far ahead of his time Jesus was, and with what difficulty modern penology, acknowledging his attitude to be right, struggles in practice to catch up with him. As for his contemporaries the gospel record bears witness to the resentment with which some of them, the grateful welcome with which others of them, and the surprise with which all of them met this characteristic attitude of Jesus—a physician, out to cure the sick. As the Fourth Gospel sums it up in words ascribed to the Master himself: "I did not come to judge the world but to save the world."[38]

While, however, this contrast between the attitude of the legalists and the attitude of Jesus is true, it must not be so sharply stated that on one side is judgment with no mercy and on the other mercy with no judgment. Every Pharisee, however strict, would have affirmed the mercy of God in the for-giveness of sinners. The Old Testament is rich in statements of God's waiting pardon for the penitent; where could one find a more moving expression of it than the Thirty-second Psalm? Rabbinical literature abounds in passages celebrating the divine forgiveness. "There is no man who is not God's debtor," wrote one rabbi, "but God is gracious and pitiful and forgives previous sins. It is like a man who borrowed money and forgot to pay it back. After a time he came to the creditor and said, I know that I owe you money. The other replied: Why remind me of the old debt? It has long ago vanished from my mind. So with God. Men sin against him; he sees that they do not repent, and that they go on sinning; yet if at last they repent, he remits them their previous sins, and if they come before him in repentance, and mention the previous sins, he says, Remember not your previous sins."[39] What Jesus faced in his contemporary Judaism, therefore, was no theoretical denial of God's forgiving mercy toward sinners. One suspects that in everything he said and did in his attitude toward the morally defeated and unworthy he thought of himself as the spokesman of the gospel of divine grace that belonged at the very heart of the Jewish faith. As one rabbinical passage puts it, with an inclusiveness that Jesus himself could not have sur-passed, "God holds no creature as unworthy, but opens the door to all at every hour; he who would enter can enter."[40]

As thus the rabbis taught God's mercy as well as his judg-ment, so Jesus taught God's judgment as well as his mercy. He pictured the terrific consequences of moral iniquity in terms as stern as any rabbi could have used; his descriptions of Ge-henna, "the eternal fire prepared for the devil and his angels,"[41] still make moderns shrink; and when one hears him say that some sinners should have great stones tied about their necks and be cast into the midst of the sea,[42] one feels the depth of indignation against evildoers from which such condemnation must have come. To be sure, just how literally Jesus thought of Gehenna is uncertain. The word means Valley of Hinnom— in Hebrew, Gehinnom—the vale outside Jerusalem where the city's refuse was burned. In the second century B.C., the word first appears as descriptive of the place of punishment into which the unrighteous dead were cast. In Jesus' day, Jewish thinking about the nature of man's post-mortem future and, in particular, about Sheol, paradise, Gehenna, was in flux, full of crosscurrents and inconsistencies. Certainly to translate "Gehenna" as meaning "hell," and then to conceive hell with all the connotations which Christian theology has put into it, is to oversimplify and modernize with a vengeance the ancient Jewish portrayal of the future world. Says one rabbinical statement: "The wicked of Israel in their bodies, and the wicked of the nations of the world in their bodies go down to Gehenna and are punished in it for twelve months. After twelve months their souls become extinct, and their bodies are burned up, and hell casts them out, and they turn to ashes."[43] It may be, therefore, that in similar fashion—true to the analogy of what went on in the Valley of Hinnom outside Jerusalem—Jesus meant to picture the "fire" as "eternal," but not the refuse which was being consumed. Nevertheless, however one may interpret his use of "Gehenna," Jesus' judgment on sin and on sinners was fearfully stern. Even in his conversation with Zacchaeus or with the woman taken in adultery—could we have the full account—one feels sure that no easygoing softness toward the sins involved characterized his dealing. No physician minimizes illness, says it does not matter, treats it lightly.

The question, therefore, rises: where was the difference between Jesus and his rabbinical opponents with regard to the treatment of sinners? To that question three answers are suggested by the available evidence.

The first seems clear: in characteristic Phariseeism, while God was willing to forgive, the initiative was left to the sinner. He, being a sinner, was under condemnation; if he would repent, God would pardon him—but that was up to him. "He who would enter, can enter." Jesus, on the contrary, sought out sinners, took the initiative himself, practiced a positive, outreaching, sacrificial saviorhood. The lost sheep is not to be left wandering in the wilderness to find the shepherd, if he can; it is the shepherd who seeks the sheep, not the sheep the shepherd. Such is the divine compassion, as Jesus proclaims and practices it. Even the analogy of the physician becomes inadequate here, for in Jesus' practice it is not the sick who seek the physician, but the physician who seeks the sick, as though, long before its time, the positive, aggressive advance of medicine into the community were presaged.

Concerning this positive, outgoing quest of Jesus for the despised and sinful—"The Son of man came to seek and to save that which was lost"[44]—Dr. Montefiore comments as follows: "That a teacher should go about and associate with such persons, and attempt to help and 'cure' them by familiar and friendly intercourse with them, was, I imagine, an unheard of procedure. That the physician of the soul should seek out the 'sick' was a new phenomenon. According to the rabbis, the visiting of the *bodily* sick was an obligation and a duty of the first order. But the seeking out of the *morally* sick was not put upon the same footing, nor, so far as we can gather, was it practised. Here Jesus appears to be 'original.' "[45]

Certainly the outcast groups in Israel felt in him an originality that made him unique. A powerful personality, concerning whom even the crowds were saying that he was Elijah, Jeremiah or one of the prophets,[46] was doing what they had never seen a religious leader of their people do—searching the mountains for one lost sheep, sweeping the house for one lost coin.[47]

Beneath this outreaching search of Jesus for the despised and outcast was a profound religious conviction that went beyond the customary thinking of the rabbis: God himself cared for these lost souls; he valued them, had compassion on them, sought after them; "There is joy before the angels of God over one sinner who repents."[48] The picture of God on a judgment seat, meting out rewards to the righteous and penalties to the wicked, was as familiar in Jesus' teaching as in the teaching of the rabbis, but Jesus, accepting such truth as he saw in this traditional analogy, went much further. His God never stayed on the judgment seat. The father of the Prodigal was moved with compassion for the lost son;[49] the king was moved with compassion for the hopelessly insolvent debtor.[50]

Religious and moral outcasts, drawn close enough to Jesus to get his message, felt not simply his human sympathy and care, but heard a message about God that must have startled them. Heaven itself was more concerned over one of them than over ninety-nine law-abiding, pious, scrupulous sons of Israel. That was shocking to the precisionists; it must have been arresting to the despised. Of all his sheep, the shepherd cares most for "the one that has strayed," said Jesus. "And if he happens to find it, I tell you he rejoices over it more than over the ninety-nine that never went astray. So it is not the will of your Father in heaven that a single one of these little ones should be lost."[51]

A new day in mankind's spiritual history began when that

was said. To be sure, the soil and rootage of Jesus' conviction about God's care for men were in his Jewish heritage. "Dear (to God) is man," said Rabbi Akiba, "in that he was created in the (divine) image."[52] The God of Israel was not simply a Judge, nor yet Father of the nation only, but Father of individual souls, and the value of the soul was the presupposition of many a noble passage in the writings of the rabbis. Why, for example, should witnesses in a trial where capital punishment might be the penalty beware of giving false evidence? Because, said the rabbis, one person is infinitely valuable: "For this reason a single man only (Adam) was created: to teach that if one destroys a single person, the Scripture imputes it to him as if he had destroyed the whole world, and if he saves the life of a single person, as though he had saved the whole world."[53] Had Jesus himself said that, we should now be taking it as the very theme of his ministry.

Nevertheless, when sinners were concerned, as the rabbis saw it, judgment was God's predominant function. Both law and gospel were present in rabbinical Judaism and in Jesus, but the difference in emphasis is unmistakable. Law's business is to define sins, announce penalties and pronounce judgment, and Jewish legalism, facing sinners, bore down heavily upon this emphasis. Jesus did not by any means neglect it, but his stress was on gospel—the outreaching mercy of God for sinners, divine grace acting not as judge but as physician.

Along with these two factors which differentiated Jesus' attitude from the rabbis'—his positive outreaching saviorhood and his conviction concerning God's searching love for sinners—went a third. Jesus believed in the savableness of sinners with extraordinary warmth and hopefulness. The lost sheep and the lost coin could be found; the Prodigal Son could come home; Zacchaeus could become a true "son of Abraham," and the adulteress could "sin no more." This confident faith in their possibilities must have astonished derelicts and outcasts. Accustomed to condemnation they faced in Jesus not alone sympathy but hope. Potentially they were valuable, although seven devils had to be cast out of Mary Magdalene, and in a tax collector Matthew's discipleship had to be discovered and set free.

Jesus was no sentimentalist about human nature; many, he said, take the broad road leading to destruction, and few the narrow road leading unto life.[54] That certainly is not easygoing optimism. Nonetheless, he came at individual men and women, disdained of others and self-disdained, with the undiscourageable assurance that here might be one more transformed character. Even the rich can become sons of the kingdom, though it be like a camel going through a needle's eye, since "all things are possible with God."[55]

The "Parable of the Prodigal Son" should be called the "Parable of the Two Sons," for the story's major impact falls not alone on the Prodigal but on his elder brother. "Now the tax collectors and sinners were all drawing near to him. And the Pharisees and the scribes murmured, saying, 'This man receives sinners and eats with them!'"[56] Thus a double audience confronted Jesus; he had both groups in front of him—scrupulous legalists on one side and publicans, *amme ha-arez*, downright sinners on the other—and he put them both into his parable.

He pictured the lawless, careless, negligent and profligate in terms of the Prodigal. That is what *you* are like, he said, deserters from your father's house. Participants in the rich heritage of Israel, you have squandered your "share of the property." With spendthrift "loose living" you have wasted your inheritance, and have landed in the defilement of a swine pasture.

We popularly stress this parable's tenderness toward sinners, but the picture of the Prodigal, as representing the outcast group in Israel, was far from tender. The strictest Pharisee might well have felt satisfaction with it—all the scathing things he had ever said about the *amme ha-arez* incorporated in this picture of a faithless profligate, false to his heritage, and landing in such pollution that "he would gladly have fed on the pods that the swine ate; and no one gave him anything." As for that listening group of sinners, facing this rude portrait of themselves, their first impression must have been not the speaker's tenderness but his sternness. Their friend he may have been, but his friendliness was not sentimental. He, too, could see them at their worst, renegades and apostates, without hope unless they recognized their lost estate and turned homeward saying, "Father, I have sinned against heaven and before you; I am no longer worthy to be called your son."

At this point in the parable the Pharisees and scribes must have been well satisfied.

Then Jesus portrayed *them* in terms of the elder son—a good son, as Jesus pictured him, meticulously obedient, so that he could say to his father, "I never disobeyed your command." Moreover, the father appreciated him, loved him, and was grateful to him: "Son, you are always with me, and all that is mine is yours."

The idea that Jesus uniformly and indiscriminately denounced the scribes and Pharisees, with no appreciation of their virtues, leaves this parable out of account. Here their virtues are acknowledged; their fidelity, their conscientiousness, their obedience, their indefatigable labor. The Prodigal's portrait is harshly drawn, but the Pharisee's portrait depicts a

[138]

man of honor and respectability, proud of his heritage, and tireless in his labors for it.

Then Jesus put his finger on the one quality in that elder brother which spoiled everything. When the younger son was in the far country, with the father day and night compassionately awaiting his return, the elder son was all condemnation without mercy, hard as nails and pitiless as pride could make him. When the younger son came home, crushed and penitent, and the father's welcome made the whole household "merry," he angrily refused to go in, though "his father came out and entreated him." In scorn he would not even acknowledge his brotherhood with the returning sinner, but brushed him off with a phrase that recognized neither penitence, forgiveness nor regeneration as possible: "this son of yours . . . who has devoured your living with harlots."

This was the main point of conflict between Jesus and the religious leaders of his people. Their many virtues he gratefully acknowledged, but still they seemed to him to be spoiling the hope of Israel. They did not seek the salvation of sinners. They despised the despicable instead of interpreting sin in terms of need and need as a call for compassion. Outreaching, sacrificial concern for the wayward and the lost was not in them. The situation, as Jesus pictured it at the parable's end, was tragic—the Prodigal restored to the father's house, while the elder son was angry, unforgiving, alienated from the very household he was so loyal to, and deaf to the father's plea: "It was fitting to make merry and be glad, for this your brother was dead, and is alive; he was lost, and is found."

As religious and moral outcasts saw Jesus, he was their friend, but he was far from being an easy friend to deal with. He faced them with high standards of ethical living—higher than any that scribal laws could require. He spared no con-

[139]

demnation of their sin, glossed over no iniquity, but along with stern requirements and judgments went a gospel. Law's business is to define sin and announce penalties, but the whole area beyond law's function—the saving of men—Jesus made peculiarly his own. Their infinite value in God's sight, their possibilities of renovation, their essential worth calling for sacrificial saviorhood—this was his specialty, and as Dr. Montefiore, speaking from the standpoint of Judaism, says, it was a "new note in religious history."

CHAPTER VI

As Women and Children Saw Him

JESUS' home in Nazareth was full of children—"his brothers James and Joseph and Simon and Judas" and "all his sisters"[1]—and Jesus' understanding and appreciation of children are evident. He recalled hungry children, asking for bread or fish.[2] He knew children's capricious moods, happy or sulky at their games.[3] He remembered neighbors disturbing the family at midnight, when all the children were peaceably in bed.[4] When his disciples jealously asked who among them was to be greatest, he set a child before them, saying, "Whoever humbles himself like this child, he is the greatest in the kingdom of heaven."[5] He identified himself with children, declaring that to welcome "one such child" is to welcome him.[6] According to Matthew, when children in the temple shouted "Hosanna" at the sight of him and indignant priests protested, he quoted the Psalmist:

> Out of the mouths of babes and sucklings
> thou hast brought perfect praise.[7]

As for his personal affection toward children, Matthew, Mark and Luke all recall how the disciples, trying to prevent parents from bringing their babes for his blessing, were rebuked: "Let the children come unto me; do not hinder them."[8]

The profound influence of family life on Jesus' thinking is evident. His words, according to the Fourth Gospel, "I am not alone, for the Father is with me,"[9] express an experience with God amply illustrated in the synoptic narratives, as when in Gethsemane Jesus addressed God with the intimacy of a Jewish child at home, "Abba."[10] Concerning Jesus' earthly father, Joseph, we know little; presumably he died in Jesus' youth; after the family's journey to Jerusalem, when Jesus was twelve years old, we do not hear of him. He must have left behind him, however, an admirable memory, for to the growing boy, Jesus, God became "Father" with an intimacy and depth of meaning that make his use of the term unique. As for his fellow men, they were his brothers. The humblest, neediest man he could imagine was "one of the least of these my brethren."[11]

Even when the break came between Jesus and his family, he retained the ideas and terminology of the home as descriptive of his divine and human relationships. For the break did come when his mother and his brothers, thinking it madness that he should so dangerously plunge into his public ministry, came to get him and bring him home. "Your mother and your brothers are outside, asking for you," he was told. "And he answered, 'Who are my mother and my brothers?' And looking around on those who sat about him, he said, 'Here are my mother and my brothers! Whoever does the will of God is my brother, and sister, and mother.' "[12] Thus forced by his mission to give up the narrower home circle, where his ideas of God and man had been nourished, he still kept the ideas themselves, extending family relationships to a wider group, and revealing by implication his ideal for mankind—a good home become universal.

One evidence of this profound influence of family life on

Jesus is seen in his attitude toward women. "He is a great champion of womanhood," writes Dr. Montefiore.[13] In all the Gospels this is evident but especially in Luke. In six important passages Luke alone records Jesus' sympathetic care for, and friendly dealing with, women. Only he reports the raising from the dead at Nain of a young man, "the only son of his mother, and she was a widow."[14] Only he narrates the scene in the home of Simon the Pharisee, where Jesus compares a sinful woman with righteous Simon to the latter's discredit.[15] Only he records the Master's conversation with Mary and Martha about the "one thing . . . needful,"[16] or the healing on the sabbath of the crippled woman, "who had had a spirit of infirmity for eighteen years,"[17] or the words addressed by Jesus to the "women who bewailed and lamented him," as he went to Calvary: "Daughters of Jerusalem, do not weep for me, but weep for yourselves and for your children."[18] In some ways most important of all stands Luke's passage about those who accompanied Jesus on one of his preaching missions: "And the twelve were with him, and also some women who had been healed of evil spirits and infirmities: Mary, called Magdalene, from whom seven demons had gone out, and Joanna, the wife of Chuza, Herod's steward, and Susanna, and many others, who provided for them out of their means."[19]

Here is detailed information, with names given, suggesting that these women were well-known members of the first church, whom Luke might have met during his stay in Jerusalem or Caesarea. Moreover, the major intent of Luke's passage is confirmed by Mark, who records that at the crucifixion, "There were also women looking on from afar, among whom were Mary Magdalene, and Mary the mother of James the younger and of Joses, and Salome, who, when he was in Galilee, followed him, and ministered to him; and also many other women who came up with him to Jerusalem."[20] Such specific facts as these are not likely to have been invented by the later church. No motive can be readily suggested to explain interest in these names of women who followed Jesus, save as they came down from early eyewitnesses as part of the original tradition. Moreover, they are notable facts, suggesting Jesus' break with oriental ideas of woman's subordination, and revealing his companionship with women on an equal basis with men. "The relation of Jesus to women," says Dr. Montefiore, "seems unlike what would have been usual for a rabbi. He seems to have definitely broken with orientalism in this particular."[21]

Here, at any rate, is a group of Jesus' contemporaries—the women—whose response to him should be worth studying.

That they found in him sensitive sympathy and understanding is clear. In view of the Gospels' brevity and the sparse selection of material from all that Jesus must have said and done, his references to the humble goings-on in a household and to women's tasks in particular are remarkable. Even when he thought of the world's end and the Messiah's advent he thought of "two women grinding together; one will be taken and the other left."[22] Even when telling a parable about an unclean spirit returning to the empty house from which he had been exiled, Jesus added, as though with a woman's insight, "When he comes he finds it swept and put in order."[23] If God's love for a sinner is like a shepherd searching the mountains for a sheep, it is also like a woman lighting a lamp and sweeping the house until she finds a coin which she has lost, possibly from her headdress.[24] The ovens heated by field-grass where women cooked,[25] the bread-making where women hid leaven "in three measures of meal, till it was all leavened,"[26]

[144]

even the moths that must be kept from the family's garments
and the rust which ruined household utensils,[27] were his
familiar figures of speech. When called upon to defend the
radical novelty of his teaching and practice, such as his dislike
of fasting, he dealt with it in terms of refusal to put new wine
into old wineskins, or to sew "a piece of unshrunk cloth on an
old garment," for "the patch tears away from it, the new from
the old, and a worse tear is made."[28] Jesus' imagination was
filled with the homely details of housekeeping. The duties
with which he had seen his mother and sisters dealing in
Nazareth, even to buying five sparrows for two pennies,[29] he
had watched and helped at with sympathetic care.

Beyond such intimate insight into woman's work in a
humble Palestinian household, Jesus was plainly aware of the
injustice women suffered, which called for rectification and
redress. There is no mistaking the compassion and indignation
with which he spoke of widow's wrongs, and if his mother was a
widow, as seems practically certain, one reason for Jesus'
sensitiveness concerning them may be sought in that fact.
Woman's estate in the oriental world was one of subordination
even at the best. Paul, a Hellenistic Jew, leaves no doubt of
that. He clung to old discriminations—such as the veiling of
women, to which he had been accustomed in Tarsus—despite
his acceptance of the doctrine which Jesus had inspired, "there
is neither male nor female; for you are all one in Christ
Jesus."[30] Even if one concludes, after studying the evidence,
that in the first century one would prefer being a Jewess to
being a Greek woman, it still remains true that it was a man's
world then, that woman's place was subservient, often humili-
ating, cramped by a long tradition of organized inferiority,
and that the situation of widows was especially difficult.

When Jesus drew a picture of an unjust judge who "had no

reverence for God and no respect even for man," it is no accident that the victim before him, pleading for redress in the inhospitable court, was a widow. "She used to go and appeal to him," Jesus said—a picture of repeated rebuffs and denials —and, in the end, she won reluctant consideration from the judge, not because he cared to be just or thought a widow's wrongs important, but only because "this widow is bothering me, I will see justice done to her—not to have her for ever coming and pestering me."[31] One wonders whether behind that parable was an occurrence of like sort in Jesus' experience in Nazareth.

Watching "the rich putting their gifts into the treasury," "he saw a poor widow put in two copper coins," and his exclamation that she had "put in more than all of them," suggests memories of his mother.[32] When he returned to Nazareth to preach, he recalled how Elijah was sent "to Zarephath, in the land of Sidon, to a woman who was a widow."[33] Even when widows had property he indignantly saw them being fleeced by unscrupulous scribes and priests, who played upon their pious generosity; they "devour widows' houses and for a pretense make long prayers."[34]

To be sure, the wrongs suffered by women in general and by widows in particular were not the sympathetic concern of Jesus only. If he valued a poor widow's gift, so did the scribe according to whom a certain priest, scornful of a woman's small offering of flour, was rebuked in a dream: "Despise her not; it is as though she offered her life."[35] Jewish civil law tried by numerous regulations to protect widows from harsh wrongs;[36] and if Jesus condemned religious leaders, using their influence to "prey upon the property of widows,"[37] so did the best of the scribes: "He who robs widows and orphans is as though he robbed God himself."[38]

[146]

These very laws and exhortations, however, emphasize the presence of the wrongs against which Jesus protested. To be sure, romantic love was prized, as in the Song of Songs; some women, from Esther to Judith, rose to positions of powerful leadership; and the praises of a good wife were sung in one of the most eloquent and lovely passages in the Hebrew scriptures.[39] Nevertheless, there was another side to the matter. Woman in that ancient world was valued altogether with reference to man; he was first and central; woman's value was rated by her meaning and service to him. She was not a person in her own right, as he was. She was at his disposal, to be regulated, suppressed, coddled or discarded as might most please him. In the current books of Jesus' time there is warm appreciation of womanhood. If a wife be beautiful and of "a gentle tongue," then

> He that acquireth a wife hath the highest possession,
> A helpmeet to him and a pillar of support.[40]

But there are other passages also whose presence in the sacred books reveals an attitude ingrained in that whole ancient world.

> A daughter is to a father a deceptive treasure,
> And the care of her putteth away sleep;
> In her youth lest she commit adultery,
> And when she is married lest she be hated, . . .
> Keep a strict watch over a headstrong daughter
> Lest she make thee a laughing-stock.
> In the place where she abideth let there be no lattice,
> And in the house where she sleepeth no entry round about.
> Let her not display her beauty before any man,
> And in the house of women let her not gossip;

For from the garment cometh forth the moth,
And from a woman a woman's wickedness.
Better the wickedness of a man than the goodness of a woman.[41]

Against such an attitude Jesus' ministry was a sustained protest. He treated women as he treated men—as persons sacred in their own right, as souls loved of God and full of undisclosed possibilities. He never condescended to women, but habitually showed them deference, and to the surprise of the attendant audience more than once came to their spirited defense.

His rebuke of those who look "at a woman lustfully"[42] is a case in point. We commonly rob the passage of its full significance, as though it were concerned only with the licentious passions of men. But to look upon a woman lustfully is to regard her as a chattel, a thing to serve man's sensual desire, not a person but a physical instrument of transient pleasure. Inwardly it is the very opposite of love, and socially it is the root of woman's many and long-continued indignities. Against this whole degrading view of womanhood Jesus protested. He stands out from the low standards of his time and of all times in his estimate of woman as a personality, to be so regarded and treated, to be loved for her whole self, and not looked on merely as a means of satisfying man's sexual desire.

Even today in the prayer book of the orthodox Jewish synagogue we read: "Blessed art thou, O Lord our God! King of the universe, who hast not made me a woman." However one may explain the persistence of this prayer, it illustrates the ancient tradition out of which we all came. The women who followed Jesus, however, saw in him another attitude. Even today the modern reader of the Gospels commonly fails to notice it. The difference between Mary and Martha,[43] for example, we modernize; it lies, we say, in the contrast between the busy service of the practically-minded and the quiet intake

[148]

of the receptive, listening soul. Martha was "distracted with much service" in preparing a meal for Jesus; Mary was absorbed in the more important matter of gaining insight into Jesus' message. This interpretation is true enough, but when Jesus said of Mary, she "has chosen the good portion which shall not be taken away from her," he meant more than that. Jesus was treating Mary as a full-orbed personality. To her, as a child of God, he was opening up the treasures of his spirit. In the presence of his gospel there was no male or female, but all were one, and probably Mary had never in her life before been so dealt with, so treated with intellectual and spiritual respect by any religious teacher. Jesus wanted Martha too to respond to his approach, and be less contented than she was with the traditional pattern of woman's status. Said one rabbi, "Better that the words of the law should be burned than delivered to women."[44] Against the whole philosophy of life involved in such a saying Jesus was in rebellion and his attitude toward womanhood which was revealed in his treatment of Mary was habitually characteristic of him.

Indeed, the record represents him as coming to woman's defense in situations where his defense needs to be defended. Mark, Matthew, and John[45] all relate the story of the grateful woman who anointed him with costly spikenard. "This angered some of those present," we read. "What was the use of wasting perfume like this? This perfume might have been sold for over 300 shillings, and the poor might have got that. So they upbraided her." Surely, their upbraiding had justification—a shilling was a day's wages then—and Jesus was the last of men either to forget the poor or to welcome extravagant adulation of himself with costly perfume. But there stood the woman who with good intent, out of a grateful heart, had done this generous, impulsive deed. He would not leave her shamefaced, humiliated, her costly reverence misunderstood, her devout motive forgotten, her sacrificial gift condemned. "Let her alone," he said. "Why are you annoying her? She has done a beautiful thing to me. The poor you always have beside you, and you can be kind to them whenever you want; but you will not always have me."[46] So he stood up for her, and if he really said the rest of what is reported—"wherever the gospel is preached all over the world, men will speak of what she has done in memory of her"—that has been fulfilled. Such championship of womanhood, distinctive of Jesus, was quite uncharacteristic of the world he lived in.

How Jesus came to the defense even of a woman taken in adultery we have seen.[47] The men who would have stoned her were grounded in an old tradition: woman was man's temptress, the creature who first in Eden had led man to sin, and their righteous wrath, backed by the Mosaic law, was ready to do away with any adulteress—as though in adultery man could ever be the mere victim, as though he is not always the equal participant, if not the probable aggressor. So Jesus turned on the men: "Let him who is without sin among you be the first to throw a stone at her." He was announcing there the single standard for men and women in the morality of sex. Once more he was denying man's right to lord it over woman with an assumed superiority not grounded in facts. As for the sinful woman, Jesus' final words to her opened the door to a transformed life: "Neither do I condemn you; go and do not sin again."

As the early records of the church, both in the New Testament and afterwards, bear witness, women were among its most ardent and effective members, and this response of womanhood to Christ and his message goes back to his own ministry. Simon, the Pharisee, seeing Jesus anointed by a sinful woman was sure he could not be a prophet; else he would have known the uncleanness of the one who touched him.[48] But here again Jesus became the woman's defender. Almost certainly she had met Jesus before, else why should she have been so grateful to him? Through him she had found forgiveness, cleansing, reinstatement as a child of God, power to amend her life and, forgiven much, she loved much. In Simon's house that day the parable of the prodigal daughter was enacted, with Simon in the part of the elder brother. Unconscious of sin, feeling little or no need of pardon, he was cold, complacent, all condescension and contempt, while the prodigal daughter, come to herself again, was penitent, thankful, adoring. To her, not to Simon, Jesus' benediction was given: "Your faith has saved you; go in peace."

While the story of Jesus' meeting with the woman of Samaria is told in John's Gospel only,[49] one thing is certain: whoever first told that story had been at the well of Sychar. Still "the well is deep," one of the deepest in Palestine. Still "this mountain," Gerizim, close at hand, rises from the plateau. Still, one has a far view across the plain and can "see how the fields are already white for harvest." In Jesus' day, however, the woman of Samaria, who had had five husbands and now was living with a man not her husband, would never have been addressed by a Jewish rabbi. When Jesus' disciples returned, we read, "They marveled that he was talking with a woman." But Jesus had no regard for such barriers, and once more he immortalized a woman who, but for him, would have lived and died in unrespected obscurity.

Such was the teacher to whom the women who followed Jesus responded. He was to them more than a teacher—a champion of womanhood in a time when a champion was needed.

If the Samaritans interpreted the Mosaic law, which was
their Scripture too, as the Jews did, that woman, who had had
five husbands,[50] had not divorced them—they had divorced
her. Divorce among the Jews, in Jesus' day, was altogether in
the power of the husband. To be sure, paganized Jewesses,
Salome and Herodias, both of the Herodian house, divorced
their husbands, but among law-abiding Jews such a scandal
would have been impossible. In Jesus' day the legal continuance of any Jewish marriage depended solely on the husband's
caprice. According to the law he could discard his wife at will
—"write her a bill of divorcement" and "send her out of his
house," if he "found some unseemly thing in her."[51] The
schools of Shammai and Hillel did indeed differ as to what the
"unseemly thing" might be. Shammai had interpreted it to
mean unchastity, but Hillel had said it might be anything
which displeased the husband, even spoiling his food, and Rabbi
Akiba added that a husband might divorce his wife for the sole
reason that he found another woman more comely than she.[52]

The consequent hardship on women, even under modern
conditions, would have been bad enough, but in Jesus' day it
was worse. Women then were regarded in effect, as by ancient
tradition they had been regarded in fact, as the possession of
men. A woman from her birth belonged to some man, first as
daughter, then as wife. She had her status in society because
she did belong to some man, and to be cast off by him, divorced, left ownerless and unattached was lamentable. Cruel
as the Mosaic law may seem, therefore, making the husband
judge, jury and executioner in dismissing his wife, a valuable
social advance over primitive custom was involved in it: it
forced the man to give her a "bill of divorcement," establishing
for her a kind of legal status and freeing her to marry another.

[152]

Nevertheless, the injustice to women involved in the divorce system of Jesus' day was monstrous, and it is fair to let a Jewish scholar state the case: "The religious position of women and the law of divorce form the least attractive feature of the rabbinical system. . . . The unerring ethical instinct of Jesus led him to put his finger upon the weak spots and sore places of the established religion. Of all such weak spots and sore places this was the weakest and sorest."[53]

Apparently the Pharisees heard that Jesus had protested against this wrong to women, and "in order to test him," Mark tells us, they asked him, " 'Is it lawful for a man to divorce his wife?' He answered them, 'What did Moses command you?' They said, 'Moses permitted a man to write a certificate of divorce, and to put her away.' But Jesus said to them, 'For your hardness of heart he wrote you this commandment. But from the beginning of creation, 'God made them male and female.' 'For this reason a man shall leave his father and mother and be joined to his wife, and the two shall become one.' So they are no longer two but one. What therefore God has joined together, let not man put asunder."[54]

The difficulties involved in this total condemnation of divorce were evident from the first. Paul knew what Jesus had said and reported it in unmitigated form to the Corinthian church: "To the married I give charge, not I but the Lord, that the wife should not separate from her husband (but if she does, let her remain single or else be reconciled to her husband)—and that the husband should not divorce his wife."[55] X By the time Matthew's Gospel was written, however, compromise had begun, and Jesus is quoted as making one exception, "whoever divorces his wife, except for unchastity, and marries another, commits adultery."[56] Indeed, the question which the Pharisees asked Jesus is so phrased by Matthew—

"Is it lawful to divorce one's wife for any cause?"—that some have thought it a demand for a decision by Jesus between the schools of Shammai and Hillel. Was Shammai right that unchastity alone was ground for divorce or was Hillel right that there were many other grounds? If such was the question, Jesus sided with Shammai. That was not Jesus' way, however —to get at important matters by defining legalistic applications and by backing one rabbinical school against another. Far more congenial with Jesus' method is it to take Paul and Mark, the earliest witnesses, as reporting what he really said, announcing without qualification that the monogamous family is right and that broken families, divorces and tandem remarriages are wrong. This he said sweepingly, without compromise or exception, basing his judgment concerning an ideal home on God's original intent in marriage.

The first disciples, according to Matthew, felt at once the impracticality of any such sweeping pronouncement—even if an exception was made in the case of unchastity—and the impossibility of enforcing it. "The disciples said to him, 'If such is the case of a man with his wife, it is not expedient to marry.' But he said to them, 'Not all men can receive this precept, but only those to whom it is given. . . . He who is able to receive this, let him receive it.'"[57] This lifts Jesus' words on divorce out of the legalistic category altogether and puts them where they belong—not a regulation to be enforced by public law courts, but the ideal of what marriage ought to be, and would be if men and women were truly his disciples. Only transformed persons can or will exercise the sexual self-control that makes true marriage possible. Only they will wish to have or can have the one kind of home which fulfills the divine intention: a household where two people love each other so much that they do not care to love anyone else in the same way, and who throw around each other and their growing children the security and affection of an indissoluble family.

Had Jesus foreseen the long evolutionary extension of society in a changing world, he would doubtless have foreseen, what indeed he never denied, the need of law codes and law courts to enforce as high a standard as at any given time was practically possible. But he still would have kept his major message unimpaired. He stood for the highest ideal of the family ever presented to mankind. He sought to re-create men and women, so right within that they were capable of having such homes. He was calling for the very best which, by God's grace, could be attained in a family.

Jesus' approach to the problem of marriage and divorce was not, however, simply a matter of his characteristic idealism. He was deeply concerned over the wrong done to woman by the existing system. Mark, writing his Gospel in Rome, where women could initiate divorce, added to Jesus' words the phrase, "if she divorces her husband,"[58] but that phrase must be Mark's, not Jesus', for among the Jews no such possibility existed. That many mitigations of the estate of divorced women had been introduced into the rabbinical regulations, some making arrangements for alimony, is true. It took ingenuity to do it, but Rabbi Jacob bar Aha deduced from a verse in Isaiah the law, "Do not withdraw help from thy divorced wife."[59] Nor, of course, was Jesus the first to deplore broken families. Had not Malachi written: "Therefore take heed to your spirit, and let none deal treacherously against the wife of his youth. For I hate putting away, saith Jehovah, the God of Israel"?[60] Nevertheless, the divorce system in the Judaism of Jesus' day was a "sore spot." Rights are not readily surrendered and men were clinging tenaciously to their traditional power over their women.

At this point Jesus became outspokenly and controversially woman's champion. The women who followed him must have recognized the new note he was striking, and they responded to his friendship with loyal gratitude.

Jesus' conviction concerning the value of marriage and the home lights up the meaning of other sayings of his about the necessity of loving the kingdom of God more than the family. "If any one comes to me and does not hate his own father and mother and wife and children and brothers and sisters, yes, and even his own life, he cannot be my disciple"[61]—this saying, reported by Luke, has shocked many by its seeming harshness. Far from being harsh, however, it comes near to being the highest tribute Jesus paid the home. He was speaking of the supreme self-sacrifice. Only one cause could rightly demand it, the kingdom of God, but that could demand the most costly self-surrender. As to the nature of this supreme sacrifice Jesus had no doubt—to break with one's family and give up one's life. These two he put together as the most costly price which devotion to the kingdom might require. In Hebrew the word "hate" was used to mean "love less,"[62] a fact which Matthew makes evident in his rendition of Jesus' saying: "He who loves father or mother more than me is not worthy of me; he who loves son or daughter more than me is not worthy of me."[63] Both come to the same issue, however: the severest self-sacrifice that can be demanded of man is to turn his back on his home folk. This is not depreciation of the family's value but its exaltation.

That this way of stating the most difficult kind of self-sacrifice came from Jesus' experience with his own family seems clear. Near the beginning of his ministry, when, having appointed the twelve disciples, he had launched his public

[156]

mission on the shores of the Sea of Galilee, and was drawing around him such crowds "that they could not even eat," we read in Mark's Gospel that "when his friends heard it, they went out to seize him, for they said, 'He is beside himself.' "[64] Who were these "friends" who thought Jesus was deranged? The Greek phrase means "those who belonged to him," and Dr. Moffatt translates it "his family." The context strongly supports this rendering, for Mark reports that it was "his mother and his brothers" who came to get him, and, standing outside, unable to reach him because of the crowd, tried to call him out to them. That call from his home folk presented Jesus with one of the most crucial tests of his vocation. He refused to go out to them, and turning to his listeners said: "Here are my mother and my brothers! Whoever does the will of God is my brother, and sister, and mother."[65]

Certainly this break between Jesus and his family was part of the tradition of the church, for John's Gospel says, "even his brothers did not believe in him,"[66] and that it was a constant factor in Jesus' own thinking seems evident. When he talked with Peter about those who specially deserved and would receive a rich reward, he singled out "one who has left house or brothers or sisters or mother or father or children or lands, for my sake and for the gospel."[67] When he saw the disruptive effect of his teaching, dividing families and alienating his followers from their own households, he exclaimed: "Do you think that I have come to give peace on earth? No, I tell you, but rather division; for henceforth in one house there will be five divided, three against two and two against three; they will be divided, father against son and son against father, mother against daughter and daughter against her mother, mother-in-law against her daughter-in-law and daughter-in-law against her mother-in-law."[68] Matthew adds that Jesus quoted a saying of Micah, uttered in one of the prophet's downcast hours, "a man's foes will be those of his own household."[69] This was Jesus' heaviest cross before he went to Calvary.

What this alienation from his family meant to Jesus such passages poignantly suggest, but what it meant to his mother, how she felt about him during his perilous ministry with its tragic ending, one can only surmise. In the synoptic Gospels she never appears again. In John's Gospel she stands so close to the cross that Jesus can speak to her, commending her to the care of "the disciple whom he loved."[70] The difficulty in accepting this late account as historical lies in the fact that Mark and Matthew give the names of women—Matthew says "many women"—who stood "beholding from afar" the crucifixion of their Lord, and the name of Jesus' mother is not among them, as it surely would have been had the earlier writers ever heard of her presence there.[71] Of only one thing can we be certain: Jesus' mission involved a tragedy in the personal relationships of the home in Nazareth.

The effect of this fact on the credibility of the story of Jesus' virgin birth is obvious. There is no evidence in the Gospels, apart from the birth stories themselves, that any member of Jesus' family or any of his first disciples ever thought of him as virgin born. Mark, who gathered from Peter the facts of Jesus' life, does not mention it. In Matthew and Luke, where the birth stories appear, are two genealogies, so inconsistent that they cannot possibly be reconciled, both of which in tracing Jesus' lineage come down to Joseph, not to Mary. These genealogies are inconceivable except on the supposition that when they were prepared Joseph was thought to be Jesus' father. Indeed, in the Monastery of St. Catherine on the traditional Mount Sinai is an ancient Syriac translation of Matthew's

Gospel, rendering, so scholars feel assured, an older manuscript of Matthew than any which we now possess, and ending the genealogy with its only logical conclusion: "Joseph begat Jesus." As for Luke, he quotes the genealogy he has before him, but destroys its meaning as a record of Jesus' lineage by his parenthesis: "Jesus . . . being the son (as was supposed) of Joseph."[72]

The category of virgin birth was alien to Jewish thinking. The passage in Isaiah,[73] in which the church, at the time Matthew and Luke were written, found prophecy of Mary's virginity—"Behold, a virgin shall conceive, and bear a son"— was taken not from the original Hebrew but from the mistaken rendering in the Septuagint, the Greek translation of the Old Testament, which even Paul and much more the later church commonly used. The original Hebrew says not "virgin," but "young woman." It was the Greek world in which virgin births were a common way of explaining unusual personalities. So Plato was said to be virgin born, and Alexander the Great, and Aesculapius, and Pythagoras and Simon Magus and Apollonius of Tyana, and many more. In the second century, when Justin Martyr stated the case, he even put Jesus' birth, for argument's sake, in the same category with such legends: "When we declare that the Word, who is the first-born of God, came into being without sexual intercourse . . . we do not report anything different from your view about those called sons of Zeus."[74]

If, then, it was in the later Hellenistic area of the church that the story of the virgin birth arose, this would explain why the early records of Jesus' first contemporaries reveal no slightest sign that they ever thought of him as physically begotten by the special act of God. Had they so thought of him, those closest to him, his "friends," his "family," would never have said that he was "beside himself" in undertaking his mission. As his first, immediate contemporaries saw him, therefore, he was not yet being explained by the category of virgin birth, and one of the strongest indications of this is the alienation between himself and his mother. One hopes that the alienation was temporary. One welcomes the account in Acts that, immediately after the ascension, the first disciples gathered in "the upper room . . . together with the women and Mary the mother of Jesus, and with his brothers."[75] One is glad of Paul's direct testimony that in Jerusalem he conferred with "James the Lord's brother," who along with Peter was in the leadership of the apostles.[76] Whatever happened in the thinking of the family in Nazareth during his earthly ministry, Jesus' mother and at least one of his brothers were at the heart of the first church.

The prominence of women among Jesus' first devoted and loyal contemporaries is notable. They were drawn to him alike by their needs and by his masterful personality and message. They came for healing, for forgiveness, for power to lead a new life, and for his benediction on their children. The timid woman who touched the hem of his garment, and when found out "came in fear and trembling" to thank him;[77] the aggressive Canaanite woman, who would not be put off by the fact that she was not of Jewish race and faith;[78] the women who provided for him out of their means;[79] and the mothers whose children he took "in his arms and blessed, . . . laying his hands upon them,"[80] are typical. There is no explaining how that first precarious movement of thought and life which Jesus started, with so much against it and, humanly speaking, so little for it, moved out into its world-transforming influence, without taking into account the response of womanhood to

[160]

Jesus. When they were sunk in sin, he forgave them; when they were humiliated, he stood up for them; when they suffered social wrongs, he defended them; when they had abilities to offer, he used them; and when they became sentimental and effusive in their devotion to him, he stopped them: "A woman in the crowd raised her voice and said to him, 'Blessed is the womb that bore you, and the breasts that you sucked!' But he said, 'Blessed rather are those who hear the word of God and keep it!' "[81]

Writes Dorothy Sayers, from the vantage-point of 1947: "Perhaps it is no wonder that the women were first at the Cradle and the last at the Cross. They had never known a man like this Man—there never has been such another."[82]

CHAPTER VII

As His First Disciples Saw Him

THE inner group of Jesus' followers numbered twelve, and we commonly assume that we know who they were. The Gospels, however, are not unanimous about the names of the disciples. Matthew, in our first Gospel, is apparently identical with "Levi the son of Alphaeus" in Mark's Gospel.[1] Thaddaeus appears in Matthew's list and Mark's, but in Luke's list, both in the Gospel and in Acts, his place is taken by "Judas the son of James."[2] The reason for this discrepancy is unknown; it may be that the personnel of the twelve was inconstant, that subtractions and additions occurred during Jesus' ministry, as after his death Matthias took the place of Judas Iscariot.

That there was an inner circle of specially chosen and commissioned disciples is clear, however, and from them must have come the earliest recollections of Jesus. The genuineness of their reminiscences is made evident, in part, by their reports about their own behavior. The later church idealized the "twelve apostles." When in the Book of Revelation the celestial city is pictured coming down out of heaven, it had twelve foundations, "and on them the twelve names of the twelve apostles of the Lamb."[3] In the Gospels, however, far from being idealized, the twelve are portrayed as acting in ways the

[162]

later church would never have made up and might well have wished to forget.

Once, when Jesus and the twelve were inhospitably received by a Samaritan village, James and John vindictively wanted to call down fire from heaven to consume the villagers, but Jesus "rebuked them," and, as some ancient manuscripts add, "he said, You do not know what manner of spirit you are of."[4] Once, when Jesus brushed aside the scribal regulations concerning diet, the disciples were as bewildered as the rest, so that Jesus said to Peter, "Are you also still without understanding?"[5] Once, James and John, with scandalous egotism, tried to secure from Jesus a promise that they should have first places in the day of his glory, so that "when the ten heard it, they began to be indignant."[6] Once, all the twelve fell to disputing about precedence, and Jesus, setting a little child in the midst of them, read them a lesson in humility.[7] According to Luke, even as they sat together at the last supper, "A dispute also arose among them, which of them was to be regarded as the greatest."[8] As for the suffering, sacrificial Christ, they so failed to understand that idea and Peter so vehemently protested against it that Jesus said to him, "Get behind me, Satan! You are a hindrance to me; for you are not on the side of God, but of men."[9] And when the final crisis came Judas' betrayal, Peter's denial, and the frightened flight of the whole band, are plainly set down without extenuation or excuse.

The church, a generation after Jesus had gone, when the glorious twelve were idealized, would never have invented such stories; they bear the mark of genuine recollection from the first disciples. Difficult though they found it to understand X and follow him, however, they were still closest to him, knew him best, entered most intimately into his thinking and experience, and what they saw in him is of paramount importance.

That they warmly felt the impact of his friendship is clear. Only in John's Gospel are the words put on Jesus' lips, "No longer do I call you servants . . . I have called you friends;"[10] but, as is often the case with the Fourth Gospel, those words make explicit what is implicit in the earlier records.

The Gospels help us little in understanding the personal experiences of the first disciples as, one by one, they surrendered to the fascination of their Master. Mark's story condenses the event until it seems incredibly abrupt. Jesus "saw Simon and Andrew the brother of Simon casting a net in the sea; for they were fishermen. And Jesus said to them, 'Follow me and I will make you become fishers of men.' And immediately they left their nets and followed him;"[11] "He saw Levi the son of Alphaeus sitting at the tax office, and he said to him, 'Follow me.' And he rose and followed him."[12] Obviously that cannot be the whole story. The Fourth Gospel explicitly says that Andrew and Simon Peter had met Jesus first in the circle around John the Baptist.[13] They and the others had certainly met him somewhere; there must have been a history behind their swift acceptance of his call.

Mark's first chapter[14] apparently records the events of a notable day in Jesus' early ministry. One is tempted to imagine Simon Peter, years afterward in Rome, telling Mark about it. Jesus calls Simon and Andrew and the sons of Zebedee from their nets and they follow him; he speaks in the synagogue the following morning with such effect that all are "astonished" at his "authority"; he heals a possessed man so that the "amazed" people question among themselves, "What is this? A new teaching! With authority he commands even the unclean spirits, and they obey him"; he enters Simon Peter's home and cures Peter's wife's mother of a fever; in the evening "the whole city" gathers about the doors and he heals many of their sick; early the next morning he goes out to a "lonely place," followed by "Simon and those who were with him," and thence—escaping the crowds, concerning which they tell him, "Every one is searching for you"—they start on a preaching tour through Galilee. This passage has been called "the memory of the greatest day in Peter's life. It was the day when his discipleship had begun."[15]

Even if imagination goes beyond the facts in such an interpretation, one suspects that the general impression is true. Those first disciples were swept off their feet, fascinated by a personality whom they could not resist, convinced that something new, unique, prophetic, was happening in Israel, carried out of themselves by a mission, only dimly understood, but incarnate in one whose call was a command.

So began a friendship with vast historic consequences. A few, at least, of its informal intimacies are remembered in the Gospels, despite the fact that when the Gospels were written informal intimacies with the Lord were not easily conceivable. The disciples critically questioned the method of Jesus' teaching in parables;[16] anxiously asked him if he understood how offensive his sayings were to the Pharisees;[17] insisted on being told what some of his difficult teachings meant—"Explain this parable to us at anyrate";[18] and once, at least, "Peter took him, and began to rebuke him."[19] They were a company of friends. He had many followers, but "He appointed twelve to be with him."[20] They were his cabinet, his counselors, his companions. When life became too hurried and hectic, he took

[165]

them away "to a lonely place," where they could "rest a while."[21] He carried their personal needs upon his heart, and what he said to Peter was doubtless typical, "I have prayed for you."[22] Even when Judas in the Garden gave him the traitor's kiss, Jesus said, "Friend, why are you here?"[23]

In understanding the motives which led the twelve to leave all and follow him, it is important to stress the fact that they joined his company during the early days of Jesus' popularity. Thinking of Jesus as despised and rejected, some picture the disciples as making a hazardous, sacrificial decision in espousing his cause. Far from being despised and rejected, however, Jesus was riding a rising tide of public favor when he called them. He was having no difficulty in securing followers. One man "begged him that he might be with him. But he refused, and said to him, 'Go home to your friends.' "[24] To another who insisted, "I will follow you wherever you go," Jesus gave a forbidding answer, describing his homeless, vagrant ministry.[25] Another who said, "I will follow you, Lord; but let me first say farewell to those at my home," found his offer declined and was frankly told that he was not "fit."[26] Many were eager to join Jesus' inner circle. The mass movement in his favor, his forceful personality, his authoritative message, his stirring deeds, constrained them. But Jesus was searching for his picked men, looking for the best reliability he could find, the hardiest characters, the most understanding minds. And then he chose the twelve. All night long, among the hills, "he continued in prayer to God," and then in the morning "he called his disciples, and chose from them twelve."[27] It was the greatest honor that had ever come to them.

To be sure, their motives were mixed. Self-seeking was there, and the crude emotions that stirred the crowd's wonderment and awe—but something deeper too. He had captured them.

[166]

They loved him. He had now honored them with his intimate confidence and trust. They were his men.

This deep personal attachment is the one factor which persisted throughout the many changes of thought and circumstance which followed, surviving crisis and hairbreadth escapes, and at last building the church. When the twelve first became Jesus' inner circle of friends they did not understand him. They were drawn to him in part because they could *not* understand him; his mystery, his strange, inscrutable authority and power, whose sources were beyond their comprehension, baffled and fascinated them. They had at first no profound discernment of his message and mission, no clear insight into who he was. A mixed lot—a tax collecter, fishermen, characters as diverse as Peter and Judas—they certainly had no common creed and probably never dreamed that they would one day believe Jesus to be the Messiah. Their faith was personal— they were drawn to *him*. The one constant factor which held them together even through the tragedy of Calvary was this personal devotion. *What* they believed they often did not know, but as the Second Letter to Timothy put it long afterward, they did know *whom* they believed.[28] The Christian movement began in friendship.

That in the end Jesus nourished this friendship with almost desperate eagerness seems evident. Apparently he planned his first appeal to Israel as a whole and was encouraged by the popular response to hope for a widespread reformation under his leadership. Then opposition grew; his powerful foes made public failure certain and his own death probable; the crowd's interest and loyalty were genuine but shallow, based on misunderstanding of his real meaning, and conditioned on terms which he could not accept. Only his disciples were left to rely upon. He must train them—upon that everything depended. Over the slender bridge of their understanding and fidelity his message must move, if it was to survive at all.

One suspects that his parable of the sower[29] was in part autobiographical. Three-fourths of the seed he sowed was wasted. It fell on trodden paths and was devoured by birds; it fell on thin soil and, springing quickly up, soon withered; it fell among thorns and was choked. Such was his disillusionment concerning his appeal to Israel as a whole. Only a little of the seed he sowed had any chance. That bit of good ground —his twelve disciples and the few more who were like them— was his only hope. If they failed to be fruitful soil, bringing forth a hundredfold, or even sixty or thirtyfold, all was lost.

As Jesus' ministry went on, three groups of auditors appeared whom he consciously distinguished from one another and addressed in specific ways. Mark's seventh chapter makes this clear. Answering a question of the Pharisees and scribes— "Why do your disciples not live according to the tradition of the elders, but eat with hands defiled?"—Jesus spoke first to his opponents. His words were caustic, biting, a scathing polemic against their casuistry. Then, turning from his opponents, Jesus called "the people" to him, "the crowd," "the multitude," and addressed them: "Hear me, all of you, and understand." When, however, his opponents and the crowd had gone and he was alone within doors with his disciples, he centered his attention upon them. "Do you not see?" he said, and with elaborate care, doubtless inadequately represented in our condensed accounts, proceeded with what became the main preoccupation of his ministry, the training of the twelve. As Mark tells us, "Privately to his own disciples he explained everything."[30]

His foes, the crowd, the inner group of his disciples—these

three he faced: the first increasingly with condemnation; the second with concern, sympathy, and deep desire to win their understanding; the third with poignant affection, eager hope, solicitously praying for them, as he did for Peter, that their faith might not fail.

They were a fallible group and he knew it, but he called them "the light of the world" and "the salt of the earth."[31] The modern reader of the Gospels often wonders at Jesus' faith in God the Father, despite his life's tragedy, but that is easier to understand than his faith in those disciples. He demanded of them a quality of life far above the average. The modern reader commonly fails to distinguish in the Gospels the passages Jesus addressed specifically to the disciples—not to the crowd or to his foes—and, in reading them, fails to emphasize the pronouns that must have had most emphatic meaning when the disciples first listened to him. Jesus, speaking privately to the twelve, pictured the rulers of the Gentiles lording it over them and said: "But it shall not be so among *you*; but whoever would be great among *you* must be your servant."[32] He pictured the self-seeking arrogance of the contemporary clergy and said to his disciples: "But *you* are not to be called rabbi, for *you* have one teacher, and *you* are all brethren."[33]

He insistently required of his disciples this excess and surplus of goodness. Many a time they must have heard that recurrent theme—not so among *you*. In his solicitude for them, thus challenged to superior and costly living, to what motives did he not appeal? He pictured their rewards, if not in this world, then in the next.[34] Conversing alone with them, he put his confidence in victory into flaming figures: "I saw Satan fall like lightning from heaven."[35] Privately, when they were discouraged by their smallness, he comforted them: "Fear not, little flock, for

[169]

it is your Father's good pleasure to give you the kingdom."[36] Scholars are correct in noting that the parables of the mustard seed becoming a tree[37] and of yeast leavening the whole lump[38] do not teach gradual growth from small beginnings to great conclusions. That concept of progress slowly achieved was not then in the minds of men. Those parables are studies in contrast—apparently insignificant littleness versus great consummations—and they were relevant to the disciples' need. Were they to carry on, they had to believe that what is vital, though small, can have large consequence.

So Jesus poured his heart out on those disciples. Their faith in him was engendered by his faith in them; their gratitude to him was matched by his thankfulness for them. Sitting at table in the upper room, "He said to them, 'I have earnestly desired to eat this passover with you before I suffer,' "[39] and as the meal ended, and farewell drew near, his grateful affection overflowed: "You are those who have continued with me in my trials."[40] John's Gospel expands this farewell scene and amplifies the words of Jesus to his friends but, in view of what the earlier Gospels tell us, there is verisimilitude in their tone and spirit: "I have manifested thy name to the men whom thou gavest me out of the world; thine they were, and thou gavest them to me. . . . I am praying for them; I am not praying for the world but for those whom thou hast given me. . . . Holy Father, keep them in thy name."[41]

In training the twelve Jesus tried especially to do two things: to prepare them for opposition, rejection, sacrifice, and to share with them adequate resources of inner power to see them through. Jesus' reported predictions concerning the disciples' future exhibit a striking contrast, not to say contradiction. On

[170]

one side, according to the record, he foresaw the speedy coming of the messianic age; within their own day,[42] suddenly like
the flood in Noah's time or like a thief in the night[43] would be
the glorious arrival of the Son of Man. On the other side, the
disciples would face, he said, ostracism, persecution, death;
they would be delivered up to councils, beaten in synagogues,
brought to trial, delivered to death by their own families and
"hated by all."[44]

However we may arrange the time schedule which was in
Jesus' mind concerning these contrasting events—about which
he is reported to have said that only God knew the "day and
hour"[45]—he certainly foresaw the sacrificial testing of his
followers. His call to them was stern, ominous, forbidding,
"blood, sweat and tears." If they were to follow him, they had
to deny themselves and take up their cross;[46] they must be
ready to disown their own families, if need be, when loyalties
clashed;[47] they must even be prepared to count themselves
"blessed" when men reviled them, persecuted them, and
uttered all kinds of evil against them.[48]

At this point we face one of the typical problems raised by
modern scholarship. Imagine Mark in Rome, around A.D. 70,
formulating his Gospel. He is certainly interested in the facts of
Jesus' historic ministry, but he is also anxiously concerned
about the contemporary church. Persecution has fallen on it.
Nero's deadly work is still fresh in memory; Paul and probably
Peter have died as martyrs; Christians are ostracized, hated,
persecuted, vile falsehoods about them popularly believed, and
mob violence a constant threat. How can Mark write his
Gospel without wishing to interject into it anything and everything that will encourage the struggling Christian community?
So, say the critics, not the historic Jesus but the harassed

church a long generation after him, is the real source of the stress which the Gospels lay on predicted suffering and persecution.

The measure of truth in this ought freely to be granted. That the circumstances of the churches when the Gospels were written affected the selection of material from the oral and written tradition which preceded them seems obvious. Moreover one can, at times, see persuasive evidence of the deliberate adaptation of such material to the pressing problems of the churches. Luke, for example, records a brief saying of Jesus: "If your brother sins, rebuke him, and if he repents, forgive him."[49] In Matthew, however, this saying is expanded into a regulation for the government of conduct in a church: "If your brother sins against you, go and tell him his fault, between you and him alone. If he listens to you, you have gained your brother. But if he does not listen, take one or two others along with you, that every word may be confirmed by the evidence of two or three witnesses. If he refuses to listen to them, tell it to the church; and if he refuses to listen even to the church, let him be to you as a Gentile and a tax collector."[50] Jesus himself could not have said that—before there was a church. That is clearly an expansion of something Jesus said to meet a need which the author of the Gospel saw in some early Christian community—early, as the reference to Gentiles and tax collectors shows.

No historian succeeds in being completely objective, even when he tries. As for the writers of the Gospels, they were not trying. They wrote, not as though a Ph.D. were the end in view, but to strengthen the churches which they loved. The persecuted church, therefore, must have directed their attention to anything Jesus ever said about persecution and must have led to the natural expansion and application of it to contemporary needs.

It is no accident, therefore, that not only is the Passion story the most emphasized feature of the Gospels, but that along with it the inevitable sufferings of the early church are stressed: "The cup that I drink you will drink; and with the baptism with which I am baptized, you will be baptized."[51] Nevertheless, to suppose that this cancels the historical validity of Jesus' warnings to his disciples, that they must count the cost, bear the cross, renounce all that they had,[52] is surely unwarranted. There was plenty of reason in the immediate situation which Jesus and his first disciples faced for such forewarning. They had joined his company when public favor brought the wondering crowds around him. Their heads were full of self-seeking dreams concerning first places in his kingdom. They were thinking of the prizes, not the costs. At no point were they less prepared for what awaited them. They needed to be told that hatred and persecution were to be their lot, flogged in the synagogues and dragged before governors.[53]

The core of such passages, therefore, whatever expansions and applications may have come later, was surely part of Jesus' training of the twelve. He was a stern taskmaster. They tried to see their discipleship to him as all glory and honor, but he insisted on destroying their illusions. They promised to follow him when he was a popular leader with multitudes about him, and the hardest lesson they had to learn was that, even if he was the Messiah, he was the suffering Messiah, and that they must suffer with him.

Facing the twelve thus with heavy demands, Jesus sought also to supply them with deep resources. At this point it is most important to note to what audience Jesus addressed any saying we wish to interpret. So approached, the Gospels reveal that Jesus' most profound and inward teaching about God's fatherhood, his intimate care for individuals and his available help through prayer was addressed to the disciples alone.

"In the morning, a great while before day," Mark tells us, "he rose and went out to a lonely place, and there he prayed. And Simon and those who were with him followed him."[54] So, from the beginning, the disciples saw Jesus in his most intimate hours, when his relationship with God meant not output but intake, and what they thus saw became one of the most indispensable factors in their training. As good Jews they had always prayed, but in Jesus' practice of prayer they saw something new, unique. Here was prayer with transforming consequence, not a form but a force. It was evident that when he prayed, he did not "heap up empty phrases as the Gentiles do."[55]

> Lord, what a change within us one short hour,
> Spent in thy presence can avail to make—

that experience they saw illustrated in Jesus in ways which awoke their wonder and their emulation. What Luke says, in describing the transfiguration, they must have witnessed more than once: "As he was praying, the appearance of his countenance was altered."[56]

In general, Jesus in his teaching of the twelve is represented as taking the initiative, challenging their prejudices, instructing their ignorance, urging upon them his ideas and ideals. In the matter of prayer, however, it was they who took the initiative. Having seen what prayer meant to Jesus they craved a share in the experience. That was the only thing the disciples are pictured in the Gospels as asking Jesus to instruct them about: "He was praying in a certain place, and when he ceased, one of his disciples said to him, 'Lord, teach us to pray.' "[57]

According to Luke, who alone records them, two of Jesus' most puzzling parables—when pleading for patience in prayer, he likens God to an apathetic neighbor in bed with his children, not wishing to be disturbed,[58] and to an unrighteous judge who regards a widow's appeal only because, as he said, she "bothers me," and "will wear me out by her continual coming"[59]—were told to the disciples alone. Granting the uncertainty which commonly attends the Gospels' circumstantial setting of Jesus' sayings, there is persuasive likelihood in Luke's ascription of these special parables to an occasion when he was alone with the twelve. With the inner group of his friends he could be intimate, frank, whimsical. To them he could say that God sometimes seems like a sleepy neighbor saying, "Do not bother me; the door is now shut, and my children are with me in bed; I cannot get up and give you anything." Prayer was no swift, easy way of getting what Jesus wanted, no magical guarantee against trouble. Did he not pray all night before selecting his disciples?—and then he picked out Judas. Did he not cry in Gethsemane, "Remove this cup from me"?—but it could not be removed. To Jesus prayer was a long-term, patient search—asking, seeking, knocking—undergirded by an undiscourageable faith, prepared to surmount denial and disappointment: "If you then, who are evil, know how to give good gifts to your children, how much more will the heavenly Father give the Holy Spirit to those who ask him?"[60]

Such insight, which the disciples were given into Jesus' experience in prayer, was not for the crowd. With the disciples alone he shared his most intimate feelings concerning God's fatherly care: "Are not five sparrows sold for two pennies?

[175]

And not one of them is forgotten before God. Why, even the hairs of your head are all numbered. Fear not; you are of more value than many sparrows."[61] He was trying to prepare his inner group of followers for the trials that awaited them, to make their resources adequate for the coming stress and strain. As one watches him, reserving for the chosen few his profoundest thoughts about prayer and about the God who responds to it, Plato's saying—despite the vast difference between Plato's aristocratic bias and Jesus' love of common folk —is lighted up: "To find the maker and father of this universe is a hard task; and when you have found him, it is impossible to speak of him before all people."[62]

So to the twelve Jesus unbosomed himself, sharing with them alike his experience of, and his thoughts about, the divine resources that would sustain both him and them. "Now it happened," we read, "that as he was praying alone the disciples were with him."[63] Thus by contagion they caught more than they understood, and when he talked about those spiritual depths which any words are insufficient to reveal, it was to them he spoke. One suspects that, in its original setting, the passage on prayer in the Sermon on the Mount was spoken when he and his disciples were alone: "When you pray, go into your room and shut the door and pray to your Father who is in secret; and your Father who sees in secret will reward you."[64]

Whether Jesus thought of himself as the Messiah, and if so, what he meant by it, is a moot question concerning whose answer scholars probably will never agree. Penetrating the self-consciousness of Jesus is a difficult undertaking. Even to the first disciples he was often inscrutable, and to us the problem of his messianic claim, whether he made it and if so what

[176]

meaning he put into it, is soluble only by conjecture. But whatever Jesus may have thought about himself, what the disciples thought about him is clear—he was the Messiah. That was the climax of their faith in him.

Had they been not Jews but Greeks, they would not have called him that. Being Jews, however, they had no other category except messiahship in which to frame a transcendent personality. They faced on one side Jesus himself, unique, original, divinely ordained and commissioned, and on the other side the inherited ideas of the Messiah with their long-accumulated and diverse meanings. The fitting of those two together was inevitably confusing and still in our Gospels it presents an all but insoluble problem.

The final outcome, however, is not dubious: they believed with flaming faith that he was the Christ. Mark's Gospel from beginning to end reveals this central conviction of the first disciples and of the early church. Jesus' marvelous deeds display his messianic power; his teachings manifest his messianic authority. John the Baptist bears witness to him, "After me comes he who is mightier than I";[65] and at his baptism a divine voice salutes him, "Thou art my beloved Son."[66] The demons know him, calling him, "the Holy One of God";[67] whenever the unclean spirits behold him, they fall down before him and cry out, "You are the Son of God."[68] At last, the disciples, slow of understanding, see the truth and Peter says, "You are the Christ."[69] At the transfiguration, a voice from the cloud says, "This is my beloved Son."[70] And after the resurrection all misgiving is ended and he is known to be the Messiah indeed, crucified, risen and coming again. This without doubt is the ardent faith that from first to last illumines Mark's Gospel.

Nevertheless, while this faith saturates the whole narrative, it is not allowed to obscure Jesus' own attitude. When the

[177]

demons acclaim him he says, "Be silent";[71] "And he strictly
ordered them not to make him known."[72] Even when Peter
makes his decisive profession, Mark says, "He charged them to
tell no one about him";[73] Luke says, "He charged and commanded them to tell this to no one";[74] Matthew says, "He
strictly charged the disciples to tell no one that he was the
Christ."[75] Not until the high priest at Jesus' trial asked him,
"Are you the Christ, the Son of the Blessed?" and Jesus answered, "I am,"[76] did he, according to Mark's record, publicly
affirm his messiahship. Considering the fact that the Christhood of Jesus was the church's first creed, and that when the
Gospels were written the church's strong conviction would
naturally urge the writers to discover or surmise the earliest
possible date for Jesus' proclamation of it, this reluctance of
Jesus to acknowledge his messiahship, this postponement of his
claim to the final hours of his life, seems clearly historical.

How, then, did the first disciples come to their faith in him
as the Christ, and what did they mean by it?

✗ They seem first to have shared the crowd's interpretation
and to have thought of him as a prophet. "A great prophet has
arisen among us!"[77] said the people, "a prophet, like one of the
prophets of old,"[78] and when Jesus asked his disciples who men
were taking him to be, they answered, " 'John the Baptist';
and others, 'Elijah'; and others, 'One of the prophets.' "[79]
Even at the end, when Jesus entered Jerusalem in triumph,
"the crowds said, 'This is the prophet Jesus from Nazareth of
Galilee' ";[80] and the chief priests and the Pharisees, planning
to arrest him, "feared the multitudes, because they held him
to be a prophet."[81] Moreover, this is what Jesus called himself—"A prophet is not without honor, except in his own
country";[82] "Nevertheless I must go on my way today and tomorrow and the day following; for it cannot be that a prophet

[178]

should perish away from Jerusalem."[83] With this interpretation of Jesus the disciples probably started.

✕ That they soon went deeper and perceived in him a unique consciousness of special relationship with God seems evident. Scholars commonly hang the discussion of this profound inner experience of Jesus upon special phrases attributed to him, such as his use of "Abba," "my Father,"[84] or upon special texts, such as "All things have been delivered to me by my Father; and no one knows who the Son is except the Father, or who the Father is except the Son and any one to whom the Son chooses to reveal him."[85] Such a text, however, can be too easily attributed to the later church's conviction about him, read back—as many a similar passage in John's Gospel was read back[86]—into the consciousness of Jesus. Here, too, penetrating Jesus' self-consciousness is difficult, but the conviction of the first disciples seems clear, that while God in one sense is Father of all, and in a deeper sense Father of right-minded, merciful men—"Blessed are the peacemakers, for they shall be called the sons of God";[87] "Love your enemies . . . so that you may be sons of your Father who is in heaven"[88]—he was in a special sense Jesus' Father and Jesus his Son. The disciples' deepening companionship with him revealed to them a spirit whose profundities they could not fathom—unique resources in prayer, a moving sense of divine vocation and mission, an emphasis upon the intimate, inward, personal meanings of God's fatherhood such as they had never met before. The flaming faith that in some special sense Jesus was *the* Son of God, without which the first church is inconceivable, and which burns throughout our present Gospels and throughout the earliest known documents used in their composition, was surely no improvisation of a later generation. Sonship to God, in Jewish thought, was not a metaphysical category; it involved

[179]

no such thinking as Hellenistic Christianity later put into the Nicene Creed; it was a matter of spiritual quality and divine vocation, involving in its supreme exhibition a unique commission to fulfill it. *That* the first disciples clearly perceived in Jesus.

That somewhere in the course of their discipleship they began to think of him in specifically messianic terms is evident. The term "Messiah," however, in Jesus' day, connoted no such clearcut idea as we moderns commonly assume. The Messiah might be a man, rising from among the people—"A man shall arise . . . like the sun of righteousness";[89] "a man working righteousness and working mercy."[90] Or he might be a military leader fomenting revolt against Rome, and more than one such violent rebel was greeted as the Expected One. Peaceable or militant, such a Messiah was human—"Nor shall he do all these things by his own will, but in obedience to the good ordinance of the mighty God."[91] The Messiah might spring from the house of David[92]—that idea is prominent in our Gospels—but there was another tradition also, that he would come from the house of Levi.[93] In conceiving the Messiah's mission, nationalistic victory might be stressed— "he shall make war against Beliar, and execute an everlasting vengeance on our enemies,"[94] or in the center of attention might be the whole world's welfare—"Neither shall there be any sword throughout the land nor battle din. . . . No war shall there be any more,"[95] and "there shall be peace in all the earth."[96] The Messiah, however, in some circles, took on superhuman aspects. He was pre-existent, at least in the sense that his name was known to God from all eternity. So Moses is represented in saying of himself: "He designed and devised me, and he prepared me before the foundation of the world, that I should be a mediator of his covenant."[97] In time, however, this Vicegerent of God was pictured by some as personally present in the heavens, ready to come in glory at God's appointed time to usher in the kingdom.[98]

Such contrasting ideas were in the air in Jesus' day. The rabbis themselves had trouble harmonizing them. How could Zechariah's picture of the Messiah—"Behold, thy king cometh unto thee . . . lowly, and riding upon an ass"[99]—be reconciled with Daniel's picture: "Behold, there came with the clouds of heaven one like unto a son of man"?[100] As late as the third century A.D., one rabbi was still tussling with that question, saying that if Israel were worthy, Daniel's picture would come true, but if unworthy, Zechariah's.[101]

When Jesus' disciples, therefore, first moved up through thinking of him as a prophet, and as in some special sense the Son of God, to thinking of him as the Messiah, what did they have in mind? Only one idea is constant through all the varied concepts of messiahship: the Messiah in some supreme sense is God's agent, his instrument and representative in saving Israel and ushering in God's kingdom. Messiahship is a category of vocation and mission. It is not primarily metaphysical but instrumental. The Messiah, human or superhuman, is a doer of deeds, a divinely appointed agent of salvation to his people.

So much, at least, the disciples saw in Jesus when first they called him the Christ. In the end they believed him to be the superhuman Son of Man ascended into heaven and waiting to come again in glory, but by what stages they reached that goal and what confused conceptions they held in the beginning it is not easy to be sure.

The contemporary confusion of thought concerning the nature of the Messiah suggests a natural explanation of Jesus' own recorded attitude. How could he declare himself openly, even if he thought he was the Messiah? To many that declaration would suggest ideas utterly alien to Jesus' concept of his mission. Even when Peter called him Christ, he turned at once to expounding an idea of his vocation which horrified the twelve. If he had reason to fear even their misunderstanding of what Christhood meant to him, how much more must he have feared the misconceptions of the multitude!

✕ As for the twelve, the Gospels record the emergence among them of an unprecedented idea of the Christ which later took possession of the church: he was the suffering servant of the Lord whom the Isaiah of the Exile had described.[102] Despite diligent research and the stretching of exegesis to its limit, there is no convincing evidence that the idea of a martyred Messiah was extant in Judaism in Jesus' day.[103] The traditional synagogue teaching, as embodied in the Targum, did on at least four occasions identify the Messiah with Isaiah's servant of the Lord, but by a triumph of evasive exegesis the sufferings in every case were taken from the Messiah and assigned either to Israel or to the heathen.[104] To be sure, the concept of vicarious suffering was in Judaism. Israel had had many sacrificial saviors in its history. The aged Eleazar, in the Fourth Book of Maccabees, prays amid his torments—"Thou knowest, O God, that when I might be saved, I am dying in fiery tortures on account of thy law. Be gracious to thy people, being satisfied with our punishment in their behalf. Make my blood a sacrifice for their purification, and take my life as a substitute for theirs."[105] Such saving martyrdom, however, ran counter to all the prevailing Jewish ideas of the Messiah, and the identification of Christ in the New Testament with Isaiah's suffering servant was a startling innovation.

Philip, presenting the gospel to the Ethiopian eunuch, started with Isaiah's fifty-third chapter, and "beginning with this scripture he told him the good news of Jesus."[106] Peter, interpreting Christian suffering, quoted from the Septuagint version of the same chapter,[107] and the Letter to the Hebrews interprets Christ's cross in terms of it.[108] There is no doubt, therefore, that the early church identified the Messiah with Isaiah's servant of the Lord, nor is there valid reason for questioning the evidence of the Gospels that this identification went back to Jesus and his first disciples. When he announced his mission in Nazareth's synagogue, he read from Isaiah's sixty-first chapter,[109] and when he answered the messages of John the Baptist he alluded to it.[110] Only one direct quotation from the fifty-third chapter is attributed to Jesus—"I tell you that this scripture must be fulfilled in me, 'And he was reckoned with transgressors' "[111]—but there are other indications that the suffering servant was influentially present in his thought. Isaiah had said that God's "righteous servant" would "justify many" and that he "bare the sin of many";[112] Jesus said that he came "to give his life as a ransom for many."[113] "How is it written of the Son of man, that he should suffer many things and be treated with contempt?"[114] said Jesus to his disciples, after the Transfiguration. "The Son of man goes, as it is written of him,"[115] he said at the Last Supper. Where else was such a suffering redeemer written about save in Isaiah's prophecies?

Whatever may have been in Jesus' mind, there can be no doubt that, in the end, the disciples' concept of messiahship moved out into this new dimension. They saw him, as their people had never seen him, as a sacrificial savior, his blood "poured out for many."[116] Nevertheless, they combined this idea of a martyred Messiah with the apocalyptic picture of a superhuman Son of Man, awaiting in heaven the appointed hour for his victorious return. Mark's Gospel frankly reveals the difficulty this juncture of ideas presented to them: "He was teaching his disciples, saying to them, 'The Son of man will be delivered into the hands of men, and they will kill him; and when he is killed, after three days he will rise.' But they did not understand the saying, and they were afraid to ask him."[117] This passage almost certainly reveals a retrospective, postresurrection view of the first disciples' thinking, but it reveals also the fact that not at first did they incorporate into their concept of Jesus' messiahship the figure of the heavenly Son of Man. That was the climax of their developing idea of Christ, and it could hardly have come to full flower until their dismay at the crucifixion had been turned into victory by their conviction that he was alive again.[118]

So Jesus' first disciples, laboring to interpret him in such inherited categories as they possessed, saw him: God's prophet, God's Son, God's suffering servant, and God's coming victorious Son of Man.

The inward struggle in the disciples' minds, involved in their endeavor to fit Jesus into their inherited mental frameworks, especially their conflicting ideas of messiahship, came to a tragic exhibition in Judas' treachery. Why Judas betrayed Jesus is still a matter of difficult conjecture. Mark and Luke picture him offering his treacherous services to the chief priests with no motive recorded; it is the priests who suggest the monetary reward, promising "to give him money." Matthew, however, changes the picture, represents Judas as saying, "What will you give me if I deliver him to you?" and under the influence of a passage in Zechariah, which he mistakenly ascribes to Jeremiah,[119] names the price that Judas received.[120] Mark's Gospel and Luke's say nothing about Judas' death; Matthew says that in remorse he returned the chief priests' bribe and "went and hanged himself," and that with the returned money the priests bought a "potter's field, to bury strangers in."[121] The Book of Acts, however, reports that Judas himself "bought a field with the reward of his wickedness; and falling headlong he burst open in the middle and all his bowels gushed out."[122]

↗ The mercenary motive for Judas' treachery is, therefore, dubious. If, as Matthew intimates, that was the controlling motive, why did Judas, as Matthew also says, at once return the money and commit suicide? There must have been something deeper going on in Judas' mind, and conjectures as to what that something was have, with general consent, centered on the conflicting notions of messiahship which must have puzzled all the disciples.

One conjecture is that for a time Judas did believe Jesus to be the Messiah—the militant Messiah of Jewish hopes. If Peter rebelled against the idea of a suffering and dying Christ, Judas may have rebelled more. He had expected Jesus to declare himself with power and, backed by superhuman authority, to seize the reins of government and usher in the glorious new era. But what could he make of this Christ, who taught humility and love for enemies and said that the Son of Man must suffer and die? Even in Jerusalem, where the triumphant revelation of Jesus' power was most to be expected, nothing but weakness and humiliation were evident. Judas had waited long enough. Doubt crept in. He had been made a fool of by this Galilean, and by as much as he had believed with ardent hope in Jesus' messiahship, by so much he now resented and was determined to destroy the one who had let him down. Such is one conjecture.

Another is that Judas did not lose faith in Jesus as the Christ. He had wagered his life on that and he clung to it to the bitter end. But if Jesus was the Messiah, he must declare himself and

[185]

manifest his glory. Now was the time, and this the place, Jerusalem, where, only a few days before, the crowds had welcomed him with palm branches and hosannas. Somehow the issue must be forced. If Jesus were faced with a dilemma, crowded into a corner where he had to choose between shameful death and the disclosure of his messianic glory, then the world would see the revelation of the victorious Son of Man. That forced issue must be arranged, and Judas would see to it. Was some such motive behind Judas' betrayal?

That such conjectures are sheer guessing is obvious, but far and away the most probable explanation of Judas' treachery connects his deed with some form of disillusionment concerning Jesus' messiahship. Moreover, while in the end Judas alone deliberately betrayed his Lord, Peter denied him and the others fled. They all were very human in their perplexities and doubts, and none of them came easily by the confident faith in Christ which later shone in the Gospels. Is there not an authentic recollection of their disappointment and bewilderment in Luke's postresurrection story of the two disciples going to Emmaus: "But we had hoped that he was the one to redeem Israel"?[123] Judas' betrayal is a window through which one sees some of the inner struggles of the twelve about Jesus' messiahship, which the later records inevitably toned down.

Nevertheless, with their complete assurance that Jesus had triumphed over death, their faith came back again. He was not dead—they were still his contemporaries—and with deepened meaning, they saw him as God's prophet, God's Son, the sacrificial Savior, and the Son of Man who soon would come in glory to bring God's kingdom in.

The modern mind has endless doubts and questions concerning the ancient frameworks of thought by means of which the first followers of Jesus interpreted him. Even when modern doubts are given full swing, however, the personality in whose interpretation they were used still remains, demanding explanation. Those who lived most intimately with him stood most in awe of him, with mingled love and adoration acknowledged in him a divine authority, felt in him the very presence of their God, gave him the supreme name they knew to express transcendent greatness, Messiah, and after Calvary they were victoriously confirmed in their adoration of him by their faith in his resurrection and their experience of his living presence. That is the astounding fact with which the Christian church began.

CHAPTER VIII

As Militant Nationalists Saw Him

TO THE casual reader our Gospels seem only slightly concerned about the political conditions in Palestine which Jesus faced. When the Gospels were written those conditions had passed away. The violent revolt against Rome had ended —or, possibly in the case of Mark, was soon to end—in Jerusalem's capture by Titus in A.D. 70. Judaism, as a political state, was ruined; the militant Zealots were decimated; the seething problems which had obsessed Palestine while Jesus lived were history. Moreover, the Gospels, written in cities of the Empire, such as Rome or Antioch, were not concerned with recording the story of Jewish politics, but were altogether intent on presenting Christ as the world's Savior. Whatever Jesus may have said about the bygone political controversies of his time and country naturally became irrelevant to the succeeding generation of Christians, and could be easily forgotten or, if remembered, could be misunderstood and referred to contexts different from the original setting. The wonder is not that the Gospels reveal so little about Jesus' attitude toward current political problems but that they reveal so much.

That Jesus took no attitude toward the public problems of his people seems incredible. We commonly think of the Jews, in their dealing with Jesus, as exclusively concerned with religion and, conceiving religion in modern fashion as altogether a matter of theology, worship, prayer, humane deeds and pious observances, we lose sight of an incalculably influential factor in the ancient scene. Jewish religion and Jewish patriotism were inextricably intermeshed. No people have ever exhibited a more passionate and sustained patriotism than the Jews and their religion was the inspiration of it. Assyria, Babylon, Persia, Greece and Rome had successively conquered and enslaved them, but still the cry of the Psalmist persisted:

> If I forget thee, O Jerusalem,
> Let my right hand forget her skill.
> Let my tongue cleave to the roof of my mouth,
> If I remember thee not;
> If I prefer not Jerusalem
> Above my chief joy.[1]

In Jesus' day in Palestine nationalistic patriotism was rampant. From the time of the Maccabees, throwing off the yoke of the Syrian Greeks, the conquerors might seize the land and work their brutal will on the bodies of the people, but they could not quell the Jewish spirit. One rebellious outburst after another had kept even the Romans uneasy on their seat of power. The predominant public problem in Jesus' day concerned the attitude which the Jews should take toward Roman rule. Should they, like the Sadducees, temporize and, for the time being, collaborate with Rome, or, like many of the Pharisees, should they wait, hating Rome but looking for the Messiah's coming to redeem the nation and crush its enemies, or should they revolt and trust in God to give victory to the right? We may call such questions political but to the Jews they were basically religious. Jewish religion was specifically organized to

[189]

protect the national life and culture from breakdown and assimilation, and Jewish patriotism was centrally dedicated to
preserve the great heritage of Judaism's faith.

As for the militant patriots who believed in armed revolt, it
is a question of small moment whether or not, in Jesus' day,
they were called "Zealots." Josephus dates the use of the name
from John of Gischala who, about A.D. 66, helped launch the
fatal revolt which ended in Jerusalem's downfall. Josephus
himself, however, records how Judas of Gamala, in A.D. 6, re-
belling against the census of Quirinus, founded a "Fourth
Philosophy" among the Jews—along with the Sadducees,
Pharisees, and Essenes—and his description of its followers
with their passionate love of liberty, their determination to
acknowledge no ruler except God, and their fanatical fearlessness whether in killing or dying, makes it evident that they
were Zealots in fact, if not in name. From their time, says
Josephus, "the nation began to grow mad with this dis-
temper."[2]

Jesus, therefore, grew up in a turbulent nation, boiling with
political unrest. Half of it was governed by a Roman Procurator, the other half by a prince of the hated family of Herod.
Even in Jerusalem, where the Sadducean priests kept the people as steady as they could, assassinations and riots were frequent, and the farther away from Jerusalem one went, the
more openly insurrection threatened. Both John of Gischala
and Judas of Gamala were Galileans, and in Galilee the militant, revolutionary movement had both its rise and its greatest
strength. "The Galileans," wrote Josephus, "are inured to war
from their infancy."[3] Into such an environment Jesus was
born, and in his childhood some of the most vivid stories told
in Nazareth's lounging places must have been memories of

tumult and bloodshed. Herod the Great, who "stole along to his throne like a fox, ruled like a tiger, and died like a dog," was still fresh in the recollections of Galilee, and many a tale of his wars there and of the furious resistance of the people must have been current in Nazareth. It was in the Galilean hill country, with its many natural caverns, Josephus tells us, that "there was one old man who was caught within one of these caves, with seven children and a wife; these prayed him to give them leave to go out, and yield themselves up to the enemy; but he stood at the cave's mouth, and always slew that child of his that went out, till he had destroyed them every one, and after that he slew his wife, and cast their dead bodies down the precipice, and himself after them, and so underwent death rather than slavery."[4]

Such were the vivid memories of Galilee from the generation preceding Jesus and, as for his own childhood, when Judas of Gamala first raised the standard of rebellion, about the time of Jesus' birth or just afterward, he marched on Sepphoris, a few miles north of Nazareth, seized the arsenal there and for a brief time triumphed, until Varus, the Roman general, defeated him, burned Sepphoris to the ground, and sold its in-inhabitants into slavery.[5]

To suppose that Jesus had nothing to say about a situation so urgent and fearful, took no attitude toward it, lived in an ivory tower and taught a religion irrelevant to his people's most critical public debates and decisions, seems most improbable. For there was little, if any, mitigation of the furious unrest during his lifetime. Driven underground it might be, but if Mommsen is right in saying that the real date for the beginning of the Jewish-Roman war may well be put as early as A.D. 44,[6] then hardly more than a decade after Jesus' death the struggle commenced. Meanwhile, what Josephus called "the madness of desperate men" was throughout Jesus' ministry preparing for the fray.

What Jesus thought about these nationalistic patriots is important to the understanding of him, and we can perhaps get at that matter best by inquiring what they must have thought of him.

That some of them thought he might become their leader in armed resistance against Rome seems evident. This was their main need—a rousing personality who would precipitate the general unrest into definite insurrection. From Judas of Gamala and Theudas[7] to Bar Cochba, concerning whom even Rabbi Akiba said, "This is the Messianic King,"[8] the revolutionists repeatedly rallied around vigorous, militant chieftains. We need not depend alone on the Fourth Gospel's statement that the crowd "were about to come and take him by force to make him king,"[9] to support the supposition that rebellious patriots thought Jesus might be the long-sought leader of their revolt.

How else can the third temptation of Jesus be explained except in terms of this possibility? "Again, the devil took him to a very high mountain, and showed him all the kingdoms of the world and the glory of them; and he said to him, 'All these I will give you, if you will fall down and worship me.' "[10] However the story of this temptation came into our records, the least probable explanation is that it was made up by the later church. The Christ in whom that church believed, by his atoning death and victorious resurrection, had become mankind's Savior. What motive could possibly have led his followers then to imagine him as tempted to worship the devil—that is, to use satanic means—to win the kingdoms of the world? In

Jesus' own lifetime, however, temptation to use bloody insurrection for the kingdom's sake was the most crucial public problem of his people.

If, as seems probable, Jesus' inner struggle concerning the nature and method of his ministry was told by him to his disciples, he let them see that he had faced the possibility of becoming a militant, revolutionary leader. He might have decided on such a messiahship as Judas Maccabaeus chose, trying to fulfill the expectations of the violent insurrectionists, who were impatiently awaiting the call of some popular leader to revolt. The pressure was on him, and it must have grown as, during the early months of his ministry, the multitudes flocked about him. When the rumor ran among the crowds that perhaps this was he who should redeem Israel, the militant spirits there were thinking, not of an apocalyptic Son of Man from heaven, but of the rebel against Rome who would lead them to triumph in a messianic war.

This expectation apparently came to its fiery climax when Jesus, having entered Jerusalem amid shouting crowds, cleansed the temple—an overt act of sedition against both priestly authority and Roman rule. The iron was hot; would he not strike then? Luke retains a recollection of that mounting hope: as Jesus drew "near to Jerusalem . . . they supposed that the kingdom of God was to appear immediately."[11] Amid Jerusalem's confusion that final week, diverse motives with reference to Jesus swayed the city. The Pharisees were indignant at him, mainly for religious reasons; the Sadducean priesthood was angry at his disturbance of public order, fearful that the uproar he was causing would bring Rome's wrath upon them; but the militant insurrectionists must have been there too, eagerly watching him and hoping that the longed for revolution was about to start. In their desire for his bellig-

erent leadership they could easily have misunderstood his real
spirit and meaning. Did not the disciples themselves have difficulty in understanding him?

It may even be that a Zealot—"Simon who was called the
Zealot" is Luke's description of him[12]—was one of the disciples. Both the Greek word, however, which Luke uses and its
Aramaic equivalent in Matthew's Gospel, "Cananaean,"[13]
mean "hot," "fervid," and if Josephus is right in saying that
this appellation's use to describe a party in Israel began later,
it may signify in Simon's case simply "zealous."[14] The meaning
of "Iscariot," attached to the betrayer's name, is also dubious.
It may indicate that his home town was Kerioth in Judea, or it
may come from "sicarii"—"dagger-men"—a group who, as
Josephus tells us, from the days of Herod the Great had practiced assassination and worked for bloody revolt. Whether or
not, however, Simon had been a Zealot and Judas a dagger-
man—as Matthew had been a tax collector—the disciples
certainly did not find it easy to understand Jesus' nonmilitant
idea of messiahship.

James and John, "sons of thunder,"[15] wanted to call down
fire from heaven on inhospitable Samaritans,[16] and conspired
to get seats on the right and the left of the king in the day of his
triumph.[17] Peter's revolt against Jesus' idea of a suffering and
dying Messiah was so vehement that the temptation which
Jesus had faced in the militant expectations of his people revived, and turning on Peter he cried: "Get behind me, Satan!
For you are not on the side of God, but of men."[18] Even at the
Last Supper his disciples offered him two swords for self-
defense,[19] and in Gethsemane one of them, drawing a sword,
cut off the ear of the high priest's slave.[20] If the disciples could
so misunderstand their Master's spirit and intent, the belligerent nationalists could utterly miss it. "I came to cast fire upon

[194]

the earth; and would that it were already kindled!"[21]—if such a saying of Jesus were known to the insurrectionists, what they would have made of it is clear.

When our Gospels were written, the Zealots were defeated and dead. Their last desperate stand on the bleak heights of Masada was over and, unlike the Pharisees, they were no longer a problem to the Christian church of the next generation. The evidence concerning them in our records, therefore, is incidental, and its meaning must be gleaned by inference. Nevertheless, that they were a dominant factor in the situation which Jesus faced is undoubted history. Windisch is justified in saying, "The most important characteristic of his messiahship, speaking negatively, is to be found in his refusal to wage the messianic war."[22]

That the militant party turned against him at last with the bitterness of disappointed hopes seems clear. That last week in Jerusalem Jesus failed them. He cleansed the temple but, so Mark reports, he said it was because the temple was meant to be "a house of prayer for all the nations."[23] He described the payment of Roman taxes as giving to Caesar what was Caesar's. When he was arrested, he surrendered with no display of messianic power. There was no violent insurrection in him. One wonders whether some disillusioned revolutionists did not swell the cry in Pilate's court for the release of Barrabbas instead of Jesus. Barabbas was one of "the rebels in prison, who had committed murder in the insurrection."[24] The Greek word used of him in the Gospels corresponds with the word Josephus repeatedly uses of the Zealots. Barabbas was a violent rebel and if, as Mark reports, the high priests, who least of all desired revolt, wished his release, how much more would the Zealots in the crowd have cried for his liberation, and for the execution of Jesus who had let them down!

That Jesus foresaw the peril of Jewish insurrection and a Roman war and that the prospect filled him with foreboding seems evident. Luke puts it explicitly:

And when he drew near and saw the city he wept over it, saying, "Would that even today you knew the things that make for peace! But now they are hid from your eyes. For the days shall come upon you, when your enemies will cast up a bank about you and surround you, and hem you in on every side, and dash you to the ground, you and your children within you, and they will not leave one stone upon another in you; because you did not know the time of your visitation."[25]

Skeptical critics may say that since the doom here foretold already had fallen on Jerusalem when Luke's Gospel was written, such a passage probably came from the early church's conviction that Jesus must have foreseen it. Such skepticism, however, faces too much contrary evidence to make it easily credible. According to Mark, Jesus said of Jerusalem's "wonderful buildings," "There will not be left here one stone upon another, that will not be thrown down,"[26] and in the early written source which scholars call "Q," and which both Matthew and Luke used, Jesus' words were recorded: "O Jerusalem, Jerusalem, killing the prophets and stoning those who are sent to you! How often would I have gathered your children together as a hen gathers her brood under her wings, and you would not! Behold, your house is forsaken and desolate."[27]

This ominous outlook of Jesus on his nation's future is expressed too frequently to be dubious. To be sure, he also foretold the end of the age, the Son of Man's coming and the last judgment, and his words about Jerusalem's destruction in a Roman war are, in our records, so confused with his words about the final arrival of the Son of Man that scholars argue

[196]

endlessly about disentangling them. Nevertheless, two future
events—Jerusalem's fall in war and the Son of Man's coming
—are plainly indicated in the Gospels.

The church of the evangelists' time was interested not so
much in the fall of Jerusalem as in the hope of the coming
Messiah, and the natural result of this would be the modification of his words about Zion's military fate to fit the last judgment. This seems clearly to have happened in Mark's so-
called "Little Apocalypse."[28] That this was a written document
which Mark incorporated in his Gospel is suggested by the
phrase, "let the reader understand."[29] That it represents a collection of predictions attributed to Jesus, modified to suit
known history when the Gospel was written—note the warning not to expect the Messiah's coming too soon—is probable.
It starts with the disciples' question as to when the temple will
be destroyed and it includes a description of the Son of Man's
coming at the end of the age. In the midst of it, however, is a
passage which, fitting the temple's destruction, does not fit the
catastrophic arrival of the messianic age at all.

But when you see the desolating sacrilege set up where it ought
not to be (let the reader understand), then let those who are in
Judea flee to the mountains; let him who is on the housetop not go
down, nor enter his house, to take anything away; and let him who
is in the field not turn back to take his mantle. And alas for those who
are with child and for those who give suck in those days! Pray that it
may not happen in winter. For in those days there will be such
tribulation as has not been from the beginning of the creation which
God created until now, and never will be.[30]

This passage plainly concerns Jerusalem's downfall; and the
details of danger and possible escape of which Jesus speaks,
while vividly applicable to the military sacking of the city, are

utterly inapplicable to the Messiah's coming. Had the apocalyptic arrival of the heavenly Son of Man been in Jesus' mind, what possible difference could it make whether or not that world-transforming event came in the winter, or how could Judeans escape it, as Jesus counseled, by fleeing to the mountains, or what relevance has his advice to escape without stopping even to pick up a garment? This passage is most reasonably explained as being a saying of Jesus about the fateful end of the coming Jewish-Roman war—a saying reset by the Gospel writers in the pattern of the later church's expectation of the woes attendant on the coming of the Son of Man from heaven.

Luke makes this reference unmistakable. Instead of the vaguer phrase "desolating sacrilege," he says, "But when you see Jerusalem surrounded by armies, then know that its desolation has come near,"[31] and, writing with the knowledge of the prediction's fulfillment, he concludes, "They will fall by the edge of the sword, and be led captive among all nations; and Jerusalem will be trodden down by the Gentiles, until the times of the Gentiles are fulfilled."[32]

Such definite forebodings concerning the threatened Jewish-Roman war light up the possible meaning of other premonitions of national doom in Jesus' thought. When he was told "of the Galileans whose blood Pilate had mingled with their sacrifices," and of the "eighteen upon whom the tower in Siloam fell," he answered, "Unless you repent you will all likewise perish."[33] One wonders whether the implication is not that they will perish in similar fashion at the hands of the Romans and under the falling towers of their city. He foresaw a storm and then "scorching heat" coming on his nation, and he rebuked the crowd who could predict the weather but who were too blind to "interpret the present time."[34] He told the nation's rulers that they were like faithless tenants of a vineyard who, having refused the owner his due and having slain his servants and his son, would themselves be destroyed and the vineyard given to others.[35] He said that upon that generation would fall the accumulated punishment for "all the righteous blood shed on earth, from the blood of innocent Abel to the blood of Zechariah the son of Barachiah, whom you murdered between the sanctuary and the altar."[36] Such was his habitual mood until, carrying his cross to Calvary, he said to the lamenting women:

Daughters of Jerusalem, do not weep for me, but weep for yourselves and for your children. For behold, the days are coming when they will say, "Blessed are the barren, and the wombs that never bore, and the breasts that never gave suck!" Then they will begin to say to the mountains, "Fall on us"; and to the hills "Cover us." For if they do this when the wood is green, what will happen when it is dry?[37]

We cannot step inside the Master's mind and see all the factors that contributed to this sense of impending national doom, but is it not reasonable to conjecture, in the light of Jesus' ethic, that he saw in his people's rejection of him, their rejection of their own national salvation? The alternative which they were choosing was the messianic war. It was brewing fearfully throughout his lifetime. When he spoke of inevitable "wars and rumors of wars,"[38] he was dealing with realistic forebodings. Sayings such as, "All who take the sword will perish by the sword,"[39] were relevant to his nation's most crucial public problem.

How the militant revolutionists must have felt toward one who thus saw the nation's future in terms of doom is evident. He was a defeatist, dashing their dearest hopes with his chill predictions. His religious faith itself was suspect, since he could so picture God surrendering his people to ruin, when they rose bravely up to defend his holy cause. What Jesus said that last week about the payment of taxes to Caesar was to the Zealots rank heresy, as well as rank lack of patriotism. Far from being, as it is often interpreted, a clever piece of repartee, evading the question asked him—"Is it lawful to pay taxes to Caesar, or not? Should we pay them, or should we not?"[40]—his answer met squarely the contention of the Zealots. They held that God alone was their rightful king; that there could not be two kings, God and Caesar; that a choice must be made, and that to pay taxes to Caesar was infidelity to God. When Jesus, therefore, said that they could pay Caesar's coin to Caesar and still give God his due, he was attacking a central article of their faith.

Worst of all, from the viewpoint of the militant patriots, was Jesus' prediction of the temple's destruction. That was heresy, indeed, too rank for priests and Pharisees, as well as for insurrectionists. They did not forget such blasphemy and at the hearing before the high priest this charge of doom pronounced against the temple was flung at him.[41] Garbled their quotations might be, but Jesus' intent was understood. He foresaw the messianic war ending in the temple's ruin.

Beyond such passages, still retained in our Gospels, despite the fact that living interest in the Jewish politics of Jesus' day had vanished from the churches out of which the Gospels came, it is reasonable to suppose that other words of Jesus, concerning the public problems of his time, must have been forgotten. One floating sentence, attached by Matthew to one context and by Luke to another, suggests what may have happened. "From the days of John the Baptist until now the kingdom of heaven has suffered violence, and men of violence take it by force"[42]—so Matthew quotes Jesus; and Luke renders it, "The law and the prophets were until John; since then the good news of the kingdom of God is preached, and every one enters it violently."[43] As the saying stands, little can be made of it, unless one sees it as an attack on violent men who sought to seize the kingdom by force as the revolutionaries did—an attack which, lacking relevance as the situation which called it out passed into bygone history, lost its context and became confused.

In any case the complete alienation between Jesus and the insurrectionists is plain, and what they must have thought of him is evident: not patriotic enough, not nationalistic enough, not belligerent enough.

The difference between Jesus and the insurrectionists, however, sprang from deeper sources than contemporary politics. His ethic was essentially incompatible with the spirit and strategy of the Zealots. That the teaching in the Sermon on the Mount concerning love of enemies was primarily directed against the legalism of the Pharisees we have seen.[44] As with prayer, fasting, philanthropic giving and a chaste life, so with reference to the treatment of foes, Jesus insisted on a righteousness exceeding that of the scribes and Pharisees. When, however, Jesus applied this principle of superlegalistic goodness to the treatment of enemies, he moved into a realm where not only the Pharisees but the militant revolutionists also, with their threatened war against Rome, were involved. That Jesus had them in mind seems evident.

When he said, "If any one forces you to go one mile, go with him two miles,"[45] he was almost certainly referring to the right of Roman officers to coerce labor. When he said, "Blessed are the peacemakers,"[46] how could he have been speaking in a vacuum with no reference to the most critical

[201]

public problem of his time? The cry of Jesus at the end, "Would that even today you knew the things that make for peace!"[47] was in his heart at the beginning. His love-ethic was shaped not only by his ideas of God, not only by his belief in undiscourageable goodwill in personal relationships, but also by his resolute opposition to the threatened messianic war.

Jesus was far from being alone in such opposition. For quite prudential reasons the Sadducean party had decided to collaborate with Rome; the Essenes were thoroughgoing pacifists, refusing even to manufacture munitions of war; and the greater portion of the Pharisees were counseling peace until God acted and the Messiah came. Notable in the leadership of the peace party was Rabbi Johanan ben Zakkai. Born some years before Jesus, he survived by a decade the fall of Jerusalem in A.D. 70. "Never did he waver," writes a Jewish scholar, "even for a moment, in his opposition to the rebellion, which he felt was destined to bring destruction on the people, the sanctuary, and the land. The romantic nationalism which was moving men to unheard-of deeds of heroism and self-sacrifice appeared to him altogether evil and irrational."[48] He too foresaw that Rome would conquer Judea, and of the temple, if war came, he said, "I know of thee that thou shalt be destroyed."[49] Even when Vespasian began the siege of Jerusalem in the winter of A.D. 68, he counseled submission. One wonders if Jesus and Johanan ben Zakkai ever met. They would have had much in common. Johanan even said, "Benevolence on the part of a nation has the atoning power of a sin-offering."[50]

Both the peace party and the war party in Israel had behind them powerful factors in the tradition of their people. On one side was the universalism of the Isaiah of the Exile, announcing Israel's mission to be "a light to the Gentiles" and God's "salvation unto the end of the earth."[51] Out of such universalism, filled with prophetic hope of a day when "nation shall not lift up sword against nation, neither shall they learn war any more,"[52] came reliance on nonviolence as the will of God. The Second Book of Enoch, written sometime between 30 B.C. and A.D. 70, says:

Endure for the sake of the Lord every wound, every injury, every evil word and attack. If ill-requitals befall you, return them not either to neighbor or enemy, because the Lord will return them for you and be your avenger on the day of the great judgment, that there be no avenging here among men.[53]

Jewish tradition, however, contained also a heritage of violence utterly contrary to such peaceful policies. The imprecatory psalms bear witness to it; the inevitable hatreds engendered against cruel conquerors strengthened it; and by the time books such as The Assumption of Moses (A.D. 7–29) and Second Esdras (A.D. 75–100) were written, it is plain what the Zealots had made of it. Says the former:

For the Most High will arise, the Eternal God alone, and he will appear to punish the Gentiles, and he will destroy all their idols. Then thou, O Israel, shalt be happy and thou shalt mount upon the neck and wings of the Eagle [i.e., the Roman eagle,] and they shall be ended and God will exalt thee. . . . And thou shalt look from on high and see thine enemies in Gehenna and thou shalt recognize them and rejoice. And thou shalt give thanks and confess thy Creator.[54]

Says the latter:

All this have I spoken before thee, O Lord, because thou hast said that for our sakes thou madest this world. As for the other nations, which also came from Adam, thou hast said that they are nothing, and are like unto spittle—and thou hast likened the abun-

[203]

dance of them unto a drop that falleth from a vessel. And now, O Lord, these nations which are reputed as nothing, be lords over us, and devour us. But now thy people, whom thou hast called thy first-born, are given unto their hands. If the world now be made for our sakes, why do we not possess for an inheritance our world? How long shall it endure?[55]

As to which of these two traditions claimed Jesus' allegiance there can be no doubt. One of the clearest distinctions in his teaching is that drawn between enduring pain and death, and causing them. The first he resolutely undertook; the second he just as resolutely refused. That there was a hard-headed, realistic motive in this refusal, so far as the threatened Jewish-Roman war was concerned, is explicit in the Gospels. His love-ethic, applied to his nation's enemies, was not altogether abstract, theologically engendered, and aloof from actual conditions. The evidence is clear that, like the peace party in general, he foresaw the tragic doom which war would bring upon his people. There was, however, in Jesus' thinking, along with this horizontal concern with present problems, a vertical conviction which carried his love-ethic up into the nature of God himself. Successful or unsuccessful, belligerent violence was essentially wrong, and all its attendant motives of vindictiveness and hatred were of the devil. As one reads the Sermon on the Mount, this seems unmistakable.

That the Gospels should have been searched to discover loopholes of escape from so difficult an ethic was inevitable. No text, for example, has been more wildly used than Jesus' saying, "Do not think that I have come to bring peace on earth; I have not come to bring peace, but a sword." The idea that Jesus meant "sword" literally, is at once shut out by the context: "For I have come to set a man against his father, and

[204]

a daughter against her mother, and a daughter-in-law against her mother-in-law; and a man's foes will be those of his own household."⁵⁶ Jesus was speaking not of war or of violence in any form but of the conflict caused in families when allegiance to him confronted hostility against him. This tragedy of divided households was beginning in Jesus' lifetime, and his comment on it was the sort of saying the later church would wish retained in the record, so applicable was it to what Christians faced everywhere in the pagan world. Indeed the metaphorical meaning of "sword" in this passage is vouched for by Luke, who drops the metaphor: "Do you think that I have come to give peace on earth? No, I tell you, but rather division."⁵⁷

A more difficult passage is Luke's description of an incident at the last supper:

And he said to them, "When I sent you out with no purse or bag or sandals, did you lack anything?" They said, "Nothing." He said to them, "But now, let him who has a purse take it, and likewise a bag. And let him who has no sword sell his mantle and buy one. For I tell you that this scripture must be fulfilled in me, 'And he was reckoned with transgressors'; for what is written about me has its fulfillment." And they said, "Look, Lord, here are two swords." And he said to them, "It is enough".⁵⁸

Jesus' general meaning is obvious: the days of happy ministry in his fellowship are over; his death and the disciples' persecution are at hand; no longer can they count on popular appreciation and the easy supply of their needs; they face hostility and want. He phrased this message with characteristic picturesqueness. They were going now to need purses, wallets, swords. The question is whether he meant "swords" literally. The disciples, thinking that he did, said: "Here are two swords"; to which Jesus retorted, as Moffatt translates it, "Enough! Enough!" or, as Goodspeed renders it, "Enough of this!" That is to say, this passage illustrates what the Gospels as a whole make clear, that, to his ministry's very end, the disciples, believing him to be the Messiah, could not get out of their heads the militant idea of the messiahship's meaning, and once more Jesus brushed it aside.

The alternative to this interpretation is to suppose that Jesus literally counseled his disciples to buy swords and fight. But, in Luke's Gospel a few verses after this incident, when one of the disciples used his sword on the slave of the high priest, Jesus rebuked him, saying, "No more of this!"[59] and Matthew, narrating the same act of violence, records that Jesus said, "Put your sword back into its place; for all who take the sword will perish by the sword."[60] The supposition that Jesus' exclamation, "It is enough!" meant that two swords were sufficient to start insurrection is fantastic in itself, as well as being a complete denial of the whole tenor of his teaching. Far from being, therefore, an admonition to militancy, this passage illustrates the very opposite—the dullness of the disciples, namely, who under the pressure of current messianic hopes could not grasp Jesus' idea of his mission. So, at any rate, the later church understood the situation: "Jesus answered, 'My kingship is not of this world; if my kingship were of this world, my servants would fight, that I might not be handed over to the Jews; but my kingship is not from the world!' "[61]

If those closest to Jesus thus misinterpreted him, the militant nationalists even more easily could have done so. Jesus could be fierce sometimes as well as gentle. His similes and parables were sometimes violent. A king in one parable cried, "As for these enemies of mine, who did not want me to reign over them, bring them here and slay them before me";[62] and another, enraged, sent his troops and burned a city.[63] Jesus drew a lesson for his followers from a king who, going to war, sat down first and counted the cost,[64] and he pointed up a truth in terms of a robber plundering a strong man's house after having bound the strong man.[65] Jesus would have been easier for his contemporaries to understand, had he been, as in modern times he has commonly been pictured, a sentimentalist. He was anything but that. His statements about the severity of God's punishments were terrific and, in human relationships, he sometimes found in violent and crooked men admirable qualities that no merely "idyllic and sweet nature," as Renan described Jesus, would have found there. He drew a lesson from an unscrupulous steward, who stole his employer's money to make friends with, and he commented: "The sons of this world are wiser in their own generation than the sons of light."[66] He drew another lesson from a domineering slaveowner who worked his servants to the limit, and then did not thank them.[67] He drew lessons from shrewd investors of capital.[68] Obviously this does not mean that he approved financial dishonesty in the steward, ungrateful tyranny in the slaveowner, or the inequities of economic greed; and if from binding a strong man and plundering his house, he could draw a lesson without approving burglary, it is clear that he could picture a wise king counting the cost of a military campaign, without approving war.

Nevertheless, Jesus was the kind of character that militant nationalists might easily have been drawn to. He had soldierly qualities in him. He met a Roman centurion once and each recognized kinship with the other. Jesus acclaimed the centurion's faith, and the centurion, feeling Jesus' "authority," said that he too was a man "with soldiers under me; and I say to one, 'Go,' and he goes, and to another, 'Come,' and he comes, and to my slave, 'Do this,' and he does it."[69] No wonder the insurrectionists hoped that Jesus might be the leader of their revolt!

As for us moderns, Mahatma Gandhi should help us to understand Jesus. Gandhi's powerful leadership swayed millions of followers and upon his will time and again hung the success or failure of Great Britain's imperial policies. He had courage and daring, a fearlessness of danger and death, that any soldier might envy. Yet with indefatigable persistence he held to his nonviolent course, refusing militant revolt, and depending solely on the might and pressure of spiritual forces. Of all the paradoxical combinations of opposing qualities in Jesus' character—self-fulfillment and self-denial, explosive enthusiam and serenity, fierce indignation and compassionate gentleness, consciousness of divine mission and profound humility—none is more amazing than this conjunction of qualities that make a great soldier with those that make a great pacifist.

One favorite method of evading the full force and meaning of Jesus' love-ethic is to say that he meant it to apply not to national policy but only to personal relationships. All the available evidence, however, contradicts that. Indeed, in the realm of personal relationships the problem concerning Jesus' probable application of his love-ethic becomes most difficult. What if, in his presence, one of the little children whom he took in his arms and blessed were viciously attacked? Would he have stood passively by, offering no forceful resistance? The supposition that by restricting the application of Jesus' ethic to personal relationships one makes it easier to practice is insupportable. As for the evidence in the Gospels, one thing is certain: he did apply his ethic to national policy. He was out and out against the Zealots and all their ways. He was their "lost leader," and in the end they hated him.

[208]

The issue turned out to be one of the strangest paradoxes in history: Jesus who so stood out against insurrection was cruci- fied as an insurrectionist. Many motives entered into the hostility which beset him that last week in Jerusalem. Early in his ministry, so Mark tells us, when crowds thronged about him in Galilee, scribes came from Jerusalem to investigate, and their fear and dislike were summed up in the worst thing they could think of saying: "He is possessed by Beelzebub."[70] From that day to the end the hostility of the rulers in the capital accumulated against Jesus, but his liquidation could not be finally achieved on religious grounds. That the Jews had been completely deprived of the right to impose the death penalty is improbable, but apparently there were limitations on that right under Roman rule.[71] At any rate, Jesus' Jewish enemies did not wish to assume the responsibility of executing him, and the Gospels make plain the reason. He was too popular. They "feared the people." Let the Romans bear the burden of resentment against his liquidation! If the Romans would execute him as a disturber of the peace, that would gain the desired end at minimum cost.

Then Jesus entered Jerusalem amid clamoring crowds and cleansed the temple. In explaining the reason for this act, Christian writers have commonly pictured the situation in the temple courts as outrageous, with the money-changers and the merchants who sold sacrificial birds and beasts fleecing pious pilgrims—a monstrous system of graft whose profits enriched the priests. The fact is, however, that much can be said in defense of the general arrangements which had been set up. The coinage of that day was notoriously unregulated; the real value of the money which pilgrims carried varied with the lands they came from; there was good reason why the authorities in

Jerusalem had ruled that before it could be used for paying the tax or making purchases in the temple, all money must be exchanged by experts into the Tyrian currency which was comparatively reliable.[72] As for birds and beasts for sacrifice, it was a public convenience to have the market organized and made easily available within the temple compound.

Nevertheless, the situation was one which readily got out of hand. The opportunity for crooked dealing was too obvious. The rate of exchange could easily be rigged in the interest of profits; and since all birds and beasts for sacrifice had to be passed by an official censor it was simple to force buyers to purchase from official merchants, and then simple for them to demand a price above the general market. Soon after the time of Jesus, Rabbi Shimeon ben Gamaliel protested vigorously against excessive charges for sacrificial birds.[73] That this factor was, in part, a cause of Jesus' act is evident. All three synoptic Gospels quote his charge that the temple courts had been made "a den of robbers."[74] His shame at the irreverent lengths to which the commercialism of the temple precincts had gone is evident too, so that "he would not allow any one to carry anything through the temple."[75]

As for the act itself, by which Jesus singlehanded stopped the traffic, the bias of interpreters has commonly made of it whatever prejudice desired, from aggressive violence comparable with war to an exhibition of spiritual power that made physical force needless. The facts, however, do not seem difficult to come at. The "whip of cords," of which so much is frequently made, is unknown to Mark, Matthew and Luke, appearing only in John's Gospel, and there so spoken of that its use in driving out "the sheep and oxen" is a natural interpretation.[76] That Jesus used force, however, is evident in all the Gospels. "He overturned the tables of the money-changers and the seats of those who sold pigeons," say Mark and Matthew; and Luke says that "he began to drive out those who sold."[77] The decisive factor, however, surely lay in Jesus' popular support. The crowd was with him. They too resented the graft of which they were the victims, so that when the chief priests and the scribes, hearing of Jesus' act, "sought a way to destroy him; . . . they feared him, because all the multitude was astonished at his teaching," or as Luke puts it, "all the people hung upon his words."[78] Without this popular backing what Jesus did, overturning the tables and driving out the hucksters and the beasts, would have proved a futile gesture, immediately and forcefully suppressed.

The cleansing of the temple gave "the chief priests and the scribes and the elders" the chance for which they had waited. Here was an overt act of insubordination. Now the charge against Jesus could be shifted from religious heresy to political subversion. He was stirring up the people.[79] He was a peril to public order, regarded by others and, it might be, regarding himself as the Messiah. If he went unstopped, he would set himself up as "king of the Jews." At first the conspirators against him intended to postpone the final stroke until after Passover. "And the chief priests and the scribes were seeking how to arrest him by stealth, and kill him; for they said, 'Not during the feast, lest there be a tumult of the people.' "[80] As their plans gathered momentum, however, they changed their minds, and events moved swiftly—the bribery of Judas, the secret arrest of Jesus in the garden, when the crowd was absent, the extralegal informal hearing in the high priest's house where Jesus acknowledged his messiahship, and then the trial before the Roman Procurator, with concocted accusations hurled at him—"We found this man perverting our nation, and forbidding us to give tribute to Caesar, and saying that he himself is Christ a king"[81]—while the hirelings and hangers-on, whom the priests had gathered, cried, as they had been told to cry, "Crucify him!" and, if John's Gospel be correct, even shouted, "We have no king but Caesar."[82]

That Jesus was executed as a political offender is certain. The Gospels so record the matter although the Christian churches, when the Gospels were written, would naturally have wished to suppress the fact. Few things were more practically important to the churches of the Empire during the latter half of the first century than to make clear to the authorities the political harmlessness of Christianity. The influence of this motive is obvious in the New Testament.[83] Luke, for example, as any reader of the Book of Acts can see, is strongly moved by it, even to the point of omitting all mention of Paul's execution at Rome. As for Jesus' trial before the Roman Procurator, Mark's picture of Pilate's desire to release him—"Why, what evil has he done?"[84]—is expanded by Luke, as thrice the Procurator, appealing against Jesus' accusers, seeks his liberation, and in an effort to escape responsibility even sends him to Herod. Matthew even records that Pilate took water and washed his hands before the crowd, saying, "I am innocent of this man's blood; see to it yourselves."[85]

This picture of Pilate, devoted to justice, conscientiously sensitive, and reluctant to order an execution is so widely at variance from all the evidence we have about his character[86] that scholars naturally question it. How, for example, could Mark have so intimately known Pilate's mind, that he could say, "He perceived that it was out of envy that the chief priests had delivered him up"?[87] And did Luke have firsthand witnesses to substantiate the story, which he alone relates, of Herod's exoneration of Jesus, and of Pilate's words: "You brought me this man as one who was perverting the people;

and after examining him before you, behold, I did not find this man guilty of any of your charges against him; neither did Herod, for he sent him back to us. Behold, nothing deserving death has been done by him; I will therefore chastize him and release him"?[88]

Whatever Pilate's attitude may have been, the urgent desire of the Gospel writers to represent him as finding no evil in Jesus and as desiring to release him as harmless to the state, is obvious. All the more the fact stands clearly out that, wishing as they did to make the charge of sedition seem false even in the Procurator's eyes, the Gospel writers could not and did not obscure the central fact: Jesus finally was executed by the Romans as a political criminal, with the offensive charge nailed to his very cross, "The King of the Jews."

So the great pacifist was crucified as a criminal insurrectionist. Some who passed by, while he was on the cross, "derided him, wagging their heads," we read, and "so also the chief priests mocked him."[89] One wonders if any "daggermen" were also there, and if they felt the irony of crucifying as a dangerous revolutionist one who so stoutly had withstood the war they wanted, and had so disappointed their hopes of his militant leadership. Were they there, they too must have "derided him, wagging their heads."

CHAPTER IX

As Jews With a World-wide Outlook Saw Him

A COMMON supposition is that Jesus' personal ministry was carried on within an exclusively Palestinian Jewish setting, and that only after the crucifixion did his movement come into contact with the larger currents of the world's thought and life.

Palestine itself, however, was far from being an isolated Jewish province. From the days of the Syrian Greeks in the third century B.C., the Hellenistic world had both surrounded and penetrated Palestine—so much so that the Maccabean revolt in particular and the Pharisaic party in general are to be explained as measures of resistance against the Hellenization of the Jewish people. In Jesus' day Palestine was set in a matrix of Graeco-Roman cities. Syria to the north; the coast cities along the Mediterranean such as Joppa, Caesarea, Tyre and Sidon; Transjordania, as the ruins of temples and theatres in such towns as Jerash and Amman still show, were all predominantly influenced by Hellenistic culture.

Moreover, within Palestine itself some areas apparently were so Gentile in population as to be out-of-bounds for stricter Jews. When Jesus, sending his disciples on their first mission, said, "Go nowhere among the Gentiles, and enter no town of the Samaritans,"[1] the implication seems plain that

[214]

there were recognized Gentile districts in Palestine—Tiberias and Taricheae, for example, cities on the Sea of Galilee, Scythopolis south of the Sea, and Sepphoris just north of Nazareth.

Galilee, thus surrounded by and infiltrated with Hellenistic influence, was certainly in some degree bilingual. Business could hardly have been carried on around the Sea of Galilee without the use of Greek. Some fifty years ago, in his *Historical Geography of the Holy Land*, George Adam Smith, perceiving that "Galilee was on the road to everywhere," confronted facts which since have been expanded, confirmed and emphasized: "The many roads which crossed Galilee from the Decapolis to the coast, the many inscriptions upon them, the constant trade between the fishermen and the Greek exporters of their fish, the very coins—everywhere thrust Greek upon the Jews of Galilee. The Aramaic dialect began now to be full of Greek words. It is impossible to believe that our Lord and His disciples did not know Greek."[2] Indeed, two of the disciples, Philip and Andrew, had Greek names; and to suppose that Matthew could have been a tax collector on the Sea of Galilee without understanding Greek seems incredible.

Moveover, Jerusalem too must have been bilingual. The most thorough study yet made of the use of Greek in ancient Palestine concludes: "The degree of a person's Hellenistic culture depended on his social standing. Probably the upper class knew Greek literature, the middle class was less conversant with it, while the knowledge of the lower class was limited to the vernacular only."[3] This seems to be confirmed by the fact that when Paul, under arrest in Jerusalem, addressed the crowd in front of the Roman barracks, they, thinking he might be an Egyptian, expected him to speak in Greek, and "when they heard that he addressed them in the Hebrew language, they were the more quiet."[4] Certainly the ruling elders in

Jerusalem needed Greek in dealing with Roman authorities. Of Rabban Gamaliel it was said, "Permission was given to the house of Rabban Gamaliel to teach their children Greek, owing to their relation with the [Roman] government." Rabbi Simeon, Gamaliel's son, even wrote, "There were a thousand pupils in my father's house; five hundred studied Torah and five hundred studied Greek Wisdom." And Simeon's son, Rabbi Juda Hanassi went further, saying, "Why speak Syriac in Palestine? Talk either Hebrew or Greek."[5]

This infiltration of Hellenistic influence into Palestinian Jewry was powerfully accentuated by the Jews of the dispersion. From Babylonia to Rome and beyond, Jews, either as forcibly displaced persons or as voluntary emigrants, had established themselves, especially in the great cities. In the time of Philo, Jesus' contemporary, Jews in Egypt were said to number a million, and Alexandria was so important a center of Jewish learning and influence that one Palestinian rabbi called it a "sister" of Jerusalem.[6] Doubtless many of these dispersed Jews fell away and were assimilated, but the tenacity with which the overwhelming number of them held to their faith and remained a distinct people is the real marvel. Nevertheless, they necessarily accommodated themselves to the Graeco-Roman world. In Egypt they so largely lost knowledge of Hebrew that the Scriptures were translated into Greek for use in the synagogues. Philo's words give a contemporary picture of the situation in Jesus' day: "No one country can contain the whole Jewish nation, by reason of its populousness; on which account they frequent all the most prosperous and fertile countries of Europe and Asia, whether islands or continents, looking indeed upon the holy city as their *metropolis* in which is erected the sacred temple of the Most High God, but accounting those regions which have been occupied by their fathers and grandfathers and great-grandfathers and still more remote ancestors, in which they have been born and brought up, as their country."[7]

That these Jews of the diaspora, though living as they often did in segregated communities, were profoundly affected by Graeco-Roman culture was inevitable. Not only in such matters as language, fashions and customs, recreations, tastes in literature and the drama, and methods in education, but in basic philosophical religious ideas, Hellenism invaded Judaism. Philo remained a loyal Jew, but the major presuppositions of his philosophy must be explained in the light of Greek thought. Though the statement is too condensed to be adequate, the fact is that Philo commonly thought as a Hellenistic philosopher and then deduced his Greek ideas by allegory from the Hebrew Scriptures.

These Hellenistic Jews of the diaspora have generally been set in sharp contrast with the strict, old-fashioned Jews of Palestine, but this distinction, while justified, can easily be exaggerated. From all over the Roman world multitudes of Jews came on pilgrimage to their holy city. Alike for financial reasons, since these pilgrims were one of the main supports of the city and the temple, and for religious motives—the maintenance of loyal faith and practice among the dispersed Jews—this and every other means of close relationship between Palestinian Jewry and the diaspora were cultivated. Hellenistic Judaism was no stranger in Palestine; Jesus must have encountered it. Early in the history of the first church in Jerusalem, "The Hellenists murmured against the Hebrews because their widows were neglected in the daily distribution."[8] These Hellenists were Jews from the Gentile world, or possibly Jewish proselytes, now Christianized, who were at home in Jerusalem, and who certainly had not all come there in the few months since Jesus died. There was, indeed, at least one Greek-speaking synagogue in the holy city—"The synagogue of the Freedman (as it was called), and of the Cyrenians, and of the Alexandrians, and of those from Cilicia and Asia."[9] The milieu in which Jesus worked was far more cosmopolitan than has generally been supposed.

Even in its central citadel Judaism had never been impervious to foreign influence. The orthodox Jewish angelology and demonology of Jesus' time had come mainly from Persia, and, as for the Essenes, "Pythagorism, Orphism, Chaldean astral religion, Parsiism and, apparently, even Buddhism all contributed ingredients much transformed on their way to the Jordan Valley."[10] The idea of a capsuled Palestinian Judaism unaffected by the world's life and thought is a myth. Some of the most important and most popular Jewish writings in the first century were from the diaspora and were deeply impregnated with Greek thought. As for Jesus himself, Dr. Klausner concludes that the reason why he "tended to set aside the ceremonial laws," was "because he had become influenced by Hellenistic Judaism through the medium of the Palestinian apocalypses."[11]

The passage in John's Gospel where "some Greeks," pilgrims at the temple festival, come to Philip, saying, "Sir, we wish to see Jesus,"[12] has been usually interpreted as representing a later situation—the Gentile world becoming the object of Christianity's mission—read back into the days of Jesus. Such may well have been the motive of this passage in John's Gospel, but in the story itself there is nothing inconsistent with the known situation in Palestine.

Jesus, while facing the narrower type of traditional Palestinian Judaism, faced, as well, the wider outlook of Hellenistic Judaism, and to suppose, as some critics hold, that words such

as, "The field is the world," could not have been his, seems
unwarranted. Putting ourselves into the place of these Jews at
home in the wider world outside Palestine, we may well ask
what they saw in him.

Jesus' views, in some important regards, were close of kin
with the more liberal outlooks of Hellenistic Judaism. The attitude of the dispersed Jews toward the Gentile world had not
been merely enmity, accommodation or self-defense. Active
proselytism had become a major concern of faithful Jews. The
ethical monotheism of the synagogue attracted many thoughtful Gentile minds, and the evidence makes clear the eagerness
with which the Judaism of the diaspora sought converts and
the success with which they were won.

This endeavor to present Judaism persuasively to Gentiles in
the Graeco-Roman world led necessarily to a rethinking of
Jewish requirements. What was essential Judaism? Were ethical monotheism and the moral law enough? How far were the
ceremonial demands of the old tradition, such as circumcision
and the observance of Kosher rules, necessary? The answers to
such questions were not unanimous. To some Jews Gentiles
were enemies of God and of his people, doomed to extermina-
tion in this world and without hope in the next; to others they
were children of the one universal God, and to teach them the
true religion and win them to its acceptance was Israel's duty
and glory. In this second group, with its evangelistic zeal, there
was a natural tendency to stress the major rather than the
minor differences between Judaism and paganism, emphasiz-
ing Jewish monotheism and its moral law, and wherever possible simplifying its ritualistic and legalistic demands. This
tendency can be exaggerated. Philo makes it clear, for example, that by "proselyte," he means one who has made a

clean break with all non-Jewish religious affiliations, has accepted fully the Jewish people as his own, and is prepared to respect its customs and to observe its basic laws. Nevertheless proselytism naturally stressed the weightier as over against the lesser matters of the law.

When Paul, after spirited debate with the stricter sort, won from the first church in Jerusalem the reduction of ceremonial requirements to abstention "from what has been sacrificed to idols and from blood and from what is strangled and from unchastity,"[13] and when as a Christian evangelist he went on his mission requiring "no greater burden than these necessary things," it has been commonly supposed that this sort of compromise was new in Judaism. Such accommodation, however, was not unfamiliar to liberal Hellenized Jews. How far such liberalism went among Jewish propagandists, facing the crucial issue of monotheism against polytheism, is evidenced even in Palestinian rabbis, saying that to reject idolatry is to acknowledge the whole Jewish law.[14]

Such liberality explains the wide divergence of opinion among Palestinian Pharisees with regard to the growing number of Gentile proselytes and near-proselytes of many sorts. In Jesus' time Rabbi Shammai's school would have no commerce with any so-called convert who was not prepared to acknowledge and obey the whole traditional law of Israel. Rabbi Hillel's school, however, was more tolerant, following their master's motto: "Be one of the disciples of Aaron, a lover of peace, following after peace, loving all mankind, and drawing them to the law."[15] This difference of attitude runs on into the Talmudic period. There, on one side, was pride in the success of Jewish propaganda among the Gentiles and in great figures such as Rabbi Akiba and Rabbi Meir, who were said to be of proselyte ancestry, and on the other side such bitter sayings as that of Rabbi Helbo that proselytes—presumably those won by liberal policies—were as troublesome to Israel as a poisonous eruption is to the body.[16]

Was it not this latter attitude which the Gospel writer had in mind when he represented Jesus as saying "Woe to you, scribes and Pharisees, hypocrites! for you traverse sea and land to make a single proselyte, and when he becomes a proselyte, you make him twice as much a child of hell as yourselves"?[17] This harsh accusation was relevant to those who, like the rabbis of Shammai's school, made acceptance of all the legalistic minutiae which Jesus discarded a *sine qua non* of any Gentile's conversion. Such Pharisees, as Jesus said, "shut the kingdom of heaven against men."

There was another kind of Pharisee, however, whose main concern was for the far-flung body of the Jewish people across the empire, and for the Gentiles who were being drawn into their fellowship. At no point is the distinction between Sadducees and Pharisees more clear than in this regard. The Sadducees were tied to the Jewish state and temple; if collaboration with Rome would help sustain even the semi-independence of the state, they were collaborationists; when war at last broke out and the state was threatened with destruction, they fought with the Zealots to preserve it; and when at last the state and temple fell, the Sadducees were finished and passed out of history. The concern of the Pharisees, however, was centered in the law, and wherever in the whole world the law was honored and obeyed they saw the hope of Israel. When, therefore, the state and temple fell, the Pharisees, far from being finished, began their greatest era of influence. In this regard, as in others, Jesus was on the Pharisee's side, his religion resting not upon transient Jewish nationalism and temple sacrifice, but upon the deep bases of ethical monotheism and the law. "The liberal party, which was strong among the Hellenistic Jews, and had influential support even in Palestine," writes G. H. Box, "was willing to divest Judaism of its accidental elements and to insist upon essentials—the profession of faith in one God, the observance of the Sabbath-rest, and the abjuration of idolatry in all its forms as well as its immoral accompaniments. In a word, all that it insisted upon was ethical monotheism."[18]

The possible relationship of Jesus with such Jews, whose attitude was so akin to his, is naturally suggested. At Pentecost, almost immediately after Jesus had gone, the audience which was reported to have heard the disciples preach in Jerusalem contained "Parthians and Medes and Elamites and residents of Mesopotamia, Judea and Cappadocia, Pontus and Asia, Phrygia and Pamphylia, Egypt and the parts of Libya belonging to Cyrene, and visitors from Rome, both Jews and proselytes, Cretans and Arabians."[19] Can it be that Jesus never met such varied folk from the ends of the known world who flocked to Jerusalem for the festivals, or that his thought never reached out to face their problems? The sharp break commonly posited between the exclusively Palestinian ministry of Jesus and the almost immediate Hellenization of the Christian movement after he had gone is difficult to imagine. Jesus could not have been so isolated from the major currents in his people's life and thought. The problem of Judaism's universality and of the terms on which it could be realized was one of the most urgent religious questions discussed in Palestine, and liberal Hellenistic Jews, hearing Jesus, must have recognized in his teaching an endeavor to state the core of their religion in universal terms.

Nevertheless, this point of view faces difficulties and Matthew, most Jewish of the Gospels, presents them in full force.

As the record stands, we confront an apparent contradiction: Jesus limited his mission to Jews only, and yet Jesus had a world vision, his aim to "make disciples of all nations,"[20] and in him Isaiah's prophecy was fulfilled, "in his name will the Gentiles hope."[21] Matthew alone quotes Jesus as saying to the twelve, "Go nowhere among the Gentiles, and enter no town of the Samaritans, but go rather to the lost sheep of the house of Israel."[22] Matthew alone records the saying, "I was sent only to the lost sheep of the house of Israel."[23] In Matthew only does Jesus say that "not an iota, not a dot, will pass from the law until all is accomplished."[24] Matthew's insistence on Jesus' Jewishness is unmistakable, but apparently with no sense of inconsistency Matthew also stresses his universalism.

Praising a Roman centurion, Jesus says, according to Matthew, "I tell you, many will come from east and west and sit at table with Abraham, Isaac, and Jacob in the kingdom of heaven."[25] Condemning the Jews as faithless tenants of God's vineyard, Jesus represents God as saying to them, "I tell you, the kingdom of God will be taken away from you and given to a nation producing the fruits of it."[26] Matthew quotes Jesus as saying to his disciples: "You are the light of the world";[27] "The field is the world";[28] "This gospel of the kingdom will be preached throughout the whole world, as a testimony to all nations."[29]

That this conflict in Matthew's Gospel between the restricted Jewishness of Jesus and his universalism reflects the later conflict in the church between the Jewish legalists and men like Paul seems certain. That Matthew's record represents the historic fact in one regard—that Jesus first offered his gospel to the Jews, that he thought of his mission as the preparation of his own people for the world-wide kingdom's coming, and that only after their rejection of him did his movement turn to the Gentiles—seems likewise certain. Behind these explanations, however, does not the record reflect a real conflict in the mind of Jesus himself? Grant him the most universal outlook conceivable, he still had to begin with the Jews. There only could he find rootage for his message. Moreover, he was himself deeply, sincerely, loyally a Jew, and through Judaism only did he see hope of God's grace coming to the world. He may well have said everything he is quoted as saying to his disciples concerning the limitation of their first preaching missions.

Nevertheless, to stress his early concentration on gaining a foothold among his immediate fellow countrymen in such a manner as to obscure his world-wide outlook is to lose the large perspective of his mission. To be sure, he conceived himself as sent to "the lost sheep of the house of Israel," but those "lost sheep" for the most part did not live in Palestine. They were scattered over the whole known world, speaking Greek, reading their Scriptures in Greek, in cities like Alexandria conducting their synagogue services in Greek, and by hundreds of thousands, as pilgrims to the holy festivals, they thronged through Palestine, had at least one synagogue of their own in Jerusalem itself, and through their writings profoundly influenced the thought of Israel. To suppose that Jesus did not have them in mind seems incredible.

Universalism was in the great tradition of the Jewish people. In books like Ruth and Jonah, in prophets from Amos saying, "Are ye not as the children of the Ethiopians unto me, O children of Israel? Have not I brought up Israel out of the land of Egypt, and the Philistines from Caphtor, and the Syrians from Kir?"[30] to the Isaiah of the Exile saying, "I will also give thee for a light to the Gentiles, that thou mayest be my salvation unto the end of the earth,"[31] Hebrew thought at its noblest had long been world-wide in its outlook. To picture Jesus as unacquainted with this or as rejecting it is unwarranted. That the later church, when the Gospels were written, when Christians were increasingly Gentile by birth and nurture, may have played up Jesus' universalism, adding new expressions to it, such as the postresurrection commission with its trinitarian formula, only with difficulty imaginable on Jesus' lips,[32] may be taken for granted. That he himself had the world in his mind, however, and that liberal Jews with a world-wide outlook found in him a kindred spirit and even during his personal ministry were attracted to his movement is the most natural explanation of the facts. The rise of Christianity from the very beginning must be explained not by reactionary Jews who rejected Jesus but by the more liberal Jews who accepted him.

This need not and should not be interpreted to mean that Jesus foresaw and commanded the early church's world-wide mission to the Gentiles. To ascribe the postresurrection words of Christ, "Go therefore and make disciples of all nations," to the historic Jesus runs counter to the attitude of Jesus himself as plainly set forth in the Gospels. To his disciples, starting on a preaching mission to their fellow countrymen, Jesus said: "You will not have gone through all the towns of Israel, before the Son of man comes."[33] Some think that this truly represents Jesus' very foreshortened view of the future at the beginning, and that he gradually changed his mind, saying later, "There are some standing here who will not taste death before they see the Son of man coming in his kingdom,"[34] and later still, "But of that day and hour no one knows, not even the angels of heaven, nor the Son, but the Father only."[35] In any case, not the long-drawn-out missionary campaign of the churches to all nations but the swift coming of the kingdom was in Jesus' mind.

It is an anachronism, therefore, to make the words "universalism" and "particularism" mean in Jesus' time what they mean to moderns now. He was both a "particularist" and a "universalist"—a loyal Jew who could even picture his twelve disciples, in the day of his coming glory, sitting "on twelve thrones, judging the twelve tribes of Israel,"[36] and at the same time an interpreter of Judaism in terms so basically human and inclusive that they were universally applicable to all mankind. The early churches were not essentially mistaken in claiming the authority of Jesus for their international, interracial mission. He almost certainly did not foresee that outcome, but he prepared the way for it. In a profound sense he universalized Judaism.

The weightiest evidence for Jesus' world-wide outlook is to be found in the essential nature of his teaching, but the incidental evidence also is so plentiful that to eliminate it would tear the gospel record to shreds. The Samaritans were special objects of disdain among stricter Jews, so that John's picture of the Pharisees, denouncing Jesus as insultingly as possible, and saying, "You are a Samaritan and have a demon,"[37] may be taken as typical. One sacred book of Jesus' time called the Samaritans, "the foolish people that live in Shechem."[38] Jesus, however, made a good Samaritan his hero, in contrast with a priest and a Levite.[39] Not postponed to the Pauline churches but in Jesus himself began the liberal outlook which Paul expressed—"When Gentiles who have not the law do by nature what the law requires, they are a law to themselves,

[226]

even though they do not have the law. They show that what the law requires is written on their hearts."[40]

In his references to the scriptures Jesus' interest in Gentiles is notable. He had pondered on Jonah's preaching to the Ninevites, on Solomon's influence on the Queen of Sheba,[41] on Elijah's service to the widow of Zarephath, on Elisha's healing of Naaman the Syrian,[42] and on Tyre, Sidon and even Sodom as having more chance in the day of judgment than Bethsaida and Capernaum.[43] That Jesus should have found in a Roman centurion more faith than he had found in Israel[44] is a single incident but it is revealing—no racial or national lines confined his appreciation and care. If John the Baptist could cry, "Do not presume to say to yourselves, 'We have Abraham as our father'; for I tell you, God is able from these stones to raise up children to Abraham,"[45] why should it be doubted that Jesus said, "I tell you, many will come from east and west and sit at table with Abraham, Isaac, and Jacob in the kingdom of heaven"?[46] If Isaiah represented God as saying, "My house shall be called a house of prayer for all peoples,"[47] why should it be doubted that Jesus quoted and enforced it?[48]

To be sure, Jesus was critical of Gentiles and their way of life: "In praying do not heap up empty phrases as the Gentiles do";[49] "And if you salute only your brethren, what more are you doing than others? Do not even the Gentiles do the same?"[50] "You know that those who are supposed to rule over the Gentiles lord it over them. . . . But it shall not be so among you."[51] Taken in conjunction with all the other evidence, however, such passages reveal in Jesus' thought not so much prejudice against Gentiles as awareness of them, interest in them, concern about them. Not Jews only but Gentiles were in the center of his attention.

Indeed, while he may have told his disciples on their first preaching mission not to approach Gentiles, he himself continually did approach them and was approached by them. If any area within Jesus' reach was thoroughly Gentile it was the Decapolis—ten Greek cities southeast of the Sea of Galilee—but Matthew tells us that "great crowds followed him from Galilee and the Decapolis,"[52] and Luke adds from "the seacoast of Tyre and Sidon."[53] Mark even describes a journey Jesus himself took into the Decapolis and his healing there.[54] The more the evidence is canvassed, the more clearly impossible it becomes to doubt Jesus' acquaintance with all sorts and conditions of people, Jews and Gentiles, and with the problems which they faced, especially the problem of universalism as against the narrower type of Judaism.

That he himself was troubled by the conflict between universalism and the endeavor to initiate his movement within Judaism, is evidenced in one of the most puzzling narratives in the Gospels:

And from there he arose and went away to the region of Tyre and Sidon. And he entered a house, and would not have any one know it; yet he could not be hid. But immediately a woman, whose little daughter was possessed by an unclean spirit, heard of him, and came and fell down at his feet. Now the woman was a Greek, a Syrophoenician by race. And she begged him to cast the demon out of her daughter. And he said to her, "Let the children first be fed, for it is not right to take the children's bread and throw it to the dogs." But she answered him, "Yes, Lord; yet even the dogs under the table eat the children's crumbs." And he said to her, "For this saying you may go your way; the demon has left your daughter." And she went home, and found the child lying in bed, and the demon gone.[55]

That Jesus thus called Jews children and non-Jews dogs—even though the word used means pet dogs—is so shocking and so inconsistent with the portrait of him in the Gospels that scholars have been tempted to suppose that Jesus has been misquoted. Some think that one of the disciples used the harsh comparison in the same spirit in which they tried to keep those who brought children to Jesus from bothering him—and that the words were mistakenly attributed to Jesus. Others think that the Syrophoenician woman herself, playfully urging her appeal, first claimed the right of the family's dogs to the children's crumbs, and that Jesus took up her words and made use of them, while all the time intending to help her. Others suppose that Jesus used the words, as he is quoted, not as an expression of his own opinion, but as a caricature of the orthodox Jewish attitude, which he discarded in helpfulness and friendliness to the woman.[56] These are only guesses whose chief value is to indicate that, if we had the whole conversation instead of the condensed narrative in the Gospels, its meaning might be clarified.

The historic setting of the narrative is of utmost importance in its interpretation. Jesus had so aroused the hostility of Herod that, facing the probability of John the Baptist's fate, he had fled from Galilee to the coasts of Tyre and Sidon. His public ministry was confronting failure; he himself in danger of death was turning to his one hope—the training of his disciples. He fled from Galilee to Phoenicia to escape publicity, and there "He entered a house, and would not have anyone know it." Even in that pagan land, however, he "could not be hid." This beseeching woman wanted him to begin there the same process that had brought the crowds swarming around him in Galilee. If he could not go on with that kind of ministry among his own people, how could he do it for the Phoenicians? He may well have been distraught, and out of his inner struggle may have come the comparison set in the picturesque speech always characteristic of him, which, put bluntly in our abbreviated record, sounds so unlike him. At any rate, whatever he said to the woman, she did not feel as badly about it as we do. Far from feeling insulted, she made a humorous answer, that brought the help she sought. Moreover, Mark and Matthew in preserving the story must have thought of it as an argument not against but in favor of the Gentile mission, for Jesus did heal the woman's daughter.

To set Jesus' universalism over against his Judaism betrays misunderstanding of what the world of Jesus' day was like and of what liberal Judaism was thinking. The Roman Empire had achieved among the nations such a degree of unity that the Stoics said, "The world is one city." To his own kind of world view Jesus came, not despite the kind of world he lived in, but as a sharer in it and in the best thinking of his people who were scattered all over it. He never doubted the primacy of Judaism in God's revelation of himself and in God's purpose for the world. No more did the New Testament churches doubt it, and whether in Pauline or Johannine thought, it still was true that "salvation is from the Jews."[57] Nevertheless, this salvation was for the whole of mankind. It was *through* Judaism that Jesus reached his conviction that "the field is the world."

His Jewish monotheism involved it. From the eighth century prophets on, the greatest of the Hebrew seers, believing in one God, had conceived of one world with all nations under the divine sovereignty and subject to the divine law. Monotheism among the Jews was not primarily speculative; it never dealt, as in modern times, with materialistic atheism as an alternative, but with polytheism; and as polytheism meant many peoples with many gods, so monotheism meant one world under one God. Let hatred and prejudice do their worst, and resentment against tyranny issue in bitter desire that the Gentiles should all perish, yet there were always those who could not escape the logic of monotheism. Among the books that almost certainly influenced Jesus was the *Testament of the Twelve Patriarchs*, in which the implications of faith in Israel's God were accepted and acclaimed: "He shall save Israel and all the Gentiles";[58] "The Lord shall reveal his salvation to all Gentiles";[59] "The Lord shall visit all Gentiles in his tender mercies forever";[60] The Gentiles shall be "multiplied in knowledge upon the earth and enlightened through the grace of the Lord."[61] Jews with such an outlook regarded the dispersion of their people across the world as providential, and heard God saying, "I will scatter this people among the Gentiles that they may do good to the Gentiles."[62]

That Jesus' God, therefore, was "Lord of heaven and earth,"[63] whose will was to be done "on earth as it is in heaven," and that his followers were to be the "salt of the earth" and the "light of the world," sprang directly from his Jewish heritage. Paul's logic was not a new discovery, revealed to him for the first time when he became a Christian, but was rooted in his spiritual tradition: "Is God the God of Jews only? Is he not the God of Gentiles also? Yes, of Gentiles also, since God is one."[64] To suppose that Paul saw this and that Jesus did not see it is incredible. Jesus was a universalist not despite his Judaism but because of it.

When Jesus, with this theological approach to his world view, dealt with God's ethical requirements, his universalism became even more evident. To the question, what does the "Lord of heaven and earth" require of men, Jesus gave an answer which only the more radical liberals, even among Hellenistic Jews, could have accepted. He described God's ethical demands in terms of righteousness so basic—sincerity, humility, self-sacrifice, inner rightness of spirit, and outward humaneness, all motivated by undiscourageable goodwill—that no racial or national lines had any relevance.

At the last judgment, said Jesus, one issue will decide the fate of men—have they fed the hungry, given drink to the thirsty, welcomed the stranger, clothed the naked, visited the sick and the inprisoned?[65] To meet this kind of requirement—to be a good Samaritan—involved nothing distinctively Jewish. A Gentile, redeemed to a right spirit, could aspire to this ideal and measure himself by this standard.

At this point also Jesus stood in the great tradition of the prophets. Had not Isaiah put ethical righteousness above all ceremonial, and had not Micah said: "What doth the Lord require of thee, but to do justly, and to love mercy, and to walk humbly with thy God?"[66] Priestly tradition and Pharisaic legalism, however, had supplemented these ethical demands of prophetic Judaism with a mass of requirements whose observance did make a Jew stand out as a Jew, distinct and unassimilable. Jesus himself conformed to many of these customary practices of his people. He was so fundamentally Jewish that Wellhausen could say, "Jesus was not a Christian; he was a Jew. He did not preach a new faith, but taught men to do the will of God; and, in his opinion, as also in that of the Jews, the will of God was to be found in the Law of Moses and in the other books of Scripture."[67] That Jesus tried his best to state his position thus in terms of the law's fulfillment instead of its abolition, and that he sought to work out his mission within the traditional culture of his people, seems clear. Was it not because of this that, after he had gone, two points of view clashed in the earliest church—one stressing Jesus' Jewishness and insisting that all Christians must be circumcised and obey all the law, and the other stressing Jesus' antilegalistic universalism? Both factors were in Jesus, their conflict necessarily unresolved while he was launching his movement in Palestine. When, however, Jesus stated the ethical requirements of God, as he saw them, he so dropped the legalistic and priestly specialties of Judaism, and so emphasized a kind of goodness to which racial and national distinctions were irrelevant that the stricter Pharisees could not miss seeing the peril with which he threatened them. He was universalizing ethics.

Men were to be humble and merciful, pure in heart and peacemakers, forgiving enemies and loving them, simple and sincere in speech and unostentatious in piety, generous without show, free from servitude to Mammon, finding life by sacrificially losing it, and so completely devoted to God's will that, having done their utmost, they still regarded themselves as "unworthy servants." Whatever one may think of such an ethic's practicability, it is certain that nothing exclusively Jewish characterizes it. Here, indeed, from the standpoint of the stricter Pharisees was the crux of Jesus' offending—he was opening the doors to the whole world on the basis of ethical monotheism and the moral law. Thus a modern Jewish scholar argues that the Jews could not have done otherwise than reject him: "A religion which possesses only a certain conception of God and a morality acceptable to *all* mankind, does not belong to any special nation, and, consciously or unconsciously, breaks down the barriers of nationality. This inevitably brought it to pass that his people, Israel, rejected him."[68]

Along with his monotheistic and ethical approach to universalism went Jesus' individualism. He cared for persons one by one, and his concern about them and desire to help them were stopped by no economic, national or racial lines. As in the case of the Roman centurion, or of the Samaritan leper, who alone of ten cured returned to thank him,[69] his ministry of healing knew no boundaries of race or nation. When little children came to him, is it conceivable that Jewish babes alone were welcomed and all others rejected?

Two major approaches to a cosmopolitan world view were in evidence in Jesus' day, as in our own: one, moving by way of overall, outward facts of political and economic interdependence to see the world as one, and the other so valuing persons, as persons, regardless of color, race or nationality that all personalities, wherever found, are equally regarded as worth living and dying for. How far the outward approach may have influenced Jesus none can tell, but that the inward approach, by way of care for individuals, led him to a universal outlook seems plain. Jesus' thought of every soul as infinitely precious in the sight of God was one of his incontestable characteristics. Adolf Harnack even said: "Jesus Christ was the first to bring the value of every human soul to light."[70]

Jesus made every profound matter which he touched intimately personal—companionship with God inward and secret, goodness a quality of the heart, moral decision an act of will from deep within the individual. As for right relationships between persons the family was Jesus' norm—God our Father, we his children, and therefore "all brethren"[71]—and a good family is the one social group we know where, no matter how many children there are, each has standing in his own right, each is loved for his own sake, each possesses distinct, inalienable worth and meaning. Jesus carried this care for individuals to a point where customary morality was shocked and ordinary commonsense rebelled. He saw value and possibility in most unlikely persons—a prodigal, an adulteress, a thieving tax collector, a beggar whose sores the dogs licked. There is joy in the presence of God, he said, over one such individual redeemed.

Such individualism is bound to have more than an individual consequence. If personality is in itself so valuable, racial and national lines must be overpassed in dealing with it. Souls, as such, are not Jewish, Gentile or Samaritan. The external approach to universalism lacks intensiveness; under its spell one cares for man but not for men. Mankind may thus be regarded as though it were one sea, the sea abiding, the waves transient. Such a world view has extension of outlook without intensity of meaning. To achieve a vital universalism involves beginning with the individual. If each person is a child of God, infinitely valuable, then all men everywhere must be that. If, however, the individual is nothing, E. F. Scott's dictum is inescapable, "Nothing may be multiplied by a hundred million, but it is still nothing."[72]

Jesus' universalism traveled the inward road. He cared for and helped persons regardless of racial, religious, economic or national lines. "Whoever" was one of his favorite words—thirty-six times in Matthew's Gospel it, or its equivalent, is reported in his sayings. "Every one then who hears these words of mine and does them will be like a wise man";[73] "Every one who acknowledges me before men, I also will acknowledge";[74] "Whoever gives to one of these little ones even a cup of cold water";[75] "Whoever does the will of my Father in heaven is my brother, and sister, and mother";[76] "Whoever would save his life will lose it, and whoever loses his life for my sake will find it";[77] "Whoever humbles himself like this child, he is the greatest in the kingdom of heaven";[78] "Whoever would be great among you must be your servant."[79] That means anybody. Color, caste, race, nation make no difference. It is human persons he is thinking of, individual souls anywhere and at any time.

Springing from his monotheism, from his idea of God's ethical demands, and from his care for individuals, Jesus' universalism was expressed in his conception of the kingdom. For a long generation now the phrase "kingdom of God"—or its equivalent, in accordance with Jewish usage, "kingdom of heaven"—has been given in modern thought a significance primarily sociological. It has been taken to mean a world-wide society, sometime in the future to arrive, utopian in its righteousness, brotherhood and peace. Present-day scholarship, however, has made clear this idea's inadequacy.

God's kingdom in the Gospels means primarily his sovereignty, and that is an eternal fact. He *is* sovereign now and forever. In its *initial* meaning the kingdom is not a new social order yet to come, not a redeemed political regime displacing the world's present empires, but an everlasting fact: "The Lord shall reign for ever and ever."[80] Acknowledged or unacknowledged, accepted by man or neglected and denied, this lordship of God is a fact.

The acceptance of the kingdom, therefore, is first of all personal. When, at his ministry's beginning Jesus faced the conflict in the world between God and Satan and, renouncing Satan, quoted Deuteronomy, "You shall worship the Lord your God, and him only shall you serve,"[81] he was acknowledging God's sovereignty, and as an ancient Jewish phrase put it, taking on himself the kingdom. When, at his ministry's end, he cried, "Not what I will, but what thou wilt,"[82] he was confirming with his willingness to die his acceptance of God as rightful sovereign.

While God's sovereignty, however, was thus an eternal fact,

its final fulfillment was yet to come. Someday this profound and in the end invincible truth of God's rightful kingship would be so asserted from on high and, whether voluntarily or forcibly, would be so accepted in the whole world, that God's will would be "done on earth as it is in heaven." From a messianic war to a superhuman Son of Man the imagination of the Jewish people canvassed the possibilities as to how God's victorious dominion would be finally achieved. Jesus surely did not think of the divine kingship as established by war, and how fully he shared any other picture of the kingdom's coming, current among his people, is now endlessly debated. Certainly he thought—at least in the early stages of his ministry—that it was coming soon.

Meanwhile—and, as his ministry continued, this apparently became more and more his emphasis—men and women could enter the kingdom now. The meaning of God's lordship, being an eternal fact, was not exhausted in its future consummation. Here and now it was operative in the world, and men and women, acknowledging it and loyal to it, could become "sons of the kingdom,"[83] and could be like leaven in the meal.[84] Though as inconspicuous as a grain of mustard seed,[85] the recognized sovereignty of God was nonetheless at work now. Wherever a victory over sin and evil was won the kingdom's presence was made evident: "If it is by the Spirit of God that I cast out demons, then the kingdom of God has come upon you."[86] However much this saying may have to be balanced by others, it certainly represents a major emphasis in Jesus' teaching. On the parchment discovered at Oxyrhynchus in Egypt Jesus is quoted as saying: "The kingdom of God is within you, and whoever knows himself will find it."[87] That this view of the present nature of God's sovereignty is not inconsistent with the apocalyptic view of its ultimate consummation is evident in

Paul who, thoroughly believing in apocalypticism, could also say: "The kingdom of God does not mean food and drink but righteousness and peace and joy in the Holy Spirit."[88]

Who, then, were qualified to enter the kingdom? Jesus' answers to that question reveal once more the universality of his idea of the divine requirements. Little children, with their trustfulness and humility—"to such belongs the kingdom of God."[89] Those who see that to love God and to love one's neighbor as one's self are "much more than all whole burnt offerings and sacrifices"—they are "not far from the kingdom of God."[90] "The poor in spirit"—"theirs is the kingdom of heaven."[91] He who "does the will" of God, instead of making pious professions only, "shall enter the kingdom of heaven."[92] Such souls are "sons of the kingdom" now, sown like seed in the world.[93] But those who serve Mammon and trust in riches, a camel can pass through a needle's eye more easily than they can "enter the kingdom of God."[94] As for those who, having put their hand to the plough, turn back when confronted with sacrifice, they are not "fit for the kingdom of God."[95]

Nothing whatever involving the legalism of the Pharisaic code or the ceremonialism of the temple is suggested as a requirement for entering the kingdom. The doors are open on terms that apply to all men and women everywhere who fulfill the conditions of ethical life and spiritual quality which Jesus lays down. Not from the later church's thinking, then, but from the essential nature of his own thinking came his admonition to all "workers of iniquity," that they would be cast out while "men will come from east and west, and from north and south, and sit at table in the kingdom of God."[96]

Had there been no receptive audience for such teaching, no good soil along with all the hard-packed, thorny, unresponsive ground for such seed to fall on, how can the consequence be explained? The earliest church we know had liberal elements in it, ready to reduce the law's requirements to the simplest terms and to proclaim a universal God and a universal ethic. Jesus' message took hold because some, at least, were prepared to understand it.

Stephen, the first Christian martyr,[97] is the kind of man whose opinion of Jesus we are trying to represent. He was almost certainly a Hellenistic Jew, well-known in the Greek-speaking synagogue in Jerusalem. He may well have seen, heard and even followed Jesus. According to an old tradition, noted by Epiphanius[98] in the fourth century, Stephen was one of the seventy disciples whom Jesus commissioned to preach,[99] and while this tradition deserves no credence, it may be true that Stephen had been won to Jesus' discipleship before the crucifixion. Certainly he dissociated himself from those who consented to the crucifixion as a "stiff-necked people, uncircumcised in heart and ears," who had "betrayed and murdered" the Christ.[100] Moreover, he understood Jesus very well and faced the enmity of the orthodox for the same reasons his Lord had faced it, accused of desire to "change the customs which Moses delivered to us," and of speaking "blasphemous words against Moses and God." Outspoken in his defense of the broader, deeper convictions of Jesus regarding the meaning of Judaism, he roused the enmity even of the Hellenistic synagogue and of Saul of Tarsus, still trying to be "a Pharisee of the Pharisees," and so died for his faith, praying as his Master had prayed, "Lord, do not hold this sin against them." Surely Stephen does not stand alone. Others, too, like him in breadth of outlook, must have recognized in Jesus their leader and their Lord.

[239]

That the stricter Pharisees had to reject him, or else surrender their whole system of thought and life, is obvious. That
there were Jews, however, often deeply influenced by Hellenistic thought, to whom his gospel brought personal liberation
and hope for the whole world seems obvious too.

Epilogue

WE HAVE not adequately described Jesus' contemporaries by classifying them, as we have done, and by noting each group's distinctive response to him. This approach, while clarifying the immediate circumstances which our Lord confronted, and throwing light upon the meaning of many of his words and deeds, may also obscure an important matter. These contemporaries were not simply members of special social and religious classes; they were first of all individual personalities with timeless spiritual needs. Analyzing the response of these contemporary groups to Jesus emphasizes the fact that he was a man of his own time, speaking to his own generation, but he has proved to be a man of all times, speaking to all generations. The reason for that goes back to depths in him and to timeless elements in his message, which these same contemporaries began discovering.

The ancient situation in Palestine, in whose matrix Jesus' ministry was set and whose traditions and ways of thinking conditioned the phrasing of his gospel, has long since been outgrown, but not Jesus himself. In one realm after another, such as war, racial relationships, economic justice, the best conscience of the world is haunted by the fact that he is ahead of us, an unattained goal. The relevance to modern need of what he believed and stood for becomes ever more apparent as powerful competing ideologies oppose it and, as for personal life, our timeless needs still find in him their abiding supply. This eternal factor in Christ and his gospel was present from the start. He appealed to profundities in human nature, which passing centuries and changing cultures do not affect. He did deal with the problems presented by current Phariseeism, legalism, nationalism, and even with special problems such as the Jewish system of divorce, but his solutions had the dimension of depth, so that they have carried over, their truth applicable to situations utterly different from first-century culture.

This timeless profundity in Jesus was felt by his first followers before it was defined. They were impressed by his "authority"; they exclaimed, "What is this? A new teaching!" They were sure he was a "prophet," speaking for God, and at last they used the most superlative patterns of thought in their possession to explain him. Putting ourselves in their places, we may surmise that this powerful impression of permanent greatness in Jesus dawned on them as they confronted the manner of his teaching, and then the substance of his teaching, and then the stature of the personality through whom the teaching came.

Jesus had a way of putting things that time does not wear out. He might have discussed neighborliness in the abstract, like a lawyer analyzing its obligations in terms of current practice. Had he done so, we probably should never have heard of it. Instead, he personified neighborliness in the good Samaritan, making him stand out in vivid contrast with the unneighborly priest and Levite, so that not only did his contemporaries grasp his meaning, but we do also. Personal incarnations have a perennial continuance in the understanding of the race. Abstract condemnations of economic greed have been both frequent and transient, but the rich man who "feasted sumptuously every day," while "a poor man named Lazarus, full of sores," begged at his gate has not been transient;[1] nor that other rich man who said to his soul, "Soul, you have ample goods laid up for many years; take your ease, eat, drink, be merry."[2] Such incarnations walk the streets of New York and London as plainly as they walked the streets of Jerusalem.

Two qualities in Jesus' manner of teaching are outstanding: the poignancy of its immediate appeal and its continuing pertinence to all men, always and everywhere. Arguments aplenty can be conjured up to excuse an unforgiving spirit when one has been wronged. The merciless steward, however, who, having been pardoned a vast debt, seized "one of his fellow servants . . . by the throat," crying, "Pay what you owe," and then, refusing his plea for patience, cast him into prison, is not easily escapable.[3] Jesus' first hearers felt that. His attack on their unwillingness to forgive was not argumentative, theoretical, abstract, but came at them in incarnate form, so forcefully personified that willy-nilly they had to make up their minds whether to be that merciless steward or not. This quality in Jesus' manner of teaching, moreover, has made all men everywhere his contemporaries. Still that merciless steward and many another character in Jesus' parables challenge our consciences.

Behind the manner of Jesus' teaching was its substance. Grant the transient, contemporary elements that necessarily entered into the Master's message, from small details reflecting current customs to prevalent ideas of Gehenna and expectations of the speedy coming of the messianic age, still the profound residue remains—truth applicable always and everywhere to man's deepest moral and spiritual needs.

The sovereignty of God with whom "all things are possible";[4] the sternness of God before whom no unrighteousness can stand; the fatherhood of God—"Your Father is merciful";[5] the availability of God's help—"If you then, who are evil, know how to give good gifts to your children, how much more will your Father who is in heaven give good things to those who ask him?"[6] the forgiveness of God—"There is joy before the angels of God over one sinner who repents":[7] with such basic ideas Jesus' teaching started. One wonders at first that his contemporaries, accustomed from youth to similar doctrines, should have found such teaching "new." But new it was. Jesus was so convinced of its truth, felt it so deeply, lived it so consistently, brought to it such fresh developments of meaning, that, when he spoke, the message became incarnate in him, novel, challenging, convincing. He did not argue about God; he revealed him. God walks through his teaching, whether as king, or as judge, or as a householder entrusting talents to his servants, or as a "Father who sees in secret,"[8] no abstraction, no hypothesis at the end of an argument, but a real Being from whose presence none can escape, in whose plenty all wants can be supplied, and to do whose will is man's glory. "His aim is not to make God an article of faith, but the object of faith," writes Dr. Manson. "We are often concerned to make God probable to men; he set out to make God real to them."[9]

Along with this basic substance of Jesus' teaching about God went his insight into eternal truths about human life. "A man's life does not consist in the abundance of his possessions";[10] "No one can serve two masters. . . . You cannot serve God and mammon";[11] "Which of you by being anxious can add one cubit to his span of life?"[12] "Whoever seeks to gain his life will lose it, but whoever loses his life will preserve it";[13] "Whoever humbles himself like this child, he is the greatest in the kingdom of heaven"[14]—such insights are timeless. As for his distinctively ethical teaching, what we have said about its relevance to all

[244]

races applies to its relevance to all generations. The framework of the Last Judgment, as Jesus pictured it—the Son of Man sitting on his "glorious throne" and, like a shepherd, parting sheep from goats—is local and contemporary, but its ethical gist is permanent: mercy to the needy as God's central requirement and love as the fulfilling of the law.[15]

Because this ethic was rooted in Jesus' faith in God, it was proclaimed in terms not alone of obligation but of hope. One of Jesus' most familiar phrases was "the will" of God. God was not primarily an object of speculation, nor even of belief, but was active purpose, the eternal Doer, immediately to be recognized in experience and wholeheartedly served. Here and now God was presently at work, revealed in nature, caring for even a sparrow's fall, the planner and achiever of all good deeds, the guarantor of a coming time when his will would be done on earth as in heaven. "My Father is working still, and I am working"[16] is John's statement of Jesus' undergirding faith. To his immediate listeners, therefore, he brought a demand for action in the name of the supreme Actor: "Go and do likewise";[17] "Which of the two did the will of his father?"[18] "Not every one who says to me, 'Lord, Lord,' shall enter the kingdom of heaven, but he who does the will of my Father who is in heaven."[19] And because divine purpose, issuing in divine action, was thus the central fact in the universe, as Jesus saw it, victory lay ahead—God's kingdom surely coming, involving the triumph of the righteous and their eternal life. His confidence was unshakable: "Every plant which my heavenly Father has not planted will be rooted up."[20]

The deep needs of human nature to which such faith is pertinent are as real today as ever. While, therefore, the forgiven sinners in the Gospels, the mended lives, the ordinary folk made extraordinary because they were carried out of themselves by a cause greater than themselves to which they gave themselves, wore first-century clothes and thought in first-century terms, they are nonetheless our contemporaries. They were subdued and mastered and enlisted by a truth that does not wear out.

It was the personality, however, through whom the teaching came, who supremely impressed the first disciples, and who still fascinates our imagination and challenges our conscience. Three names by which Jesus is called are familiarly remembered: a "physician" who cares for the sick; a "bridegroom" rejoicing with his bridal party; an incendiary, who has come "to cast fire upon the earth," to consume evil things whose doom God has decreed. But Jesus and his truth are thought of in a fourth way also, as a stone: "Every one who falls on that stone will be broken to pieces; but when it falls on any one it will crush him."[21] So those first disciples began to see him—impregnable, permanent, the decisive arbiter of what will last and what will pass away. Despised and rejected, crucified and hated, all the evil in men and nations arrayed against him and his gospel, he still maintains that position in the faith of his followers—a rock on which evil falling will yet be broken.

That he taught humility and impressed those who knew him best with his humble spirit is evident in the Gospels. As Ruskin said of the supreme artists, they could not be proud because "the greatness is not *in* them, but *through* them."[22] As Jesus saw the matter, it was not himself but God who was good, and who was using him in every good work he did. So John interpreted his self-consciousness: "The Father who dwells in me does his works."[23] But while thus humble about himself, he was uncompromising in affirming and defending the truth he stood for and in asserting his supreme authority as its representative:

[246]

"He who receives you receives me, and he who receives me receives him who sent me";[24] "So every one who acknowledges me before men, I also will acknowledge before my Father who is in heaven."[25] The earliest Christianity of the first disciples was thus devotion to a person—"Follow me," he said. It was not a formal creed nor an ethical code but a Man they believed in. He was to them that most powerful force in human experience, an incarnation, embodying and revealing in his own person the truths he represented. When they thought of God, it was more and more in terms of Jesus; when they thought of goodness, it meant likeness to him. So he became to them not only Teacher, but Lord and Savior, revealer of the divine, ideal of the human, who having died for their sakes still lived, and to whom, in God's good time, the future belonged.

This, too, has stood the test of passing centuries and, amid the many conflicts which divide his followers today, one constant element alone binds them together—loyalty to a Personality.

Jesus, as his contemporaries saw him, cannot be thought of, therefore, in his stark historicity as an uninterpreted person. His very first disciples began interpreting him and, so far as the four Gospels are concerned, this theological rendering of Jesus, which came to its climax in John, began in Mark. By various paths those first followers came to him, wanting renewed faith, forgiveness of sin, healing of body and spirit, a leader to follow, a cause to serve, a hope to give them courage; and, finding these timeless needs supplied by Jesus, they began asking, Who is he? and answering in terms of the mental categories they had inherited. This, too, is a perennial process and still goes on. For the deep and abiding needs of man, in the twentieth century as in the first, call for a living, personal revelation and symbol of God, for pardon, power, faith in divine

[247]

purpose and courage in serving it, for inward peace, a cause worth ultimate self-sacrifice, and for hope here and hereafter. The process which started in the experience of the first disciples has proved to be endless: man's profoundest spiritual wants finding their satisfaction in this Eternal Contemporary, with the question rising, Who is he?

> Yea, in the night, my Soul, my daughter
> Cry,—clinging Heaven by the hems;
> And lo, Christ walking on the water
> Not of Gennesareth, but Thames![26]

REFERENCES

CHAPTER I

A REAL MAN, NOT A MYTH

1. Acts 5:33–39.   2. Sanhedrin, 43a.
3. The soldier's name, according to this tale, was *Pantheras;* the word for virgin is *Parthenos.* Jewish scholars like Klausner and Christian scholars like Goguel agree that this Jewish canard was at first a wordplay on "Son of the Virgin." See *Jesus of Nazareth,* by Joseph Klausner, p. 23 f.; *The Life of Jesus,* by Maurice Goguel, p. 73 f.
4. See *Christianity in Talmud and Midrash,* by Robert Travers Herford.
5. See e.g., Klausner, *op. cit.,* p. 56 ff.   6. *Annals* XV. 44.
7. *Life of Claudius,* 25.
8. *The Search for the Real Jesus,* by Chester Charlton McCown, p. 69.
9. *Encyclopaedia Britannica,* article on Buddha.
10. The First Epistle of Clement, chaps. 5 and 47: *The Ante-Nicene Fathers,* ed. by Roberts and Donaldson, I, 5; cf. I Corinthians 11, 17 ff.
11. II Corinthians 5:16 (A.R.V.).   12. Galatians 1:18–19.
13. Acts 12:12.   14. Acts 12:12.   15. Galatians 4:4.
16. I Corinthians 11:23 f.   17. Galatians 2:20.
18. Cf. the "we" sections of Acts, chaps. 16:10–17; 20:5–15; 21:1–18; 27:1–28.
19. Philemon 24.   20. Colossians 4:14.   21. II Timothy 4:11.
22. II Corinthians 10:1.   23. Romans 15:1–3.
24. II Corinthians 3:18 (Henry Drummond).   25. Luke 14:11.
26. Romans 12:16.   27. Matthew 25:40.   28. II Corinthians 11:29.
29. Matthew 5:10.   30. II Corinthians 12:10.   31. Matthew 6:25.
32. Philippians 4:6.   33. Mark 7:15.   34. Romans 14:14.
35. Matthew 7:1.   36. Romans 14:13.   37. Mark 11:23.
38. I Corinthians 13:2.   39. Matthew 5:44.   40. Romans 12:14, 17.
41. Mark 12:28 f.   42. Romans 13:10.   43. I Corinthians 11:1.
44. Ephesians 4:21 M.   45. Galatians 4:19.   46. Philippians 2:3–5.
47. Matthew 5:3.   48. Luke 6:20, 21, 24.
49. Roberts and Donaldson, eds., *op. cit.,* I, pp. 154–5.   50. Mark 10:18.
51. Matthew 19:17.   52. Mark 11:12–14, 20–21; Matthew 21:18–19.
53. Mark 5:1–20; Matthew 8:28–34.
54. Mark 10:46–52; Matthew 20:29–34.
55. Mark 14:47; Luke 22:51.   56. John 2:1–11; 9:1–7; 11:1–44.

REFERENCES

57. Mark 13:30 f; 9:1.   58. Roberts and Donaldson, eds., *op. cit.*, I, 153.
59. Mark 2:27.   60. Matthew 19:14.   61. Mark 2:17.
62. Luke 6:32 f.   Cf. *The Poetry of Our Lord*, by Charles Fox Burney.
63. Luke 1:1–4.   64. Roberts and Donaldson, eds., *op. cit.*, I, 155.
65. Luke 1:1–4.   66. Mark 6:1–6; Luke 4:16 f.
67. Matthew 21:12–13; Mark 11:15–17; Luke 19:45; John 2:13–17.
68. Matthew 6:9 f; Luke 11:2–4.   69. Matthew 7:12; Luke 6:31.
70. Matthew 27:51–53.   71. Church History, Eusebius, 6, 14, 6.
72. E.g., Mark 5:41; 7:11, 34; 14:36; 15:34.   73. Mark 12:42.
74. Mark 11:13.   75. Mark 7:3.   76. Mark 10:11 f.; cf. Matthew 5:31 f.
77. See *The Gospel of Luke*, by William Manson, p. xi.
78. *Ibid.*, p. xxvii f.   79. Acts, chap. 21 ff.   80. Acts 21:17–18.
81. Acts 21:8–9.   82. Colossians 4:10, 14; Philemon 24.
83. Church History, Eusebius 6, 14, 7.   84. Matthew 15:24.
85. Cf. *The Gospel before the Gospels*, by Burton Scott Easton, chap. iv.

CHAPTER II

AS THE CROWDS SAW HIM

1. John 6:2.   2. John 6:15.   3. John 1:11.
4. John 7:1; cf. 7:11, 30; 8:48–59.   5. Mark 1:28.   6. Mark 2:2.
7. Mark 3:9.   8. Mark 3:31, 32.   9. Mark 3:20.   10. Mark 1:33.
11. Mark 5:31.   12. Mark 3:7–8.
13. Josephus, *History of the Jewish War*, 3:2; *Life*, 45.
14. *Itinerarium Antonini Placentini: Corpus Scriptorum Ecclesiasticorum Latinorum*, Vol. 39, p. 162.   15. Strabo 16:2, 34.   16. Mark 6:14–16.
17. Luke 13:31.   18. Luke 13:32.   19. Luke 13:33.   20. Mark 7:24.
21. Matthew 21:9.   22. John 12:19.   23. Mark 12:37 M.
24. Luke 22:2.   25. Luke 23:27.   26. Luke 23:48.
27. H.D.A. Major, in *The Mission and Message of Jesus*, p. xxx.
28. *The Jewish Encyclopedia*, V, 522.   29. Mark 6:56 M.   30. Luke 4:16.
31. Acts 23:8.   32. Matthew 11:19.   33. M. Sota 3, 4.
34. Sota 22b.   35. Deuteronomy, Rabba 2, 24.   36. Mark 4:10–13.
37. Mark 1:27 M.   38. *Antiquities* 17:2, 4.   39. Matthew 23:24.
40. Matthew 7:3–5.   41. Matthew 7:6.   42. Matthew 5:29–30.
43. Matthew 18:6.   44. Matthew 18:23 f.   45. Mark 11:23.
46. Luke 17:6.   47. Matthew 10:16.   48. Matthew 19:24.
49. Matthew 8:22.   50. Mark 10:21.   51. Matthew 8:10.
52. Matthew 7:16.   53. Matthew 10:30.   54. Matthew 7:9, 10.
55. Berachoth 55b; Baba Mezia 38b.   56. Matthew 7:28.
57. Romans 11:24.   58. δύναμεις, δύνατα ἔργα, τέρατα, σημεῖα.
59. Luke 11:15.   60. Mark 13:22.   61. Luke 11:19.
62. See Joseph Klausner, *Jesus of Nazareth*, p. 266.   63. Acts 13:6 f.

64. Klausner, *op. cit.*, p. 266.   65. Mark 1:44; 3:12; 5:43; 7:36.
66. Matthew 12:28.   67. Matthew 11:4–6; Luke 7:20–22.
68. Luke 5:26.   69. Mark 2:12.   70. Mark 5:1–20.
71. Luke 6:6–11.   72. Matthew 9:34.   73. Matthew 11:20–24.
74. Mark 5:43.   75. Luke 11:29 M.   76. Luke 11:29–32.
77. Mark 8:11, 12.   78. Mark 5:22–24; 35–43.   79. Matthew 12:39 f.
80. *The Apocryphal New Testament*, by M. R. James; especially *The Gospel of Thomas* and *The Gospel of Pseudo-Matthew*.   81. Matthew 21:18–21.
82. Mark 16:18.   83. Major, Manson and Wright, *op. cit.*, p. 107.
84. Luke 16:31.   85. Luke 10:17–20.   86. Mark 8:27–28.
87. Acts 15:5.   88. Epistle of Ignatius to the Magnesians, X.
89. *Jesus the Nazarene, Myth or History?* by Maurice Goguel, p. 38.
90. E.g., John 8:37–59.   91. Mark 14:61.   92. Matthew 11:20–24.
93. Matthew 23:37.
94. See *The Historic Mission of Jesus*, by C. J. Cadoux, p. 183 f.

CHAPTER III

AS THE SCRIBES AND PHARISEES SAW HIM

1. *Antiquities* 13:10, 6; 18:1, 4.   2. *Antiquities* 13:10, 6.   3. **Mark 7:8.**
4. Mark 12:18–23.   5. Matthew 2:4; 16:21; Luke 19:47; 23:10.
6. Mark 11:18; cf. 11:27; 14:1.   7. Mark 2:16.
8. Matthew 12:34; 23:33; cf. Matthew 3:7.   9. Acts 15:5.
10. Acts 23:6.   11. Mark 12:28–34.   12. John 3:1 f.
13. Galatians 2:12 f.   14. Acts 21:18–26.   15. *Antiquities* 20:9, 1.
16. Matthew 13:52.   17. Matthew 8:19.   18. Matthew 5:17, 18.
19. Matthew 23:2, 3.   20. II Enoch 42:13.
21. *Testament of the Twelve Patriarchs*, Benjamin 5:4.   22. *Ibid.*, Joseph 18:2.
23. *Ibid.*, Issachar 7:2.   24. *Ibid.*, Benjamin 8:2.
25. Judith 16:16.   26. Mark 2:18–20.   27. Luke 6:1–5.
28. Mark 7:1–5.   29. Luke 15:1, 2.   30. Mark 7:14–19.
31. Galatians 5:6.   32. *Jesus of Nazareth*, by Joseph Klausner, p. 376.
33. *Saints and Strangers*, by George F. Willison, p. 47.
34. *The Churchman*, January 15, 1944, letter in protest against *Churchman's* liberality.   35. Matthew 23:23.   36. Matthew 23:24.
37. Mark 7:1–5.   38. Mark 7:6–8 M.   39. Sota, 4b.
40. Numbers 30:2.   41. Matthew 5:34, 37.   42. Matthew 23:16–22 M.
43. Mark 7:9–13 M.   44. Shabbath 22, 6.
45. See *The Pharisees and Jesus*, by A. T. Robertson, p. 45 f; *The Jewish World in the Time of Jesus*, by C. A. H. Guignebert, p. 796; *The Jewish People in the Time of Jesus Christ*, by Schuerer, Div. II, Vol. II, pp. 96–105.
46. Magnalia, Bk. III, p. 178 (London, 1702).
47. *The Puritan Oligarchy*, by Thomas Jefferson Wertenbaker, p. 170.

REFERENCES

48. *The Memorial History of Boston,* by Justin Winsor, II, 470 n.
49. Shabbath 31a.   50. *Judaism,* by George Foote Moore, I 80 f.; see *The Jewish Encyclopedia,* III, 115 f.
51. *The Mission and Message of Jesus,* by Major, Manson and Wright, p. 99.
52. M. Hagigah 1, 8.   53. M. Sota 3, 4.   54. Moore, *op. cit.,* II, 194, n. 2.
55. Mark 2:27.   56. See Klausner, *op. cit.,* p. 278.
57. *History of the Jewish War,* 1:5, 2.   58. Yoma 85 f.   59. Mark 2:23 f.
60. Mark 3:1–6.   61. Matthew 12:12 M.   62. Luke 13:14 M.
63. Yoma 85 f.   64. Luke 13:10–17 M.   65. Matthew 12:1–4 M.
66. Mark 10:2–9 M.   67. Matthew 9:10–13.
68. Matthew 12:1–8; Hosea 6:6.   69. *Abot de Rabbi Nathan,* IV, 5.
70. Luke 4:25–27.   71. Exodus 3:6.   72. Mark 12:18–27.
73. Matthew 5:21–22.   74. Mark 2:22.   75. Luke 15:1–32.
76. Mark 9:33–37.   77. Luke 10:25–37.   78. Luke 7:36–50.
79. Luke 11:2.   80. Matthew 7:6.
81. *The Complete Works of James Whitcomb Riley,* V, 124, ed. by Edmund Henry Eitel.   82. Matthew 23:4.   83. Jer. Sota, 19a.   84. Luke 18:11.
85. Berakoth 28b.   86. Leviticus, Rabba 1, 5.   87. Matthew 7:18 M.
88. Matthew 23:26.   89. Luke 11:39 G.
90. *The Teaching of Jesus,* by T. W. Manson, p. 300.   91. Baba Kamma 83b.
92. Acts 26:5.

Chapter IV

As the Self-complacent Saw Him

1. Philippians 3:6.   2. Luke 15:29.   3. Mark 10:17–22.
4. Luke 19:1–10.   5. Luke 10:38–42.   6. Mark 5:18–19.
7. Luke 18:12 f.   8. Luke 7:36–50.   9. Matthew 5:21, 22.
10. Luke 11:42.   11. Luke 5:14.   12. Psalm 51:10.
13. Jeremiah 31:33.   14. Revelation 1:10.
15. Song of Songs, Rabba 1, 2.
16. *Studies in Pharisaism and the Gospels,* by Israel Abrahams, second series, p. 12.
17. Hebrews 4:15.   18. Mark 10:18.   19. Mark 10:21.
20. Luke 10:30–37.   21. Matthew 25:42, 43.
22. Matthew 21:28–31.   23. Matthew 12:43–45.   24. Matthew 23:15.
25. Josephus, *History of the Jewish War,* 2:10, 4.   26. Luke 18:11.
27. Abodah Zarah 20b.   28. Matthew 23:5–7.   29. Luke 15:7.
30. Sota 5a.   31. Luke 18:9.   32. Matthew 21:31.
33. Matthew 5:38–48 M.   34. Proverbs 25:21.   35. Job 31:29–30.
36. Discourses of Epictetus, IV, 1.   37. Plato's *Georgias,* 468 f.
38. Samyutta Nikaya 7.1.2; 11.1.4.   39. Dhammapada 197.
40. Kakacupama Suta: Majjhima Nikaya 1.129.   41. Matthew 5:20.
42. Romans 12:21.

43. *Rabbinic Literature and Gospel Teachings*, pp. 103 f.
44. Luke 19:41 f.   45. Matthew 23:37.
46. *The Life of Jesus*, by Ernest Renan, chap. 5.   47. Matthew 5:39.
48. Matthew 6:34.   49. John 12:27.   50. Matthew 5:48.
51. Luke 6:36.
52. *The Four Gospels*, a New Translation, by Charles Cutler Torrey.
53. Hebrews 5:14.   54. Ephesians 4:13.   55. I Corinthians 14:20.
56. E.g., Matthew 18:23–35.   57. E.g., Luke 7:36–50.
58. Matthew 6:29.   59. Mark 10:13–16.   60. Matthew 9:14, 15.
61. Matthew 6:16.   62. Matthew 22:2.   63. Luke 15:7, 10.
64. Matthew 6:1.   65. Matthew 5:14–16.   66. Matthew 11:28–30.
67. Matthew 16:24.   68. Matthew 6:34.   69. Matthew 25:1–13.
70. Luke 6:35.   71. Matthew 5:9.   72. Luke 12:51.
73. Matthew 5:45.   74. Luke 12:5.   75. Matthew 5:17.
76. Matthew 5:21, 22.
77. *Akiba, Scholar, Saint and Martyr*, by Louis Finkelstein, p. 103.
78. *Ibid.*, pp. 138–139.   79. pp. 15–16.   80. Luke 17:7–10.
81. *Othello*, Act II, scene 3.   82. Luke 6:22–23.   83. Yoma, 86b.
84. Matthew 18:21–22.   85. Aboth 11, 9.   86. Matthew 7:1.
87. Matthew 26:63.   88. Matthew 7:24 M.

CHAPTER V

As Religious and Moral Outcasts Saw Him

1. Sota 22a.
2. *The Beginnings of Christianity*, by Jackson and Lake, Pt. I, Vol. I, Appendix E, p. 439 f.   3. Pesachim 49a.   4. Kethuboth IIIb.
5. Pesachim 49b.   6. Aboth 11, 6.   7. Pesachim 49b.
8. Jackson and Lake, *op. cit.*, Pt. I, Vol. I, p. 444.   9. Mark 2:15.
10. Baba Bathra, chap. I, 8a.   11. John 7:48, 49.   12. Matthew 7:28.
13. Mechilta 57b.   14. Matthew 9:33.   15. John 7:15.
16. Cf. *The Teaching of Jesus*, by T. W. Manson, p. 47 f.
17. Mark 12:14, 32.   18. *Against Apion* 1, 12; 2, 18.
19. *Life In Palestine When Jesus Lived*, by J. Estlin Carpenter, p. 53 f.; *Rabbinic Literature and Gospel Teachings*, by C. G. Montefiore, p. 6.
20. Matthew 9:36.   21. Luke 7:34.   22. Cf. Carpenter, *op. cit.*, p. 83.
23. Luke 3:12, 13.   24. Luke 19:8.   25. Luke 18:9.
26. Matthew 5:46.   27. Carpenter, *op. cit.*, p. 83.   28. Luke 19:9.
29. Matthew 9:9.   30. Matthew 23:23 M.   31. Matthew 11:25 M.
32. *The Jewish Encyclopedia*, I, p. 484.   33. Luke 7:34.
34. John 7:53–8:11.   35. *Church History*, Eusebius, 3, 39.
36. de conjug. adult. 2, 7. Cf. *The Mission and Message of Jesus*, by Major, Manson and Wright, pp. 793–796.   37. Luke 5:30–32.   38. John 12:47.

39. Exodus, Rabba 31.   40. Midrash on Psalm 120.   41. Matthew 25:41.
42. Matthew 18:6.
43. Tos. Sanhedrin 13³; cf. *Judaism*, by George Foote Moore, II, 387.
44. Luke 19:10.   45. Montefiore, *op. cit.*, p. 222.   46. Matthew 16:13, 14.
47. Luke 15:1–10.   48. Luke 15:10.   49. Luke 15:20.
50. Matthew 18:27.   51. Matthew 18:12–14 M.   52. Aboth 3, 14.
53. M. Sanhedrin IV, 5.   54. Matthew 7:13, 14.
55. Mark 10:23–27.   56. Luke 15:1, 2.

CHAPTER VI

AS WOMEN AND CHILDREN SAW HIM

1. Matthew 13:55, 56; Mark 6:3.   2. Matthew 7:9, 10.
3. Matthew 11:16, 17.   4. Luke 11:7.   5. Matthew 18:1–4.
6. Matthew 18:5, 6.   7. Matthew 21:15, 16.
8. Matthew 19:13–15; Mark 10:13–16; Luke 18:15–17.   9. John 16:32.
10. Cf. *The Mission and Message of Jesus*, by Major, Manson and Wright, p. 460.
11. Matthew 25:40.   12. Mark 3:31–35.
13. *Rabbinic Literature and Gospel Teachings*, p. 47.   14. Luke 7:11–17.
15. Luke 7:36–50.   16. Luke 10:38–42.   17. Luke 13:10–17.
18. Luke 23:27, 28.   19. Luke 8:1–3.   20. Mark 15:40–41.
21. *Op. cit.*, p. 217.   22. Luke 17:35.   23. Luke 11:25.
24. Luke 15:8–10.   25. Matthew 6:30.   26. Matthew 13:33.
27. Matthew 6:19–21.   28. Mark 2:21, 22.   29. Luke 12:6.
30. Galatians 3:28; cf. I Corinthians 11:2–15; I Timothy 2:11–15.
31. Luke 18:1–8 M.   32. Luke 21:1–4.   33. Luke 4:25, 26.
34. Mark 12:40.   35. Leviticus, Rabba III, 5.
36. Cf. *The Jewish Encyclopedia*, XII, 514.   37. Luke 20:47 M.
38. Exodus, Rabba, XXX.   39. Proverbs 31:10–31.
40. The Wisdom of Ben Sira (Sirach) 26:21–24.   41. *Ibid,.* 42:9, 11–14.
42. Matthew 5:28.   43. Luke 10:38–42.
44. Major, Manson and Wright, *op. cit.*, p. 748.
45. Mark 14:3–9; Matthew 26:6–13; John 12:1–8.   46. Mark 14:4–7 M.
47. John 7:53–8:11 (cf. chap. IV).   48. Luke 7:36–50.
49. John 4:5–30.
50. On the possibility that the five husbands may be allegorically interpreted, see Major, Manson and Wright, *op. cit.*, p. 746 f.   51. Deuteronomy 24:1.
52. *Studies in Pharisaism and the Gospels*, by Israel Abrahams, first series, p. 72.
53. *The Synoptic Gospels*, by C. G. Montefiore, Vol. 1, p. 235.
54. Mark 10:2–9.   55. I Corinthians 7:10–11.   56. Matthew 19:9.
57. Matthew 19:10–12.   58. Mark 10:11.
59. Abrahams, *op. cit.*, first series, p. 76.   60. Malachi 2:15–16.
61. Luke 14:26.   62. Genesis 29:30–31.   63. Matthew 10:37.

REFERENCES

64. Mark 3:21.   65. Mark 3:31–35.   66. John 7:5.   67. Mark 10:29.
68. Luke 12:51–53.   69. Matthew 10:36 (Micah 7:6).
70. John 19:25–27.   71. Mark 15:40; Matthew 27:55, 56.
72. Luke 3:23.   73. Isaiah 7:14.   74. *First Apology*, 21.
75. Acts 1:13–14.   76. Galatians 1:18–19.   77. Mark 5:25–34.
78. Matthew 15:21–28.   79. Luke 8:1–3.   80. Mark 10:15–16.
81. Luke 11:27–28.   82. *Unpopular Opinions*, p. 148.

Chapter VII

As His First Disciples Saw Him

1. Matthew 9:9; 10:3; Mark 2:14; 3:18.   2. Luke 6:16; Acts 1:13.
3. Revelation 21:14.   4. Luke 9:51–56.   5. Matthew 15:16.
6. Mark 10:35–41.   7. Mark 9:33–37.   8. Luke 22:24.
9. Matthew 16:23.   10. John 15:15.   11. Mark 1:16–17.
12. Mark 2:14.   13. John 1:40–42.   14. Mark 1:16–38.
15. *The Life and Teaching of Jesus The Christ*, by Arthur C. Headlam, p. 11.
16. Matthew 13:10.   17. Matthew 15:12.   18. Matthew 15:15 M.
19. Mark 8:32.   20. Mark 3:14.   21. Mark 6:31.   22. Luke 22:32.
23. Matthew 26:50.   24. Mark 5:18–19.   25. Luke 9:57–58.
26. Luke 9:61–62.   27. Luke 6:12–13.   28. II Timothy 1:12.
29. Matthew 13:3 f.; Mark 4:1 f.; Luke 8:4 f.   30. Mark 4:34.
31. Matthew 5:13–14.   32. Mark 10:42–44.   33. Matthew 23:8.
34. Mark 10:29 f.   35. Luke 10:18.   36. Luke 12:32.
37. Mark 4:31 f.   38. Matthew 13:33.   39. Luke 22:15.
40. Luke 22:28.   41. John 17:6–11.   42. Matthew 10:23.
43. Matthew 24:36–44.   44. Mark 13:9–13.   45. Matthew 24:36.
46. Luke 14:27.   47. Luke 14:26.   48. Matthew 5:11.
49. Luke 17:3.   50. Matthew 18:15–17.   51. Mark 10:39.
52. Luke 14:25–33.   53. Matthew 10:17–18.   54. Mark 1:35–36.
55. Matthew 6:7.   56. Luke 9:29.   57. Luke 11:1.
58. Luke 11:5–8.   59. Luke 18:1–8.   60. Luke 11:9–13.
61. Luke 12:6–7.   62. *Timaeus:* VIII.   63. Luke 9:18.
64. Matthew 6:6.   65. Mark 1:7.   66. Mark 1:11.   67. Mark 1:24.
68. Mark 3:11.   69. Mark 8:29.   70. Mark 9:7.   71. Mark 1:25.
72. Mark 3:12.   73. Mark 8:30.   74. Luke 9:21.   75. Matthew 16:20.
76. Mark 14:61–62.   77. Luke 7:16.   78. Mark 6:15.
79. Mark 8:27–28.   80. Matthew 21:11.   81. Matthew 21:46.
82. Mark 6:4.   83. Luke 13:33.
84. E.g., Matthew 7:21; 15:13; 16:17; 18:19; 18:35, etc.
85. Luke 10:22; Matthew 11:27.   86. John 3:35; 10:15; 13:3; 17:25.
87. Matthew 5:9.   88. Matthew 5:45.   89. Testament of Judah, 24:1.
90. Testament of Naphtali 4:5.   91. Sibylline Oracles 3:655, 656.

REFERENCES

92. Testament of Simeon 7:2; Testament of Issachar 5:7; The Book of Jubilees 31:18 f.   93. Testament of Reuben 6:7 f.; Testament of Levi 8:14.
94. Testament of Dan 5:10.   95. Sibylline Oracles 3:653.
96. Testament of Levi 18:4.   97. Assumption of Moses 1:14.
98. Daniel 7:13–14; I Enoch 48:2–6; 49:2.   99. Zechariah 9:9.
100. Daniel 7:13.   101. Sanhedrin 98a.
102. Isaiah 42:1–4; 49:1–6; 50:4–9; 53: 1–12.
103. See *Judaism*, by George Foote Moore, I, 551.
104. See *Jesus the Messiah*, by William Manson, Appendix B, the Targum on Isaiah 53.   105. IV Maccabees 6:27–29.   106. Acts 8:27–39.
107. I Peter 2:22–25.   108. Hebrews 9:29.   109. Luke 4:16 f.
110. Matthew 11:2 f.; cf. Isaiah 35:5.   111. Luke 22:37.
112. Isaiah 53:11–12.   113. Mark 10:45.   111. Mark 9:12.
115. Mark 14:21.   116. Mark 14:24.   117. Mark 9:31–32.
118. On the difficulties involved in interpreting the phrase "Son of man," as used in the Gospels, see *Jesus the Messiah*, by William Manson, p. 158 f.; *The Historic Mission of Jesus*, by C. J. Cadoux, p. 90 f. On problems associated with Jesus' resurrection see *The Mission and Message of Jesus*. by Major, Manson and Wright, p. 211 f.; also. the author's book, *A Guide to Understanding the Bible*, chap. vi.   119. Zechariah 11:12–13.
120. Mark 14:10–11; Matthew 26:14–16; Luke 22:3–6.
121. Matthew 27:3–10.   122. Acts 1:16–19.   **123. Luke 24:21.**

Chapter VIII

As Militant Nationalists Saw Him

1. Psalm 137:5–6.   2. *Antiquities* 18:1, 6.   3. *History of the Jewish War*, 3:3, 2.
4. *Antiquities* 14:15, 5.   5. *Antiquities* 17:10, 9.
6. *The Provinces of the Roman Empire*, II, 203.   7. Acts 5:36–37.
8. *Akiba, Scholar, Saint and Martyr*, by Louis Finkelstein, p. 269.
9. John 6:15.   10. Matthew 4:8–9.   11. Luke 19:11.   12. Luke 6:15.
13. Matthew 10:4.   14. Cf. Acts 21:20; Galatians 1:14.   15. Mark 3:17.
16. Luke 9:54.   17. Mark 10:35 f.
18. Mark 8:33 (cf. "Begone, Satan!" Matthew 4:10).
19. Luke 22:35–38.   20. Mark 14:47.   21. Luke 12:49.
22. Windisch, Der Mess. Krieg, p. 95.   23. Mark 11:17.   24. Mark 15:7.
25. Luke 19:41–44.   26. Mark 13:2.
27. Matthew 23:37–38; cf. Luke 13:34–35.
28. Mark 13:1–37; Matthew 24:1–44; Luke 21:5–36.   29. Vs. 14.
30. Mark 13:14–19.   31. Luke 21:20.   32. Luke 21:24.
33. Luke 13:1–5.   34. Luke 12:54–56.

35. Mark 12:1–11; Matthew 21:33–46; Luke 20:9–19.
36. Matthew 23:34–36.   37. Luke 23:28–31.   38. Matthew 24:6.
39. Matthew 26:52.   40. Mark 12:13–17.   41. Mark 14:56–59.
42. Matthew 11:12.   43. Luke 16:16.   44. Chaps. III and IV.
45. Matthew 5:41.   46. Matthew 5:9.   47. Luke 19:42.
48. Finkelstein, *op. cit.*, p. 60.   49. Yoma, 39b.   50. Baba Bathra 10b.
51. Isaiah 49:6.   52. Micah 4:3.   53. II Enoch 50:3 f.
54. The Assumption of Moses 10:7–10.   55. II Esdras 6:55–59.
56. Matthew 10:34–37.   57. Luke 12:51.   58. Luke 22:35–38.
59. Luke 22:50–51.   60. Matthew 26:51–52.   61. John 18:36.
62. Luke 19:27.   63. Matthew 22:7.   64. Luke 14:31–32.
65. Mark 3:27.   66. Luke 16:1–9.   67. Luke 17:7–10.
68. Matthew 25:14–30.   69. Matthew 8:5–9.   70. Mark 3:22.
71. Cf. *The Gospel of Mark*, by B. Harvie Branscomb, pp. 271–277.
72. *Studies in Pharisaism and the Gospels*, by Israel Abrahams, first series, chap-XI.   73. Kerithoth 1:7.
74. Mark 11:17; Matthew 21:13; Luke 19:46.   75. Mark 11:16.
76. John 2:13–15.   77. Mark 11:15, Matthew 21:12; Luke 19:45.
78. Mark 11:18; Luke 19:48.   79. Luke 23:5.
80. Mark 14:1–2; cf. Matthew 26:4–5.   81. Luke 23:2.
82. John 19:15.   83. Eg., Romans 13:1–7; Titus 3:1–2; I Peter 2:13–14.
84. Mark 15:14.   85. Matthew 27:24.
86. E.g., Philo. Leg. ad. Caium, 38.   87. Mark 15:10.
88. Luke 23:14–16.   89. Mark 15:29–31.

CHAPTER IX

As Jews with a World-wide Outlook Saw Him

1. Matthew 10:5.
2. Eighth ed., chap. 28.
3. *Greek in Jewish Palestine*, by Saul Lieberman, p. 21.   4. Acts 22:2.
5. T. B. Sota 49b.
6. *A Social and Religious History of the Jews*, by Salo Wittmayer Baron, I, 156.
7. *Against Flaccus*, 7, 46.   8. Acts 6:1.   9. Acts 6:9.
10. Baron, *op. cit.*, I, 222.   11. *Jesus of Nazareth*, by Joseph Klausner, p. 117.
12. John 12:20 f.   13. Acts 15:22–29.
14. Sifre (Midrash) Numbers, Sec. 111; Deuteronomy, Sec. 54. cf. *Judaism*, by George Foote Moore, I, 325.   15. Aboth 1, 2.   16. Yebamot 47b.
17. Matthew 23:13–15.
18. *The Journal of Theological Studies*, XIII, 324.   19. Acts 2:9–11.
20. Matthew 28:19.   21. Matthew 12:18–21.   22. Matthew 10:5–6.
23. Matthew 15:24.   24. Matthew 5:18.   25. Matthew 8:11.

26. Matthew 21:43.   27. Matthew 5:14.   28. Matthew 13:38.
29. Matthew 24:14.   30. Amos 9:7.   31. Isaiah 49:6.
32. Matthew 28:19.   33. Matthew 10:23.   34. Matthew 16:28.
35. Matthew 24:36.   36. Matthew 19:28.   37. John 8:48.
38. The Wisdom of Ben-Sira (Sirach) 50:25; 26.   39. Luke 10:30 f.
40. Romans 2:14–15.   41. Luke 11:30–32.   42. Luke 4:25–27.
43. Matthew 11:20–24.   44. Matthew 8:5 f.   45. Matthew 3:9.
46. Matthew 8:11.   47. Isaiah 56:7.   48. Mark 11:17.
49. Matthew 6:7.   50. Matthew 5:47.   51. Mark 10:42.
52. Matthew 4:25.   53. Luke 6:17.   54. Mark 7:31 f.
55. Mark 7:24–30.
56. Cf. *The Gospel of Mark*, by B. Harvie Branscomb, p. 132.   57. John 4:22.
58. Testament of Asher VII, 3.   59. Testament of Benjamin X, 5.
60. Testament of Levi, IV, 4.   61. Testament of Levi, XVIII, 9.
62. Baruch, 1.1.4.   63. Matthew 11:25.   64. Romans 3:30.
65. Matthew 25:31–46.   66. Micah 6:8.
67. *Einleitung in die drei ersten Evangelien*, p. 113. Berlin, 1905.
68. Klausner, *op. cit.*, p. 390.   69. Luke 17:11 f.
70. *What is Christianity?* tr. by Thomas Bailey Saunders, 1912, p. 73.
71. Matthew 23:8.   72. *The Ethical Teaching of Jesus*, by Ernest Findlay
     Scott, p. 13.
73. Matthew 7:24.   74. Matthew 10:32.   75. Matthew 10:42.
76. Matthew 12:50.   77. Matthew 16:25.   78. Matthew 18:4.
79. Matthew 20:26.   80. Exodus 15:18.   81. Matthew 4:10.
82. Mark 14:36.   83. Matthew 13:38.   84. Matthew 13:33.
85. Mark 4:30 f.   86. Luke 11:20–21.
87. *The Sayings of Jesus from Oxyrhynchus*, by H. G. E. White.
88. Romans 14:17.   89. Mark 10:14, 15.   90. Mark 12:32–34.
91. Matthew 5:3.   92. Matthew 7:21.   93. Matthew 13:37 f.
94. Mark 10:23 f.   95. Luke 9:62.   96. Luke 13:27–29.
97. Acts 6:8–8:3.   98. Haer. XX.4.   99. Luke 10:1.
100. Acts 7:51–53.

Epilogue

1. Luke 16:19–31.   2. Luke 12:13–21.   3. Matthew 18:23–35.
4. Matthew 19:26; Mark 10:27.   5. Luke 6:36.   6. Matthew 7:11.
7. Luke 15:10.   8. Matthew 6:4.
9. *The Teaching of Jesus*, by T. W. Manson, p. 72.   10. Luke 12:15.
11. Matthew 6:24.   12. Matthew 6:27.   13. Luke 17:33.
14. Matthew 18:4.   15. Matthew 25:31–46.   16. John 5:17.
17. Luke 10:37.   18. Matthew 21:28–31.   19. Matthew 7:21.
20. Matthew 15:13.   21. Luke 20:17–18.

REFERENCES

22. *Modern Painters*, chapter on "Of Modern Landscape." 23. John 14:11.
24. Matthew 10:40. 25. Matthew 10:32.
26. "In No Strange Land" in *The Collected Poetry of Francis Thompson*, *p.* 412.
Reprinted by permission of Sir Francis Meynell and the publishers, Messrs.
Burns, Oates & Washbourne, Ltd.

Selected Bibliography

MATHEWS, SHAILER. *New Testament Times in Palestine*, 175 B.C.–135 A.D. Macmillan, 1934.

CHARLES, R. H. *Religious Development between the Old and New Testaments*. Thornton and Butterworth, 1934.

MOORE, GEORGE FOOTE. *Judaism in the First Centuries of the Christian Era*. Harvard University Press, 1927–30.

BARON, SALO WITTMAYER. *A Social and Religious History of the Jews*. Columbia University Press, 1937.

GUIGNEBERT, CH. *The Jewish World in the Time of Jesus*. Kegan Paul, Trench, Trubner & Co., 1939.

GRANT, FREDERICK. *The Economic Background of the Gospels*. Oxford University Press, 1926.

HERFORD, ROBERT TRAVERS. *Christianity in Talmud and Midrash*. Williams and Norgate, 1903.

WALKER, THOMAS. *The Teaching of Jesus and the Jewish Teaching of His Age*. George Allen and Unwin, 1923.

MONTEFIORE, C. G. *Rabbinic Literature and Gospel Teachings*. Macmillan, 1930.

CHARLES, R. H. *Apocrypha and Pseudipigrapha of the Old Testament*. Clarendon Press, 1913.

JAMES, M. R. *The Apocryphal New Testament*. Clarendon Press, 1926.

BRANSCOMB, B. HARVIE. *Jesus and the Law of Moses*. R. R. Smith, 1930.

McCOWN, CHESTER CHARLTON. *The Search for the Real Jesus*. Charles Scribner's Sons, 1940.

[261]

SELECTED BIBLIOGRAPHY

SCHWEITZER, ALBERT. *The Quest of the Historical Jesus*. A. & C. Black, 1910.

CASE, SHIRLEY JACKSON. *The Historicity of Jesus*. University of Chicago Press, 1912.

SCOTT, ERNEST FINDLAY. *The Validity of the Gospel Record*. Charles Scribner's Sons, 1938.

LIGHTFOOT, R. H. *History and Interpretation in the Gospels*. Harper & Brothers, 1935.

EASTON, B. S. *The Gospel before the Gospels*. Charles Scribner's Sons, 1928.

TAYLOR, VINCENT. *The Formulation of the Gospel Tradition*. Macmillan, 1935.

GRANT, FREDERICK. *Form Criticism: A New Method of New Testament Research*. Willett, Clark & Co., 1934.

GOGUEL, MAURICE. *The Life of Jesus*. Macmillan, 1944.

KLAUSNER, JOSEPH. *Jesus of Nazareth*. Macmillan, 1925.

MACKINNON, JAMES. *The Historic Jesus*. Longmans, Green & Co., 1931.

STRACHAN, R. H. *The Historic Jesus in the New Testament*. Student Christian Movement Press, 1931.

MAJOR, MANSON AND WRIGHT. *The Mission and Message of Jesus*. E. P. Dutton & Co., 1946.

CASE, S. J. *Jesus: A New Biography*. University of Chicago Press, 1927.

CADOUX, C. J. *The Historic Mission of Jesus*. Harper & Brothers, 1943.

KNOX, JOHN. *The Man Christ Jesus*. Harper & Brothers, 1942.

MANSON, T. W. *The Teaching of Jesus*. Cambridge University Press, 1943.

BRANSCOMB, B. HARVIE. *The Teachings of Jesus*. Abingdon-Cokesbury Press, 1931.

LINDSAY, A. D. *The Moral Teaching of Jesus*. Harper & Brothers, 1937.

SCOTT, ERNEST FINDLAY. *The Ethical Teaching of Jesus*. Macmillan, 1936.

MANSON, WILLIAM. *Jesus, the Messiah*. The Westminster Press, 1946.

CADBURY, HENRY J. *Jesus, What Manner of Man*. Macmillan, 1947.

COLWELL, ERNEST CADMAN. *An Approach to the Teaching of Jesus*. Abingdon-Cokesbury Press, 1946.

SELECTED BIBLIOGRAPHY

WILDER, AMOS NIVEN. *Eschatology and Ethics in the Teaching of Jesus.* Harper & Brothers, 1939.

SIMKHOVITCH, V. G. *Toward the Understanding of Jesus.* Macmillan, 1921.

CADBURY, H. J. *The Peril of Modernizing Jesus.* Macmillan, 1937.

SMITH, B. T. D. *The Parables of the Synoptic Gospels.* Cambridge University Press, 1937.

DODD, C. H. *The Parables of the Kingdom.* Charles Scribner's Sons, 1936.

ABRAHAMS, ISRAEL. *Studies in Pharisaism and the Gospels.* Macmillan, first series, 1917; second series, 1924.

HERFORD, ROBERT TRAVIS. *Pharisaism: Its Aim and Its Method.* G. P. Putnam's Sons, 1912.

MONTEFIORE, C. G. *Some Elements of the Religious Teaching of Jesus.* Macmillan, 1910.

OTTO, R. *The Kingdom of God and the Son of Man.* Zonderman Publishing House, 1938–39.

SHARMAN, H. B. *Son of Man and Kingdom of God.* Harper & Brothers, 1943.

MCNEILE, ALAN HUGH. *The Gospel According to St. Matthew.* Macmillan, 1915.

SMITH, B. T. D. *The Gospel According to Matthew.* Cambridge University Press, 1927.

RAWLINSON, A. E. J. *St. Mark.* Methuen & Co., 1931.

BRANSCOMB, B. HARVIE. *The Gospel of Mark.* Harper & Brothers, 1937.

CREED, J. M. *The Gospel According to St. Luke.* Macmillan, 1930.

EASTON, BURTON SCOTT. *The Gospel According to St. Luke.* Charles Scribner's Sons, 1926.

LUCE, H. K. *The Gospel According to St. Luke.* Cambridge University Press, 1933.

MONTEFIORE, C. G. *The Synoptic Gospels.* Macmillan, 1909.

STREETER, B. H. *The Four Gospels.* Macmillan, 1930.

SCOTT, ERNEST FINDLAY. *The Fourth Gospel, Its Purpose and Theology.* T. & T. Clark, 1908.

COLWELL, ERNEST CADMAN. *John Defends the Gospel.* Willett, Clark & Co., 1936.

SMART, W. A. *The Spiritual Gospel.* Abingdon-Cokesbury Press, 1945.

[263]

MacGregor, G. H. C. *John*, in *The Moffatt New Testament Commentary*, Harper & Brothers, 1928.

Strachan, R. H. *The Fourth Gospel: Its Significance and Environment*. Student Christian Movement Press, 1941.

INDEXES

INDEX I

NAMES AND SUBJECTS

INDEX II

Passages from the Old Testament

INDEX III

Passages from the New Testament

INDEXES

INDEX IV

PASSAGES FROM THE APOCRYPHA AND PSEUDEPIGRAPHA